Strategy-Driven Talent Management

The Professional Practice Series

The Professional Practice Series is sponsored by The Society for Industrial and Organizational Psychology, Inc. (SIOP). The series was launched in 1988 to provide industrial and organizational psychologists, organizational scientists and practitioners, human resources professionals, managers, executives and those interested in organizational behavior and performance with volumes that are insightful, current, informative, and relevant to *organizational practice.* The volumes in the Professional Practice Series are guided by five tenets designed to enhance future organizational practice:

1. Focus on practice, but grounded in science
2. Translate organizational science into practice by generating guidelines, principles, and lessons learned that can shape and guide practice
3. Showcase the application of industrial and organizational psychology to solve problems
4. Document and demonstrate best industrial and organizational-based practices
5. Stimulate research needed to guide future organizational practice

The volumes seek to inform those interested in practice with guidance, insights, and advice on how to apply the concepts, findings, methods, and tools derived from industrial and organizational psychology to solve human-related organizational problems.

Previous Professional Practice Series volumes include:

Published by Jossey-Bass

Customer Service Delivery
Lawrence Fogli, Editor

Employment Discrimination Litigation
Frank J. Landy, Editor

The Brave New World of eHR
Hal G. Gueutal, Dianna L. Stone, Editors

Improving Learning Transfer in Organizations
Elwood F. Holton III, Timothy T. Baldwin, Editors

Resizing the Organization
Kenneth P. De Meuse, Mitchell Lee Marks, Editors

Implementing Organizational Interventions
Jerry W. Hedge, Elaine D. Pulakos, Editors

Organization Development
Janine Waclawski, Allan H. Church, Editors

Creating, Implementing, and Managing Effective Training and Development
Kurt Kraiger, Editor

The 21st Century Executive: Innovative Practices for Building Leadership at the Top
Rob Silzer, Editor

Managing Selection in Changing Organizations
Jerard F. Kehoe, Editor

The Professional Practice Series

To the innovators and seekers who see possibilities and have the courage to challenge the status quo to pursue them

—R.F.S.

To my wife, Viki, who has been my understanding partner for over forty years; my daughter, Meggan, who brings me joy every day; and my grandsons, Ben and Quinn, who are the future

—B.E.D.

Strategy-Driven Talent Management

A Leadership Imperative

Rob Silzer and Ben E. Dowell, Editors

Foreword by Allan H. Church and Janine Waclawski

JOSSEY-BASS
A Wiley Imprint
www.josseybass.com

Published by Jossey-Bass
A Wiley Imprint
989 Market Street, San Francisco, CA 94103-1741—www.josseybass.com

Library of Congress Cataloging-in-Publication Data

Strategy-driven talent management: a leadership imperative/edited by Rob Silzer and Ben E. Dowell; with foreword by Allan H. Church and Janine Waclawski.—1st ed.

    p. cm.

   Includes bibliographical references and index.

   ISBN 978–0–7879–8847–0 (cloth)

    1. Personnel management. 2. Leadership. 3. Employees—Recruiting. I. Silzer, Robert Frank. II. Dowell, Ben E., 1947-

  HF5549.S888 2009

  658.3—dc22

2009020126

Printed in the United States of America
FIRST EDITION
HB Printing 10 9 8 7 6 5 4 3 2 1

Contents

FIGURES, TABLES, AND EXHIBITS

Figures

Tables

Exhibits

Foreword

Talent management is arguably one of the most important topic areas in organizations today. Although there has always been an emphasis both in industrial-organizational (I-O) psychology and among human resource (HR) professionals in identifying, selecting, developing, and retaining the best and the brightest people, as Rob Silzer and Ben E. Dowell note in their Preface, we truly have entered the age of strategic talent. Between the continuous war for talent (which has only increased in urgency rather than decreased, unlike what some predicted would happen in the early part of the decade), the changing demographic nature of the workforce, the aging of the boomers and entrance of the millennials, and the ever increasing pace of change in technology and the financial marketplace, organizations and their leaders are under tremendous pressure to get the talent equation right. They are also burdened with increasing reviews and intrusion from their boards of directors to ensure that robust succession plans are in place and the bench is strong at all levels of leadership.

As a result, talent management as an HR functional area of practice has expanded tremendously over the past five to ten years, with annual conferences, articles in popular outlets, the creation of new roles and shifts in corporate job titles, various practice-based books, and even the introduction of a dedicated monthly magazine, *Talent Management.* Interestingly enough, however, the field of I-O psychology has lagged somewhat behind the curve of the talent management craze. A quick scan and search of past Society of Industrial and Organizational Psychology (SIOP) conference listings regarding the term *talent management* in session titles showed only one session on the topic in 2005 and just four in 2006. Thankfully, the numbers have been increasing since then, along with a fall conference and recent SIOP workshops in this area as well.

Given the absence of an informed I-O psychologist point of view on talent management, however, and following a very well-attended early Saturday morning session on talent management at SIOP a few years back in Dallas, titled, "Talent Management: Will the High Potentials Please Stand Up?" we felt that it was time for the Professional Practice Series to tackle this important and timely topic. To this end, we discussed the idea with Rob and Ben, both of whom were also part of that fateful 2006 session, and asked them to put this book together.

What you have here, *Strategy-Driven Talent Management: A Leadership Imperative,* is the outcome of their efforts. These were considerable efforts; in fact, this is one of the largest volumes in the Professional Practice Series to date. Rob and Ben, and their collection of very high-caliber contributors, have done an excellent job of first defining the strategic talent management landscape and then reviewing a number of key areas of practice, including everything from attracting and recruiting, onboarding, high-potential identification, the different ways of developing leaders, to the engagement of those leaders. Having these practices examined together in one book and discussed in the context of talent management makes this a unique and seminal contribution to the field right out of the gate. That said, Part Three of the book contains a review of a number of critical issues in the area, and Part Four provides applications and case examples from various organizations as well. We are convinced these contributions will make this a coveted resource for HR, I-O, and OD (organization development) practitioners for years to come. The chapter on critical research questions in the talent management area should appeal to academics as well, and the extensive annotated bibliography will be a handy resource for those in the field.

In the end, this book fills a critical and, in our opinion, a rather gaping hole in the I-O practice arena. It brings existing theory and research together from different elements of I-O into one compendium on talent management, which to date has not been directly addressed by the field. We hope that both practitioners and academics alike will find it useful and stimulating, and perhaps even provocative in some areas. It's a job very well done, and we extend our sincerest appreciation to Rob and Ben for bringing this book to life.

■ ■ ■

September 2009

Allan H. Church
Janine Waclawski
Series Editors

Preface

The Imperative of Talent

Talent is becoming recognized as a core competitive asset in business organizations and as the currency of business. Over recent years, companies have widely adopted talent management programs and processes in an effort to attract, select, develop, deploy, engage, and retain talented employees who can help achieve business objectives. At first glance, the broad adoption of talent management programs and initiatives seems to be a blind rush into a new Human Resource (HR) framework. However, based on our own lengthy experience in organizations, we sense that the new focus on talent management is potentially a significant paradigm shift for both organizations and human resources. In working on this book, we leveraged our network of professional colleagues in an array of organizations to see how others are viewing the emerging field of talent management.

Organizations are beginning to understand the strategic value of talent and the impact that strong talent can have on financial outcomes. This represents a major shift in how business executives view the value of Human Resources. In the 1980s and 1990s, effective Human Resource planning was a step in the direction of better utilizing and leveraging talent for business objectives. Companies came to realize that the sustaining element through the ups and downs in business was the critical talent in the organization. Out of that process emerged the idea of actively managing that talent for the organization rather than depending on the ability of the organization to find and hire critical talent just when needed. In addition, organizations discovered that their need for talent, particularly leadership talent, was growing faster than the available supply. These companies realized that successfully buying or building critical talent would create competitive advantage in the global marketplace.

As a result, many organizations started creating and implementing programs, processes, and systems that built the internal talent pool. These efforts included various programs on leadership development, high-potential identification and development, engagement, retention, and others that became known as talent management. At first these programs were just a collection of various existing programs that were clustered together under one function. This would probably describe many current talent management efforts.

Some more ambitious and farsighted organizations saw the value in coordinating efforts across these programs to improve effectiveness and efficiency. They were given common goals and became aligned with each other. This represented an important step forward for HR in integrating these previously independent programs. The directors of these programs and processes now had shared goals and were being evaluated on their combined effort to produce the desired talent. For many companies this is seen as the current leading edge for Human Resource efforts and has made the term *talent management* almost ubiquitous in business organizations today. However, based on our experience, we know that there is an even more significant HR evolution on the horizon. There has been an emerging interest in making Human Resources a strategic function in business. Currently, only a few HR professionals know how to make that happen.

We believe that the coming significant paradigm shift for HR is to *strategic talent management,* which we define as:

- Driven by business strategy
- Integrated with other processes
- Managed as a core business practice
- Engrained as a talent mindset

Organizations are learning how to design and implement talent management programs processes and cultural norms to attract, develop, deploy, and retain the talent that is needed to achieve current and future strategic business objectives. Some leading-edge companies, such as 3M, Microsoft, PepsiCo and GE, are already doing this. In some companies, talent reviews are now a core business process along with strategic business reviews and annual operations reviews. But in the future, even these companies are likely to go further in more strongly connecting talent decisions to financial outcomes. Talent management will also be engrained as a talent mindset that will be adopted as a pervasive cultural norm and expectation.

We are in fact entering the "age of strategic talent," where human capital and talent decisions will be seen as highly critical business decisions. Strategic talent management will evolve into a more rigorous discipline with supportive evidence for making various talent decisions. CEOs and executives will see talent as an asset equally important to financial assets. Chief Human Resource Officers will gain equal status and influence to Chief Financial Officers in organizations. The impact of strategic talent management on financial outcomes will be well known and respected. Both HR professionals and line managers will be expected to have expertise in strategically managing talent. Candidates for executive positions will be evaluated on their expertise and experience in talent management.

Premise of the Book

Organizations are at various stages of this transformation to strategic talent management. The objective of this book is to uncover how organizations are developing and implementing strategic talent management and managing this transformation. We wanted to draw on the experiences and expertise of organizations and professionals who are leading this transformation. The objectives for the book are:

- To identify the leading-edge organizational practices in strategic talent management
- To link business strategies with strategic talent management practices.

We recruited many of the leading-edge talent management experts in business and consulting organizations to be resources and chapter authors for the book. The book includes numerous examples of talent management practices in business organizations, including five chapters that focus on specific companies.

All of the chapter authors have been actively involved in talent management efforts in a range of organizations and are highly experienced in their field, with over 500 years of combined professional experience in organizations. In each chapter, authors were asked to discuss the link between business strategy and talent management efforts and to provide organizational case examples where possible.

The chapter structure is organized around five parts:

- *General Frameworks:* Two introductory chapters discuss the strategic foundation of talent management.
- *Key Practices:* Eight chapters provide insight into key talent management practices such as attracting, recruiting, onboarding, identifying, assessing, developing (through programs, experiences, and coaching), managing, and engaging talent.
- *Critical Issues:* Four chapters discuss talent management in organizational functions, in global organizations and in China, and measuring talent management effectiveness.
- *Different Perspectives:* Six chapters provide five organizational case studies (PepsiCo, Microsoft, Home Depot, Allstate, and Cargill) and interviews with two CEOs and three Chief Human Resource Officers.
- *Future Directions for Practice and Research:* Three chapters that discuss the future of talent management practice, outline key research issues, and provide an Annotated Bibliography that contains 58 core references on strategy-driven talent management.

This book is designed to provide a broad view of talent management practices in organizations. It is not designed to be encyclopedic because of space limitations. The field of talent management is very broad and growing, touching almost all aspects of Human Resource practice. We tried to include many of the key components of talent management but could not include everything (for example, performance management and compensation are not discussed in depth). Nevertheless, we think the book provides a broad leading edge view of how organizations are developing and implementing strategic talent management.

Organizational managers and executives, human resource professionals, and industrial-organizational psychologists will benefit from this book. Organizations will see how other companies are transforming HR and talent management. In addition, professors and graduate students will likely see how this book can guide future research and be added to graduate level courses in psychology departments and business schools. The chapters have over 650 references on talent management and frequently include a discussion of related research issues. A separate research chapter outlining some of the broad research issues related to talent management has also been added to the book to stimulate thinking on issues that need to be further investigated.

We hope that this book will significantly advance the field and support the transformation to strategic talent management by sharing leading-edge thinking and practices.

Acknowledgments

This book is the result of a great deal of hard work by a large number of colleagues, including those developing and implementing talent management strategies and processes in organizations, those who are active in sharing their work with others in the field, and the dedicated chapter authors.

Human resource professionals and industrial-organizational psychologists have been working for many years to introduce leading-edge practices and strategic talent management into their organizations. Often they are bringing significant positive change to their organizations and transforming Human Resource contributions to the business. They often are the unheralded change agents who are building organizations for the future.

Many of our colleagues have shared their leading-edge practices with us and with other organizations. We particularly recognize our colleagues who over the years we have engaged in extended discussions about talent management issues and practices and who have taught us a great deal. They include Seymour Adler (Aon), Steven Ashworth (Sempra Energy), Marcia Avedon (Ingersoll Rand), Bob Barnett (MDA Leadership Consulting), Judy Blanton (RHR), Stephen Cerrone (Sara Lee), Allan Church (PepsiCo), Sandra Davis (MDA Leadership Consulting), Robert Eichinger (formerly with Lominger), John Fulkerson (formerly with PepsiCo), Tim Gartland (Corporate Insights and Development), Karen Grabow (Land O'Lakes), Mirian Graddick-Weir (Merck), George Hollenbeck (formerly at Harvard Business School and Merrill Lynch), Mike Hopp (Lockheed Martin), Dick Jeanneret (Valtera), Leslie Joyce (formerly with Home Depot), Andrea Konz (S. C. Johnson), Mary Lewis (PPG), Dennis Lieberson (formerly with Capital One Financial), Morgan McCall (University of Southern California), Cindy McCauley (Center for Creative Leadership), Mike McDermott (T. Rowe Price), Lance Miyamoto (Comverse), Karen Paul (3M), Pat Pedigo (IBM), Mike Piergrossi (W. R. Grace), David Rodriguez (Marriott), Jeff Schippmann (Balfour Beatty), Gillian Scholes (formerly at Ingersoll Rand), John Scott (APT), Rosemary Slider (formerly at BellSouth), Peter Wentworth (Adams Respiratory Therapeutics, formerly at Pfizer), and Paul Yost (Seattle Pacific University).

We also acknowledge the contributions of the business executives (such as Wayne Callaway of PepsiCo, Larry Bossidy at Allied Signal, and Herb Henkel at Ingersoll Rand) who had the foresight to ask the questions and create the expectations that made the evolution of the field of talent management necessary. They saw how talent management could add strategic value and encouraged ethical practices that contributed to the growth of their businesses and, in turn, the evolution in our field of practice.

This book rests almost entirely on the expertise and commitment of the chapter authors. We applaud their dedication to seeing this project through to the end, despite their heavy work responsibilities. They are the leading-edge thinkers who are moving the field forward in their own organizations.

Thanks are also due for the ongoing support of the SIOP Professional Practice Book series editors, Allan Church and Janine Waclawski, both at PepsiCo. They have remained enthusiastic and supportive from the initial idea to the final book. Also our liaisons at Jossey-Bass, Matt Davis and Lindsay Morton, have been very helpful in coordinating production and marketing efforts.

We thank our mentors along the way. In particular, we are indebted to Marvin Dunnette, who showed us how the science and practice of industrial-organizational psychology can work together to build successful organizations and advance science while simultaneously helping individuals. Our deep gratitude to you, Marv: *We'll be seeing you in all the old, familiar places.*

And finally to our family and friends, who have tolerated our focus on completing this book. They have been patient with the long hours of writing and editing and have been wise enough to pull us out of our obsession with the book when we needed a distraction back into the real world of life.

■ ■ ■

Greenwich Village, Manhattan, New York City   Rob Silzer
Austin, Texas   Ben E. Dowell
April 2009

The Editors

Rob Silzer is Managing Director of HR Assessment and Development, a corporate consulting business, and has consulted with business executives and managers in over 150 organizations, focusing on leadership assessment and development, selection, executive coaching, talent management, and other strategy-driven HR programs. After receiving his Ph.D. in industrial-organizational psychology and counseling psychology from the University of Minnesota, Rob served as Senior Director of Personnel Research for Fieldcrest-Cannon and President of Personnel Decisions–New York before founding his own consulting firm.

Rob is a Fellow of the American Psychological Association (APA), the Association for Psychological Science (APS), the Society of Industrial and Organizational Psychology, and the Society of Consulting Psychology. He has taught Ph.D. courses in industrial and organizational psychology and been Adjunct Professor at the University of Minnesota, New York University, and Baruch College–City University of New York. Currently he is on the doctoral faculty in industrial-organizational psychology at the Graduate School of the City University of New York. Rob has served on the editorial boards of *Personnel Psychology, Industrial and Organizational Psychology: Perspectives on Science and Practice,* and *The Industrial-Organizational Psychologist,* and on the board of Personnel Decisions Research Institute. He has been president of the Metropolitan New York Association of Applied Psychology and cofounder of the Minnesota Industrial Organizational Psychology Association.

Rob has written numerous articles and book chapters in the field of industrial-organizational psychology and has edited several books, including *The 21st Century Executive: Innovative Practices for Building Leadership at the Top* (Jossey-Bass) and, with Dick Jeanneret, *Individual Psychological Assessment: Predicting Behavior in Organizational Settings* (Jossey-Bass). He has frequently delivered workshops and presentations at professional conferences and in client organizations. He enjoys adventure travel, high-altitude mountain trekking, alpine snow skiing, and scuba diving and travels frequently around the world. He lives in Greenwich Village, Manhattan, New York City.

■ ■ ■

Ben E. Dowell is an independent talent management consultant. He retired from the Bristol-Myers Squibb Company in 2006 where he was Vice President of Talent Management. His experience spans 30 years, working primarily within companies to align talent management actions, systems, and processes with the strategic needs of the enterprise. He was with Bristol-Myers Squibb from 1989 to 2006 in a variety of human resource generalist and development roles.

Prior to that, Ben held a number of management development and human resource generalist positions in various divisions of PepsiCo, including Frito-Lay, PepsiCo Foods International, and Pizza Hut. Prior to PepsiCo, he was Assistant Professor of administrative sciences in the Graduate School of Business, Kent State University, and Managing Partner of the Kent Group, a consulting firm he cofounded. Ben received his Ph.D. in industrial-organizational psychology from the University of Minnesota and his B.A. in psychology from the University of Texas.

His writing, speaking, and consulting engagements have focused on talent management processes for senior leaders, integrated leadership development systems, succession planning and management, high-potential development, performance management, integration of new executives, executive coaching, and ethical decision making. Ben enjoys woodworking, metal smithing, golf, and sharing experiences with his family and friends. He now lives in Austin, Texas.

The Contributors

Seymour Adler is Senior Vice President of Talent Solutions consulting at Aon Consulting, where he directs the development and implementation of assessment, talent management, and leadership development programs for clients, many of them global organizations, in the corporate sector as well as with large public sector agencies. After receiving his doctorate in industrial-organizational psychology from New York University, he cofounded Assessment Solutions Incorporated, a firm he helped take public in 1997 and which was acquired by Aon in 2001. In addition to his consulting career, Seymour has taught in graduate industrial-organizational programs at Purdue University, Tel Aviv University, Stevens Institute of Technology, New York University, and Hofstra University. His empirical research has been in the areas of personality, leadership, global mindset, customer service, and onboarding.

Seymour is a Fellow of the Society of Industrial-Organizational Psychology, has served as President of the Metropolitan New York Association of Applied Psychology, and has published widely in both the academic and practitioner literatures.

■ ■ ■

Pooja Anand joined the talent management and learning group at Siemens Corporation in June 2007; her area of focus encompasses talent validation methods of key corporate positions, analysis of employee survey data, and the design and development of communications to high-potential employees. Previously she has worked in India at the World Bank and the Bank of America. Her functional concentration was on marketing and operations—primarily developing strategies to increase and retain market share.

Pooja received her bachelor's degree in industrial psychology from Delhi University, India, and her master's in human resource management from Rutgers University.

■ ■ ■

Marcia J. Avedon is the Senior Vice President of Human Resources and Communications for Ingersoll Rand, a global diversified industrial and technology company with over 60,000 employees. She joined Ingersoll Rand from Merck & Co., where she had companywide responsibilities for all human resource strategies, programs, and policies globally. Previously Marcia was Vice President of Talent Management and Organization Effectiveness for Merck. Marcia has held a variety of HR and communications leadership positions with Honeywell (formerly AlliedSignal), including Vice President of Corporate Human Resources; Vice President of Human Resources and Communications for the Performance Polymers & Chemicals business group; and Director of Organization and Leadership Development for the engineered materials sector. She also held corporate and division human resources and organization development roles with Anheuser-Busch Companies. She began her career with Booz-Allen & Hamilton, spending six years as a management consultant specializing in human capital and organizational development practices.

Marcia holds an M.Phil. and a Ph.D. in industrial-organizational psychology from George Washington University and a B.A. in psychology from the University of North Carolina–Wilmington. She serves on the advisory boards for Cornell University's Center for Advanced Human Resources Studies and the Rutgers Center for Human Resource Strategy. Marcia is a member of the Society for Industrial and Organizational Psychology, HR50, and the HR Policy Association. Marcia served as a board member for Lincoln National Corporation and board president for a nonprofit agency, Jersey Battered Women's Services.

Marcia and her husband, Charles Farrar, have two children and reside in Charlotte, North Carolina. They enjoy traveling, outdoor activities, and the arts.

■ ■ ■

Robert C. Barnett is the Executive Vice President and a Partner at MDA Leadership Consulting in Minneapolis. Bob joined MDA in 1985 and has over 20 years of experience consulting in the areas of organizational psychology and organizational development. At MDA, he specializes in providing executive selection, succession, leadership development, and organizational change services.

Bob earned his B.A. and Ph.D. in psychology from the University of Minnesota and has an M.S. in organizational development from Pepperdine University. He is an Adjunct Associate Professor of management at St. Mary's University of Minnesota, is the author of a number of articles and book chapters, and is a frequent presenter at psychological, management, and human resource professional meetings and conferences. He is a licensed psychologist in the State of Minnesota and a member of the Society of Industrial-Organizational Psychology, and volunteers as a board member for Big Brothers/Big Sisters of the Greater Twin Cities.

■ ■ ■

John W. Boudreau, Professor and Research Director at the University of Southern California's Marshall School of Business and Center for Effective Organizations, is recognized worldwide for breakthrough research on the bridge between superior human capital, talent, and sustainable competitive advantage. His research has won awards from the Academy of Management in human resource management and organizational behavior.

John consults on and conducts executive development with companies worldwide that seek to maximize their employees' effectiveness by discovering the specific strategic bottom-line impact of superior people and human capital strategies. His recent books include *Beyond HR: The New Science of Human Capital,* with Peter M. Ramstad (2007); *Investing in People,* with Wayne F. Cascio (2008); and *Achieving HR Strategic Excellence,* with Edward Lawler (2009).

■ ■ ■

Stephen Cerrone is the Executive Vice President of Global Human Resources and Communications for Sara Lee Corporation, a global manufacturer and marketer of high-quality, brand-name products for consumers throughout the world. Previously he was the head of human resources for retail financial services at JP Morgan Chase, a position he held after the merger between JP Morgan Chase and Bank One in July 2004. Prior to the merger, he was the head of human resources for Bank One.

Stephen joined Bank One in September 2003 from Burger King Corporation, where he was Executive Vice President of Worldwide Human Resources. He started at Burger King Corporation in 1989 and was named head of worldwide human resources there in 1999. During his decade-long career at Burger King, Stephen served as the head of HR for Burger King's Europe/Middle East/Africa unit. He also spent two years as the head of senior leadership training and executive development for GrandMet, Burger King's parent company, in the United Kingdom.

Stephen has a B.A. degree in psychology from Providence College in Rhode Island and an M.A. and Ph.D. in industrial-organizational psychology from the University of Houston. He has served as an adjunct faculty member at the University of Houston and at the University of Miami. Since relocating to Chicago in 2003, he has been elected a member of the board of trustees for Roosevelt University and the board of directors for Hubbard Street Dance Chicago. He is the 2006 recipient of the Academy of Management Distinguished Executive Award.

■ ■ ■

Allan H. Church is Vice President of Talent and Organizational and Management Development for PepsiCo. He is responsible for leading the design of the enterprisewide talent management and people development processes. He joined PepsiCo in December 2000. Previously Allan spent nine years as an external organization development consultant working for Warner Burke Associates, where he designed 360-degree feedback and organizational survey interventions for Fortune 100 clients. He also spent several years at IBM.

Allan has served as an Adjunct Professor at Columbia University, and a Visiting Faculty Scholar at Benedictine University, and is a past chair of the Mayflower Group. He is on the editorial board of several journals, including *Personnel Psychology, Journal of Applied Behavioral Science, Organization Development Practitioner,* and *Team Performance Management.* An active writer, he has authored 4 books, 20 book chapters, and over 120 practitioner and scholarly articles.

Allan received his B.A. in psychology and sociology from Connecticut College and his M.A. and Ph.D. in organizational psychology from Columbia University. He is a Fellow of the Society for Industrial-Organizational Psychology and the American Psychological Association.

■ ■ ■

Jay A. Conger is the Henry Kravis Chaired Professor of Leadership at Claremont McKenna College in California and a visiting professor at the London Business School. In recognition of his extensive work with companies, *BusinessWeek* named him the Best Business School Professor to Teach Leadership and one of the top five management education teachers worldwide. As a management educator and consultant, Jay has worked with over three hundred companies in his 25-year career.

Author of over one hundred articles and book chapters and fourteen books, Jay researches leadership, organizational change, boards of directors, and the training and development of leaders and managers. His most recent books include *Boardroom Realities* (2009), *The Practice of Leadership* (2007), *Growing Your Company's Leaders* (2004), and *Shared Leadership* (2002). He received his B.A. from Dartmouth College, his M.B.A. from the University of Virginia, and his D.B.A. from the Harvard Business School.

■ ■ ■

Sandra L. Davis is the CEO of MDA Leadership Consulting, which she cofounded in 1981. Her extensive consulting experience spans talent management and selection, executive coaching, and leadership development. She focuses on services to MDA's Fortune 100 clients, where she specializes in executive succession, CEO selection, and board development.

Sandra earned her B.S. from Iowa State University and Ph.D. in psychology from the University of Minnesota. A licensed psychologist in the State of Minnesota, an author, and an active member of the Society for Industrial and Organizational Psychology, she speaks regularly at its annual conferences. Sandra currently serves on the boards of the Saint Paul Chamber Orchestra and the Jeremiah Program and is an Iowa State University Foundation governor. A member of Minnesota Women's Economic Roundtable, she has been recognized as a Woman Changemaker by the *Twin Cities Business Journal.*

■ ■ ■

Erika D'Egidio is Director of Talent Management for the Bristol-Myers Squibb Company. She is responsible for partnering with the business to design systems, processes, and programs focused on the identification, selection, development, engagement, and retention of talent within the organization. Since joining Bristol-Myers Squibb in March 2004, she has been responsible for the development and implementation of a variety of functional talent systems.

Previously Erika worked for Jeanneret & Associates, a consulting firm based in Houston, Texas, for nine years. Her work there focused on designing and validating selection systems, providing advice and counsel to clients regarding a variety of human resource processes, and litigation support regarding a variety of employment issues. She has been the coauthor on a number of book chapters related to the O*NET and job component validation. Erika received her Ph.D. and M.A. in industrial-organizational psychology from the University of Houston and her B.A. in psychology from the University of Texas.

■ ■ ■

Joshua B. Fyman is a doctoral candidate at Baruch College–City University of New York. His research has focused on predictors of work team performance, and he has also contributed to research involving the evaluation of work teams, personality testing, job analysis, and bias in the evaluation of managers. As a consultant, Josh has worked with private companies on selection systems at various levels. He has also worked in government as an organizational analyst, designing and conducting organizational surveys as well as providing organizational evaluations. He is currently working on selection and organizational issues at Aish International, a nonprofit organization. In addition, Josh has been an Adjunct Lecturer at Baruch College and Touro College and taught industrial-organizational psychology, work motivation, group dynamics, and research methods.

■ ■ ■

Mirian Graddick-Weir joined Merck & Co. as the Senior Vice President of Human Resources in September 2006. She has responsibility for all aspects of global human resources. She joined Merck from AT&T, where she was Executive Vice President of Human Resources and Employee Communications since 2004. Prior to that, she held a number of human resource positions, including Chief Human Resource officer for the consumer services company, Vice President of Human Resources for business effectiveness, and Vice President of multimedia products and executive HR.

Mirian earned a bachelor's degree in psychology from Hampton University, and a master's degree and a Ph.D. in industrial-organizational psychology from Penn State. She is a member of the board of the Harleysville Group Insurance Company, Jersey Battered Women's Services, National Academy of Human Resources, Human Resources Policy Association, Cornell CAHRS, National Medical Fellowships, Personnel Roundtable, and Kent Place School.

Among her many awards, Mirian received the Distinguished Psychologist in Management award in 2003, the HR Executive of the Year in 2001, and the AT&T Catherine B. Cleary Woman of the Year in 1990. In 2009, she was named in *Black Enterprise Magazine*'s 100 Most Powerful Corporate Executives in America issue. Mirian is married and has five children and one grandchild.

■ ■ ■

Leslie W. Joyce served as Vice President and Chief Learning Officer for The Home Depot, the world's largest home improvement retailer, from 2004 through 2008. She had responsibility for all aspects of designing, developing, and delivering learning and leadership development solutions for Home Depot's 300,000 associates. Her areas of expertise include executive and leadership development, technical training, learning technology, and organizational effectiveness. Leslie joined The Home Depot in 2002 as a Director of Organization Effectiveness, with responsibility for individual, team, and organizational assessment; leadership and competency modeling; selection processes; and organization design and development.

Prior to joining The Home Depot, Leslie was Global Director of Organization Effectiveness for GlaxoSmithKline and responsible for global organizational research and effectiveness programs and processes to include change effectiveness and organization development. Prior to GlaxoSmithKline, she held the role of Vice President of Human Resources and Organizational Development at ClinTrials Research.

Leslie is President of the Atlanta Human Resources Forum and serves on the advisory board for the Executive M.B.A. program at Kennesaw State University, the Atlanta Human Resources Leadership Forum, and the Atlanta chapter of ASTD, and is a founding member of ASTD's Learning Executives Network. She is an active member of the Society of Industrial and Organizational Psychology. Leslie holds a Ph.D. in industrial-organizational psychology from North Carolina State University.

■ ■ ■

Brent W. Mattson is Vice President and Chief Talent Development Officer for the London-based Invensys plc. He has responsibility for all aspects of talent development for Invensys's 25,000 employees. Prior to joining Invensys in 2009, Brent was Senior Vice President of Executive Development and Talent Management at Bank of America and also held a variety of human resource and six sigma leadership roles in GE's Commercial Finance division and with Wells Fargo & Company.

In his consulting, Brent has provided support to public and private sector clients in the areas of change management, acquisition integration, facilitative leadership, conflict resolution, team dynamics, and coaching. He holds a bachelor's degree from St. John's University and master's and doctoral degrees from the University of Minnesota. In addition, Brent served as an adjunct instructor at the University of North Carolina and the University of Minnesota, where he taught graduate courses in psychology and organization development. He is the author or coauthor of over a dozen academic and practitioner-focused articles and book chapters.

■ ■ ■

Suzan McDaniel is Vice President of Talent Management at Hewlitt Packard. She is responsible for identifying and defining talent management strategies and solutions. She joined Hewlitt Packard in July 2009. Previously, she spent eight years at Bristol-Myers Squibb, where she was most recently Vice President of Global Talent Management acquisition and diversity and accountable for designing end-to-end talent-management processes, including the development and implementation of functional talent systems. Suzan has also been a Human Resources business partner and a leadership development specialist at Bristol-Myers Squibb.

Prior to joining Bristol-Myers Squibb, Suzan was a consultant at Hogan Assessment Systems for five years. She began her career at Ford Motor Company Glass Division as a learning and development specialist. Suzan received her Ph.D. and M.A. in industrial-organizational psychology and her B.A. in psychology from the University of Tulsa.

■ ■ ■

Mary Mannion Plunkett has more than 18 years of experience in the field of leadership and organization development, including roles with The Boeing Company, Ernst & Young LLP, and McDonnell Douglas Aircraft Company. She most recently served as the head of talent management for Lehman Brothers

Europe and the Middle East and as Vice President of Executive Development for BP plc. Mary received a Ph.D. in organizational psychology from St. Louis University.

■ ■ ■

Steven G. Rogelberg is Professor of organizational science and Professor of psychology at the University of North Carolina at Charlotte. In addition, he serves as Director of organizational science, and is the founder and Director of the Organizational Science Consulting and Research Unit. He has produced over 50 publications and 25 invited addresses or colloquiums addressing issues such as team effectiveness, health and employee well-being, meetings at work, organizational research methods, and organizational development. Steven served as Editor-in-Chief of the two-volume *Encyclopedia of Industrial and Organizational Psychology* (2006) and the *Handbook of Research Methods in Industrial and Organizational Psychology* (2002, 2004). He currently serves as Editor of the Talent Management Essentials book series and the *Journal of Business and Psychology*.

Recent honors include serving as program chair for the Society of Industrial and Organizational Psychology (SIOP); chair of the SIOP Education and Training committee and of SIOP's Katrina Relief and Assistance effort; and receiving the 2001 Bowling Green State University (BGSU) Psi Chi Professor of the Year Award and the BGSU Master Teacher Award. His research has been profiled on public television and radio, and in newspapers and magazines. Companies for which he has provided consulting services include IBM, Grace Cocoa, Vulcan Materials, Procter & Gamble, Toledo Area Regional Transit Authority, Mid-American Information Services, and Marshall-Qualtec. He received his Ph.D. in industrial and organizational psychology from the University of Connecticut.

■ ■ ■

Thomas Ruddy joined Becton Dickinson (BD) in April 2008 as Vice President of Talent Management and Learning and Development. He is responsible for identification, assessment, development, and advancement of leaders to drive BD's future business growth. Previously Tom was the senior director of talent management and learning campus for Siemens, USA. His responsibilities included the identification, development, and movement of talent within Siemens United States. He joined Siemens in June 2000. Tom previously had responsibility for the first wave of Siemens's HR transformation, including the deployment of Siemens global employee portal as well as e-enabling HR processes. He had HR business partner responsibility for Siemens Corporation USA.

Prior to joining Siemens, Tom was the manager of knowledge management for Xerox Worldwide Customer Services. He was appointed to that position in September 1997. At Xerox, he was responsible for developing knowledge management strategies for customer services, including the global deployment of Eureka, a system for the authoring and sharing of technical knowledge. In addition, he had responsibility for Xerox empowered team strategy for worldwide customer services in over 35 countries. Prior to his time in customer services, he worked for six years in Xerox human resources in a variety of areas, including employee selection, employee engagement, and succession planning. Tom has conducted extensive research in the areas of knowledge management, team effectiveness, total quality management, organizational structure, performance evaluation, employee retention, customer satisfaction, leadership development, and employee selection and assessment. He joined Xerox in 1984 as the manager of selection research for Xerox U.S. customer operations.

Tom received his doctorate in industrial-organizational psychology from Bowling Green State University in 1989. Tom and his wife, Nancy, daughter Natalie, and son Sean live in Mountain Lakes, New Jersey.

■ ■ ■

Jeff Schippmann is the Senior Vice President of Human Resources and Chief People Officer for the U.S. segment of Balfour Beatty plc (Balfour Beatty Construction), where his responsibilities include oversight of all aspects of human resources. Previously he was the Vice President of Global Talent

Management for the Hess Corporation, where he managed all succession planning, performance management, talent assessment, and management development and training activities for this $30 billion global oil and gas company. Previous to Hess, Jeff was the Director of Organization and Management Development for PepsiCo. In this role, he was responsible for a broad range of talent management activities and internal consulting projects over a six-year period, including significant work to refocus managers on people development activities and restructuring the PepsiCo "employment deal." Jeff was also in consulting with Personnel Decisions International in a variety of roles focusing on selection and staffing solutions, executive assessment and development, assessment centers, and competency modeling.

Jeff is the author of two books describing best practices in executive assessment and competency modeling, and his research has appeared in a number of scholarly journals, including *Journal of Applied Psychology* and *Personnel Psychology*. He received his Ph.D. from the University of Memphis.

■ ■ ■

Gillian Scholes is an independent consultant specializing in organizational strategy, succession management, and executive development. She has held leadership positions in high-technology and industrial firms, including roles in strategic business planning, organization development, and talent management. She began her career with Digital Equipment Corporation in the United Kingdom and was most recently Vice President of Organization and Leadership Development for Ingersoll Rand Company.

Gillian has extensive experience in leading strategic organizational change, creating talent management processes, and selecting and developing senior leaders. She has managed succession plans at the senior executive level and built global pipelines of talent to meet future business needs. Her focus is on helping organizations and executives implement their goals and achieve their full potential.

Gillian holds a B.A. from London University, an M.B.A from the London Business School, and an M.S in applied behavioral science from American University/NTL Institute. She is a founding board member of the Global Leadership Program, an international consortium for executive development managed by MESA Research.

■ ■ ■

John C. Scott is Vice President and cofounder of APT, a human resource consulting firm based in Darien, Connecticut. He directs consulting services in the area of talent management and has implemented human resource solutions for Fortune 100 companies and market innovators across a broad range of industries, including pharmaceuticals, electronics, consumer products, retail, telecommunications, hospitality, transportation, electric and gas utilities, aeronautics, and financial services. John is the chief architect of APT's HR platform, APTMetrics, which has yielded APT's suite of automated Web-based talent management solutions.

John is an expert in the field of human resource evaluation. He is an author and frequent lecturer on the subject. He is coeditor of *The Human Resources Program Evaluation Handbook,* a guide to human resource evaluation, and coauthor of *Evaluating Human Resources Programs: A Six-Phase Approach for Optimizing Performance.* He has also authored numerous chapters and articles in the areas of assessment, selection, and organizational surveys.

John is the past conference program chair for Division 14 of the American Psychological Association and the 2009 Society of Industrial-Organizational Psychology convention program chair, and he serves on several Professional Practice Book Series editorial boards. John received his Ph.D. in industrial-organizational psychology from the Illinois Institute of Technology in 1985.

■ ■ ■

Lorraine Stomski is a Senior Vice President and practice leader for leadership development and executive coaching in Aon Consulting's human capital group. She is responsible for the design and delivery of global leadership development and executive onboarding programs for top talent in a wide variety of organizations. Her areas of expertise include leadership development and retention of top talent, executive coaching and onboard-ing, and talent management strategy. Lorraine holds a Ph.D. in industrial-organizational psychology from Stevens Institute of Technology and has been an I-O practitioner for over 20 years.

■ ■ ■

Janine Waclawski is Vice President of Human Resources for the PepsiCo Foodservice Division, a $3 billion division of PepsiCo. She is the chief personnel officer for the division and a member of the senior leadership team. Prior to this role, she was Director of HR for Pepsi Cola North America, partnering with marketing, joint ventures, public affairs, corporate devel-opment, and finance. She joined PepsiCo in 2002 as the direc-tor of organization and management development. Previously Janine was a principal consultant in the strategic change practice of PricewaterhouseCoopers and a senior consultant at Warner Burke Associates. As a consultant, she specialized in organization development and change and executive development through the use of data-driven methods.

Janine has been an Adjunct Professor at Columbia University and Hunter College and has published over 25 articles and book chapters. She has also coauthored two books with Allan Church— *Designing and Using Organization Surveys* and *Organization Development: A Data Driven Approach to Organizational Change*— both published by Jossey-Bass. Janine received her B.A. in psy-chology from the State University of New York at Stony Brook and her M.Phil. and Ph.D. from Columbia University

■ ■ ■

Elizabeth Weldon is Professor of management and Academic Director of Custom Executive Education at the China Europe International Business School (CEIBS) in Shanghai, China. Previously she served as an Adjunct Associate Professor at the Hong Kong University of Science and Technology and as the H. Smith Richardson, Jr. Visiting Fellow at the Center for Creative Leadership (CCL). She was also Professor of organization behav-ior at IMD International in Lausanne, Switzerland, where she taught and designed executive programs focused on leadership, corporate renewal, and strategic human resource management. Elizabeth has served on the faculties of Indiana University, the Kellogg Graduate School of Management at Northwestern University, and the University of Illinois; worked as an invited professor in the Executive M.B.A. program at Beijing University in the People's Republic of China; and taught executive courses at the China Europe International Business School in Shanghai.

In addition to teaching awards, Elizabeth has received awards for her research from the Organization Behavior Division of the Academy of Management and the Society for Industrial and Organizational Psychology, a division of the American Psychological Association. She is the coeditor of Volume 4 of *Advances in Global Leadership* (2006) and *Management and Organizations in China* (2000). She is doing research in three areas: the design of fast, agile organizations; the effectiveness of Western leadership development practices in Asia; and leadership development in Chinese companies.

■ ■ ■

Paul R. Yost is Associate Professor of industrial-organizational psychology at Seattle Pacific University. He previously served as a senior research specialist at Microsoft with responsibilities in talent management and executive assessment and as manager of leadership research with the Boeing Company, where his work focused on leadership development, learning from experience, training program design and evaluation, and employee surveys. Other experience includes positions at GEICO Insurance and Battelle Research, with responsibilities in managerial training, assessment and selection, and team development.

Paul's ongoing research and writing focus on experience-based leadership development including *Real Time Leadership Development*, coauthored with Mary Mannion Plunkett. Paul received his Ph.D. in industrial-organizational psychology from the University of Maryland.

Part One

General Frameworks

CHAPTER 1

STRATEGIC TALENT MANAGEMENT MATTERS

Rob Silzer, Ben E. Dowell

A Leadership Imperative

Why do organizations succeed or fail? Ultimately it comes down to talent. Did the organization have the talent to make the right decisions regarding where to invest financial and human resources, how to innovate and compete, and how to energize and direct the organization to achieve the business strategy? For good or ill, people make the decisions and take the actions that result in the success or failure of their organization. Many times CEOs (chief executive officers) get all the credit or all the blame, but in our experience, it is the quality of talent throughout the organization that ultimately leads to the creation and effective execution of successful strategy. Gary Hamel argues that "people are all there is to an organization" (cited in Sears, 2003). Collins (2001) suggests that having the right people comes before having the right strategies.

Have you ever asked a CEO or senior executive what issues he or she spends the most time on and worries about the most? Based on our sixty years of combined business experience across many corporations, our answer is that the most effective CEOs and senior executives focus as much on talent issues as they do on financial issues. Jack Welch (2006) made the point that talent management deserves as much focus as financial capital management in corporations. Larry Bossidy (2001) concludes that "there is no way to spend too much time on obtaining and developing the best people." Other CEOs in a recent interview study seem to agree, suggesting that talent management takes as much as 50 percent of their time (Economist Intelligence Unit & Development Dimensions International, 2006; Silzer, 2002a). Similar conclusions are reached on the critical importance of talent and talent management by other professionals and thinkers in the field and by various executive and corporate surveys (Bernthal & Wellins, 2005; Hewitt Associates, 2005; Michaels, Handfield-Jones, & Axelrod, 2001; Corporate Leadership Council, 2006; Morton, 2004; Lawler, 2008; American Productivity and Quality Center, 2004).

Financial resources may be the lifeblood of a company, but human resources are the brains. It has long been accepted that sound financial management is critical to business survival. This is especially true in challenging economic times. However, having strong talent and sound talent management is equally critical to business survival.

Linking Talent and Talent Management to Financial Outcomes

There has been some agreement that having strong talent in the company has a positive impact on business outcomes (Lawler, 2008; Michaels et al., 2001). A McKinsey survey of 4,500 senior managers and officers at 56 U.S. companies (Axelrod, Handfield-Jones, & Welsh, 2001) found that senior executives report that "A" players, (defined as the best 20 percent of managers) who are in operational roles raise productivity by 40 percent over average performers; those who are in general management roles raise profitability by 49 percent over average performers; and those who are in sales roles raise sales revenues 67 percent more than average performers.

One manufacturing company found that the best plant managers increased profits by 130 percent, while the worst managers brought no improvement. It should be noted that the productivity ratings were survey estimates by senior executives, so the estimates may include some subjective bias.

Business executives have suggested that talent management practices need to lead to measurable financial business results.

Gubman (1998, p. 294) reviews the "large and growing body of evidence from a variety of sources that shows being an employer that values its workforce, demonstrates it, and tries to improve talent management practices tied to business strategy pays off with better long term financial performance." He suggests that "more than 100 pieces of research have been conducted in the last 10 to 15 years trying to connect management practices with financial success."

Some studies connect having a people-oriented culture with financial gains. For example, Collins and Porras (1994) found that the cumulative stock return since 1926 for visionary companies, defined as "role models for management practices around the globe," outperformed the general stock market by more than 15 times. However companies matched to the visionary companies on other factors outperformed the general market by only two times. When they investigated how these visionary companies "construct their culture," they found differentiating criteria that include these talent management practices:

- Extensive new employee orientation
- Use of selection and rewards to align employees with company values
- Formal management development programs
- Careful succession planning and CEO selection
- Investment in human capabilities through recruiting, training, and development

Pfeffer (1994) first identified companies with the highest total return to shareholders (stock appreciation plus dividend yield) and discovered that they differ from other companies on the way they managed people, with some specific distinctions in selection, training, labor relations, or staffing.

A number of studies looked at how the number of talent management practices used might relate to financial performance. Huselid (1995) rank-ordered 700 companies and grouped them by quintiles based on the number of basic talent management practices (such as recruiting, selection, training, performance appraisal, and pay practices) they used in their company. He demonstrated a significant and progressive increase in annual shareholder return and gross return on capital, with higher-quintile companies showing progressively larger returns. A follow-up study on 986 companies with a more refined list of management practices found a significant increase in sales per employee, market value per employee, and cash flow per employee and a decrease in turnover for companies that used more of the human resource (HR) practices (Huselid, 1995).

McKinsey followed up their original research, *The War for Talent* (Michaels et al., 2001), with several more extensive survey studies. In a 2000 McKinsey survey of 6,900 managers, including 4,500 senior managers and officers at 56 U.S. companies, Axelrod et al. (2001) concluded that the companies doing the best job of managing talent (in the top 20 percent on self-identified talent management practices) outperform their industry's mean return to shareholders by 22 percent.

McKinsey also looked at the impact of global talent management practices. In a study of 22 global companies and 450 CEOs, senior managers, and HR professionals, Guthridge and Komm (2008) sorted the companies into three groups based on their combined company score on ten dimensions of global talent management practices. The research found a significant relationship between a company's global talent management score and financial performance. Companies scoring in the top third based on a combined talent management score earned $168 average profit per employee compared to $93 for the bottom third of companies. The following are the talent practices that most distinguished the companies in the top and the bottom thirds on the combined talent scores:

1. Creating globally consistent talent evaluation processes
2. Achieving cultural diversity in global setting and
3. Developing and managing global leaders

Companies achieving top third scores for any one of these three practice areas had "a 70 percent chance of achieving top third financial performance" (p. 4). In other words, doing any one of these practices seemed to relate to higher financial performance. Other talent practice areas that also distinguished the top third from the bottom third were translating human resources information into action, creating internal talent pools, and sourcing and recruiting global talent.

Several researchers have looked at the link between a specific talent practice and financial measures. Danielle McDonald at Hewitt Associates studied 432 companies (cited in Gubman, 1998) and looked at the impact of having a formal performance management process versus having no process, or a simple informal one, on financial measures. She found a significant link to higher return on equity (ROE), return on assets (ROA), return on investment (ROI), total shareholder return, sales per employee, and income per employee over a three-year period. The study concluded that companies with a formal performance management process had higher profits, better cash flows, stronger market performance, and greater stock value. In addition, McDonald looked at financial indicators before and after performance management process implementation and found statistically significant improvements after implementation in total shareholder return (24.8 percent increase) and sales per employee (94.2 percent increase) over a three-year period.

Other studies found similar links to financial results for other practices. Bernthal and Wellins (2005) showed a relationship between having stronger leadership development systems and higher ROE and profit for companies when compared to competitors. A 1999 study by the Sibson & Company and McKinsey Associates (cited in Wellins, Smith, & McGee, 2006) showed a link between the quality of the company's succession management program and increased shareholder returns. And studies by Lawler, Mohrman, and Ledford (1995) found a significant relationship between the use of employee involvement programs in a company and larger ROA, ROI, ROE, and return on sales, but the use of the programs had only a modest impact on employee productivity measures and no impact on total return to investors. However, one study by Watson Wyatt Worldwide (2001) found that the use of a multirater feedback survey had a negative correlation with organizational performance. Perhaps poorer performing companies saw a greater need to improve management performance by giving competency ratings feedback to managers.

In general, the relationship between the implementation of talent management practices and an impact on business results is a difficult area to study because of the confounding list of other variables that might also have an impact on these financial outcomes. From our perspective, there does seem to be a link between talent practices and financial outcome measures, but it would be premature to conclude that it is causal.

In many successful business corporations, talent management receives attention similar to that given to financial management. It is a leadership imperative for them. For many years, leading companies have seen effective talent management as a competitive advantage over other companies that give limited attention to their talent. Leading corporations, among them, PepsiCo, Microsoft, Home Depot, Ingersoll Rand, Cargill, and Allstate (all explored in individual chapters in this book), understand that talent management is more than just a competitive advantage; it is a fundamental requirement for business success. These corporations tend to have talent management systems and processes that are both integrated and strategic—focused on achieving specific business objectives. A frequent and comprehensive talent review is now often seen as one of the core business processes in the corporation, along with operational reviews and financial reviews.

Business Reasons for Talent Management

Talent management is now more than a desirable HR program: it is a leadership imperative. It is difficult for any business corporation to succeed in the long term without making talent central to the business model. This is particularly true because of the complex business challenges that need to be addressed.

The business environment since the early 1990s has gone through a significant expansion with falling trade barriers and the globalization of business. For many companies, growth has come through global expansion, particularly into China and India. This expansion has put a premium on having the global talent needed to support these initiatives (McCall & Hollenbeck, 2002; Sloan, Hazucha, & Van Katwyk, 2003) and has provided great visibility to successful global leaders (Kets DeVries & Florent-Treacy, 1999). This has resulted in greater competition for the best talent (Michaels et al., 2001). The growing worldwide demand for talent, along with the shrinking availability of exceptional talent, has made talent acquisition, development, and retention a major strategic challenge in many companies.

The business world is changing in many ways and there are a number of factors that have contributed to the critical significance of talent:

- An increasing worldwide demand for talented leaders and executives with the growth of emerging markets in Asia and Latin America
- A shrinking pool of experienced and talented leaders in the Americas, Europe, and Japan
- The complexity and faster pace of global business and the need to have talent available to adapt quickly to changing business conditions
- The realization that within an industry there are specific organizational capabilities necessary to achieve competitive advantage and a need to recruit and retain the leading talent with specialized competence to build that capability
- The difficulty of retaining critical talent due to a shift to self-managed professional careers where talented individuals aggressively pursue their careers and actively seek advancement by moving across different companies and geographic boundaries

Corporations have gone through several business cycles since the 1980s and have learned some lessons about being successful. One major trend has been to look carefully at internal costs and expenses and identify as many ways as they can to make sure the organization runs as efficiently and lean as possible. For example, this has led to centralized shared services, outsourced functions, and an ongoing expectation that a compelling business case needs to be made to retain or invest in a function, program, or initiative to determine if it continues to add value or will add value in the future to the corporation. The strategic objectives of the company are now central to most business decisions. Executives want to clearly see how a function, program, or initiative contributes to achieving their specific business strategies.

Strategically Driven Human Resources

Most organizational functions and capabilities must now demonstrate their strategic value to the company. The Human Resources function is now under the same scrutiny. HR, like other corporate functions, has increasingly been judged by its contributions to the company's strategic objectives (Guthridge, Komm, & Lawson, 2008; Hewitt, 1997; Ulrich, 1997; Beer, 1997). Some of the expectations of Human Resources include:

- Playing a critical role in identifying, developing, and protecting core organizational capabilities, and the supporting individual competencies, that enhance or establish competitive advantage
- Identifying and delivering the talented individuals who have the competencies required to achieve competitive advantage
- Finding global talent and pursuing talent strategies that support entering or surviving in other geographic markets
- Considering outsourcing to external vendors or handling by information technology some traditional HR functions, particularly administrative activities, that do not provide competitive advantage
- Ensuring that compensation, benefits, and other HR areas play significant roles in making the challenging decisions involved in designing systems to attract and retain talent while minimizing unnecessary costs
- Improving HR productivity by shifting to a more consultative role, advising line managers on how to better align their management approach, systems, and processes to achieve business objectives

As a result, senior executives are learning how to effectively leverage Human Resources and talent management for greater strategic impact. Programs and initiatives are increasingly expected to align with and be driven by specific business objectives and strategies.

Matching Executive Talent to Business Strategy

One example of how human resource efforts have become more strategically driven is in the selection of senior executives. Companies that are having business problems or a lack of financial success often face significant public scrutiny of the executives running the company. Frequently these concerns lead to the termination of the CEO or other associated executives. The 2008 financial industry crisis, although an extreme example, shows that senior executives are increasingly held personally accountable for poor company performance and are severed from the company. Boards of directors are now more likely to step up to their own accountability to various stakeholders by changing the senior management. The actual rate of executive turnover is not precisely known (Hollenbeck, 2009), but there is some general agreement that it is high.

There may be several reasons for executive turnover. Hollenbeck (2009) suggests that executive selection techniques may be at fault. We have been observing executives for many years, and it has become apparent to us that executive failure can also be caused by poorly matching candidates to the business situation and strategy. Few executives are equally effective in dealing with different business environments and challenges, and different business strategies may require different leadership approaches (for example, high-growth versus restructuring and cost-control business environments). Few would argue against the observation that executives now face a constantly changing business environment. Simultaneously financial analysts and stockholders in public companies now insist on faster organizational responses to changing business conditions in order to maintain steady financial returns.

Our experience suggests that most individual senior executives are more likely to be successful in some environments than others. A senior executive who is hired specifically for the skills and abilities to drive business growth may be less well matched for undertaking a major corporate restructuring or cost-reduction effort. An executive with a strong track record of financial management and analysis may be more effective in a business cycle that requires strong financial control than one that requires a focus on product or service innovation.

Increasingly we are getting more effective at identifying the type of talent needed for different strategies. Talent management professionals are becoming more skilled at determining which talent profiles would be more successful than other profiles for accomplishing certain strategies. We can better match individual executives to particular executive positions and companies. There is an increasing expectation that the talents of an individual or executive team need to match business strategies and organizational demands. While this has been suggested in the past

(Gerstein & Reisman, 1983; DeVries, 1992; Silzer, 2002b), it is now being given more attention in executive selection decisions. Corporations are now more likely to carefully outline the specific business environment and business strategies and identify the specific executive skills and abilities required in the position. An effort is made to select executive candidates whose talent profile matches the position and business situation.

There is some risk that a match to near-term requirements may ignore longer-term executive requirements. If a candidate is well matched to the immediate executive opportunity and business strategy, the individual may be less well matched for new strategies and situations as the business evolves and changes. The decision to focus on fidelity to current needs, or maximizing the short-term match, can result in a mismatch over the longer term when the business requirements later change.

Executive failure can occur sooner if the candidate is not a good match for the immediate business situation and later if the candidate is not well matched to different future challenges. Either way, the talent must be the right fit for the situation and the strategies. Unfortunately, there are few executives who can be equally effective in a range of business situations, which is one reason executive tenure, particularly CEO tenure, is declining.

In general, corporations are beginning to better match talent with longer-term business strategy. However, the quality of the match may last only as long as the business strategy and business environment stay the same. For some companies in some industries with little change, this approach works well. Some leading companies, particularly those in fast-changing industries or global markets, now recruit or identify internal executives who have fungible skills and abilities that can adapt to different business situations and demands. This still focuses on identifying and matching individuals to the business environment and strategy but tries to identify broadly talented, fungible individuals who can learn and adapt to new business requirements. For example, some companies such as Bristol-Myers Squibb are enhancing their executive selection methods by supplementing assessments of an executive's ability to achieve short-term strategic objectives with an assessment of the executive's ability to learn and adapt to new strategies and business conditions.

This ability to adapt to future needs is receiving significant weight in selection decisions.

Talent management efforts must produce the talent needed to achieve specific business strategies. Numerous examples throughout this book show the link between talent and business strategies. Although generally the business strategy drives the talent strategy, sometimes the reverse happens. Some companies are becoming more sophisticated in assessing the existing talent in the organization and developing business strategies that best leverage that talent (companies with entrepreneurial talent starting new businesses or companies that are good at customer service starting new service businesses). At other times, companies have realized that they had a shortage of talent in a particular area and were unable to pursue a desired strategic initiative.

What Is Talent?

The term *talent* dates back to ancient Greeks and biblical times, starting out as measure of weight, then becoming a unit of money, and later meaning a person's value or innate abilities (Michaels et al., 2001). We might now refer to a person with innate abilities as a "gifted" individual.

We could make a distinction between individuals who have innate abilities in an area (who are gifted) and those who have learned their skills and knowledge. Of course, people have a mix of natural and learned abilities and skills. That distinction, however, is not common in organizations, so our use of the term *talent* includes people with both innate and learned skills.

In organizations *talent* can refer to:

- An individual's skills and abilities (*talents*) and what the person is capable of doing or contributing to the organization
- A specific person (*she is a talent*, usually implying she has specific skills and abilities in some area) or
- A group (*the talent*) in an organization

In groups *talent* can refer to a pool of employees who are exceptional in their skills and abilities either in a specific technical area (such as software graphics skills) or a competency (such as consumer marketing talent), or a more general area (such as general managers or high-potential talent). And in some cases, "the talent" might refer to the entire employee population. Many companies now have multiple talent pools, beyond their high-potential pool. Other versions have been called *acceleration pools* (Byham, Smith, & Paese, 2002) and *pivotal talent pools* (Boudreau & Ramstad, 2005), which are different ways to define a talent pool and guide decisions about talent and on how much to invest in them.

Over the years as companies have delayered, eliminated bureaucratic systems, and globalized, the nature of organizational talent has changed (see Sears, 2003, for a summary) from a focus on division of labor distinctions to an evaluation of strategic contributions. Sears suggests that "talent is knowledge" (as a competitive advantage) and that it is shaped by what customers value. For the purpose of this discussion, we will use the three definitions of talent listed above.

Defining Talent Management

Talent management is an emerging concept in corporations. Although the term *talent management* is becoming more widely used, it does not have a single, clear definition. Discussions about talent management often focus on what processes or components are included and what types of talent are managed. The term is often used informally without any specific definition. Lewis and Heckman (2006) found a variety of definitions for talent management—as a process, as an outcome, and as a specific decision—which adds to the confusion.

Some people use *talent management* as a synonym for *human resource management* and nothing more. This meaning essentially includes all of the traditional human resource processes: recruiting, selection, development, human resource planning, performance management, retention, and others. There are even suggestions that some organizations are considering renaming the human resources department as the talent management department, although we know of no actual examples where this has been done. The title of Director or Vice President of Talent Management is becoming common in major organizations. With each of the past name evolutions, from employee relations, to personnel, to human resources, there has been a reconceptualization of the function, resulting in a different approach to the function. Similarly, the introduction of the term *talent management* may provide the business world with an opportunity to establish a new definition and expectation for HR performance and effectiveness. While we are not advocating that HR change its name, we do think that talent management represents something much more than just a collection of existing HR processes.

Talent management has been used more narrowly either as a new term for an existing HR function (as a substitute for succession planning, human resource planning, or leadership development) or to focus on a select group of employees (individuals who are seen as having exceptional skills and abilities or having the potential to handle greater responsibility). We think the use of *talent management* to refer to only a small group of employees or a singular process is too narrow and potentially damaging to an organization. Both approaches can exclude large groups of employees from the talent management process.

This issue is related to the current discussion among human resource professionals on where to invest employee development funds. One argument is to make significant investments in the broad group of employees and not just in a select group (such as the high-potential pool) since their continued strong performance and personal growth is important to the organization. Others (Boudreau & Ramstad, 2005) argue that organizations should differentially invest in special groups of employees—the "pivotal talent"—that are more strategically important to the organization and invest much less, if at all, in other less critical employee groups.

The term *talent management* could include a long list of HR processes and components and cover only some, most, or all employees. Varied definitions are being used. (See the sample definitions in Table 1.1.) Some definitions are very narrow and focus only on a single process or employee group, while other definitions are so broad and all inclusive that it is difficult to know what they intend to include.

Lewis and Heckman (2006) criticize many definitions of talent management as having no clear meaning or not being sufficiently

Table 1.1. Sample Definitions of Talent Management

Source	Definition of Talent Management
Avedon (see Chapter 20, this book)	Talent Management: " . . . is an integrated set of processes and procedures used in an organization to attract, onboard, retain, develop and move talent, as well as to exit talent, to achieve strategic objectives."
Graddick-Weir (see Chapter 20, this book)	" . . . is our ability to attract, develop and retain key diverse talent to meet critical current and future business needs."
Cerrone (see Chapter 20, this book)	" . . . is attracting, retaining, and developing the right people with the right skills in the right roles."
Cappelli (2008b)	" . . . is the process through which employers anticipate and meet their needs for human capital . . . " (p. 1). " . . . the goal is the more general and important task helping the organization achieve its overall objectives" (p. 5).
Lawler (2008)	" . . . an outstanding talent management system . . . attracts the right talent and helps them understand exactly what to expect from their work experience with the company. . . . also provides employees with the kind of development experiences that build the organization's capabilities and core competencies so they retain the right talent" (p. 63).
Morton (2004)	Focuses on a series of eight categories of individual initiatives and how they fit together to comprise TM. Talent is defined as "individuals who have the capability to make a significant difference to the current and future performance of the company" (p. 10).

Wellins et al. (2006)	" . . . is the recruitment, development, promotion and retention of people, planned and executed in line with your organization's current and future business goals" (p. 2).
Sloan et al. (2003)	" . . . is managing global leadership talent strategically, to put the right person in the right place at the right time" (p. 236).
American Productivity and Quality Center (2004)	. . . is "the cradle to grave processes to recruit, develop, and retain employees within an organization" (p. 1).
Jackson & Schuler (1990)	Human resource planning is to "ensure the right person in the right job at the right time" (p. 235).

strategic. However, we think there is great value in the term and suggest that it can be useful, strategic, and grounded in business reality. Our definition of talent management can be found in Exhibit 1.1.

Our definition does not focus on any single HR process but rather includes a range of activities that attract, develop, deploy, and retain. We think this definition captures the core objectives and components of talent management.

Talent Management Components

There is some emerging agreement on which HR activities should be included under the umbrella of talent management, and includes activities that benefit or focus on individuals such as recruiting, staffing, development, performance management and retention. These seem to most clearly connect with managing the talent in the organization. However many, if not most, HR activities and processes are somewhat connected to talent management. See Table 1.2 for this list.

Exhibit 1.1. Core Talent Management Definition: Silzer and Dowell

Talent management is an integrated set of processes, programs, and cultural norms in an organization designed and implemented to attract, develop, deploy, and retain talent to achieve strategic objectives and meet future business needs.

A recent HR executive interview study by the Conference Board identified the components of talent management as recruitment, retention, professional development, leadership and high-potential development, performance management, feedback and measurement, workforce planning, and culture (Morton, 2004). Others might argue that additional HR activities and systems should also be included as components or that some activities on the Conference Board list might not always be directly connected to talent management.

For example, compensation systems are often leveraged to attract and retain talent in organizations. One could argue that this is the main purpose of compensation: to attract, motivate, and retain particular individuals or groups of employees, such as sales representatives or engineers. So for specific groups and specific individuals, the compensation system is often used to manage talent in an organization. However, compensation is not usually seen as part of talent management. There are other HR activities, (see Table 1.2) such as organization culture initiatives, employee engagement programs, and employee surveys that at times might contribute to attracting, developing, deploying, and retaining talent.

There is another group of HR activities and processes that few people would specifically include in talent management. These activities, such as organizational development, focus more clearly on organizational issues and seem only tangentially related to talent issues. Employee benefits usually falls in this category as well, primarily because of federal regulations and labor agreements

Table 1.2. Talent Management Components

Included Under Talent Management?	*Human Resource Activities and Functions*
Usually included	Recruiting
	Selection, promotion
	Placement, assignments
	Onboarding, assimilation
	Retention initiatives
	Reward and recognition programs (other than compensation)
	Training, development, learning opportunities
	Coaching, mentoring
	Leadership and executive education and development
	Performance management
	Career planning and development
	High-potential identification and development
	Employee diversity efforts
	Succession management and planning
	Organizational talent reviews
	Measurement and evaluation of talent management efforts
Sometimes included	Compensation systems, recognition programs
	Organizational culture initiatives
	Organizational values initiatives
	Organizational capability development efforts
	Organizational structure changes
	Workforce planning
	Employee engagement
	Employee surveys
	Work and job design

(Continued)

Table 1.2. Talent Management Components (*Continued*)

Included Under Talent Management?	Human Resource Activities and Functions
Usually not included	Labor relations strategies
	Employee and labor negotiations
	Organizational development
	Organizational change efforts
	Organizational design
	Employee benefits
	Lifestyle initiatives (such as flextime)
	Termination and severance processes
	HR information systems

that dictate certain required components. However, organizations have begun to offer employees some benefit options. For example, there are choices around flextime, when to take personal holidays, and level of health coverage. Some employees are now making career decisions based on the attractiveness of benefits offered at different companies. Kalamas, Mango, and Ungerman (2008) argue that employee benefits should be seen as a competitive weapon and clearly linked to talent management efforts.

Some people might argue that all HR activities and processes contribute to and should be included under the umbrella of talent management. They are likely to see *talent management* and *human resource management* as synonymous. Most HR professionals, however, see these as different from each other (see a related discussion in Chapter 20) and view human resource management as the larger umbrella including essentially everything listed in Table 1.2.

Talent Management Model

Talent management must not just coexist with many other organizational programs and systems but also support and coordinate with them. It must be driven by the business strategies and in turn help drive business results. This relationship is represented

Figure 1.1. Talent Management Framework

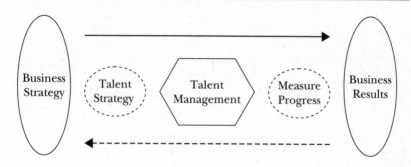

in Figure 1.1 The business results should then in turn influence setting new business strategies and talent strategies. The business results in many organizations are used as a broad outcome measure of whether the talent management effort is effective.

The talent management framework in Figure 1.1 shows the relationships among business strategy, talent management, and business results. We suggest that organizations use five main processes to ensure that the necessary talent is available to achieve their business strategies, and most HR programs, systems, and processes are related to these five talent processes:

1. **Attract and select** talent to the organization.
2. **Assess** competencies and skills in talent.
3. **Review** talent **and plan** talent actions.
4. **Develop and deploy** talent.
5. **Engage and retain** talent.

These talent management components are more than just independent activities and processes. Later we will discuss why they need to be connected and integrated. Most HR professionals are very aware of the natural flow of talent through the organization, beginning with efforts to attract and recruit talent and moving through various HR assessment and development processes to retention efforts. A model of how talent flows through a company is represented in Figure 1.2.

The talent management model in Figure 1.2 illustrates how talent moves through an organization and through various talent management systems and processes. Ultimately the success

Figure 1.2. Talent Management Model

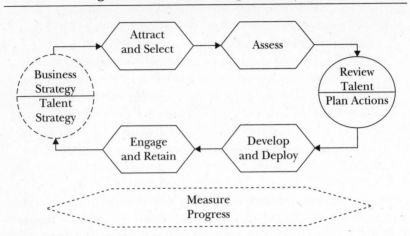

of each of the components and the system as a whole should be measured and the results used to guide both the business strategy and the talent strategy.

Talent management, however, is more than a string of HR programs and processes, which Gubman and Green (2007) describe as a programmatic approach to managing talent in an organization. It is a new of thinking about, designing, and implementing talent processes and systems. In some ways, it is a systems approach to thinking about talent. Boudreau and Ramstad (2007) argue that managing organizational talent and human capital should become a decision science like financial management. We support the use of evidence-based decision making regarding talent; however, because of the complex individual differences among people, it will be difficult for talent management to become a precise decision science.

Talent management systems and processes need to be strategically driven and fully integrated with each other. These qualities and others can take talent management efforts to much higher levels of effectiveness and greater organizational contributions.

Talent Management Success Factors

Talent management efforts are becoming more widely known and used in many business organizations. We are interested in finding out what separates effective and successful talent management systems—the ones that add true value to an organization—from the less effective systems. We discussed this with many colleagues in a wide range of companies and asked them to share their experiences and their views on which companies have the most effective talent management efforts and why those efforts are successful. Many of these companies are mentioned in this book, and some of our colleagues, who are doing leading-edge work in talent management, agreed to write chapters for this book about their insights and experience.

For many years, human resource departments have been working hard to make sure they had effective recruiting efforts, staffing departments, leadership development programs, succession planning reviews, and other HR programs. Since the early 1990s the focus for many organizations has been on building solid human resource functions, programs, and systems. Some organizations achieved their goal of being highly effective in specific areas of HR and established a reputation for being a leading edge HR group. However, a higher level of performance expectation is now being set that requires both an integrated and a strategic talent management effort. Many organizations are now working toward this objective.

Based on our experience and the perspectives of others, we think there are four distinctions that characterize the most successful talent management efforts. The four success factors for talent management distinguish more advanced talent management efforts from those that are made up of effective but independent HR programs, systems, and initiatives—a programmatic approach. The four distinctive success factors for talent management, or the DIME model, are presented in Exhibit 1.2.

Exhibit 1.2. DIME Model of Talent Management Success

- Driven by Business Strategy
- Integrated with Other Processes
- Managed as a Core Business Practice
- Engrained as a Talent Mindset

1. Driven by Business Strategy

In most organizations, there is widespread understanding of the company's business strategies and a strong focus on achieving them. Due to increased competition and limited financial resources, organizations are making tough choices on where to invest those resources and which strategies and products to pursue. The days of the broad conglomerates may be waning as companies divest businesses that are not core to their mission or split into multiple independent companies. Organizational functions have had to demonstrate that their structures, processes, initiatives, and people are aligned with a clear set of business objectives. Anything that does not clearly and directly support those strategies does not get funded. Like other functions, HR has had to become much more strategic, and at the center of that effort is the strategic role of talent management.

The connection between talent management and business strategy has its roots in two trends that have emerged since the mid-1990s:

- The emergence of talent as strategic resource and competitive advantage
- The evolution of the Human Resources function as a strategic business partner

Talent as a Strategic Resource

The idea of viewing talent as a strategic resource has been discussed for decades. For example in the 1960s, engineering talent was seen as a strategic resource needed for the United States to remain competitive with the Soviet Union in the space race. There was a rush to establish, fund, and promote engineering education in the United States.

In the 1990s, executive talent was beginning to be seen as a strategic resource and competitive advantage to business. This was evident in their high public profiles and the media attention they attracted, as well as the extraordinarily high compensation packages they were paid. There was also more visible attention paid to CEO turnover, with some companies, such as AT&T, having multiple CEOs in a relatively short time period. The individual differences in the skills, abilities, and experience of CEOs were often seen as directly affecting the financial results of a company. The business world and financial analysts paid attention to the way the business press depicted the impact of corporate leaders on company results and the "great man" theory of leadership seemed to regain some currency (Organ, 1996).

During this period Zuboff (1988) and Stewart (1997) were discussing the relationship between talent and business strategy by outlining the impact of technological innovations on the value of talent with specific technical skills and pointing out the difficulty of replacing that specialized talent from the marketplace. High-value, difficult-to-replace technical talent was beginning to be seen as a strategic asset. Their approach helped to identify the strategic talent in the organization, that is, those individuals or groups of individuals who create a competitive advantage for the company. Zuboff (1988) argued that talent is critical to business strategies, and Stewart (1997) suggested that this strategic talent might be found at all levels in the organization. Boudreau, Ramstad, and Dowling (2003) now call these *pivotal talent pools*.

In the same vein, Gubman (1998) was making the case that "your workforce is the only thing that is both necessary and sufficient to execute strategy" (p. 15). He argues "the real strategic opportunities for becoming a singular success, achieving uniqueness, and moving quickly lies in your most unique and potentially most powerful resource—your workforce" (p. 16).

Some companies, such as GE, gained a reputation for developing and producing successful corporate executives who were then highly sought after by other companies and moved into CEO positions in many other organizations. GE's executive leadership talent was seen as a strategic asset and a competitive advantage.

Others companies focused on different strategic talent pools. Capital One Financial created a huge corporation, almost from scratch, that put talent at the center of its business strategy. The objective was to build the business analyst and business entrepreneur talent pools, which in turn could start, build, and lead a wide range of businesses. Merck, a pharmaceutical company, gives a lot of attention to identifying and recruiting the leading scientific researchers in particular medical areas, such as diabetes, in order to capture the premier talent and become the leading provider of pharmaceutical products in that area. Honeywell, a wide-ranging manufacturing firm, focused on building a talent pool of general managers who could run a range of businesses. Strategic talent, in a variety of roles but particularly leadership talent, has moved to the center stage in the business world as a critical resource. Collins and Porras (1994) suggest that effectiveness in developing internal leadership talent is one of several factors that predict an organization's performance and longevity.

Companies are starting to see that some talent is not easily replaceable. The demand for leadership talent, particularly global leadership, is rising as the large baby boom generation of leaders is beginning to retire. More companies are chasing and competing for a shrinking resource (Michaels et al., 2001; Bartlett & Ghoshal, 2002). The McKinsey global surveys in 2006 and 2007 (McKinsey & Company, 2007; Guthridge, Komm, & Lawson, 2008) found that global respondents "regarded finding talented people as likely to be the single most important managerial preoccupation for the rest of this decade" and "expect an intensifying competition for talent— and the increasingly global nature of that competition—to have a major effect on their companies over the next five years" (p. 5).

Talent is seen as a scarce resource. And as Barney (1995, 2001) suggests, companies gain sustained competitive advantage when they develop "resources that are valuable, rare and hard to imitate." Some companies have tried to leverage their existing internal strategic talent for new business development, such as when an industrial company leverages its internal high-performing customer service function to start a separate customer service business. However, most companies, such as GE and Capital One Financial, build their strategic talent to match their business model and strategy.

Borrowing a phrase from Andy Grove (1999) at Intel, McKinsey Associates suggest that the "war for talent is a *strategic inflection point*" for business (p. 2). It is one of those turning points in business when something, such as a technological innovation or the emergence of a major new competitor, significantly changes the way everyone approaches their business. They argue "that talent is now a critical driver of corporate performance and that a company's ability to attract, develop and retain talent will be a major competitive advantage far into the future" (Michaels et al., 2001, p. 2).

Lawler (2008) notes that "increasingly, companies in a wide variety of businesses are finding that people can be their number one source of competitive advantage" (p. 1). In fact talent issues need to be carefully considered when developing business strategies. He suggests that "talent considerations are central to both the development and the implementation of business strategy" (p. 9).

In a recent global survey, senior executives from around the world indicate that their two most important management challenges are recruiting high-quality people from multiple territories and improving the appeal of the company culture and work environment. Over 85 percent of these same executives said "that people are vital to all aspects of their company's performance particularly their top strategic challenges: increased competition, innovation and technology" (Deloitte Touche Tohmatsu & Economist Intelligence Unit, 2007).

Some argue that selecting top performers makes a big difference in business results. Axelrod et al. (2001) suggest that the "top performing 20 percent or so of managers . . . were twice as likely as average ones to improve operational productivity and to raise sales and profits" (p. 2). Some argue that organizations should get the very best available talent in every position (Smart, 1999), and McKinsey (Michaels et al., 2001) seems to support the view of hiring only star players. But that approach may be counterproductive for organizations in some positions. We would argue that in an era of limited resources, organizations cannot afford to have the most talented individuals in every position: it would be costly and may even be detrimental to employee engagement and motivation. Highly talented individuals in strategically unimportant positions are likely not to receive the attention, work challenges, career opportunities, and rewards that they require to stay engaged. Boudreau and Ramstad (2005) suggest that resources should be focused on the strategic talent and not invested equally across all employees.

Strategic Human Resources

The most effective HR programs are designed to support and achieve specific business strategies. Each program must be able to clearly outline how it directly supports a strategy. In many cases, this is measured by specific concrete outcomes. Corporations are becoming leaner and wiser about where to invest limited resources, and HR is being required to demonstrate the value that human resource programs add to the business. As a consequence, we are getting much better at deciding where investment in talent management programs will create the most value and in measuring the impact of HR programs and contributions to the business strategy. This book is full of business examples of the connection between talent management initiatives and business strategy.

Converting Business Strategy into HR Strategy

Clear organizational attention has been given to translating business strategies into human resource and talent strategies. Increasingly these efforts include establishing an HR or talent brand for the company, establishing company values and an aligned internal culture, and building the broad organizational capabilities and competencies needed to achieve business objectives.

The process of aligning HR strategies with business strategies can be complex and challenging, particularly if HR efforts are only considered after the business strategies are already set. Many argue that HR needs to be involved in setting the business strategies as well (Beer, 1997; Ulrich, 1997). Lawler (2008) goes further and argues that talent strategies are business strategies.

Numerous people (Gubman, 1998; Sears, 2003) have outlined how business strategies can be translated into human resource and talent strategies. Gubman (1998) also suggests that the "lead" talent management practice may change depending on the business strategy or "strategic style." For example, he recommends a "selection for fit" approach for a customer strategy and a "performance-based compensation" approach for an operations strategy. Being aligned with the business strategy typically means more than just knowing what to do; it also means acting in ways that focus on and advance the business strategy.

Human Resource Professionals Need to be Strategic

Human Resource professionals increasingly are considering their work to be strategic. In the distant past, only some HR executives had the strategic and analytical thinking skills and the broad business experience to understand the strategic implications of their work or perhaps the personal motivation and ambition to step up to a strategic role. In addition, business executives may have been hesitant to include HR executives in strategic discussions.

This is now changing with the advent of a new wave of HR professionals who have the required business experience and the strategic skills to get accepted as business partners. Chief financial officers went through a similar evolution in their roles. HR executives are now seeking opportunities to make strategic contributions at the executive level and are earning a seat at the strategic table as they demonstrate their added value.

Strategic Links

Once Human Resources decides to align processes, systems, and activities with the business strategies, then the next step is to pursue strategic talent management. How can your organization best attract, develop, engage, and retain talent to achieve those business strategies? The strategic links between these are not easily made (see Figure 1.3). While there is usually a strong link between the business environment (external market, competitors, customers, etc.)

Figure 1.3. Strength of Talent Management Links

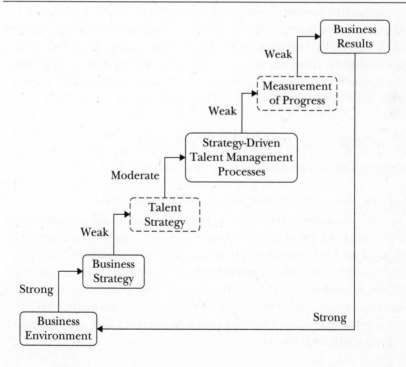

and the business strategy, the next link to a talent strategy is often much weaker. This is often a result of the insufficient experience of many talent management professionals in translating business strategy into talent strategy. Once the talent strategy is understood, then talent management professionals seem to be more effective in translating it into specific talent programs, processes, and systems. For many talent management professionals, their primary expertise and experience are in developing systems, programs, and processes to achieve a specific HR or talent objective.

Once the talent systems and programs have been developed and implemented, HR has not been highly effective in measuring outcomes and progress against business and talent strategies. So the links to measuring progress and business results are weak. However, most organizations have fairly strong links from business results back to business strategies, and of course external financial analysts always seem ready to remind them of this link.

If the goal of HR is to align with the business strategies, to focus on deliverables, to be judged on impact, and to add measurable corporate value, then the corporation needs to have a clear and robust business strategy (Hewitt, 1997; Ulrich, 1997). If the strategy is clear, then, Hewitt (1997) suggests, HR can link to it by building the core strategic competencies, developing a process for leveraging those resources, and building a global strategic mindset in the organization. Of course, this may be easier said than done.

2. Integrated with Other Processes

Companies are learning that having a selection system pursue specific objectives and having a leadership development program pursue very different objectives leads to a waste of both financial and human resources. The various talent management initiatives and HR activities, systems, and processes need to be aligned at a minimum, but they are most effective when they are fully integrated.

Most organizations, however, do not have fully integrated talent management systems, but are operating at a more basic talent management stage. We suggest five stages of talent management integration: (1) reactive, (2) programmatic, (3) comprehensive, (4) aligned, and (5) strategic (see Table 1.3).

Table 1.3. Five Stages of Talent Management

Stage	Definition
5. Strategic	Talent management systems and processes: Collaboratively pursue shared goals and are driven by business strategies and talent strategies Are synergistic and fully integrated with other HR systems and processes Are managed as a core business practice in the organization and deliver the strategic capabilities and competencies that are required Are engrained in the organization as part of a talent mindset
4. Aligned	Talent management systems and processes: Coordinate and link with other HR systems and processes Are coordinated with the talent objectives and efforts of other systems and processes May be linked together using similar language and talent models
3. Comprehensive	Each talent management system and process: Is fully and rigorously developed Is carefully implemented to achieve specific program objectives Focuses independently on its own specific program objectives and a single aspect of talent needs
2. Programmatic	Each talent management system and process: Is sufficiently designed to be repeatable and consistent across multiple implementations Includes a defined process that allows a reliable implementation and delivery
1. Reactive	This talent management approach: Focuses on addressing short-term, immediate talent issues Often quickly adopts popular, available, and off-the-shelf programs to meet an urgent need Gives little attention to long-term needs or to building enduring programs and processes

Source: Adapted from American Productivity and Quality Center (2004) and Gubman & Green (2007).

Reactive—Stage 1

The most primitive stage of talent management puts an emphasis on quickly addressing immediate and urgent talent issues. This often means finding a quick and readily available program that appears to be a solution. This approach relies on the broad range of packaged off-the-shelf programs from outside consulting firms. These plug-and-play programs and tools are designed to be generic and quick fixes. Unfortunately, they rarely take into account the organization's culture and strategic issues, often do not adequately address the initial problem, and have a short life in most organizations.

Programmatic—Stage 2

Most large business organizations have built professional Human Resource functions that establish programs and processes that are at least consistent over time. They may not be well developed, but they are repeatable, which gives the perception, often false, of being effective (tradition is sometimes mistaken for proven). Many staffing programs in the past were very consistent—recruiting at the same schools, asking the same selection questions, relying on a single decision maker—but they were not always effective. They often failed to update the selection process and techniques to adapt to changing talent needs and candidate populations. These habits thrived in many industries, such as the textile industry, that had significant difficulty adapting to the changing business environment.

Comprehensive—Stage 3

Many organizations have tried to build and implement talent programs and processes that are rigorously developed and represent state-of-the-art thinking in the area. For example, in the 1990s there was a rush to build leading-edge leadership development programs in many companies, following the GE model. Many companies hired leadership development specialists to do this. The results were comprehensive programs and processes that were seen as very effective in achieving their specific and narrow development goals. Often, though, these programs were independent, freestanding efforts that were unconnected with other talent management efforts.

Aligned—Stage 4

Since the mid-1990s, there has been a great deal of effort in some companies to have an aligned talent management approach. In this stage, HR professionals link their HR systems and processes with other HR systems and processes and are aware of the range of talent objectives and efforts. The various efforts may be linked together using similar language and talent models. They also may work toward a shared goal when there seems to be a connection, but they are not all driven by larger business and talent strategies.

For example, those executing a sales recruiting program and those executing a sales training program are often aware of each other's goals and work to make sure their efforts are aligned, that is, they are not working against each other's objectives. However, their efforts may not be fully integrated, that is trainee performance results from the training program may not be used to adjust or modify the recruiting efforts. Similarly, the recruiting outcomes may not be used to modify the training approach. While they both may support producing high-quality sales staff in general, they are not taking advantage of the potential synergy between the two programs. Although they may have well-developed and comprehensive programs and are aware of their connection, they are not sufficiently integrated to realize the full possible synergistic benefits to the organization.

An organization might have recruiting, assessment, and development programs that are separately comprehensive and rigorous and that coordinate with each other. However, they may all have different goals. *Alignment* suggests separate components "forming a line" or "being arrayed on the same side of a cause" (Merriam-Webster, 2002). However we think a higher stage of talent management is to be both strategically driven and fully integrated.

Strategic—Stage 5

Ultimately the talent management approach should be strategically driven to be most effective. It is more than just being on the same side of a cause (alignment); it is actually intensely focusing on achieving the business and talent strategy. This requires that the talent management programs and processes have the same shared strategic goals as the recruiting and staffing processes. In this stage, HR programs and processes are synergistic and multiply their effectiveness across and through other systems, programs, and processes.

For example, a corporation may be interested in forming a business development unit to create innovative approaches to satisfy customer demand. From a talent strategy perspective, it needs to be staffed with entrepreneurial people who have the potential to start and lead new businesses. All of the HR systems and processes, from recruiting to assessment, development, retention, and compensation, need to fully understand and work together to achieve that business strategy and the talent strategy of hiring and building entrepreneurial talent. The type of talent needs to be specifically defined, and each HR area needs to identify its interface and shared responsibility with every other HR area. For example, a discussion of an individual who failed soon after moving into the new unit would need to be addressed by the larger team (recruiting, selecting, development, onboarding, and retention), not just by the selection staff.

A failure in one part of the talent effort is a failure for the strategy, and everyone should have some responsibility to correct it. In some ways, the strategy (business or talent) defines the team rather than the specific HR system or program. These systems and processes are strategically driven and fully integrated.

Other Approaches to Integration

Avedon and Scholes (see Chapter 2) discuss the importance of being integrated at three levels in the organization:

- Integration with business strategy and human resource strategy
- Integration within the talent management processes
- Integration with the culture of the organization

All three are important integration components, and an organization needs to do all three to have a fully integrated, strategically driven talent management system. Being integrated within talent management processes suggests alignment (stage 4) within HR.

But to be strategic (stage 5) also requires being integrated with both the human resource strategy and the business strategy. Being integrated with the culture suggests that the values embedded in talent management programs and processes are consistent with the cultural values of the organization and that they have been not only accepted but engrained in the culture (Strategic, stage 5). An "up or out" career philosophy might work in an organization that does not value having long-tenured employees but would probably not work in an organization that values the development of deep relationships between employees.

Gubman and Green (2007) suggest four stages of talent management: Programmatic, Systemic, Strategic, and Cultural (see Chapter 2 by Avedon and Scholes for a more complete description). Earlier Gubman (1998) also discussed alignment with business results and strategy but used the term *alignment* similarly to how we use the term *strategic*. The distinguishing feature of his *alignment model* is "a clear line of sight from strategy to people," which is similar to our Strategic, stage 5 (p. 33).

Sloan et al. (2003) discuss how a company's globalization strategy (global, international, transnational, or multidomestic) can link to defining leadership roles and requirements and to designing a talent management system. They also point out the importance of aligning three core talent management processes:

- Drawing people into the company (attract and retain)
- Assisting people to take on new roles (select and transition)
- Encouraging people to develop new skills and maintain high performance (mobilize and develop)

Others who have studied or written about talent management tend to use the term *integrated* to mean connected or aligned and not strategically driven (American Productivity and Quality Center, 2004; Morton, 2004; Smilansky, 2006). They suggest that talent management can be integrated by making the "right connections" between programs and processes. Some suggest that having a centralized competency model is the integration cornerstone for a company rather than the business strategies. In our opinion, being connected or aligned is a worthy goal but falls short of being strategically driven (that is, integrated with the strategies).

In a Conference Board survey (Morton, 2004), approximately one-third of 75 "HR-related executives" viewed their talent management initiatives as integrated or having "connections made to all critically related aspects in the organization" (p. 22) (for example, connected or aligned processes). The respondents suggest that this connection occurs primarily through the talent management processes (cited by 49 percent) and talent management professionals (cited by 49 percent). The HR areas that are mentioned most frequently as connected are performance management, recruitment and leadership, and high-potential development. The areas mentioned as the least connected are workforce planning, retention, feedback, and measurement. The survey respondents said the talent management initiatives that were the most important were leadership development and high-potential development (cited by 73 percent), performance management (cited by 44 percent), culture (cited by 21 percent), and retention (cited by 16 percent). Based on the survey data and corporate interviews Morton proposes a "road map to talent management maturity" and recommends a specific order for bringing HR processes into talent management maturity: (1) recruitment, (2) professional development, (3) culture, (4) retention, (5) performance management, (6) feedback and measurement, (7) leadership and high-potential development, and (8) workforce planning.

In discussing executive talent, Smilansky (2006) advocates integrating talent management with the core components that underpin these HR processes such as: an understanding of jobs and the hierarchy of managerial positions, the definition of managerial competencies, and culture and values. Although his focus is on executive talent, he does not emphasize business strategy as the foundation for talent management, even at the executive level.

Another talent management consortium benchmarking study (American Productivity and Quality Center, 2004) surveyed 21 companies and concluded that companies should "integrate the various elements of talent management into a comprehensive system—an overall talent management framework, a competency model consistently used across elements, opportunities for the various stakeholders to work together, the use of data from one process as input to other processes, and partnerships between HR and line managers are all mechanisms used to foster integration" (p. ii). This study (like those by the Conference Board and Smilansky) emphasizes coordination between HR programs and processes, but does not suggest that talent management processes need to be determined and driven by the business and talent strategies.

We think, however, that talent management systems need to be fully integrated with and driven by business and talent strategies. In addition, talent management programs and processes need to be integrated with each other and not just connected or aligned.

3. Managed as a Core Business Practice

In the past, senior executives in many organizations had limited contact with talent programs and processes. Frequently they attended annual replacement planning meetings that focused on discussing impending retirements and potential replacements for those positions. Over the years, these meetings have evolved through different phases, from replacement planning to human resource planning to full strategic talent management (see Table 1.4).

In the 1970s and early 1980s, some leading companies, notably Exxon and AT&T, moved from single position staffing and replacement planning to longer term Human Resource planning. This initially involved elaborate replacement plans and succession wall charts that identified not only individuals who were the likely near-term replacements for specific leadership positions but individuals who could be developed over one to three years to be viable future candidates. In the 1990s and 2000s, there was an evolution in organizations to talent management that focused on aligning Human Resource programs and processes in order to identify and develop talent, both leadership talent and specialized talent.

The talent planning and management process is now becoming a core business practice, driven by business strategy and talent strategy. Both Dowell (see Chapter 9) and Avedon and Scholes (see Chapter 2) make a clear case for the central business role of strategic talent management in organizations. Dowell argues that the talent review process "forms the third leg of the organization planning process along with reviews of the organization's strategy and operating plans." Avedon and Scholes suggest that it should be one of three core business practices along with the strategic planning process (including financial goals) and the annual operating review. Dowell points out, "The organization's strategy provides the foundation for identifying future talent needs, and the operating

Table 1.4. Evolution of Talent Management and Planning

	Framework	*Characteristic*
2010s–future	**Strategic talent management**	• Is driven by and fully integrated with business and talent strategies • Is managed as a core business process • Planning cycle matches business strategy and operation timelines • Engrained with a talent mindset throughout the organization
2000s	**Talent management**	• Focus is on developing and managing talent pools • Aligns HR programs and processes to meet talent needs • Considers time needed for recruiting and developing needed staff
1980s–1990s	**Human resource planning**	• Focus is on planning and managing staffing needs over time and includes succession planning • Planning usually covers next one to three years of leadership moves and management development • Involves forecasting staffing levels to meet business needs
1960s–1970s	**Replacement planning**	• Focus is on short-term continuity and filling likely, near-term, open positions • Planning usually covers next 12 months
1950s–1960s	**Single position staffing**	• Focus is on filling immediately open positions • Reactive approach to requests

plan provides the mechanism for allocating resources (financial and human) to support the actions identified during the talent review process (such as, new recruiting efforts, developmental programs for high potentials, and retention programs)." He makes the case that talent can be central to gaining competitive advantage:

> Organizations put their future at risk if they do not apply the same discipline to planning the development of their talent as they do

to planning the development of products and services. The ability to formulate and execute strategy depends on having the necessary talent in place. An organization's talent is one of the sources of sustainable competitive advantage. When an organization has highly talented individuals in strategically critical positions, this talent becomes a source of competitive advantage that is one of the most difficult to replicate by competitors.

In fact, in leading organizations these three business processes form the foundation for effectively managing a corporation. They place as much emphasis on the strategic talent reviews as they do on the strategic planning process and the annual operating reviews.

Over the years, others have also suggested that talent planning should be considered an important business process. Walker (1980) makes a clear case for the long-range planning of human resources and argues for linking it with three levels of organizational planning: strategic planning, operational planning, and annual budgeting. Ulrich (1997) advocates for a strategic approach to Human Resources that puts an emphasis on adding corporate value, gaining impact, delivering results, and integrating HR practices into the business strategy.

Mohrman and Lawler (1997; Mohrman, Lawler, & McMahan, 1996) propose that Human Resources be a full business partner and an integral part of the management team. They include in the partnership role "developing strategy, designing the organization, change implementation and integrating performance management practices ... (goal setting, performance appraisal, development practices and rewards) ... with each other and with the business management practices of the organization" (Mohrman & Lawler, 1997, p. 246).

However, it has taken some time for organizations to see these links and to see Human Resources as a business partner. Some progressive companies, such as GE, PepsiCo, Bristol-Myers Squibb and Ingersoll Rand, have made these links and are leveraging their talent approach for their own business advantage. Other companies seem to be slow to make this transition. Hewitt (1997) suggests that this may be due to the false assumption that the corporation has "a robust concept and process of competitive strategy" (p. 39). He also suggests that an organization's strategic planning process is often little more than annual budgeting and that many current executives have limited strategic skills. Others note the weak links between the strategic planning apparatus in an organization and superior competitive performance (Ashkensas, Ulrich, Jick, & Kerr, 1995).

Some senior executives may have difficulty viewing HR as a strategic function. However in many organizations, such as at Ingersoll Rand and PepsiCo, both the Chief Executive Officer and the Chief Human Resource Officer see a critical strategic role for Human Resources and talent management.

4. Engrained as a Talent Mindset

Most companies, and most managers for that matter, rely on Human Resources to design, implement, and monitor various talent management programs and processes. In leading companies, such as PepsiCo, Microsoft, Bristol-Myers Squibb, and Ingersoll Rand, senior executives take an active role in linking talent management to business success. They now have or are building a talent mindset, or what Avedon and Scholes in Chapter 2 call *talent stewardship* in the company. As talent management becomes integral to the organization culture, every supervisor, manager, and leader in the company is expected to take responsibility and accountability for attracting, developing, deploying, and retaining talent. Everyone is expected to take an active role in talent management, from identifying and recruiting exceptional talent to coaching employees and guiding the careers of individuals with the potential to assume greater responsibility.

Many years ago companies discovered the value of using quality circles in manufacturing operations—an idea borrowed from Japanese companies that involved manufacturing plant employees taking responsibility for the product quality in their group or department. These groups later evolved into employee involvement groups (self-directed work groups), which had decision-making responsibility over the work in their group. Over the years, executives and managers became used to giving employees greater decision-making authority. This approach was seen as a way to improve product quality, empower employees, attract more talented people, and lower costs at the same time.

First-level supervisors were perhaps the last organizational level to fully accept shared decision making with their employees—and perhaps with some justification, since the process restricted their direct control and their span of responsibility and often led to a significant reduction in the number of supervisors.

By the time talent management emerged, employees, managers, and executives were used to the idea of pushing responsibility down into the organization. One of the last holdouts of tightly held responsibility was, and still is, the talent planning process. Executives often hold these meetings in private and are cautious about sharing their conclusions or even the process or decision rules or guidelines. Most corporations are still hesitant to let individuals know if they have been designated as high potential (see Chapter 5 by Rob Silzer and Allan Church in this book).

As organizations have made talent management a central focus across the whole company, and not just in HR, there is a need to involve and engage all managers and leaders in talent management activities. One trend that supports this distribution of talent responsibility is the emergence and use of organization-wide competency models (Hollenbeck, McCall, & Silzer, 2006) as a central organizing framework for talent management.

For example, Capital One Financial in the early 1990s developed a comprehensive research-based competency model, based on the business strategy of the company, that was widely shared with employees (Silzer, 1996; Silzer & Douma, 1998). Also developed with the actual competency model were many supporting programs and materials—selection tools, 360-degree feedback instruments, development catalogues, training programs, and performance management rating systems, for example—that were widely distributed to employees for self-directed use. The objective was to put as much talent-related information as possible in the hands of employees, managers and leaders, so they could take responsibility to improve their own performance, advance their own careers and improve the performance of their group. This was an early, and quite successful, attempt to push talent responsibility down into the organization and even to individual employees. One of the reasons this worked so well was that employees saw it as an opportunity to take some responsibility for their own development and careers.

Talent management became engrained in the Capital One organizational culture and became a manager responsibility and mindset. Ulrich (1997) suggests the "shared mindset of common culture represents the glue that holds an organization together" (p. 68). Leading talent companies such as PepsiCo and Capital One Financial understand that to successfully achieve business and talent strategies, talent management efforts must be a core business process that is the responsibility of all managers throughout the company.

McKinsey (Michaels et al., 2001) reinforced the importance of adopting a talent mindset in an organization in order to successfully compete in the war for talent. They described talent mindset as "a deep conviction that better talent leads to better corporate performance" and "the belief that better talent is a critical source of competitive advantage." Guthridge et al. (2008, p. 8) describe it as a "a deep commitment to talent throughout the organization, starting at the top and cascading through the ranks . . . a conviction among business unit heads and line leaders, that people really matter." Avedon and Scholes in Chapter 2 define it as "a frame of mind, or a culture, where every manager feels ownership and accountability for talent on behalf of the organization."

McKinsey (Michaels et al., 2001) proposed that talent management needs "to be a central part of how to run the company" and "a huge and crucial part" of every leader's job (p. 27). Gubman and Green (2007, p. 1) advise that talent management should be a "top-of-mind priority that becomes second nature to executives" (p. 1). Michaels et al. (2001, p. 22) go further and suggest that managers need to "commit a major part of their time and energy to strengthening their talent pool and helping others strengthen theirs." Jack Welch modeled this mindset when he said, "I view my primary job as strengthening our talent pools. So I view every conversation, every meeting as an opportunity to talk about our talented people" (Michaels et al,, 2001, p. 31).

Guthridge et al. (2008, p. 8), McKinsey consultants, point out that they "consistently see that top performing companies instill the mindset and the culture to manage talent effectively." Lawler advocates building a human capital-centric organization, where "every aspect of the organization is obsessed with talent and talent management" (2008, p. 10). He suggests that human capital–centric organizations "do everything they can to attract, retain, and develop the right talent" and that "talent management deserves at least as much focus as financial capital management" in a company.

McKinsey argues for a top-down approach (Michaels et al., 2001) that requires "the CEO's leadership and passion" and suggests that a leader "establish a gold standard for talent, get actively involved in people decisions deep within the organization, drive a simple, probing talent review process, instill a talent mindset in all managers, invest real money in talent and hold themselves and their managers accountable for the strength of the talent pools that they build" (p. 27).

Sears (2003, p. 140) suggests that there are two types of talent mindset: the first "clearly comes from the top," where the CEO champions a commitment to talent, while the second comes from "talent athletes" or "leader-managers," who "ultimately conceived, built, implemented and sustained" the business strategies and talent strategies (p. 140).

We think talent management must be championed by the CEO with the full commitment of senior leaders, but ultimately talent must be owned by managers and leaders at all levels. In the Capital One example, the mindset was easier to establish than in most mature organizations because the company had a limited history, the senior executives had a strong talent orientation at the beginning, the culture had a data-based learning orientation, and almost all associates (selected through rigorously developed selection tools) were hired with limited or no prior organizational experience. The associates were bright, highly motivated, ambitious, and committed to learning and using the talent management tools to improve their competencies and advance their careers. It should be noted that during the first ten years, Capital One Financial grew from 300 to 28,000 associates and had outstanding financial performance.

The creation of a talent mindset does need to start at the top with the CEO's commitment. In many organizations, this is probably the biggest hurdle to establishing a talent mindset. CEOs often do not understand it, are not interested, or have their own outdated view of talent. Their interest and involvement are based to some degree on their past organizational experience. If they had worked in a company committed to talent management at some time in their career, they would be more likely to understand it and actively support it. Larry Bossidy, for example, who spent many years in GE leadership before becoming CEO of Allied Signal and later of Honeywell, states, "There is no way to spend too much time on obtaining and developing the best people" (Bossidy, 2001, p. 46).

Executive commitment seems to be a starting point. McKinsey Associates, in a 2000 survey of corporate executives (reported in Michaels et al., 2001), revealed that talent was much more likely to be seen as a top priority by officers from high-performing companies (49 percent) than officers from average-performing companies (30 percent). However, while 93 percent of the officers surveyed think managers should be held accountable for the strength of the talent pool that they build, only 3 percent of the surveyed officers think their companies actually do this. Gaining CEO and executive commitment may be the greatest hurdle that Human Resource executives and talent management professionals face in establishing a talent mindset in their organization.

These four talent management success factors (the DIME model as presented in Exhibit 1.2) run through this book and show up in many of the chapters:

- Driven by business strategy
- Integrated with other processes
- Managed as a core business practice
- Engrained as a talent mindset

These are the design criteria for outstanding talent management systems and critical to the future success of talent management.

Other Talent Management Approaches

Other talent management frameworks have proposed similar and different design and implementation approaches. Avedon and Scholes (in Chapter 2 in this book) and Wellins et al. (2006) outline talent management models similar to ours (see Figures 1.1 and 1.2) and include common elements such as business strategy; attract, select, and identify; assess; develop and deploy; and retain. Wellins et al. (2006) describe their model as focusing exclusively on leadership talent, while in comparison, the

Avedon and Scholes model is more broadly applicable and lists connections to specific HR programs and processes. The American Productivity and Quality Center (2004) reported on a benchmarking study on talent management and found that the "best practice organizations" excelled at recruiting, identifying, developing, performance management, and retention.

Gubman (1998, p. 33) presents the Hewitt Associates alignment model, which is called the "Improving Business Results with People Model" and is designed to "line up all the critical elements in talent management." It takes a broad strategic approach emphasizing how business strategies get translated to business capabilities, people requirements, and workforce strategies. Gubman discusses how the strategic style of a company—its products, operations, and customers—can determine the lead talent management practice for the organization. Gubman identifies five key talent management practices (staffing, organizing, learning, performing, and rewarding) and gives company examples of each.

Sloan et al. (2003) discuss the strategic management of Global Leadership Talent, although their recommendations seem equally relevant for nonglobal talent. They propose five steps for designing a talent management system: (1) define the value proposition for employees, (2) identify talent gaps, (3) choose the source for needed talent, (4) align talent management processes, and (5) build organizational support mechanisms. They also identify six core talent management processes grouped in three clusters:

- Attract and retain—drawing people to the organization
- Select and transition—helping people take new roles
- Mobilize and develop—encouraging development and high performance

Smilansky (2006) focuses on the management of executive talent. His book is based on in-depth interviews with the heads of HR at 14, mostly European, companies. He outlines six key steps to effective talent management: (1) focus on critical jobs, (2) develop high-performance talent pools, (3) assess potential, (4) develop capabilities of high-potential executives, (5) reduce the impact of organizational silos, and (6) develop solid performers who may not be high potential.

Others discuss talent management in general or narrow ways. Lawler (2008) sees outstanding talent as critical to having a human capital–centric organization but discusses talent management only generally. He supports the importance of establishing management priorities and an employer brand but only briefly mentions identifying talent needs, selection, development, or retention. Similarly, Sears (2003) provides a more general discussion of talent management and focuses on strategy formation, delivery, and performance. He discusses six key talent processes: relating (establishing relationships), recruiting, retaining, performance management, learning, and rewarding.

Several thinkers in this area advocate applying models from other functional areas to talent management. Cappelli (2008a, 2008b) focuses on the "uncertainty of talent demands" in an organization and cautions against having an oversupply of talent because of costs and other factors. To address the risk uncertainty, he suggests using a supply chain management model and proposes a "talent on demand framework," similar to just-in-time manufacturing, and that companies should undershoot their estimates of the talent that will be needed. While this theoretically may make sense for reducing costs it seems unlikely that companies will tolerate much risk in not having or being able to quickly attract the right talent when it is needed. Many companies, however, are already thoughtfully weighing the risks in make or buy decisions around specific talent groups.

Boudreau and Ramstad (2005, 2007) propose a decision science for managing talent resources and determining talent strategies that they call *talentship*. They offer an analytical approach, based on a financial management model, to understanding the impact of business strategy on talent planning and talent management and how investments in talent can provide strategic opportunities. Their model is complex and may be difficult to apply in practice. Underlying the approaches by Capelli (2008a, 2008b), as well as Boudreau and Ramstad (2005, 2007), is the premise that organizations should differentially invest in critical or pivotal talent capabilities and pools in an organization and focus on talent groups that can have the greatest impact on strategic success. This is not a new idea. Some leading companies have been selectively investing in critical functions, career paths, or positions for some time.

In addition, much has been written on the various components of the talent management process. The following are the relevant chapters in this book related to specific talent management components.

- Attracting and selecting (Chapters 3 and 4)
- Assessing (Chapter 5)
- Reviewing and planning (Chapter 9)
- Developing and deploying (Chapters 6, 7, and 8)
- Engaging and retaining (Chapter 10)
- Measuring progress (Chapter 12)
- Specific talent pools (Chapters 11, 13, and 14)
- Company approaches (Chapters 15, 16, 17, 18, and 19)
- General talent management discussion (Chapters 2, 20, 21, and 22). There is also a large body of literature on each of these components (Jeanneret & Silzer, 1998; Hollenbeck, 2002; Silzer, 2002a, 2004, 2005; Silzer & Adler, 2003).

Issues in Talent Management

Organizations face a number of issues and obstacles to the effective implementation of strategic talent management. They can be grouped into three areas: the nature of talent, design and execution issues, and influences and challenges.

The Nature of Talent

Organizations have to decide whom to include as talent and what they mean when they discuss "talent." This raises a few choices that can affect the design of the talent management approach and the organizational culture and brand.

Natural or Developed Talent

A core question in designing talent systems is whether there is a dominant view in the organization, and among the senior executives, about whether talent is something you are born with or whether talent can be developed. While most experienced industrial-organizational psychologists believe that the answer is "both," many executives, and even many HR professionals, have strong opinions and biases for one alternative or the other. This is usually due to their limited exposure to the research in this area and their own personal experiences. These beliefs can directly affect organizational decisions on whether to build or buy talent and whether to emphasize recruiting and selection programs or to create extensive training and development programs.

Believing only in natural talent leads an organization to focus heavily on a selection approach to talent, since it is assumed that there would be little development or learning on the job. Once the job requirements change, the job incumbent is moved out, and another individual is selected into the position as a better match to the new requirements. The result is frequent recruiting of talent from outside the company, and the resulting high turnover is considered a cost of doing business. Some companies pursued this approach (and some still do) when there was a ready and available supply of external talent to hire and the compensation was high enough to attract the specific talent needed. This is more of a "just in time" approach to talent (see Cappelli, 2008b). These organizations often develop a reputation for giving individuals a lot of early responsibility, but their tenure is generally short. The financial industry has developed a reputation for this approach over the years.

Believing only in developed talent leads to bringing in a large group of individuals early in their careers and using an extensive development effort to build their skills over time and sort out those individuals who learn and develop the most. The difficulty with this approach is that it is costly and time consuming and is generally seen as a luxury that few corporations can continue to afford. This approach may result in prematurely placing individuals in stretch roles with the hope that they will grow into the role. Although some people can do this, there typically are costly failures, which can be a financial drain on the corporation. Research suggests that a person's natural talent or abilities generally set a range of how much they can be developed in an area. Consider, for example, intellectual, interpersonal, and motivation skills. Individuals typically have different levels of natural talent in each of these areas, which can set limits on how much the individual can further develop in each area.

Many business organizations today have a selection or development bias, although not to the total exclusion of the other. Sometimes this is generated from the attitudes and beliefs of the CEO and senior executives or by the history of the company. Enlightened executives and HR professionals realize the need for a mix of selection and development efforts, and understand that well-designed development efforts can significantly build on and extend an individual's natural talents. Selection and development need to be closely integrated and driven by shared goals. The right mix depends on the specific situation and a range of considerations, such as the type of talent needed, the availability and cost of external talent, and the competitive advantage of having unique internal talent.

Broad or Narrow Inclusion

Some organizations have put a good deal of effort into identifying and developing only high-potential talent (see Chapter 5). Other organizations try to raise the talent level in all positions by developing a much broader group of employees. This raises the question of which way is best for building a more effective organization: a broad inclusion or a narrow inclusion of employees in development programs.

High-potential programs typically focus on identifying individuals who have the potential to advance several levels in the organization and then differentially invest in their development. This talent pool is often seen as the future of the company. Greater consideration is now being given to selectively focusing on the specific talent that will have the greatest impact on achieving strategic objectives and giving little, if any, development resources to other employees, who are seen as replaceable and not critical to achieving business objectives (Boudreau & Ramstad, 2005). The decision to restrict who receives developmental resources can be seen as a rational and strategic use of limited development resources.

Other organizations are interested in improving the effectiveness of all employees and broadly include larger numbers of employees in development efforts. There are several reasons to use this approach. One might argue that all employees can contribute to improving company performance through their own work efforts, even if in small ways. Some HR professionals are concerned about having only a select group of individuals get development attention and suggest that this is demotivating and feels exclusionary to those not included. They argue that development is an effective tool for engaging and motivating most employees. In addition, there is the risk that the individuals who are not included in the development efforts may decide as a result that their career will be limited at the company and may leave for better career opportunities and more development support at other companies, and they could turn out to be strong long-term contributors.

Most companies have a mixed approach, offering specialized and advanced development opportunities for select talent pools while also providing some level of development support for other employees. Selective investment but not exclusive investment seems to be a common approach. The choices that organizations make on this issue partially define their culture. Our experience is that effective talent organizations balance these two approaches, providing basic learning and development opportunities for most employees while having specialized and extensive development programs for individuals in strategically critical areas or with the greatest potential to contribute at higher levels in the organization.

Satisficing or Maximizing Talent

This issue focuses on the type of talent mix that is desired in the organization. Some organizations want the best talent available in every position, while others are comfortable hiring individuals in most positions who have just enough talent to satisfy the job requirements, and then hiring the best talent available in only a select few positions.

The maximizing organizations and consultants (Smart, 1999) suggest that the organization benefits in many ways by hiring the best talent possible in every position. They argue that only the best talent can bring new thinking and innovative ideas for improving effectiveness and efficiency in every position. GE famously pushed for managers to identify and turn over the bottom 10 percent of performers every year in an effort to constantly upgrade talent. Although there have been some employee lawsuits over this approach, it continues to be used in some business organizations.

Others take the satisficing approach and argue that hiring only the best talent available in every position can be an inefficient and wasteful use of corporate resources, given the high compensation costs associated with this approach (Boudreau & Ramstad, 2005). Boudreau and Ramstad suggest that the improvement in effectiveness is small, and the return does not justify the financial investment. Rather, they say, hiring people who can perform the job competently is all that is needed in many positions.

HR professionals again see the need for a mixed approach depending on the situation. If you are staffing an entire pharmaceutical research group, it might be smart to hire only the best research talent you can in order to maximize the likelihood that they will discover a medical breakthrough in treating a disease. But if you are staffing a customer call center with customer representatives, it might be wiser to bring in a mix of people: some who can advance to be call center supervisors and others who will be very happy being a solid, high-performing call representative for many years and who are not pushing for greater responsibilities or to redesign and upgrade their work.

Talent decisions around these issues are rarely easy and often require careful consideration of the situation, the culture, the strategic needs of the organization, and the talent brand that the company has or wants to establish. Only rarely can organizations make a clear, absolute, and companywide decision on any of these three talent issues.

Design and Execution Issues

Many functional areas in organizations, including HR, have trouble getting the right balance between design complexity and comprehensiveness and between execution ease and effectiveness. For example, the design of IT software programs and HR succession planning processes are known for being overdesigned, adding many extra features and complexities that often make them difficult to implement and use. They often crash (software programs) or are ignored (elaborate succession planning notebooks). Design and execution decisions can make or break a talent management program or process.

Comprehensive Design or Effective Implementation

Many HR professionals have read with great interest about the latest advances, tools, and programs for talent management programs. Often these features or ideas are promoted by external consulting firms or academics as essential to having an effective and leading-edge system. While some of these ideas make sense, others are short-lived fads that often soon prove to be unnecessary and distracting.

Less experienced HR professionals are more likely than experienced talent management professionals to get enamored with being on the leading edge of the field and can be more easily influenced by an aggressive consultant. Often the downside is that the programs take a long time to develop, are complicated to explain, are impractical, and ultimately are ineffective in addressing the business need. The most effective organizations and HR professionals know how to balance design and execution issues and always draw a clear line to solving a business need. Often simpler design leads to more effective execution.

Focusing on the Needs of the Individual or the Needs of the Organization

Most programs and processes are designed and implemented to meet specific business needs and strategies. In general, this has been a widely accepted approach, with little attention given to the interests and needs of individual employees. However, it is now recognized that employees are more motivated and effective when their needs and interests are considered in organizational decisions. Employees are often encouraged to take command of their own career and pursue their own career interests and goals. People have learned to manage their careers and make their own career choices.

However, this often comes in conflict with organizational plans and decisions. It is not uncommon for organizations to carefully plan out a series of leader moves, with one person replacing another in a chain of moves, when someone in the middle of the sequence turns down the offer (often because of their own interests or ambitions) and disrupts the whole series of moves. Frequently the individual's career interests, willingness to move, or personal life needs were not adequately known or considered beforehand. Executives and leaders who know their employees well enough to understand their individual interests and needs are more likely to make decisions that are consistent with the needs of both the organization and the individual.

Tell No One or Widely Communicate

On many issues, executives and HR professionals have to carefully decide what information can be shared and what information needs to remain confidential or closely managed. This is particularly true when dealing with sensitive HR and talent information. But where should the line be drawn between what must remain confidential and what can be shared? In the past, it seemed that everything was considered confidential, and the executive suite often resembled a locked fortress.

But a more open, transparent environment has evolved in some organizations that supports sharing certain information because it can motivate and engage employees to improve performance. The argument is that employees are more likely to set higher performance and career goals if they are aware of the possible benefits and rewards available to them. While some personal information, such as compensation level, is still considered confidential, other information, such as the development opportunities given to high potentials or high achievers, is seen as serving as an incentive for others. (See Chapter 5 by Rob Silzer and Allan Church for a discussion on what information gets shared with high-potential individuals.)

A balance must be found between protecting private individual data while communicating the talent processes and programs in enough detail so they can be understood and serve as incentives for all employees. High ethical standards need to be maintained when implementing and communicating talent programs and processes so that resources are allocated based on merit, not relationships or some other bias, and information is shared based on reasonable guidelines that consider both the organization's and the individual's needs. Transparency helps assure employees that developmental resources are being allocated fairly.

Influences and Challenges

The world is getting more complex and interconnected, and change is happening rapidly. These changes can be distracting or even defeating for some organizations. Others see them as an opportunity to gain competitive advantage and take the view that if "you are not changing, then you are falling behind." Here are some influences and challenges that can be seen as obstacles or opportunities for organizations.

Looking Forward or Looking Back

Many organizations are pushing HR and other functions to be more strategic in their view, processes, and decisions. Often this means looking into an ambiguous and quickly changing future to try to predict future situations and dynamics and then make the right decision for those circumstances. Years ago, these decisions were made intuitively, based on some fuzzy understanding of past experiences and current circumstances. More recently, there has been a movement toward analytical decision making based on solid data. Capital One Financial, primarily a credit card company but more recently a bank holding company, has had more than a decade of strong financial performance by relying on a data-based decision-making approach to business management and HR.

There is now an emergence of evidence-based HR approaches that rely on concrete data to guide decisions. Making talent decisions based on data analysis can be a big step up from a fuzzy intuitive approach to talent. For example, measuring and analyzing past leadership turnover rates and reasons may be more helpful in guiding talent system development than having a 20-year company veteran provide his personal intuitive views of what to do.

However, data analyses collect data from the past, look back at what happened, and are constrained by the circumstances of that past. For example, if the turnover data were collected during a strong economic period when switching companies to advance a career was both attractive and easy to do, then the data may not be entirely relevant to a slow economic period.

In psychology, one basic accepted premise is that the best predictor of future behavior in an individual is past behavior under similar circumstances. This is also true in predicting the future behavior of individuals and making future-oriented decisions about talent. Relying solely on an analysis of the past is looking backward and only captures the reality of the past. Looking forward, predicting the future, is frequently not just an extension of past. Looking forward should involve both careful analysis of the past and some judgment about how the future will be different from current or past circumstances.

Thinking strategically and making future-oriented decisions is different from analytical thinking and extrapolating the future from the past. The design of talent programs and processes, as well as the assessment of talent, needs to be based not only on past organizational and individual data but also on judgments of how business requirements might be different in the future and how individuals may change and grow in the future. The future belongs to those who can perform successfully in the future, not to those who duplicate the behaviors of the past.

Short-Term or Long-Term View

Over the years business cycles seem to be getting shorter, quarterly financial reports seem to be turning into monthly reports, executives are moving around financial assets to serve short-term balance sheet needs, and a CEO's survival seems to be increasingly based on quarter-to-quarter results. At the same time talent system cycles are getting much longer, often three to five years or more. The career paths of high-potential or early-career talent can bridge 10 to 20 years or longer in an organization. This presents a dilemma on how to effectively and simultaneously manage both of these fundamental business processes.

Some organizations force the talent system into the short-term business cycle. This involves addressing short-term talent needs and ignoring longer-term talent planning and management. This could be called replacement planning. It is often driven by a CEO who is either totally preoccupied with quarterly business results or is not capable of long-term thinking.

Other organizations understand the need to have different time cycles. They can readily deal with short-term talent issues and decisions while also maintaining a focus on long-term talent development. The companies that are known for developing talent, such as GE, are equally well known for the time and attention given to long-term talent reviews and planning.

A study by Hewitt Associates and the Human Resource Planning Society (2005) found that the top twenty companies for producing leaders, such as 3M, GE, and Johnson & Johnson, when compared to 350 other companies, are much more likely to have succession plans for the CEO and other executives. They also are much more likely to have their CEOs involved in the planning and to hold their leaders accountable for developing their direct reports. They do not succumb to the pressure of focusing only on short-term issues and crises. When they make short-term talent decisions, they also consider the long-term implications and try to satisfy both at the same time.

Expanding or Integrating into Global Markets

Most companies have global market opportunities and are facing global competitors, a situation that presents complex talent challenges. Senior executives are asking whether they have the talent to enter these global markets and whether they have the talent who can compete against the new competition. In the face of these challenges, some companies retreat into familiar markets and products. Most initially address these challenges by sending familiar internal talent into the new global markets to compete. While this offers a conservative entry approach, over time it often leads to limited success or even business failures. What this approach misses is the importance of having business leaders who understand and can execute within local culture and business practices. Most companies eventually move to hiring and developing local talent who are capable of running the business without compromising the organization's fundamental culture and principles.

Influencing or Being Influenced by the CEO

In most corporations, the CEO has a tremendous amount of authority to influence a wide range of decisions. Since the late 1990s, there has been an increase in the cult of the CEO in the business world. Whether the CEO is revered or reviled, there is little question about the CEO's clout in an organization. As a result, the CEO's views and biases regarding talent are often clearly reflected in talent policies, processes, and programs. In the past, the CEO exerted enormous control over the talent in organizations, which often resulted in either taking ownership over talent issues, delegating them (usually to other business executives), or ignoring them entirely. Because of the power of CEOs, many HR professionals have been hesitant to challenge their views or even voice alternative perspectives. So the talent system in most organizations has been heavily shaped by the CEO.

More recently (and throughout this book) human resource and talent professionals are being asked to take a more strategic role and be a business partner to the CEO. This means proactively influencing the CEO and educating him on talent issues rather than just simply implementing the CEO's talent views and biases. The most effective CEOs will recognize the value of this partnership and the seasoned views of others. This becomes a particularly critical issue when a company has a new CEO. Depending on the circumstances, it is often important to convince the CEO not to make rash changes to the existing talent approach while she gains perspective on this new role and organization.

Talent Roles

In order to develop and implement the talent practices, program, and culture that we have been discussing, different people in the organization should have talent management responsibility and accountability:

- Board of Directors
- CEO, senior executives
- Human Resource and talent professionals
- Line managers
- Individual employees—the talent

Corporate Board of Directors

The Board of Directors for corporations has historically not spent much board time on talent matters. Although the board members have usually been involved in the selection process and compensation packages for the CEO and other senior executives, they have had limited interest or involvement in broader talent management efforts. However, as talent management grows in strategic importance, there have been calls for more active board involvement in managing organizational talent (Michaels et al., 2001; Lawler, 2008).

McKinsey consultants (Michaels et al., 2001) find that boards have a limited knowledge and involvement in talent issues, and they advocate for the corporate board to take a more proactive role in managing the internal talent pool. They found that only 26 percent of 400 corporate officers somewhat or strongly agreed that "the Board of Directors really know the strengths and weaknesses of the company's top 20 to 100 executives" and only 35 percent thought that the "Board plays an important role in strengthening the overall talent pool of the company" (p. 172).

The American Productivity and Quality Center benchmarking study on talent management (2004) found that the 16 corporations sponsoring the study (with the surveys likely completed by HR and talent professionals) think the Chairman of the Board and the Board of Directors have the highest accountability for talent management in the organization. Others are rated as having lower talent accountability—in decreasing order, the CEO, the COO, Human Resources, the leadership development function, and other senior-level executives.

At about the same time a Conference Board survey of 75 HR talent professionals in 35 companies (Morton, 2004) found that 72 percent of respondents think their boards of directors take a direct interest in talent management integration. This suggests that HR and talent professionals think the board has primary accountability for talent management and takes some interest in talent management (although this could be an interest only for the most senior talent, that is, the top 5 to 20 executives).

Lawler and his colleagues at the Center for Effective Organizations have regularly surveyed corporate board members about their organizational role (Lawler, 2008). In 2006 they found that only 32 percent of board members say they track measures of human capital or talent to a great extent. In addition, they find that board members have little involvement in the development of key executives. In comparison, a survey of chief financial officers (CFO Services and Mercer Human Resource Consulting, 2003) found that only 23 percent of the 191 CFOs say that their boards are highly involved in human capital issues, even though the CFOs report that 49 percent of investors are beginning to ask about human capital issues to at least a moderate extent.

Lawler (2008) and Michaels et al. (2001) clearly advocate for much greater involvement by the boards of directors in talent issues. Lawler suggests that boards need the "power, knowledge, motivation, information, and opportunity" in order to take more responsibility for managing talent and human capital. and he challenges boards to spend as much time on talent as they do on financial and physical asset allocation and management.

We agree that boards should take a more active role in monitoring talent management efforts in the company, particularly now that talent management is accepted as a critical corporate strategy. Table 1.5 presents some talent responsibilities we recommend for the Board of Directors and other key roles in the organization. The board should be as involved in talent as it is in business strategy, financial management, and CEO effectiveness.

CEO and Senior Executives

The CEO probably has the single greatest influence on talent management effectiveness in an organization. In many studies, it is common to find that the commitment and involvement of the CEO and senior leadership are foundational requirements for successful talent management. They are expected not only to champion the efforts and role-model talent management behaviors to others but also to take responsibility for talent results.

Michaels et al. (2001) concluded from their 2000 executive survey that 49 percent of corporate officers at high-performing companies say that improving the talent pool is one of their top three priorities. In a benchmarking study at 16 corporations (American Productivity and Quality Center, 2004), 38 percent of the respondents said that the CEO is the primary champion of talent management in their organization, followed closely by senior-level executives (31 percent) and more distantly by HR (19 percent), the leadership development function (13 percent), and the board of directors (6 percent). In addition, 60 percent of the organizations say that their CEO and senior leaders spend 11 to 25 percent of their time on talent management, with one company, Celanese, reporting 30 percent of executive time. A Conference Board survey (Morton, 2004) concludes that during the 2000–2001 weak economy, two-thirds of corporate respondents reported that their companies did not significantly reduce any of their talent management initiatives. Some CEOs spend more time than others dealing with talent issues. Jeff Immelt,

Table 1.5. Talent Management Roles and Responsibilities

Role	Talent Responsibilities
Board of Directors	• Review and provide input on the organization's talent strategy and plans • Evaluate how well the CEO and senior executives manage talent • Take personal accountability for ensuring the quality of the talent in the top two levels of the organization, including selection and coaching • Establish a board-level talent committee with accountability beyond executive compensation • Advise the CEO and senior executives on how to strengthen the talent pool
CEO and senior executives	• Set clear talent policy, and provide strategic guidance in talent management • Conduct and involve executives in frequent talent reviews, planning, and development • Stay actively involved in talent management processes and programs: recruiting, assessment, development, retention • Serve as a role model to others, and develop talent management skills in others • Proactively reach out and get to know employees in critical positions • Take personal accountability for talent results • Hold managers and executives accountable, and reward them for talent management success

Human Resource and talent professionals	• Actively participate in the development and execution of talent strategy and business strategy • Be a subject matter expert on attracting, developing, and retaining talent • Help the CEO, the Board of Directors, executives, and line managers make better talent management decisions • Staff HR with the best talent professionals available who understand the link between talent and business strategy • Facilitate talent reviews and talent action planning • Be the architect for the development strategy for the top managers and executives • Use valid metrics to monitor talent management effectiveness • Act as a change agent for building and sustaining an effective talent management approach
Line managers	• Take responsibility and be held accountable for talent decisions and development • Take an active role in people decisions throughout their organization • Develop expertise in recruiting, managing, developing, and retaining the right talent for business needs • Establish a clear and high standard for talent • Use sound principles and metrics to make talent decisions that are rigorous and strategically relevant • Instill a talent mindset in others

(Continued)

Table 1.5. Talent Management Roles and Responsibilities (*Continued*)

Role	Talent Responsibilities
Individual employees—the talent	• Work to understand the talent requirements and business strategies in the company • Set a clear and high standard for your own performance • Know your own skills, abilities, development needs, and career interests • Take responsibility for pursuing your own development, and hold yourself accountable for development progress • Honestly communicate your career interests and limitations to your management • Find companies and career opportunities that are a good fit with your values, skills, abilities, and interests

Source: Partly based on Michaels et al. (2001), Lawler (2008), and Ulrich (1997).

GE's CEO, stated in GE's 2005 annual report, "developing and motivating people is the most important part of my job. I spend one third of my time on people" (see Lawler, 2008, p. 210).

CEOs and senior executives are also held accountable for talent. In the 2004 Conference Board study (Morton, 2004), 52 percent of respondents (human resource and talent professionals) said that the entire senior leadership team was accountable for talent management results, while 45 percent held human resources primarily responsible for results.

There is some evidence that senior leaders also hold themselves accountable. In an interview study with 50 CEOs, business unit leaders, and HR professionals, McKinsey Associates (Guthridge et al., 2006) conclude that senior managers blame themselves and business line managers for failing to give talent management enough time and attention and suggest that the failures are "largely human" or, as one executive stated, "Habits of the mind are the real barriers to talent management" (p. 1). The top obstacles cited by those interviewed are: "1) senior managers do not spend enough high quality time on talent management, 2) line managers are not sufficiently committed to people development, 3) the organization is siloed and does not encourage constructive collaboration, sharing resources, 4) line managers are unwilling to differentiate their people as top, average and underperformers and 5) senior leaders do not align talent management strategy with business strategy" (p. 2).

Clearly the CEO and senior executives have the authority and responsibility to significantly influence the talent management process and results in an organization. They need to understand and role model the talent mindset in the organization. Both Lawler (2008) and Michaels et al. (2001) discuss the talent responsibilities for senior executives. See Table 1.5 for CEO and senior executive responsibilities related to talent. The CEO in particular must be committed and involved, although we have seen talent champions in other senior executive roles who can help compensate for an unwilling or disinterested CEO.

Human Resource and Talent Professionals

A good deal of attention has been given to suggestions on ways to redirect and reshape the Human Resources function to make it more relevant and strategic (Lawler, 2008; Michaels et al., 2001; Ulrich, 1997). In some ways, it is part of a predictable evolution (similar to the finance function moving from financial reporting to strategic partner), but it also reflects frustrated expectations of Human Resources by executives and managers. Michaels et al. (2001) in the 2000 McKinsey survey found that 88 percent of officers thought "it was critical or very important that HR should be a high-impact partner to line managers in strengthening the talent pool" (p. 32); however, only 12 percent of the officers thought their HR leader actually played this role. Officers and line managers seem to want help from HR with talent issues. With the emerging organizational interest in talent management, it seems likely that HR is now stepping up to this challenge.

Part of the issue is deciding the talent accountability for HR. The Conference Board survey (Morton, 2004) found that HR was held accountable for talent management integration by 66 percent of the respondents, while the leadership team was seen as having the accountability by 30 percent of the respondents (compared to almost equal accountability between HR and the entire senior leadership team for talent management results). The strategic role of Human Resources is also being advocated. In a 2006 survey (Lawler, Boudreau, & Mohrman, 2006), 39 percent of senior Human Resource executives in Fortune 1000 companies thought their function was a full partner in developing their company's business strategy. However, only 24 percent of the line managers in the same companies agreed that HR actually was a full partner. Not only is there a difference in HR versus line manager perceptions, but as Lawler (2008) points out, there was agreement in 60 to 75 percent of these companies that HR is not yet a full partner in formulating and implementing business strategy.

Michaels et al. (2001), Lawler (2008), and Ulrich (1997) argue that the Human Resource function should be as strategically important to an organization as the finance function is. Michaels et al. (2001, p. 32) suggest that "attracting, developing and retaining talented people is the stuff of competitive advantage— more so than financing strategies, tax tactics, budgeting or even some acquisitions. Hence the HR leader has a much more strategic role to play in years ahead, arguably one equal to that of the CFO." Jack Welch, former CEO of General Electric, agrees: "If your CFO is more important than your CHRO [Chief Human Resource Officer], you're nuts!" (see Lawler, 2008, p. 180).

The discussion has focused on what HR should be doing in the future. Lawler (2008) advocates for three major responsibilities:

- HR administration (provide high-quality, low-cost services)
- Business support (help managers become more effective and make better human capital management decisions)
- Strategy development and implementation (align human capital management, organizational development, and organizational design with the company's business model)

Over the years, HR departments have been moving beyond HR transactions and administration (including outsourcing some operations) to working closely with business managers to make better talent decisions. The current transition for HR departments is to become more fully integrated and driven by shared strategic goals. Lawler (2008, p. 166) argues, "In HC [human capital] centric organizations nothing is more basic to the formulating of business strategy and to its implementation than talent and organizational effectiveness." Ulrich (1997) concurs that HR should be a strategic partner, which occurs "when they participate in the process of defining business strategy, when they ask questions that move strategy to action, and when they design HR practices that align with business strategy" (p. 27).

Despite these calls, a more strategic role for HR has been slow to develop. In 2000 only 7 percent of managers surveyed said that their companies "link business strategy to specific talent pool requirements" (Michaels et al., 2001, p. 32). We can only hope that that is noticeably improving with the current interest in strategically driven talent management.

The Human Resource function has some logical and obvious talent management responsibilities. Some of them are outlined in Table 1.5. To accomplish this, HR should have an exceptionally strong staff—the "best talent" (Lawler, 2008)—of talent professionals, industrial-organizational psychologists, and other subject matter experts who have the expertise in talent and can strengthen the link between business strategy and talent strategy.

Line Managers

Senior executives have a history of wanting to make most, if not all, of the talent decisions in a company. More recently, HR has been pressed to take a more active role, beyond just transactions and administration, to become talent experts. Human Resource and talent professionals have started to develop the skills and the motivation to fill that role. The next step in the evolution is for all managers to take personal responsibility and accountability for talent. We, and others, have called this a *talent mindset* throughout the organization.

In 2000 only 26 percent of 6,900 managers surveyed in a McKinsey survey (Michaels et al., 2001) strongly agree that talent is a top priority at their company. We suspect that more managers are now likely to see the importance of talent. In a more recent survey by Lawler et al. (2006), 56 percent of managers indicate that the business leaders' decisions that affect talent are "as rigorous and logical" as the decisions that affect other key organizational resources. But in the same survey, only 42 percent of human resource executives agreed. The conclusion is that there needs to be better objective and rigorous decision making regarding talent.

Michaels et al. (2001) found that 93 percent of corporate officers believe that line managers should be held accountable for the strength of their talent pool, but only 3 percent of the officers think that actually happens. In a later McKinsey article (Guthridge et al., 2006), 50 CEOs, business unit leaders, and HR professionals identified a number of obstacles related to line managers that prevent talent management programs from delivering business value including, "Line managers were not sufficiently committed to people development; . . . were unwilling to differentiate top performers [from] average performers and underperformers; [and] . . . did not address chronic underperformance" (p. 2).

The most successful talent companies, such as Johnson & Johnson and GE, have effectively created a talent mindset or culture in their organization where all managers are responsible and accountable for talent management. (Some of the talent responsibilities for line managers are listed in Table 1.5.) It seems obvious that if all managers have responsibility for managing financial resources in their area, then they should have equal responsibility for talent resources. As Michaels et al. (2001) suggest, "Once a manager believes that talent is his or her responsibility, the other imperatives (talent objectives) seem the logical and natural thing to do" (p. 22).

Individual Employees: The Talent

Most of the discussion on talent management focuses on what the organization, the leaders, and the managers can do to build and implement an effective talent management approach. However, in order for these efforts to be successful, they require the involvement and commitment of the talent: the employees who will be selected, assessed, reviewed, developed, deployed, and retained. As individuals take more responsibility for their own careers, they want to participate in the decisions that will affect them. Their interests, needs, and life preferences need to be understood and considered in the talent decisions in order for the decisions to be successful.

Of course they have some responsibilities as well in the talent process. (Table 1.5 lists a few of them.) Ultimately an effective talent management effort is a partnership between individuals and the organization, and both need to be committed to its success.

Talent Management Going Forward

This chapter has provided an overview of the key issues and challenges organizations face in pursuing strategy-driven talent management. It will require HR to have a more sophisticated understanding of business strategies and talent strategies and to develop, implement, and evaluate the talent systems, processes, and programs that will achieve those strategic objectives. We expect that HR will continue to step up to these challenges and become a full business partner to the CEO and senior executives. This book presents a range of approaches that organizations are taking to these challenges and an array of ideas and solutions that will guide the future of talent management.

References

American Productivity and Quality Center. (2004). *Talent management: From competencies to organizational performance: Final report.* Houston: American Productivity and Quality Center.

Ashkensas, R., Ulrich, D., Jick, T., & Kerr, S. (1995). *The boundaryless organization.* San Francisco: Jossey-Bass.

Axelrod, E. L., Handfield-Jones, H., & Welsh, T. A. (2001, May). The war for talent, part two. *McKinsey Quarterly.* Retrieved January 5, 2009, from http://www.mckinseyquarterly.com/The_war_for_talent_part_two_1035.

Barney, J. B. (1995). Looking inside for competitive advantage. *Academy of Management Executive, 9*(4), 49–61.

Barney, J. B. (2001). Is the resource–based "view" a useful perspective for strategic management research? Yes. *Academy of Management Review, 26*(1), 41–56.

Bartlett, C. A., & Ghoshal, S. (2002). Building competitive advantage through people. *MIT Sloan Management Review, 43*(2), 36–44.

Beer, M. (1997). The transformation of the human resource function: Resolving the tension between a traditional administrative and a new strategic role, In D. Ulrich, M. R. Losey, & G. Lake (Eds.), *Tomorrow's HR management: 48 thought leaders call for change* (pp. 84–95). Hoboken, NJ: Wiley.

Bernthal, P. R., & Wellins, R. S. (2005). *Leadership forecast 2005–2006: Best practices for tomorrow's global leaders.* Pittsburgh, PA: Development Dimensions International.

Bossidy, L. (2001, March). The job no CEO should delegate. *Harvard Business School,* 46–49.

Boudreau, J. W., & Ramstad, P. M. (2005). Talentship and the new paradigm for human resource management: From professional practice to strategic talent decision science. *Human Resource Planning, 28*(2), 17–26.

Boudreau, J. W., & Ramstad, P. M. (2007). *Beyond HR: The new science of human capital.* Boston: Harvard Business School Press.

Boudreau, J. W., Ramstad, P. M., & Dowling, P. J. (2003). Global talentship: Toward a decision science connecting talent to global strategic success. *Advances in Global Leadership, 3,* 63–99.

Byham, W. C., Smith, A. B., & Paese, M. J. (2002). *Grow your own leaders: How to identify, develop, and retain leadership talent.* Upper Saddle River, NJ: Financial-Times Prentice Hall.

Cappelli, P. (2008a). Talent management in the twenty first century. *Harvard Business Review, 86*(3), 74–81.

Cappelli, P. (2008b). *Talent on demand: Managing in an age of uncertainty.* Boston: Harvard Business Press.

CFO Services and Mercer Human Resource Consulting. (2003). *Human capital management: The CFO's perspective.* Boston: CFO Publishing.

Collins, J. (2001). *Good to great.* New York: HarperCollins.

Collins, J. C., & Porras, J. I. (1994). *Built to last.* New York: HarperBusiness.

Corporate Leadership Council. (2006). *Upgrading the organization's talent management strategies.* Washington, DC: Corporate Executive Board.

Deloitte Touche Tohmatsu & the Economist Intelligence Unit. (2007). *Aligned at the top.* New York: Deloitte Touche Tohmatsu.

DeVries, D. L. (1992). *Executive selection: Why do we know so little about something so important?* Working paper. Greensboro, NC: Center for Creative Leadership.

Economist Intelligence Unit & Development Dimensions International. (2006, May). *The CEO's role in talent management: How top executives from 10 countries are nurturing the leaders of tomorrow.* London: Economist Intelligence Unit.

Gerstein, M., & Reisman, H. (1983). Strategic selection: Matching executives to business conditions. *Sloan Management Review, 19,* 33–49.

Grove, A. S. (1999). *Only the paranoid survive.* New York: Currency Doubleday.

Gubman, E. L. (1998). *The talent solution: Aligning strategy and people to achieve extraordinary results.* New York: McGraw-Hill.

Gubman, E. L., & Green, S. (2007). *The four stages of talent management.* San Francisco: Executive Networks.

Guthridge, M., & Komm, A. B. (2008, May). Why multinationals struggle to manage talent. *McKinsey Quarterly.* Retrieved January 5, 2009, from http://www.mckinseyquarterly.com/Organization/Talent/Why_mulitnationals_struggle_to_manage_talent.

Guthridge, M., Komm, A. B., & Lawson, E. (2006, May). The people problem in talent management. *McKinsey Quarterly.* Retrieved January 5, 2009, from http://www.mckinseyquarterly.com/Talent/The_people_problem_in _talent_management.

Guthridge, M., Komm, A. B., & Lawson, E. (2008, January). Making talent a strategic priority. *McKinsey Quarterly.* Retrieved January 5, 2009, from http://www.mckinseyquarterly.com/Talent/Making_talent_a_strategic_priority.

Hewitt, G. (1997). Corporate strategy and human resources: New mind sets for new games. In D. Ulrich, M. R. Losey, & G. Lake (Eds.), *Tomorrow's HR management: 48 thought leaders call for change* (pp. 39–47). Hoboken, NJ: Wiley.

Hewitt Associates. (2005). *How the top 20 companies grow great leaders.* Lincolnshire, IL: Hewitt Associates

Hewitt Associates & Human Resource Planning Society. (2005). *The top companies for leaders study.* Lincolnshire, IL, and New York: Hewitt Associates and the Human Resource Planning Society.

Hollenbeck, G. P. (2002). Coaching executives: Individual leader development. In R. Silzer (Ed.), *The 21st century executive: Innovative practices for building leadership at the top* (pp. 77–113). San Francisco: Jossey-Bass.

Hollenbeck, G. P. (2009). Executive selection—what's right . . . and what's wrong. *Industrial and Organizational Psychology: Perspectives on Science and Practice, 2*(2), 130–143.

Hollenbeck, G., McCall, M., & Silzer, R. (2006). Do competency models help or hinder leadership development? A debate. *Leadership Quarterly, 17,* 398–413.

Huselid, M. A. (1995). The impact of human resource management practices on turnover, productivity, and corporate financial performance. *Academy of Management Journal, 38*(3), 635–672.

Jackson, S. E., & Schuler, R. S. (1990). Human resource planning: Challenges for industrial/organizational psychologists. *American Psychologist, 45*(2), 223–239.

Jeanneret, R., & Silzer, R. (Eds.). (1998). *Individual psychological assessment: Predicting behavior in organizational settings.* San Francisco: Jossey-Bass.

Kets DeVries, M.F.R., & Florent-Treacy, E. (1999). *The new global leaders.* San Francisco: Jossey-Bass.

Lawler III, E. E. (2008). *Talent: Making people your competitive advantage.* San Francisco: Jossey-Bass.

Lawler III, E. E., Boudreau, J. W., & Mohrman, S. A. (2006). *Achieving strategic excellence: An assessment of human resource organizations.* Stanford, CA: Stanford University Press.

Lawler III, E. E., Mohrman, S. A., & Ledford Jr., G. E. (1995). *Creating high performing organizations.* San Francisco: Jossey-Bass.

Lewis, R. E., & Heckman, R. J. (2006). Talent management: A critical review. *Human Resource Management Review, 16,* 139–154.

Kalamas, J., Mango, P. D., & Ungerman, D. (2008, September). Linking employee benefits to talent management. *McKinsey Quarterly.* Retrieved January 5, 2009, from http://www.mckinseyquarterly.com/Linking_employee_benefits_to_talent_management.

McCall Jr., M. W., & Hollenbeck, G. P. (2002). *The lessons of international experience: Developing global executives.* Boston: Harvard Business School Press.

McKinsey & Company. (2007, December). The organizational challenges of global trends: A McKinsey global survey. *McKinsey Quarterly.*

Retrieved January 5, 2009, from http://www.mckinseyquarterly .com/Organizational_challenges_of_global_trends.

Merriam-Webster Inc. (2002). *Merriam-Webster's Collegiate Dictionary* (10th ed.). Springfield, MA: Merriam-Webster.

Michaels, E., Handfield-Jones, H., & Axelrod, B. (2001). *The war for talent.* Boston: Harvard Business School Press.

Mohrman, S. A., & Lawler III, E. E. (1997). Transforming the human resource function. In D. Ulrich, M. R. Losey, & G. Lake (Eds.), *Tomorrow's HR management: 48 thought leaders call for change* (pp. 241–249). Hoboken, NJ: Wiley.

Mohrman, S. A., Lawler III, E. E., & McMahan, G. (1997). *New directions for the human resources organization: An organization design approach.* Los Angeles: Center for Effective Organizations.

Morton, L. (2004). *Integrated and integrative talent management: A strategic HR framework.* New York: Conference Board.

Organ, D. W. (1996). Leadership: The great man theory revisited. *Business Horizons, 39*(3), 1–4.

Pfeffer, J. (1994). *Competitive advantage.* Boston: Harvard Business School Press.

Sears, D. (2003). *Successful talent strategies: Achieving superior business results through market focused staffing.* New York: AMACOM.

Silzer, R. (1996). *Companywide integrated human resource system.* Richmond, VA: Capital One Financial Corporation.

Silzer, R. (Ed.). (2002a). *The 21st century executive: Innovative practices for building leadership at the top.* San Francisco: Jossey-Bass.

Silzer, R. (2002b). Selecting leaders at the top: Exploring the complexity of executive fit. In R. Silzer (Ed.), *The 21st century executive: Innovative practices for building leadership at the top* (pp. 77–113). San Francisco: Jossey-Bass.

Silzer, R. (2004). Executive development and coaching. In C. Spielberger (Ed.), *Encyclopedia of applied psychology* (Vol. 1, pp. 853–860). Oxford, UK: International Association of Applied Psychology and Academic Press/Elsevier.

Silzer, R. (2005). *Playing three dimensional chess: The Complexity of executive success.* Presentation at the SIOP Leading Edge Consortium: Leadership at the Top: The Selection, Globalization and Ethics of Executive Talent, St. Louis, MO.

Silzer, R., & Adler, S. (2003). Selecting managers and executives: The Challenge of measuring success. In J. Edwards, J. Scott, & N. Raju (Eds.), *The human resources program evaluation handbook* (pp. 130–152). Thousand Oaks, CA: Sage.

Silzer, R., and Douma, R. (1998). *Partnership of strategic selection and development: Building a high growth, high technology, Generation X company.*

Presentation at a Practitioner Forum at the Annual Conference of the Society of Industrial and Organizational Psychology, Dallas.

Sloan, E. B., Hazucha, J. F., & Van Katwyk, P. T. (2003). Strategic management of global leadership talent. *Advances in Global Leadership, 3*, 235–274.

Smart, B. (1999). *Topgrading: How leading companies win by hiring, coaching, and keeping the best people.* Upper Saddle River, NJ: Prentice Hall.

Smilansky, J. (2006). *Developing executive talent: Best practices from global leaders.* San Francisco: Jossey-Bass.

Stewart, T. A. (1997). *Intellectual capital: The new wealth of organizations.* New York: Doubleday.

Ulrich, D. (1997). *Human resource champions.* Boston: Harvard Business School Press.

Walker, J. W. (1980). *Human resource planning.* New York: McGraw-Hill.

Watson Wyatt Worldwide. (2001). *Watson Wyatt's Human Capital Index.* Arlington, VA: Watson Wyatt Worldwide.

Welch, J. (2006). *Winning.* New York: HarperCollins.

Wellins, R. S., Smith, A. B., & McGee, L. (2006, July). *The CEO's guide to talent management: Building a global leadership pipeline.* Pittsburgh, PA: Development Dimensions International.

Zuboff, S. (1988). *In the age of the smart machine: The future of work and power.* New York: Basic Books.

CHAPTER 2

BUILDING COMPETITIVE ADVANTAGE THROUGH INTEGRATED TALENT MANAGEMENT

Marcia J. Avedon, Gillian Scholes

The business world is more dynamic today than ever before with an accelerating pace of new technologies, increasing globalization of markets and competition, changing regulatory requirements, and increasingly commonplace mergers, acquisitions, and divestitures. In this tumultuous environment, organizations must continually renew their organizational capability to achieve competitive advantage. However, it is increasingly challenging to find the talent needed to compete in this dynamic business environment.

The availability of educated, working-age talent is shrinking in many of the world's labor markets (Zolli, 2007). Multinational companies are moving work to developing lower-cost countries, only to find the talent wars and wages subsequently escalating in those countries (Qihan & Denmat, 2006). Skilled leaders and other professionals, with the capabilities to enter new markets, create new business models, and innovate new technologies, are highly sought after (Michaels, Handfield-Jones, & Axelrod, 2001). Consequently, the demand for talent is outstripping the supply. As a result, top performers in key talent pools typically have multiple employment opportunities at any point in time. In addition, senior leaders, including CEOs, are in their jobs for shorter periods of time (Lucier, Kocourek, & Habbel, 2006), and employees generally no longer expect lifetime employment with one company. Leadership and employee development, through experience and education, still takes considerable time and effort and will never be a quick fix. This set of complex, changing business and talent realities creates the imperative for companies to focus on talent in a strategic, systemic, and customized manner.

The ability for a firm to create an integrated system that yields a continual flow of talent ready to address specific strategic and operational opportunities may be the single-most enduring competitive advantage. While organizations often find that their strategies, products, services, or markets require change, the need to have relevant, differentiated talent to achieve these business goals remains constant. However, the specific talent strategies need to adapt accordingly. Several recent surveys of both chief executive officers and chief human resource officers confirm that attracting, developing, and retaining talent is a top concern (Donlon, 2007; HR Policy Association, 2007). One CEO identified the point well (Donlon, 2007): "We are the most highly regulated industry in the world, and we have the most compliance issues in the world. So, those are risks, but our single biggest issue is human capital. We are losing it really fast and that is really scary."

This chapter provides definitions, models, and examples for creating a dynamic, customized, and integrated talent management system. We do not provide a set of absolute "best practices" or optimal solutions that will work for all companies. The focus is on creating a framework and the inherent logic of a talent management system for the particular company at a certain point in time. Also, approaches are presented to ensure that the talent management processes are sustainable but adaptable and, most importantly, are integrated into the business management system and organizational culture. Specifically the integration of talent management is discussed at three levels: (1) integration with business strategy, including human resource (HR) strategy; (2) integration of the talent management system; and (3) integration with the culture of the organization. Also provided are "learnings" and examples of how to make these connections in the talent management framework in order to achieve the greatest impact on business outcomes.

Talent Management Defined

Only in the last several years has the term *talent management* become popular, although it is defined in a variety of ways (Lewis & Heckman, 2006). These talent management definitions include:

- "Rebranded human resource management," that is, taking the traditional HR functions and doing them better
- Human resource planning and succession planning
- Talent as an attribute—either focusing on developing the inherent talents in all employees or focusing on "highly talented" individuals in general, usually high-performing or high-potential individuals

In this chapter we use the term *talent* to mean those individuals or groups that are strategically important to the purpose and goals of the organization. Specifically, *talent* refers to those individuals and groups with the strategic competencies that enable a company to achieve its short- and long-term goals. They exhibit the competencies that will add the most value to customers and in doing so, help to differentiate the organization from its competition. We define *talent management* as a subset of human resource (HR) processes, programs, and tools designed to identify, assess, develop, and retain talent.

Boudreau and Ramstad (2002) have proposed focusing on what they call *pivotal talent,* that is, the pools of talent where improvements in capabilities will make the most significant impact on competitive advantage. Business strategy involves making choices about resources and investments to create competitive advantage. When talent management is integrated into strategic business planning, there is an opportunity to discuss the capabilities and skills needed to execute the plan. This helps leaders create proactive plans to ensure that they have the talent they need to achieve the strategy.

Zuboff (1988) further defines *talent* in terms of the value that the talent segment brings to satisfy the needs of the customer and the degree of difficulty to replace the talent. This concept can be extended to segmented pools of talent by considering their strategic value to the organization and by their internal or external availability. This approach leads to the conclusion that given limited resources, the investment in people needs to be skewed toward the pools of talent that will provide the biggest value to the enterprise. Although all employees should be developed and engaged in order to achieve a sustainable organization, some groups of talent should be identified for additional focus. Therefore, the primary purpose of talent management is to define which groups and individuals are key to the organization's future, and then design and deliver processes, programs, and tools that grow this talent base.

Taking a targeted approach can be disconcerting to those who believe that organizations should invest in all employees. This does not mean that development is only confined to the strategic talent pools, but that additional investment should be made in strategic talent. This is really no different from a classic market segmentation approach, where investments in markets and brands vary depending on the strategic importance to the organization. This is captured in the philosophy of one large financial services company that advocates providing "good development for all, great development for some."

Making decisions about which talent pools are strategic is the first step in creating an integrated talent management strategy. We have identified four broad categories of strategic talent that should be considered:

- Leadership talent
- Talent for strategic functions
- Talent for strategic technologies
- Talent for strategic geographies

Leadership Talent

Leadership talent is generally an area of strategic importance for most organizations. As business becomes increasingly complex, the leadership competencies that are necessary for success have become harder to find and develop. In an environment where leaders no longer stay with one company for their entire career, it is critical to ensure leadership continuity and a flow of leaders through all career stages (Charan, Drotter, & Noel, 2001).

Executives must look not only at their current leadership teams to assess whether they have the performance levels and competencies needed for the short term, but also to the future needs of the organization. It is important for them to ask the questions:

- Where will the next generation of leaders come from?
- Are we grooming leaders early in their career and facilitating their career progression?
- Do we have talent shortages in early career, midcareer, or senior leadership talent?

Once these questions have been answered, then targeted programs can be created to grow leadership at the different stages within the pipeline. Leadership capability is a key differentiator between companies with sustained success and other less successful companies (Holstein, 2005). Therefore, identifying and developing employees with leadership potential is a major area of focus and investment in leading companies. Also, attracting and retaining leadership talent is a priority in top-performing companies.

Talent for Strategic Functions

Every organization has key functions that are of critical importance to the organization's strategy at a given time. Typically these functions become dominant in the culture, while other functions play a secondary or supporting role (Hewitt, 2000). For example, in technology companies, the hardware and software engineers fuel product development and innovation (the core goal of the company), while marketing, finance, and operations are essentially supportive functions. As their markets mature, some technology companies may find that they need to shift their focus to marketing and field service, in which case their talent strategy needs to be adjusted to increase the attention given to those functions.

When a company embarks on a new business strategy it is particularly important to identify which functions need to be strengthened and supported by the talent strategy. Treacy and Wiersema (1995) proposed that although companies need to be good at three fundamental business strategies—product innovation, operational excellence, and customer intimacy—they should aim to excel at only one, in which case, the company's focus will be reflected in the dominance of certain functions in the organization (see Table 2.1). For example, when one diversified manufacturing conglomerate moved toward a strategy of accelerated revenue growth from developing existing products and markets as well as acquiring new companies, it started to hire and develop business presidents from different functional backgrounds. Traditionally all business presidents in this company had come from either the finance or operations functions, but seven years later, over a third of these roles had leaders with sales, service, or marketing backgrounds. This represented a significant shift in the general management capabilities inside the company, and one that was more in line with their new market orientation and growth strategy.

Table 2.1. Identifying Talent Needs to Achieve Business Strategy

Strategic Forces	*Dominant Function*	*Samples of Specific Talent Needs*
Product Innovation	Engineering, Research, Technology	Electronics engineers, Biochemists
Operational Excellence	Manufacturing, Finance, Logistics	Procurement and sourcing specialists, Lean Six Sigma experts, Cost accountants
Customer Intimacy	Marketing, Sales, Customer service, Field service	Market researchers, Brand managers, Customer service representatives

Source: Treacy & Wiersema (1995).

Talent for Strategic Technologies

In many instances, products or services rely on a particular technology for a competitive advantage in the marketplace. As technologies develop and change, it may be necessary to recruit or develop talent with different experience. This can be a challenge, particularly if a company has built its culture around one technology and now needs to incorporate new approaches. In the energy industry, for example, large petroleum companies are investing in new technologies such as geothermal energy and biofuels in order to meet society's demand for renewable energies. They are partnering with different universities and researchers, and finding ways to attract talent who can commercialize the new technologies in new areas of the world. Often this creates tension between the traditional parts of the organization and the new start-up businesses because the expectations of the new talent for compensation, benefits, and work environment may be very different from the prevailing norms. The organization will have to develop new strategies to attract and retain talent with different skills and aspirations in order to be successful with the next generation of product and solutions.

Talent for Strategic Geographies

A growth strategy often requires geographic expansion, either within the domestic market or into other countries of the world. It is particularly hard to build organizational capability in rapidly developing economies (Boston Consulting Group, 2005) and requires a targeted talent strategy to build success. The emphasis for talent management will likely be very different when the organization is attempting to build a strong talent pool in these economies than when it is entering a more economically mature country.

Starting up in a new geography can be an expensive undertaking, and so a well-planned talent strategy, along with the right level of investment, is crucial. Identifying which geographies are the top priorities and then developing the appropriate talent strategy for each particular market is an essential first step toward business expansion. Without a targeted approach, it is likely that the business strategies will not be implemented as quickly or as successfully as envisioned. When foreign companies enter a new geography, they are competing for talent against each other, sometimes in markets where there is a lack of an educated workforce or an existing workforce that has developed under very different political or economic models, such as communism versus capitalism. This requires tailored hiring and development plans in order to have the skills that are needed to grow the business.

For example, in China some companies found that although they were able to find manufacturing and business managers to start up their operations, they were unable to find a distribution channel for sales and marketing to effectively bring their products to market. Since midcareer managers typically came from government-owned enterprises in a communist system, they had no experience in the use of dealers and other channels that could market products and services to end customers. Companies that wanted to grow through product distribution had to find ways to identify, educate, and support independent dealers in order to create a channel. This took time and investment before they could achieve their growth plans.

Three Levels of Talent Management Integration

The model of talent management that we propose integrates business and human resources strategy, talent management processes, and organizational culture; provides a systemic approach; and results in having talented leaders and individuals available to accomplish the mission of the organization.

Most of the published literature on talent management refers to the integration of talent management processes relative to other elements of human resource management or within the talent management system itself (Corporate Leadership Council, 2005; Morton, 2004). While these definitions may be of interest for certain purposes, focusing on this level of integration alone will not succeed in producing real value for the organization. The only way talent management will truly succeed is by being in support of, and part of, the business strategic plan and ultimately part of the culture or mindset of the organization. This is supported by recent research by Gubman and Green (2007) for Executive Networks on their members' experience with the evolution of talent management in their organizations. In their model, described in Figure 2.1, talent management evolves from a programmatic approach, where the focus is on the alignment of initiatives and activities, to a culture where managing talent is "an unquestioned, top-of-mind priority that becomes second nature to executives (and line managers)" (p. 1).

The discussion of approaches to integrated talent management should consider integration with strategy—both business strategy and human resource strategy—as the starting point. This is consistent with Lewis and Heckman's (2006) talent management decision architecture and Boudreau and Ramstad's (2007) human capital bridge decision framework. Both models start with strategy, or sustainable competitive advantage for the enterprise, as the critical input into the design of the talent management system.

Integration with Strategy: Business Strategy

Most organizations have a strategic planning process, but many do not explicitly incorporate organization and talent strategy

Figure 2.1. The Stages of Talent Management

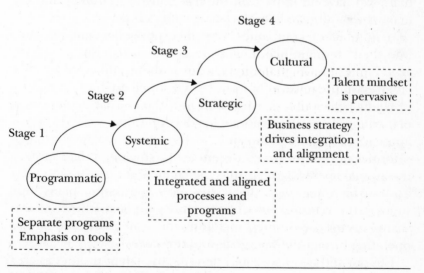

Source: Based on Gubman & Green (2007).

development into their strategic planning. Organizations that have embedded the talent strategy into their strategic planning process on a recurring, systematic basis ensure that they have the talent to execute the strategic plan. Ulrich and Lake (1990) discuss organizational capability as one of four ways an organization differentiates itself in the eyes of the customer. For a company to succeed, it must be capable (that is, have the capacity and competence) in four areas:

- Economic and financial
- Strategic and marketing
- Technological
- Organizational

Their model asserts that building organizational capability must be given the same level of attention as the other three.

Specifically, the integration of talent management plans into strategic plans answers the key question, "How do we ensure that the organization has the competencies and capacity to achieve its goals?" This question needs to be asked at the time of strategy development, not left until it is time to implement the business plans. The availability and readiness of talent, internally or externally, will have an impact on the feasibility of a strategy and can make the difference between success and failure.

A number of companies have incorporated talent planning into their strategic planning cycle as a formal business subprocess. For example, many have written about and tried to emulate General Electric's "Session C," GE's well-established process of talent review that is integrated into the annual management planning processes (Corporate Leadership Council, 2001). These approaches are successful only to the extent that the strategic priorities or themes are consistent across the long-range strategy, the annual operating plan, and the talent and organization plan. To be truly integrated, the talent and organization plans must support the requirements of the strategic plans (three- to five-year plans for the business including financial goals) and annual operating plans (one-year goals and objectives).

Charan and Bossidy (2002) describe the talent process as critical to successful execution of business strategy. They specifically emphasize the talent process as "making the link with strategy and operations" (p. 141). Some companies prepare the strategic plans and talent plans simultaneously to ensure integration. Regardless of whether the talent planning is a component of the strategic plan or a direct outgrowth of it, an integrated talent management system must be focused on determining the specific talent needs critical to achieving the business goals and on identifying the actions that will have the greatest impact on gaining strategic competitive advantage.

In addition to alignment with the business planning processes, an effective talent management process must include an honest, critical analysis of how well the company is currently achieving its talent goals to meet the business needs. Sophisticated, evolved talent management systems have both strong "look-forward" and "look-back" components to learn from mistakes or gaps and to build on successes. This approach also allows thoughtful decisions to be made about investments in strategic hiring, training, or other talent development activities.

When the talent management system is not well integrated with the business plan, there is often an excessive focus on the forms, programs, and process. For talent management to be truly integrated into the business planning and review system, the focus must be on achieving the strategic talent goals and on candid talent conversations at both the strategic and operational levels. Once the business strategy is translated into a talent strategy with measurable actions and goals, then there must be a process to follow up on commitments just as with other aspects of the business plan.

Talent Management Integration with Strategy: A Current Case

A current example of the integration of the talent planning into the strategic business plans is in Ingersoll Rand's security technologies business. Traditionally this business created value from the design, manufacturing, and marketing of mechanical locks primarily in North America under the Schlage brand. The strategic planning process a few years ago identified growth opportunities and goals through acquisitions and market expansion into electronic access control and electronic security. It was clear that this strategic shift required new skills in electronics and electrical engineering, software development, and global market development.

The new talent requirements demanded a shift in how talent was sourced, recruited, assessed, and assimilated. Through the strategic plan, it was determined that many of the new hires will come from "high-tech companies with human resource practices and work environments different from those at Ingersoll Rand."

The strategic plan defined the specific business opportunities in electronic locking and security by geographic market segment over the next five years. In addition, the business leaders identified the numbers and expertise levels of software, electronics, and electrical engineers needed; the sources of this talent; and the strategies for recruitment. New leaders with experience in global markets and the new technologies were also identified, as well as plans for developing internal high potentials. The plan also identified the potential retention risk if the cultural issues, including differing work environment expectations, were not addressed with the change in the talent base. Interestingly, the company was not abandoning the mechanical locking segments, so while there was a disproportionate investment in the new strategies, it was important to also keep the current, traditional talent pools engaged. Once the strategic plan was approved, including the talent goals, detailed action plans were established and reviewed quarterly.

Companies that have their talent management system highly integrated into their strategic management system will evaluate leaders' effectiveness based on their ability to develop and implement organizational and talent strategies to achieve sustainable performance. Leaders in these companies understand that achieving their talent plans is as important as achieving their financial plans. For example, Ingersoll Rand Security Technologies has the highest profit margins in the company and outperforms competitors in many markets, success that can be partially attributed to its talent strategy.

Integration with Strategy: Human Resources Strategy

An organization's human resources strategy is necessary to support the accomplishment of the business strategy and must explicitly address areas such as employee relations, compensation, benefits, recruitment, and development in order to create an HR environment that is aligned with organizational goals. In addition to the need to integrate talent management into the business strategy, it must be integrated with the rest of the HR strategy. The integration of talent management within the HR strategy may be accomplished in a number of ways, including through using common HR principles, philosophy, mindset, and HR systems and data, or by having shared competency models as an integrating framework. Once the requirements for talent are identified from the business strategy, strategic human resources programs should be designed with flexibility to differentiate strategic talent. For example, within an overall budget for annual merit raises in pay, leaders need to be able to give significantly higher increases to deserving individuals who meet the criteria for strategic talent.

HR Principles for Integration

Companies have implied or explicit philosophies or principles underlying their HR strategy. For example, one company may have a principle to strive to have top talent in all positions or talent pools. This is similar to the philosophy that Smart (2005) describes in his book *Topgrading*. He defines an "A" player as one who qualifies among the top 10 percent of those available for a position. This talent principle could be inconsistent with the HR philosophy if the compensation approach is always to bring people into the organization at or below the median pay level in the market. Although they may be among the top 10 percent of those willing to accept that level of pay, they may not be getting the true top 10 percent of those qualified, since others may have been available if the pay was higher.

On the other hand, if the overriding principle in a company is top pay for top talent or pay for performance, with a focus on distinguishing individual contributions, then the topgrading philosophy for talent management may fit very well. This philosophy also requires a strong performance management system and training for managers in order for them to distinguish performance levels. Again, alignment across HR processes or functions is essential so that the principles are consistently applied. Otherwise HR processes may be working at cross-purposes from the talent management goals.

The connection between leadership potential and equity compensation is another opportunity for integration within the

HR strategy. Often the principle is that annual incentives such as bonuses should tie directly to an employee's performance in the prior year (assuming consistent business performance). Whereas the overriding principle for long-term incentives, such as stock options or restricted stock awards, is often to have the awards linked to employees' potential for future contributions. Employees who are seen as the future leaders of the company and critical to the long-term success of the company are given larger grants of equity than those who do not have as much potential, even if their performance levels are the same. This type of linkage sends a powerful message to the high-potential talent about their value to the organization for the long term. Also, this approach assists with retention since equity grants typically vest several years into the future. These linkages between long-term incentives and talent management practices of performance management and succession planning are good examples of an integrated HR strategy.

Another HR principle that illustrates integration with the HR functions is in the area of benefits, specifically health and welfare and retirement programs. Some companies view benefits simply as a cost of doing business, almost like keeping the lights on. These companies want to be on par with their competition but not highly differentiated. Often this is not explicit but is the result of their investment in and positioning of their benefits offerings relative to benefits of other employers. In contrast, other companies view benefits as a key part of the HR strategy, not just from a cost management standpoint but also as a component of the value proposition for attracting and retaining talent.

In addition, the approach to integration of benefits and talent management may be segmented by career stages. For example, after identifying the critical talent issues, benefits changes may be made that will help attract early career talent or retain experienced talent. Given the demographic shifts in the workforce, with baby boomers retiring in large numbers, some companies are reexamining the early retirement provisions in their pension programs. Adjustments can be made to the formulas and credits to ensure they do not provide too great an incentive for experienced critical talent to retire early. Other companies have created "phased retirement" programs that allow experienced workers with key knowledge or skills to move from full-time to part-time status in lieu of full retirement without penalties to their pension calculations. These approaches allow better planning for transfer of knowledge to other workers, prolong key talent contributions, and may reduce recruitment costs.

Another area of integrated talent management within HR is in the health benefits arena. This has become a more critical part of the HR strategy for many companies as the workforce ages and the cost of health care escalates for employers and employees. Some organizations have developed creative "wellness" programs to keep employees healthy and productive. These initiatives may include on-site fitness centers or reimbursements for private fitness center memberships, health diagnostics and resources and free physicals and screenings, or even incentives for healthy behavior such as not smoking. Companies with a well-integrated HR strategy use such investments to improve the company's employment brand by promoting these benefits during the recruitment process and strongly linking benefits with talent acquisition.

HR Technology for Integration

In addition to philosophical or principle-based linkages between the components of the HR strategy, technology can help to align decision making and ensure the philosophy is executed as planned. For example, with well-designed information systems, managers can access individual performance and potential data at the same time they are allocating rewards, such as bonuses and equity grants. Decision makers can look at the differences between the average awards for top performers and average performers to ensure they achieved the desired differentiation. Such reports can be predesigned and user friendly, allowing the talent logic to be embedded into the work of every line manager as they manage their talent. In the initial years, the system can teach and reinforce the talent principles.

Another example of information systems that facilitate integration is when a company expects its leaders to create a positive work environment and measures employee engagement. Employee engagement survey scores can be included in the database as an additional planning tool for managers when evaluating annual performance of their own managers. Many companies state that performance evaluations, promotions, and rewards are a function of both results and leadership behaviors. Well-designed HR systems, data, and analytical tools can help managers reinforce these connections by making both leadership information, such as engagement scores or leadership competency ratings, and traditional results on financial or other business metrics readily available for talent management decision making.

Competency Models for Integration

Competency models can be effective tools to define the critical skill requirements for the business strategy and to align the various talent management and HR processes accordingly. Such models can also help to transform the culture of a company to the extent that new competencies are defined and valued for future success. For example, if a company wants to become more customer focused and emphasize innovation to a greater extent, these competencies should be part of the competency model. Then selection systems, performance management processes, succession and talent reviews, training, and development programs can all be linked to the same critical competency needs.

Many companies have also found that a well-defined competency framework is helpful to give managers a new language to describe and communicate expectations. For example, in the 1990s when Larry Bossidy was CEO of Allied Signal, the company had a competency labeled "bias for action," and it became clear that this was one of the attributes that was highly valued in leaders. Action orientation and drive were preferred over being methodical and highly analytical. Bias for action was a well-articulated, discussed, and understood competency. It became a defining aspect of the company culture and helped fuel the rapid transformation of the corporation.

Talent Management Integration with Human Resources Strategy: A Current Case

One global company had grown through acquisition over the years and had been managed as a holding company. While some product lines and business processes were integrated, several HR processes were allowed to remain disparate, including the core compensation structure that differed across businesses and within the same geographic locations. Talent movement for development and succession was relatively rare across businesses and countries.

When a change in business strategy required moving talent across the company, the inconsistencies in pay grades became a barrier to movement and development. The corporate HR group was charged with developing a global grading system to ensure a consistent pay classification structure for all professional jobs around the world. The structure was implemented over several months by evaluating jobs using a common methodology. This standard structure laid the foundation for easier movement and succession of talent across the entire company. This was an example of the need for integration between the HR processes of compensation and talent management to achieve the business strategy.

Integration Within the Talent Management Processes

Once the business and talent strategy has been determined and the human resources strategy has been aligned, a talent management process needs to be in place that integrates programs and initiatives to drive the desired outcomes. Talent management is most effective when it is a system, where the process itself is integrated so that activities form a logical flow, and the output from one step becomes the input to the next. Talent management activities need to follow a cycle just like any other business process. This ensures that strategic and tactical decisions are addressed every year and that they are timed to have the most impact on the success of the business plan. Functional talent management and other HR initiatives are then selected to close gaps between the current state of talent capability and the desired state. Establishing these linkages is a critical step in designing a talent management system because it ensures that the gathered information gives a complete picture of the strengths and weaknesses of talent at both the individual and the organizational level.

We propose a model of talent management that aligns programs and operates as a core business management process and is driven by a process around four steps:

1. Identify strategic talent requirements.
2. Assess individuals against required competencies.

3. Develop their capabilities.
4. Retain key talent.

After talent pools have been identified, they are assessed, and the results of the assessment lead to development actions, including career moves for individuals. At the enterprise level, succession plans are created for key functional roles or talent pools, and the assessments are used to validate and develop succession candidates. Also, strategies for internal and external staffing are developed based on the availability of qualified internal candidates.

In our experience, the value from the talent management system comes from the integration and alignment of the whole process rather than in the design of any particular program or initiative. Even if an organization cannot afford sophisticated programs and tools, having an integrated system around a few core programs will have a tremendous impact on the ability to create a culture where the value of the talent is fully realized. Ultimately, as a Conference Board study proposed (Morton, 2004), the primary integrating mechanism "is truly a merging of the hearts and minds around the power of talent and the importance of connecting the talent mindset to all aspects of the business" (p. 5).

Integration Within Talent Management Processes: A Current Case

During the long-range plan, the senior team of a multinational company realized that they needed to reduce their time to market for new products in order to achieve their growth and innovation goals. They decided to evaluate how product engineering was being managed and determine whether their engineering center in India, which had been used mainly for routine engineering work, could do some of the new product development process.

Their initial assessment of the capabilities of the India engineering group led them to recruit a new leader for that group from outside the company—someone who had led new product development for a peer company. In his first six months with the company, he developed a proposal for how the India engineering center could participate in the design and development of certain new products for global markets. He and his talent management specialist then used a third-party firm to conduct in-depth assessments of the senior engineering leaders, using interviews, testing, and simulations, built on the competencies that were identified as critical to success for the center as a global innovator. Each leader received a detailed report of the findings from the assessment, along with developmental suggestions. One-on-one development discussions were held between each participant and her manager to review the assessment findings and to consider the participant's career interests. Development plans were created, and a process was outlined for monitoring the completion of specific development actions.

During the course of this process, new product development roles were designed, and the company moved individuals into these roles based on the assessment results. The assessments ensured that leaders were placed based on their fit for new product development work and their ability to manage and motivate teams of newly hired engineering graduates.

Because of the competitive market for engineers in India, some changes were made to compensation programs and the work environment. The company invested in a major new design center with the latest technologies in order to support new product development, but also to attract and retain the best new engineers. By offering them a state-of-the-art environment, the company was able to assure engineers that they would have exciting work and would continue to learn and develop as engineers.

By the time of the next long-range plan review, the company was feeling confident that a significant piece of the new product development process could be managed from India, and the domestic group felt confident about the capabilities of their colleagues in India. As a result, they were able to manage more projects, improve their time to market, and reduce the cost of development.

Integration with Organizational Culture

Schein (1985) proposes that culture and leadership are "two sides of the same coin" in that the behavior of leaders creates and reinforces the basic assumptions and beliefs of the organization. Often without realizing it, leaders communicate what they consider important through the issues and activities that they spend time on. Members of the organization observe this behavior and draw conclusions about what is important. Schein identifies five ways in which the behaviors of leaders embed and reinforce the underlying culture of the organization:

1. What they pay attention to, measure, and control
2. Their reactions to critical incidents and organizational crises
3. Their deliberate role modeling, teaching, and coaching
4. Their criteria for allocating rewards and status
5. Their criteria for recruitment, selection, promotion, retirement, and excommunication

In lay terms, the culture of an organization is "how things are done around here." Nothing defines success better than when the talent management practices are so ingrained in the organization that they are part of the management culture. For example, a benchmarking team evaluated the talent management metrics of companies who had been identified as having the best talent management practices. In many cases, the team could not find any elaborate scorecards or dashboards. When these benchmark companies were asked how they knew that their talent management practices were working, they replied that employee development and talent management were just part of the culture.

This resonates with our experience working in several large companies. The talent management tools and processes were not too different across companies, but the success of talent management differed considerably. As others have observed (Hewitt Associates, 2005; RBL Group, 2007), what seems to have the most meaningful impact are the levels of commitment, ownership, and time that managers at all levels spend on talent management. So a key learning about talent and culture is that while mindset, methods, and metrics all matter, mindset matters most.

The focus initially must be on creating a talent mindset in all leaders, starting at the top. Before any discussion on programs and processes, the senior leadership of the organization must come to believe in the value of talent and their role in the creation of a culture where strategic talent is identified and actively managed for the long-term success of the organization.

Talent Management Integration with Culture: A Current Case

At Ingersoll Rand, after nearly three years of focus on talent management by the chief executive and the senior management team, it was clearly time to make talent management a business accountability for all managers. Although the human resources and talent organization was driving a comprehensive talent management process, it was not going to achieve full impact until all managers understood their role and acted as stewards of talent. The senior team decided to ask a group of high-potential leaders enrolled in the company-sponsored M.B.A. program to create a way of assessing the current management culture and providing an action plan for creating a culture of talent stewardship.

Drawing from their experience in business operations, the team used a methodology from lean manufacturing called the *maturity path*. This approach defines specific behaviors that will lead to process excellence at four levels of performance: from beginning through improving, succeeding, and leading. By creating a simple grid of behaviors, they could score the effectiveness of a plant on inventory management, for example, and show what concrete steps they can take to achieve best-in-class performance in that area over time. The team took the five elements of Ingersoll Rand's talent management model—identify, assess, develop, move, and engage—with the nine subprocesses associated with those elements and placed them on the vertical axis of a grid. They placed the four generic stages of process excellence—beginning, improving, succeeding, and leading—on the horizontal axis. This tool became known as the "leader/manager index" (LMI) (Ingersoll-Rand Company Limited, 2007).

The next step was to identify the specific behaviors at each stage of the maturity path as a manager demonstrated process excellence in talent management. Working with the talent organization, they completed the cells of the grid with behavioral descriptions of effectiveness at each stage. This tool allowed managers to clearly determine what they need to do to be effective in the specific talent management processes. Figure 2.2 shows excerpts of the progression in behaviors in the LMI to assess talent stewardship.

LMI scoring is either 0 or 1 in each subcategory, and it is not possible to score 1 unless all the behaviors in that cell can be verified. The total LMI score indicates the stage the manager has

Figure 2.2. Excerpt from the Ingersoll Rand Leader/Manager Index

	Sub Category	Beginning	Score (0 or 1)	Improving	Score (0 or 1)	Succeeding	Score (0 or 1)	Leading	Score (0 or 1)	Totals
Identify	Talent Review	• Manager understands the IR Talent Review process and how to use it to identify high potential talent. • Manager can recognize the difference between a high performer and a high potential employee.	0	• Manager assesses high potential talent using learning agility, competencies, and career motivation, as defined. • Manager is able to identify and document strengths, development needs and potential next role for high potentials.	0	• Manager demonstrates significant knowledge of talent within organization at all levels. • Manager calibrates high potential identification with other IR orgs. • Manager identifies and implements actions to accelerate the development of high pots.	0	• Manager is building the leadership pipeline through targeted development assignments and other development activities. • Manager ensures that individuals receive formal assessment and results are documented and used for development and planning next move.	0	0
	Organization Leadership Review	• Manager can articulate the purpose of the OLR Process, and use tools appropriately. • Manager can describe capabilities and resources needed to deliver business/department goals. • Manager assesses the strengths and weaknesses of his/her team relative to long term business/functional goals.	0	• Manager completes OLR process for his/her department. • Manager demonstrates an understanding of organization capability needs, and develops specific actions to build those capabilities.	0	• Manager assesses the organization on current and future competencies needed to achieve business strategy. • Manager has a near term succession plan for all positions, two levels below, with ready and available talent.	0	• Manager refers to and updates his/her OLR throughout the year to plan and build capability for his/her organization. • Manager reviews OLRs within organization. • Manager has a viable "ready now" succession plan for all positions two levels below.	0	0
Assess	Performance Management	• Manager can explain and lead the team through the Performance Management process. • Manager works with reports to complete PMPs identifying SMART goals for business and competency objectives. • Manager holds performance discussions mid-year and end of year, and provides feedback and reinforces company values, business ethics and integrity.	0	• Manager works with all direct reports as a team to align SMART individual and competency objectives with business objectives. • Manager provides performance feedback on an ongoing basis in addition to the midyear and year-end reviews. • Manager provides coaching, resources and training enabling direct reports to achieve objectives.	0	• Manager ensures that all employees have a clear line of sight between their goals and Enterprise goals. • Manager provides effective feedback and coaching on strengths, development needs, values, business ethics and integrity, to all reports both formally and in the moment. • Manager takes timely, documented action on poor performance.	0	• Manager ensures coordination in goal setting between his/her group and other groups where goals are interdependent. • Manager tracks the results of feedback based on visible impact on individual and business performance, and all behaviors related to company values, business ethics and integrity. • Manager holds meetings with his/her team to calibrate performance of individuals.	0	0
	Selection	• Manager prepares for interviews by reviewing resumes, and assessing required leadership and functional competencies. • Manager documents his/her assessment of candidates, and can articulate the rationale for selecting the final candidate using behavioral-based interview techniques.	0	• Manager seeks diversity of experience, gender, ethnicity etc. in candidate slate. • Manager selects for functional and leadership competencies as well as work experience. • Manager conducts a structured competency based behavioral interview process that includes multiple interviewers.	0	• Manager uses multiple interview methods and applies them appropriately. • Manager rigorously seeks diversity in candidate slates and selects individuals who bring new capabilities into the organization. • Manager leads and facilitates the interview team through final selection.	0	• Manager role models behavior-based interviewing skills, and coaches others in the process. • Manager hires candidates with potential beyond current organizational needs. • Manager is continuously prospecting for external talent and proactively makes referrals to the Enterprise.	0	0
	Totals		0		0		0		0	0

reached in the execution of the processes and gives the person a clear guideline on how to improve. Scores across managers can be aggregated to determine a total LMI score at the group or organizational level.

During the annual goal-setting and performance management process, managers assess themselves using the LMI tool and then review their self-assessment with their managers. They establish a score and an improvement goal for the year, which is then linked to 10 percent of their annual incentive. Ultimately employee feedback from the employee engagement survey will also be incorporated into the process. Since the LMI tool is a device for continuous improvement and managers are measured on improvement rather than by an absolute score, it has become an effective way of teaching Ingersoll Rand managers how to excel at talent management.

The LMI has become accepted across the company as a way to make progress toward the company's goal of creating a culture of exceptional global leadership. The expectation is that by building talent management into the measurement and reward system for leaders in this way, talent stewardship will soon become an integral part of the management culture.

A Model of Integrated Talent Management

The need to proactively build strategic capabilities has led to the emergence of talent management as a function within HR organizations. This function focuses human resource processes, programs, and tools on the critical groups of talent that are required for organizational success—perhaps no more than 20 percent of the workforce at any point in time.

From reviewing current literature and from our own experience in a variety of businesses, we have identified six generic components common to any integrated talent management model, which are depicted in Figure 2.3. Starting with strategy, the core talent management processes are identification, assessment, development, and retention, all supported by a culture of talent stewardship. These components all need to be in place and reinforcing of each other for talent management to add the highest value and impact to the business.

Figure 2.3. Talent Stewardship Model

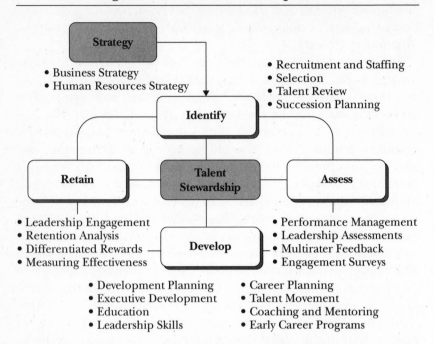

* Business Strategy
* Human Resources Strategy

* Recruitment and Staffing
* Selection
* Talent Review
* Succession Planning

* Leadership Engagement
* Retention Analysis
* Differentiated Rewards
* Measuring Effectiveness

* Performance Management
* Leadership Assessments
* Multirater Feedback
* Engagement Surveys

* Development Planning
* Executive Development
* Education
* Leadership Skills

* Career Planning
* Talent Movement
* Coaching and Mentoring
* Early Career Programs

This is a generic model that can be customized to suit specific organizations. Although the generic components will be present, the implementation of the model may look very different from one company to another as one or more components are emphasized over others. Each component of the model is discussed in turn.

Business Strategy

For a talent management system to be of value it must be driven by the short- and long-term needs of the business. Linking the talent management process to the business planning processes of the organization ensures that the talent strategy stays aligned, and is monitored and measured throughout the annual planning cycle.

Business strategies have a tendency to be aspirational and not take into account the realities of implementation that depend on the capabilities and capacities of the people of the organization. While leaders usually think in terms of whether they have the physical and financial assets to execute a new strategy, they often forget to assess their leadership capabilities. For example, it is not unusual to find a leadership team talking excitedly about venturing into developing markets, but without recognizing that neither they, nor their teams, have any experience in the new geography.

A review of organizational and talent capability during the discussion of long-term strategy provides an important opportunity to assess the feasibility of strategy implementation. For example, one company uses a tool (see Table 2.2) that asks business leaders to translate their top three strategic business priorities into the specific organizational competencies that will be needed in order to implement each priority successfully. They then identify their current gaps and the actions that they need to take to close the gaps. These actions become business initiatives that are monitored and measured throughout the year. The power of this tool is in creating a thought process that forces leaders to develop the capabilities that will ensure that they can achieve their business aspirations.

Talent Identification

After having determined the talent requirements that are strategically important to the organization, the next step is to consider whether there is a sufficient internal pipeline for the short- and long-term talent needs. Inevitably the talent strategy will require some mix of external hiring and internal promotion. Even in organizations that have a philosophy of promoting from within, there still is some percentage of talent that needs to be brought in from the outside to meet strategic needs. This could be at the executive level, or it could be in a relatively obscure technical discipline, such as writing architectural specifications, which is crucial to how the products are sold.

Depending on the business strategy and the competencies required, the organization needs to determine the ratio of internal to external hires. The "make versus buy" decision will vary by strategic talent pool. For strategic technologies, such as a bench scientist for new pharmaceutical research, the only answer may be to acquire those skills externally, whereas it may be feasible to develop general management talent from within the organization.

Table 2.2. Strategic Business Priorities and Organizational Implications

Key Strategic Business Priorities	Competencies Required for Success	Current Gaps That Could Impact Achievement of Business Objectives	Actions to Address Gaps
1. Become a solutions organization focused on customer productivity	A. Assessment of customer's productivity barriers and opportunities B. Consistent methodology for calculating total cost of ownership	A. Solutions selling skills and business acumen B. Each individual takes his own approach to the calculation	A1. Assess competencies of senior account managers A2. Create specialized account teams and staff with best talent B. Design PC-based tool, and train all account managers
2. Improve profitability for retail business	A. Sales channel competencies B. Lean processes in retail business management	A. Channel management capabilities B. Lack of service productivity program	A1. Develop selection model for channel management hiring A2. Develop training curriculum for sales organization B. Reengineer business process
3. Low-cost country sourcing and manufacturing	A. Procurement and engineering skills B. Supply base quality assessment C. Manufacturing footprint aligning to market growth	A. No sourcing or engineering organization in Asia B. No manufacturing facilities in China	A1. Hire engineering team in China A2. Hiring and sourcing expert for Asia B. Build new facility in China

Internal Sourcing

Being in a position to promote from within for the majority of openings requires strong succession planning, career planning, and talent movement processes. Overcoming barriers to moving talent across organizational boundaries, such as business sectors or functions, can be difficult, but with the right level of leadership commitment, it will reap benefits. It may mean creating a culture where jobs are posted and individuals are encouraged to apply for positions outside their current organization and where moving to another part of the enterprise is viewed positively rather than as a lack of loyalty to their current group.

This process may need to be actively managed at certain levels, using the succession plan to develop qualified slates of candidates from across the company. At these levels, individuals are invited to interview for new roles after obtaining the support of their manager. The match between individual development needs and career plans can also be used to proactively drive movement, where time in position is tracked and talent is declared available for a cross-business or cross-functional move. In this way, it may be possible to create an opportunity that will be developmental for the individual. This requires a culture of talent movement, where managers are willing to "offer up" talent, knowing that this will build bench strength for the whole company and that they will receive talent in return.

Choosing to hire externally because you want to, rather than because you have to, is an aspiration that many companies have in today's talent wars. But this will be a reality only if all the components of the talent management system are working together to create a pipeline of available internal talent for critical positions.

External Sourcing

The external sourcing and recruitment strategy will have to be adjusted to source talent that might not have been considered before. This is an opportunity to integrate diversity and inclusion into the talent management agenda by making the business case that the company cannot afford to be missing out on any talent sources in today's competitive talent market. This requires examining the aspects of the culture or work environment that support or create barriers to inclusion. For a multinational company or one planning to expand internationally, the mix of local hires and expatriate hires is an important decision. Decisions should be made regarding the aspects of talent management that are global, that are regional, and those that can be unique to a local market or specific business need.

Whenever possible, it is advisable to hire ahead of the need, and certainly hire for future, not just for present job requirements. This may be easier to do in businesses where profit margins or business growth are high. For example, one high-growth computer technology company was known for hiring talented individuals whenever it found them, knowing that the growth in the business would ensure productive roles for them within a matter of months. In this way, they were able to keep up with the growth of the business; however, as the industry slowed, this talent strategy needed to change. Even a highly cost-controlled organization can identify creative ways to do anticipatory hiring. In industrial companies, where costs are tightly managed, many companies have adopted an approach where the bottom 10 percent of performers are managed out of the organization and the resulting vacancies are used to hire strategic talent (Smart, 2005).

Setting aside a budget to invest in even a handful of strategic positions will create a buffer of talent and enable the organization to be more agile. Traditionally companies have used graduate rotational programs to build their leadership pipelines, with the intention that the majority of those hired will spend their entire career with the organization. Although career-long employment with one company is no longer likely, early-career rotational programs can be an excellent source of talent. These hires may be used for enterprisewide initiatives and can be particularly useful in strategic geographies as a way of attracting and developing a local pipeline of talent for the midterm. What is critical is that the retention of these early-career hires is long enough to provide a return on the investment.

Talent Assessment

Implementing selection systems that are built on the organization's strategic competencies and used for both external and internal selection is a critical component to the talent management system. Teaching managers to use behavior-based interviews is a valuable first step toward building an understanding of the science of talent management. If managers can learn to assess competencies during the selection process, they will start to use these skills when assessing their employees for development and potential.

Once individuals have been placed, there is still a need for a formal assessment process to indicate their current and future capabilities against business performance, strategic competencies, and career potential. A good performance management system, one that assesses individuals not just on what they do but also on how they do it and also on their development of strategic competencies, is an important foundation. However, the performance management system is truly effective only if managers are objective and are skilled in the assessment of results, behaviors, and competencies. Often there is a lack of calibration across the organization, making it extremely difficult to get a true sense of the capability of the organization as a whole.

Incorporating the use of validated instruments for particular job families provides additional objective assessments of individuals for both development and selection into high-potential talent pools or into new roles. The management of these data becomes extremely critical, and organizations need to establish which data are to be "owned" and used by the organization and which data are "owned" by the individual for developmental purposes and not shared for decision making by management. Some companies have implemented policies that essentially create a "firewall" between the assessments used in learning programs and the assessments used for validation of potential or for internal selection. This gives the individual the safety to experiment and take risks in a learning environment without worrying that the data may be used in the selection process. Ultimately organizations strive to have an open environment where strengths and development needs can be discussed without defensiveness, but this is hard to achieve.

Formal leadership assessments that are designed and conducted by qualified individuals, either internal or external to the organization, are invaluable when evaluating the capabilities of strategic talent. These assessments are time intensive and typically include in-depth background and career history, cognitive and personality tests, and peer and manager interviews. They can be particularly helpful when assessing high performers for their potential to be successful at the next level in the organization. Such assessments will lead to a "three-way" discussion with the individual, his manager, and the assessor, to validate the findings and agree on the priorities for a development plan. This type of assessment may be used as part of selection for promotional opportunities, and in this case, the data are owned by the organization. A critical element that can be captured by this approach is in the "fit" of the individual with the role the person is being considered for. Silzer (2002) notes that the question of fit is too often ignored, leading to a mismatch between the capabilities of the individual and the needs of the environment. Ignoring the question of fit can lead to costly mistakes that damage the individual, the organization, and the business.

Talent Development

Development planning for both current and future roles is one of the most important activities that managers can do to accelerate the growth of capabilities in their organization. The Corporate Leadership Council (2004) found that development planning was one of the strongest drivers of employee engagement. By having an effective development plan—one that is challenging but allows sufficient time to complete the plan—managers can significantly improve the engagement of their employees. Leaders need to engage all employees in development but need to be especially focused on targeted development for strategic talent.

To be effective, development requires a three-way partnership focused on creating development actions tied to business needs and competency requirements (Kaye, 2002). As Figure 2.4 shows, the individual, the manager, and the organization each have specific accountabilities to make development successful. First, the organization's role is to provide processes, tools, and investment and encourage a culture of continuous development. Next, managers need to be skilled in identifying areas for development,

Figure 2.4. Development as a Three-Way Partnership

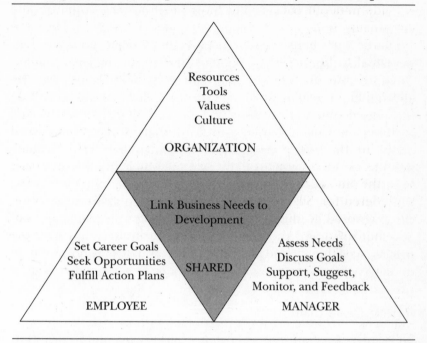

Resources
Tools
Values
Culture

ORGANIZATION

Link Business Needs to Development

Set Career Goals
Seek Opportunities
Fulfill Action Plans

SHARED

Assess Needs
Discuss Goals
Support, Suggest,
Monitor, and Feedback

EMPLOYEE

MANAGER

Source: Adapted from Kaye (2002).

helping to find the appropriate resources and opportunities and providing coaching and feedback on an ongoing basis. Third, individuals must take responsibility for their own development by following through on development suggestions and committing to improving their skills and developing new competencies. Finally, the development actions and plans must be linked to the needs of the organization and the opportunities inherent in the business plan.

Development plans must include the appropriate mix of activities and the appropriate level of challenge for the individual. The Center for Creative Leadership (McCall, Lombardo, & Morrison, 1988) asked executives, "What has had the greatest impact on your development in your career?" The results were that 70 percent of their responses described experiences, 20 percent described relationships, and 10 percent described formal training. Many practitioners have used this research to suggest that development plans should include activities from all three areas, with roughly 70 percent of the development plan geared toward experience (projects and assignments), 20 percent to relationships (learning from managers and peers), and 10 percent to formal training programs. We also propose that managers should determine the appropriate degree of challenge for the individual when identifying a developmental activity.

Managers have a tendency to think that formal training programs are the most appropriate development solutions, but they need to be made aware of the ways in which individuals could broaden their learning through on-the-job experiential activities, which may have an even stronger developmental impact. Ideally, the development plan will use all three types of activities for one development goal: for example, providing training on strategic pricing, coaching by a pricing expert, and the opportunity to develop a pricing proposal for a product or service that is then presented to the marketing team.

Another common pitfall is identifying development actions that have too little or too much challenge or risk. What must be evaluated is both the importance of the assignment or job to the organization and the degree of "stretch" or previous experience required for success (see Figure 2.5). Sometimes organizations are reluctant to take a risk in providing an individual with an assignment that is a first-time learning and repeatedly rely on those who are proven in a given area. This is not developmental for either the person who has done the role many times or for the person never given the opportunity. What is critical is to find an opportunity that is not of the highest importance level to allow the first-timer to develop skills or to provide support from the more experienced person. Conversely, a person who is given a highly important role with many "firsts" and little support is being set up for failure. For example, moving someone to a new business and a different country as a promotion will have a lower probability of success than promoting this person in a business that he knows or that is in his own country. Figure 2.5 is a useful tool to find the optimal level of challenge for developmental assignments or moves. This optimal level, or "sweet spot," encompasses the development actions or moves that provide sufficient

Figure 2.5. Planning Optimal Development Assignments

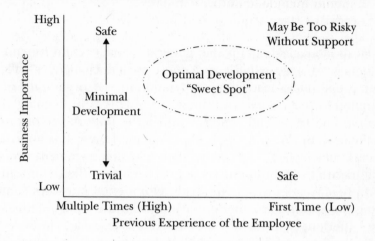

challenge for growth without undue risk to the individual or the organization. The tool can also be used to determine which person is best for an open role from a development standpoint.

Development Through Experience

Broad functional and business experience is essential in today's business world. Companies need leaders who have the ability to make sound decisions in a rapidly changing environment, and so the experience of having been in diverse business situations can build the confidence and judgment necessary for the challenges of the future. Herb Henkel, Chairman and Chief Executive Officer of Ingersoll Rand Company, captured his expectations for development as "$2 \times 2 \times 2 + 5$" (Ingersoll-Rand Company Limited, 2004), which is company shorthand for experience in:

- Two businesses
- Two functions
- Two geographies

and with the five stages of a business life cycle:

- Starting up a business
- Turning a business around

- Growing a mature business
- Implementing an enterprise initiative
- Leading a large acquisition or divestiture

Herb Henkel's belief is that general managers and functional leaders who have experienced these varied challenges will be best prepared to lead complex, multinational organizations to sustainable success over the long term. This is in keeping with the findings of McCall et al. (1988) on the importance of varied challenges and development experiences. Taking this approach necessitates having an effective succession management process that identifies high-potential talent from across the organization and proactively moves them for developmental purposes considering the specific learning opportunities in the assignments and the experiential needs of candidates. This approach to development through experiences, including cross-business, cross-function, and cross-geographies, has become a well-understood part of the talent management model in his company.

Development Through Relationships

Role models, whether they are direct managers or peers, have a significant impact on development. As the Center for Creative Leadership research showed, we learn by observing the behavior of others who are successful, so having effective leaders with the right values at all levels of the organization is critically important.

The relationship with the direct manager is particularly significant as we learn which behaviors to emulate and which not to emulate. Having a relationship where the manager gives the appropriate balance of challenge and support creates an environment where talented individuals can learn and grow. Having the opportunity to discuss weaknesses candidly and to have regular feedback and coaching can accelerate the development of leaders at all stages in their career.

Learning from peers through cross-functional, cross-business teamwork also gives developmental opportunities, as does membership in functional councils, where specialists come together to share best practices. Other networks, such as affinity groups, organized by gender, ethnicity, or business interest, also provide opportunities to learn from role models. Anecdotally we often get feedback from participants in training and education programs indicating that they learned as much from their peers as from the instructor. This suggests that selecting the optimal group of peers for a class can have a significant impact on the quality of the learning experience. Peer networks have been found to be critical in retention of talent. Recently such networking has become virtual through online groups or communities of practice (Wenger, McDermott, & Snyder, 2002).

Development Through Formal Training

Although formal training programs may have a relatively small percentage of impact on development, the value can be increased by (1) focusing training and development on the strategic competencies, (2) having a widespread rollout of specific strategic programs, and (3) getting leadership participation.

Having a curriculum and a delivery strategy that focuses on reaching targeted groups with the strategic competencies that they need to drive the business agenda can be highly effective. This means developing programs that address the competency gaps that have been identified as being critical to the organization's strategy (Meister, 1998). Some companies organize their programs around a core business curriculum, with the addition of "colleges" that specialize in specific functional or technical areas. Those "colleges" are selected based on the strategic competencies and are targeted to the relevant segment of the population.

The delivery strategy for a particular program can affect the impact on both the individual and the organization. One company wanted to build a more entrepreneurial mindset in general managers, and developed a two-week program that was cascaded through the organization. This meant that concepts and behaviors were reinforced after the participant left the classroom because the managers of the participants had also gone through the program. In this way, the program had an impact on the leadership capabilities across the company.

The corporate university can also provide learning opportunities through participation in its own governance. Creating a strategy board consisting of a cross-section of business leaders has the benefit of increasing ownership for the university, ensuring alignment with business needs, and providing a developmental experience for high-potential leaders. Similarly involving line managers in design teams and having them teach parts of the curriculum builds their competency and confidence as leaders (Tichy, 1997).

Talent Retention

Over the past few decades, the approach to retention in many organizations has evolved from a focus on measuring overall turnover to measuring voluntary versus involuntary turnover in order to get a better sense of the reason for the losses. More recently, companies have segmented this further by identifying the turnover of high-performing or high-potential talent in order to address the specific issues for these critical employees.

We believe that organizations should go beyond the macromeasures of turnover to look at turnover within strategic talent pools. This is the talent that is most important to the future of the organization and where retention is the most critical. Cappelli (2000, p. 100) proposes "a market driven retention strategy that begins with the assumption that long-term, across-the-board employee loyalty is neither possible nor desirable. The focus shifts from broad retention programs to highly targeted efforts aimed at particular employees or groups of employees."

Effective retention efforts require examining each strategic talent pool to identify who is at risk and why, so that individualized retention plans can be created. Sometimes this involves accelerating a career move or providing a key individual with visibility to senior executives in other parts of the business. The retention action could include the expansion of current responsibilities or the invitation to participate in a significant learning program. Invariably the retention strategy will go beyond compensation and will be tailored to what is likely to motivate and engage the individual or groups of key talent.

Compensation and benefits strategies need to be monitored for external competitiveness and internal equity, but as we know, compensation and benefits alone will not solve retention issues. Targeted "stay bonuses" can be effective but are not sufficient for long-term retention. Capelli (2000) suggests that in addition to compensation, companies should consider how job design, social ties, location, and hiring can be used in designing effective retention strategies.

Developmental assignments or special projects are often given to the top performers or high-potential talent as part of a retention or engagement plan. Although this may generally be a good practice, it points to the need for the manager to truly understand what is important to an individual employee and customize the approach accordingly. The assignment could be seen as highly valuable to meet the employee's career goals or just additional workload. If travel is required, the employee could see it as either an interesting experience or personal sacrifice.

It is equally important for managers to recognize when adding special projects or developmental assignments will be counterproductive. It is usually the case that the very individuals whom we want to retain are the ones who are under the most pressure, are given the most challenging assignments, and are turned to for participation in activities that go beyond the scope of their role. This can lead to stress and burnout, which may make the individual more susceptible to calls from recruiters. It is important for the manager to pay attention to overall workload and challenge to make sure that the individual is supported and will be able to sustain performance over long periods of time.

People are said to join companies and leave managers, which is why effective management is so important to the development and retention of strategic talent. Having an effective relationship means that the leader knows what motivates and engages her employees and is able to assess retention risk and develop a customized retention plan for key talent. While the formal retention analyses and plans are important, the informal leadership behaviors are equally important. Through the leader's actions, employees judge whether their contributions are valued and appreciated or not, and to what degree the company is committed to their future. If the manager understands the employee's goals, aspirations, and personal circumstances and builds a supportive relationship with a two-way dialogue, then the specific retention action plans will be more effective.

Even if the retention strategy is ultimately ineffective, the best talent stewards remain in contact even after the individual has left the organization. Today we cannot interpret a resignation as an act of disloyalty; it may very well be the best move for the development of that individual. It is also true that the grass is not necessarily greener in other pastures and sometimes it is possible to recruit and persuade talent to return at a later date. This can send a very positive message to the organization if those who were seen as great talent choose to return to the company. All in all, there are many benefits to staying connected to alumni, not least of which is to make them part of the organization's extended network of advocates.

Talent Stewardship

The first five elements—strategy, identification, assessment, development, and retention—enable the organization to put appropriate process and programs in place and ensure integration across the enterprise. However, at the heart of the model is talent mindset, or what we call "talent stewardship": a frame of mind, or a culture, where every manager feels ownership and accountability for talent on behalf of the organization. This means that the manager takes responsibility not only for managing today's talent, but also for strengthening the team or the organization for the future. Once talent stewardship is engrained in the management disciplines of the organization, it transforms the talent management strategy from a functional initiative to a competitive business advantage.

This type of culture does not happen overnight. Some companies have invested heavily in leadership development for decades and have built supporting systems, processes, and programs that are embedded in the fabric of the organization. For companies that are just embarking on this journey, it may take time, but progress can be accelerated by clearly establishing talent management expectations for line managers, by providing them with development and support, and by evaluating and rewarding their results.

In a best-in-class company, every manager must feel ownership for talent within their own organization and for the larger enterprise. Constantly scouting for talent internally and externally, coaching and mentoring others, providing performance feedback, developing and teaching: these are all part of the day-to-day accountabilities of today's best managers. Managers who are talent stewards have a commitment to developing others and supporting them for promotional opportunities.

Customized Talent Management Systems

A talent management system should be designed around the six components described above (and presented in Figure 2.3), with strategy being a critical input to the system and talent stewardship being the cultural underpinning. However, within this model there is tremendous opportunity for customization. The specific talent management strategies will vary, depending on the business strategy, the stage in the life cycle of the business, the level of leadership commitment, and the culture of the organization. This will also vary by company, and so it is possible to see two successful talent management strategies that are very different. In Figure 2.6, company A is operating in an emerging market, with a talent strategy that is focused on external hiring (identification) and retaining talent (retention). Company B is focused on building an internal leadership pipeline and is putting additional effort into formal assessments (assessment) and talent movement (development). The key point is that the talent management tactics of each company are fully aligned with their

Figure 2.6. Customized Talent Management

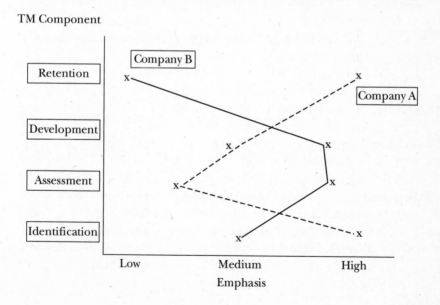

TM Component

business strategies and they are making the appropriate decisions about investments in programs.

Companies should select from a menu of programs that are designed to work within the strategic framework of their organization. Most companies cannot implement a talent management system all at once and must pick strategically from the menu to create a system that will have the most impact. Table 2.3 provides some examples of how specific programs support the different components of a talent management system. This is not an exhaustive list but illustrates that practitioners must make strategic choices about program investment across all components, starting with the areas that will have the most impact on the organization.

Table 2.3. Talent Management Menu

Identification	Talent Planning	Competency Models
	Staffing	Leadership, Technical, Functional
	University Recruitment and Selection	Behavioral Interviews
	Succession Planning	Talent Reviews
Assessment	Performance Management	Behavioral Interviews
		Multirater Surveys
	Leadership Assessments	Upward Appraisals
Development	Development Planning	Development Dialogues
	Career Planning	Career Progression Models
	Succession Management	Early Career Rotational Programs
	Talent Movement	Educational Programs
		Learning Events
Retention	Employee Engagement	Employee Engagement Surveys
	Compensation and Benefits	Recognition Programs
		Differentiated Rewards
		Work Environment Initiatives

It typically takes many years to fully design and implement a talent management process, but once the basic architecture is established and priorities are set, the system can be built out and adapted to meet the changing needs of the organization. The work of alignment with strategy and integration with culture is ongoing and cannot be overemphasized. It is when these two elements are in place that the true power of talent management can be realized.

Implementation of Talent Stewardship

Creating an integrated talent management system that is driven by strategy and supported by a culture of talent stewardship takes a partnership between three key stakeholders:

- Executive management, including the board of directors
- Line management
- Human resource and talent management practitioners

Executive Management

Chief executive officers and boards of directors must provide oversight and direction to the talent management process. They set the tone and signal the importance to the business success. The CEO demonstrates talent stewardship behaviors for other leaders. A significant driver for effective talent management is also the interest that boards of directors take in the talent capabilities of the organization. For decades, boards have reviewed executive succession plans focused primarily on the CEO and the top officer positions. Increasingly they are asking questions about the availability of talent to support strategies in new markets, technologies, and geographies. Progressive boards—those that understand the importance of effective talent management—are moving from an annual to a semiannual review. Also, their topics for discussion in these reviews are going beyond questions about executive retirements and succession to a much deeper conversation with the chief executive officer about strategic talent at multiple levels in the organization.

Line Management

Talent stewardship is a line management accountability. Accountability for attracting, developing, and retaining strategic talent is more than a priority for the best leaders; it is the way they operate on a daily basis. The best leaders know that they, and their organizations, cannot lead in the marketplace without highly talented individuals, and so the cultivation of talent is an essential aspect of being a line manager in business today.

Block (1993) defines *stewardship* as "the willingness to be accountable for the well-being of the larger organization by operating in service, rather than in control, of those around us" (p. xx). Another aspect of stewardship is leaving a legacy: an organization or team stronger than it was initially, "to hold something in trust for another" (p. xx). This is not merely an altruistic notion. Talent stewards know from experience that they will always be able to attract the best talent to their teams because of their reputation for successfully developing others. Also, they understand that their business performance will be stronger as a result of their personal focus on talent management.

Human Resource and Talent Management Professionals

The human resources and talent management function is the enabler. In an organization that has a talent stewardship culture, the role of the human resources and talent function is to bring subject matter expertise and consultation to address the talent needs of the organization. They design and manage processes and programs, and provide advice and counsel to managers and individuals, but managers personally make the final talent decisions. The role of talent management is to help managers make the best talent decisions in both the short and long terms. In this way they use data from assessments, performance appraisals, behavioral interviews, and observation to make recommendations on an individual's strengths, areas of development, and potential. As specialists in talent management, HR should be able to provide insight and recommendations, but managers have the responsibility to make the final decisions for hiring, promotions, development, and retention.

Finally, we must always remember that talent management is a high-touch activity. We cannot forget that talent is composed of individuals who have their own unique aspirations and motivations. Although talent management requires tremendous process discipline and the thoughtful analysis of data, the reality is that we are working with individuals and attempting to match their needs with the needs of the organization. Effective talent management is about relationships and requires the establishment of trust among all parties involved. The organization has to trust the talent manager's assessment of individuals and fit; individuals have to trust that confidentiality will be maintained appropriately and that the organization is vested in the fairest outcome for their career. Each individual in the talent pool has a set of personal needs and aspirations. Issues of mobility, family issues, work/life balance, and career aspirations often come into play. It typically takes significant counseling and coaching to orchestrate one succession move. Each situation has to be managed with the individual, and often the family, in mind. Effective talent management cannot be orchestrated purely from a database; it requires a combination of process and relationship to achieve the best results.

Future Challenges and New Directions

We have presented a model of integrated talent management that is driven by business and human resources strategy and fueled by a pervasive culture of talent stewardship. The specific components of an integrated talent management system are supportive and connected but may vary in emphasis across companies. We believe that this model of integrative talent management is compelling to achieve superior business outcomes. These views are based primarily on our practical experience across multiple businesses, companies, and industries. Currently there is little research that demonstrates the benefits of a more integrated or systemic approach to talent management.

One research effort attempted to link talent management to financial outcomes (Holstein, 2005) and found that companies evaluated as the "Best Companies for Leaders" had 22 percent greater return to shareholders than the other companies studied.

However, the results of this study could have been contaminated because company financial performance was known to the investigators and could have influenced the choices as best companies for leaders. We challenge researchers and practitioners to collaborate in order to empirically demonstrate that companies with greater alignment between their business strategies and talent management approach achieve stronger financial performance. Also, we encourage researchers to better define and measure the stages of talent management evolution in organizations. Such work could also more rigorously specify the definitions, attributes, and signs that an organization has moved its culture toward a talent stewardship model of management.

In the field of talent management, we also know relatively little about why certain organizations are able to sustain an effective integrated talent management process over the long term while others falter. We understand that the CEO and Board of Directors play key roles. However, some organizations manage to maintain a focus on integrated talent management even when top leaders and business strategies change. Practitioners must focus more of their efforts on embedding the talent management mindset into the management model in the organization rather than on merely designing and implementing programs. Programs, by their nature, come and go. We will be successful as a discipline when it is no longer the exception, but common practice, to have sustainable integrated talent management as a core aspect of effective management. As Boudreau and Ramstad (2007) ask, how do we move to a true decision science, like the evolution from accounting to finance? How do we create organizations where managers could not imagine running their business without the necessary data and processes to be effective talent stewards, just as they could not run their business without strong financial data and processes to be effective financial stewards?

Other chapters in this book provide in-depth reviews of specific aspects of talent management. Our view is that the most promising new directions for the field of talent management are less about specific components per se, but in selecting the strategically relevant areas to pursue, in managing and measuring the interconnections and business impact, and in evolving to a talent stewardship culture.

References

Block, P. (1993). *Stewardship: Choosing service over self-interest.* San Francisco: Berrett-Koehler.

Boston Consulting Group. (2005). *Navigating the five currents of globalization: How leading companies are capturing global advantage.* Boston: Boston Consulting Group.

Boudreau, J. W., & Ramstad, P. M. (2002). *From "professional business partner" to "strategic talent leader": What's next for human resource management.* Working Paper, Cornell University, Center for Advanced Human Resource Studies, Ithaca, NY.

Boudreau, J. W., & Ramstad, P. M. (2007). *Beyond HR: The new science of human capital.* Boston: Harvard Business School Press.

Cappelli, P. (2000). A market-driven approach to retaining talent. *Harvard Business Review, 78,* 103–111.

Charan, R., & Bossidy, L. (2002). *Execution: The discipline of getting things done.* New York: Crown.

Charan, R., Drotter, S., & Noel, J. (2001). *The leadership pipeline: How to build the leadership powered company.* San Francisco: Jossey-Bass.

Corporate Leadership Council. (2001). *GE's "session C" leadership talent assessment.* Washington, DC: Corporate Executive Board.

Corporate Leadership Council. (2004). *Engaging the workforce: Focusing on critical leverage points to drive employee engagement.* Washington, DC: Corporate Executive Board.

Corporate Leadership Council. (2005). *Integrating performance management and talent review processes.* Washington, DC: Corporate Executive Board.

Donlon, J. P. (2007). *Best companies for leaders.* Retrieved November 8, 2007, from http://www.chiefexecutive.net.

Gubman, E. L., & Green, S. (2007). *The four stages of talent management.* San Francisco: Executive Networks.

Hewitt, G. (2000). Presentation at the Executive Development Program, Honeywell International, Morristown, NJ.

Hewitt Associates. (2005). *How the top 20 companies grow great leaders.* Lincolnshire, IL: Author.

Holstein, W. J. (2005). Best companies for leaders. *Chief Executive Officer, 113,* 24–29.

HR Policy Association, (2007). *Annual chief human resource officer survey.* Presentation at the HR Policy Association annual meeting, Boca Raton, FL.

Ingersoll-Rand Company Limited. (2004). *2 × 2 × 2 + 5: The development equation.* Unpublished company document, Montvale, NJ.

Ingersoll-Rand Company Limited. (2007). *Leader-manager index.* Unpublished company document, Montvale, NJ.

Kaye, B. (2002). *Up is not the only way: A guide to developing workforce talent.* Palo Alto, CA: Consulting Psychologists Press.

Lewis, R. E., & Heckman, R. J. (2006). Talent management: A critical review. *Human Resource Management Review, 16,* 139–154.

Lucier, C., Kocourek, P., & Habbel, R. (2006). CEO succession 2005: The crest of the wave. *Strategy + Business,* 1–14.

McCall, M. W., Lombardo, M. M., & Morrison, A. M. (1988). *The lessons of experience: How successful executives develop on the job.* New York: Free Press.

Meister, J. C. (1998). *Corporate universities: Lessons in building a world-class work force.* New York: McGraw-Hill.

Michaels, E., Handfield-Jones, H., & Axelrod, B. (2001). *The war for talent.* Boston: Harvard Business School Press.

Morton, L. (2004). *Integrated and integrative talent management: A strategic HR framework.* New York: Conference Board.

Qihan, J., & Denmat, K. (2006). Building talent in new economies. In Cornell University Center for Advanced Human Resource Studies, *The talent management challenge: A collection of white papers.* Ithaca, NY: Cornell University.

RBL Group. (2007). *Top companies for leaders study.* Retrieved November 8, 2007, from http://www.rbl.net/resources/research/top-companies-for-leaders.

Schein, E. H. (1985). How leaders embed and transmit culture. *Organizational culture and leadership: A dynamic view* (pp. 223–243). San Francisco: Jossey-Bass.

Silzer, R. F. (2002). Selecting leaders at the top: Exploring the complexity of executive fit. In R. F. Silzer (Ed.), *The 21st century executive: Innovative practices for building leadership at the top* (pp. 77–113). San Francisco: Jossey-Bass.

Smart, B. (2005). *Topgrading: How leading companies win by hiring, coaching, and keeping the best people.* New York: Portfolio.

Tichy, N. (1997). *The leadership engine: How winning companies build leaders at every level.* New York: HarperCollins.

Treacy, M., & Wiersema, F. (1995). *The discipline of market leaders. Choose your customers, narrow your focus, dominate your market.* Reading, MA: Addison-Wesley.

Ulrich, D., & Lake, D. (1990). *Organizational capability: Competing from the inside out.* New York: Wiley.

Wenger, E., McDermott, R., & Snyder, W. (2002). *Cultivating communities of practice: A guide to managing knowledge.* Boston: Harvard Business School Press.

Zolli, A. (2007). *HR 2012: Demographics and talent.* Presentation at the meeting of the Human Resource 50, New York.

Zuboff, S. (1988). In the age of the smart machine: The future of work and power. New York: Basic Books.

Part Two

Key Practices

CHAPTER 3

BUILDING THE TALENT PIPELINE
Attracting and Recruiting the Best and Brightest

Leslie W. Joyce

The War for Talent Starts with Attraction

Romance and relationships start with attraction. One party is attracted to another party because of certain attributes. One learns about these attributes through a wide variety of sources, both personal and public. This is true regardless of whether one is searching for a relationship with another person or another employer. Getting someone interested in your organization is the first step in attracting and retaining top talent. Attraction is where the decision to explore a relationship is made. The challenge is to ensure that your attributes are attractive, clearly stated, and communicated. This chapter discusses the key steps you should take to make your organization, and not your competitors, attractive to top talent.

In recent years, the phrase "the war for talent" has been used most often in conversations about the challenges in retaining top talent. But before you can talk about the challenges of retaining talent, you have to overcome the challenges of acquiring talent. Acquiring talent can be the tougher of the two challenges.

With retention, you have "familiarity" on your side. In acquisitions, the unknown can be frightening. The challenge for employers is to make their organization both known and attractive in order to create a level of familiarity that will offset the fear of the unknown. There are six steps to creating and communicating a compelling argument that top talent cannot ignore:

1. Identifying the talent acquisition strategy that best supports your business strategy and will result in meeting your talent needs
2. Creating a compelling employment value proposition that clearly articulates what is different about your organization versus other organizations
3. Capturing the employment value proposition in a memorable employment brand that states simply what makes your organization a great choice
4. Detailing the employment brand into a talent brand and a leadership brand that clearly articulates the caliber of talent and leadership working for your organization
5. Determining the most productive channels to the talent you want to use
6. Measuring your success

Of course, each of these six steps is comprised of many smaller steps and a litany of critical business decisions. Each step and each decision is important in its own right and essential to the effectiveness of the overall approach.

Remember that what you are asking someone to do is change her life and the lives of her family for you, for your organization. That is an enormous request, and the responsibility of every organization is to make that choice, and that change, worthwhile. Your responsibility is to ensure that every potential employee who considers your organization does so with eyes wide open and heart full of anticipation. This chapter focuses on how you can do that, step by step.

Step 1: Identifying Your Talent Acquisition Strategy

Effective talent acquisition starts with a sound talent strategy: a conscious decision regarding what methods and approaches to use to identify, source, and secure the best talent in the market.

A sound talent strategy starts with the organization's strategy and a thorough understanding of the organization's competitive position. Why start with the strategy? Because it is imperative to know and understand the business plans in order to ensure that you have talented employees and leaders who can make those plans a reality.

Organizational strategy serves to align the organization's functions around a common set of goals and objectives. Strategy sets direction and establishes guidelines for decision making and investment. For talent acquisition, organizational strategy drives key decisions about who—what kinds of talent—is needed, when they are needed, and for what purpose they are needed.

For example, a small, rapidly growing entrepreneurial company may determine that strategically, it needs to compete more directly with established companies in the same space in order to be taken seriously as a contender. In this case the company strategy would lead to a talent strategy seeking to acquire talent, and hence competitive intelligence, from its larger competitors. The company might also determine that its best talent strategy is to gain competency by acquiring other smaller companies and their talent, and as a result optimizing innovation and entrepreneurial energy as competitive advantage.

Another example might be a consolidation strategy for a highly diversified business. If consolidation is the result of divestiture, the talent strategy would be to retain top talent from the divested division without eroding the value of the divested asset. And in a company with an aggressive growth strategy, finding the best talent, both internally and externally, and being able to deploy that talent in key business segments would be critical.

From a competitive advantage perspective, it is imperative to know where your organization is in terms of market maturity, what the core competencies of success are, and where you stand relative to your closest competitor. The answers to these questions and the essence of the organization's strategy will guide your choice of a talent acquisition strategy.

Talent Strategy Choices

Organizations face many choices about how they will recruit and acquire talent. Basically, these choices can be distilled down to four fundamental strategies. Will you buy, build, borrow, or bind the talent to realize your business strategy? Each talent strategy works best in certain business conditions, and each has specific pros and cons. Perhaps most beneficial is that each strategy complements the others, enabling an employer to use multiple strategies at once, or in succession, as business conditions and strategies evolve. In this section, we identify the conditions in which each strategy may be most effective, the pros and cons of each, and common recruiting methods that align with each strategy. A more detailed look into each recruiting method is provided later in the chapter.

Buy Strategy

A buy strategy is one in which an organization decides that the needed talent exists outside the organization and must be acquired to realize the business strategy. It can also apply to instances when the internal talent to the organization is already fully utilized, and there is a significant cost in moving that talent to a new business unit or function. Buying talent is an effective strategy in these situations:

- Your organization needs or wants to get talent quickly.
- Your organization is in a significant and rapid growth mode that exceeds the capability of your internal pipeline to produce talent.
- Your organization is engaged in a substantial transformation, in which new ideas and perspectives are essential to changing the culture and where bringing in new and different perspectives is an accelerator to change.

Each strategy has pros and cons—things that work well and things that are challenging. Some of the pros of a buy strategy are:

- *Speed.* Top talent in the market can be identified and screened quickly because recruiters contact only those who are clearly qualified for the role and choose the best among them.
- *Focus.* Attention to specific needs by a dedicated recruiting team that is not distracted by other day-to-day recruiting responsibilities.

- *No "domino effect."* Hiring external top talent does not create an opening in another part of your organization that you then have to fill.

Some of the cons are:

- *Expense.* Retained search firms tend to be an expensive choice.
- *Resource intensity.* To stay focused and move quickly requires staff and hiring managers who are willing to make key candidates a top priority for attention.
- *Sustainability.* Due to the expense and intensity, buy strategies are best put in place for short durations or for specific talent segments—for example, senior leaders and organization officers.

Common methods for buying talent are traditional employment advertising, job boards, recruiting firms, and referrals.

Build Strategy

In a build strategy, the organization commits to training and developing internal talent to meet the needs of the business strategy. This process is dependent on a good workforce forecasting and planning process and access to development resources. Building talent is an effective strategy in these situations:

- Your organization is focused on "promoting from within" to ensure an "organization way" of working.
- Your organization is capable of sustaining a rich internal pipeline.
- Your organization can make significant and sustainable investments in the training and development of incumbents.

Some of the pros of a build strategy are:

- *Building culture.* Investing in internal resources ensures that the existing culture continues to thrive and the ways of working are understood, especially with leadership candidates.
- *Known quantities.* The capabilities of internal candidates are typically well known. Knowing capabilities is especially important in filling leadership roles where changes in leaders can

be quite disruptive or when their true capabilities fall short of what was promised.

- *Test driving.* Promoting from within allows the organization, and the employee, to try out the role and the talent, often without the negative consequences suffered by an external hire. If the fit is not optimal, incumbents can return to their prior role or move to another role within the organization, whereas an external hire would face the challenge of finding another employer.

A build strategy has these cons:

- *Duration.* It takes a long time to build internal capability. This is especially true for leadership skills since effectiveness is so dependent on experiential learning.
- *Infrastructure requirements.* Committing to promotions from within the organization means providing consistent opportunities to develop. Leadership development programs should be created to ensure the leadership pipeline is progressing and that development can happen in "a safe environment" that allows leaders to take risks in decisions and actions.
- *Sense of entitlement.* In some instances, a build strategy will create a sense among employees that they are entitled to promotions even if they are not the most qualified candidates.

One other consideration with adopting a build strategy is that it can sometimes be a difficult strategy to change. For instance, if an organization finds it needs talent more quickly than it can build it, hiring from the outside can be hard to start up and it can be very difficult for external hires to be accepted by internals. This is especially the case when external hires are placed in leadership positions. They may be coming into a role in which team members, subordinates or peers, may have been internal contenders for the same role. This requires significant relationship building skills on the part of the newly hired employee and a commitment by the hiring leader to actively support the new person through the assimilation process.

Common methods for building talent include creating college and university alliances and partnerships, developing and sustaining on-campus recruiting programs (to hire entry-level college graduates), robust job rotation programs, a focus on facilitating internal career transitions, and job retraining. One additional benefit of a build strategy is that it avoids the costly practice of hiring experienced people.

Borrow Strategy

A borrow strategy is one in which an organization determines that the talent gaps must be filled quickly but the duration of the need may be short term or unknown. In these cases, the organization must access capable talent for a defined time frame without a commitment to long-term or permanent employment. A "borrow" strategy is effective in these situations:

- Your organization is in a dynamic market with constantly changing business conditions or competitors.
- The need for talent waxes and wanes based on market conditions, seasonality, or business strategy.
- Your core business is providing labor to other businesses whose talent needs are dynamic.
- Your organization is entering new markets or businesses and needs to move key talent from one market or business to another to sustain the culture and quickly transfer capability.

A borrow strategy has these benefits:

- *Cost control.* Staffing costs can increase or decrease in alignment with changing business conditions.
- *Rapid response.* There can be quick responses to unanticipated needs or changes in tactics and strategy.
- *Workforce flexibility.* There is greater flexibility for employees when it comes to work schedules and work locations. For instance, contingent workers may want and need to work only part-time or be willing to live in new locations for specific durations of time.

A borrow strategy has these cons:

- *Competitive markets.* If competitors in your sector also adopt a borrow strategy, then available flexible employees may become scarce quickly. If the skills you are seeking are in short supply in general, then competitors may beat you to the talent or drive up the cost of talent.

- *Impact on organization culture.* Since borrowed employees are not part of the organization, they may be less inclined to conform to or bolster the organization culture.
- *Expense of expatriate programs.* In the case of global movement of leaders, this is a very expensive proposition and requires a well-developed "reentry plan" for the employee when the assignment concludes.

Common methods for borrowing talent include contract or contingent workers and rotational assignments. Contingent or temporary workforces can be highly specialized and very flexible, responding easily to changing business conditions.

Bind Strategy

A bind strategy is one in which an organization seeks to keep talent with the organization by rewarding them for remaining for defined periods of time. Common methods for binding talent are employment contracts, retention bonuses, noncompete clauses, expatriate programs, rotational assignments, and temporary assignments. Binding can be effective in these situations:

- Your organization is involved in mergers, acquisitions, or divestitures that make it difficult to retain key talent as human capital synergies are explored.
- Your organization is in a highly competitive market, where talent is scarce but portable from organization to organization, division to division.
- You are facing a large number of retirees and the potential knowledge drain that may come with that, and you have not yet created a process for knowledge transfer.

A bind strategy has these pros:

- *Competency protection.* It may be important to keep talent at critical times or in critical competency areas during transitions or transformations.

- *Knowledge management.* The organization may need to accelerate the transfer of knowledge from experienced employees to newer, less experienced employees.

A bind strategy has these cons:

- *Expense.* Retention bonuses and other incentives can be expensive in the short term for companies that are trying to control costs.
- *Requires a clear plan.* The decision to bind people to the organization should be accompanied by a clear plan for building new talent and honoring the retention agreements.
- *Negative impact to overall morale.* In some instances, keeping people with the organization who would rather be elsewhere can result in resentment that transfers to remaining incumbents. A clear plan should be in place to address this issue should it occur.

Choosing the Strategy

It is likely that companies will engage in each of these strategies at some point and in some circumstance. In fact, it is not uncommon for an organization to be engaged in multiple approaches simultaneously depending on the business growth strategy. The most important thing is to consciously decide and to use a plan that optimizes the effectiveness of the chosen strategy. The effectiveness of each strategy can be optimized by (1) thinking critically about what makes your organization different from others, (2) creating a credible, exciting value proposition that articulates those differences, and (3) ensuring that the organization can deliver on and sustain the promises it makes through that value proposition.

Step 2: Creating a Compelling Employment Value Proposition

Successful products have a compelling value proposition—one that represents the features and benefits of the product. This proposition must make it obvious why consumers should buy that product and not one of the others on the shelf.

Successful companies have a compelling customer value proposition, which clearly articulates what makes this organization a better place to shop at or invest in than its competitors, and specifies the kind of relationship a customer can expect with that organization. Increasingly, successful companies also have a compelling employment value proposition: one that clearly represents the benefits of working for this organization versus its competitors. This proposition has three key elements: differentiation, credibility, and sustainability.

Differentiation

This first consideration may be the most important. How will you, or do you, differentiate your organization from others? When others consider your organization, can they articulate what the organization does and, more important, what it stands for? Are you clear and specific about the attributes of the organization that create the foundation of attraction—the foundation that will get top talent interested in you? These attributes are commonly referred to as your *employment value proposition.* What is the value that your organization offers to potential employees, and how does that value proposition exceed the value proposition of others? The employment value proposition is the employee parallel to the organization's customer value proposition. What is it about your organization that makes candidates choose it above all the others in the marketplace?

The marketplace is enormous, and the ability to stand out, to differentiate oneself, is critical to attracting top talent. Think about how Southwest Airlines differentiates itself and its staff from other airlines. Individuals familiar with the airline will immediately cite "fun" as a key characteristic of flying with Southwest. So powerful is the "fun proposition" that it overshadows long lines and middle seats. Southwest's customer value proposition flows to its employment value proposition: a fun customer experience is created by employees who have fun at work. If it is important to you to have fun at work with others who value the same thing, then Southwest Airlines may be a better employment choice for you than a more traditional airline. This is the value proposition that helped propel a small, regional airline into a force to be reckoned with. The same might be said for Virgin Atlantic or any of the businesses in the Virgin brand. How Virgin differed from others was a clear focus for the businesses leaders.

Credibility

Once they are identified and defined, these attributes—your employment value proposition—must be real, pervasive, and here and now, not an aspired to or eventual one. It is essential that a potential candidate is confident that what you see is what you get and that what you hear is how it is. As with personal credibility, employment credibility is the cornerstone of trust. In an employment market noted for free agency, trust can be a powerful binding factor for talent. Consider companies such as REI and the Body Shop, which gained widespread regard for their stated commitments to the environment. Communicating their position and how that translates into the organization's culture is essential to attracting people who share their values. Substantiating their stance on environmentalism with commitments and publicity on product sourcing, contributions to conservation causes, and giving back to their communities have been just a few of the tools the organization used to support the credibility of their employment value proposition (Corporate Leadership Council, 2006).

Sustainability

Sustaining the employment value proposition can be extremely challenging. Challenging economic conditions or a highly competitive landscape can put key elements of the proposition at risk as companies look to control costs and optimize the use of capital. But sustainability is critical. Talent, especially top talent, expect their employer to honor the promises made. Sustaining the value proposition begins with top leadership and works its way through the organization until it becomes part of the DNA of the organization. It is imperative to avoid the "bait and switch"—cases in which candidates are led to believe one thing and then when hired experience something very different. In the same sense that customers will change suppliers if the promises made are not kept, talent will change companies when employment promises are not kept.

Possibly three of the best examples of sustainability are Ritz-Carlton Hotels, Nordstrom, and Maytag. Each organization has set an incredibly high bar for service and has maintained that level for decades. It has consistently hired and retained talent who reflect that standard. Consistency, sustainability, and realization of mutual expectations are effective levers for success.

Clearly stated, supported with resources, and sustained over the years, an organization's employment value proposition—the trusted characteristics that consistently differentiate one employer from another—can be the most powerful element in creating attraction. The challenge is that the proposition can be complex and detailed, with elements that take time and space to fully describe. Few sourcing channels have that much space, and few passive candidates have that much time. Recently companies have begun to distill their employment value proposition into a shorter, punchier, and more provocative "employment brand": a simple phrase or statement that creates a compelling argument to consider an organization for employment. A statement that is powerful, present, and pervasive.

Step 3: Creating a Memorable Employment Brand

In its simplest form, an employment brand is a "tag line" of sorts that grabs the job seeker's attention and compels him or her to consider the employer. In actuality, the employment brand and the marketing campaign that supports it are the embodiment of the employment value proposition. The employment value proposition, the employment brand, and all supporting recruiting material are the foundation of an employment marketing campaign, whose purpose is to put the employer front and center with the talent it seeks.

Possibly the best way to understand the employment brand and employment branding is to consider some examples:

■ ■ ■

- *McDonald's.* When the organization had its first quarterly loss in 47 years of operation, it began the development of a revitalization plan. Part of that plan was the creation of the "My

First" campaign, which highlighted that many of its top executives started their career success by working at the restaurants. The recruiters and all their recruitment materials emphasized the extraordinary career opportunities that existed at McDonald's. The employment brand became about building skills and instilling pride in their employees (Marquez, 2006).

- **The Home Depot.** When the organization began struggling to meet its recruitment goals and attrition started to rise, an emphasis was placed on determining why talented candidates would want to work for The Home Depot instead of its competitors. Out of the process came a clear understanding, as at McDonald's, that many of its most senior people had progressed rapidly through the ranks after starting out in entry-level jobs like "lot associates"—the individuals who load customer cars and maintain the parking lot. In addition, it knew that the core business, home improvement, drew certain types of candidates. Out of those conversations and realizations came the employment brand of "Build Something." These two words became the simple message that you could come to The Home Depot and build a great career while helping others build their dream homes.

- **Honolulu Police Department.** Facing the fact that in the coming years many of the department's senior officers would be reaching retirement age, the department launched a massive recruiting campaign built around its commitment to *Ohana*—Hawaiian for "family" and a key element of Hawaiian culture. The recruiting campaign paid off, drawing unprecedented numbers of candidates (Regan, 2004).

- **Enterprise Rent-a-Car.** The organization depends heavily on new college graduates, hiring as many as 6,000 college graduates a year. To keep this pipeline full, Enterprise decided to build its employment brand around its long tradition of promoting from within. The message the organization decided to send to recruits came from talking with successful associates about what was exciting about their jobs. The answer back from them was the resounding appreciation for the variety of activities and the high levels of responsibility they had, supported by Enterprise's commitment to train and reward associates. This resulted in the "My Personal Enterprise" employment brand, launched in 2000. The brand clearly communicated a recruit's ability to join the organization and make it his own (Wellner, 2004).

■ ■ ■

You can see from these examples that employment brands are important to organizations that hire large numbers of people in competitive markets where the differentiating aspects of the culture of the organization may not be well known. It is possibly even more important for small to medium-sized organizations that do not have a well-established product brand or may be a niche player in a broad field. In these instances, creating and communicating an employment brand can set the organization apart by highlighting opportunity and the broadness of experience that can be gained in smaller companies. In summary, it is critical that the employment brand flows from the employment value proposition and authentically reflects the organization, the work, and the experiences of the organization's employees.

Creating the employment brand itself is just the first step. The remaining steps focus on ensuring that all materials used for recruiting purposes are developed with the message of the brand in mind and the elements of the employment value proposition included. One particularly important tool for recruiting is the organization's career website. This is the richest opportunity to share the brand and all the elements behind it. This is a great place to include employee testimonials that illustrate what the brand means and how it comes to life every day at work. Organizations use all sorts of collateral materials in employment campaigns, including brochures, posters, referral cards, postcards, and flyers. A consistent and compelling "look and feel" to the materials is essential to supporting the employment brand.

Step 4: Crafting Your Talent Brand

At this point you have identified the talent acquisition strategy that best fits your business strategy, you have determined what it is about your organization that sets it apart as an employer, you have translated that into a compelling employment brand, and you have featured the brand and the employment proposition prominently in your recruiting materials. So what is left to do? You have a great place to work and a great message. The next question is, To whom do you want to tell it? What kinds of people do you want working in this great place?

The talent brand is a description that simply and efficiently describes the kinds of people who work for an organization, the kinds of talent the organization seeks, and the kinds of talent who succeed. This brand is an essential element of attracting, recruiting, and hiring superior talent.

"If the reputation of a company's products and services is its face, the talent brand is its heart and soul," say Hank Stringer and Rusty Rueff, the authors of *Talent Force* (Rueff & Stringer, 2006). They suggest "that the talent brand builds over time and it can engender the same feelings of desire and dreams that a compelling product message brings to life. It can bring tremendous loyalty and, through word of mouth, more traffic to your door."

A talent brand is the characterization or personification of what it means to be a member of a particular organization. How is it that others describe people who work for your organization? Why is it that your employees are targeted by recruiters? Answers to these questions can often be found in your talent brand: the perceptions and beliefs about the kinds of people who work for your organization.

A quick test when the following phrases are mentioned, what companies come to mind: *fun; blue suits; edgy and competitive; entrepreneurial; visionary and imaginative; ladies and gentlemen; green and eco-friendly?* Do you get images respectively of Southwest Airlines, IBM, GE, Microsoft, Apple, Ritz-Carlton, and Whole Foods? Even if you did not get these specific images, some images came to mind. These words describe an organization you know, one you have worked for, or maybe even the one for which you currently work. The point is that just as impressions of products, companies, and people are formed, impressions of talent are formed too. Those who interact with your employees are forming impressions about them and creating generalizations about your employee population as a whole from this sample of interactions. Consider a few more examples:

- Home Depot built its reputation on knowledgeable people who could help people solve common home improvement problems. Its talent brand is *knowledgeable and helpful.*

- Google has built its reputation on innovation and risk taking. Its talent brand is *young, smart, and free thinking.*
- Microsoft built its reputation on a single-minded focus on market domination. Its talent brand is *smart, highly competitive people with an unbridled work ethic.*

Think back to your employment value proposition and the meaning behind the words and images of your employment brand and the employment campaign. Who are the people you are seeking? What kinds of people are successful at your organization? What kinds of people are needed to make the business strategy successful? These characterizations are the beginnings of your talent brand.

The Leadership Brand

Recently much has been written about a specific type of talent brand: the leadership brand. As a result of the work of Dave Ulrich of the University of Michigan and his colleagues at Results Based Leadership (Ulrich & Smallwood, 2007; Younger, Smallwood, & Ulrich, 2006), an organization's leadership brand is becoming a focus in leadership recruitment and leadership development.

Just as the talent brand is the *personification* of what it means to be part of an organization, a leadership brand is the *personification* or characterization of the consistent traits and behaviors of the organization's leaders. It is a description of the kinds of leaders who are successful in your organization—the kinds of leaders who make the organization successful. It is a shared identity that separates your leaders from the leaders of your competition.

When discussing the leadership brand, Intagliata, Ulrich, and Smallwood (2000) specifically cite Microsoft and Apple as prime examples of companies with well-known leadership brands—a clear set of characterizations that describe leaders in those companies: "Microsoft leaders are known for their attributes of high intelligence, their desire to dominate competitors and their high technical competence. Microsoft leaders embody a desire to win in every industry" (p. 13). When mentioning Apple, Intagliata et al. (2000) make clear the connection between a visionary and imaginative CEO and "visionary and imaginative" as the leadership brand. Another organization with a strong leadership brand is GE. Talented leaders at GE are often characterized as highly competitive, results-focused, aggressive leaders who emphasize getting things done. Of course, this is in complete alignment with GE's strategy of being number one or number two in each business it is in or getting out of that business altogether.

Here are a few more examples from Ulrich's work:

- Wal-Mart, which is dedicated to providing low prices to consumers, requires leaders who are frugal, manage costs efficiently, get things done on time, and are relentless negotiators.
- FedEx, which has an organization brand that ensures absolutely and positively on-time delivery, requires leaders with singular focus on meeting deadlines and solving problems quickly.
- Lexus, which is known for the pursuit of perfection, requires leaders who are facile in lean manufacturing and six sigma and in the leadership discipline that comes with a commitment to data-based decision making.
- McKinsey, known for offering high-paying, extremely demanding jobs to only the best and the brightest, is incredibly selective even within those ranks. This results in leaders who are highly intelligent, ambitious, and extremely confident in a wide range of demanding environments.

So you can see the clear connection between the nature of the organization, the organization's strategy, and the talent brand that is created. Talent is attracted to places that reflect themselves and the things that are important to them. Your talent brand captures the kinds of people who are successful in your organization and communicates that to others.

Developing a Leadership Brand

Just as with the employment value proposition and the employment brand, organizations must be deliberate in creating their leadership brand. Perhaps the first step in developing a leadership brand is in realizing what benefits a leadership brand can bring to the organization. It is clear that it can help in recruiting talent to your organization, especially if the brand is a powerful one that candidates see as desirable. As Wall Street pays more and more attention to *intangibles* when valuing companies, the quality and consistency of its leadership, the leadership brand, have become even more important.

Developing the leadership brand closely follows the process for creating and articulating the employment value proposition and the talent brand. Think critically about what leadership capabilities, competencies, traits, and characteristics the business needs in order to excel. What kinds of leaders have been successful so far, and will this same success profile be the one that takes you to the next level? What should leaders be, what should they know, and what should they do to ensure the business strategy is realized and you are set apart from your competitors?

Clearly articulating what leaders know, do, and deliver sets the standard for expectations of behavior and results on Wall Street and Main Street. Once leadership standards are set, processes for assessing, selecting, and developing leaders who reflect the standard should be put in place. Here are some things to consider:

- *Assessing and selecting leaders.* Ensure that processes for assessing leadership capability and competence are constructed around the key elements of the leadership brand. This includes interview templates, assessment center profiles, developmental assessments like 360-degree surveys, and other processes for promotion and executive placement. It may seem very basic, but make sure that those selected for hire, promotion, or placement reflect the leadership brand.
- *Developing leaders.* Use all the development processes at your disposal—training, on-the-job experiences, off-the-job experiences, coaching, mentoring, and others—to allow leaders to develop the skills to be successful. Ensure that these programs and processes teach and reinforce the key elements of your leadership brand.

The leadership brand is built over time through consistency and commitment. It is important to publicize the leadership brand so that stakeholders know and understand the caliber and quality of leaders who are making the business a success.

Step 5: Determining the Most Productive Talent Channels

One could easily argue that the 21st century job seeker's options are bigger and brighter than ever before. There are more channels to market—ways to communicate, contact, and interact—than ever before. This is true for both talent and talent seekers. These channels take a variety of forms, from traditional media-based processes to more innovative web-based processes. They range from traditional, person-based networking to the increasingly popular practice of virtual social networking. Channels are available to job seekers every minute of every day and anywhere. They allow employers to connect to local talent or to global talent. In a mere click of a mouse, an organization can become a major player in the talent war.

But as every combatant knows and as every suitor knows, success begins with strategy. In the war for talent, it begins with a sound and comprehensive talent acquisition strategy that takes advantage of all the tools and channels available and a strategy that is broad but tailored to the specific business challenges. The wonderful thing about our times is that all the channels have value, allowing an organization to be targeted and comprehensive in its approaches to talent acquisition. The good news is that in the field of employment marketing and advertising, there have never been more choices. The bad news is that there have never been more choices! Choosing well is important.

Talent Channels

Talent channels are more prolific than ever before. The range includes familiar methods like media (print and radio), agencies, and professional groups and newer methods such as job boards and virtual social networks like MySpace and LinkedIn with which we are getting more familiar. And there are truly cutting-edge methods like multiplayer gaming and virtual worlds (for example, Second Life), with which we have taken only tentative steps so far.

An important element in making great talent choices is having lots of talent from which to choose. Diversifying your recruiting channels is critical to creating this situation. With so many channels to choose from, it is important to know which channel excels in what situations and which channels line up with your talent acquisition strategy. Will you buy, build, borrow, or bind to get the talent you need? According to a recent Morgan Stanley report (Ruiz, 2007a), employers spent an estimated $6.4 billion for help wanted ads in the United States in 2006 alone. So being thoughtful about your investments is critical.

Print Media

Some may suggest that print media are old-fashioned and ineffective, given the proliferation of job boards. But this is an erroneous conclusion. In fact, print media (newspaper and magazine classifieds) have seen a resurgence in recent years. As recently as March 2006, *Workforce Management* magazine (Hansen, 2006) reported the results of a study of forty name-brand companies, each with a workforce population in excess of 5,000, revealing that print advertising was reversing a downward trend. In fact, survey respondents cited print advertising as the channel for 7.0 percent of external hires in 2006, up from just 4.6 percent in 2005. Sponsors of the survey say these are the highest numbers they have seen in decades for this media. Print media are effective in the buy, build, and borrow acquisition strategies. For instance, advertising in the *Wall Street Journal* may help with your buy strategy (because of its reader profile of seasoned professionals) while advertising in the local paper may help with your build strategy.

Referrals

Estimates are consistent that approximately 26 percent of new hires come from employee referrals, making this the most prolific channel of all (Ruiz, 2007b). Employee referral programs have a long history in organizations and take many forms, from simple to sophisticated. At one end is the simplicity of just asking incumbents to refer friends and family in return for modest cash awards. At the other end are highly sophisticated approaches that include providing incumbents with referrals cards, pamphlets, and posters. This fully equips them to reach out not only to their friends and family but also to situations in which they may come across a person who gives superior service or demonstrates interest in the organization. SAS Institute, a software and services organization based in North Carolina, relies heavily on its employees to locate outstanding software engineers and salespeople. The organization works with its employees to elicit the names of talented people they have worked with in the past who might fit into SAS, and then HR takes over as the recruiter (Munson, 2006).

In addition, referrals can be particularly fruitful when sourcing leadership candidates, especially if they are provided by incumbent executives. Some companies have been very successful in "mining" the rolodexes and networks of their new executives since most executives have long work histories and great networks. Referrals are a helpful *build* channel, in that most talent in this channel have a good idea about the organization and the people who work there and are looking to build a career there.

Job Boards

Job boards like Monster and Career Builder remain popular because of their ease of access, geographic diversity, flexibility, and comprehensiveness. They remain the easiest channel to exploit. However, this ease does not appeal to all populations and is, of course, dependent on computer ownership or access to a computer and the Internet, which not all job seekers have and not all jobs require. This is especially true for companies that look to take advantage of older workers looking for opportunities to continue working during retirement. Many organizations have found that this talent pool is rich in knowledge, experience, and positive work habits—traits that all employers value. Ensuring you have a channel they can access will be important to realizing your strategy. Job boards are helpful in fulfilling most talent acquisition strategies, with the possible exception of a buy strategy, in that many experienced senior professionals are already contentedly working in companies and not surfing the job boards.

Recruiting Firms

Recruiting firms remain a popular option for many employers. This is especially true for leadership roles and hard-to-fill specialist roles. However, this is typically the most expensive channel available.

A recruiting fee is often 20 to 30 percent of the candidate's total compensation for the first year. According to a 2007 talent report (Workforce Management, 2007), the five biggest recruiting firms had combined sales in excess of $2 billion. Keep a couple of things in mind as you work with recruiting firms:

- Negotiate your fees. You may get some resistance, but it is a great place to start.
- Watch out for the "indirect fees" in your contract (fees that cover the recruiting organization's overhead and should not be your responsibility).
- Have a detailed engagement letter or contract so that all parties are very clear about what happens at all points along the way of a search.

It is also a good idea to ensure that the firm(s) chosen are specialists in your industry, your organization, or the type of job(s) you are trying to fill. Look specifically at the number of similar positions they have filled in the recent past. This activity can be an indication of an existing "ready now" talent pool and accelerate your time to fill the job. Also, for decentralized organizations, ensure that you check with your corporate teams to determine if there are already strategic alliances or preferred partnerships with some firms that can reduce your search fees, or if there are firms you should avoid based on corporate direction.

A couple of other choices you may want to make concern whether to work with a small boutique firm or a large, established firm and if you should go with a contingency-based or retained search. Here are a couple of points to consider:

- *Large firms.* They have name recognition, making it more likely that candidates will call them back. However, they also are more likely to have "exclusivity or hands-off agreements" with existing clients, which will not allow them to search in the companies where those agreements exist.
- *Boutique firms.* They offer flexibility and reach because they are less likely to have agreements that make many of your target companies off limits to them, particularly large companies that lean toward large recruiting firms. Also, smaller

firms tend to be able to focus deeply on your organization, its business, and key elements of culture and leadership fit.

- *Contingency search.* In this scenario, the firm is hired to source candidates and does not get paid if you do not hire someone it has sourced. Often this is a useful way to get lots of résumés sent in your direction, but you still do a lot of the screening work yourself.
- *Retained search.* In this case, there is an arrangement for an exclusive search with a firm and a pay arrangement that requires payments for the search as it progresses. These are often helpful when you are looking for executives or talent with a specific skill set.

This channel is particularly helpful if you are choosing to "buy" your talent and need to do it quickly and with limited risk. Finally you can use the Association of Executive Search Consultants (www.aesc.org) as a reference guide for maximizing your relationship with your chosen firm.

College and University Alliances

These alliances are a particularly beneficial channel if you have a comprehensive "build" strategy. It is important that you support that strategy with well-formulated and well-executed development programs that support the onboarding and assimilation of new college graduates.

University alliances are common sources of graduate-level talent, most commonly M.B.A. graduates from top-tier schools. Some organizations have expanded these programs to include other specialties, like finance, audit, labor relations, and HR. For instance, Capital One, whose business strategy calls for starting up new businesses from the inside, focuses heavily on finding highly capable people early in their career and fast tracking them to business leaders. This strategy requires them to excel at recruiting the best and the brightest out of the best business schools. Procter & Gamble, another example, has been a "staple" on the campuses of the top-tier business schools and has excelled at establishing a campus identity, an employment value proposition, and a talent brand that draws the best to the organization. Some large retailers have established key relationships with colleges that offer retail management degree programs and use those programs as funnels for moving talent into store leadership positions.

Initiating a presence on campus is a fairly easy activity, since placement offices have very well-developed processes. Establishing your organization as a viable competitor to other organizations already present on campus takes both a time and a financial commitment and should be done for the long term. Companies that do well on campus are those like P&G that are known, predictable, and respected. Building deep, long-term relationships with universities can provide a "first-pick" advantage, enabling the employer to attract and hire the best of the best and the brightest.

Virtual Social Networks

Virtual social networks are the newest channel to emerge, and as with all new channels, there is a mix of excitement and trepidation. This option seems to have great potential for companies that figure out how to do it right. Virtual networks like Facebook, MySpace, and LinkedIn are connecting people virtually who might never have had the opportunity to connect in person. They provide an avenue of conversation and discovery that is faster than any other talent channel.

Fay Hansen (2006) has described the tack taken by Osram Sylvania's Towanda plant, where the demands for chemical engineers are quite high and the local talent pool cannot meet them. According to Hansen, the real power of the networking technology is its ability to reach passive candidates with special skills. The recruiter's profile on LinkedIn specifies that she is always looking for chemical engineers. As a result, she receives inquiries and interest from people with whom she would not normally be able to network.

Networks like Jobster allow recruiters to establish specific networks for individual positions or skill sets. This is particularly helpful for companies that recruit consistently for the same types of positions, like hospitals, retailers, and service firms. As a final example, you can visit www.myspace.com/marinecorps to see how the Marine Corps has been successful in signing up more than 22,000 MySpace friends.

Virtual worlds, like *World of Warcraft, America's Army,* and *Second Life,* bring together thousands of people in ways that could not possibly happen in the real world. In these virtual worlds, many of which are quest based, people meet, form teams, and work together for a common goal. They learn about one another's talents far more quickly than would happen in the normal work world. John Seely Brown (Brown & Thomas, 2006), author and founder of Xerox PARC, suggests that these games are a potentially superior training ground for talent, particularly in the key areas of leadership and relationship building. He convincingly cites the success profile of a "guildmaster" in comparison to effective work team leaders. He suggests that guildmasters are actually learning to be leaders by playing, as opposed to trainees who might be learning about leading through more traditional methods.

As another example, *Second Life* is a virtual world created by California-based Linden Labs in which investors purchase property and build their homes, their businesses, and their communities. A number of respected companies—Nike, Nissan, Toyota, IBM, Reuters and Reebok, to name a few—have established storefronts, portals, or other presences to market their products and services to the inhabitants of this virtual world. The added benefit is that these employers are now visible to an expanded talent pool that they may not otherwise connect with and have an image that is attractive to this specific segment. This could be particularly effective for smaller companies or more locally known international organizations that do not yet have a global footprint.

It is important to use as many channels as necessary to get the job done. More innovative approaches like social networks and virtual worlds are certainly new tools that should be investigated. However, many in the recruiting profession are cautious about the long-term viability of something that is so new and so early in the adoption curve. Creating and maintaining a diverse set of channels (job boards, media, networking, associations, recruiters, and others) remains the most prudent approach.

Talent Pool Segmentation

People in marketing and advertising think about product segments, market segments, and customer segments. This allows marketers to develop strategies that are targeted to specific customer or market subgroups, or segments, in the hope of maximizing that group's interest in their product or service.

In talent attraction and recruitment, it is also helpful to think like marketers and advertisers, where your product is your organization and your market is talented people. In talent segmentation, think like a product manager. Who do I want to buy this product (my organization)? Where are they, and how do I get to them? How do I get this specific population interested in coming to work for my organization?

Talent segments do not necessarily have clear definitions but are mostly reflective of the core competencies or attributes you want to present in your organization. For instance, you may want to ensure that your organization population is as diverse as your customer population, so you will want to determine where your minority talent segments are. What is important to them in an employer? What is the best channel to get your message to them? It may be that your focus talent segment is women or technologists or bioethicists. Segmenting your needs and focusing your efforts on channels that reach each segment is a fruitful approach.

One good example of segmentation is The Home Depot and its focus on hiring older workers. Once the organization realized that its older workers were more dependable, more productive, and stayed with the organization longer than other part-time populations, it focused its recruiting efforts on finding and hiring older workers. The key channel in this effort was a strategic alliance with the American Association of Retired Persons (AARP), an organization whose members are 55 years and older and spread throughout the United States. This created an exclusive, dedicated path to an enormous pool of qualified candidates— members of AARP—who at the time exceeded 40 million. The organization, in partnership with AARP, was able to take its employment proposition to a huge talent segment it otherwise would not have reached. In addition, the reputation of AARP gave credibility to The Home Depot as an employer, and its endorsement created a trusting foundation for employment.

The relationship with the AARP was the first step in a practice that The Home Depot has perfected and expanded. In fact, over only a few years, the company also established hiring partnerships with the Department of Defense, the Department of Labor, and a confederation of Hispanic nongovernmental agencies. Each partnership represents a key talent segment The Home Depot sees as critical to meeting its hiring needs. For an organization that hires tens of thousands of people each year, productive channels and partnerships are vital.

Protecting the Brand

An important consideration as an organization spreads out and diversifies its recruiting channels is ensuring "channel integrity." It is important to ensure that each and every channel is one that the organization benefits from and that the performance and reputation of that channel are consistent with the performance and reputation of the organization.

Specifically, if one is committed to a certain job board, make sure that board is an organization that you want to be associated with—one that shares your approach to candidates. Make sure it is well respected by the candidate population and that its system performance is the best in the industry. This is also true with whichever applicant tracking system (ATS) an organization chooses to use. A slow, cumbersome, forgetful ATS system can easily be construed as the "face" of a slow, cumbersome, forgetful organization—not exactly the sought-after branding that you want!

Watch the circulation rates of the print media in which you advertise. If rates begin to decline, talk with your media partner to understand what is happening and to determine whether to continue the relationship. With other channels such as associations and search firms, consider creating exclusive partnerships or alliances so that the associations and firms know your organization and your talent needs and are committed to you and not your competitors. You also want to be very selective in the search firms you use to ensure that their reputation is sound and they have a proven track record. Word travels fast about "deals gone bad," especially in leadership populations.

Finally, it is important to know when to end a relationship. Partnerships can run their course, and the benefits may no longer be mutual. Your talent needs may have changed or your focus has realigned. It is also possible that the original premise of the partnership is no longer valid (exclusivity, prohibitions against working with competitors, and the reach of the partner). In the face of such changes, it is wise to exit the relationship, regardless of how long it has existed.

Each channel has value. The key is using multiple channels, matching the channel to the talent segment you are seeking to attract and then determining how successful you have been. Performance metrics are a key part of the attraction and recruitment equation.

Step 6: Measuring Your Success

"If you don't measure it, it doesn't matter," "you get what you measure," and various other common sayings underscore the importance of measurement and metrics. Measuring the effectiveness of attraction and recruitment efforts is important to continuously improving performance. For the purposes of this section, the metrics are split into two categories: tactical metrics and strategic metrics. We also discuss what should be reported, to whom, and when.

Tactical Metrics

Number of job requisitions, applicants per requisition, time to fill a vacancy, and selection ratios are all tactical metrics (see Table 3.1). They are typical metrics that will tell you how you have done in the past, and what is important to know. Tactical measures help you fine-tune processes, evaluate people, maintain current applicant flow, and make on-the-spot adjustments. They are the primary components of your performance scorecard or set of indicators that tell you how you are doing at any point in time or across multiple points in time such as hiring peaks and valleys.

Tactical metrics tend to be widely used and relatively easy to collect. They can be found in existing HR information systems and applicant tracking systems and can be validated and recreated. Their utility is in knowing what is happening at the current moment so that you can adjust quickly to changes by creating new job requisitions, extending the life of a requisition, posting more advertising, or diversifying the channels that are used.

Table 3.1. Tactical Metrics

Metric	Description
Days to fill a job requisition	The days elapsed from the day the job requisition was opened until the day the position was filled
Number of open requisitions	A simple count of the number of positions in active recruitment
Lift in the qualified pool	The extent to which the pool of qualified candidates increases following a recruiting event
Hits to organization career website	The number of online visits to your career website
Offer-to-acceptance ratio	The ratio of offers made to offers accepted
Candidates in the qualified pool	The number of qualified applicants in the pool of interested applicants
Selection ratio	A comparison of the number of persons who are considered before a qualified person is hired
Turnover rates (voluntary and involuntary)	Voluntary: The annualized percentage of the employee population that leaves the organization by choice
	Involuntary: The annualized percentage of employees who are released from the organization by the organization's decision
Cost per hire	The fully loaded cost of hiring a single employee. This may vary by job level, but includes lost productivity, lost sales, and recruitment costs.
Productivity of talent channels	The extent to which an identified talent channel consistently provides qualified candidates
Tenure by channel	The length of time people hired through a particular channel stay with the organization
Promotion rates	The percentage of employees sourced through a certain channel who are later promoted and whether the rate is different from other channels

Strategic Metrics

Strategic metrics (see Table 3.2), on the other hand, are less common and often harder to collect. These metrics provide a glimpse into what the future might hold (for example, workforce demographics, attrition, seasonality, job growth) and are typically found in external databases or publications. They have to be collected, collated, analyzed, and interpreted by internal resources. Seeking and finding trusted sources of strategic metrics is an important activity.

Strategic metrics help the organization anticipate and prepare for important shifts in workforces and workplaces. For example, recent demographic shifts caused by a growing Hispanic population result in an increased need for bilingual employees and therefore bilingual attraction and recruitment tools, and the aging of the population has led to a renewed interest in older workers and concerns about the workforce readiness of the next generation of leaders to succeed those who will retire.

Staying current is important and can be accomplished by keeping up with a variety of trade and academic journals, recently published books, publicly accessed government reports and research, and trend reporting from various foundations and nongovernmental organizations. Memberships in associations and professional networks are also useful sources of information and ideas.

It is important to have both kinds of metrics—tactical and strategic. Having both will allow you to perfect your performance in the short term and determine tools and channels that need to be created to be ready for the future. Do not hesitate to collect data just because they might not be exact. Data that are in the ballpark are often useful in order to know what is happening, at least directionally. One can always get started and then perfect the processes and measures as you go.

Performance Reporting

Creating a performance scorecard is a valuable activity. However, finding a way to easily and accurately display key metrics is sometimes challenging. It is best to focus on the vital few: the metrics that are of interest to you and to your senior leadership. Getting

Table 3.2. Strategic Metrics

Metrics	Definition
Annual brand study	A yearly assessment of talent or organization brand awareness in targeted populations
Demographic changes	The extent to which the demographic mix of talent or customer populations is changing
Search firm perceptions	The perceptions of the organization by talent search firms
Organization engagement index	The extent to which an organization's employees are engaged as measured by the organization's preferred metric
Workforce planning results	The success of workforce planning in predicting the types and amounts of talent and competencies that will be needed by the organization in the next 12 months and beyond
Unemployment rates and trends	The unemployment rate within the total population or within certain talent segments and the extent to which it is increasing or decreasing
Global workforce trends	The shifts that are occurring in the workforce on a global basis and how they affect your business
Candidate focus groups	The conclusions that come from talking with candidates who accepted and rejected jobs in order to determine the reasons for their decisions
Employment brand perception	Different from the annual brand study, this is solely the perceptions of various talent segments of the organization's talent brand
Gaps in capabilities	The differences between existing capabilities and the capabilities needed for the future
Competitive capability analysis	The comparison of the organization's capability gaps with those of competitors to determine who has the advantage
Competitors for talent	The other employers who are the most significant competitors for talent
Depth of talent segments for niche roles	The extent of talent in the organization for highly specialized roles and highly critical talent segments
Surveys of high-potential talent	The collection of the views of current high-potential talent to determine what brought them to the organization and what keeps them in the organization

into the habit of collecting and reporting data on a scorecard ensures that talent acquisition is front and center in your organization and provides an efficient way to keep talent acquisition at the top of the agenda for your executives.

It is also important to have a way of reporting progress and performance to your clients. Let them know that you are looking for their talent all the time, keeping pace with the progress of the search, and always looking for ways to accelerate talent acquisition for the enterprise.

Having the same expectations for any third party is also appropriate and well advised. When an organization is just starting out on the metrics path, benchmarking with established and respected search firms can be a good source of ideas for the composition of the scorecard.

In summary, there are three primary audiences for metrics reports: the talent acquisition team members, their clients, and the senior leadership team. Each report may be different, but the message will always be about looking backward at past performance and forward for optimizing future efforts.

Alignment Is the Secret Sauce

The basic requirement of an effective talent acquisition process is sending a consistent message to your talent segments. The secret sauce, if you will, is the total integration and alignment of all the efforts within the organization. It is through alignment and integration that you will ensure consistency and sustain a talent pipeline.

As with friendships and romances, confidence that *what you see is what you get* and that *what is promised is provided* are critical to building sound relationships with talent segments. In today's highly connected world, it takes very little time for failures (such as not delivering on promises) to be discovered and shared with others. Once trust is lost, it is very hard to rebuild. This is certainly true of the relationships we want to build with talented people.

There are two critical areas of alignment. The first is the alignment between the organization brand and talent brand. Keep in mind that if the reputation of an organization's products and services is its face, the talent brand is its heart and soul. If the talent brand and the organization brand are even slightly inconsistent, then the credibility of both is in question. Credibility is the key to trust, and trust is at the core of every positive and productive relationship in life. Trust in a potential employer is at the core for those who are considering a job change. To ensure that alignment is created and sustained, it is useful to work closely with the marketing and public relations departments. These are professionals who craft and protect the organization brand and can be an enormous help in creating and protecting the talent brand.

The other alignment is that between the talent brand and the organization's selection and development processes. This alignment starts with ensuring that the parties responsible for selection, staffing, training, and development are fully aware of the organization's existing or desired talent brand. It also involves partnering with others to ensure that:

- The success profiles for jobs reflect the characteristics of the brand.
- There is optimal configuration and functionality of the applicant tracking system.
- Any realistic job preview reinforces both the organization brand and the talent brand.
- The onboarding and assimilation processes reflect and reiterate the promises of opportunity made by the value proposition and the brand.
- Development tools and programs are consistent with the promises made for growth opportunities.

It is vital that the external view of the organization and the perceptions of what it means to work in the organization are realized once the external candidate has become an internal team member.

What happens when you are out of alignment? As noted, one of the most fruitful talent channels is employee referrals. If the promise and the reality are out of alignment, referrals will cease to be a useful channel. In a world as connected as the one we all live in, disconnects, misalignments, and untruths are communicated widely and quickly and are difficult to overcome.

A Research Agenda

Although the science of employee selection is well developed, the science of attraction and recruitment is not (Trank, Rhynes, & Bretz, 2002). Given all that we know about current and future workforce demographics, it is critical for employers to understand exactly what it is that attracts talent to their organization. It may be even more important to know what attracts high-ability and high-achieving talent to an organization and what they expect in a work environment (Rhynes, 1991). Are these the same things or different things, and what makes the difference? Trank et al. (2002) have begun this work, but there is more to do.

Additional questions abound, and answering these questions would be time well spent for industrial-organizational psychologists—for example:

- Given the increasing diversity of the workforce, what are the best ways of connecting with such a diverse group of people?
- What are the business implications of *mass customization* of the talent strategy if one size truly does not fit all? How does an organization truly connect with such a diverse workforce?
- What are the key HR practices that support or erode effective attraction and recruitment processes, and how long does it take for them to have negative impact?
- What is the relative effectiveness of the virtual networks and the virtual worlds when they are compared to more traditional methods? Do the rules of the real world hold true in the virtual world?
- How important is an employment brand? Is it a true differentiator for companies? How does it connect with or support the organization's commitment to employee engagement?
- Does a leadership brand make a real difference in organization performance, and if yes, where and how?

Conclusion

Today's workforce has unprecedented variety. They have at their fingertips extraordinary tools for job search. A one-size-fits-all attraction and recruitment strategy no longer serves today's employers well. Employers now need to know and understand what is important to today's workforces and reflect that in their employment value proposition. They need to be clear about their talent brand and their leadership brand (the attributes and behaviors that support the organization's strategy and lead to success for team members and leaders). They need to exploit all the talent channels that are available to them and challenge their recruiting staffs to find new and even more productive channels. They need to be "educated consumers" about the pros and cons of every talent channel and hold those channels to a high standard of effectiveness. Employers need to take a thoughtful, scientific approach to setting their talent acquisition strategy. That starts with a full understanding of the business and the business strategy.

Talent is the great differentiator—the one thing that cannot be copied quickly by other organizations. Winners in the talent war will have sound talent strategies and rich productive talent channels. They will ensure that excellence in attracting and recruiting talent continues into their selection and placement processes. The linchpin for organizational effectiveness is having the right talent in the right place at the right time. Sourcing the right talent is only the beginning of the equation. It is just the beginning of the relationship.

References

Brown, J. S., & Thomas, D. (2006, April). You play World of Warcraft? You're hired! *Wired, 14*(04).

Corporate Leadership Council. (2006). *Attracting and retaining critical talent segments: Building a competitive employment value proposition for in-store employees, Special supplement.* Washington, DC: Corporate Executive Board.

Hansen, F. (2006, December). Using social networking to fill the talent acquisition pipeline. *Workforce Management Online.* Retrieved August 21, 2007, from www.workforce.com.

Intagliata, J., Ulrich, D., & Smallwood, N. (2000). Leveraging leadership competencies to produce leadership brand: Creating distinctiveness by focusing on strategy and results. *Human Resource Planning, 23*(3), 12–23.

Marquez, J. (2006, March 13). When brand alone is not enough. *Workforce Management,* 39–41.

Munson, H. (2006, August). *How to hire top performers.* Washington, DC: Conference Board.

Regan, K. (2004, September). Recruiting for paradise. *Workforce Management Online.* Retrieved November 15, 2007, from www.workforce.com.

Rhynes, S. L. (1991). Recruitment, job choice and post hire consequences: A call for new research directions. In D. Dunnette & L. M. Hough (Eds.), *Handbook of industrial and organizational psychology* (2nd ed., Vol. 2, pp. 399–444). Palo Alto, CA: Consulting Psychologists Press.

Rueff, R., & Stringer, H. (2006). *Talent force: A new manifesto for the human side of business.* Upper Saddle River, NJ: Prentice Hall.

Ruiz, G. (2007a, March). Print ads see resurgence as hiring source. *Workforce Management,* 16–17.

Ruiz, G. (2007b, July). Special report: Talent acquisition. *Workforce Management,* 39–45.

Trank, C., Rhynes, S., & Bretz, R. (2002). Attracting applicants in the war for talent: Differences in work preferences among high achievers. *Journal of Business and Psychology, 16*(3), 331–345.

Ulrich, D., & Smallwood, N. (2007). *Leadership brand: Developing customer-focused leaders to drive performance and build lasting value.* Boston: Harvard Business School Press.

Wellner, A. (2004, July). The pickup artists. *Workforce Management Online.* Retrieved November 5, 2007, from www.workforce.com

Workforce Management. (2007, June 24). *Leading executive search firms,* p. 24.

Younger, J., Smallwood, N., & Ulrich, D. (2006). Developing your organization's brand as a talent developer. *Human Resource Planning, 30*(2), 21–29.

CHAPTER 4

ROPES TO SKIP AND THE ROPES TO KNOW

Facilitating Executive Onboarding

Seymour Adler, Lorraine Stomski

> *They brought me into the organization to implement change. I had the background, the experience, and the enthusiasm. What they did not tell me was that they were just kidding. They were not ready at all for genuine change. I failed miserably.*

These words, expressed with a mixture of exasperation and sadness, were recently shared during a coaching session that one of us had with a senior executive at a Fortune 100 company. Newly hired employees often have such mistaken expectations. They may face challenging, unfamiliar situations at work and cling to erroneous notions of how they fit the new position and culture, with no specific short-term goals and milestones, and with no one assuming responsibility for helping them to assimilate. Not surprising, then, that costly failures of new employees frequently occur, especially at the executive level, during the onboarding process. That cost is paid by:

- The newly hired employees themselves, who have gambled their careers and are now associated with failure
- Their families, who may have uprooted their lives, only to have to move once again

- The work team members, who now have to adjust to yet another new leader and whose trust in future leaders may be eroded by their experiences with a short-tenured leader
- Customers, who may be concerned about "revolving door" leadership and account management in the organization
- The organization as a whole, of course, whose substantial investment in recruiting, hiring, and socializing the new employee has been wasted

Given the initial investment in the search efforts, the interview process, and the compensation negotiations, it is not surprising that organizations have high expectations for their new executives. Organizations often expect the new leader to be perfectly prepared to be productive from day 1. However, this is rarely the case. A great deal of effort and cost is initially invested in the executive search and selection process. But then the new leader is typically just left to "figure it out" and master the challenge of taking on a new role and navigating the onboarding experience on his own.

Onboarding failures for new leaders are all too common. Downey, March, and Berkman (2001) report that half of all newly hired executives in the United States will quit or be fired within the first three years and that most will actually fail within the first 18 months on the job. Similarly, a 2003 Corporate Executive Board study (Corporate Leadership Council, 2003) cited data from the Center for Creative Leadership indicating that 40 percent of external hires fail within 18 months. This risk of failure exists even at the chief executive officer (CEO) level (Nadler, 2007) and is exacerbated by the increasing trend of hiring CEOs from outside the company. Over one-third of the CEOs at Standard & Poor's 500 firms today were hired from the outside, up from 10 percent 25 years ago ("Turning to outside candidates to find chiefs," 2007), raising the risk of failure. A study at American Express (Corporate Leadership Council, 1998) found that the turnover risk for external executive hires after three years was three times higher than the turnover risk for internal executive promotions. Even at executive levels below the CEO position, the cost of each failure can be in excess of $500,000 dollars (Bauer, Erdogan, Liden, & Wayne, 2006). The Aberdeen Group (2008) recently surveyed over 700 human resource (HR) and business leaders on their onboarding processes. Of these 86 percent stated that they believe new hires make their decision to stay or leave the organization within the first six months on the job. At the same time, onboarding itself occurs all the time; it is estimated that the average American employee will change jobs 10.2 times over a 20-year time span (Bauer, Bodner, Erdogan, Truxillo, & Tucker, 2007). The pressure on organizations to retain and accelerate a new hire's time to productivity is increasing in intensity.

In this chapter, we describe the onboarding process using organizational examples to illustrate key stages in the process. Our objective is to integrate and enhance both science and practice in this area in order to help readers:

- Assess the existing onboarding process in their organizations
- Describe what is learned during onboarding
- Address potential derailers to the successful assimilation of new employees
- Identify trends in the relevant research literature on the subject of onboarding
- Identify the activities, critical success factors, and milestones that need to occur in the preboarding and initial 90-day onboarding period
- Apply tools and metrics to add discipline to the onboarding process
- Make a business case for an investment in a more disciplined onboarding process

Our focus is primarily on the assimilation of executive- and professional-level talent, since the risk of failure associated with poor onboarding efforts is greatest with these populations. Recruiting and replacement costs at this level are high—conservatively estimated at two to four times the executive's annual salary. The impact of a failed senior executive on the organization and its customers—and on the reputation of the organization— is large and often long lasting. However, most of our discussion applies to onboarding efforts at all job levels, including entry levels. Although our emphasis will be on the onboarding of new executives hired from outside the organization, much of what we discuss also applies to employees moving across internal organizational boundaries through promotions, lateral transfers, expatriate assignments, and mergers and acquisitions.

The Onboarding Challenge

Picture our client, Amanda, a new executive vice president, brought in to manage an $80 million business unit within a $1 billion global organization. There is a laptop computer on her desk when she arrives for her first day at work, but it does not yet allow her to access the company's internal network or to set up her own e-mail account. She is supposed to travel over her first two weeks on the job to meet some of the senior leaders on her team, but her Blackberry will not be ready and functional until her third week.

She has heard about some of the key players in the broader organization and met a few during the selection interviewing process, but no one has taken responsibility for introducing her to other employees or identifying the priorities for her meetings. Amanda's new boss has sent her an organizational chart with a note that says, "Let me know who you want to meet, and I'll have my administrative assistant set up those meetings for you." Amanda stares at the organizational chart for a while but cannot figure out with whom it is most important for her to connect at this point in her assimilation into the organization.

She is sharing an administrative assistant with another executive while she is in the process of hiring her own assistant. Indeed, HR has already called with the news that there are three candidates for that position for her to interview: two from outside the company and one from another internal department. The insider was just notified that her position in that other department was eliminated, and she is desperately looking for a new position elsewhere in the company. Amanda wonders: Is it better to hire an insider or an outsider as her administrative assistant? Should she call Ann, her former trusted assistant, and bring her over or hire an insider who knows her way around the organization?

Amanda's team is geographically dispersed; none of her direct reports are actually in her location. In addition, her boss is buried in end-of-year budgetary planning with little time or attention to help Amanda get assimilated. Amanda has enough talent and focus to overcome these initial obstacles, but even though she only just arrived, she is already a derailment risk.

Potential Derailers

Amanda is not an isolated case. Based on our experience in coaching newly hired executives and their managers and in conducting workshops on onboarding with Human Resource practitioners, the onboarding efforts of talented newcomers frequently get derailed by:

- A lack of alignment with the immediate manager regarding performance expectations
- A failure to fully identify the key stakeholders both inside and outside the organization who ultimately affect the new executive's success
- A failure to form internal networks early in the process
- Little or no feedback and coaching during onboarding
- The hiring manager not taking responsibility for the successful onboarding of the new leader, which is often seen as "HR's job"
- The hiring manager focusing the new leader on quickly addressing an immediate work need rather than on formulating a long-term vision for the new leader's role
- Not identifying during the interview process the new executive's past difficulties in dealing with challenging work transitions to better predict and address potential onboarding derailers
- A preemployment assessment process that focuses on the candidate's competency to manage the business once he has mastered the demands of the position ("learned the ropes"), but ignores the candidate's limited capacity to actually learn those ropes
- The subtle but profound cultural gaps between the environment in which the candidate thrived in the past and that of the new organization

Ropes to Learn

Most newly hired executives like Amanda face enormous ambiguity when stepping into new roles, with an enormous amount to learn. Louis (1982) identified a number of what she called "transition tasks" that comprise "the ropes" that a newcomer needs to learn.

Our own model is based on Louis's work and sorts the transition tasks that need to be addressed by newcomers into five categories:

1. *Mastering the position.* What are the work objectives of the position, what day-to-day activities are performed, what information is needed to perform effectively, and where can that information be found?
2. *Mapping the organization.* What names, faces, titles, roles, and reporting relationships need to be learned, and how can new employees establish their own position in the organizational network? In other words, how can the organizational chart get converted into a mental map that is accurate and that can guide behavioral navigation? To whom does the employee go to inside the organization to get something done (approvals, resources)?
3. *Building relationships.* How can a newcomer establish a social identity or reputation (Hogan, 2007) in the web of relationships within and outside the organization?
4. *Understanding the culture.* What is the normative code of conduct in the organization, what are the organizational values, what do the symbols mean, and what are the unstated assumptions? How does one learn the organizational language, including the unfamiliar acronyms?
5. *Handling the tools.* How can a newcomer learn to use the technology (computer log-in procedures, passwords, programs, systems) to understand the layout and components of the financial reporting system, to determine the logistics required to get the work done (from dealing with security issues to scheduling international conference calls), to choose and enroll in a personal benefits plan, and to get administrative support?

As in all other learning processes (see Chapter 8 by Sandra Davis and Bob Barnett), the rate and style at which the newcomer learns these ropes varies based on individual differences in ability and motivation and on situational factors such as the specific socialization tactics (Jones, 1986) used in the organization. One key benefit from thinking about onboarding as a learning process is that it reminds us that assimilation takes time; for each newcomer, there is a distinct learning curve. There is much to learn, many ways that we can learn what we need to know, and learning occurs over a period of time, through distinct stages. Indeed, one of the metrics that Watkins (2003) uses to track the onboarding process is the net contribution of the newcomer over the first weeks at work. Initially that newcomer is a net consumer of resources, taking time and the resources of the organization to accomplish the five transition tasks listed above and contributing little in return back to the organization. Hopefully over time, the newcomer reaches a breakeven point, where the net value of her contributions is greater than the net value consumed. Effective organizational onboarding processes accelerate the time it takes to reach and stay above that breakeven point. Ineffective or haphazard processes retard newcomers from becoming net contributors to their organizations. Later in this chapter, we describe the stages of the onboarding process, highlighting the challenges associated with each stage and suggesting ways to facilitate onboarding.

The Science of Onboarding

The science of onboarding is rooted in theory and research on the topic known in the industrial-organizational psychology literature as organizational socialization. In the first comprehensive treatment of this subject, in the very first volume of the *Research in Organizational Behavior* series, Van Maanen and Schein (1979) defined organizational socialization as "the process by which an individual acquires the social knowledge and skills necessary to assume an organizational role" (p. 211). They developed a comprehensive and influential model that uses six dimensions (for example, formal-informal, collective-individual, sequential-variable) to describe the tactics organizations use to socialize new members.

In the wake of this pioneering treatment, the 1980s saw rich conceptual development, with authors drawing on a number of theoretical perspectives. Nicholson (1984) drew on role theory to describe how people transitioning to new roles learn and absorb role requirements. Louis (1980) drew on an information-processing perspective to describe the newcomer's surprise when the person's expectations run into organizational reality. In her model, this inevitable surprise motivates the person to try to make sense of the situation, as the newcomer works to match his own behaviors, attitudes, and perceptions with the new organizational circumstances. Ashforth and Mael (1989) used social identity theory to describe how the newcomer develops an identity in the new organization. Elements of that new identity include the adoption of characteristics (for example, dress, work habits, styles of speech) typical of organizational members. Weiss (see Weiss & Shaw, 1979) used social learning theory to shed light on how the attitudes of newcomers are shaped by modeling the attitudes of the organizational incumbents they encounter.

The rich conceptual development of the 1980s created a foundation for significant advances in empirical research conducted since 1990. A recent meta-analysis of the literature on newcomer adjustment (Bauer et al., 2007) identified studies on 70 distinct samples. All but seven of the empirical studies included in the meta-analysis were published after 1990. Particularly impressive is that fully 83 percent of these studies employed a longitudinal experimental design. In addition, several of the studies sampled across organizations, allowing greater generalizability of findings. Several recent studies examined newcomer socialization at midcareer positions rather than at entry-level positions. The findings of this body of empirical work are thoroughly synthesized in recent publications by Bauer and her colleagues (Bauer et al., 2007; Bauer & Taylor, 2001). Here, we simply want to extract what we see as key findings from this literature and some trends in the recent research that can be used to inform onboarding practice.

Newcomer Adjustment

Early on, Van Maanen (1978) described the process of transitioning into or across significant organizational boundaries as "break points that thrust one from a state of certainty to uncertainty; from knowing to not knowing; from the familiar to the unfamiliar"(p. 19). The literature highlights four aspects of the newcomer experience as particularly critical to assimilation.

The first aspect is primarily a function of the preboarding process, and the other three are related to the onboarding process itself:

■ ■ ■

1. *Reality shock.* Executive talent is actively recruited, especially in tight markets. It is likely that the negative features of the new position are rarely mentioned when "selling" the talented recruit on the position and the new organization. No job is perfect, and the reality of those negative aspects associated with the new role often comes as a shock to the new executive. The extensive literature on realistic job previews for entry-level positions (Hom, Griffeth, Palich, & Bracker, 1998) demonstrates that providing an honest and detailed picture of the position during the pre-employment process—negative aspects and all—will reduce this reality shock and significantly improve employee retention and assimilation once the new hire is on board.

2. *Role ambiguity.* Newcomers often do not have a clear definition of the full scope of their responsibilities and objectives. Indeed, they may not know whose expectations, beyond those of their immediate supervisor, they are required to meet in order to be successful. Newcomers who are successfully assimilated develop a clear view of their role. They understand the tasks they are expected to perform and the work priorities that should govern how they allocate their time and other resources. For this to occur, the key stakeholders with whom they interact need to be clear, specific, and in general agreement in the expectations they communicate to the newcomer.

3. *Social marginality.* As a recent arrival into a new social structure, the new executive feels the insecurity of not having an existing network of trusted colleagues. Building relationships and getting socially integrated takes time and effort. It often requires guidance from an experienced colleague with whom the newcomer must connect in regard to how to establish those connections. Successful assimilation produces an executive who feels socially secure, trusted, and liked (Feldman, 1981).

4. *Ineptness.* There is much for the newcomer to learn when entering the organization. Not knowing the rules, roles, names,

faces, where the restroom is located, or how to make travel arrangements leaves the new executive feeling inept. The risk of feeling inept extends even to the performance of core tasks that the newcomer has always executed expertly in the past, but in an often vastly different context and with different resources available. Systematic processes that teach newcomers what they need to know and equip them to meet expectations and perform effectively allow them to demonstrate job mastery and replace those initial feelings of ineptitude with a sense of self-confidence. Rather than just inferring from their own past successes that they are likely to perform effectively in the new role, new executives need to develop genuine self-confidence in their ability to do the new job, based on concrete accomplishments in that role.

■ ■ ■

In their meta-analysis on newcomer adjustment, Bauer et al. (2007) show that successfully meeting the three challenges of the onboarding experience—role ambiguity, social marginality, and ineptness—predicts a number of key socialization outcomes. Newcomers who develop stronger role clarity demonstrate stronger job performance, job satisfaction, organizational commitment, and intention to remain with the organization. Newcomers who gain social acceptance are higher than those who do not on all five outcomes studied: job performance, job satisfaction, organizational commitment, intentions to remain, and actual retention. Newcomer self-confidence predicts performance, intention to remain, and retention. Moreover, with only a few exceptions, the socialization tactics used by the organization on the one hand and the corresponding information-seeking activities of newcomers on the other also affect these outcomes through their impact on newcomers' feelings of role clarity, social acceptance, and self-confidence. These results suggest that how well newcomers are adjusting along these three dimensions needs to be considered and tracked when designing the onboarding process as a whole and when managing, mentoring, and coaching individual newcomers.

Emerging Findings

There are three other noteworthy themes emerging from the organizational socialization literature.

The Newcomer as Active Sense Maker

Louis (1980), building on earlier work by Weick (1979), argued that newcomers are not merely passive recipients of messages from recruiters, hiring managers, and others telling newcomers what they should or should not be thinking and doing. Nor do they just model what others are doing and saying. Rather, newcomers take an active role in trying to figure out "the ropes to skip and the ropes to learn" (Ritti & Levy, 2007).

A recent study across seven Korean organizations by Kim, Cable, and Kim (2005) illustrates this emerging perspective. Kim et al. investigated the impact of the organization's use of a systematic, planned set of socialization activities on the resulting perceptions of person-organization fit held by newcomers three to twenty-four months in the organization. As expected, systematic institutionalized socialization efforts facilitated effective assimilation ($r = .51$). However, the actions of the newcomers themselves were also found to play an important, and often complex, role in their own assimilation. Among the proactive newcomer behaviors examined were feedback seeking, information seeking, positive framing, general socializing, building a relationship with the supervisor, and network building. Some of these proactive behaviors interacted with organizational tactics to significantly affect assimilation. For new employees who energetically work to build a positive relationship with their boss, the influence of the organization's socialization tactics is weak. In this case, the employee's own socialization efforts replace those of the organization. Other newcomer initiatives serve to enhance or neutralize organizational tactics. As an example, for employees who see the onboarding experience as positive, then the better the organization's socialization process is, the better the adjustment is. For those who see the experience more negatively, institutionalized socialization efforts have no effect on perceived person-organizational fit.

This and similar recent studies remind us that the newcomer's own initiative, mindset, and actions play a major role in determining successful assimilation. Systematic onboarding programs need to acknowledge and support the new leader's own responsibility in the assimilation process.

Socialization as a Multiphase Process

Early research on socialization looked at individual and direct predictors of assimilation. More recently, researchers have proposed and tested multiphase process models that examine the chain of influences on successful socialization. Figure 4.1 presents the elements that characterize many of these newer models. The antecedents represent individual difference factors that newcomers bring to their new position. Researchers have examined how such antecedents in turn both affect and interact with the socialization experiences imposed by the organization to produce both near-term (proximal) and longer-term (distal) effects on newcomer behaviors, capabilities, performance, and attitudes.

Developing and then testing these process models provides rich and more fine-grained insight into what actually happens during onboarding, which can help better inform practice. Three examples from the recent empirical literature that unravel elements of the onboarding process illustrate that insight:

- Newcomers who receive intense socialization on the organization's politics, values, and people from veteran organizational

Figure 4.1. Socialization as a Multiphase Process

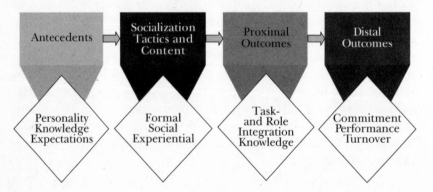

members are more likely to absorb these values and in turn, develop a stronger sense of organizational commitment and satisfaction (Wesson & Gogus, 2005).

- While the tactics used to socialize newcomers directly affect whether the newcomer feels satisfied on the job or not, these tactics affect employee retention only if they first help the newcomer feel socially accepted and self-confident (Bauer et al., 2007).
- Over time, the extent to which newcomers ask coworkers for technical information decreases; the extent to which they ask supervisors for technical information, however, remains constant (Chan & Schmitt, 2000).

These studies reflect both the complexity and the usefulness of a more nuanced understanding of the elements of onboarding. Accordingly, those designing onboarding programs need to make sure they carefully think through how each planned intervention (for example executive coaching) links to other elements in the onboarding process.

Personality Plays a Role

Van Maanen and Schein (1979) explicitly ruled out a role for personality in their theory: "We assume that a theory of organizational socialization must not allow itself to become too preoccupied with individual characteristics (. . . personality)" (p. 216). This reflected in some measure the general skepticism in our field at that time about the value of personality in the study of organizational behavior (Weiss & Adler, 1984). However, with the revival of interest in personality (Morgeson, Campion, Dipboye, Hollenbeck, Murphy, & Schmitt, 2007) has come a more serious consideration of how the newcomer's personality influences the socialization process.

Three personality constructs that have recently been explored in relationship to socialization processes are self-monitoring, proactive personality, and extraversion.

Self-monitoring refers to personality-based differences in an individual's sensitivity to external social cues in shaping his own behavior. Those who are high in self-monitoring are motivated to seek social acceptance and social status. Newcomers who are high self-monitors have been found to more proactively seek out and be influenced by mentors and role models (Day & Kilduff, 2003). Not surprisingly, in a five-year follow-up study of newly minted M.B.A.s going into managerial jobs (Kilduff & Day, 1994), self-monitoring was a significant predictor of career mobility, including internal and cross-organizational promotions.

Crant and his colleagues (Seibert, Kraimer, & Crant, 2001) have been studying a construct they call *proactive personality*. This construct represents the degree to which people take initiative to identify and seize opportunities to improve things in their lives and in their environment. Managers with a more proactive personality have been found to develop better knowledge of the organization's politics, take more career initiative, and show more innovation in their organizational roles. As a result, they are more likely over a two-year period to receive promotions and salary increases and to experience greater career satisfaction.

Bauer et al. (2006) examined the role of extraversion in executive onboarding in a Fortune 500 pharmaceutical company. They found that new executives who were extraverted, as compared to those who were socially introverted, were performing more effectively in their role after six months and were more likely to have been retained after three and a half years, regardless of the quality of the relationship they had formed with their boss over their first 90 days at work. In contrast, the work performance and tenure of relatively introverted new executives was strongly determined by the quality of the relationship they initially formed with their boss. The more positive and supportive the supervisor-subordinate relationship experienced by introverts, the better their performance and retention.

In the case of all three of these personality factors, the relationships found with other variables are complex, often subtle, and reflect multiphase processes, with personality factors interacting with situational factors to determine longer-term outcomes of socialization. Consideration of these subtleties should guide the practice of managing, coaching, and mentoring newcomers.

More generally, what we see from this overview of the emerging literature on organizational socialization is that the relevant science is maturing rapidly and that onboarding practitioners would be well served to pay close attention to that science.

The Executive Onboarding Process: A Five-Stage Model

- Come in and change our world, BUT adapt to our culture.
- We know you are on a learning curve, BUT hit the ground running.
- Here are your new or expanded responsibilities. Go perform, BUT keep doing your *old job* until a replacement can come up to speed.

These are just a few of the challenges that executives can face during onboarding. This section examines onboarding as a six-month, multiphase process that, if effectively designed and executed, allows the newcomer to successfully navigate these countervailing tensions. Our five-phase model is presented in Figure 4.2. Two of the phases of onboarding actually occur prior to the newcomer's first day at work. This reflects our belief in the value of careful preparation to successful assimilation. The onboarding model we propose for organizations does not place the accountability for onboarding solely on the organization or solely on the new executive. Our model explicitly recognizes that effective onboarding requires the commitment and engagement of multiple partners in the organization.

Figure 4.2. Five Stage Onboarding Process

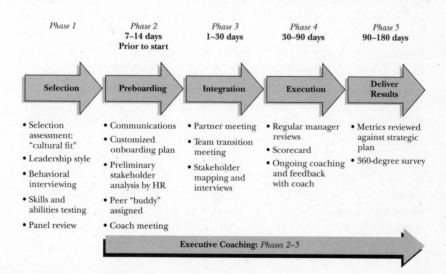

Phase 1	Phase 2 7–14 days Prior to start	Phase 3 1–30 days	Phase 4 30–90 days	Phase 5 90–180 days
Selection	**Preboarding**	**Integration**	**Execution**	**Deliver Results**
• Selection assessment: "cultural fit" • Leadership style • Behavioral interviewing • Skills and abilities testing • Panel review	• Communications • Customized onboarding plan • Preliminary stakeholder analysis by HR • Peer "buddy" assigned • Coach meeting	• Partner meeting • Team transition meeting • Stakeholder mapping and interviews	• Regular manager reviews • Scorecard • Ongoing coaching and feedback with coach	• Metrics reviewed against strategic plan • 360-degree survey

Executive Coaching: *Phases 2–5*

We acknowledge that there are situational contingencies unique to organizations and to particular newcomers that require customization of the length and the components of the onboarding process. Indeed, formal onboarding programs across organizations range considerably in length—from one month to one year—and in content. As discussed later the state of the business and the culture of the organization affect the tactics and content of the socialization process. Moreover, we recognize that many organizations will not have the resources or focus to design and implement all phases of the onboarding process described in our model. Nonetheless, we argue that any disciplined, structured process that provides onboarding support—even if not as comprehensive as that outlined here—will yield more positive benefits than the haphazard, "sink or swim" experience of most newcomers.

Phase 1: Selection

Much has been written about selecting executive talent (Silzer & Adler, 2003; Chapter 5, this book). However, from an onboarding perspective, two critical characteristics of executive candidates appear to be missing in many executive assessment processes: cultural fit and learning agility.

Culture Fit

Despite recent research on the importance of person-organization fit (Kristof-Brown, Zimmerman, & Johnson, 2005), organizations rarely systematically assess the external candidate's fit to the new culture. Not surprisingly, in a recent survey of 53 Human Resource managers, 75 percent cited poor cultural fit as the main reason for the derailment of new leaders (Watkins, 2007).

How does an organization measure an individual's cultural fit? In order to develop a culture fit assessment, we recommend first bringing together a panel of individuals who have history with, and deep knowledge of the organization, its culture, and its core values. These cultural subject matter experts should be asked to identify those elements that uniquely define the organizational climate and how work gets done within the organization. For example, how are decisions made? Is the organization consensus driven? Is it hierarchical? Do individual business units have autonomy, or is the organization more centralized?

Cameron and Quinn (2006) have developed a model of cultural fit that examines the dimensions of the organization's culture as it exists *now* and the culture that is "preferred." The model and the assessment tool they have developed, called the OCAI (organizational culture assessment instrument) could be used to assess the organization's current culture and the culture in which an external candidate prefers to operate. The instrument identifies six aspects of organizational culture:

1. *Dominant characteristics.* Questions target the overarching attributes that drive the organization. For example, is it focused on results? Innovative? Controlled and structured?
2. *Organizational leadership.* What defines the approach of leadership? Is it nurturing and mentoring? Does it foster risk avoidance, or is it more aggressive and encouraging of risk?
3. *Management of employees.* What is the predominant management style? Is the organization driven by teamwork and consensus? Or is it more competitive and oriented toward individual achievement?
4. *Organizational glue.* What are the values of the organization? Is the emphasis on loyalty and trust or on formal rules and structure?
5. *Strategic emphasis.* What does the organization emphasize in its strategy? Efficiency and control? Meeting revenue targets and being dominant in the market? Being innovative?
6. *Criteria of success.* How does the organization measure success? Is it by having unique products and services? Or by having dependable delivery and lowest cost production?

We suggest there is value in having subject matter experts use a tool like the OCAI or some similar instrument to identify which attributes uniquely define what the organizational culture currently is and in what direction these cultural experts want to see the culture develop. This scan of the cultural "DNA" of the organization has three main applications in phase 1 of onboarding:

- It provides a realistic preview to the candidate that goes deeper than the superficial descriptive factors typically communicated during the pre-hire stage. Watkins (2007) recommends that companies be very explicit in communicating to the executive job candidate the aspects of culture that most impact leader behavior. Watkins claims that when companies do this systematically, early executive failure rates drop to less than 10 percent. Shell Oil's comprehensive onboarding program explicitly incorporates customized and highly realistic simulation exercises in the selection phase in order to give candidates an experiential feel for the target executive role and the culture surrounding that role (Corporate Leadership Council, 2003).

- A culture scan is particularly helpful to a candidate being recruited from outside the organization specifically to bring in a new perspective and change aspects of the current culture. For such a candidate, the scan can be a gauge of whether the organization's expectations are realizable and, if they are, the scan can serve as an initial road map for change.

- Candidates can complete a tool like the OCAI during the selection process to assess their own preferred culture. Those who are evaluating the candidate (for example, recruiters and hiring managers) can then judge where the candidate's cultural preferences match those of the organization's existing or desired culture and where they do not, in arriving at a candidate suitability decision. Alternatively, after candidates have completed the assessment tool, they can be provided with the culture scan results so they can make their own judgment of their fit to the organization.

At one major U.S.-based pharmaceutical company, an in-depth structured interview is administered by a third-party assessment firm that specifically focuses on culture fit. This organization's culture has historically been very collaborative. Accordingly, a section of the structured interview focused intensely on the executive candidate's preference for "going it alone" and taking individual initiative. Mavericks were screened out.

While trying to assess the person-culture fit of external candidates at the pre-hire stage, organizations often are caught in cross-purposes. Hiring managers and recruiters describe the changes they desire and the urgent need for change when speaking to candidates, but in the end, organizational inertia works against the individual's efforts to change the culture once the person is on board. Judy Allen, of Agilent Technologies, refers to the resistance an organization shows to a newly arrived change champion as the organization's "cultural antibodies" (personal communication, 2006). At the executive level, organizations often want "fresh blood" infused into the leadership ranks from the outside specifically to initiate cultural change. In fact, change leadership is often a major reason that organizations look to "the outside" to fill senior positions. However, in looking for candidates who fit the culture, companies decrease the likelihood of identifying leaders who have the ability and courage to walk into an organization and constructively initiate material change in the culture. The pharmaceutical company that assessed fit to its collaborative culture and screened out mavericks discovered to its chagrin that newly hired senior leaders lacked innovation and entrepreneurship. The company has more recently revised the structured interview to reflect the need for more independent leaders.

Learning Agility

An important part of the executive selection process, given all that has to be learned during onboarding, should be the measurement of learning agility. Learning agility has been discussed primarily in the context of identifying high potentials (Eichinger & Lombardo, 2004). However, it is critical to ensure the success of a new leader's onboarding, given the learning curve that is required early in the job.

Based on work at the Center for Creative Leadership (Eichinger & Lombardo, 2004), this construct refers to the ability and willingness to learn, change, and gain from life experiences. There is some evidence from work at the Center for Creative Leadership that a newcomer's ability to learn how to effectively deal with first-time or changing work situations is predictive of long-term potential and performance. There is, of course, overwhelming empirical evidence that the capacity to learn, as reflected in general mental ability, is predictive of success in training and on-the-job performance, especially in complex, challenging positions (Schmidt & Hunter, 2004).

Eichinger and Lombardo (2004) have defined four factors that in their model comprise learning agility:

- *People agility*: Describes people who know themselves well, learn from experience, treat others constructively, and are cool and resilient under the pressures of change
- *Results agility*: Describes people who get results under tough conditions, inspire others to perform beyond normal, and exhibit the sort of presence that builds confidence in others
- *Mental agility*: Describes people who think through problems from a fresh point of view and are comfortable with complexity, ambiguity, and explaining their thinking to others
- *Change agility*: Describes people who are curious, have a passion for ideas, like to experiment with test cases, and engage in skill-building activities

Each of these elements of learning agility can be assessed through behavioral interview questions that explore candidates' past actions and emotions under conditions of change and ambiguity, their commitment to growth and learning, and their reactions to failure. Agile learners tend to demonstrate in their interview responses that they are:

- Problem solvers
- Voracious readers
- Multidimensional thinkers who are comfortable with complexity
- People who enjoy the learning process
- Intelligent risk takers
- Focused on learning to do what they do not yet know how to do
- People who like figuring out something new or different in advance in order to perform well under first-time conditions
- Good at coping with the discomfort of change

Information derived from interviews can be complemented with measures of personality traits such as the big five factor of openness or Hogan's (2007) dimension of intellectance (Hogan's name for open-mindedness and refers to curiosity, openness to experience, and imagination). Additionally, assessment protocols could include inventories that measure traits such as initiative and tolerance for ambiguity, general mental ability, as well as learning (versus performance) orientation (Dweck, 2006).

Broadening the Use of Assessment

Even more fundamental than adding a systematic evaluation of culture fit and learning agility to executive preemployment assessment, is that organizations need to take into account more fully the rich data they have gathered at the selection stage to create an onboarding plan for the individual. Instead, hiring managers and recruiters now tend to have the expectation that new leaders, especially given their high level of compensation, should be able to get assimilated quickly and on their own with seemingly no areas of risk.

We recommend that once a selection decision is made, the selection team share relevant assessment information and clearly identified areas of strength and development opportunity with those accountable for the newcomer's assimilation (for example, the hiring manager and the HR manager, as well as the newcomer). Areas of assimilation risk identified in assessment can be closely monitored and coached in order to anticipate and prevent derailment. In our work as practitioners, when we conduct a debriefing after a new leader fails in her role, one of the first questions we ask the hiring manager is: "How did you plan for managing the risks you identified in the hiring process?" Typically the need to plan the onboarding efforts based on the identified onboarding risks gets lost in the transition from the selection phase to the integration phase.

For the newcomer, comprehensive assessment data create a dilemma. On the one hand, no candidate is "perfect," everyone comes to the organization with strengths and weaknesses. Yet, in particular for the newly hired talented executive, there often is an expectation that the individual is in fact coming as a perfect package, carrying the high expectations of the hiring manager (at the most senior levels, including the board of directors itself). As such, the new leader may hesitate to ask for help from others to address the risk areas identified in assessment. This is where the use of a professionally qualified executive coach can be particularly beneficial. Having an external or an appropriately placed internal coach provides the new leader a *safe haven* to discuss these risks and to get an objective perspective. The ability to share with a trusted coach that "these people operate in a very different way from my prior organization" or "my manager is giving me mixed messages about learning versus producing" can help address some of the inevitable tensions of a new role.

Phase 2: Preboarding (Beginning 7 to 14 Days Prior to Start Date)

A key activity that should occur in the preboarding phase, 7 to 14 days prior to starting the new job, is to identify the onboarding team and review the responsibilities of every member. Each of the team members serves a unique role in the process. Below we outline what we believe are the roles that comprise the onboarding team and the major responsibilities of each role over the course of the onboarding process. We recognize that many organizations may not be able to take the holistic approach advocated here; minimally the Human Resource leader should have a discussion with both the new leader and the hiring manager, reviewing the onboarding process and articulating each person's responsibilities at each phase. We also recognize that often these conversations may not actually take place until the newcomer arrives at work in phase 3.

Hiring Manager

- Defines key performance expectations for the new leader
- Prepares onboarding plan, which identifies key resources and stakeholders (with assistance from the Human Resources leader)
- Establishes clear and focused work objectives with the new leader that support business priorities
- Provides ongoing coaching, feedback, and guidance

Human Resource Leader

- Facilitates overall executive onboarding process
- Meets with the hiring manager to create the onboarding plan
- Provides regular coaching and support for plan execution
- Supports new leaders in their role as change agents

New Leader

- Acquires necessary knowledge to understand the organization's business and market strategies within the first 90 days
- Executes the onboarding plan, including meetings with manager, staff, colleagues, and customers, as well as site visits and all-employee communication events
- Develops performance objectives and personal development objectives with input from the hiring manager and others
- Solicits feedback, coaching, and development support

Administrative Assistant (or Sometimes the Hiring Manager's Administrative Assistant)

- Serves as key link to provide a positive and welcoming first impression
- Provides support for office and equipment setup, especially of technology required to communicate (PDA or personal digital assistant, e-mail)
- Gathers and provides background information resources (organizational charts, strategic plans, contact lists, and so forth)
- Coordinates new leader's schedule for first week and beyond
- Provides moral support

Recruiter

- Provides pre-job start information on the job offer, salary, benefits, company culture, and other information
- Previews the culture and relevant information about key stakeholders—especially that of the hiring manager—and any historical information about the role that may be relevant

Mentor or Buddy

- Provides technical support and cultural assimilation information in a nonthreatening, peer-to-peer relationship

Coach

- Serves as an objective sounding board and a source of best-practice advice. Guides the newcomer through the learning process, encouraging him to discover new sources of information and develop his own understanding of the organization and his role within it
- Maintains the new leader's focus on cultural assimilation and personal development in the face of pressures to produce immediate results

In the days leading to the new leader's first day on the job, the hiring manager and HR manager should create a comprehensive draft onboarding plan for the new leader, assigning resources and providing critical support from day 1. Components of this plan are customized to the needs of the new leader and include information about the business, the culture, the team, and available resources, including administrative support and key activities that need to occur early during the first two weeks on the job. For example, as part of the onboarding plan, initial meetings should be scheduled with key team members and stakeholders. The plan also includes a preliminary stakeholder analysis (described below) along with more general organizational information such as a listing of all the team members, business goals, performance objectives, and key initial priorities.

Exhibit 4.1 represents a sample format for an onboarding plan. It can be made more or less elaborate and detailed depending on the needs and objectives of the organization and the newcomer. The plan lays out the key objectives, activities, and responsibilities for each phase of the onboarding process. The onboarding plan is a "living document" that is revised and updated regularly during the newcomer's first 180 days with the new organization.

A unique aspect of the onboarding plan is that it focuses on learning as opposed to doing. In other words, instead of starting the job by implementing new approaches and activities, new

Exhibit 4.1. Sample Onboarding Plan

Purpose of the Onboarding Plan

This plan should be used to help identify and define what is expected of a new leader in a new role. This plan contains a road map for the first six months on the job, including:

- Responsibilities and Decision-Making Authority
- Preboarding Activities

Strategic Objectives for the first 30, 60, 90, and 180 days

New Leader Onboarding

Accountabilities and Performance Standards/Metrics

Partner Meeting Agenda and Outcomes

Development Plan

New Leader: Title: Reports to:	Responsibilities:
Stakeholders: 1. 2. 3.	Decision-Making Authority:

ONBOARDING CHECKLIST:

❑ Selection information reviewed by hiring manager (e.g., interview information, comments from hiring panel, issues and concerns, and key areas of strength)	❑ Administrative Assistant is assigned and Office/IT requirements are fulfilled
❑ Discuss any potential issues around cultural fit	❑ Formal orientation is conducted
❑ Potential derailers identified	❑ Stakeholder interviews are set up through Admin Assistant
❑ Preliminary development plan is created based on hiring informaion	❑ Peer "Buddy" or Mentor is assigned
	❑ Partner Meeting scheduled, pre-work sent out and completed prior to the meeting

(Continued)

Exhibit 4.1. Sample Onboarding Plan (*Continued*)

PARTNER MEETING AGENDA:

Date and Time:	Attendees:
Note: This is the first formal meeting of all partners involved in directly onboarding the new leader. This is typically a half-day meeting with pre-work completed by all attendees.	1. New Leader 2. Hiring Manager 3. HR 4. Coach (may be the same as HR or external coach)
Agenda: • Review Onboarding Plan • Discuss Development Plan and agree to objectives • Discuss potential derailers and plan to overcome • Use of Peer "Buddy" or Mentor	Outcomes: • Alignment with Hiring Manager and sign-off on strategic objectives and goals • Development plan and action items agreed upon • Metrics of success clearly defined (the "Scorecard") • Next steps identified

Strategic Objectives:

This document is intended to be formally reviewed on a monthly basis.

First 30 Days: Outline New Leader's Onboarding Accountabilities, Results, and Metrics

Describe your key onboarding accountabilities for the first 30 days. Describe the objectives and expected results, and define the minimally acceptable metrics as well as the key activities to be performed.

Accountability 1:	Actual Performance/ Results:	Minimally Acceptable:	Key Activities:
Accountability 2:	Actual Performance/ Results:	Minimally Acceptable:	Key Activities:

KEY ACTIVITIES DURING FIRST 30 DAYS

- Partner meeting
- Stakeholder mapping and interviews
- Team transition meeting

First 60 Days

Describe your key accountabilities for the first 60 days. Describe the objectives and expected results, and define the minimally acceptable metrics as well as the desired key activities to be performed.

Accountability 1:	Actual Performance/Results:	Minimally Acceptable:	Key Activities:
Accountability 2:	Actual Performance/Results:	Minimally Acceptable:	Key Activities:

KEY ACTIVITIES DURING FIRST 60 DAYS

- Hiring Manager reviews (monthly)
- Scorecard (metrics) reviewed
- Coaching sessions with New Leader
- Partner Review Meeting

First 90 Days

Describe your key onboarding accountabilities for the first 90 days. Describe the objectives and expected results, and define the minimally acceptable metrics as well as the key activities to be performed.

Accountability 1:	Actual Performance/Results:	Minimally Acceptable:	Key Activities:
Accountability 2:	Actual Performance/Results:	Minimally Acceptable:	Key Activities:

(Continued)

Exhibit 4.1. Sample Onboarding Plan (*Continued*)

Key Activities During First 90 Days

- Hiring Manager reviews (monthly)
- Scorecard (metrics) reviewed
- Coaching sessions with New Leader
- Partner Review Meeting

First 6 Months

Describe your key onboarding accountabilities for the first 6 months. Describe the objectives and expected results, and define the minimally acceptable metrics as well as the key activities to be performed.

Accountability 1:	Actual Performance/Results:	Minimally Acceptable:	Key Activities:
Accountability 2:	Actual Performance/Results:	Minimally Acceptable:	Key Activities:

KEY ACTIVITIES DURING FIRST 6 MONTHS

- Hiring Manager reviews (monthly)
- Scorecard (metrics) reviewed
- Coaching sessions with New Leader
- Formal Review at end of 6 months with specific emphasis on progress against strategic plan

Development Plan

Identify knowledge, skills, and abilities required to be successful in role:

- How can the New Leader maximize strengths to achieve objectives?
- No New Leader comes into a role perfect. What development needs to take place to improve and apply specific knowledge or skills? (Consider coaching, mentoring, structured on-the-job development, as well as formal training.)
- Are there any derailers or cultural fit issues that need to be addressed or to be aware of?

Critical Knowledge, Skills, Abilities Required to Meet Priorities:	Actions	Resources/Support Required
Development Goal 1:		
Development Goal 2:		
Strength Area to Leverage 1:		
Strength Area to Leverage 2:		
Potential Derailer 1:		
Potential Derailer 2:		

Additional comments:

_____

_____

Signatures:

New Leader   Hiring Manager   HR   Coach

_____   _____   _____   _____

_____

leaders should focus first on the five key learning tasks: mastering the position, mapping the organization, building relationships, understanding the culture, and handling the tools. Some companies have created standardized onboarding plan templates. For example, at American Express, the HR leader provides each new executive hire with a "First 100 Days" plan that covers all key learning objectives, lists all relevant contacts, and has a checklist of onboarding activities that need to be accomplished. At a major pharmaceutical company, a new executive is actually handed a 90-day road map by the hiring manager or HR leader. The road map has a schedule of prearranged meetings with key stakeholders, provides a brief background on each stakeholder, and suggests questions that the newcomer may want to ask during the meeting. The road map provides a structure for what needs to be learned during the onboarding, from whom, and in what sequence. It also sets the newcomer on a path of networking and relationship building.

Preferably as part of the preboarding process, the newcomer should be connected with a coach. We advocate the use of external coaches for onboarding because of the objective, external perspective they can bring to coaching and the enhanced safety required in a coaching relationship by a newcomer. Organizations that are reluctant to use a professional external coach should consider an appropriately placed and trained internal coach—one who is not within the newcomer's immediate business unit. Whether the coach is external or internal, a coaching contract should be created early on.

Drawing on the assessment information collected in the selection phase, a development plan is drafted by the coach and discussed with the new leader either in the days just prior to the job start date or in the first days after starting. The learning objectives in the final plan, agreed to by the new leader and coach, are reviewed with the hiring manager and the HR leader. The developmental plan addresses ways to develop weak areas or identify ways to compensate for them. Also, ways to leverage the newcomer's strengths are identified. This plan is integrated into the coaching contract and agreed to by the onboarding team. Consistent with a philosophy that puts the primary accountability for onboarding on the new executives themselves, Shell Oil has newcomers convene their own developmental and onboarding planning meetings with the coach, hiring manager, and HR leader (Corporate Leadership Council, 2003).

In addition, organizations should do as much as possible to provide more realistic job preview information in this preboarding phase. For example, at Agilent Technologies, new leaders are assigned a peer buddy. This individual meets with the newcomer for lunch a few days before the start date to provide a welcome, share insights into the culture, and, on an ongoing basis during onboarding, help the new leader make connections. For an externally hired new leader, it may be particularly beneficial to identify a peer who was also externally hired and has successfully transitioned to the new culture. By honestly sharing the challenges that newcomers face in the organization, the peer buddy can help prepare the newcomer for the initial "surprises."

Finally, effective preboarding planning includes ensuring that the basics of corporate life are in place for the new executive on day 1. These include an office assignment, badge or access card, office keys, telephone extension, e-mail and PDA set-up with associated user IDs and interim passwords, and business cards. Typically the administrative assistant has responsibility for these arrangements with some oversight by the hiring manager (or her administrative assistant) or the HR leader.

Phase 3: Integration (Days 1 to 30)

Phase 3, which extends over the first 30 days, is usually the most intense phase in the new executive's transition. Three events in this phase can accelerate the assimilation of the individual into the team and organization:

■ ■ ■

1. Partner meeting. The partner meeting consists of the new leader, the hiring manager, the HR manager, and the coach. During this meeting, the hiring manager articulates his expectations and the critical goals and objectives to be achieved by the newcomer in the short term (that is the first 90 days), as well as over the longer term (the first year). This meeting serves to prevent one of the most common derailers of onboarding: a misalignment of expectations between the new leader and the manager. In addition, the onboarding plan is updated to document agreed-upon objectives and milestones. The HR manager is present to help facilitate the conversation as well as serve as a resource to the new leader and hiring manager. The coach is present to identify and help raise any issues that could potentially prevent the new leader from achieving her goals. In addition, the coach can discuss how coaching will address the derailers that all newcomers typically face, as well as help the new leader manage through the inevitable mood swings that accompany such major life transitions as moving into a new role.

2. Team transition meeting. Onboarding a new leader is not just simply transitioning the individual into the new role. It transforms the entire work team, and indeed the business unit as a whole. To help facilitate this transformation, one large high-tech company mandates a half-day team transition meeting within the first week of an executive's start date. This meeting has two objectives: it enables a new leader to observe the dynamics of the team, and it gives the leader an opportunity to hear the team's issues and concerns, thus creating a two-way dialogue between the team and the new leader. The process works as follows. First, the team meets with a facilitator without the presence of the new leader. Typically the facilitator is the HR manager or the coach, or both. The team is asked to come up with a list of the key information about the team that they collectively feel it is important for the new leader to know. One example might be a description of situations where the team has functioned particularly well in the past and situations where it seems to stumble as a team. They are also asked to develop some questions they would like to ask their new leader—for example:

- What are your expectations of us as a team?
- What goals and objectives do you have for us over the next three months? six months?
- How often do you like to meet with us individually and as a team?
- How do you like to make decisions?
- Can you describe your "work style" for us?
- What do you view as your key strengths?
- How will you be seeking our help as a team?
- What would you like to see us focus on immediately?

This brainstorming session typically takes two to three hours. After the information and questions are gathered and posted on the wall or flip chart, the new leader joins the team. At that point, the posted information is shared and questions are asked. The new leader responds only to those questions with which he is comfortable. Of course, he is encouraged to come to the meeting with questions for the team. The result of this session is more clarity around what the team expects of their new leader and, in turn, what the new leader expects of the team.

At a large pharmaceutical company and at a large bank, similar processes are used to integrate the newcomer into her peer network, especially where the newcomer's role will be tightly integrated with a peer team. The new peer integration meeting uses a facilitator from HR or an external coach to surface questions and concerns that the newcomer can then address. The objective is to accelerate the new leader's integration into a peer network and begin building peer working relationships.

3. Stakeholder mapping and interviews. Another important component of the integration phase is conducting stakeholder mapping and interviews. This is a critical activity regardless of whether the new executive was promoted from within or hired externally. A common mistake occurs when an internal hire sees no need to go through the stakeholder process since, she reasonably thinks, *I know all the players and have good relationships with each of them.* The faulty logic here is that too often, newly promoted executives do not realize that they need to build new kinds of relationships with these individuals. With the executive now operating at a different level, the interface needs, power balance, and operational scope of the stakeholders shift in both obvious and subtle ways.

The goals of the stakeholder mapping and interviews are twofold: to build key relationships and to gather critical information about how the new leader can meet stakeholders' needs. We use a two-step process to conduct a stakeholder analysis. First, a visual stakeholder map is created. The initial stakeholder map, particularly in the case of an external hire, should be developed by the HR manager. Using that as the template, the HR manager or coach (or both) takes a more in-depth look at the relationships the individual currently has in place and those that need to be developed further. The coach then asks the new executive to evaluate the strength of each relationship and estimate how critical each stakeholder is likely to be to the success of the new leader's team and organization. After this process is completed, the new leader identifies the people with whom it is most critical to build stronger relationships. If the new leader is an external hire, the HR leader or hiring manager is brought into this process of identifying stakeholders and assessing the criticality of the relationship to the new leader's success. Stakeholder interviews are then scheduled and conducted—all within the first 30 days on the job. This timing is essential. As individuals move up in the organization, the strength of relationships they build with key stakeholders—their personal social capital—becomes more and more critical to success. Building relationships early on and soliciting help from stakeholders in pursuit of work objectives increases the likelihood of a successful assimilation.

One company that takes stakeholder networking especially seriously is American Express. Part of the onboarding plan for each new executive is a meeting with the CEO and subsequent meetings with a number of the CEO's direct reports within the first 30 days. Later, during phase 4, the onboarding plan is updated to include additional scheduled meetings and forums that give the newcomer exposure to internal and external customers.

■ ■ ■

Apart from these individualized activities, many organizations have a formal orientation program for new executives. These programs typically run from two hours to several days (Corporate Leadership Council, 2004). At their most basic, these programs include a welcome address from a senior leader; an overview of the business, its strategy, culture, and values; benefit options and enrollment instructions; a description of the performance management process; and a summary of ethical guidelines and other policies.

One objective of some orientation programs is to provide an integrated perspective on the business as a whole from day 1. To that end, bringing new executives together from different parts of the business and different geographic regions creates a networked "incoming class" or cohort that can continue to provide the new executives with informal relationships that transcend the individual business unit. Some organizations go beyond the orientation program to expand the new executive's perspective from the start. For example, for many years at Xerox, newly hired engineers would spend their first two or three weeks working in the sales department, while newly hired salespeople spent the first two or three weeks in manufacturing.

It is also important to make the new executive feel welcomed. The first step in fostering a welcoming atmosphere is alerting the organization as soon as possible to the newcomer's arrival. Since 2006 in our own company, Aon Consulting, the business unit HR leaders have been sending out weekly announcements of all new hires in each location to all employees at that location, encouraging the incumbents to welcome the newcomer. At Vision Service Plan, fellow workers are assigned to call newcomers a few days before they start, welcome them aboard, and set a date for coffee or lunch sometime during Week One.

Phase 4: Execution (Days 30 to 90)

During phase 4, which extends from 30 to 90 days, the organization begins to expect results. This means that the new executive needs to demonstrate early mastery of the target learning tasks and begin developing a detailed strategic business plan that outlines in specific terms the actions and changes that will be implemented in the 90- to 180-day period. A typical derailer at this stage is an increasing disconnect between the manager and new leader as the newcomer attempts to produce early results. Regularly scheduled meetings with the hiring manager are key to keeping onboarding on track. The HR manager and coach can serve as catalysts during this stage to ensure that communication between the newcomer and the manager occurs on a regular basis, despite the distractions and hectic calendars that make communication difficult to schedule. In addition to the manager meetings, the new leader should be meeting regularly during this phase with the coach to keep focused on learning, especially in the face of internal and external pressures to produce tangible results, and developing ways to leverage strengths and prevent derailment.

In order to ensure the onboarding process is producing the expected outcomes, a large West Coast manufacturer conducts a brief six-question, web-delivered bimonthly *pulse survey* during phase 4. The survey takes only a minute or two to complete but can provide an early indication of derailment. The pulse survey captures the perspective of the new executive as well as, through a parallel version of the survey, that of the hiring manager and

HR leader. Using a 5-point agree-disagree scale, the survey asks the new leader such questions as, "My coach has helped to increase my time-to-productivity in my new role" and "My manager has been engaged in and supportive of my onboarding process." At this manufacturer, the hiring manager and HR leader's version of the survey focuses on the mentoring element of onboarding and asks them to agree or disagree that:

- The mentor provides appropriate support in creating a development plan that will support the new leader's success.
- The mentor works with the new leader and his team to help identify and address potential issues in working effectively together.
- The mentor helps to increase the new leader's time to productivity.
- The mentor helps the new manager avoid or address potential derailers.
- The new manager has been included in the onboarding mentoring process appropriately.
- The onboarding mentoring program is a worthwhile investment.

Of course, the hiring manager can evaluate mentoring only if she has regular conversations about the mentoring process with both the newcomer and the mentor. This format can easily be adapted to address coaching and other elements of the onboarding process.

The results of the pulse survey should be entered into a simple electronic dashboard to help alert the new leader and the HR manager to whether onboarding is on track or not. The dashboard, updated at least monthly during the first 90 days, should indicate whether milestones were reached on each of the key steps of the onboarding process—for example:

- Onboarding plan completed by day 15
- Coaching relationship started by day 15
- Buddy or peer relationship started by day 15
- Team transition meeting held by day 20
- Stakeholder analysis completed by day 30

- Coaching contract, including development plan, completed by day 30
- Strategic business plan completed by day 90

A second section of the dashboard can track ongoing onboarding activities such as the frequency of the new leader's meetings with the manager, the coach, and the buddy or peer. A simple red (not meeting goals), yellow (at risk of not meeting goals), or green (meeting goals) rating can be assigned for each required area. A monthly review of this scorecard during phases 4 and 5 can help ensure the onboarding process stays on schedule.

Phase 5: Settling in (90 to 180 Days)

Over the first six months, it is important to take comprehensive stock every 12 weeks or so of what has occurred during the onboarding process. It should be noted that research on onboarding consistently points to inadequate feedback to the new leader as a major early derailer (Corporate Leadership Council, 2006). For the new hire, it is simply too long to wait a year or more for the first comprehensive performance review. We describe three types of metrics that can be used at both the 90-day and 180-day points to provide valuable feedback.

■ ■ ■

- *Operational metrics.* Operational metrics measure the usefulness of the onboarding tools. They assess whether the prescribed activities are actually being executed in a timely fashion, at recommended frequency, and are seen by the newcomer and others as helpful to the newcomer's assimilation. Examples of operational metrics are:
  - How many of the prescribed coaching sessions were held?
  - Did the partner and stakeholder meetings occur in the first 90 days?
  - Ratings by the newcomer of the usefulness to assimilation of each key onboarding activity (for example, coaching, mentoring, formal orientation, manager meetings).
- *Management metrics.* Management metrics are indices of how productive the new leader is during the first 90 days.

These metrics assess the degree of the newcomer's early performance in her new role. Here the key performance dimensions (influence, team building, innovation, productivity) that will be part of the new manager's annual performance appraisal are evaluated (most typically by the hiring manager) on an interim basis at the 90- and 120-day marks to assess how productive the newcomer is becoming.

- *Strategic metrics.* These metrics look at longer-term outcomes of the onboarding process. Measures examined often include an assessment of the degree to which the onboarding plan was executed, whether a strategic business plan was submitted by the 180-day mark, and retention of the newcomer past milestone dates (90 days, 180 days, 1 year). The hiring manager is most commonly the primary source of evaluations of the newcomer's strategic contribution. However, in some organizations, the hiring manager's own manager, as well as peers and customers of the newcomer, provide ratings through a multirater survey.

■ ■ ■

One key question that the HR leader may want to ask the hiring manager at the 3-, 6-, and 12-month milestones to assess whether the newcomer is assimilating well is: "Would you hire this individual again, knowing what you know now?" The HR leader should see whether the answer elicited is a definitive and enthusiastic yes.

Figure 4.3 illustrates some of the measurements in each of the three categories that can be used to track onboarding success. For most new executives, by the end of phase 5, the intense learning period should be over and the break-even point (Watkins, 2003) should have been reached; by then the newcomer is expected to be delivering results to the organization.

As part of taking stock during this phase, Bank of America conducts a review with key stakeholders at the four-month mark. The HR leader (someone from the learning and development organization fills this role at the bank) interviews key stakeholders about the new leader, capturing the newcomer's emerging reputation—positive and negative—within the organization.

Figure 4.3. Onboarding Program Metrics

Operational Metrics ‖➡ (process performance measures)	Management Metrics ‖➡ (leading status indicators for line managers)	Strategic Metrics (results and outcomes)
Usefulness of the Onboarding Tools	**Productivity of New Leader**	**Successful Integration Within Organization**
• Positive evaluation by stakeholders	• Immediately productive with tools, information, resources, and contacts	• Effective execution of the 90-day plan
• Use all resources available	• Creation of effective 90-day plan within the first 30 days	• No unwanted attrition within 12 months
• Frequency of use		• 100 percent "would hire again" in response at 6- and 12-months follow-up
• Follow up with new leader at 3, 6, and 12 months	• Check-in evaluation conducted by hiring manager and HR	• Leader meets his business and people goals within 18 months

A report is prepared for the new leader and the hiring manager that provides feedback on what these key stakeholders are saying about the newcomer "behind his back." On one level, the key stakeholder check-in helps identify the strengths, developmental needs, and possible derailers that have become apparent during the onboarding process and helps in the design of an action plan to address emerging opportunities for development. On another level, this process surfaces stakeholder perceptions and attitudes that are often corrosive to the newcomer's image and reputation and are difficult to overcome later. In addition, the interviews engage potential critics in the constructive process of contributing to the newcomer's successful onboarding.

Ending the Formal Onboarding Support

We recommend that at the end of phase 5, the structured onboarding process be formally closed. For the most part, new leaders at this point should be fully integrated into the organization and their new roles. If there are areas that the individual is still working on from a development standpoint, the nature of the coaching engagement shifts from an onboarding relationship to a more defined developmental coaching relationship.

How is this determined? A final meeting is conducted at the 180-day point with the newcomer, manager, HR leader, and coach to close out the onboarding support. The purpose of this meeting is to look back at the transition progress, ensure goals and objectives were met, and to transition into the next phase.

At Shell Oil, the conclusion of phase 5 is marked by a centralized, celebratory workshop that brings together all new external executive hires after approximately six months on the job in one central location (Corporate Leadership Council, 2003). The workshop gives participants exposure to senior leaders of the corporation, an opportunity to learn directly about evolving company business strategies, an appreciation of the support available to help them continue to grow, and the chance to share onboarding experiences and network with peers from around the globe. The workshop also creates an occasion to celebrate early success.

Of course, whether formal or informal, the conclusion of the official onboarding is not the end of learning and development for the newcomer. The talent development strategies discussed throughout this book should engage the new leader in a career-long process that nurtures the growth of skills and knowledge through learning experiences embedded in the work and in more structured *off-line* educational and training activities.

Onboarding Contingencies: It All Depends

Which ropes need to be learned during onboarding, indeed how much focus should be dedicated to learning at all during onboarding, depends in part on situational contingencies. We touch on three key contingencies.

The State of the Business

Watkins (2003) has proposed a model that identifies four types of business situations a new executive might face: start-up, turnaround (the business or unit is in deep trouble), realignment (where things have started to decline), and sustaining success. The challenges faced by the newcomer, the skills that need to be acquired and applied, and the leader's balance between learning and doing differ sharply across these situations. For example, the need to turn around a poorly performing unit requires that the new executive quickly make tough decisions and reenergize employees and other stakeholders. Difficult decisions may have to be made before the new executive has mastered all the nuances; initial decisions may need to be refined later as the newcomer learns more about the situation. For the newcomer, in Watkins's terms, the situation is "ready-fire-aim." What needs to be mastered quickly during onboarding is the basic technical information: financials, products, markets. The selection phase of onboarding needs to fully assess the candidate's confidence, learning agility, and stress tolerance. In contrast, sustaining success affords the incoming executive time to master the full range of learning tasks: the position, organization, relationships, culture, and tools.

Table 4.1, based on Watkins's (2003) contingency model, outlines some of the key challenges and opportunities facing a new leader depending on the state of the business or business unit she is managing. Beyond differences in the overall state of the business the newcomer is entering, the business's strategy may influence aspects of the onboarding process. Market-driven organizations, for instance, need to build extensive contact with external customers into the onboarding plan.

Furthermore, whether the new leader is replacing a terminated executive or the hiring manager who has been promoted, this clearly will affect the onboarding process. A hiring manager who is the newcomer's predecessor can share detailed information on the position and its challenges in ways that another hiring manager or recruiter could not. Also, the predecessor may have a very defined view of the role, which may constrain the ability of the newcomer to innovate. In designing an onboarding plan, it is critical that stakeholders realistically appraise the state of the business and succession situation the newcomer is entering and adjust the onboarding strategy accordingly.

Organizational Culture

The organization's culture will influence how an onboarding should be designed. For example, organizations with a more externally focused culture will have a very different set of key stakeholders than one that is more internally focused for the

Table 4.1. Contingency of Onboarding Challenges and Opportunities

State of Business	Onboarding Challenges	Onboarding Opportunities
Start-up	Absence of internal role models and mentors Pressure to create new structures and systems quickly Limited resources No HR infrastructure	Freedom to be creative No burden of preexisting structures, procedures, and precedents Openness to transfer of prior experience and expertise to new setting
Turnaround	Demoralized stakeholders may not be reliable sources of information to newcomer Pressure to have quick and decisive impact Mandate for painful personnel cuts places barrier between new leader and team Past practices are delegitimatized	Openness to newcomer's contributions Acceptance of change Internal and external stakeholders likely to be supportive
Realignment	Ingrained cultural norms and practices that may no longer contribute to high performance Pressure to create and implement new strategy quickly Organization may be resistant to change initiatives	Pockets of strong internal and external stakeholders who can provide useful guidance Existing HR infrastructure to support onboarding
Sustaining success	Replacing successful leader creates unachievable expectations Strong, confident team in place that views newcomer as outsider Stakeholders present existing practices and norms as immutable keys to success Skepticism about value of newcomer's past experience and expertise	Suitable models and mentors Strong HR infrastructure and other resources to support onboarding

Source: Based on Watkins (2003).

newcomer to meet and build relationships. In their model of organizational socialization, Van Maanen and Schein (1979) distinguish between investiture and divestiture tactics. Essentially investiture tactics ratify the skills, expectations, beliefs, work orientation, and style that the newcomer brings to the new role. Cultures that are open and flexible will employ investiture tactics to welcome newcomers and reinforce their value to the new organization. Onboarding in these cultures is intended to make the transition as smooth as possible. Our onboarding model assumes a primarily investiture-focused orientation.

However, Van Maanen and Schein remind us that there are cultures that are more closed, suspicious of unproven outsiders, and perhaps more paranoid. These organizations tend to employ divestiture tactics during onboarding. The newcomer may be repeatedly and systematically tested both formally and informally. There may be direct or indirect communication that denigrates the relevance of the newcomer's prior experience or credentials. Divestiture tactics tend to be used in organizations that feel unique or embattled in a highly competitive marketplace or that are developing a product or using a technology that the organization believes is highly proprietary. The intent of divestiture-oriented onboarding is, in some way, to strip away some of the newcomer's prior identity and facilitate the assumption of a new identity, with new company-focused values and narrowly focused engagement and commitment.

In reality, all onboarding reflects a tension between investiture and divestiture. At times, newcomers excessively emphasize how things were done in their prior organization, provoking a strong divestiture response from members of the new organization and stressing differences in the new organizational context. Those designing effective onboarding processes need to consider both the openness of the culture as a whole and the degree, and the areas, where divestiture, versus investiture, strategies are desired and desirable. Even, and perhaps especially, in more closed cultures, a systematically designed onboarding process will articulate exactly where the newcomer has to have access to information and people and will specify avenues for the newcomer to build the relationships and establish herself in the organizational network. Such a plan will enhance the newcomer's likelihood of success.

National Culture

A full treatment of onboarding across national boundaries is beyond the scope of this chapter (for a meta-analysis of some key factors, see Bhaskar-Shrinivas, Harrison, Shaffer, & Luk, 2005). However, with larger corporations operating with an increasingly global scope, newcomers are transitioning across both organizational and national boundaries. Recent findings, and especially those emerging from the massive GLOBE consortium research effort—170 researchers from 62 societies over a 10-year period with data from over 17,000 managers—have identified some important cross-cultural differences in work values and in culturally rooted management and leadership practices (Javidan, Dorfman, de Luque, & House, 2006). The GLOBE research defined a number of dimensions on which national cultures differ and to which newcomers in a multinational setting need to be sensitive, including these:

- *Performance orientation*—the degree to which the culture emphasizes performance improvement and excellence
- *Future orientation*—the degree to which people in the culture take a planful rather than opportunistic approach to the future
- *Gender egalitarianism*—the extent to which men and women are treated equally
- *Institutional collectivism*—the degree to which group performance rather than individual performance is stressed and rewarded
- *Humane orientation*—the extent to which society values caring, generosity, and kindness
- *Uncertainty avoidance*—the extent to which the culture emphasizes rules, order, and structure to minimize unpredictability
- *Power distance*—the degree to which unequal power between leaders and subordinates is expected and accepted

An awareness of these dimensions of cross-national cultural variations can be useful at several points in the assimilation process, particularly for new leaders taking on multinational assignments for the first time (Bhaskar-Shrinivas et al., 2005). In the preboarding and integration stages, a profile of each national culture comprising the multinational team the newcomer will manage can help clarify potential areas of conflict. Benchmark profiles of many national cultures are presented by the GLOBE researchers (Javidan et al., 2006), who also found a universal set of attributes that are associated with effective (honest, decisive, a team builder) and ineffective (ruthless, egocentric, asocial) leadership. However, at least three leadership attributes are seen differently across national cultures as effective or ineffective: individualism, status consciousness, and risk taking.

In some cultures, these three leadership attributes are required to be effective. In others, they virtually guarantee failure in a leadership role. When onboarding into an organization across cultures, newcomers have to:

- Develop self-awareness on where they score on these culturally critical attributes
- Learn about the explicit and implicit values and preferences of their new stakeholders (team, manager, peers, customers)
- Communicate clearly and explicitly about both common ground and gaps
- Work to bridge the gaps by balancing their own preferences, values, and strengths with those of the local culture in what Javidan et al. (2006) call "a collective learning journey that can be enriching, educational, and productive for both sides" (p. 85).

Investing in Onboarding

The five-stage onboarding process we describe requires investment on the part of the organization and its members. The organization's initial investment includes designing and implementing the metrics, dashboard, pulse survey, branding, and communication and providing training for the HR partners and mentors. In our experience, the initial investment, even in a large global organization (over 20,000 employees), rarely exceeds $100,000, and in smaller or less complex organizations, it is often considerably less. Ongoing fixed costs include a program manager, dedicated on a full-time or part-time basis to the onboarding effort, and the system support and maintenance needed for the technology-enabled elements. These fixed operational costs can range, in our experience, from $25,000 to $100,000 a year. Finally, there are variable costs associated with the onboarding activities of individual newcomers related to: coaching, training, mentoring, facilitation, hiring manager time, and networking and discovery-related travel. Here the investment could—and, in our view, should—vary considerably based on a differential investment model, where the scope of onboarding support provided to an individual new executive is based on business risk and need.

To illustrate the potential return on this investment, we will draw on an actual high-tech organization where the failure rate of newly hired executives in their first two years was 20 percent—not particularly high (Downey et al., 2001). In a typical year in the early 2000s, this organization hired about 100 executives a year from the outside. The cost of each failure was conservatively estimated at $400,000, based on twice the average executive's total compensation. This is actually lower than the costs for executive attrition reported by American Express in 1998 (Corporate Leadership Council, 2000); there, direct executive search-related replacement costs alone were $187,000, which, in turn, were estimated at only 31 percent of total attrition cost. On the whole, then, at the high-tech company, the cost of newcomer failure at the executive level for a given year's hires was $8 million, with that cost spread over two years. The company spent $75,000 to design and launch a more systematic onboarding process. Based on assessments and discussions held by the onboarding partners during phases 1 to 3, half the new executives received intensive onboarding support, including professional coaching over their first 90 days and mentoring over the first 180 days. The costs of these onboarding investments averaged $12,000 for each of the 50 new executives selected, for a total of $600,000. At the two-year mark, the failure rate had dropped from 20 percent to 15 percent—clearly better, although onboarding is no panacea and more data are needed before these results can be considered stable. Nonetheless, for that cohort of executives, the first-year investment of $675,000 yielded a net return of $1,325,000.

Admittedly, as in much of utility analysis, these estimates are based on assumptions and approximations, though we have tried to be conservative. We present this analysis primarily to lay out the elements of a utility analysis for onboarding so that readers can build the business case for better onboarding in their own organizations. At American Express the introduction of a more disciplined onboarding process incorporating many of the elements described in our model resulted in a 30 percent increase in the success rate for new external executive hires (Corporate Leadership Council, 2003). Even more dramatic, the introduction of a systematic onboarding process reduced six-month turnover for all new hires from 70 percent to 16 percent at Hunter Douglas, and from 26 percent to 8 percent at Neumann Homes (Corporate Leadership Council, 2006). Our own work in this area has convinced us that given the cost and risk associated with bringing on board high-priced, high-impact, high-risk executive talent, the business case for investing an additional $10,000, $20,000, or $30,000 to mitigate that risk is easily justified. Moreover, a branded onboarding program, with a proven track record of accelerating the assimilation of new leaders, can become a valuable recruitment tool as organizations pursue executive talent in a shrinking market.

Some Lessons Learned and Some Questions

We conclude by highlighting some key lessons learned from our own work implementing onboarding programs, from coaching newcomers, speaking to colleagues responsible for designing and implementing onboarding programs, and reviewing the published literature. Key common denominators of effective onboarding programs included a number of key factors:

- *Leadership commitment.* Executives at the most senior levels appreciate the value of disciplined assimilation and the folly of a "sink or swim" approach. These executives endorse the program at appropriate opportunities, invest the resources to sustain the program over the years, and express their patience to new leaders and their managers as newcomers learn the ropes that will make them long-term contributors to the organization's success.
- *Strong program management.* Someone, typically from the Human Resources organization, should be responsible for

the onboarding program, certainly in its initial development and implementation. Having Human Resources (staffing, learning and development, talent management) take responsibility helps to ensure that onboarding is embedded in and integrated with the organization's talent management activities. But no matter who is responsible, managing the onboarding process needs to be someone's job.

- *Clear accountabilities.* The new leader, hiring manager, HR leader, coach, mentor, and administrative assistant should all be clear about their roles in onboarding each newcomer. The activities and timetables associated with each role should be put in writing and assigned as a formal responsibility. That means that each person's job performance evaluation at the end of the year should reflect how effectively he executes that responsibility. People on the onboarding team who do not fulfill their responsibility are putting at risk the investment the organization has made in recruiting, selecting, and assimilating a new leader. They should be dealt with promptly.

- *Skillful and engaged execution.* All parties need to be trained in their respective roles. Mentor training is often a full-day program, with certification assessment at its conclusion. Stakeholders should understand the business case for executing the onboarding plans, and all parties can stay engaged by being actively involved in shaping the plan. To be engaged, all participants need to understand the benefits to themselves enough so they do not push onboarding activities aside in the face of day-to-day work pressures. Many organizations with effective programs brand their onboarding program ("Fast-Start" is a popular choice). The newcomer should receive a clear message, one reinforced especially by the hiring manager, that the organization values learning and relationship building during onboarding and that there is less urgency for producing concrete business results from day 1.

- *Tracking.* Metrics need to be in place that provide early detection of possible derailment. Results should be available to management on both the aggregated group and individual levels. The organization then can use an intervention process if an executive's assimilation is getting off track.

This chapter has glossed over a number of factors that relate to successful onboarding. Although it is beyond our scope to cover these in any detail, at least one is worth mentioning: the role of the newcomer's family in affecting the new leader's successful assimilation. This is a particularly important issue when onboarding involves, as it often does, relocation. There is a fairly extensive literature on the influence of family-related factors—particularly the adjustment of spouses and children—on the success of expatriate assignments (Caligiuri, Hyland, & Joshi, 1998). There is almost no empirical work—but much anecdotal discussion—on the family's role in newcomer adjustment. At one large pharmaceutical company, a coach is specifically assigned to help the families of newcomers with both the logistics (finding appropriate schools, day care, and so on) and the stresses of relocating to a new community and supporting the newcomer in adjustment to a new organization.

Many open questions remain to be addressed through systematic research that guides the refinement of practice. We end with some questions that we would like to see studied:

- What are the best ways to assess learning agility and culture fit?
- Which competencies are more easily developed in midcareer, and which need to be screened more rigorously during selection?
- How does the pace of change occurring generally in the organization have an effect on the onboarding process?
- In the individualistic climate of the American executive suite, what are effective ways to develop social networks?
- When is it appropriate to employ divestiture-oriented socialization tactics that attack the newcomer's old identity and approaches?
- What predicts oversocialization, resulting in excessive conformity to existing norms and processes?
- How do we account for generational shifts in values when designing onboarding? For example, millennials (those born between 1977 and 2002) are thought to be less stable and less loyal to their employers. For many of that generation, there may be no long-term work commitments, during which an organization can get a return on the investment in recruiting,

hiring, and onboarding. Should companies dispense with formal onboarding programs for the millennials?

- How should the onboarding process differ across national cultures? How should it be adapted for expatriates serving in other countries?
- Do onboarding practices really work? Most of the onboarding practices described here have not been rigorously evaluated through systematic research.

References

Aberdeen Group. (2008). *All aboard: effective onboarding techniques and strategies*. Retrieved April 4, 2008, from www.aberdeen.com/summary/report/benchmark/4574-RA-effective-onboarding-strategies.asp.

Ashforth, B. E., & Mael, F. (1989). Social identity theory and the organization. *Academy of Management Review, 14,* 20–39.

Bauer, T. N., Bodner, T., Erdogan, B., Truxillo, D. M., & Tucker, J. S. (2007). Newcomer adjustment during organizational socialization: A meta-analytic review of antecedents, outcomes, and methods. *Journal of Applied Psychology, 92,* 707–721.

Bauer, T. N., Erdogan, B., Liden, R. C., & Wayne, S. J. (2006). A longitudinal study of the moderating role of extraversion: Leader-member exchange, performance, and turnover during new executive development. *Journal of Applied Psychology, 91,* 298–310.

Bauer, T. N., & Taylor, M. S. (2001). A globalized conceptualization of organizational socialization. In N. Anderson, D. S. Ones, H. K. Sinangil, & C. Viswesvaran (Eds.), *International handbook of industrial, work, and organizational psychology* (Vol. 1, pp. 409–423). Thousand Oaks, CA: Sage.

Bhaskar-Shrinivas, P., Harrison, D. A., Shaffer, M. A., & Luk, D. M. (2005). Input-based and time-based models of international adjustment: Meta-analytic evidence and theoretical extensions. *Academy of Management Journal, 48,* 257–280.

Caligiuri, P. M., Hyland, A., & Joshi, A. (1998). Families on global assignments: Applying work/family theories abroad. *Current Topics in Management, 3,* 313–328.

Cameron, K. S., & Quinn, R. E. (2006). *Diagnosing and changing organizational culture.* San Francisco: Jossey-Bass.

Chan, D., & Schmitt, N. (2000). Interindividual differences in intraindividual changes in proactivity during organizational entry: A latent growth modeling approach to understanding newcomer adaptation. *Journal of Applied Psychology, 85,* 190–221.

Corporate Leadership Council. (2000). *Workforce turnover and firm performance.* Washington, DC: Corporate Executive Board.

Corporate Leadership Council. (2003). *Models and methodologies for on-boarding programs.* Washington, DC: Corporate Executive Board.

Corporate Leadership Council. (2004). *Coordinating new hire onboarding.* Cat # CLC11C9EU5. Retrieved May 25, 2008, from www.corporate-leadershipcouncil.com.

Corporate Leadership Council. (2006). *Implementing and managing onboarding programs.* Washington, DC: Corporate Executive Board.

Day, D. V., & Kilduff, M. (2003). Self-monitoring, personality, and work relationships: Individual differences in social networks. In M. R. Barrick & A. M. Ryan (Eds.), *Personality and work* (pp. 205–228). San Francisco: Jossey-Bass.

Downey, K., March, T., & Berkman, A. (2001). *Assimilating new leaders: The key to executive retention.* New York: AMACOM.

Dweck, C. S. (2006). *Mindset: The new psychology of success.* New York: Random House.

Eichinger, R. W., & Lombardo, M. M. (2004). Learning agility as a prime indicator of potential. *Human Resource Planning, 27,* 12–15.

Feldman, D. C. (1981). The multiple socialization of organization members. *Academy of Management Review,* 6, 309–318.

Hogan, R. (2007). *Personality and the fate of organizations.* Mahwah, NJ: Erlbaum.

Hom, P. W., Griffeth, R. W., Palich, L. E., & Bracker, J. S. (1998). An exploratory investigation into theoretical mechanisms underlying realistic job previews. *Personnel Psychology, 51,* 421–451.

Javidan, M., Dorfman, P. W., de Luque, M. S., & House, R. J. (2006). In the eye of the beholder: Cross-cultural lessons in leadership from Project GLOBE. *Academy of Management Perspectives, 20,* 67–90.

Jones, G. R. (1986). Socialization tactics, self-efficacy, and newcomers' adjustments to organizations. *Academy of Management Journal, 29,* 262–279.

Kilduff, M., & Day, D. V. (1994). Do chameleons get ahead? The effects of self-monitoring on managerial careers. *Academy of Management Journal, 37,* 1047–1060.

Kim, T., Cable, D. M., & Kim, S. (2005). Socialization tactics, employee proactivity, and person-organization fit. *Journal of Applied Psychology, 90,* 232–241.

Kristof-Brown, A. L., Zimmerman, R. D., & Johnson, E. C. (2005). Consequences of individuals' fit at work: A meta-analysis of person-job, person-organization, person-group, and person-supervisor fit. *Personnel Psychology, 58,* 281–342.

Louis, M. R. (1980). Surprise and sense making: What newcomers experience in entering unfamiliar organizational settings. *Administrative Science Quarterly, 25,* 226–251.

Louis, M. R. (1982). Managing career transitions: The missing link in career development. *Organizational Dynamics, 10,* 68–77.

Morgeson, F. P., Campion, M. A., Dipboye, R. L., Hollenbeck, J. R., Murphy, K., & Schmitt, N. (2007). Reconsidering the use of personality tests in personnel selection contexts. *Personnel Psychology, 60,* 683–729.

Nadler, D. A. (2007). The CEO's second act. *Harvard Business Review, 85*(1), 66–72.

Nicholson, N. (1984). A theory of work role transitions. *Administrative Science Quarterly, 29,* 172–191.

Ritti, R. R., & Levy, S. (2007). *The ropes to skip and the ropes to know* (7th ed.). Hoboken NJ: Wiley.

Schmidt, F. L., & Hunter, J. (2004). General mental ability in the world of work: Occupational attainment and job performance. *Journal of Personality and Social Psychology, 86,* 162–173.

Seibert, S. E., Kraimer, M. L., & Crant, J. M. (2001). What do proactive people do? A longitudinal model linking proactive personality and career success. *Personnel Psychology, 54,* 845–874.

Silzer, R., & Adler, S. (2003). Selecting managers and executives: The challenge of measuring success. In J. E. Edwards, J. C. Scott, & N. S. Raju (Eds.), *The human resources program-evaluation handbook* (pp. 130–152). Thousand Oaks, CA: Sage.

Turning to outside candidates to find chiefs. (2007, November 6). *New York Times.*

Van Maanen, J. (1978). People processing: Strategies of organizational socialization. *Organizational Dynamics, 7,* 18–36.

Van Maanen, J., & Schein, E. H. (1979). Toward a theory of organizational socialization. *Research in Organizational Behavior, 1,* 209–264.

Watkins, M. (2003). *The first 90 days.* Boston: Harvard Business School Press.

Watkins, M. (2007). Help newly hired executives adapt quickly. *Harvard Business Review, 85*(6), 26–30.

Weick, K. E. (1979). *The social psychology of organizing* (2nd ed.). New York: McGraw-Hill.

Weiss, H. M., & Adler, S. (1984). Personality and organizational behavior. *Research in Organizational Behavior, 6,* 1–50.

Weiss, H. M., & Shaw, J. B. (1979). Social influences on judgments about tasks. *Organizational Behavior and Human Performance, 24,* 126–140.

Wesson, M. J., & Gogus, C. I. (2005). Shaking hands with a computer: An examination of two methods of newcomer orientation. *Journal of Applied Psychology, 90,* 1018–1026.

CHAPTER 5

IDENTIFYING AND ASSESSING HIGH-POTENTIAL TALENT

Current Organizational Practices

Rob Silzer, Allan H. Church

Mediocrity knows nothing higher than itself, but talent instantly recognizes genius.
Sir Arthur Conan Doyle

With the recognition of the strategic role of talent in organizations comes an interest in effectively finding, building, and leveraging talent. This has led to a huge talent industry that provides programs and services in talent recruiting, selection, development, assessment, compensation, and retention. Talent has become the lifeblood of organizations. It is often seen as a primary reason for organizational success and failure and the key source of competitive advantage. As organizations spend more time and resources on talent, interest in identifying and developing the needed talent inside the organization has been growing. For many organizations, this means trying to determine what talent already exists in the organization and which employees have the potential to be effective in larger roles.

The attention given to talent issues leads organizations to focus on identifying and developing high-potential individuals as part of succession planning and leadership development. Once organizations realized that people could be developed to improve their current individual performance, there was an interest in developing them for the next position in their career path. It was only a matter of time for this effort to extend from development for current performance to development for performance in the next position to development for long-term future performance.

Today organizations are creating sophisticated systems and programs for identifying, assessing, and developing high-potential talent, that is, individuals who are seen as having the capability to develop further and be effective in larger future roles. *Potential* refers to the promise or possibility of an individual becoming something more than what he is currently.

Our interest is in exploring the current practices and approaches that organizations use to identify and assess high-potential talent and build on the work of previous efforts in this area (Executive Knowledgeworks, 1987; Slan & Hausdorf, 2004; O'Connell, 1996; Corporate Leadership Council, 2005a). There are a few distinctions to make to clarify the practice of identifying high-potential talent:

■ ■ ■

1. *This discussion does not include job selection decisions, replacement planning, or even successor planning.* All of these areas are related but involve selecting or matching an individual to specific known positions. In identifying high potentials a specific job or position is not known. Rather, a person is considered for designation as a high potential based on whether the individual has the capability and fungibility to develop and grow in order to handle a range of positions (such as executive positions) at some point in the long-term future. Consequently a list of specific job requirements is not available when making decisions about high potentials.

2. *There is a difference between performance and potential.* While we find that many organizations look at a person's past performance record as a qualifier to be a high potential, there is agreement that past or even current performance does not always lead to

effective performance in broader future roles. We make a distinction between individuals with high performance and individuals with high potential.

3. *We start with an assumption that potential is a dynamic state, not an end state.* Individuals who are seen as high potential generally have the capability to learn, grow, and develop. So we assume that the high-potential person is a dynamic person who will develop beyond her current skills and abilities. One key challenge is to assess a person's growth potential. There is some disagreement, however, on whether the potential factors themselves, such as learning ability or adaptability, can be developed. Rogers and Smith (2007, p. 7) conclude, "Given that these [potential] factors are essentially personality factors, the likelihood of dramatically developing them through training or other development means is quite slim." We think that the potential factors, like most other skills and abilities, may have both natural innate components and components that can be developed.

4. *Identifying potential is different from assessing development needs.* Many organizations use a variety of assessment tools and programs (assessment centers, individual assessment, 360-degree feedback instruments, and others) to assess an individual's current leadership, management, or executive skills and to determine the person's development needs. Often this assessment is based on a set of competencies that try to capture what it takes to be effective in specific roles. This type of assessment measures the individual against end-state competencies. However, the individual is dynamic and a "work-in-developmental-progress." Most developmental assessments do not evaluate the person against potential factors such as learning ability and do not identify the person's potential to grow further and develop. The job-related competencies are focused on performance in specific jobs, while the potential factors are indicators of a person's capability to grow into a wide range of career opportunities.

■ ■ ■

Our discussion focuses on current organizational practices in identifying and assessing high-potential talent. It is a relatively new field that has emerged as organizations developed a strategic view of talent (Michaels, Handfield-Jones, & Axelrod, 2001). The prediction challenge related to identifying high potentials is fundamental to this discussion.

Prediction Challenge

One of the challenges of identifying high-potential individuals is the inherent complexity of making predictions about how successful a person might be in the long-term future. It involves defining what you are trying to predict, assessing a person against the appropriate criteria, and making predictions about future performance. A wide range of issues needs to be considered, including the person's capabilities and motivations and the challenges and opportunities associated with future positions in the organization. This is different from a selection decision where there is a clear understanding of the specific job requirements for the position to be filled.

Managers and executives need three key skills in order to make successful predictions regarding high potentials:

- The ability to see into the future and anticipate the types of future leaders (or experiences, skills, and abilities) that will be needed for future organizational success
- The ability to accurately assess current employees in the organization
- The ability to gauge an individual's potential for future growth and development

Seeing into the Future

This book contains numerous examples of how business strategy can drive talent management decisions. But knowing the current organizational strategies is different from anticipating the organization's future strategies. For companies that operate in a relatively stable market, this may be easier than for most companies that have to contend with dynamic business markets that are subject to constant change. The future is less clear for them.

As a result, executives and human resource (HR) professionals need to anticipate the types of leaders who will be needed to implement the future unspecified strategies. This requires that the executives running the business and the HR professionals have visionary skills (not a common skill) to see how the company and the business market will evolve in the future. Most managers and executives are best skilled at understanding short-term, concrete business issues and have not needed to develop the visionary skills to see the long-term future of their business.

Accurately Assessing Talent

The second step in high-potential identification is to assess current employees on their potential. In the past, strong assessment skills in managers have not been widely valued or developed. However, as talent becomes a core strategy of an organization, assessment skills are becoming more highly valued. Useful assessment techniques and tools have been around for many years (Bray, Campbell, & Grant, 1974; Thornton & Byham, 1982; Jeanneret & Silzer, 1998), but they typically have been used for selection decisions and for diagnosing development needs.

It is common in many organizations for decisions about high potentials be made by untrained managers and executives using informal ratings or nomination forms. However, because of the strategic and critical nature of talent in an organization, it is increasingly important for managers and executives to have or develop their assessment skills to accurately assess a person's potential. Organizations are beginning to teach assessment skills to managers or are using outside professional assessments to improve assessment accuracy. We suggest that a combination of both internal and external assessments increases the objectivity and relevance of those judgments. Now that building organizational talent is seen as a core manager responsibility, managers are expected to assess and build their own talent, and organizations are increasingly interested in evaluating how well they do it.

As with almost every other skill, assessment skills are probably a mix of natural and developed abilities. Some managers are naturally much more insightful and interested than others about the abilities, skills, and motivations of people. It might be said that talented individuals are more likely to recognize talent in others. On the other hand, assessment skills can be developed to a limited extent in some managers. There has been a history of training managers to serve as assessors for assessment centers, but even after extensive training, many managers are never able to develop more than basic assessment skills.

Learning how to assess in an assessment center, with structured behavior rating guidelines for observing behavior in controlled and carefully designed situations, is one level of assessment skills, but assessing individuals for their long-term future performance is a much more difficult challenge. Numerous problems and biases can complicate assessment judgments, such as deciding what to observe, determining how to categorize the observations, and being influenced by the assessor's own biases and preferences (Ruderman & Ohlott, 1990).

Predicting Potential to Develop

Often managers and executives confuse assessing an individual's current skills and abilities with the person's potential, just as they confuse past performance with future effectiveness. Current skills and abilities are different from potential and need to be considered separately. Accurately assessing a person's current knowledge, skills, and abilities is an important first step, but it should not be confused with determining the person's ability to grow, adapt, and develop enough to handle more complex future work challenges and responsibilities. Unfortunately this difference is not typically recognized or discussed in most organizations, even when they understand the difference between past performance and future effectiveness. This may be due to a poor understanding of the difference but also to a poor definition and measurement of potential. Unfortunately the judgment about a person's future potential is often left to a hasty discussion at the end of a long succession planning meeting, and the decision is frequently made by a single executive. Few organizations have specifically defined what they mean by potential or how potential differs from past performance or current abilities and skills.

Even when potential is clearly defined, the judgment can be difficult. How do you evaluate a person's ability to grow and develop in the future? Making predictions about the future is more complex than assessing a person's current skills and abilities. It may be similar to predicting progress on other developmental variables. What does early career stage potential look like in comparison to later potential? Are there basic signs or indicators that suggest later development? How do you gauge the developmental progression line toward an end state and determine where the person should be along that line at this stage in his career? Should there be different expectations for someone early in their career than for someone in midcareer? These are complex issues. It seems likely that the ability to make accurate predictions about a person's future development requires sophisticated assessment skills that are not widely present in organizations.

Executives and HR professionals also need to make judgments about where to best invest limited development resources. Which individuals are the most likely to benefit from the training? What is their development ROI (return on investment) or RODI (return on development investment)?

Given this complexity, judgments of potential can lead to many poor and costly decisions. Perhaps some of the prediction pitfalls and biases can be avoided by strengthening these assessment skills in managers and leaders.

Corporate High-Potential Survey

In an effort to understand current organizational practices in identifying and managing high-potential talent, an organizational survey was sent to 30 large corporations in 2008 asking about their current practices and approaches. The objective of the survey was to understand the talent management practices related to high potentials at major business organizations. The survey covered a range of topics, including the definition of high potential, identification and selection factors and tools, and approaches to managing high-potential talent. It builds on previous efforts to investigate how organizations identify high-potential talent (Executive Knowledgeworks, 1987; O'Connell, 1996; Corporate Leadership Council, 2005a, 2005b; Hewitt Associates, 2008). The survey results are summarized throughout this chapter.

Twenty major business corporations completed the survey electronically (one company preferred to remain anonymous).

Exhibit 5.1. Organizations Participating in the High-Potential Survey

- AOL
- Bristol-Myers Squibb
- D&B (Dun & Bradstreet)
- The Home Depot
- Ingersoll Rand
- JP Morgan Chase
- Levi Strauss
- Maersk
- Marriott
- Merrill Lynch
- Microsoft
- PepsiCo
- PPG
- Sara Lee
- Sempra Energy
- Siemens
- T Rowe Price
- Tyco
- W.R. Grace & Co.

Definitions of Potential

The term *high-potential talent* is a widely used term in most organizations. There is often great interest by Human Resources as well as line leadership in finding and developing talented individuals who have the potential to contribute to the organization in the future, usually in a different capacity, doing different and broader kinds of work. In most cases, the search for potential is connected to either talent management or succession planning processes. For some organizations, high potentials are only those who might move into C-suite roles running the organization—the CEO and other chief officers of an organization such as the chief operating officer (COO), chief financial officer (CFO), chief human-resources officer (CHRO), chief marketing officer (CMO), and chief information officer (CIO).

In other organizations there is concern about whether high potentials should be identified at all. Some managers and leaders believe that singling out a distinct group of employees for special designation, attention, and development is detrimental to an organization's talent management efforts. They think it endorses an exclusive rather than inclusive approach, and worry that it sends a signal to other employees that they are not important to the organization. This issue is actively discussed in many organizations and encourages managers to keep in balance how much attention and investment is given exclusively to high potentials. Another concern is that the identification process is subjective and not only can reflect the biases of current leaders but also might miss some employees who can later make significant contributions to the organization. These missed individuals may be more likely to leave the organization if they feel they are being excluded from career opportunities.

In many organizations, however, much time and many resources are devoted to defining, identifying, and developing high-potential talent. All of the 20 surveyed organizations have identification and development efforts focused on high potentials. This suggests an increasing interest from previous corporate studies. Silzer, Slider, and Knight (1994) found that only 42 percent of 21 major corporations studied had some type of program for high potentials. Slan and Hausdorf (2004) found that only 31 percent of 71 Canadian organizations surveyed had an identification and development effort for high potentials. Hewitt Associates (see Wells, 2003) found that only 55 percent of the 100 companies they surveyed had a formal approach to identifying high potentials, while 100 percent of the top-performing companies among the 100 companies (as measured by total shareholder return) had a formal approach.

However, it is not always clear what people mean when they say that someone is "high potential." Organizations often differ from each other in their definitions, and it is not uncommon for there to be significant differences of opinion within the same company among senior leaders. If an organization cannot agree on a defintion of high potential then it is unlikely to agree on who should be included in the high-potential group. The underlying definitional question often asked is, "Potential for what?" The "what" usually suggests specifying the ultimate position or group of positions that may be likely for the individual. Sometimes the "what" relates to being effective in future senior management roles or at higher levels in general. At other times, the "what" might relate to having the potential to contribute to specific strategic capabilities in the organization (for example, entrepreneurial skills for starting up businesses) or having talent to fill key positions, functions, or areas (such as sales manager positions).

Our corporate survey identified several different definitions of *high potential* (see Table 5.1). Most of the organizations are divided among definitions of By Role, By Level, and By Breadth.

Table 5.1. Definitions of High Potential

In Surveyed Organizations	
35%*	**Use By Role**—the potential to move into top or senior management roles
25%	**Use By Level**—the ability to move and perform two positions or levels above current role
25%	**Use By Breadth**—the capability to take on broader scope and a leadership role and develop long-term potential
10%	**Use By Record**—a consistent track record of exceptional performance
5%	Unknown

Other Definitions

By Strategic Position—Key positions that may be at the core of the organization's success (perhaps a subset of *By-Level* definitions but targeting specific positions)

By Strategic Area—Functions, business units, or geographic areas that are central to the organization's strategic objectives

*% of the 20 participating organizations

By Role

The definition of *By Role*, favored by 35 percent of the organizations surveyed, is perhaps the clearest definition. It identifies people who could be effective in senior management roles independent of the individual's current role or level. This means the high-potential person could be one, two, three, or even more levels away from the target role. The further away the individual is in level from the target role, the more challenging it can be to apply this definition because the target role is further into the future. The other challenge with this definition is specifically determining the target role. Someone might be a high potential for a chief financial officer role, but that might be a very different profile for a high potential for a general management role. With the definition of *By Role*, it is important that others look at the senior management roles in the organization and reach some agreement on the target role requirements for each and the KSAs (knowledge, skills, and abilities) needed to be effective in those roles. Of course, the senior roles and the related requirements may be poorly defined or may be constantly changing, which raises additional issues.

By Level

A less specific definition is *By Level,* which usually targets the ability to be effective in positions two levels above the individual's current position. Used by 25 percent of the organizations surveyed, this approach avoids the concern that some people have with the definition of *By Role* that it is difficult to identify C-suite talent four or five levels away. However, since the individuals being considered are often at different levels in the organization, the target positions (two levels higher) change accordingly, depending on the current level of the individual. For example it could mean that the target positions could be at the department manager level, the vice president level, or even a senior executive level. This results in a shifting definition and suggests that several different pools or groups of high-potential individuals, depending on their current level in the organization, will need to be identified. The pool at each level may include a wide swath of different positions across each of the levels in the organization. Also, the requirements for each of these different levels may be poorly defined or constantly changing.

By Breadth

The definition of *By Breadth,* also used by 25 percent, seems the least specific definition employed by the surveyed organizations. It provides a significant amount of latitude to accommodate a range of different views about the requirements for being a high potential, but could also include anyone who might be seen as promotable or who could take on some additional responsibilities. It is a vague answer to the question, "Potential for what?" Since the definition is vague, it can lead to further difficulty in assessing for it and to disagreements about who can be included in the high-potential group. It also does not provide any guidance for using the designation when making talent-related decisions (for example, the other two definitions focus on either an end state or target level).

All three of these definitions risk being backward looking, that is, basing identification decisions on past or current requirements rather than being forward looking and defining future-oriented requirements of the business. When using any of these three definitions, it is important that the requirements and the assessment process focus on future-oriented capabilities.

Two of the twenty organizations (10 percent) use a definition of having a consistent track record of exceptional performance. While past performance does give some indication of future performance (in similar circumstances) and is usually reviewed when making talent decisions, it is less effective in predicting future success in new situations or when dealing with new business challenges. However, if the past successful performance was in a number of different jobs with different challenges, then it might indicate the person's ability to adapt and perform in new situations. This definition does not distinguish between high performance and high potential, which is the common practice in most organizations.

By Strategic Position

Other organizations use a definition of *By Strategic Position* of high potential, which emphasizes the ability to effectively perform in specific key positions (also called critical positions or strategic positions). At Honeywell, for example, one key position is the general manager of a business unit. Individuals are reviewed for their potential to effectively handle a general management position. These positions are seen as core to the organization's future success. A good deal of attention is paid to recruiting, evaluating, and developing individuals for these roles across the organization.

By Strategic Area

It is not uncommon to find definitions of *By Strategic-Area*, which focus on the capabilities required in specific organizational functions, business units, or geographic areas that are central to the company's strategic objectives. This is similar to identifying a function-specific talent pool. For example, in consumer product companies, the marketing function is often the dominant function and seen as the most central to the organization's strategies. These organizations place a clear emphasis on identifying, evaluating, and developing marketing talent (see Chapter 15 by Allan Church and Janine Waclawski for PepsiCo's approach). Another example is geographic talent. Currently many American firms are expanding their business into China and India, and those geographic areas are seen as core to the organization's growth strategies. Therefore, they are bringing significant attention to identifying talent that has the potential to effectively deliver on those geographic strategies (see Chapter 14 by Elizabeth Weldon).

Definitional Challenges

Many organizations are hesitant to specify too clearly what it takes to be high potential, for several reasons. First, they want some flexibility in the definition so they can adapt it to changing organizational talent needs and business conditions. Second, they may not want to be locked into a concrete definition that individuals can hold them accountable to in order to push for their own inclusion into the high-potential group. Third, some organizations prefer not to share their talent decisions with employees and like to keep close control over the entire process (particularly who is included and who is not). Organizations do not like to be constrained and usually want as much latitude as possible when making decisions. However, it clearly is an advantage to the organization to have a clear and consistent definition of *high potential,* particularly among leaders and managers making those talent classifications, so that everyone can reach agreement on who qualifies for the extra organizational attention and development resources that are not widely available. Some might argue that these are not clear advantages and that development should be broadly available. They would also suggest that since we cannot accurately identify high potentials, then focusing on high potentials is a waste of time and resources.

Other research efforts find a range of definitions. The Corporate Leadership Council study (2005a, 2005b) of 59 organizations concludes that a "high potential employee is someone with the *ability, engagement, and aspiration* to rise to and succeed in more senior, more critical positions"(that is *By Role* and *By Strategic Position*). The Executive Knowledgeworks study (1987) surveyed 225 organizations and discovered that 83 percent of companies define a high-potential manager as "someone who can rise two (organizational) levels in five years" (*By Level*) (p. xii). In addition, about 60 percent of the companies in this study indicate that high potentials are people identified to fill key jobs (*By Strategic Position*). After talking to eight organizations and six consulting firms, O'Connell (1996) concluded there was no universal definition of *high potential.*

In a succession management survey, Slan and Hausdorf (2004) found that only 31 percent of 71 surveyed Canadian organizations had identification and development efforts for high potentials in 2004. They identified three major components of a definition for *high potential.* Of the 22 companies with these programs the most common definitional elements were:

- "demonstrates organizationally defined leadership capabilities" (that is *By Breadth*)—36 percent
- "can move two levels higher within the next couple of years" (that is, *By Level*)—23 percent
- "can take on more responsibility or work in a different function" (that is, *By Breadth*)—18 percent

Phases of Definitions

So the "potential for what?" question does get answered, but in different ways across organizations. Over the years, the definition of high potential has moved through three phases, from being *past looking* (emphasizing past performance track record), to focusing on the near-term future (capability to handle specific known positions), to predicting a longer-term future (capability to handle unspecified ambiguous future roles).

We suggest that past-looking definitions, such as *By Record*, were the first widely used definitions because the individuals who met this definition were the known exceptional performers. At the time, organizations were not rapidly changing, so future positions often were similar to past or current positions. The high potentials at this time could easily be identified based on their past performance record using annual performance appraisals. Definitions of *By Record* are still used in some organizations, but a strong past performance track record is now typically seen as a basic requirement or entry hurdle to even be considered as a high potential rather than the defining decision factor.

In the next phase, the *near-term* definitions started being more forward looking (after it was discovered, for example, that past sales performance did not accurately predict future sales management performance). Many organizations started using definitions of *By Level*, which required them to match candidates to existing, specific, known positions at higher organizational levels. This was forward looking but rested on matching a known person to known positions. This approach is still widely used, particularly in organizations where there is not a lot of change in organizational structure and roles. The definitions that emphasize *By Strategic Position* may be a subset of definitions of *By Level*, since the focus is on matching individuals to specific and well-defined roles in the organization, such as general manager or marketing manager.

The third phase, long-term definitions, emphasizes trying to predict success in ambiguous future roles. Definitions of *By Breadth* and *By Role* are more long term and future oriented; they try to predict performance success in broader or senior leadership roles that may look very different in the future from how they look today. It requires organizations to identify the factors or characteristics that will predict future success in a range of future roles and situations. It is a much more difficult prediction challenge from the previous two phases. Definitions that emphasize *By Strategic Area* are usually matching individuals to specific functions or business units but to relatively undefined roles and positions. So these are probably a subset of this third phase.

Many organizations use multiple definitions for different groups or talent pools. For example, a company may be looking for individuals to fill specific key positions (*By Strategic Position*), to develop individuals for senior executive roles (*By Role*), and to identify who should get special development attention and support (*By Breadth*). It is not uncommon to find some disagreement, or at least different interpretations, in an organization over the definition of *high potential*. Some managers and executives like to use their own definition and may have enough power and influence in the organization to openly use them. Of course, it is very helpful if there is some agreement on the definition in order to easily identify, move, and transfer talent across the organization.

High-Potential Categories

Many organizations have multiple categories or groups of high-potential talent; some call them talent pools (see Chapter 9 by Ben Dowell). They are often differentiated based on band level (different organizational compensation levels or responsibility levels). Some talent pools are defined by functional area, key positions, or special target groups such as diversity talent pools based on gender or ethnicity.

Of the surveyed organizations, 65 percent have multiple categories of high-potential talent (see Table 5.2). Talent categories used in organizations include Global Leaders/Senior Management, Mid-Management, General Management, Functional Management, and Early Career talent. Some organizations include a HiPro category for individuals who are highly valued high performers and who could handle expanded responsibilities in their current role, but are not seen as having potential to advance to other roles in the organization. Several organizations use the *Top, Turn, Grow,* and *Mastery* distinctions noted in Table 5.2.

The use of talent pools in organizations probably started with replacement planning efforts. At first, immediate replacements for more senior positions were identified and typically focused on direct reports in the same department or function to the target position. This *successor pool* was later expanded to include candidates outside the same department. When management development efforts became popular in the 1980s, the successor pool broadened to distinguish candidates in different categories depending on how soon they would be ready for the position and how much more development they needed.

For many organizations, the concept of talent pools expanded to multiple talent pools that were distinctively defined, such as executive potential talent pool, functional talent pool, diversity talent pools, and supervisory talent pools. Frequently they are defined by the future role or organization level that the talent might achieve; some call them *acceleration pools* (Byham, Smith, & Paese, 2002).

Table 5.2. High Potential Categories

In Surveyed Organizations	
65%*	*Have more than one category of high potential* and cluster high-potential individuals based on band differences.
	Band-Level Categories
	Global leaders/senior executive potential
	Middle management or technical/functional potential
	"High Value" or "HiPro" performers (keep in role and develop for expanded responsibilities)
	Typical designations include:
	Top Potential (senior level potential)
	Turn Potential (next level potential)
	Grow Potential (same level but expand)
	Mastery Potential (same work, same level)
15%	*Establish expected time frames* for band promotion
	Next Band—Can perform at next band level in 1–2 years
	Same Band—Able to have larger "scope, scale, and strategic importance" at the same band level in the next one to two years (horizontal movement)
	Same Functional level—Continue to do the same work within the same functional level, only more effectively in the next one to two years

*% of the 20 participating organizations

Others have proposed talent group variations. Boudreau and Ramstad (2005), for example, suggest segmenting talent and identifying *pivotal talent*—the talent essential for an organization to remain strategically competitive.

High-Potential Time Frames

Time frames are commonly used in organizations to designate how soon a high-potential individual will be ready to advance to the target position, level, or band. In some cases, the time frame can actually have an impact on the talent decision itself; for example, some companies remove the label of high potential after promoting someone to a higher band position until that person effectively performs in the higher role. This is most common in organizations using definitions of *By Level.* The typical time frames used are "ready now," "ready in one year," and "ready in two to three years."

These are subjective estimates of when a high-potential individual will be ready to assume another, usually higher or broader, role. It is typically determined by a group of senior managers at a talent review meeting and is a quick estimate based on matching the individual's profile of strengths and development needs against the requirements and demands of the target role or level. The time line decision usually involves estimating how much time it will take for the individual to learn some specific knowledge or skills or to get additional development experience that would prepare her for the target role. For some individuals, it may mean taking a temporary assignment during the time period, while for others it might mean participating in a specific leadership development program, task force, special project, or other critical experience that would answer a specific question about the individual's potential (for example, "How well would this person handle a multifunctional team?").

Of the 13 organizations in our survey that used bands to distinguish multiple categories of high-potential talent, 23 percent of them (three companies) identify the expected time frame for promotion to the next band for each individual (see Table 5.2). The typical time frame in these organizations is usually one or two years for either promotion to the next level, movement to a larger role at same band level, or continued but more effective work at same functional level.

Size of High-Potential Pool

The size of the high-potential pools or groups may depend on the business situation, the strategies of the organization, and the general culture of the organization (such as being inclusive versus selective). An organization with a high growth strategy probably needs a much larger number of high-potential individuals to staff future business expansion than an organization that is facing significant competitive challenges and needs to resize (or downsize) the workforce. Different types of capabilities might also be needed. Organizations need to consider the expected turnover and potential retirements in senior management or key positions (particularly in today's aging workforce), past success in retaining high-potential talent, and the talent requirements for the business strategies. In addition, because of the resources that are needed to develop high-potential talent, an organization may limit the number of high-potential individuals in order to focus scarce resources on individuals with the greatest potential.

Most organizations in our survey do not set a target number or size for the high-potential group (see Table 5.3). Only 20 percent of the organizations identify a target distribution, and their typical goal was set in the range of 5 to 20 percent of the overall salaried employee population. The most common guideline is 10 percent of the population. PepsiCo, for example, does not have a formal percentage of high potentials required as part of the talent management process for any group, division, or function. Rather, the following guidance is given to leaders and Human Resource managers involved in determining the talent decisions: "While there is no set goal, based on a normal distribution of talent we would expect somewhere between 10 percent to 20 percent of people to be high potentials." Byham et al. (2002) suggest that the talent pools typically range from 1 to 2 percent of the total population (all employees, not just those in management or professional roles).

In addition, 25 percent of the surveyed organizations set goals for ethnic and gender representation in the high-potential group.

Table 5.3. Target Distributions for High Potentials

In Surveyed Organizations	
20%*	*Identify general target distribution or %.*
	Ranges from 5 to 20% of the overall salaried employee population
	The most common guideline is 9 to 10%
25%	*Establish representation goals* to promote gender and ethnic diversity; a few other organizations monitor the representation

*% of the 20 organizations surveyed

Many organizations monitor diversity representation in the group but do not have set goals. Some have separate diversity talent pools for these individuals to ensure they are adequately developed. It is likely that in the future, there will also be diversity talent pools for global representation as well.

Identification Process for High Potentials

Organizations often have a standard process that is used for identifying high-potential talent. This can be a formal, structured process with carefully defined steps and deadlines, or it can be a semiformal, or even informal, process that tries to ensure that senior managers are at least aware of the exceptional talent in the organization. Larger organizations are more likely to formalize the process to make sure all business units are meeting identification goals and time lines and discussing developmental moves. They have a need for more talent and want to make sure they are not overlooking anyone currently in the organization. The formal process also helps to ensure that all managers are taking responsibility for identifying talent. Smaller organizations are likely to take a more informal approach since there is less need to coordinate broadly across many business units and because the talented individuals are more likely to already be known by senior management. The typical steps are outlined in Exhibit 5.2.

Agreement on Categories and Definitions of Potential

The identification process usually starts at the top of the organization, with senior managers agreeing on the categories and definitions of *high potential* (see Table 5.4). Senior managers must first decide on the high-potential categories to consider (bands, key positions, strategic areas, or others), the definitions of potential for each of the categories, and a process for identifying high-potential talent in each category. They also must decide how far down in the organization the talent decisions will be applied.

The identification process may vary depending on the category of potential. More general categories, such as those defined by band or level, usually involve a process that spans the breadth of the organization. More narrowly defined categories, such as those focusing on strategic positions or strategic areas, have more narrowly defined populations to scan and involve a more customized approach. Typical steps in the identification process can be found in Exhibit 5.2.

Exhibit 5.2. High-Potential Identification Steps

Typical Identification Steps

1. *Agreement on Potential Categories and Definitions*
   A key first step is to reach agreement on the definition of potential and to identify the specific categories of potential (Role, Level, Breadth, Performance Record, Strategic Position, Strategic Area, etc.) and how deep in the organization the definition and categories will be applied.

2. *Solicitation*
   Senior managers ask for nominations of high-potential candidates.

3. *Nomination*
   Individuals are identified and nominated by a manager who is familiar with the individual's performance, abilities, and career aspirations. Nominations often include current and past performance evaluations, career, and educational history and reasons for the nomination.

4. *Assessment*
   Additional assessment data is collected on the nominated candidates. This may include data from leadership competency ratings, interviews, tests and inventories, assessment centers, and individual assessments.

5. *Review and Acceptance*
   Candidates and their portfolio are reviewed by one or more levels of senior management, often first at business unit or functional review meetings and if accepted then reviewed again at the corporate senior management level. Discussions often eliminate some nominated candidates.

6. *Development*
   Once accepted, the high-potential individuals are often given accelerated development opportunities and experiences, and are slated for future roles.

Solicitation

Most organizations have a set annual timetable for the solicitation of high-potential candidates. For broad potential categories, all managers or managers at specific levels in the organization are asked to identify candidates and submit their nominations to the business unit or corporate HR staff by a specific date. For more specialized potential categories, managers at specific levels, in specific functions, or in particular geographic areas are asked for nominations. General managers are often asked to identify individuals in their business unit who have general management potential. Similarly senior global or international managers may be asked to identify talent with the potential for global management roles. For example, an organization may decide that the business units operating in China are strategically significant and may review all managers at all levels in those business units to identify global management talent. This targeted approach frequently gets used in functional areas, such as finance or human resources. Sometimes candidates for these more specialized potential categories also emerge from the process focused on identifying candidates in the broader potential categories.

Nomination

Nominations for high potential usually are advanced up the organizational hierarchy. They can be reviewed by individual senior leaders or in successively higher groups of peers. Some organizations use a process called calibration, where each manager reviews the nominations for high potential from her team with peers, HR, and the group manager for feedback on the nominations. As a result of this review process, nominations may get rejected by managers at the next levels for various reasons. In some cases, higher-level managers may not think the person is ready for the accelerated development and advancement, or they may want to keep the individual in his own business unit longer to accomplish a specific business goal and not want to risk losing a talented person (this is known as hoarding talent). There are often differences of opinion on the individual's potential.

The candidate's nomination, or portfolio, often includes:

- Career and educational history, including tenure in current position and tenure with the company
- Recent and past performance evaluations, including significant accomplishments and failures
- Past developmental experiences and programs
- Current development plans and an indication of recent developmental progress
- An evaluation of the person's leadership strengths and development needs
- The individual's career interests and mobility
- Critical experiences already gained and experiences needed for career progress
- Reasons why the person is being nominated

Today, with the additional information technology and systems capabilities that are available, organizations are collecting and including a wider array of data on an individual's employee profile, such as engagement survey results, functional competency ratings, and 360-degree feedback summaries. This provides more extensive background information on the candidate and helps to improve decision making by leaders and managers (see Chapter 15 by Allan H. Church and Janine Waclawski, Chapter 16 by Paul R. Yost, and Chapter 17 by Leslie Joyce for organizational case studies on PepsiCo, Microsoft, and The Home Depot). Only rarely does a company allow individuals to self-nominate themselves as high-potential candidates. In some organizations, individuals can self-nominate into an assessment center pool, and the outcome of that assessment might determine whether the individual is nominated as a high-potential candidate.

Assessment

The next step is often for the individual to go through an assessment process, although it is common for this step to occur after the decision is made about an individual's potential. Assessments might include a range of assessment tools, such as leadership competency surveys, 360-degree interviews, functional competency measures, career background interviews, cognitive ability tests, personality inventories, assessment centers, or individual assessments. Some data can be collected quickly and efficiently, through interviews, competency measures, and inventory data,, while other information may take longer to obtain, for example, assessment center data or background interviews with prior colleagues. There are also significant differences in the costs associated with these different assessment approaches ranging from minimal costs for one-on-one interviews with internal staff to a more expensive outside executive assessment. Some organizations collect these data to help make the high-potential decisions, while other organizations assess individuals only after they have been reviewed and accepted as high-potential talent. In this case, the purpose of the assessment is to facilitate their further development. See Silzer and Davis (2010) for a more comprehensive discussion of assessing potential. High-potential talent predictors and assessment tools are discussed later in this chapter.

Review and Acceptance

The nominations are then reviewed and discussed at senior management review meetings. (See Chapter 9 by Ben Dowell for a full discussion of the review meetings.) In large organizations, candidates may be reviewed first at business unit or functional talent review meetings, and if they are accepted, the nominations are then sent on and reviewed again at the corporate senior management review meetings. These talent review meetings often have a number of objectives besides identifying high-potential individuals. They may also include reviews of all managers at particular organizational levels, in strategic key positions, in strategic business areas, or on slates of specific candidates as potential backfills for succession planning purposes.

Frequently these discussions eliminate some nominated candidates. If there is a plethora of strong candidates, then solid but not outstanding candidates may get rejected in the interest of investing limited corporate resources in the strongest candidates. If the pool of nominated candidates is less competitive, then good but not outstanding candidates may get accepted into the high-potential pool. If the roles being discussed are highly strategic in nature and the pool is weak, the decision instead may be made to conduct an external search to find high-potential candidates for those roles from outside the company.

Organizations may also have a range of reasons for designating people as high potential:

- An interest in retaining specialized or scarce talent for current business strategies
- An interest in retaining core individuals in specific functions or business units
- An expected future strategic need for specific skills and abilities or cultural knowledge and experience
- An interest in having a more diverse high-potential talent pool
- Expected growth in part of the business
- An anticipated turnover in senior managers
- A concern over pending retirements
- A recent problem retaining individuals in strategic positions

Talent review meetings are regularly held by 75 percent of the surveyed organizations (see Table 5.4); 60 percent hold annual meetings, while 15 percent hold semiannual meetings. Some major organizations that emphasize leadership talent development are showing more interest in having semiannual review meetings in order to more closely monitor the developmental progress of high-potential individuals and to more effectively hold managers and the individuals accountable for making sure development plans are being implemented. It also encourages senior managers to get more personally and frequently involved in leadership talent development as a strategic organizational priority.

Rejected candidates in 50 percent of the surveyed organizations can be renominated and reconsidered for status as a high potential in one year (usually as part of the next cycle of talent reviews). Individuals who are promoted after they are in the high-potential group are allowed to stay in the group after promotion at 50 percent of the surveyed companies. At other companies they must later be renominated, often for a higher-level talent pool. Some of this depends on the nature of the definition of *high potential* while in other cases, it depends on organizational practice. Nonetheless, this is a hotly debated issue in

Table 5.4. High-Potential Status

In Surveyed Organizations	
75%*	*Conduct High-Potential Status Reviews*
60%	Review annually (15% review semiannually)
50%	Reconsider someone annually after initial rejection
50%	Leave person on list following promotion until next review
	Turnover in High-Potential Group
60%	Report annual turnover of 3 to 11% annually
40%	Do not know or do not track
	Primary turnover reasons are:
	More attractive career opportunities elsewhere
	Mobility
	Poor performance
	Change in boss relationships
Most	*Tell Individuals Their Status*
	Do not release information to individual
	Concerns about misinformation, shifts in performance, labeling biases, retention, and creating culture of entitlement
	Status communicated indirectly through assignments and development opportunities
	Some growing interest in having open, honest, and transparent conversations

*% of the 20 organizations surveyed

industry (particularly in organizations that share the selection decision with the employee) because leaders fear that if a high potential learns that he is no longer in that group after being promoted, he may become demotivated and inclined to leave the organization.

Only 60 percent of the surveyed organizations track the turnover among high potentials. The turnover rate ranges from 3 to 11 percent annually in these organizations. Turnover in the high-potential group can be due to a range of causes:

- Diminished performance by the individual
- Failure of the individual in an important development opportunity
- Key individuals (such as a mentor, sponsor, or colleagues) have left the organization
- Change in standards and requirements for high potentials
- Closing, shrinking, or outsourcing a business unit or function
- Significant change in business strategies
- Change in senior leadership (for example, a new CEO or function head)
- An interest in moving faster in their career (for example, leaving for a bigger job at another company)
- Individual has restricted mobility to move to internal advancement opportunities
- A new manager has different views on identifying high potentials

Whether to tell individuals their status as a high potential is a highly contested issue in organizations today, particularly given the preference for greater transparency among both Generation X and the new millennial employees entering the workforce. Most of the organizations we surveyed do not release this information to the individual primarily for these reasons:

- The information may get misinterpreted by the individual and lead to expectations for promotions, development opportunities, and resources that the organization might not be prepared to provide to the individual.
- It may lead to a decline in job performance by an individual who believes he has achieved an unassailable and permanent status in the organization.
- The person may be interested in leveraging her status and start looking for promotion opportunities outside the company.
- It will leak out to others who are not seen as high potential (usually the majority of the population) and act as a demotivator for them.

Although organizations may not directly tell an individual her status as a high potential there are some good reasons to let the individual know that the organization is interested in her and her career. With the current competition in the marketplace for leadership talent, it would a real loss if the individual left the company because no one told her how much she was valued or discussed future career opportunities with her. Aside from the career conversation, many organizations are likely to communicate status as a high potential indirectly through special assignments, leadership programs, coaching and mentoring, and other development opportunities given to the person. Getting sent to China on a special task force, working on writing the corporate values statement, or participating in the company's executive leadership program led by the CEO are cues that the organization is investing in the individual's career. Because individuals are now more in control over their own career and the social contract of lifetime employment is long gone, organizations are showing a growing interest in having open, honest, and transparent conversations with talented individuals.

Development

The final stage in the identification process is development. Once an individual is formally or informally designated as a high-potential individual then typically he will be given opportunities for accelerated development. Among the surveyed organizations, 50 percent have preestablished and standard development programs and opportunities for high-potential individuals (see Table 5.5). The other 50 percent indicate that their programs and activities are evolving or still in development.

During the talent review meetings, senior managers usually take the time to discuss possible development opportunities for high-potential individuals. These often include formal leadership programs, providing a coach or mentor, in-depth executive assessment, career planning, special work assignments (projects, task forces, temporary assignments), or executive education courses. Often these opportunities are identified based on the individual's specific development needs, but some companies have individuals go through more standard development activities, for example, an executive assessment, an executive leadership development program, or a university-based executive education

Table 5.5. High-Potential Development Activities

In Surveyed Organizations	
Standard or Evolving Programs/Activities	
50%*	Evolving, being developed
50%	Preestablished and set
Programs/Activities	
35%	Development experiences and rotational assignments
35%	Leadership development programs (internal)
35%	Special projects, task force assignments
35%	One on one interactions with senior leaders, such as lunches, dinners
25%	Mentors, coaches
20%	Attend annual senior leadership offsite meetings
15%	Executive education programs (external)

*% of the 20 organizations surveyed

program. However, organizations are using university-based education programs less and giving more emphasis to special assignments and work experiences inside the company (see Chapter 6 by Jay Conger and Chapter 7 by Paul Yost and Mary M. Plunkett).

In the surveyed organizations, the most frequent activities cited were work assignments and experiences, internal leadership programs, and interactions with senior leaders. Coaches and mentors are still used, but organizations are now more selective in using those resources and more closely managing the high costs in hiring external executive coaches. Some organizations, particularly in difficult economic times, have significantly cut back on the expense of external coaches. There has also been a switch at some companies to using internal coaches, often HR and line managers trained to coach others. Interaction with senior leaders is growing in popularity and serves two purposes: it gives the individuals more opportunity to build relationships with senior leaders and helps senior leaders get to know the rising talent in the organization.

Many different development activities are used with high potentials across organizations, but not all of them are effective.

The Corporate Leadership Council (2005b) reviewed more than 300 "drivers of employee potential" and found that fewer than 80 of them actually build potential. The highest-rated drivers were the quality and skills of the current manager and a customized, achievable development plan. The top 80 had three general themes: leveraging employee relationships, supporting organization commitment, and structuring the job challenges. The drivers that are least effective, and actually diminish potential, are frequent manager changes, working with team members you dislike, working without clear goals or objectives, dealing with organizational politics, and frequent rotations across business units.

Predictors of Future Performance

Predicting future behavior is a difficult challenge. It becomes easier if we can accurately define the future situation or position requirements. Then it would be more of a typical selection problem where the position is clearly known, the job requirements can be identified, and candidates can be assessed against those requirements. However, in identifying high-potential individuals, the future is often not very well known for several reasons:

- Business strategies change over time in reaction to changing business conditions.
- The capabilities and leadership roles needed to accomplish those strategies may also change.

Consider the business conditions that have changed over the past 10 to 20 years. How well could we have predicted the current global business competition, the financial challenges and the need for global leadership skills?

The challenge in predicting high potentials for organizations is to identify individuals who are highly likely to be effective in future leadership positions five to ten or more years into the future. What particular cues or indicators should be used to separate out future high performers from other individuals? Organizations want to use their limited development resources and experiences with individuals who have the greatest likelihood of succeeding at higher levels, in senior leadership positions and in broader roles. How well can senior managers, HR professionals and industrial-organizational psychologists accurately predict future behavior?

The first step is to define the organizational capabilities and individual competencies that will be needed in the future. That is why talent review meetings are most effective when they follow the strategic planning process in an organization. Once the business strategies have been determined or adjusted, then the organizational capabilities and leadership talent can be identified that are needed to achieve those strategies. (Most of the chapters in this book discuss the connection between strategy and talent; however, readers might pay particular attention to Chapter 20 by Marcia J. Avedon, Stephen Cerrone, Mirian Graddick-Weir, and Rob Silzer for the views of chief human resource officers.)

The organizational capabilities needed for the future might involve specific business situations (growth, turnaround, acquisition), specific competitive environments (new market, highly competitive), specific products and technology (new technology, redefining existing product space), specific cultural initiatives (entering China market, pursuing Hispanic market), or specific business functions (opening customer service call centers, outsourcing back office functions, implementing a new supply chain system). With proper guidance, senior managers can then identify the individual competencies and characteristics (experiences, knowledge, skills, abilities, such as entrepreneurial skills, work motivation, career ambition) that will be needed to achieve those strategies. Of course, near-term business strategies are usually easier to translate into specific talent needs than longer-term strategies. For example, starting up customer service call centers over the next three years will be easier to translate into talent needs than moving into the China and India markets over the next ten years. Customer service leaders have been widely studied and have a known competency profile, while the leadership skills needed to be successful in China in the next five to ten years are much more ambiguous and unknown.

Once the future organizational and leadership capabilities have been determined, the organization can specify the characteristics and requirements that will be used to identify high-potential individuals for those opportunities. The factors used by the surveyed companies are presented in Table 5.6.

Table 5.6. Factors Used for Identifying High Potentials

100%*	*Leadership Competencies*
	Evaluate some leadership competencies
	Emphasis is on people leadership skills such as engaging, motivating, developing others
	90% use a leadership competency model
100%	*Performance Record*
	60% review past performance record
	50% say it is a critical factor
	Current performance is particularly important
90%	*Career Drive/Motivation to Advance*
80%	*Mobility*
	Important to prepare for career opportunities
	Utilized more at senior levels
	May not be a disqualifier
75%	*Adaptability/Flexibility*
70%	*Specific Experience/Tenure*
	Such as work, functional, technical, and leadership experience; also education and knowledge, skills, and abilities
65%	*Learning Ability*
60%	*Commitment to Company*
	Related to engagement and retention

55%   *Personality Variables*

     25% identify interpersonal skills beyond competency model

     20% match behavior to organizational, cultural, and team fit/values

     Such as trust, integrity, respect, relationship skills, humility, positive attitude, self-awareness

45%   *Specific Abilities*

     Seen as somewhat important; importance varies by role

     30% assess technical, business, and functional expertise

     20% evaluate intellect and cognitive skills

     10% look at ability to handle ambiguity or complexity

30%   *Career Growth Potential for Future Requirements*

     Probably consist of other factors listed above

Other Identification and Selection Factors

- Development Orientation
- Cultural Fit
- Fungibility

*% of the 20 organizations surveyed

Performance Record

All the surveyed companies use past performance as one identification factor. Some use it as a "price of admission," noting that
individuals need to have a strong performance track record to
even be considered for further development. Others see it as a
critical indicator of an individual's ability to successfully perform
in a variety of roles. Several issues are related to using performance as an identification factor.

First, how much variety has there been in the work challenges
that are faced by the individual? If, for example, the person has
always been in the accounting or auditing department in the
finance function, it raises the question of whether the individual
has demonstrated the ability to effectively handle a range of challenges and work situations. It may suggest that the person needs
to develop more versatility. So the range of an individual's past
work experiences should be considered.

Similarly the person's past work experiences need to be
matched against future strategic needs in the organization. For
example, an individual may have only worked in the customer
service operation. If the organization has decided to outsource
customer call centers in the future, it may raise the question of
whether the individual has the skills and abilities that will be
needed in the future.

A third issue with performance track records is that some
individuals might actually be more effective in some higher-level
jobs than lower-level positions. Working as a first-line supervisor
might be a poor job match for someone who has the skills and
abilities to be an effective marketing manager. Performance in
the lower job, with the associated constraints and structure, may
not be indicative of the person's ability to handle a more conceptual and creative manager role. So organizations need to be cautious about overrelying on performance track record.

There is some agreement that past performance behavior can
be an indicator of future performance providing the future role
is in similar circumstances and requires similar skills. The classic
case of outstanding sales representatives later failing when they
are promoted to sales managers is an example of when a past
performance track record does not predict future effectiveness.

The same issue is particularly prevalent in technical functions such as R&D. Not only do highly trained scientists sometimes make poor managers, they often do not want to be managers at all.

Some organizations place particular importance on recent performance effectiveness. The significant recent achievements (and failures) by each individual are reviewed in the context of classifying someone as a high potential. Often these achievements are indications of particular skills or lessons that the person has learned or the person's ability to handle particular business situations (such as an operational assignment, a product repositioning, or a turnaround). Noticeable failures should also be reviewed to determine if they reveal some limitation or development need in the individual (or if they were beyond the control of the individual). In many companies, poor performance often derails high potentials regardless of the circumstances.

Leadership Competencies

All of the surveyed organizations consider the leadership skills (such as engaging, motivating, and developing others) of high-potential candidates. Leadership competency models (Hollenbeck, McCall, & Silzer, 2006) are commonly used, and 360-degree feedback surveys (Tornow & London, 1998; Bracken, Timmreck, & Church, 2001; Tornow & Tornow, 2001) are frequently used to collect the competency ratings. There are some mixed views on using leadership competency models specifically for identifying high potentials (see Hollenbeck et al., 2006), but they have generally been widely accepted despite some validity and legal concerns. For example, using a leadership competency model that has not been carefully developed and 360-degree ratings from peers and direct reports to help select high-potential individuals may open an organization to legal challenges. Since this can be seen as a selection process, these tools need to be reliable and valid if they are going to be used as selection instruments.

There is some agreement that a person's current leadership skills are relevant to predicting his future leadership capability. However, it is important that the organization use future-oriented leadership standards that anticipate the skills needed in the future. Few leadership competency models or 360-degree feedback instruments take this approach. Instead, they are usually reflections of past behavioral standards or, at best, are based on current standards and expectations. It does present a selection dilemma that in order to predict an ambiguous future, organizations need to be able to anticipate what capabilities will be needed in five or ten years in the future. Yet most of our selection guidelines and tools rely on past or current performance standards.

One exception is the effort made with future-oriented job analyses (see Schippmann, 1991). Future-oriented standards need to estimate both the business context and situations as well as the needed skills and abilities. Then a person's demonstrated leadership skills in specific situations could be matched to the future requirements. Unfortunately the current art and science in this area is not advanced enough to let us do this with much precision. So in practice this often means that senior managers give some thought to the business strategies, discuss the organizational and individual capabilities that will be needed, and discuss how well an individual might currently have or develop those capabilities over time. The process relies on group discussion and consensus.

Motivation Issues

Another key factor in many prediction models is the individual's level of ambition, motivation, and drive. An individual has to be motivated to advance her career in order to effectively deal with all the challenges and setbacks along the way and still want to be in a senior leadership position. This is usually gauged by two factors: motivation to advance and commitment to the company.

In the surveyed companies, 90 percent consider a person's motivation to advance his career as an indicator of high potential. This is often reflected in the person's demonstrated work effort above and beyond what is expected (which could also be linked to being highly engaged) and a clear and often formally stated commitment to doing what it takes to advance his career. Often immediate managers and past performance track record can be used to verify this commitment. We have also found that having a high energy level is a good predictor of engagement level and work capacity as well. And our experience is that the work demands significantly increase as a person moves up an organization. Also considered is the individual's specific career interests and aspirations: What type of work and career is the person interested in pursuing? This is why, in practice, it is critical for managers and HR professionals to have honest discussions with employees to fully understand their career interests and ambitions. Highly ambitious individuals, who for whatever reason are not identified as high potentials, are likely to leave the organization for other opportunities that will advance their careers.

Commitment to the company is considered an important factor by 60 percent of the surveyed organizations. However, this is a difficult construct to accurately measure since most employees profess a high degree of commitment, and it would not be wise for them to voice any doubts or intentions to leave (unless someone was trying to use that as a bargaining tool to obtain a more senior position, which works in some cultures but not in many). Frequently leadership turnovers come as a surprise to the organization because the person leaving usually keeps her intentions quiet and only covertly pursues other career opportunities. That said, evaluating a person's retention risk is a general consideration in talent reviews, but the available data are not always accurate. Some of the factors that organizations use in identifying turnover intentions include:

- Length of time without a promotion or significant change in role (often two years or more is a key indicator of retention risk)
- Performance history (if a high potential received an average performance rating in the prior evaluation cycle while learning a new job)
- Verbal statements regarding a general level of dissatisfaction with the organization, the person's manager, or career situation made to colleagues (usually not to managers or human resources)
- Indicators of potential burnout in the job, such as the extent to which the role requires extended hours or lacks supporting resources

- Situations where a perceived devaluation of the person's capability or potential future opportunities occurs as the result of organizational changes (structure, job design, reward systems, strategy, policy)
- Clear indicators of issues or conflict with the direct manager (it is well understood that people join companies but leave managers)

When identifying high-potential talent, it is often assumed that the nominating manager or the human resources professional can vouch for the individual's commitment to the company. The manager and HR professional have some responsibility for knowing the individual's level of commitment.

Mobility

The relevance of a person's mobility—the willingness and ability to move to new locations for career opportunities—to being designated as high potential has shifted in significance several times over the last few decades. Forty years ago, most leaders did not have to move geographically to advance their career, unless it was to corporate headquarters from a remote location. Then as organizations began to restructure more frequently, leaders were expected to change locations accordingly, in order to obtain broader experience and to more quickly advance their careers. In some organizations, particularly in the 1980s, individuals were simply "tapped on the shoulder" one day and told to pack up and take a new position in another location or lose any hope of ever getting another advancement opportunity. In the 1990s this trend expanded to include moving individuals across functions, business units, and even countries as companies diversified and developed global businesses. As a result of all this movement, mobility has often historically been seen as a key indicator (even a requirement in some cases) of a high-potential individual.

However, more recently a subtle shift seems to be occurring. While leaders may still need experience working in another business or culture, the key leadership positions in other countries (particularly in the emerging markets) are increasingly being filled with individuals from that culture, who may spend some time doing a developmental assignment at the corporate head-quarters before returning to their native country.

There also has been a growing resistance from many leaders to the frequent moves required to progress and a greater interest in balancing career opportunities with family priorities. This trend is particularly evident among the millennials now entering the workforce, and has many organizations scrambling to determine how best to respond. Going forward, it is less likely that organizations will be able to require high mobility from high-potential individuals, and they will need to become more tolerant and understanding of family issues that may require the individual to stay in one location for awhile. Even in China there is some clear resistance to moving to another city and away from a person's larger family (see Chapter 14 by Elizabeth Weldon).

Some organizations look for more local career opportunities for individuals who want to advance their career but who do not want to move their family. Others may need to rely more heavily on technology solutions that allow people to take on new roles while remaining in the same location (although this raises the question of whether remote virtual responsibilities provide sufficient experience and development). Exhibit 5.3 presents the PepsiCo response to a question about mobility and high-potential individuals. PepsiCo takes a more nuanced and thoughtful approach to the issue than many other companies.

Adaptability and Flexibility

Many HR professionals and industrial-organizational psychologists have considered a person's ability to adapt to different situations and work demands as a key predictor of job performance. It is related to an individual's openness to new experiences and ability to learn from new situations. Flexibility can be defined as a person's mental and behavioral openness and willingness to consider and try different ideas and approaches. Experience has demonstrated that people who are inflexible and unable to adapt to change have great difficulty handling new and broader responsibilities. Their tendency is to handle things the same way they have in the past without having any insight into the differences in situations or problems. Typically these individuals experience

**Exhibit 5.3. PepsiCo View on Mobility
as a Requirement to Be High Potential**

*If a high-potential individual is not mobile (i.e., cannot relocate to
another city for PepsiCo) should they still be coded as high potential?*

In general, YES. While mobility plays a key role in making
internal staffing decisions in some cases (particularly as roles
open in Plano, Chicago, or New York), the fact that someone
is not mobile should not automatically eliminate them from
being classified as a high potential if they have the talent. It is
entirely possible to have a successful career at PepsiCo while
remaining in the same location (depending on the number of
opportunities available there).

We recognize that people go through different stages in
their lives and their careers when moving to another country, city or state is simply not possible. That said, it is critical
that we operate with truth and candor on this issue. There are
three points to consider here:

First, it is extremely important that PepsiCo knows an
employee's true preferences (i.e., fully mobile, somewhat limited mobility, no mobility whatsoever) so that we can effectively
plan for filling roles.

Second, it is incumbent upon us (whether as line leaders
or HR professionals) to communicate to employees if mobility is
a necessity for certain roles.

Third, there are certain examples of individuals in truly
remote locations or countries who have indicated that they will
never relocate. In these types of cases the individual might be
better classified as a Key Contributor, Critical Professional or
Concern (if blocking a key developmental role), since their lack
of mobility would limit them from gaining the critical experiences expected of a high potential.

Source: Personal communication, Allan Church, March 1, 2009.

a number of problems performing in their new roles. One exception,
however, is when an inflexible person follows a single manager or
mentor up the organization. The manager has come to rely on
the person for very specific, and often narrow, skills and continues
to depend on those specific skills as the manager gets promoted.

Frequently this person survives as long as the manager is around to protect him; however, once the manager leaves, the person's lack of flexibility becomes apparent and his perceived value to the organization is significantly diminished.

In our survey, 75 percent of the companies consider the individual's level of adaptability. This might be determined based on the person's ability to be effective in a variety of situations and working for different types of leaders. Having a track record of "landing on your feet" and performing well in different roles over time often is a good indicator of adaptability.

Specific Experience and Tenure

Of the surveyed organizations, 70 percent also focus on specific work experiences in selecting high potentials. The nature of the specific experience may be unique to the company or the industry and related to company strategies or culture. In some companies, this might involve working in the dominant function or in the leading business of the organization. In specialized high-potential groups (such as functional or geographic groups), there may be very specific experience requirements, such as work on a manufacturing plant floor. In many organizations, this can also refer to having had some significant leadership experience overseeing a task force or building a team. There might even be some educational expectations such as a Ph.D. or M.B.A. or a C.P.A. certification.

In some organizations, these specific experiences can be gained after the individual is identified as a high potential. For example, in some consumer product companies, it is critical to spend some time in the marketing function before a person can be considered as high potential, while in other companies, an individual can gain this experience after being identified as a high potential. It depends on which experiences are seen as qualifiers and which are seen as later development opportunities.

Learning Ability

In many organizations, learning skills and ability are used as a screening factor. In our survey sample, 65 percent of the organizations reported using some type of learning indicator. (Different names are used by different organizations, such as *learning ability, learning skills,* and *learning agility.*) A consensus is emerging that learning ability and skills are important to fulfilling future career potential (see Chapter 7 by Paul Yost and Mary M. Plunkett; McCall, 1994; Spreitzer, McCall, & Mahoney, 1997; Lombardo & Eichinger, 2000). However there is not yet a consensus on how to define or measure it. Various definitions are used. Many definitions contain some common elements:

- The ability to learn
- The motivation to learn
- An openness to new information and ideas
- The cognitive ability to process and understand the information
- A willingness to integrate the information with what a person already knows and apply it to new situations and contexts

Here are a few definitions from organizations in the survey:

- "Ability and willingness to assimilate and use new information"
- "Learning quickly from feedback and new experiences, adapting effectively and applying learnings to new challenges"
- "Responding constructively to feedback and coaching, being open to new ideas, a willingness to change direction when faced with setbacks"
- "Seeking feedback and new opportunities to learn, regularly challenging self to develop new approaches"
- "Seeking new experiences, learning required skills and behaviors, integrating new skills into repertoire"

Learning ability is a future-oriented capability that allows the individual to quickly understand and adapt to new and changing situations. It seems to improve the chances that a person can handle future unknown challenges and is one of the bridging capabilities to an ambiguous future, like adaptability and flexibility. It is difficult to measure, however, and most surveyed organizations use an internally developed assessment approach, since there is no well-developed, validated instrument currently available in the market. In some organizations, cognitive ability tests are used as a measure of learning ability. However, there may be some sensitivity around using cognitive ability tests, such as the Watson Glaser Critical Thinking Test, as a screening tool for identifying internal high-potential candidates. Although a solid argument could be made for using a cognitive abilities assessment as a screening tool, it would need to be validated for that purpose. Currently learning ability measures are most likely to be used internally for developmental assessments, while cognitive ability tests are generally used for selection of external candidates.

One component of learning that often is overlooked in this area is a person's ability to observe and recognize cues in the environment. While some individuals may be cognitively smart, they can have a limited ability to read situational cues and interpersonal signals. They often miss critical, defining cues in the environment and fail to recognize and understand the situation-specific, person-specific, or problem-specific information that would help them effectively deal with an issue. This ability to observe and interpret the situational and people cues is an underappreciated skill. It has been referred to as social intelligence. This term was temporarily displaced by the term *emotional intelligence* but has more recently been properly restored as the preferred term (Albrecht, 2006; Goleman, 2006).

Personality Variables

Personality variables are used as high-potential indicators in 55 percent of the surveyed organizations. Related variables specifically mentioned by surveyed companies include interpersonal trust, integrity, respect for others, interpersonal relationship skills, humility, positive attitude, and self-awareness. Interpersonal skills are the most widely used personality variables. Some companies assess personality variables using standardized personality inventories, while others observe behaviors that are indicative of certain personality variables. Also 20 percent of the organizations consider how well the individual's behavior matches organizational, cultural, and team values. There is growing interest in determining an individual's fit to the organizational values and norms.

Often the behavioral manifestations of personality variables are measured in a 360-degree behavioral competency survey or by management observations on the job. Some organizations use formal personality inventories, such as the California Psychological Inventory and the Hogan Personality Inventory, to measure these variables. However, using these tools for identifying high potentials may introduce some concerns for the organization.

While personality instruments are gaining again in popularity, there are legal risks, as there are with all selection tools, in using them for a selection process without fully validating their use for the target positions. Also, showing some selection preference for certain personality types (such as being socially extroverted) over others is not yet fully accepted in the U.S. culture, even though it is a widespread latent practice (for example, preferring extroverted individuals over introverted individuals for certain positions such as customer service representative). It might be hard to legally defend the use of personality inventories for selection (or even identification) of high potentials without solid construct validity or empirical validity support. As a result of these issues, many organizations either administer personality inventories after the individuals have been identified as high potential (and use for development purposes) or they use work behavior observation rating scales instead, which measure personality variables (such as interpersonal skills) by evaluating the person against clearly identified and relevant work behaviors (such as collaboration on a team). Although the use of personality variables has gained in popularity, organizations still use caution to make sure the variables are related to relevant work behaviors.

Specific Abilities

Organizations may also look at specific abilities when they have a clear rationale for why they are needed. For some high-potential groups, such as for functional talent pools, there may be specialized abilities that a person needs to have to progress in that function, such as understanding accounting principles or labor relations. In companies with dominant functions, such as marketing or sales, some qualifying abilities in that function may be expected (for example, having consumer, customer, competitive, and channel insight skills). In other companies, expertise in the main product or service line might be needed. In our sample, 45 percent of the organizations look for specific abilities, and 30 percent look for technical, business, or functional expertise.

Some surveyed organizations look for more general abilities such as intellectual or cognitive skills (20 percent) or the ability to handle complexity or ambiguity (10 percent). These might focus on critical thinking, conceptual thinking, logical thinking skills, numerical reasoning, or reasoning through complex problems and are related to some of the other factors discussed already, such as learning ability. These abilities are often seen not as situation or function specific but as broad fundamental abilities that help individuals in a wide range of situations. These general abilities are also seen as bridging capabilities to the future that give the individual some ability to understand and reason through new problems and situations. They can be helpful, like learning skills, in dealing with undefined future challenges.

Sometimes the organization has a clear understanding of the individual capabilities that will be needed to achieve future business strategies. Included in these capabilities may be the need for specific abilities such as business turnaround leadership abilities, six sigma black belt analysis skills, or acumen in new product development. These might be added to the list of variables that are considered when selecting high-potential individuals.

Career Growth Potential

Some organizations (30 percent in our sample) try to determine the future career growth for an individual, that is, identifying how far up the organizational hierarchy the individual might go in his career. Sometimes referred to as *future back thinking,* it allows organizations to theoretically plan future development moves by gauging what the end goal is and laying out a development plan to help the person get there. Although often not very accurate, it typically relies on senior manager judgment of a person's past career growth, where the person is now in her career, and how far she might go in the remainder of her career.

Developmental Orientation and Progress

Organizations expect individuals to further develop their skills and abilities after they are identified as high potential. In fact, development progress is usually expected to be steeper and more intense than the person's past development experiences. One indicator of the person's ability to progress rapidly in the future is his prior developmental track record. What is his developmental history? What major developmental objectives has he achieved in the past? What is his current development plan and recent development progress?

Cultural Fit

Every organization has cultural and organizational values and behavioral norms. For example, is it a team-oriented culture where everyone is expected to be cooperative and collaborative, or is it more of an entrepreneurial individual achievement culture, where independent accomplishments are encouraged and rewarded? Is there a focus on aggressively pursuing revenue growth at all costs, or is there a central focus on showing respect for others and building relationships? Does the culture take a strong selection approach and emphasize hiring the best talent from the outside or a development approach by building talent internally? Most organizations have identified their key values and core principles. Employees and managers are expected to behave in ways that are consistent with those values and behavioral norms.

Organizations are becoming increasingly interested in determining whether external and internal selection candidates for positions and internal candidates for high-potential designation are a good fit or match to the organizational values and norms. There are many examples, some of them quite high profile, of external candidates who were hired into a visible leadership role and brought needed capabilities to the company but failed in their first year or two and ultimately left the organization.

One visible example of a cultural misfit to an organizational culture was when AlliedSignal acquired Honeywell. Larry Bossidy, the CEO and chairman of AlliedSignal, agreed to retire so that Michael Bosignore, CEO of the former Honeywell, could become CEO of the combined companies. The leadership style of the two CEOs was significantly different. It became clear in six months after the merger that Bosignore was a poor match for the AlliedSignal culture. The organization floundered under him, and his leadership approach was questioned by the organization and the financial community. One year after the merger, Bosignore retired and Bossidy returned as CEO and Chairman of the new combined Honeywell Corporation. The company stock price reflected the executive transitions of the two CEOs.

Often a primary reason for a cultural mismatch is that an executive usually sticks with his own leadership and execution style, and neither may be consistent with the norms and culture of the new company or business. So while there may well be a need for someone to drive cultural change in an organization, sometimes that change is the wrong one or too much change occurs too quickly, and the leader fails. Hiring managers are so focused on adding particular capabilities for the company that they often overlook the lack of fit to the culture. For example, the aggressive sales leader who increases revenues but offends everyone around her with her insensitive interpersonal style, or the IT manager with strong technical skills who is autocratic and controlling in his leadership approach. These failures are often seen as obvious cultural mismatches after the fact. With an increasing understanding of the direct and indirect costs associated with these failures, based on better ROI metrics, more organizations are calculating the costs of cultural mismatches and attempting to prevent them with more rigorous identification and selection processes.

Similarly with high-potential candidates, senior managers often want some assurance that the individual will support and even role model the existing cultural norms and values. It does present something of a dilemma for senior managers, however, as they need to balance promoting and supporting the existing culture with the need for organizational change to meet future business challenges. The need for consistency in the present sometimes may be at odds with the need for change in the future. How does an organization balance both points of view?

Fungibility

Some organizations focus on the need for fungible talent, that is, individuals who can be effective in a broad range of roles and be somewhat interchangeable with others at the same level in other functions (often these individuals show both adaptability and learning ability). Allied Signal (and later Honeywell) put an emphasis on building general managers who could lead a variety of businesses for the company. Capital One Financial looked for individuals who could start up and lead a range of future businesses. Both companies wanted to avoid having people who specialized in one business and would have difficulty moving across businesses or sectors. This puts a focus on identifying individuals with general leadership skills who can be effectively used in a broad range of business situations.

Other Identification Models

In addition, some consulting firms have developed their own models for identifying high potentials. One well-known model was developed by the Corporate Leadership Council (2005a) and is used by three of the surveyed companies (15 percent). In many ways, this model incorporates a number of the factors discussed above. The model has three core components:

- *Ability*: "A combination of innate characteristics (mental cognitive agility and emotional intelligence), and learned skills (technical/functional skills and interpersonal skills) that an employee uses to carry out his/her day to day work."
- *Engagement:* "Consists of four elements: emotional commitment, rational commitment, discretionary effort, and intent to stay."
- *Aspiration*: "The extent to which an employee wants or desires: prestige and recognition in the organization, advancement and influence, financial rewards, work-life balance, and overall job enjoyment" (p. 5).

The Corporate Leadership Council (2005a) argues that "to rise and succeed in more senior, more critical positions, employees must have the aspiration, engagement and ability to do so" (p. xi). The CLC argues that "71 percent of *high performers* have limited potential for success at the next level" and identifies three common profiles of high performers who are not high potential:

- *Engaged dreamers:* Employees with a great deal of engagement and aspiration but only average ability. They represent 10 percent of the high performers who are not high potential and have 0 percent probability of success at the next level.
- *Unengaged stars:* Employees with a great deal of aspiration and ability but lack engagement. They represent 43 percent of the high performers who are not high potential and have 13 percent probability of success at the next level.
- *Misaligned stars:* Employees with great ability and engagement but lack drive and ambition. They represent 47 percent of the high performers who are not high potential and have 44 percent probability of success at the next level.

An organization can evaluate its talent against these benchmarks and determine what development areas to emphasize. For example, if an organization has significantly more unengaged stars and far fewer misaligned stars (perhaps they already left the organization) compared to other companies, the organization might initiate action plans that focus on increasing engagement levels of high performers.

Other consulting organizations have also proposed leadership potential models. DDI's executive leadership potential model (Rogers & Smith, 2007; Wellins, Smith, & McGee, 2006) has four cornerstones of executive potential:

- *Leadership promise:* ". . . defines a person who shows certain inherent abilities to lead others" (p. 3).
- *Personal development orientation:* . . . defines a person who "never stops trying to become an even better leader" (p. 4).
- *Mastery of complexity:* ". . . touches on an individual's ability to excel in a work environment rife with constant, rapid change, swirling ambiguity, and competing demands from many quarters" (p. 5).
- *Balance of values and results:* ". . . reflects a senior leader's ability to work within a company's culture and still get the desired results" (p. 6).

MDA Leadership Consulting has proposed a model of high potential (Barnett, 2008) with three core factors:

- *Personality characteristics*: Dominance, sociability, drive, versatility, and stability
- *Successful intelligence*: The capacity to analyze, evaluate, and accurately and insightfully solve problems effectively and apply what they know to adapt, to positively influence others and impact their environment
- *Attitudes and values*: Attitudes toward learning and a positive disposition toward their team and organization.

Predictor Summary

So what factors predict high potential? A summary of possible high-potential identification factors identified by the surveyed companies is presented in Table 5.7. Predictor data can be either supplied by other people (through ratings, evaluations, interview data, observations) or by the individual (through self-ratings, inventories, assessments, assessment centers, achievements). The data can also come from the past (career and educational history) or the present (current performance, current abilities), or can be focused on future behavior (career growth, career aspirations). For a further discussion of high-potential predictors see Silzer and Church (2009).

Short-Term Versus Long-Term Prediction

It is commonly accepted that past behavior is the best predictor of future behavior. However that is not always true. It is important to look at past behavioral patterns over time and whether the behavior is in past situations or contexts that are similar to what the person may face in the future. So, for example, past sales management success in a cooperative supportive environment, where significant company resources are available to the individual for support, may not predict the individual's future sales success in an independent environment, where the sales manager is expected to provide her own resources and do everything on her own.

An example is the study of stock analysts in the financial industry who switch companies (Groysberg, Nanda, & Nohria, 2004). The failure rate in the new company with a different environment

Table 5.7. High-Potential Predictor Data

Data	From the Past	From the Present	Future Oriented
From others (for example, observations, ratings)	• Past performance ratings • Competency ratings • Performance appraisals • 360-degree surveys	• Current performance ratings • Boss nomination • Senior manager review • Evaluation of • Cultural and values fit • Career motivation • Commitment to company • Drive for results	• Evaluation of: • Career growth potential • Development orientation • Capabilities for future strategies
From self (for example, self-ratings, self-report behavior, inventories, tests)	• Performance achievements • Career history • Educational history	• Current performance • Specific abilities • Cognitive • Technical knowledge • Mobility • Personality variables	• Desire to advance • Career aspirations • Learning ability • Adaptability

is quite high. The authors suggest that differences in the organizational situation and context significantly affect performance in the new company. This problem is also evident with individuals who have successfully worked under a single manager for most of their career and then fail when assigned to a new manager. In order for past behavior to be a useful predictor of future behavior, there need to be several similarities:

- The required behavior itself has to be similar and require similar skills and abilities.
- The behavior has to be long-standing or at least demonstrated over some significant time period.
- Behavior demonstrated in the recent past is more predictive of future behavior than behavior demonstrated in the distant past.
- The situation or context in which the behavior was demonstrated is similar to the future situation.

It is also easier to predict behavior in the near future because recent past behavior is more relevant, and the near-term future situation may be knowable. Short-term predictions of behavior are more likely to be accurately based on recent behavior. However, longer-term predictions are more difficult because of the longer time period between predictor and criterion behavior and because situations that are further into the future are less knowable.

Some might argue that past and current behavior, as measured by performance track record, more accurately predict the near-term future behavior in similar situations (next few years) than the longer-term future, while leadership characteristics (measured by competency ratings, personality inventories, and ability measures) are more likely to predict longer-term behavior across a range of situations. A person's basic personality characteristics and leadership abilities are more likely to be stable over time than a situation-specific skill or behavior. Some personality measures have been designed to capture consistent patterns of behavior (also known as personality characteristics) over time and across situations. Longer-term performance may be more accurately based on enduring characteristics than any specific behaviors.

Of course, understanding a person's true potential is based on predicting both short-term and long-term performance, so organizations might be advised to use a mix of predictors, for example, combining personality factors, skills and abilities measures, and understanding performance over time, while factoring in the needs of the future. As Ben Dowell notes in Chapter 9 in this book, "A combination of different assessments may be the best approach, using one type of assessment for judging potential to assume specific roles in the short term and another assessment for judging the potential to assume future roles as the organization's strategy evolves over the longer term." Short-term and long-term predictions of potential are probably sufficiently different that they require different predictors and assessment tools.

Assessment Techniques and Tools

As part of the identification of high-potential individuals, organizations today use a variety of assessment techniques and tools (see Table 5.8). All of the surveyed companies considered immediate manager ratings and recommendations as a key tool and indicator of potential. Half of the companies indicate that those recommendations are critical to the identification process, while 20 percent view them primarily as entry hurdles to being considered.

Similarly 100 percent of the surveyed companies used senior management review meetings as a component of the identification process as well. Many companies (35 percent in our sample) also use management calibration meetings (often used in the performance evaluation process) to ensure that candidates across an organization are evaluated using the same calibration standards. This usually involves peer groups of managers at the same level in the organization comparing and contrasting individuals from different parts of the organization against a common measure or scale.

Past performance is often seen as a key predictor of future effectiveness. In our sample, 100 percent of the companies considered the last performance review and looked for performance trends over the last several years.

Many organizations now use 360-degree competency feedback surveys, primarily for providing development feedback

Table 5.8. Tools Used to Identify High-Potential Candidates

In Surveyed Organizations	
100%*	*Immediate Manager Ratings and Recommendations*
	50% view as critical to the process
	20% view as entry requirement
100%	*Senior Manager Review*
	35% use management calibration meetings
100%	*Last Performance Review*
	Usually from last two to three years to identify trends
65%	*360-Degree Feedback Instrument or Competency Ratings*
	Typically used to identify development needs
	Most are internally developed or customized tools
30%	*Interviews*
	Usually behavioral or competency based
30%	*Personality Instruments*
	Used for developmental purposes
15%	*Ability Tests*
	Used for identification or development
	Focus is on cognitive ability tests
15%	*Assessment Centers*
10%	*Individual Psychological Assessment*

*% of the 20 organizations surveyed

to individuals, although there is still significant debate in the field around using these tools for development only versus using them for selection decision making (Bracken et al., 2001; Tornow & Tornow, 2001). The typical competencies that are evaluated are strategic thinking, building relationships, setting the agenda, motivating others, being inclusive, demonstrating integrity and ethics, and encouraging teamwork. Competency feedback surveys have become a widespread practice (Tornow & London, 1998). In our sample, 65 percent of the companies collect competency ratings on high-potential candidates. They use them primarily for determining development plans after the high-potential individuals have already been identified.

Although many consulting firms have their own well-established frameworks, the best approach for using 360-feedback ratings for internal development of high potentials is for organizations to develop their own customized leadership competency model that is carefully developed and specific to the organization's culture and strategies. These models should be built to incorporate the organization's values, reflect the business strategy, and either reinforce the current culture or outline through behavioral examples what the new culture should look like. Often they include future-oriented competencies where appropriate. For example, if fostering innovation is a particularly important competency that will be needed in the next ten years for an organization to thrive, the leadership competency model used for 360-degree feedback should include and define that dimension with much greater specificity than other more generic (but still important) elements.

Interviews, particularly behavioral or competency focused interviews, are used by 30 percent of the surveyed organizations as an assessment tool. In some organizations, the interviews are used as a screening device to understand the individual's career preferences, to identify past accomplishments, and to determine the lessons the individual has learned from prior experiences. Other companies use in-depth career interviews as part of an extensive developmental assessment for individuals after they have been designated as high potential. In some cases, these are long and very in-depth background interviews lasting up to several hours (Silzer, 2002b; Smart, 1999).

Psychological tests are thoughtfully used in some organizations. In our sample 30 percent of the companies use personality inventories—such as the California Psychological Inventory and the Hogan Personality Inventory—but almost always for development purposes. Few organizations use personality tests for the identification and selection of high-potential individuals, although they typically are included in assessment centers and individual assessments that might be used for identification and selection purposes.

Ability tests, particularly cognitive ability tests, are used by only 15 percent of the surveyed companies for both development and selection purposes. However, mental "horsepower" is an important and relevant individual difference, so these tools can be useful at certain levels and for certain purposes in an organization. When an organization is looking to identify high-potential individuals at more junior levels or with external candidates, they can be important tools, within limits, to distinguish the long-term potential of individuals. They also can be useful in development and coaching programs to identify the person's cognitive and learning capacity. At senior levels, they might be somewhat less useful because cognitive ability is not as clear a distinguishing variable among senior managers (most senior managers have solid cognitive skills). Senior leaders usually have a clearer performance track record that reflects cognitive ability, and there are other equally important factors related to identifying senior-level high-potential candidates (Silzer 2002a). Similar in their use to personality inventories, they often are included in assessment centers and individual assessments as a component of the process.

Both assessment centers and individual psychological assessments (Jeanneret & Silzer, 1998) are used by surveyed organizations (15 percent and 10 percent, respectively), which reflects an increase in popularity for high-potential identification and development from the 1980s and 1990s. Both approaches often include behavioral interviews, behavioral exercises, personality measures, and cognitive tests. Some companies also include 360-degree survey results in the assessment, collected by written surveys or in face-to-face interviews. They are used for both identifying and selecting high-potential individuals, as well as for their later development after they have been identified.

Although these approaches can provide a helpful external evaluation of an individual's potential, companies often combine the results with internal evaluations and reviews. There are both validity and cultural reasons for making sure that a person's past behavior and achievements inside the organization are fully considered and evaluated when determining if the individual has future potential. Companies might limit the accuracy of their high-potential predictions and lose some internal credibility if they relied too heavily on external evaluations to identify candidates. Some consulting firms recommend these approaches as identification and selection tools since they can produce useful

assessment data that add to longer-term predictions. They probably are best used as part of a larger set of predictor data that
includes and weighs internal data, and not used as stand-alone
predictors. The exception may be for the selection of external
candidates. External individual assessments can provide a helpful balance to the internally collected data, particularly when
there might be some question about the validity or usefulness
of the internal data. When used in this way, it is important to
ensure that the assessments are based on behavioral standards
that are reflective of the particular organization and the future
expectations of the organization.

Assessment Versus Prediction

It is important to distinguish between accurately assessing specific
variables and predictors (data collection) and making predictions about future behavior and performance (data evaluation).
The high-potential identification process needs to effectively do
both. The key steps in this process are:

1. *Identify predictor variables.* First carefully define the concept
   of a high potential in the organization, and then identify
   the right variables and predictors based on the current and
   future business strategy. They should be carefully chosen to
   make sure they contribute to, and not distract from or diminish, accurate prediction.
2. *Assess for predictor variables.* The assessment tools and
   approaches should be thoughtfully chosen to make sure the
   identified predictors are accurately measured and that valid
   and relevant data are collected. Keep in mind that not all
   tools are equally valid or useful, and there is no single "magic
   bullet" predictor despite the fact that many senior leaders
   want one or overrely on just one.
3. *Predict future behavior.* The assessment data should be
   thoughtfully evaluated, weighed, and combined into an overall prediction. This step can introduce a good deal of error
   and personal biases into the process. Whenever possible,
   there should be some clear standards for interpreting the
   data and a structured process for weighing and combining

the data into a reliable and valid prediction. During implementation, organizations and leaders should agree on how prescriptive they want the prediction process to be. Is the assessment and prediction process going to result in a clear yes or no decision, or will the information be used as input for a broader discussion?

Identify Predictor Variables

Many organizations do not adjust their definition of *high potential* as the business strategies and context changes. The decision process used in organizations to identify the predictor variables that best reflect the high-potential definition is often subjective, based on what data are readily available and what variables HR professionals and senior leaders think are relevant. Unfortunately it is rarely based on valid data or evidence. (Traditional validity is established using historical backward-looking data.) Much greater attention and research should be given to this decision process and how to predict a discontinuous future. Selecting the best variables to include is the critical first step that can help or hinder the organization's ability to successfully predict future behavior. Of course, the most predictive variables will probably vary for different organizations, based on the strategic objectives, the desired organizational and individual capabilities, and the organization's culture and values.

Assess for Predictor Variables

Most of the assessment tools and techniques mentioned in this chapter can be used to reliably and validly assess specific skills, abilities, and characteristics. Many of them have supporting research that demonstrates that they effectively measure what they say they are measuring. This is probably truer for the structured approaches (such as structured interviews, personality instruments, ability tests, assessment centers, and individual psychological assessment) than for less structured approaches (such as unstructured interviews, manager ratings and recommendations, senior manager reviews, and performance reviews). For example, much has been written about why performance evaluations do not accurately reflect actual performance (Murphy, 2008). In general, it is important to consider the reliability, validity, and usefulness of the data that are being used.

Predict Future Behavior

The step that often is overlooked in the high-potential identification process is how the data are combined to predict future behavior. Frequently it is a subjective decision based on the judgments of senior managers and human resource professionals. The judgments may not be consistent (reliable) across managers, across times, or across candidates. There may not be much discussion about the strength of the evidence on the predictor variables. Moreover, in some organizations, there may not be any formal facilitated discussions by either an internal talent owner or an external consultant.

Also, the data may be more valid for some predictor variables than others. There is a long history of outlining the limitations of human judgment in combining large sets of data (Dawes, 1988; Meehl, 1954; Silzer, 1984). This suggests a research and a practice opportunity to improve the accuracy of identifying high potentials by using mechanical methods of combining data into overall predictions. There is evidence that the mechanical combination of data, with the opportunity for some adjustment by human judgment, may significantly improve prediction accuracy above and beyond human judgment data combination alone (Silzer, 1984).

Tracking Progress

Organizations are increasingly interested in collecting outcome data to determine the effectiveness of HR programs and systems. In evaluating high-potential identification efforts, organizations are most likely to track the ongoing performance and career moves of high-potential individuals over time. Most of the companies in our survey (75 percent) do track high potentials (see Table 5.9), although many of these efforts are very informal (they are not systematically evaluated) or are new efforts in the company (with no historical data).

Table 5.9. Tracking High-Potential Progress

In Surveyed Organizations	
75%*	*Track High Potentials*
	Track High Potential progress
	Many efforts are new or informal
	Tracking Metrics
	Promotion rates
	Movement to new assignments
	Performance
	Time spent in position
65%	*Monitor Speed of Moves*
	Report that High Potentials progress at faster rate than others
	Other companies do not know

*% of the 20 organizations surveyed

The tracking measures that the surveyed organizations use focus on:

- Promotion rates for high potentials
- Movement of high potentials to new assignments
- Performance of high potentials
- Time spent by high potentials in positions
- Attrition and churn rates of high potentials

These metrics are often compared to similar measures for a comparative group of managers—perhaps high performers. Frequently companies report the promotion rate of high potentials compared to other groups. This measure and the others listed above are not pure measures but are contaminated since the individuals making some of these decisions are almost always aware that the individual is a high potential. Some organizations report that their—high-potential list is dynamic and that individuals move on and off the list frequently. However, it does seem that being labeled a high potential may bring some expectations with it—often that the person has passed the hurdle and may be given the benefit of the doubt in the future. Organizations may take some risk when focusing on a select group of high potentials and giving them extensive and costly development experiences. The risk is voluntary attrition or turnover in this group when individuals become more ambitious and decide to move to another organization, usually to advance their career. For organizations that have had a high-potential program for awhile, it is common to have twice as many individuals in the high-potential group as the projected needs in order to accommodate this anticipated turnover. However, Dowell and Elder at Bristol-Myers Squibb (2002) found "no difference in turnover between a high potential group who received unusual and extensive development opportunities and a control group of high potentials who received normal development opportunities." A follow-up study by them confirmed the initial results, although the type of turnover varied between the groups.

One of the emerging trends in human resources is to follow up on talent decisions and measure later outcomes. Ideally we should be measuring the impact on business outcomes and objectives. Although the field has been advancing in recent years (see Chapter 12 by John C. Scott, Steven G. Rogelberg, and Brent W. Mattson), it continues to be difficult to measure the direct impact of HR systems and programs on business outcomes. Once we figure out how to accurately measure this impact, HR will gain significantly more influence in business corporations.

Conclusion

The science and art of predicting potential for future roles and responsibilities in an organization is complex and challenging. The organizations in this survey all have, or are developing, programs and approaches for identifying and assessing high potential talent. The summary conclusions from the survey (see Table 5.10) suggest that this is a Human Resources practice area that is in transition.

Organizations are giving greater time and resources to developing their high-potential processes. We anticipate that in the next five years, major advances will be made in accurately defining, identifying, assessing, and developing high-potential talent. The seeds for those innovations can be found throughout this book.

Table 5.10. General Conclusions

Based on Surveyed Organizations

General Conclusions

Organizations give a lot of attention to the identification, development, and retention of high-potential talent

The most widely used identification factors are:

- Leadership competencies
- Past performance
- Career aspiration

Other frequently considered factors are:

- Adaptability
- Commitment
- Specific experience
- Mobility
- Learning ability

- Most organizations use a mix of data for identifying high potentials. There is no single measure or *silver bullet* that captures all aspects of potential.
- Although using standardized assessment tools are better than using nothing, it might be more effective to use tools that reflect the organization's culture, values, and behaviors.
- The most common assessment tools are management ratings, 360-degree competency instruments, calibration discussions, and talent review discussions.
- High-potential turnover is typically 3 to 11% annually.
- Most organizations do not tell individuals their status as a high potential.
- High-potential individuals are given a wide range of development activities and work experiences.

Future Directions

The field of identifying and assessing high-potential talent in organizations is evolving. Based on our experience working inside and externally to business corporations, we believe several key issues in the area need to be addressed in the future in order to advance the field. Here are ten important issues:

■ ■ ■

1. *How can we build a more comprehensive model of high potential?* We need a broadly useful model that identifies the core components of potential and how they interact and goes beyond the existing variables and frameworks. The model should be applicable across people, cultures, and situations.

2. *What are more effective measures of high potential?* We need better measures and assessments of potential. Can we build assessment tools that are valid and still work across multiple organizations (perhaps with some customization)? We also need to do a better job of measuring even the existing potential factors such as learning ability and learning motivation. Should we focus more on behavioral observation measures than self-report measures? How do we find and collect the best data on high potentials?

3. *Is potential immutable or something that can be developed?* Some colleagues argue that potential is an innate, immutable characteristic in people. But is it really so unchangeable to the point that it cannot be developed or at least encouraged in people? Is it destiny, or can it be nurtured with focused attention? Should we focus on only the identification, and not the development, of potential? Are there both nature and nurture components of potential?

4. *How does the situation or context affect potential?* What factors in situations or experiences might influence the expression or the development of potential? Is potential a general construct that is portable across corporations, or is it situationally specific? Does "Potential for what?" ask the wrong question? Does the what (the outcome goal) really matter if we are discussing a general construct independent of situations and specific jobs? Or are there several different categories of potential, such as potential to be effective in a specific role (selection oriented) versus potential to be effective in a broad range of roles (a broader construct)? Is high potential a relative concept (depending on the company, situation, strategy, or time period), or is it truly an innate portable capability that can be effective across many different situations? What causes potential to diminish or flourish: a bad boss, a life crisis, a failure, a supportive family, a strong mentor, landing a challenging job?

5. *How does the person's motivations and career aspiration affect potential?* Are an individual's motivations and aspirations part of his potential or separate from it? As a person's motivation ebbs

and flows during a career, does her potential rise and fall at the same time? If motivation and aspiration affect potential (from either the inside or from the outside of the construct), wouldn't that suggest that the situational factors that affect motivation and aspiration also affect potential?

6. *Are there different maturity levels of potential?* Does potential look the same regardless of the career level of the person? Does it look different at different career stages? Would we expect potential to look different among recent college graduates, early career managers, and midcareer leaders? Are there maturity profiles for potential factors? How early in someone's career (or life) can we gauge potential? Do people advance in their potential at different rates? Do some people show more advanced levels of potential early, and are they seen as precocious or arrogant? What separates the exceptional potential from the merely good potential?

7. *What is the real impact of communicating high-potential status?* There has long been an unverified legend in organizations that telling people that they are seen as high potential leads to all sorts of negative consequences: such as entitled crown princes and turnover in those not selected. But we are not aware of any empirical research (beyond Dowell & Elder, 2002) that measures the consequences of telling or not telling people they are high potential. Are the effects real or just rumored?

8. *How can we improve the assessment and prediction skills in leaders?* Over the years, there has been good progress in teaching managers and leaders how to more effectively use performance evaluation rating scales and how to improve their coaching and feedback skills. Can we be equally effective in teaching them assessment skills and how to make accurate and insightful potential predictions and decisions about people? These are far more complex skills than the assessor skills in assessment centers. In assessment centers, assessors are given highly structured behavioral dimensions, definitions, and rating guides, usually tailored to specific, highly structured assessment exercises. And even then, after days of training, many managers do a poor assessment job. Yet now we often rely on a single untrained executive to make the final decision call on the potential of a person. How can we improve the reliability and validity of these predictions and decisions?

9. *What are the best outcome measures for potential?* What are we actually trying to predict? General success? Advancement level? What would be the criterion measure for potential in a predictive empirical study? How will we know if a person's potential ever pays off for the organization? Should we fall back on the more concrete outcomes, such as advancement and successful performance at two levels higher in the organization?

10. *How can potential be developed in others?* If we conclude that potential can be developed in people, then what are the most effective and efficient development approaches? Will certain experience-based approaches work best (on variables such as learning ability or fungibility), or are other approaches more effective? Is there a conflict between developing skills and abilities that are critical for a person's current job and developing the person's longer-term potential? Could they naturally interfere with each other in time constraints and development focus?

■ ■ ■

With the attention that organizations are giving to high-potential talent, we believe that others share our interests in exploring these issues and identifying effective solutions.

References

Albrecht, K. (2006). *Social intelligence: The new science of success.* San Francisco: Jossey-Bass.

Barnett, R. (2008). *Identifying high potential talent.* Minneapolis, MN: MDA Leadership Consulting.

Boudreau, J. W., & Ramstad, P. M. (2005, April). Where's your pivotal talent? *Harvard Business Review,* 23–24.

Bracken, D. W., Timmreck, C. W., & Church, A. H. (Eds.). (2001). *The handbook of multisource feedback.* San Francisco: Jossey-Bass.

Bray, D., Campbell, R., & Grant, D. (1974). *Formative years in business: A long term AT&T study of managerial lives.* Hoboken, NJ: Wiley.

Byham, W. C., Smith, A. B., & Paese, M. J. (2002). *Grow your own leaders: How to identify, develop, and retain leadership talent.* Upper Saddle River, NJ: Financial-Times Prentice Hall.

Corporate Leadership Council. (2005a). *Realizing the full potential of rising talent* (Vol. I). Washington, DC: Corporate Executive Board.

Corporate Leadership Council. (2005b). *Realizing the full potential of rising talent* (Vol. II). Washington, DC: Corporate Executive Board.

Dawes, R. (1988). *Rational choice in an uncertain world.* Orlando, FL: Harcourt.

Dowell, B. E., & Elder, E. D. (2002). *Accelerating the development of tomorrow's leaders.* Presentation at the annual conference of the Society of Industrial–Organizational Psychology, Toronto, Canada.

Executive Knowledgeworks. (1987). *The identification of development of high potential managers: A benchmarking report on the practices and trends in America's major and mid sized corporations.* Palatine, IL: Anthony J. Fresina & Associates.

Goleman, D. (2006). *Social intelligence: The new science of human relationships.* New York: Bantam Books.

Groysberg, B., Nanda, A., & Nohria, N. (2004, May). The risky business of hiring stars. *Harvard Business Review,* pp. 92–100.

Hewitt Associates. (2008). *Getting to high potential: How organizations define and calibrate their critical talent.* Lincolnshire, IL: Author.

Hollenbeck, G., McCall, M., & Silzer, R. (2006). Do competency models help or hinder leadership development? A debate. *Leadership Quarterly, 17,* 398–413.

Jeanneret, R., & Silzer, R. (Eds.). (1998). *Individual psychological assessment: Predicting behavior in organizational settings.* San Francisco: Jossey-Bass.

Lombardo, M., & Eichinger, R. (2000). High potentials as high learners. *Human Resource Management, 39*(4), 321–329.

McCall, M. (1994). Identifying leadership potential in future international executives: Developing a concept. *Consulting Psychology Journal, 46*(1), 49–63.

Meehl, P. E. (1954). *Clinical versus statistical predictions: A theoretical analysis and review of the evidence.* Minneapolis: University of Minnesota Press.

Michaels, E., Handfield-Jones, H., & Axelrod, B. (2001). *The war for talent.* Boston: Harvard Business School Press.

Murphy, K. (2008). Explaining the weak relationship between job performance and the rating of job performance. *Industrial and Organizational Psychology: Perspectives on Science and Practice, 1*(2), 1–35.

O'Connell, D. (1996). *High potential identification.* Boston: Executive Development Roundtable, Boston University School of Management.

Rogers, R. W., & Smith, A. B. (2007). *Finding future perfect leaders.* Bridgeville, PA: Development Dimensions International.

Ruderman, M. N., & Ohlott, P. J. (1990). *Traps and pitfalls in the judgment of executive potential.* Greensboro, NC: Center for Creative Leadership.

Schippmann, J. (1999). *A strategic job modeling: Working at the core of human resources.* Mahwah, NJ: Erlbaum.

Silzer, R. F. (1984). *Clinical and statistical prediction in a management assessment center.* Unpublished doctoral dissertation, University of Minnesota.

Silzer, R. F. (Ed.). (2002a). *The 21st century executive: Innovative practices for building leadership at the top.* San Francisco: Jossey-Bass.

Silzer, R. F. (2002b). Selecting leaders at the top: Exploring the complexity of executive fit. In R. Silzer (Ed.), *The 21st century executive: Innovative practices for building leadership at the top.* San Francisco: Jossey-Bass.

Silzer, R. F., & Church, A. H. (2009). The pearls and perils of identifying potential. *Industrial and Organizational Psychology: Perspectives on Science and Practice, 2*(4).

Silzer, R. F., & Davis, S. L. (2010). Assessing the potential of individuals: The prediction of future behavior. In J. C. Scott & D. Reynolds (Eds.), *The handbook of workplace assessment: Selecting and developing organizational talent.* San Francisco: Jossey-Bass.

Silzer, R. F., Slider, R. L., & Knight, M. (1994). *Human resource development: A benchmark study of corporate practices.* St. Louis, MO, and Atlanta, GA: Anheuser-Busch Corporation and Bell South Corporation.

Slan, R., & Hausdorf, P. (2004). *Leadership succession: High potential identification and development.* Toronto: University of Guelph and MICA Management Resources.

Smart, B. D. (1999). *Topgrading.* Upper Saddle River, NJ: Prentice Hall.

Spreitzer, M. S., McCall, M. W., & Mahoney, J. D. (1997). Early identification of international executive potential. *Journal of Applied Psychology, 82*(1), 6–29.

Thornton, G., & Byham, W. (1982). *Assessment centers and managerial performance.* Orlando, FL: Academic Press.

Tornow, W. W., & London, M. (1998). *Maximizing the value of 360-degree feedback: A process for successful individual and organizational development.* San Francisco: Jossey-Bass.

Tornow, W. W., & Tornow, C. P. (2001). Linking multisource feedback content with organizational needs. In D. W. Bracken, C. W. Timmreck, & A. H. Church (Eds.), *The handbook of multisource feedback.* San Francisco: Jossey-Bass.

Wellins, R. S., Smith, A. B., & McGee, L. (2006). *The CEO's guide to talent management: Building a global leadership pipeline.* Bridgeville, PA: Development Dimensions International.

Wells, S. J. (2003). Who's next: Creating a formal program for developing new leaders can pay huge dividends, but many firms aren't reaping those rewards. *HR Magazine, 48*(11), 44–64.

CHAPTER 6

Developing Leadership Talent

Delivering on the Promise of Structured Programs

Jay A. Conger

It has long been argued that most organizations suffer from a shortage of leadership talent. As a result, a broad range of formal initiatives has appeared over the past two decades to address this dilemma. That said, most managers believe they learn leadership best on the job (McCall, Lombardo, & Morrison, 1988) through work assignments. This belief is due in part to the haphazard and sporadic deployment of formal leadership development initiatives (Ready & Conger, 2003). Many organizations commit limited time and resources to formal leadership development initiatives. Training for managers may be only a few days a year. In some organizations, a single leadership development program may be offered once every several years. A one-time administration of a 360-degree feedback assessment may be the scope of a manager's formal developmental feedback. Opportunities for professional coaching are often limited. Multiple leadership frameworks may be present in the organization, sending a confusing message about what the appropriate leadership behaviors are. A new CEO may radically alter leadership development initiatives, undermining prior investments in development. For these and other reasons, formal approaches to leadership development may not have the impact that their designers and sponsors hope for.

However, when formal leadership education and development initiatives are deployed in a comprehensive manner with an eye toward a long-term commitment, they can play a critical role in deepening the bench of leadership talent (Conger & Fulmer, 2003). At a minimum, programs can heighten an individual's appreciation for leadership and in turn strengthen his resolve to develop certain leadership capabilities. In the ideal case, initiatives can facilitate the development of leadership skills that are trainable. Initiatives can facilitate a common and widespread understanding of the organization's vision and its culture, and clarify the leadership roles and responsibilities required to advance both. Programs can foster continuity among leaders by socializing new or up-and-coming leaders to an organization's values and culture. They can also help with critical leadership transitions by integrating training with job promotions and working to address derailing behaviors. They can help to build champions to lead critical strategic transitions.

Given their potential, this chapter explores how formal leadership education and development initiatives can best be deployed. It examines the range of approaches and their trade-offs, as well as the practices that enhance an initiative's effectiveness, and identifies common pitfalls facing programs.

Before we dive into the approaches and practices, it is helpful, however, to first explore the historical roots to today's approaches. This examination will frame the dynamism of leadership development approaches and how they are a reflection of the demands of the times and current notions or paradigms of leadership. It will also illustrate how much more sophisticated the approaches to leadership development have become.

Leadership Education and Development: A Historical Perspective

Looking back thirty or forty years ago, leadership development for front-line and middle-level leaders consisted largely of workshops offered by specialized training organizations or in-house training departments. Many of these were built around a simple leadership model, such as "Situational Leadership," developed by Paul Hershey and Kenneth Blanchard (1984). Guided by a diagnostic questionnaire, participants would learn that successful leadership involves tailoring one's style to the dynamics of a particular situation. For example, in certain situations, leaders needed to focus more on the task at hand. In other situations, they needed to be more people oriented. Training, in essence, was designed to help managers assess their situations and then apply the appropriate leadership behavior.

For the more senior levels of leadership, development typically consisted of attending a university-based program outside the corporation. Individual managers would attend these programs, which could range anywhere from one week to several months. The learning experience was largely teacher or professor centered, using off-the-shelf case studies, readings, and exercises as instructional vehicles. Participants learned about the latest theories and research by studying what other companies had done and listening to lectures on faculty research. The content was determined primarily by the faculty or training organization and was often more of a mini-M.B.A. than a pure focus on leadership.

Program Goals

During this time, leadership education had primarily a dual role. One was to help managers transition into upcoming roles by broadening their understanding of business disciplines (outside their functional silo) and understand the impact of their leadership style. The second was as a reward for "up and comers" for their strong performance. At the same time, there was limited customization of learning materials to either organizations or managers, and the leadership models they introduced were relatively simplistic. Executive coaching did exist, but it was primarily reserved for executives whose management styles were dysfunctional. Job assignments were considered the primary grooming grounds for leadership. Formal developmental feedback was provided in performance reviews by superiors. Peers and subordinates had few vehicles to provide direct feedback to an individual leader unless it was solicited by individual managers themselves.

Also popular during this time period was a more radical form of leadership education called sensitivity training, in the form of encounter groups or T-groups. While university training focused on conceptual or cognitive learning, sensitivity training targeted the manager's interpersonal behavior. In small groups at retreat centers, managers engaged in group dialogue under the supervision of facilitators. There was often no set agenda other than self and group discovery. Participants learned about themselves as they dealt with group members through the dialogues that emerged. They learned directly from experiencing and reflecting on the needs, attitudes, and interpersonal behaviors that participants demonstrated in the group setting. In contrast to university learning, this was a highly learner-centered experience and relied to a large degree on intense reflection of one's interpersonal style. These experiences were forerunners to the more structured and less emotionally demanding self-assessment tools and action learning experiences of the 1990s and beyond. The experiences also had parallels to the development of what we today call emotional intelligence (Goleman, 1996).

Critical Shifts

Leadership development began to change starting in the 1980s. Important shifts were induced as a result of intensifying global competition in the business world. This caused companies to search for educational experiences that would simultaneously build leadership capability as well as source and speed solutions to the organization's strategic challenges. Under these conditions, the idea of sending one or two managers to a university program to study cases written about other industries appeared to be a poor choice. The open enrollment character of university-based programs meant that course work and materials could not be tailored to a single company or industry. Interest therefore grew dramatically in highly customized, in-company programs.

Economics also played a role. As the drive for greater operating efficiencies encouraged corporate cost cutting, budgets for education and development received more scrutiny. There was strong pressure to show more immediate and tangible paybacks for investments in formal development programs. The economics of custom-built in-company programs quickly became more attractive. After all, bringing four university professors in to teach 50 managers was a significantly less-expensive proposition than sending 50 managers to open enrollment programs. Indeed the growth in customized programs was so strong that by the middle 1990s it was estimated that more than 75 percent of all executive education dollars was spent on these programs (Fulmer & Vicere, 1995).

Other benefits followed with customized programs. Topics and materials could be tailored to the company's needs. CEOs began to realize that programs could be deployed to reinforce company's cultures and to further their strategic agendas. By combining relevant learning, hands-on experience, and corporatewide commitment, top management could create a cadre of change agent leaders. A growing focus on using programs to drive change also helped to promote another leadership education trend—action learning—an approach popularized by General Electric in programs run at the corporate university in Crotonsville, New York. These programs placed managers in team-based experiential exercises aimed at solving real-life problems of immediate relevance to the company (Noel & Charan, 1988). For example, if a business unit was considering new markets in Malaysia, action learning teams would conduct market research on these emerging markets. Participants would test out ideas for business development, address implementation issues, and present recommendations for company initiatives. Action learning also incorporated another more general trend in leadership education, team-based learning, whose roots could be found in the earlier sensitivity training.

During this time, 360-degree feedback tools rose in popularity. As leadership concepts and education gained greater currency, it became clear that the followers (subordinates) of leaders should share their views on their leader's effectiveness. With the rise of the organizational matrix and greater cross-functional collaboration, it also became clear that peers would have useful views on the effectiveness of a manager's leadership style. The rise of 360-degree feedback assessments also encouraged greater use of competency models built specifically around leadership behaviors. Organizations soon had lists of the leadership behaviors they expected from their managers.

In conclusion, the role and scope of formal leadership development has changed dramatically over the past two decades.

Initiatives are now far more pervasive and less elitist. They are increasingly designed around understanding that leadership development is a continuous, lifelong process rather than a single training event. They deploy more interventions: action learning, coaching, education, feedback assessments, and formal mentoring (Fulmer & Conger, 2004). They are more ingrained in the actual doing of work and more integrated with organizational support systems such as performance management, rewards, and succession. They also involve far more stakeholders than the approaches of yesterday. The best initiatives strive to advance the strategic and cultural objectives of the organization while simultaneously developing a deep bench of leadership talent.

The following sections examine how the deployment of formal leadership initiatives has evolved from a more singular emphasis on individual development skill to more sophisticated approaches with broader impact. A typology of today's approaches is presented along with guidance on best practices and common implementation pitfalls.

A Typology of Formal Leadership Development Approaches

Formal leadership development initiatives can be organized into four general categories: (1) individual skill development, (2) socialization of the corporate vision and values, (3) strategic interventions that promote a major change throughout an organization, and (4) targeted action learning approaches to address organizational challenges and opportunities.

Historically the most popular of these four approaches has been individual skill development. This approach is focused on helping managers learn the essential concepts and skills of leadership. The second approach seeks to socialize the corporate vision, values, and mission of an organization throughout its leadership ranks. In recent years, this has become a far more widespread approach. Learning in this case involves the need for organizational leaders to embody and role model certain behaviors and values and to actively translate the corporate vision into local visions for their own units. The third approach, facilitating strategic change, is the least common of the three but potentially one with significant payoffs for the organization. These educational experiences focus on action learning, task forces, and facilitated group discussions to identify organizational initiatives that can facilitate and accelerate a major strategic change. The emphasis is on having participants take ownership for leading strategic change initiatives at their own level. The final approach, action learning, is a targeted one. It uses team-based projects that explore opportunities or dilemmas facing the organization as a development vehicle for mid- to senior-level leaders. We examine each of the four approaches in the discussions that follow (see Table 6.1).

Table 6.1. Design Success Factors by Approach

Individual Skill Development	Socializing Leadership Vision and Values	Strategic Leadership Initiatives	Action Learning Initiatives
• A single well-delineated leadership model • Precourse preparation assignments • Multiple learning methods • Multiple sessions to reinforce learning • Organizational support systems to reinforce and reward learning	• Careful selection of participants • Well-articulated organizational vision and philosophy in place • Practicing leaders provide instruction • Systems approach emphasizing integration and support for demonstration of leadership behaviors	• Clear strategic framework drives program content • Curricula designed to elicit group discussion between levels and units • Trained facilitators provide process assistance • Learning experiences cascade across multiple levels • Active participant feedback mechanisms	• Projects directly linked to business imperatives • Clearly defined project deliverables • Multiple opportunities for reflective learning • Active senior management involvement in projects and teaching • Expert facilitation and coaching for learning teams

Individual Skill Development Interventions

Leadership is first and foremost an individual capability, and leadership development is first and foremost an individual experience. Leadership experts like James Kouzes and Barry Posner (1987) argue that leadership development is very much about finding your own voice. It is therefore not surprising that leadership development has historically been concerned with advancing the individual's latent leadership talents (Conger, 1992). The objective of this approach has been to teach developing leaders the essential dimensions of leadership, have them reflect on their leadership capabilities, and in turn stimulate their desire to seek out developmental experiences. These individually oriented formal programs tend to be relatively short and employ a variety of development methods. They can provide one of the few windows for managers to objectively look at their own leadership style. Well-designed programs afford opportunities for detailed feedback from facilitators and others and give leaders a chance to reflect on their strengths and weaknesses. Studies have shown that these programs can encourage self-evaluation and insight (Schmitt, Ford, & Stults, 1986), factors that in turn can lead to improved individual performance.

A program developed for a manufacturing business provides an illustration of the design of a program focused on individual development. Two professors, experts in leadership, were hired to design and deliver the program. The leadership framework for the course was derived from research by the professors. It consisted of four dimensions: leadership vision, communications capabilities, role modeling behavior, and motivational and empowerment approaches. On the first day of the program, a 360-degree survey feedback assessment based on the four dimensions provided participants with benchmark data on their own capabilities related to each dimension. Case studies, practice sessions, and reflective exercises conveyed and taught the four dimensions in some depth. The emphasis was on the individual participant's learning and mastery of the leadership framework.

Best Practices for Individual Development Programs

The following best practice dimensions are important for success in the deployment of these types of programs.

1. Build the Program Around a Single Well-Delineated Leadership Model
Research confirms that a well-defined and simple model or framework of leadership improves participants' learning (Conger & Benjamin, 1999). In contrast, the use of multiple models increases the probability that participants will forget essential components or find themselves confused about the different frameworks. Multiple models make it more difficult to cover individual dimensions in depth. In other words, the number of different dimensions hinders a genuine and deep understanding of any one. This results in participants having difficulty gaining mastery over individual dimensions. In contrast, a single model provides a clear focus for both participants and designers, makes for tighter alignment of learning materials as well as assessment tools, and removes the probability of conflicting points of view.

The more effective models are typically built around a set of tangible leadership behaviors or competencies. Competencies, in turn, form the skill categories that participants learn in exercises and on which they receive personalized feedback. Later we will discuss the distinct advantages and disadvantages of competency-based programs.

2. Conduct Precourse Preparation
By sending exercises and materials in advance that encourage participants to reflect on their leadership precourse preparation can heighten an appreciation for the upcoming learning experience. It can also facilitate potential links between the daily challenges of participants and the development program that lies ahead. While an obvious point, it is of course critical that the course experiences link directly to the prework. Ideally the prework is a combination of reflective and workplace application exercises, as well as preparation for actual course experiences.

3. Use Multiple Learning Methods
Adult learning theory shows that individuals differ in their learning styles. Some learn best from experiential exercises, others from reflective methods, and others from traditional classroom methods. Multiple learning methods increase the likelihood that at least one method (if not several) will be compatible with an individual participant's style. Also, learning occurs at several levels. For instance,

it is useful to have a conceptual and cognitive understanding of the basic roles and activities of leadership. At the same time, there are behavioral skills that the learner can acquire through actual practice and experimentation. Personalized feedback is useful to target the learners' attention and awareness. Learning that taps into the psychological and emotional needs of individuals is also necessary to stimulate their interest in seeking out developmental experiences after a formal program.

4. Conduct Extended Learning Periods and Multiple Sessions

Research on the transfer of learning from training shows that information gleaned over distributed periods of training is generally retained longer than in a one-time formal program (Naylor & Briggs, 1963). As well, feedback-oriented programs that span multiple periods appear to move participants from awareness to an increased probability of effecting change in their behavior and perspectives (Young & Dixon, 1996).

The research that sheds the greatest light on why extended and multiple periods of learning are required for developing leadership comes from a growing body of research on how individuals become experts in different fields. Becoming an expert takes time. Ten years of preparation appears to be the norm, and often the period is longer (Ericsson, Krampe, & Tesch-Romer, 1993). During this extended time, a developmental experience must take place that includes deliberate, focused, and repeated practice (Ericsson & Charness, 1994). Practice ensures the acquisition of critical tacit knowledge. It must be learned through multiple and varied exposures to the area in which one is to become an expert. The literature on expertise makes an important distinction between exposure to knowledge and deliberate practice or application. Exposure does not suffice. Training built around a few days of practice is insufficient. It takes a longer-term orientation with multiple, focused sessions occurring over a period of years.

5. Put Organizational Support Systems in Place

One of the common dilemmas facing participants who return from formal programs is a lack of reinforcement for exhibiting the leadership behaviors taught in the program. To succeed organizations must align their performance management systems to incorporate the demonstration of leadership behavior. There must be extrinsic and intrinsic rewards for exhibiting leadership behavior.

The attitudes and styles of superiors are a critical factor in the transfer of learning. In fact, studies (Huczynski & Lewis, 1980) that examine the factors that facilitate or inhibit learning show that the participant's application of new learnings on the job is largely dependent on his or her superior's support. Through praise, incentives, coaching, feedback, and challenging assignments, the supervisor can reinforce the leadership behavior of subordinates. To further motivate learning, superiors can discuss program learnings and benefits both before and after the program, as well as set action goals for the individual around learning and implementing specific behaviors or actions. The superior's own role modeling can also influence a subordinate's behavior (Sims & Manz, 1982). In the ideal case, superiors would model behavior that is congruent with the development initiative's emphasis. Finally, supervisors can support new behaviors by providing rewards and opportunities to practice new skills. Work assignments following training experiences can reinforce and deepen learnings. Yet rarely is this connection made.

Dilemmas with Individual Skill Development Approaches
The individual development approach can be a relatively slow path to expanding the cadre of leaders in an organization. Skills-based programs may focus so much on personal development that they overlook opportunities to instill company philosophies or to tie leadership to new company strategies and their implementation. These are but a few of the common shortcomings of initiatives focused on individual development. Many of the most common design pitfalls are also problems for the other types of leadership development initiatives.

1. Failure to Build a Critical Mass
One of the principal drawbacks of individual development programs is that they are not always geared to cohorts of individuals from a single workplace; this is especially true for programs offered on the outside, such as at universities. When participants return, they may discover that their learnings are little appreciated or understood by others. The dilemma is tied to the fact that

work is a collaborative experience. As Brown and Duguid (1991) have shown, an individual's learnings are inseparable from the collective learning of her work group.

What gives new learnings and insights the potential for taking hold is that one's work group also endorses, promotes, and reinforces them. Without social support and group pressure, new ideas and behaviors may receive neither sufficient reinforcement nor rewards to survive for long. Moreover, an integral part of a workplace learning community is a shared language and a set of stories about what is valued (Brown & Duguid, 1991). If only a single individual or handful of individuals attend a program, there may not be a sufficient mass of participants to fully spread the learnings when they return to the workplace. Having no experience with the development lessons, coworkers will have little comprehension or appreciation for the knowledge and language that participants might share with them. As a result, the normally powerful influence of the workplace community is hindered from both spreading and reinforcing an individual's learnings.

2. Limits of Competency-Based Leadership Programs

While competency models are the foundation for most initiatives, at least three characteristics of competency-based programs pose dilemmas for leadership development. Their dimensions can be complicated, conceptual, and built around past or current realities (Conger & Ready, 2004). Because many of the frameworks are based on research on a wide range of managerial and leadership behaviors, they have a tendency to be complicated and contain many dimensions. For example, it is not uncommon for some competency frameworks to contain between 30 and 50 or more different behaviors. This creates a program with complicated content. Yet it is far from clear whether managers can focus developmentally on more than a few behaviors at a time. Certain coaching experts argue that managers can and should focus on only one to two behaviors at most (Goldsmith, 2003). Although programs built around multiple competencies may capture the complex reality of leadership, they dilute not only the attention they get but also an understanding of which competencies are priorities for the individual's current role or situation.

From a program design perspective, a large number of competencies may similarly lessen an appreciation for the real priorities. In a recent biography Louis Gerstner Jr. (2002), who was chairman and CEO of IBM from 1993 until 2002, describes his experience with the firm's use of a competency model to drive changes in leadership behavior within the company. IBM used a set of 11 competencies (customer insight, breakthrough thinking, drive to achieve, team leadership, straight talk, teamwork, decisiveness, building organizational capability, coaching, personal dedication, and passion for the business). Training and evaluation was designed to reinforce these behaviors with the aim of producing a new culture at IBM. Although Gerstner did witness changes in behavior and focus, he concluded there were simply too many competencies, and in the end, they were clustered into three categories: win, execute, and team. So although competencies played a role in developing a new generation of leaders at IBM, the model was simplified. That said, Gerstner did find that they created a common language, a sense of consistency, and a basis for performance management and rewards.

The second limitation is that competency-centric programs are based on an idealized concept of leadership—in other words, the concept of a universal best-in-class leader capable of functioning across all situations. Few managers, however, are outstanding examples of the full range of leadership behaviors that these models promote. As a result, they reinforce the notion that there is a "perfect" leader; however, such individuals rarely exist. Moreover, to ensure the advantage of consistency, organizations have moved toward universal competency models for their leadership development programs. Yet a "universal" model fails to recognize that leadership requirements vary by level and by situation. For example, leadership skills at the executive level are often significantly different from those at the midranks. Different functions and operating units may also demand different leadership capabilities given their unique requirements.

Most important, the underlying assumption behind the conceptualization of competency models of leadership is that an effective leader is the sum of a set of competencies (Hollenbeck & McCall, 2002). This does not reflect the reality of the manager's world (for a debate of this issue, see Hollenbeck, McCall,

& Silzer, 2006). The logic of these models follows that if we develop each competency to the point of mastery, one after the other, a manager will emerge as a successful leader. Morgan McCall and George Hollenbeck, two experts on leadership development, argue that there are myriad ways to accomplish a leader's job, especially at the executive level. "No two CEOs do the same things much less in the same ways, or have the same competencies. To define especially executive leadership around nine or ten universal behavioral dimensions over-simplifies a highly complex role. This conclusion is not only obvious on its face, it is evident when we observe outstanding leaders, whether military officers, heads of states, or CEOs—one cannot but be struck by the differences rather than the similarities in their makeup" (Hollenbeck & McCall, 2002).

At best, there is a loose coupling between the results a leader achieves, along with the means to those results and any specific set of behaviors and competencies. McCall and Hollenbeck argue that the focus of developmental needs must move away from behavioral models to strategic demands. Organizations need their senior leaders to define the strategy of the business and from there identify the leadership challenges implied by these objectives. Experiences could then be identified that provide sufficient preparation for managers to meet such strategic challenges. Succession management processes would begin by focusing on the essential question: what types of jobs, special assignments, bosses, and education are needed to build the leadership capability to successfully achieve the business strategy? These experiences would be identified and safeguarded by the senior team as essential to the succession management process.

The last concern is that competency-centric programs tend to be focused on past or current leadership behaviors. In other words, their frameworks are developed using today's high-performing leaders as benchmarks. Moreover, the models themselves tend to stabilize themselves in organizational systems; after all, they require extensive resource and psychological investments as performance and feedback systems are revised, managers are educated in the new models, and new expectations are set for the behavior that will be rewarded. Yet unfortunately, the competencies that helped current leaders succeed may not be appropriate for the next generation of leaders. Younger leaders may require different competencies for the challenges ahead, and yet they may be trained and rewarded for today's competencies.

3. Insufficient Time Spent on Developing Individual Skill Areas

One of the most common dilemmas facing individual leadership development initiatives is the lack of follow-up. When the program ends, there may be no additional experiences to reinforce learnings or ongoing programs of feedback to gauge their development efforts around specific leadership competencies. Many of the problems related to follow-up initiatives can be traced back to the issues of ownership, time, and rewards. For example, who claims responsibility for learning after a program is over? Who makes certain that learnings are extended throughout the organization?

Often the burden of ownership falls on either the program designers and leaders or on the participants. But in many cases, these groups do not control the needed resources or have the political clout necessary to make changes in the structures and systems of the organization. In addition, follow-up assignments are commonly done in one's spare time, beyond normal working hours. As a result, they rarely receive the time and dedication needed to succeed. Rewards may be limited or nonexistent for one's follow-up efforts. It is critical that organizations accept greater responsibility for postprogram activities. It means providing a method of monitoring participants' progress toward meeting certain prescribed development goals. One solution to the follow-up dilemma is to provide participants with formal coaching and mentoring. Another is to hold the boss accountable for the individual's development progress.

Socializing Leadership Vision and Values Interventions

One of the most important functions of senior leaders is defining the strategic parameters and cultural values that will guide the decisions of organizational members. Executive leaders instill these by building a shared understanding of what the organization is about and how it should operate. It is important that the next generation of leaders accurately understands and embodies the vision and values that they are expected to perpetuate. Recognizing this, more leadership development initiatives focus on socializing crucial strategic and cultural elements. They do so with two broad objectives in mind: to indoctrinate leaders to the company's core vision and the cultural values and to facilitate career transitions by involving leaders in a dialogue about their upcoming roles and responsibilities. These initiatives try to build a shared interpretation of the organization's key strategic objectives and a commitment to the values and assumptions that underlie its culture. Consequently they focus less on developing individual skills and talents and more on imparting a collective culture and a leadership philosophy that are acted on as much as they are acknowledged.

The U.S. Army's approach to leadership development exemplifies this particular model. For example, the U.S. Army strongly emphasizes its leadership culture in almost every program and operational assignment that officers take part in. More important than its formal doctrine and programs, the informal mentoring and role modeling by army officers, along with on-the-job training experiences, instill the leadership in the culture and daily activities of army life. Through an extensive socialization process, officers learn and internalize the army's leadership creed through years of direct interaction with more experienced leaders. Through this integrated approach of formal classroom instruction, on-the-job training, informal mentoring, role modeling, and self-development, the army leadership development system clarifies and reinforces the army's vision and leadership values, along with the duties and expectations associated with carrying them out at each level of management.

Certain design features enhance the effectiveness of such initiatives designed for socialization of an organization's leaders.

Best Practice Features of the Socialization Process

The following are descriptions of the best-practice features and their contribution to the socialization process.

1. Careful Selection of Program Participants

Leadership programs aimed at socialization must pay particular attention to the selection of participants. These programs ideally seek to provide leadership development primarily to individuals who have demonstrated significant leadership potential through their past performance and who embody the values and styles consistent with the existing leadership culture. As we will later see, there are other approaches that try to move the general population of leaders—not just those currently on the right path. Selectivity increases the probability that participants will hold values similar to the stated values of the corporation. Such consistency serves to strengthen communication and inquiry both within the learning environment and later, when the participant returns to the job. Second, selecting only individuals who consistently demonstrate certain traits and values confirms that such characteristics are important to the organization and will be rewarded. This encourages others to develop similar capabilities.

2. Ensure a Well-Articulated Organization Vision and Philosophy

While this point seems obvious, I have seen organizations fail on this dimension of design effectiveness. Programs cannot effectively socialize a corporate vision and philosophy if the organization itself is conflicted about its own vision and values or if they are in flux or in question. It is therefore crucial that the organization possesses a vision and value set that are reasonably well articulated and well lived by leaders.

3. Practicing Leaders Provide Instruction

While a well-known leadership expert can provide insight into the latest theories on leadership, outside experts typically have less to say about the strategies and practices that work well for one's own firm. Moreover, outsiders are likely to have superficial knowledge about the firm's culture and history.

Using organizational leaders as instructors facilitates the socialization of junior leaders in a number of ways. First, by providing interaction with leaders who embody the company's values and live its philosophy, the company offers living role models of the ideology it hopes to perpetuate through successive generations. Second, using practicing leaders ensures that learning remains grounded in the reality of the workplace and culture. Leaders directly convey their beliefs, experience, and expectations to program participants, thereby facilitating the transmission of cultural knowledge. Finally, a system of leaders teaching leaders creates a two-way exchange of information and learning. By increasing interaction between new and existing leaders, leadership development programs can improve the probability that new information and insight will be properly integrated within the firm's culture.

4. A Systems Approach Emphasizing Integration and Support

To be truly successful, socialization of leadership capabilities depends on continual, progressive, and sequential development. A single program cannot be sufficient. In addition, organizational leaders must be unified in their understanding of the corporate vision and the values considered important in achieving the vision. Organizational systems need to be properly aligned to send consistent messages about what is valued and what is not. Consistent work processes, performance metrics, succession systems, promotions, and reward systems must maximize the probability that the values and assumptions instilled during the development program will be reinforced and supported once leaders return to the job.

Problems and Pitfalls Facing Socialization Initiatives

Socialization programs hold the promise of embedding a company's vision and values deep into its cadre of leaders, but they are difficult to implement and require a long-term commitment from senior executives. They can also be expensive, as they are often supported by an in-house educational center such as GE's Crotonville and FedEx's Leadership Institute. Below are descriptions of common problems facing these types of programs.

1. Hidden Challenge in Using Company Leaders as Teachers

It would be a mistake to assume that company leaders do indeed make the best instructors or that their use is not without special challenges. Several important dilemmas must be addressed with executive instructors. They need to be world-class leaders with icon status within the organization. In contrast when executives who are poor role models are used for instruction in programs they often generate cynicism among program participants and undermine the credibility of the program itself. In addition to problems associated with poor role models, there is the risk that company insiders will reinforce organizational paradigms and worldviews. If the external environment is changing rapidly and moving away from the organization's paradigm, this reinforcement from senior leaders can inhibit the organization's ability to adapt. One approach is to choose iconoclastic leaders with a track record of being at the front of important trends. Executive instructors and their message should also not be the driving factor behind a program design. Rather, the internal and external leadership needs of the organization should be the primary design drivers.

Preparation of the executive, their materials, and instruction formats all need careful attention. The program designer must be prepared to coach the executive on certain common problems. For example, the executive often feels a burden to carry the full weight of the program on his or her shoulders. Part of the designer's task is to convince the executive instructor that effective learning best occurs when the participants are involved. Also, executive instructors must learn to allow participants to reach their own conclusions rather than to simply feed them information and points of view. Program designers need to sit in during program sessions and provide executive instructors with feedback on their teaching style, participant reactions to content, how discussions are progressing, and session timing.

2. Participant Selection Criteria Are Poorly Defined or Enforced

Participants for these types of programs are selected for their ability to demonstrate leadership behaviors and embody the organization's values. In reality, selection criteria are often poorly defined or poorly enforced. Maintaining a focused selection process means that those responsible for nominating and selecting participants must clearly understand and support the selection criteria and the rationale behind them. They must be able to apply these criteria reliably and concretely when making judgments about potential candidates.

Selection often becomes muddied as programs begin to develop a reputation. People watch to see who attends programs and what opportunities present themselves to graduates. Once a program is perceived as a critical marker that participants are on a fast track, managers can begin to plot how to get themselves into programs. At the other end of the spectrum, programs may be viewed as a fad or simply a waste of time. In this case, managers work hard to exempt themselves from nominations to a program. Who is chosen to nominate can also pose a challenge. For example, senior executives may be the nominators, but they may have limited information on those they nominate, especially if candidates are several levels below them. Similarly, programs that focus on new directions may involve senior-level nominators who themselves are not necessarily advocates of the new direction.

3. Corporate Ownership Supersedes Division Ownership

Most socialization programs are "owned" by the corporate center, and there are clear advantages to corporate ownership of leadership development. For example, in tough times, corporate centers are often immune to cost cutting. It is not uncommon for the corporate center to be the principal guardian of an organization's vision. Finally, support from the very top powerfully reinforces what is valued in an organization. But there are trade-offs to program ownership centralized at the corporate level. For one, programs owned by a division can more effectively tailor their learning content around specific market and organizational issues facing the operating division, especially if action learning is used. With program ownership at the division level, competency models can also be tailored to the specific leadership demands facing that part of the organization. For these reasons, there should be some degree of divisional ownership.

4. Organizational Downturns or Serious Challenges Undermine Programs

It is not unusual in a business downturn for leadership development budgets to be among the first to be cut. As a result, the socialization initiative usually dies out. Most important, a symbolic message is sent throughout the organization that the values and leadership behaviors were perhaps not as essential as employees were led to believe. Crises can produce events that undermine the very behaviors and values that organizations are socializing.

Strategic Leadership Development Initiatives

Leaders today face a marketplace characterized by change and great complexity. There are strong indications that learning how to lead the direction, intensity, and speed of strategic and organizational change will be the key driver of corporate success in the years ahead. Moreover, this learning will be required not only of the organization's most senior leaders but of leaders at all levels. No longer will executives be able to rely on simply top-down command-and-control tactics. A more collaborative form of leadership is required.

As a result, some organizations are deploying leadership development initiatives to address strategic shifts and the leadership capabilities required for their successful implementation. This approach is more customized and tightly integrated to the organization's strategic agenda. These programs facilitate efforts to communicate and implement the corporate strategy, to build strategic unity throughout the organization, and to create a cadre of change agents. In other words, they simultaneously build leadership capabilities while facilitating progress toward key strategic objectives.

An illustrative example is an initiative deployed by a European technology company for the radical repositioning of its strategy to close performance gaps with its competition. The company wanted to engage approximately a quarter of a million employees spread across 52 countries. The leadership initiative was built around three components. First was an effort to translate the new corporate vision into local goals and programs. Some 30,000 leaders representing the top four levels of the company were brought together in groups of 30 to 70 for a three-day program. These leadership team meetings translated the company's new strategic vision of the change process into actions and goals for the business units and product divisions. In the second component, twenty-two task forces examined important aspects of the company's strategy, marketing, research, products, and management skills. This initiative identified and addressed issues that were the key drivers for the future strategy. Each task force was headed up by a champion who had a track record of performance in the area being examined. This component reached some 200,000 employees using up to 400 town meetings at each plant to discuss the implications of the strategic change for individual work situations. The third component consisted of two separate days of interactive satellite discussions for the entire European workforce.

The first session was held soon after the start of the overall initiative, and the second session occurred 18 months later. These sessions focused on how the company could become more customer focused and quality driven. As this example illustrates, these types of strategic initiatives are ambitious and often involve the entire organization.

To the extent that an organization's senior leaders have a clearly defined change agenda and the accompanying change leadership requirements, these programs can be extremely effective mechanisms for rapidly building a shared sense of the new strategic vision and a cadre of change agents. Certain design elements, however, are critical for success.

Critical Design Elements

1. A Clear Strategic Framework Driving Program Content

The foundational feature of these programs is a clearly articulated strategic framework that guides the organization's collective efforts. If the new strategy is vague or clouded by competing initiatives, the development effort will simply surface underlying conflicts, create frustration, and ultimately increase opposition to the change effort. In short, these programs should be undertaken only when there is a consensus around the strategic agenda or vision.

2. Curricula Designed to Elicit Group Discussions Between Units and Across Levels

These initiatives are highly dependent on individuals coming together, sharing experiences, and jointly constructing a common interpretation of the information and events around them. Group discussions across functions and levels are critical for developing a common understanding of a firm's larger strategic vision and, in turn, a shared interpretation of how that vision can be adapted at the local level. Because strategic implementation efforts require a complicated transition from abstract ideas to clearly defined directives and goals, facilitated group discussions are essential for determining how an organization's strategy can unfold to become an effective course of action. The best programs therefore include multiple sessions built around discussions that generate support for the new strategy and its leadership requirements but also effectively translate the over-arching strategy into tangible local initiatives.

3. Trained Facilitators Provide Critical Process Assistance

Given that much of what occurs in these initiatives is through discussion, well-designed programs employ trained facilitators. With discussions centered on issues that are complex and charged, facilitators keep the participants focused and constructive in their conclusions. They are also instrumental in organizing and codifying group discussions and keeping groups from getting distracted by tangential issues. The facilitators ideally not only enhance group process but challenge and push participants to think in different ways. In particular, outside facilitators can challenge status quo thinking and implicit assumptions when participants may be unable or uncomfortable to do so. Moreover, facilitators can model for the participants effective team facilitation skills. Finally, they can serve as nonthreatening providers of information across the organization. They can bridge gaps in information and disseminate information more broadly through their sessions with participants.

4. Learning Experiences Cascade Across Multiple Levels

A multilevel approach is necessary and ensures that all levels of the organization have a consistent understanding of the organization's strategic direction, the leadership demands in light of that direction, and the implementation steps essential to moving the organization forward. This is called cascading initiatives. In other words, there are similar initiatives running at each level of the organization's hierarchy, often in tandem. They use the same methodology but are seeking outcomes specifically tailored to each level. In the best cases, these initiatives overlap levels so that senior and middle-level leaders are interacting with one another in the same program. Cascading initiatives powerfully help to translate what a particular vision or change initiative means to leaders at each level. Research (Finkelstein & Hambrick, 1996) shows that senior leaders are generally too far removed from day-to-day operations to determine the best ways to implement the vision in every unit, function, and situation. By cascading an initiative down into the organization, frontline leaders can determine the most appropriate local structures, strategies, and tactics for their level and in turn feel a greater sense of ownership. Cascading can also ensure better integration across levels when senior leaders actively participate in conveying their own understandings to those below them. Finally, by discussing the vision, encouraging comments, answering questions, and incorporating feedback, senior leaders demonstrate their commitment to the change agenda and to model for others the types of behavior necessary for interactions with the next level.

5. Active Feedback Mechanisms

It is critical to be able to monitor the reactions of program participants to implementation challenges and to track the progress of initiatives in meeting objectives and time lines. Active feedback approaches can take a variety of forms, including direct interaction, follow-up interviews, and surveys. Methods that allow a greater flow of information and ideas are the best. Regardless of its form, it is critical to gather feedback from a representative sample of participants across the organization. This ensures that the information gathered provides an accurate picture of how the program is being received and adapted. Technology can play an important role in this feedback process with online discussions and intranet forums and surveys.

Pitfalls and Problems Facing Strategic Intervention Initiatives

These types of initiatives tend to be extremely complicated and demanding. The greatest risk is that they will be seen as a discrete event or set of events rather than as part of an ongoing change process. They also raise expectations. Employees leave with a sense of momentum that places a burden on the program sponsors and designers to maintain its energy and focus. Following are additional pitfalls common to strategic leadership initiatives.

1. Poor Modeling by Corporate Leaders

Given the overriding emphasis on the strategic direction of the organization, these programs tend to raise expectations about the organization's senior leaders. They raise expectations that senior leaders will model the very behaviors that the program aims to instill in others. In addition, immediately following each stage of the initiative, employees will watch to see what initiatives emerge from the executive suite as tests of the senior team's commitment to the overall initiative. Modeling by top leaders becomes critical. In one organization, the CEO emphasized his commitment to two-way communications at the start of a strategic leadership initiative. The program itself contained exercises illustrating how best to implement two-way communications. The CEO himself, however, failed to change his own behavior. As managers down the line continued to experience top-down, one-way communications, they discounted the initiative and in turn reinforced the old behaviors.

2. Entrenched Managers and the Legacy of Past Relations Limit Program Impact

Any change effort has supporters of and resisters to the change. Because strategic intervention designs rely on local managers and their work groups, resisting managers can block the impact of learning initiatives in their units and create intractable problems for an intervention initiative. For example, they may have a history of past relationships that prevent the interaction and dialogue needed to effect learning and change. In one company, supervisors in one unit boycotted a kickoff event and follow-up sessions. Their subordinates concluded that their own efforts to participate and develop a local vision would be futile. It is therefore critical to both identify and engage managers who are likely to resist the initiative.

3. Competing Initiatives Detract from Sponsor Support

The initial momentum created by these strategic initiatives may begin to wane as time passes. Senior leaders may turn their attention elsewhere even if they consider the program important. As the firm's top leaders become less directly involved, momentum behind the program can begin to stall. It is critical that senior leaders continually communicate their commitment and demonstrate it in follow-up initiatives. Otherwise employees will see it as a one-time event or fad.

4. Lack of Consistent Reinforcement

For a number of reasons, many of these strategic development initiatives lack systematic follow-up and reinforcement. Program sponsors may be promoted or transferred or leave the organization. The daily challenges and time demands of a major change effort, added to a person's regular work, can make individuals less supportive of subsequent events that require additional time and energy. The natural rhythms of the business cycle, as well as unexpected events such as mergers or market downturns, may divert attention to more immediate pressures. Finally, top management naiveté about the need for follow-up can lead to a lack of reinforcement. The best programs succeed because they ensure systemic change across a number of important support systems. Incentive systems, job assignments, performance measures, reporting relations, training, and organizational structures all may need to be realigned to support the larger change initiative.

5. Limitations of Facilitators

Despite their advantages, facilitators are often in a precarious position. If they challenge too strenuously, they may jeopardize their own employment. They are also asked to help address issues yet are given few resources or formal power. Many facilitators are not strategy consultants and are generally limited in their ability to help teams develop more of a strategic mindset.

Action Learning Leadership Development Initiatives

Action learning describes developmental approaches where participants learn by working on issues from their own organization. These formats involve a continuous process of learning and reflection built around working groups of colleagues. Most therefore emphasize learning by doing, are conducted in teams, address actual organizational challenges or opportunities, place participants in a problem-solving mode, and require that teams formally present their decisions. For example, a typical action learning project might have participants conduct a team-based investigation of new markets for the organization's products or services.

The stages of an action learning experience are fairly standardized (Dotlich & Noel, 1998). Typically, after receiving project assignments and background materials, learning teams travel to locations where the issues or information reside and conduct other forms of field research. The participants have access to key managers involved in the issue. As their findings and recommendations progress, they are reviewed by consultants or advisors who identify gaps in the analysis and assist in mapping out concrete and viable recommendations. The conclusion of this effort results in presentations, often to the senior leaders of the business unit involved and sometimes to the organization's executives. From the standpoint of leadership development, the projects are used to ensure that up-and-coming leaders are exposed to the next generation of emerging issues and challenges facing the organization that require a broad enterprise perspective.

Critical Design Features

Five design features are essential: (1) careful selection of projects, (2) clearly defined project outcomes, (3) multiple opportunities for reflection, (4) active involvement by senior management, and (5) expert facilitation, coaching, and consultation.

1. Careful Project Selection

A thorough and rigorous approach to selecting projects is an imperative. Projects must have a direct link to a business imperative. The most valued experiences are those where teams are given responsibility for initiating a significant organizational change or a new venture. It is also important to ensure that projects are structured for success. In the ideal case, projects would be chosen so that individual leadership development can be addressed simultaneously while tackling the business imperative. Finally, in selecting projects, there must be a clear project sponsor who is highly motivated to take a team approach on the issue. There needs to be a high probability that this individual will act on the recommendations of the team.

2. Clearly Defined Project Outcomes

On the dimension of clearly defined outcomes, it is best to ensure that the sponsors are very clear at the front end about their outcome expectations for a successful project. Problems around outcomes often arise when there are joint sponsors because each party may communicate different expectations. There can also be too many objectives or else the objectives are hidden or in dispute among sponsors.

3. Multiple Opportunities for Reflection

From the vantage point of participant learning, it is important that program designers incorporate multiple opportunities for reflective learning. Coaches, facilitators, company leaders, and teammates are all sources of useful feedback in action learning experiences. Feedback and reflection should be focused on as many different levels of learning as possible, from lessons about the issue being explored to team processes to individual reactions and styles. Reflections should also be staged at regular intervals rather than just at the end of the program.

4. Active Involvement by Senior Management

The importance of active senior management direction, support, and feedback cannot be overemphasized. Participants often expect some form of special recognition for their investment of time and energy in their projects, and visible recognition by executives is one powerful form of recognition. Senior management participation signals the importance of the programs, rewards participants, and conveys to the larger organization that such programs are valued.

5. Expert Facilitation and Coaching

Since a significant portion of the learning experience occurs in team-based discussions, facilitators and coaches play a vital role. Participants often find themselves bombarded by information. Facilitators help them process and structure information. They can also help the group more effectively use frameworks and concepts that coursework may introduce and reflect on the process.

Pitfalls Facing Action Learning Programs

The pitfalls that action learning programs face are numerous, from "make-work" projects that have little or no real meaning to a lack of follow-up on a team's recommendations. The business units providing the projects must be committed to taking some form of action, which ranges from providing access to critical information and resources to get the project accomplished, to the actual implementation of recommendations. A lack of either can completely undermine the meaningfulness of the initiative.

Dysfunctional team dynamics are another common pitfall. Teams that do not develop strong norms of candor and include a diversity of perspectives typically produce inferior outcomes. Teams where one individual or function dominates tend to produce far less insightful and innovative recommendations.

Finally, a failure to include follow-up learning is a common fault of many programs. Often when the action learning project ends, it is assumed that the learning ends, quite literally. There is an assumption that the learning has fully taken place. Yet nothing could be further from the truth. Participants need to learn what actually happens to their recommendations. Which ones are implemented, and why? Which ones are not implemented, and why? What were common implementation challenges with the various recommendations, and how did the recommendations need to be adapted to be useful?

Conclusion

If we return to the earlier notion that leadership is another form of expertise, we can begin to appreciate the long gestation period required to successfully develop leaders. The formal developmental approaches described in this chapter are only some of the complex and rich ways in which leaders are developed. Supplementing them are the organization's succession processes, performance management and reward systems, culture and core values, and the behaviors and actions of the senior team (Ready & Conger, 2007). These all profoundly influence leadership development. As a result, we cannot think of leadership as the product of an event or a particular program but rather as a deep commitment embodied in ongoing actions, systems, and values of the organization.

While our knowledge of leadership development has advanced greatly in the past decade and a half, we still have much to learn. Research is needed that explores how robust the program design and derailment factors identified in this chapter are in terms of truly influencing positive or negative outcomes. There are also likely to be numerous other design elements that have been overlooked. Future research is needed to rigorously tease apart as many contributing factors to successful leadership development as possible and provide a deeper sense of the impact of individual dimensions.

In addition, we need to examine far more carefully the role of follow-up interventions. These include after-program initiatives such as 360-degree feedback or coaching or boss-subordinate activities. Participants, their bosses, and their organizations often lose their attention to development soon after a program ends. This is a great tragedy since we know that development is an ongoing process. It never ends when a program ends. We must identify new and more enduring means for after-program development.

References

Brown, J. S., & Duguid, P. (1991). Organizational learning and communities-of-practice: Towards a unified view of working, learning, and innovation. *Organizational Science, 2*(1), 40–57.

Conger, J. A. (1992). *Learning to lead.* San Francisco: Jossey-Bass.

Conger, J. A., & Benjamin, B. (1999). *Building leaders: How successful companies develop the next generation.* San Francisco: Jossey-Bass.

Conger, J. A., & Fulmer, R. (2003). Developing your leadership pipeline. *Harvard Business Review, 81*(12), 76–84.

Conger, J. A., & Ready, D. A. (2004). Rethinking leadership competencies. *Leader to Leader, 32,* 41–47.

Dotlich, D. L., & Noel, J. L. (1998). *Action learning.* San Francisco: Jossey-Bass.

Ericsson, K. A., & Charness, N. (1994). Expert performance. *American Psychologist, 49*(8), 725–747.

Ericsson, K. A., Krampe, R. T., & Tesch-Romer, C. (1993). The role of deliberate practices in the acquisition of expert performance. *Psychological Review, 100*(3), 363–406.

Finkelstein, S., & Hambrick, D. C. (1996). *Strategic leadership.* St. Paul, MN: West Publishing.

Fulmer, R. M., & Conger, J. A. (2004). *Growing your company's leaders: How organizations use succession management to sustain competitive advantage.* New York: AMACOM.

Fulmer, R. M., & Vicere, A. A. (1995) *Executive education and leadership development: The state of the practice.* University Park: Penn State Institute for the Study of Organizational Effectiveness.

Gerstner, L. (2002). *Who says elephants cannot dance.* New York: HarperCollins.

Goldsmith, M. (2003). Helping successful people get even better. *Business Strategy Review, 14*(1), 9–16.

Goleman, D. (1996). *Emotional intelligence: Why it can matter more than IQ.* New York: Bantam Books.

Hershey, P., & Blanchard, K. H. (1984). *The management of organizational behavior.* Upper Saddle River, NJ: Prentice Hall.

Hollenbeck, G., & McCall, M. W. (2002). *Competence, not competences: Making global executive development work.* Working paper, Center for Effective Organizations, University of Southern California.

Hollenbeck, G., McCall, M. W., & Silzer, R. F. (2006). Leadership competency models. *Leadership Quarterly, 17,* 398–413.

Huczynski, A. A., & Lewis, J. W. (1980). An empirical study into the learning transfer process in management training. *Journal of Management Studies, 17*(2), 227–240.

Kouzes, J. M., & Posner, B. Z. (1987). *The leadership challenge.* San Francisco: Jossey-Bass.

McCall, M., Lombardo, M., & Morrison, A. (1988). *The lessons of experience: How successful executives develop on the job.* Lanham, MD: Lexington Books.

Naylor, J. C., & Briggs, G. E. (1963). The effect of task complexity and task organization on the relative efficiency of part and whole training methods. *Journal of Experimental Psychology, 65,* 217–224.

Noel, J. L., & Charan, R. (1988). Leadership development at GE's Crotonville. *Human Resource Management, 27,* 433–447.

Ready, D., & Conger, J. A. (2003). Why leadership development efforts fail. *Sloan Management Review, 44,* 83–88.

Ready, D., & Conger, J. A. (2007). Make your company a talent factory. *Harvard Business Review, 85*(6), 68–77.

Schmitt, N., Ford, J. K., & Stults, D. M. (1986). Changes in self-perceived ability as a function of performance in an assessment center. *Journal of Occupational Psychology, 59,* 327–335.

Sims, H. P., & Manz, C. C. (1982, January). Modeling influences on employee behavior. *Personnel Journal,* 45–51.

Young, D., & Dixon, N. (1996). *Helping leaders take effective action.* Greensboro, NC: Center for Creative Leadership.

CHAPTER 7

DEVELOPING LEADERSHIP TALENT THROUGH EXPERIENCES

Paul R. Yost, Mary Mannion Plunkett

It has been known for nearly two decades that experience plays a critical role in the development of leaders (McCall, Lombardo, & Morrison, 1988; Quinones, Ford, & Teachout, 1995; Robinson & Wick, 1992; Wick, 1989). And while most organizations acknowledge that on-the-job experiences play a critical role in developing talent, they continue to rely heavily on classroom training programs to develop the next generation of leaders and employees in the company. The American Society for Training and Development reported in 2006 that organizations spent over $109 billion the previous year on workplace learning and performance programs (Ketter, 2006). The past several years have seen significant gains in our understanding of how to make traditional training programs more effective (Salas & Cannon-Bowers, 2001). However, we have failed to make advances at the same speed in our empirical understanding of on-the-job development and our ability to systematically leverage it to improve performance.

When organizations do build experiences into development programs, the efforts tend to be piecemeal and tactical. For example, some organizations simply encourage employees to include on-the-job activities in their development plans. Other organizations might introduce job rotational programs for their high-potential leaders or use accelerator job assignments for leaders—those that are rich developmental experiences designed to speed up a leader's growth in targeted areas, such as leading one of the organization's strategic business initiatives. Although these programs are useful, they seldom achieve the potential that could be attained with a rigorous, comprehensive approach that systematically builds experiences into the very heart of the organizational talent management system. Given the important role that work experience plays in development, it should be a major component of any talent management system. In fact, we suggest that experiences can serve as one of the primary integrating mechanisms for human resource (HR) systems.

In this chapter, we focus on the development of leadership talent to simplify the discussion and because of the rich body of research on the topic. However, all of the principles discussed could be expanded to promote the development of all employees in the organization. (See Chapter 16 by Paul R. Yost for a discussion of talent management at Microsoft.) Our discussion is organized into four sections:

- Why experiences are so important
- How to build a talent management taxonomy that leverages experience
- How to embed experiences into talent management systems
- Future directions for research and practice

Why Experiences Are So Important

The strategies that organizations use to leverage experiences fall along a continuum, from doing nothing to the strategic use of job experiences. At the lowest end are organizations that do little or nothing to take advantage of on-the-job development opportunities. Morgan McCall (1998, p. 1) relates the story of an executive who lamented, "We don't do much to develop our people." However, he notes that the executive was wrong. Leaders were being developed all of the time through experiences and selection decisions, from watching good and bad role models, from making mistakes, and from dealing with work challenges. McCall suggests a more relevant question is, "Were these the types of leaders that the company wanted to develop?"

A slightly more sophisticated approach is to rely on a survival-of-the-fittest strategy by putting leaders in stretch positions and then promoting the ones who succeed. A problem with this approach is that leaders with high potential may be lost along the way because they were not placed in the right challenges to develop their strengths or improve in significant areas where they are weak. Other leaders can be lost because they find themselves in situations where they do not have the organizational support to be successful. For those who do survive, the lessons they learn are likely to be haphazard and not focused on their development needs. Other leaders may be so concerned about just surviving the experience that they fail to learn key lessons or they take away the wrong lessons. For example, a leader who is repeatedly put in turnaround situations may learn how to be tough and autocratic but may not learn how to be flexible or appropriately adapt his leadership style to situations. This leader may then generalize the tough and autocratic behaviors to situations where other management styles are needed, such as driving corporate initiatives that require the leader to influence other groups without any official authority.

Other ways to more fully leverage experience include the use of experience-based training programs, action learning projects, job rotations, and strategic job assignments. As noted in Chapter 6 by Jay Conger in this book, classroom-based leadership development programs today are more likely to explicitly link the program content to business strategy and are often tied more directly to leaders' ongoing work responsibilities. Action learning leadership development initiatives (Dotlich & Noel, 1998; Marquardt, 2004) focus even more explicitly on learning through experience by requiring participants to address actual strategic business challenges in the organization. Expanding on this model, job rotations (Campion, Cheraskin, & Stevens, 1994; Ortega, 2001) could be considered a series of extended action learning experiences, where participants are systematically engaged in short-term work assignments across a wide range of jobs. When taken to its logical extreme, this approach becomes a series of logically ordered job assignments where high-potential leaders are systematically given increasing challenges in different strategic or operational areas of the business to develop the expertise, capabilities, and perspective needed to perform effectively in future leadership roles.

Now imagine an organization at the highest end of this continuum: a company that relies only on the strategic use of job experiences to develop organizational talent. This is what some have called a shift from a training to a learning orientation (Poell, van Dam, & van den Berg, 2004). What would have to be put in place in the organization to make this work?

To begin, we propose that there would need to be a framework or taxonomy in the organization that identifies the experiences, competencies, relationships, and learning capabilities that people will need as they move through job assignments in the organization. Table 7.1 provides an example of a leadership taxonomy built on these four dimensions. As noted later, the elements contained in each of these dimensions will vary by organization. For example, in the experiences column, an information technology company might value technical experience or managing a technical group as one of the key experiences. In contrast,

Table 7.1. Sample Talent Management Taxonomy for Leaders

Experiences	Competencies	Key Relationships	Learning Capabilities
Start-up business	Strategic thinking	Senior executives	Intellectual horsepower
Sustaining business	Building organizations	Key customers	
		Key suppliers	Openness to experience
Turnaround business	Integrity	Board of directors	
	Business acumen		Integrity
Corporate staff role	Technical expertise	Government relations	Comfort with ambiguity
Sales and marketing role	Judgment and decision making	Union relations	Openness to feedback
		Community relations	
Global experience	Drive for results		
		Mentor/ champion	

an aerospace company might emphasize the value of having experiences on the commercial aircraft side and on the government contracts side of the business. Once established, individual leaders could use the taxonomy to assess their own strengths and weaknesses in each of the areas and seek assignments and experiences that will challenge them in the areas where they need development. Likewise, organizations could use the taxonomy to assess the extent to which various leadership positions in the company provide key developmental experiences for leaders (that is, the positions contain the experiences, competencies, relationships, and learning capabilities dimensions that are needed by future leaders). Today, companies tend to focus only on moving high-potential leaders to more senior levels in the company. In the same way, they tend to focus on only a few key positions in the company that have been identified as the most important., However, real development occurs in the interaction between people and the jobs; that is, development happens when leaders are put in experiences that force them to build new skills. This means that almost any job could be developmental. The key is to find a leader who will be stretched by the job and who could develop new skills in areas of deficiency. The taxonomy of experiences, competencies, relationships, and learning capabilities dimensions gives the organization and individual leaders the framework to make intentional and strategic placement choices and to find assignments that will challenge leaders to grow in areas they have targeted for development.

Furthermore, if organizations relied solely on job assignments to develop talent, the importance of several talent management processes would be magnified. Development plans would become the most critical mechanism for developing talent throughout the company. Development plans would focus on projects and assignments that stretch the leader. Candid, regular feedback would become indispensable, providing people with real-time feedback to evaluate how they are doing, to self-correct their behavior, and to develop new capabilities. Performance reviews would be an assessment of a person's performance and a measure of whether or not the person is developing her potential. Mentors and peers would be viewed not only as an important network to help the person reach business goals, but also as important sources of developmental feedback. Interestingly, most of these elements (development planning, performance management, feedback) exist in companies today, yet they are seldom used to strategically support experience-based development. The first step in more fully using on-the-job development is to build the taxonomy that aligns talent management processes with the business strategy and with each other.

How to Build a Talent Management Taxonomy that Leverages Experience

Experience-based talent management systems start with the business strategy. From this, a taxonomy can be constructed that includes the work experiences, competencies, key relationships, and learning capabilities elements that are most critical for leaders in the organization. Learning capabilities are included as a separate dimension because they are so important. In increasingly dynamic organizations, raw leadership talent is almost never enough. The leaders who succeed over time are the ones who know how learn and develop as they are performing their jobs in ways that allow them to apply those lessons to future challenges (Argyris, 1991; Lombardo & Eichinger, 2000).

Business Strategy

As noted throughout this book, effective talent management practices are always designed and implemented in the context of the business strategy (Boudreau & Ramstad, 2005; Lewis & Heckman, 2006; Ulrich & Brockbank, 2005). Establishing a foundation of talent management tools and processes that support the business strategy requires a thorough knowledge of the strategy and an ongoing partnership between senior business leaders and human resource (HR) professionals. Strategic talent management systems are integrated vertically with the business strategy and horizontally with HR systems that complement and reinforce each other (Wright & McMahan, 1992: Wright, McMahan, & McWilliams, 1994). This requires HR professionals to reorient their thinking from more internally focused organizational issues such as cost management to more strategic external factors such as customers, competitors, and emerging markets (Delery & Doty, 1998; Seibert, Hall, and Kram, 1995).

Although it is beyond the scope of our discussion to discuss strategy in detail (see, for example, Barney, 2001; Collins, 2001; Porter, 1985), the following questions represent a sample of those that should be asked before creating talent management systems and experience-based development practices:

- What is the company's sustainable, strategic advantage? What can the company do better than any other company?
- What are the critical business challenges that the organization will face in the next five years? In the next ten years?
- What are the barriers to entry in our business space that we can use to protect our competitive advantage?
- Who are our key customers, suppliers, partners, and competitors?

Once the business strategy has been articulated, organizations can analyze the talent management implications. Unfortunately, some organizations immediately start building new talent management processes (such as leadership development programs, succession planning processes, or performance management systems) without first building an underlying framework that can be used to align all elements of the talent management system. Other organizations may build a taxonomy that relies solely on competency models. However, both approaches are incomplete. A rigorous talent management system does not focus on single programs or rely solely on competencies as the aligning framework, but rather incorporates the experiences, relationships, and learning capability elements that will be needed to develop future talent.

Experiences

Identifying the experiences that are most important in the development of future leaders is the first place to start. Several of these experiences have been identified in previous work. McCall et al. (1988) identified 16 key experiences in the development of leaders (for example, starting something from scratch, business turnarounds, role models, failures and mistakes). Subsequent work (McCall & Hollenbeck, 2002; Yost, Mannion-Plunkett, McKenna, & Homer, 2001) has confirmed the importance of these events and highlighted additional experiences that may play an important role for other leader populations, such as negotiations, joint ventures, alliances, and mergers and acquisitions.

The critical experiences within an organization could build on taxonomies created by others (Byham, Smith, & Paese, 2002; Lombardo & Eichinger, 1988; McCall et al., 1988) or might be built from scratch in the organization. The former allows the company to build on previous research, and the latter highlights experiences that may be unique to the organization. The best method is likely a combination of the two approaches. For example, start-up and turnaround business experiences tend to be consistent across businesses and industries. Ignoring this existing body of knowledge would be foolish. However, tailoring the experience definitions to reflect the unique language used in the company is often critical to getting the new processes accepted in the organization.

There are also likely to be some key experiences that are unique to each organization. For example, an organization that is planning to expand production worldwide might identify supplier management and global experience as critical for future leaders. A company that is primarily product based but is planning to expand the current services business might identify leading a services business as a critical experience. Companies may want to include some simpler experiences in their taxonomies that are accessible to many leaders, such as introducing a process that will be used across the organization, turning around a failing team, or taking on a short-term global assignment. It should be acknowledged that these will not be as developmental as the larger experiences, but they can teach several valuable lessons and prepare leaders to successfully take on bigger challenges in the future.

Practitioners are probably wisest to begin with experiences identified in past research in other companies and conduct open-ended interviews with senior leaders and high-potential leaders in the company to refine the list. Questions to ask might include:

- What have been three key events in your development as a leader?
- Given our strategic direction, what challenges will future leaders face?
- What kinds of job experiences would best prepare the next generation of leaders to meet these challenges?
- Consider one or two leaders who are great in today's environment but are not prepared to meet future business challenges. What job experiences or capabilities are they lacking?
- Identify in your own mind one or two high-potential leaders in your organization. What job experiences or assignments have been critical in making them the high-potential leaders that they are today?

These questions provide guidance on what was significant in the past and what will be most critical in the future. Together they create a map of how leadership development is changing and evolving in the organization. Once the experiences have been identified, they can be written up and used to develop future leaders. Descriptions should include a summary definition of the experience, distinctions of what constitutes a limited versus a thorough experience, the competencies most likely to be developed in the experience and lessons that will be learned, and some ways to assess the development of leaders in the experience. A global experience example is provided in Exhibit 7.1.

Other dimensions that could be part of an experience definition include:

- The types of job assignments in the organization that map to this experience
- A list of smaller development-in-place assignments that also might be available or created
- Strategies to navigate through the experience
- A description of the key elements that must be present to make the experience strongly developmental (for example, supervisory support, risk, profit and loss responsibility)

Exhibit 7.1. Sample Experience Definition

- *Global experience:* Work assignments requiring the leader to live and work outside his home country.
  - *Limited:* The leader remains in his home country but is required to work in partnership with and through people in other countries. The leader lives and works abroad but only for a limited length of time (less than one year).
  - *Moderate:* The leader is in a support role that requires her to manage business projects, interact regularly with residents of the country, and get things done through others. The leader lives and works outside her home country for a moderate length of time (one to three years).
  - *Deep:* The leader is in a senior position that requires him to drive significant change, manage multiple business projects, and get things done through others. The leader has held the position for an extended length of time (three or more years).
- *Competencies developed:* Strategic thinking, adapting to change, customer focus, negotiations and influence skills, working across organizations.
- *Lessons to be learned:* Dealing with cultural issues, dealing with key stakeholder groups (foreign governments, the media, unions, corporate headquarters), entering new markets, and interpersonal relations.
- *Things to watch to assess ongoing development:* Relationships with coworkers, direct reports, partners, customers, and the home office; formal business metrics (productivity, market growth, customer satisfaction, and others); personal adjustment and work/life issues.

In any discussion about experiences, it is important to remember that leaders who go through an experience can fail to learn the lessons along the way. It is important to ensure that leaders are in an environment that supports and helps them identify their learning. This includes ensuring the assignment stretches the leader and provides the right support. McCauley, Ruderman, Ohlott, and Morrow (1994) identified job challenges that promote development—for example, unfamiliar responsibilities, inherited problems, and the need to influence without having the authority. Several support factors also play a critical role in on-the-job development, including managerial support, a feedback-rich environment, team support, and reward systems (Maurer, Weiss, & Barbeite, 2003; Tracey, Tannenbaum, & Kavenagh, 1995; Yost et al., 2001).

As leaders are asked about the key events in their development, they could also be asked the following questions:

- What about the event made it so developmental? That is, why was this event so critical in your development compared with other events in your career?
- What challenges in the experience allowed, or forced, you to learn during the event?
- What support during the experience allowed you to learn and grow during the event?

Identifying the elements of the situation that maximize learning will help the organization ensure that the guidance and processes are in place that people need to grow and develop. Our experience suggests that learning is the greatest when leaders are neither overwhelmed nor overly comfortable, but when they are right at the edge of their comfort zone. When people are outside their comfort zone, their anxiety can interfere with learning. Conversely, leaders who are overly comfortable may tend to hold onto old habits and fail to try new approaches. Leaders may be at their best when they are confident they can perform at a minimum level but are forced to face new problems in new ways. This is reminiscent of the Yerkes-Dodson law (1908), which notes that performance is maximized at moderate stress levels. Some of the leaders we have worked with describe these as points in their careers when they were simultaneously excited and fearful.

Competencies

The second dimension of the taxonomy represents the competencies (general leadership skills) and capabilities (industry- or organizational-specific skills) that current and future leaders will need to achieve the business strategy. Many organizations have adopted formal competency models for their leaders that identify the explicit behavioral standards expected of current and future leaders. The competency list should be as simple and as focused as possible. If too many competencies are used, they are hard to communicate and can get diluted, as Jay Conger notes in Chapter 6 in this book. If a large number of competencies must be used, they can be grouped into a memorable number of factors (for example, the rule from cognitive psychology that people generally can only remember seven, plus or minus two, items; Miller, 1956).

Many techniques are currently used to identify and build competency models. They vary widely in how rigorously they were developed. Competencies can be based on interviews with senior leaders by asking a broad sample of leaders throughout the company to identify the business challenges that they face and the leadership competencies required to meet those challenges. More empirically based techniques might include formal job analysis methods or criterion-validity studies that assess leadership capabilities in formal assessment centers and compare scores against performance ratings. Commercially available competency taxonomies also exist (Byham et al., 2002; Gebelein et al., 2000; Lombardo & Eichinger, 2001). Whatever approach is used, leadership competencies should be built on the characteristics that research suggests are related to leadership effectiveness in an organization (Bass & Stogdill, 1990; Borman & Brush, 1993; Judge, Bono, Ilies, & Gerhardt, 2002; Yukl, 2005) and the specific needs of the business.

In many organizations, the competency framework serves as the foundation for connecting organizational processes such as training, succession planning, and performance management. In our view, competencies and experiences together provide the most useful framework to integrate talent management processes. Focusing only on competencies tends to reinforce the "great person" view of leadership; that is, leaders succeed or fail because of their skills. But this approach tends to overlook the situational factors that could be causing their behavior (a phenomenon so common in psychology that it has been labeled "the fundamental attribution error"). Over time, organizations that rely solely on competencies risk focusing so much attention on selecting the right people that they neglect the same rigor needed to ensure they are in the job experiences that will maximize their development with the right development support. When experiences are included with competencies, the focus shifts from the person alone or the experience alone to the dynamic interaction between the person and the situation. Talent management processes like succession planning no longer focus just on identifying individuals; rather, they are more likely to focus on the ongoing development of leaders in assignments.

Relationships

The relationships that leaders build are critical to their development and their performance. The original research conducted by the Center for Creative Leadership (CCL) found that approximately 20 percent of the key events in a leader's development were related to other people, most commonly bosses who served as good or bad role models (Lindsey, Homes, & McCall, 1987). The Corporate Leadership Council (2001) also found that relationships were one of the most critical factors in a leader's development.

The relationships that are most significant often include working with senior leaders, key customers, suppliers, particularly effective or ineffective teams, the board of directors, government relations staff, community relations staff, and union representatives. Interactions with these groups can provide leaders with important feedback, unique challenges, and support (McCauley & Douglas, 2004). Each of these groups offers a unique perspective. Together, they can help leaders better understand the organization and themselves. Several of these relationships are important for leaders to start building early in their careers since they often take time to develop. The following questions can be used to identify the most important relationships in the organization:

- What relationships will be most important for future leaders in this organization?
- Who will be the critical customers? Who will be the critical suppliers in the organization's value chain? Who will be the key strategic partners? Who will be the organization's major competitors?
- Which government and regulatory agencies will have the most impact on the organization's success?

- What departments, functions, and business units inside the organization will be most important?
- Do labor unions represent any employee groups in the organization? How can leaders begin building lasting relationships with their membership and their leadership?

Relationships are important for two reasons. First, they are often important determinants of the leader's success; that is, they are the way that leaders get their work done (Balkundi & Kilduff, 2006; Brass, 2001). Second, they are important in the development of leaders. Relationships help leaders see new perspectives (for example, how do senior leaders view the organization and what are the biggest priorities and challenges from their perspective? How do our customers view the organization? How do employee groups view the organization?). The multiple perspectives allow leaders to consider more alternatives when making decisions and exercising judgment. Relationships are also rich sources of feedback that help leaders learn, self-correct, develop, and refine their leadership capabilities. Future research might focus on how organizations can systematically identify the most critical relationships and ways to assess the depth and quality of these relationships.

Learning Capabilities

Learning capabilities can be defined as a leader's ability to capture the lessons of experience and apply them to future challenges. These capabilities are more than simple learning ability but also include the behaviors, skills, and resilience that leaders need to step into new challenges, navigate through them, capture the learning, and emerge as better leaders after the challenge. Learning capabilities are qualitatively different from competencies, in the sense that the competencies represent end states while learning capabilities represent the self-regulatory strategies that allow people to develop competencies.

The importance of learning capabilities will only increase as markets and organizations become more dynamic. In highly dynamic environments, the future may not be predictable. For example, disruptive technologies can severely limit the ability of organizations and leaders to predict the future (Christensen, 1999), and in highly dynamic markets, the future may in fact be unknowable. In this kind of environment, organizations cannot predict the competencies that future leaders will need. What becomes important is the ability of leaders to learn and develop as they go. This includes the ability to identify the leadership skills that are needed to meet current and emerging challenges, to develop new skills while executing against performance goals, to manage their emotions, and to capture lessons and apply them to future business challenges. An even higher-level skill is the ability to observe one's own learning tactics and apply these to future challenges. In educational psychology (Derry & Murphy, 1986), these are sometimes referred to as executive learning skills. Others have referred to them as metacognitive activity (Ford, Smith, Weissbein, Gully, & Salas, 1998) or self-regulation (Bandura, 2001).

Several research domains point toward the characteristics that allow leaders to capture and learn the lessons of experience. In this section, we briefly review five of them: learning agility, self-management, cognitive ability, personality characteristics, and leadership derailment factors.

General measures of learning agility are reported in Lombardo and Eichinger (2000) and in Spreitzer, McCall, and Mahoney (1997). Both measures emphasize the importance of openness to experience, treating other people well, openness to feedback, the willingness to take risks, and comfort with ambiguity.

The self-management literature suggests several strategies related to making behavioral changes, including goal setting, self-monitoring, self-evaluation, and self-reward (Bandura, 2001; Kanfer & Gaelick-Buys, 1991; Manz, 1986). For example, leaders who set high goals for themselves, build strong feedback systems, and assess their ongoing development and performance should be more likely to successfully navigate through experiences and capture relevant lessons along the way.

Research suggests that cognitive ability is also a good predictor of performance, especially as job complexity increases (Howard & Bray, 1988; Hunter & Hunter, 1984; Judge, Colbert, & Ilies, 2004). Beyond raw cognitive ability, meta-learning or meta-cognitive skills may be even more important (Ford et al., 1998;

Marshall-Mies et al., 2000; Sternberg, 2007). That is, individuals who "learn how to learn" should improve their learning capabilities over time, progressively improving their performance and adaptability. These leaders are able to engage in double-loop learning (Argyris, 1991): they have developed the ability to learn as they go, not only solving an immediate problem but using their experience to figure out how to approach and solve future problems. Interestingly, there is some evidence that this ability to learn is developed through experiences in stretch positions (Howard & Bray, 1988; Jacques, 1986).

The personality literature suggests that several personality dimensions are related to leadership progression and effectiveness. Dimensions that appear to be particularly important include openness to experience and extraversion (Judge et al., 2002). The importance of openness is consistent with constructs assessed in the learning agility measures. The relationship between extraversion and learning capabilities is less apparent; however, extroverted leaders may be more likely to build stronger networks that enable them to navigate the organization and get relevant feedback. As the workplace becomes more complex and dynamic, these two personality variables are likely to become even more significant.

Leadership derailment research highlights the dimensions that get in the way of leadership effectiveness and advancement (McCall & Lombardo, 1983). These factors include clusters of behaviors that lead to problems with interpersonal relationships, failure to meet business objectives, an inability to build and lead a team, and an inability to develop or adapt to changes (Van Velsor & Leslie, 1995), or negative personality dimensions such as being narcissistic, overly cautious, or mischievous (Hogan, Curphy, & Hogan, 1994; Hogan & Hogan, 2001; Maccoby, 2000). The reason some of these attributes are so damaging is that they prevent leaders from learning from experience. For example, we would expect that leaders who have problems with interpersonal relationships are less likely to get feedback and support from others.

As we look across these research domains, several important factors emerge that can affect a leader's ability to grow from experiences: cognitive ability, learning strategies, openness to experience, treating other people well, creating an environment rich in feedback, setting and monitoring development goals, and the ability to adapt. These can have a direct impact on a leader's ability to grow from experiences. They also are likely to predict those who will develop and expand their capabilities over time.

Putting It All Together

Once the four dimensions (experiences, competencies, relationships, and learning capabilities) and the key elements contained in each of these categories have been identified for a given organization, they can be ordered in a taxonomy that defines what is required of future leaders. Some organizations use competency models as their aligning framework, but very few include the other three dimensions. We believe that sole reliance on competencies focuses too much attention on the characteristics of people and downplays the importance of the situation and experience. The advantage of considering all four dimensions together is that it creates a more comprehensive picture of what is needed in future leaders and emphasizes the dynamic nature of talent development.

Once established, the taxonomy can be used as a tool to:

- Identify which experiences, competencies, relationships, and learning capabilities are most important and can be developed in different business units and functions in the company
- Assess and develop individual leaders
- Evaluate and enhance the developmental potential of job assignments
- Measure the collective breadth and depth of the leadership talent across the organization

For example, divisions within the organization can use the taxonomy to identify the experiences, capabilities, and relationships that are most important to their business. Likewise, organizations can use the taxonomy to assess their leaders against the dimensions to identify gaps. In succession planning, the taxonomy can be used to identify positions that are key accelerator roles, that is, assignments that will expose high-potential leaders to critical areas of the business. Without the taxonomy, many of these key roles could be overlooked. For example, in one company, a plant located outside corporate headquarters emerged as a critical stop for future leaders. Although it was relatively small, the remote plant was the major employer in the state where it was located. The plant manager had responsibility for all functions, government affairs, press relations, and profit and loss at the plant. In the past, the company had primarily rotated high-potential leaders through corporate roles, but these roles never included the span of experiences, the variety of relationships, or the level of responsibility required at the remote site.

At the individual level, leaders can use the taxonomy to assess themselves against the elements that fall in each of the four dimensions and to identify gaps in their development. Likewise, they can also compare the breadth and depth of their experiences, competencies, relationships, and learning capabilities to the demands of their current jobs to identify areas where they will be stretched. Leaders can use this kind of analysis to proactively look for assignments that will stretch them to improve in the areas they have targeted for their own development.

The taxonomy can play a central role in making experience-based learning a critical element of the organization's talent management system. Without a common taxonomy across the organization, experiences tend to be overlooked or used haphazardly. However, for the full value to be realized, the elements of the taxonomy also have to be designed into the HR systems so they become part of the organization's DNA.

How to Embed Experiences in Talent Management Systems

Talent management systems take on a fundamentally different structure when experience-based development is explicitly built into them. This section provides some examples of how experiences can be integrated into a variety of talent management processes. Further ideas can be found elsewhere (Yost & Plunkett, 2009).

Succession Planning

Succession planning tries to ensure that a sufficient number of leaders are identified and developed over time for key roles in an organization (Garman & Glawe, 2004). Creating a match between the organization's future talent needs and the career aspirations of individuals is one of the key indicators of an effective succession management system. Another key indicator is overcoming the fundamental weakness of most succession management systems: that organizations spend the majority of time and energy on identifying succession candidates, while devoting little energy to the development of these individuals once they have been identified (Karaevli & Hall, 2003). Assessing candidates on experiences can explicitly build development into the process in three ways. First, a list of the experiences that leaders will need to meet future business challenges can be used to highlight experience gaps in succession plan candidates. The experience gaps highlight where future development is needed and what development is needed.

Second, a simple matrix can be created (see Table 7.2) that links leadership competencies with each of the key experiences. Such a matrix can be based on linkages found in past research (McCall et al., 1988; Yost et al., 2001) or can also be built from scratch, relying on senior leaders or subject matter experts in the company, or both, to identify the competencies that are most likely to be developed in each experience. As will be discussed later, building research-based and validated linkages represents a fertile area for future research. Once established, this matrix can be used to support development in two ways. First, leaders can be assigned to experiences that will develop them in the targeted competency area, either to further enhance strengths or to address areas of weakness. Second, leaders can use the matrix to identify the competencies that are most likely to be developed in their current experiences.

For example, using Table 7.2, leaders who need to improve their *strategic thinking* skills could be assigned to start-up businesses, turnaround businesses, strategic task forces, or role models known for their strong strategic thinking skills. The matrix suggests that other experiences are unlikely to provide development in this area. Starting with experiences in the matrix, a leader in a staff role will be challenged to develop his negotiation and influence skills and ability to work across organizations. The leader is less likely to be challenged to further develop

Table 7.2. Experiences and Competencies Matrix

	Strategic Thinking	Building Organizations	Adapting to Change	Business Acumen	Technical Knowledge	Customer Focus	Negotiation and Influence Skills	Empowering Others	Drive for Results	Working Across Organizations
Business experiences										
Start-up business	X	X	X	X		X	X	X	X	
Sustaining business		X		X		X		X		X
Turnaround business	X			X		X	X		X	
Key disciplines										
Engineering and technical organization					X	X			X	X
Sales and marketing role				X		X	X		X	
Staff role								X		X
Perspective-building experiences										
Strategic task force	X								X	X
Global experience	X		X				X	X		X
Role model								X	X	X

competencies in any of the other areas. The matrix allows even more sophisticated approaches. For example, leaders who need to improve their strategic thinking skills and their ability to build organizations could be assigned to a start-up business where both competencies are likely to be developed.

A third way that experiences can be used to enhance succession management systems is to explicitly identify outcome measures that can be used to assess whether or not learning has occurred in the assignment. In most organizations, there are numerous examples of leaders who "succeeded" in an assignment but failed to grow from it or learned the wrong lessons along the way, destroying departments and leaving a mess for their successor to clean up. Detailed experience definitions (see Exhibit 7.1) can include measures for assessing not only a leader's performance but also whether she developed her leadership ability.

All three strategies enhance succession management processes by better aligning them with the business strategy, tailoring succession assignments with individual leader needs, and moving succession planning from a one-time event to an ongoing process. These strategies focus greater attention on the ongoing development of leaders and on the relationships between senior leaders and individuals in the talent pool. They also can help establish accountability in advance for learning the expected lessons.

Development Plans

The development planning process offers one of the greatest opportunities to systemically leverage experiences in a company. Unfortunately, in many organizations this is a missed opportunity. In many organizations, the only focus is on improving performance in the current job, or development plans are filled with training courses and do not leverage on-the-job development. In other organizations, individuals are held accountable for completing the planning form rather than being held accountable for achieving the learning objectives in the plan. A development planning process that focuses on getting key experiences that are aligned with the business strategy minimizes these shortcomings.

Three relatively simple strategies can be used to build experiences into development plans. First, in the action steps section of the development plan, individuals could be required to indicate if the activity is best categorized as on-the-job development (70 percent), other people (20 percent), or training (10 percent). These percentages refer to CCL's original research conclusions on where development is most likely to occur (Lindsey et al., 1987). Something as simple as these check boxes can underscore for employees where development should be occurring.

A second strategy is to provide a checklist at the end of the development plan that gives people a way to self-assess the quality of their plans for the coming year. The checklist should not be worded using typical administrative language that is all too common (for example, "This development plan includes all the required signatures and approvals"). Instead, it should be compelling, drawing on people's personal self-interests ("I am developing skills that will be in demand three to five years from now"). When people read the checklist, their reaction should be, "I would be crazy not to do this!" Exhibit 7.2 provides a sample development plan checklist that we created and used at the Boeing Company (Yost & Mannion-Plunkett, 2005; Learning & Development Roundtable, 2005).

As a third strategy, organizations can track measures that raise the visibility of the development planning process and the importance of experience-based learning in this process. This could include tracking the percentage of employees who completed their development plans, tracking employee survey items that are related to career development, or completing development plan audits. For example, an audit might look at the average percentage of development activities that are on-the-job development versus classroom training and the quality of the development goals. Are they specific and challenging goals, with deadlines, and with outcome measures for success?

Performance Management

If experiences are where the majority of development occurs, then ongoing job assignments become the critical development activities. Are assignments stretching the leader in the expected ways and in the person's development areas? As work goals are set for the coming year, do managers and employees consider both the business objectives (the results that need to be achieved to make the business successful) *and* the employee's development goals (the assignments and projects that will stretch the employee)? Is the leader given ongoing feedback and coaching throughout the year? Likewise the performance management discussion should also focus on the performance results, how the results were achieved, and the employee's ongoing development.

Exhibit 7.2. Sample Development Plan Checklist

How Good Is Your Development Plan?

Directions: This assessment can measure the quality of your development plan. Put an X next to the statements that are true for your development plan. A scoring key is provided at the end of the form.

ALIGNING WITH THE BUSINESS

_____ My development plan will help develop my skills and achieve my business goals at exactly the same time.

_____ At least 70 percent of my development actions are linked to on-the-job development.

_____ I am developing skills that will be in demand three to five years from now.

_____ This development plan will push me to the edge of my comfort zone in the areas I have targeted for development.

FINDING YOUR POTENTIAL

_____ I get excited when I look at my development plan for the coming year.

_____ My plan focuses as much energy on developing my strengths as it does on improving my weaknesses.

_____ I feel like I am making a difference in my work.

(Continued)

335

Exhibit 7.2. Sample Development Plan Checklist (*Continued*)

HOLDING YOURSELF ACCOUNTABLE

_____ For each development goal, I have included a metric to assess whether the goal has been reached.

_____ I have recruited at least two people to hold me accountable to my goals.

_____ I have identified milestones throughout the year to ensure that I am on track.

Your Score	*What It Means*
0 to 4 points checked	You are in danger of finishing the year less employable than when you began. Look for a block of time (at least two hours) over the next two weeks when you can seriously focus on your development and discuss it with your manager. Your future is worth it!
5 to 7 points checked	You have a good development plan, but it needs some work. Look at the items you did not check, and modify your plan accordingly.
8 to 10 points checked	You have created a strong development plan that will challenge you to develop your skills in important areas, positioning you to take advantage of future opportunities in your career.

Thinking about how the performance management system can support development opens up new possibilities. There are also some dangers if it is not done well. For example, when organizations try to use 360-degree feedback ratings for both development and evaluation, employees tend to inflate their ratings and provide less developmental feedback. (For a broader discussion of the complexities of performance feedback, see Alvero, Bucklin, & Austin, 2001, and Kluger & DeNisi, 1996.)

Training and Development

As Jay Conger notes in Chapter 6 in this book, training programs today are increasingly likely to ask participants to work on real business and organizational problems during the program. The more that these programs are based on job-related challenges, the more opportunity exists to tie the training to experience-based development and the greater opportunity for the training to move outside the classroom and be a catalyst for continued development. There is still an important place for formal training when new ways of thinking are required (for example, when introducing new concepts like value chain analysis, lean manufacturing, or reengineering). However, training alone is seldom enough to spark individual or organizational change.

Leadership development programs that are experience based challenge participants to apply new models to current work challenges. Training programs that emphasize on-the-job development are more likely to include practice sessions that incorporate the ideas back on the job, followed by feedback and coaching. Training sessions become an opportunity to integrate learning and to share best practices. Similarly, in experience-based development programs, building networks with other participants is not just an unrelated by-product but an important part of the program content. The interactions between participants and the new networks that are formed become valuable outcomes by themselves (Burt, 2004). Participants can serve as peer coaches in the program. The process uses co-learning rather than instructor-directed learning. In addition, senior leaders are frequently brought in to teach part of the program, building their experience and current organizational challenges into the content.

Accountability is another way to initiate and support experience-based learning in programs. This might mean requiring participants to share their development action plans with their boss, bringing participants back together after six months to report on lessons learned, or establishing measurable outcome goals as part of the development program. Both Day (2000) and Bolt (2004) note that evaluation and metrics continue to be one of the weakest areas of leadership development. As training programs become more experience based, training evaluations and business performance metrics should increasingly overlap. Participants should be able to use their own performance measures to determine if the training program is successful and integrated with the business strategy. For example, if the training program helps them achieve their performance goals, they should be able to see the results in the measures of productivity, quality, service, cycle time, and safety that they already track.

Mentoring and the Role of Other People

Past research has highlighted the importance of other people in a leader's development (McCauley & Douglas, 2004). Important relationships can include role models, mentors, peers, direct reports, customers, and people outside the organization who provide social support. Having role models can be one of the most critical developmental experiences for leaders. Interestingly, research suggests they can be either positive or negative role models (McCall et al., 1988; Yost et al., 2001) and most often are a person's immediate boss. They can appear early in a leader's career to set the stage for his future development or at critical inflection points in a leader's development. Some organizations have translated this into formal and informal mentoring programs (Ragins & Cotton, 1999). Evidence suggests that these relationships can have a significant positive impact on a person's career success (Allen, Eby, Poteet, Lentz, & Lima, 2004).

The most powerful developmental situations are often experiences that push leaders to the edge of their comfort zone. Bosses, colleagues, peers, customers, and others, inside and outside the organization, can provide important guidance, feedback, and support to the leader (McCall et al., 1988; McKenna & Yost, 2004). Immediate managers appear to play a particularly important role in developing leaders (McCall, 1998; Tracey et al., 1995; Yost et al., 2001).

Staffing and Workforce Planning

There are opportunities for experiences to play a much larger role in staffing and workforce planning decisions. For example, past experiences are the foundation for behaviorally based interviewing techniques designed to assess the breadth of a candidate's knowledge, skills, and abilities. Asking candidates to describe past work experiences has proven to be one of the most powerful structured interviewing techniques (Huffcutt, Conway, & Roth, 2004; Taylor & Small, 2002). As an extension of this approach, asking candidates to identify past lessons and apply them to future situations could begin to tap into their learning strategies and capabilities. This could assess candidates not only on their ability to perform well in the immediate job, but also assess their ability to perform well in future jobs.

Thinking beyond individual jobs, organizations are often equally concerned about the skill mix of a team, division, or organization. For example, rather than focusing on the skills and experiences of individuals, it may be more important to have the right mix of skills and experiences in the team (someone with engineering expertise, someone with budgeting and finance skills, someone with operations expertise, and so forth). Information technology systems have made it feasible to assess the talent mix across an organization if the data are available. For example, it is much easier now for organizations to track the current number of people in different job categories and professions and compare those numbers across divisions or geographic locations. If this is done well, talent can be transferred from divisions that are downsizing to divisions that are growing. However, most talent data in organizations are still captured at a very high level (for example, the number of people in a job category such as the number of electrical engineers). Having organization-wide measures on the competencies, experiences, relationships, and learning capabilities of employees in different parts of the organization could be very powerful. This information could also be used to develop people.

McCall (1998) has proposed that different divisions and functions could be utilized as "schools" that develop leaders in predictable ways. For example, the corporate finance department might be the best place for leaders to develop their business acumen and get experience in driving cross-organizational initiatives. In contrast, the sales division may be the best place for leaders to learn how to drive results, hold people accountable, and gain experience in customer relations. Some companies have adopted this methodology at the leadership level, but applying this concept of "schools" across the company to all employees has yet to be done. One could imagine a taxonomy similar to the one discussed earlier: helping employees at all levels find the jobs where they can develop the skills and gain the experiences that are important to them and to the organization.

Future Directions for Research and Practice

Talent management work is challenging. Organizations today are extremely dynamic. Global markets, mergers and acquisitions, new technology, and new business models make change the rule rather than the exception (Drucker, 1999; Friedman, 2006; Powell & Snellman, 2004; Rousseau, 1997). People are also dynamic. Talented people are likely to be in high demand and are often part of dual-career families with allegiances to both careers. In addition, the "new employment contract" reduces the stability of talent populations in companies (Hall, 1996); that is, long-term employment is no longer guaranteed. Companies and employees maintain a relationship only as long as each perceives value in a continued partnership. In this dynamic environment, sustainable, systemwide talent management systems are needed more than ever before.

The potential of leveraging on-the-job development in organizational talent management systems has barely begun to be realized. Technology makes several new things possible that could not have been considered even ten years ago. For example, the accessibility of organizational intranets makes it possible for managers and employees to update their performance goals, capabilities, experience, and development goals throughout the year with continuous data feeds into companywide talent management systems. Of course, all of this depends on the quality of the information, the people who use the system, and the depth of our knowledge in this emerging field. Significant work remains, especially in the use of on-the-job experience to drive development.

Future Directions for Research

Future research is needed to validate and extend the list of critical experiences in the development of leaders and other professionals. One important next step would be for industrial-organizational psychologists to invest as much effort in operationalizing experiences (that is, defining the experiences so they can be measured and assessed) as they have in identifying and defining competencies. Research suggests that several key experiences cross leadership populations (for example, starting something up, turning around a failing business) while others differ between leadership populations including experiences needed for global leaders (McCall & Hollenbeck, 2002) and for non-profit leaders such as clergy (McKenna, Yost, & Boyd, 2007). A cross-organizational list of critical experiences that are defined and behaviorally scaled would be extremely useful and create a common language and foundation for future research. Tesluk and Jacob (1998) proposed this more than ten years ago, yet little systematic work has been done so far. Large consulting firms may be in the best position to do this work since they have access to leaders and employees across multiple organizations.

Once a list of critical experiences has been established, then a progressive ordering of the experiences over a career for maximum development could be constructed. This might help answer several questions. What are the critical experiences, and what is the best order of experiences needed to develop a general manager versus an entrepreneurial leader versus a technical leader? For example, to develop a general manager, is there a short list of "must-have" experiences (for example, start-up, turnaround, and role model), or will different combinations of experiences work as well? What is the best sequencing for these experiences? Likewise, a global experience may be most powerful if it is presented early in a leader's development when her cognitive model of leadership is still forming (McCall & Hollenbeck, 2002).

Furthermore, relatively little work has been done to validate the lessons learned from each experience, strategies that individuals can use to capture the key lessons in an experience, the situational factors that are most significant, or the measures that should be used to assess if learning has occurred. The original research linking experiences to lessons was based on the past recall of the research participants (Lindsey et al., 1987). Future research could be done to more rigorously assess what is actually learned in the experiences using pre- or post-research designs to measure actual changes that have occurred as a result of the experience. At the same time, situation-based factors such as management support and feedback and person-based factors such as openness to experience, learning goals, and comfort with ambiguity should be identified that enhance or hinder a person's development.

Research on learning agility could benefit from more rigorous research as well. To date, the research has largely been concurrent survey data, correlating learning agility ratings against managerial ratings of potential. Longitudinal studies are needed to assess if learning dimensions are in fact predictive of future performance, advancement, and success at more senior management levels.

Future Directions for Practice

Organizations could benefit if they had a systematic, standard process to identify the experiences needed to develop key talent pools within the organization. When experiences are quantitatively defined and measured, an organization can compare the experience-based capabilities of the current workforce against what will be needed in the future. For example, a company might have leaders with considerable experience running stable businesses and managing turnarounds, but very few with start-up experience. If the business strategy is dependent on growth in new products or services, this information may have important implications for both recruiting and development efforts. External leaders can be recruited who have start-up experience, and internal succession planning processes can be used to place high-potential leaders in charge of new ventures. The organization-wide experience data can also be used to evaluate the current mix of talent in the organization. Today most companywide talent management systems at best focus on ensuring they have the right mix of functions, but they seldom assess if they have the underlying capabilities associated with each function (for example, rather than just focusing on the number of software development engineers, they can assess the software engineers on the underlying critical competencies and experiences that can make them effective). A taxonomy of competencies and experiences would allow organizations to address a far broader range of talent management issues.

We end our discussion where we began. Imagine an organization that had no formal training but relied solely on developing leaders and other employees through on-the-job experiences. What systems or knowledge would need to be in place to make this successful? There will always be a place for formal, structured development programs. It is time that we, as researchers and practitioners, help leaders figure out how to fully leverage the other 70 percent of their development opportunities.

References

Allen, T. D., Eby, L. T., Poteet, M. L., Lentz, E., & Lima, L. (2004). Career benefits associated with mentoring for protégés: A meta-analysis. *Journal of Applied Psychology, 89*, 127–136.

Alvero, A. M., Bucklin, B. R., & Austin, J. (2001). An objective review of the effectiveness and essential characteristics of performance feedback in organizational settings. *Journal of Organizational Behavior Management, 21*, 3–29.

Argyris, C. (1991). Teaching smart people how to learn. *Harvard Business Review, 69*(3), 99–109.

Balkundi, P., & Kilduff, M. (2006). The ties that lead: A social network approach to leadership. *Leadership Quarterly, 17*, 419–439.

Bandura, A. (2001). Social cognitive theory: An agentic perspective. *Annual Review of Psychology, 52*, 1–26.

Barney, J. B. (2001). Is the resource-based "view" a useful perspective for strategic management research? Yes. *Academy of Management Review, 26*, 41–56.

Bass, B. M., & Stogdill, R. M. (1990). *Handbook of leadership: Theory, research, and managerial applications.* New York: Simon & Schuster.

Bolt, J. F. (2004). *The future of executive development.* Oklahoma City: Executive Development Associates.

Borman, W. C., & Brush, D. H. (1993). More progress toward a taxonomy of managerial performance requirements. *Human Performance, 6,* 1–21.

Boudreau, J. W., & Ramstad, P. M. (2005). Talentship, talent segmentation, and sustainability: A new HR decision science paradigm for a new strategy definition. *Human Resource Management, 44,* 129–136.

Brass, D. J. (2001). Social capital and organizational leadership. In S. J. Zaccaro & R. J. Klimoski (Eds.), *The nature of organizational leadership: Understanding the performance imperatives confronting today's leaders* (pp. 132–152). San Francisco: Jossey-Bass.

Burt, R. S. (2004). Structural holes and good ideas. *American Journal of Sociology, 110,* 349–399.

Byham, W. C., Smith, A. B., & Paese, M. J. (2002). *Grow your own leaders: How to identify, develop, and retain leadership talent.* Upper Saddle River, NJ: Development Dimensions International & Prentice Hall.

Campion, M. A., Cheraskin, L., & Stevens, M. J. (1994). Career-related antecedents and outcomes of job rotation. *Academy of Management Journal, 37,* 1518–1542.

Christensen, C. M. (1999). *The innovator's dilemma: When new technologies cause great firms to fail.* Boston: Harvard Business School Press.

Collins, J. C. (2001). *Good to great.* New York: HarperCollins.

Corporate Leadership Council. (2001). *Voice of the leader: A quantitative analysis of leadership bench strength and development strategies.* Washington, DC: Corporate Executive Board.

Day, D. V. (2000). Leadership development: A review in context. *Leadership Quarterly, 11,* 581–613.

Delery, J. E., & Doty, D. H. (1998). Issues of fit in strategic human resource management: Implications for research. *Human Resource Management Review, 8,* 289–309.

Derry, S. J., & Murphy, D. A. (1986). Designing systems that train learning ability: From theory to practice. *Review of Educational Research, 56,* 1–39.

Dotlich, D. L., & Noel, J. L. (1998). *Action learning: How the world's top companies are recreating their leaders and themselves.* San Francisco: Jossey-Bass.

Drucker, P. F. (1999). *Management challenges for the 21st century.* New York: HarperBusiness.

Ford, J. K., Smith, E. M., Weissbein, D. A., Gully, S. M., & Salas, E. (1998). Relationships of goal orientation, metacognitive activity, and practice strategies with learning outcomes and transfer. *Journal of Applied Psychology, 83,* 218–233.

Friedman, T. L. (2006). *The world is flat: A brief history of the twenty-first century* (updated and expanded). New York: Farrar, Straus & Giroux.

Garman, A. N., & Glawe, J. (2004). Succession planning. *Consulting Psychology Journal: Practice and Research, 56,* 119–128.

Gebelein, S. H., Stevens, L. A., Skube, C. J., Lee, D. G., Davis, B. L., & Hellervik, L. W. (2000). *Successful manager's handbook.* Minneapolis, Minn.: Personnel Decisions International.

Hall, D. T. (1996). *The career is dead—long live the career: A relational approach to careers.* San Francisco: Jossey-Bass.

Hogan, R., Curphy, G. J., & Hogan, J. (1994). What we know about leadership: Effectiveness and personality. *American Psychologist, 49,* 493–504.

Hogan, R., & Hogan, J. (2001). Assessing leadership: A view from the dark side. *International Journal of Selection and Assessment, 9,* 40–51.

Howard, A., & Bray, D. W. (1988). *Managerial lives in transition: Advancing age and changing times.* New York: Guilford Press.

Huffcutt, A. I., Conway, J. M., & Roth, P. (2004). The impact of job complexity and study design on situational and behavior description interview validity. *International Journal of Selection and Assessment, 12,* 262–273.

Hunter, J. E., & Hunter, R. F. (1984). Validity and utility of alternative predictors of job performance. *Psychological Bulletin, 96,* 72–98.

Jacques, E. (1986). The development of intellectual capability: A discussion of stratified systems theory. *Journal of Applied Behavioral Science, 22,* 361–384.

Judge, T. A., Bono, J. E., Ilies, R., & Gerhardt, M. W. (2002). Personality and leadership: A qualitative and quantitative review. *Journal of Applied Psychology, 87,* 765–780.

Judge, T. A., Colbert, A. E., & Ilies, R. (2004). Intelligence and leadership: A quantitative review and test of theoretical propositions. *Journal of Applied Psychology, 81,* 542–552.

Kanfer, F. H., & Gaelick-Buys, L. (1991). Self-management methods. In F. H. Kanfer & A. P. Goldstein (Eds.), *Helping people change: A textbook of methods* (4th ed., pp. 305–360). New York: Pergamon Press.

Karaevli, A., & Hall, D. T. (2003). Growing leaders for turbulent times: Is succession planning up to the challenge? *Organizational Dynamics, 32,* 62–79.

Ketter, P. (2006). Investing in learning: Looking for performance. *Training and Development Journal, 60*(12), 30–33.

Kluger, A. N., & DeNisi, A. (1996). The effects of feedback interventions on performance: A historical review, a meta-analysis, and a preliminary feedback intervention theory. *Psychological Bulletin, 119,* 254–284.

Learning and Development Roundtable. (2005). *Setting leaders up to succeed: Tactics for navigating across critical upward career transitions.* Washington, DC: Corporate Executive Board.

Lewis, B. L., & Heckman, R. J. (2006). Talent management: A critical review. *Human Resource Management Review, 16,* 139–154.

Lindsey, E. H., Homes, V., & McCall, M. W. Jr. (1987). *Key events in executives' lives.* Greensboro, NC: Center for Creative Leadership.

Lombardo, M. M., & Eichinger, R. W. (1988). *Eighty-eight assignments for development in place.* Greensboro, NC: Center for Creative Leadership.

Lombardo, M. M., & Eichinger, R. W. (2000). High potentials as high learners. *Human Resource Management, 39,* 321–329.

Lombardo, M. W., & Eichinger, R. W. (2001). *For your improvement: A development and coaching guide.* Minneapolis, MN: Lominger Limited.

Maccoby, M. (2000). Narcissistic leaders. *Harvard Business Review, 78*(1), 68–77.

Manz, C. C. (1986). Self-leadership: Toward an expanded theory of self-influence processes in organizations. *Academy of Management Review, 11,* 585–600.

Marquardt, M. J. (2004). *Optimizing the power of action learning: Solving problems and building leaders in real time.* Mountain View, CA: Consulting Psychologists Press.

Marshall-Mies, J. C., Fleishman, E. A., Martin, J. A., Zaccaro, S. J., Baughman, W. A., & McGee, M. L. (2000). Development and evaluation of cognitive and metacognitive measures for predicting leadership potential. *Leadership Quarterly, 11,* 135–153.

Maurer, T. J., Weiss, E. M., & Barbeite, F. G. (2003). A model of involvement in work-related learning and development activity: The effects of individual, situational, motivational and age variables. *Journal of Applied Psychology, 88,* 707–724.

McCall, M. W. (1998). *High flyers: Developing the next generation of leaders.* Boston: Harvard Business School Press.

McCall, M. W., & Hollenbeck, G. P. (2002). *Developing global executives.* Boston: Harvard Business School Press.

McCall, M. W., & Lombardo, M. M. (1983). *Off the track: Why and how successful executives get derailed.* Greensboro, NC: Center for Creative Leadership.

McCall, M. W., Lombardo, M. M., & Morrison, A. M. (1988). *The lessons of experience: How successful executives develop on the job.* New York: Free Press.

McCauley, C. D., & Douglas, C. A. (2004). Developmental relationships. In C. D. McCauley, R. S. Moxley, & E. Van Velsor (Eds.), *The Center for Creative Leadership handbook of leadership development* (pp. 85–115). San Francisco: Jossey-Bass.

McCauley, C. D., Ruderman, M. N., Ohlott, P. J., & Morrow, J. E. (1994). Assessing the developmental components of managerial jobs. *Journal of Applied Psychology, 79,* 544–560.

McKenna, R. B., & Yost, P. R. (2004). The differentiated leader: Specific strategies for handling today's adverse situations. *Organizational Dynamics, 33,* 292–306.

McKenna, R. B., Yost, P. R., & Boyd, T. N. (2007). Leadership development and clergy: Understanding the events and lessons that shape pastoral leaders. *Journal of Psychology and Theology, 35,* 179–189.

Miller, G. A. (1956). The magical number seven, plus or minus two: Some limits on our capacity for processing information. *Psychological Review, 63,* 81–97.

Ortega, J. (2001). Job rotation as a learning mechanism. *Management Science, 47,* 1361–1370.

Poell, R. F., van Dam, K., & van den Berg, P. T. (2004). Organising learning in work contexts. *Applied Psychology: An International Review, 53,* 529–540.

Porter, M. E. (1985). *Competitive advantage: Creating and sustaining superior performance.* New York: Free Press.

Powell, W. W., & Snellman, K. (2004). The knowledge economy. *Annual Review of Sociology, 30,* 199–220.

Quinones, M. A., Ford, J. K., & Teachout, M. S. (1995). The relationship between work experience and job performance: A conceptual and meta-analytic review. *Personnel Psychology, 48,* 887–910.

Ragins, B. R., & Cotton, J. L. (1999). Mentor functions and outcomes: A comparison of men and women in formal and informal mentoring relationships. *Journal of Applied Psychology, 84,* 529–550.

Robinson, G. S., & Wick, C. W. (1992). Executive development that makes a business difference. *Human Resource Planning, 15,* 63–76.

Rousseau, D. M. (1997). Organizational behavior in the new organizational era. *Annual Review of Psychology, 48,* 515–546.

Salas, E., & Cannon-Bowers, J. A. (2001). The science of training: A decade of progress, *Annual Review of Psychology, 52,* 471–499

Seibert, K. W., Hall, D. T., & Kram, K. E. (1995). Strengthening the weak link in strategic executive development: Integrating individual development and global business strategy. *Human Resource Management, 34,* 549–567.

Spreitzer, G. M., McCall, M. W., & Mahoney, J. (1997). Early identification of international executive potential. *Journal of Applied Psychology, 82,* 6–29.

Sternberg, R. J. (2007). A systems model of leadership: WICS. *American Psychologist, 62,* 34–42.

Taylor, P. J., & Small, B. (2002). Asking applicants what they would do versus what they did do: A meta-analytic comparison of situational and past behaviour employment interview questions. *Journal of Occupational and Organizational Psychology, 75,* 277–294.

Tesluk, P. E., & Jacob, R. R. (1998). Toward an integrated model of work experience, *Personnel Psychology, 51,* 321–355.

Tracey, J. B., Tannenbaum, S. I., & Kavenagh, M. J. (1995). Applying trained skills on the job: The importance of work environment. *Journal of Applied Psychology, 80,* 239–252.

Ulrich, D., & Brockbank, W. (2005). *The HR value proposition.* Boston: Harvard Business School Press.

Van Velsor, E., & Leslie, J. B. (1995). Why executives derail: Perspectives across time and cultures. *Academy of Management Executive, 9*(4), 62–72.

Wick, C. W. (1989). How people develop: An in-depth look. *HR Reporter, 6*(7), 1–3.

Wright, P. M., & McMahan, G. C. (1992). Theoretical perspectives for strategic human resource management. *Journal of Management, 18,* 295–320.

Wright, P. M., McMahan, G. C., & McWilliams, A. (1994). Human resources and sustained competitive advantage: A resource-based perspective. *International Journal of Human Resource Management, 5,* 301–326.

Yerkes, R. M., & Dodson, J. D. (1908). The relation of strength of stimulus to rapidity of habit-formation. *Journal of Comparative Neurology and Psychology, 18,* 459–482.

Yost, P. R., & Mannion-Plunkett, M. (2005). Building individual and leadership capacity at Boeing. In D. Day (Chair), *Leadership development: Integrating individual and organizational development.* Symposium conducted at the annual conference of the Society for Industrial/Organizational Psychology, Los Angeles.

Yost, P. R., Mannion-Plunkett, M., McKenna, R. B., & Homer, L. (2001). Lessons of experience: Personal and situational factors that drive growth. In R. B. McKenna (Chair), *Leadership development: The strategic use of on-the-job assignments.* Symposium conducted at the annual conference of the Society for Industrial/Organizational Psychology, San Diego, CA.

Yost, P. R., & Plunkett, M. M. (2009). *Real time leadership development.* Cambridge, MA: Wiley-Blackwell.

Yukl, G. (2005). *Leadership in organizations* (6th ed.). Upper Saddle River, NJ: Prentice Hall.

CHAPTER 8

CHANGING BEHAVIOR ONE LEADER AT A TIME

Sandra L. Davis, Robert C. Barnett

The argument about whether leaders are born or made has been answered resoundingly by the market. Currently, the leadership development, executive coaching, and management training markets account for several billion dollars of corporate expense. Recent estimates about the executive coaching market alone suggest that it has already topped $1 billion and is still growing (Sherman & Freas, 2004). Clearly there is a widespread belief that leadership can be taught, that emerging leaders can learn, and that organizations can develop individual leaders.

Social trends have also fueled the business demand for individualized behavior change strategies. As consumers, we demand customized and personal attention. Witness the burgeoning market for personal trainers and coaches of all kinds. If Tiger Woods has his own coach, why shouldn't CEOs also have one? If we can order computers configured to our personal specifications and buy jeans custom-made to our own measurements, why not expect learning to be individualized as well? As the authors of *The Experience Economy* point out, we have entered a new era in which the economic winners know how to pay attention to the customer experience (Pine & Gilmore, 1999).

The focus of this chapter is on how individual leaders change, the predictors of change, what can or cannot be changed, the process of change, and what the research on coaching tells us about the effectiveness of individual change interventions. The Hellervik,

Hazucha, and Schneider's (1992) chapter on behavior change in the *Handbook of Industrial/Organizational Psychology* provides a good foundation. Since then, others have contributed helpful summaries and reviews (see, for example, London & Maurer, 2004; McCauley & Hezlett, 2001; and Van Velsor, Moxley, & Bunker, 2004). This chapter builds on these with a view toward helping managers and executives make well-informed choices and toward helping practitioners (those providing developmental services) understand and use best practices as they work to change individual leader behavior.

Organizations are spending considerable amounts of time and money to change individual leaders, but are the investments leading to the payoffs they expect? The CEO of a Fortune 100 global manufacturing business was interested in discovering the answer for her own organization. She asked the simple question: "How much are we spending on executive coaching, and what are the benefits to the business?" The line and human resource (HR) executives could easily add up the costs of executive coaching: as a company, they found they were spending more than $20 million per year on external coaches. They had a more difficult time specifying payoffs in quantifiable terms. Although they reported powerful examples of significant gains in individual leader effectiveness, no one could articulate the formula for success.

Leaders can change—some more than others—but just because they can does not guarantee they will. Some behaviors can be changed, while others seem more resistant. Some coaches have a special ability to be a catalyst for change; others may do more harm than good. Some, but not all, organizations actively support individual change. How does an organization, an executive, or an HR professional know whether and when to spend money to try to change an individual leader's behavior? Organizations and HR leaders would benefit from better understanding how to get the most from the dollars they invest.

Leadership Matters

Why is changing leader behavior and developing leadership talent so important to organizations? We believe it is because people know and understand that leadership matters. Although this is taken for granted by many, there is ample evidence that strong leadership and effective management are related to the following:

- Hard measures of organizational performance, such as increased productivity, revenue growth, profit, market value, long-term returns, and shareholder wealth
- Customer satisfaction and retention
- Positive outcomes for the organization, such as decreased turnover, increased employee commitment and engagement, and enhanced high-potential talent retention and development

Powerful research exists from studies conducted with large samples and across industries, countries, cultures, and organizational types that provides convincing evidence that skilled managers or leaders are a key factor, if not the key source of competitive advantage and organizational success. For example, the Centre for Economic Performance and McKinsey and Company conducted a study of 731 manufacturing organizations in Europe and the United States and found that well-managed firms performed significantly better than poorly managed firms and had higher levels of productivity, profit, and sales growth (Bloom, Dorgan, Dowdy, Van Reenen, & Rippin, 2005). Differences in management effectiveness, measured by a standardized interview process evaluating 18 key management practices, accounted for as much as 10 to 20 percent of the differences in company performance across industries and countries.

A study of 968 firms representing all major industries in the United States found that organizations with more skilled managers and more effective people management strategies achieved $27,044 more in sales, $18,641 more in profits, and $3,814 more in market value per employee than organizations without effective leadership (Huselid, 1995; Pfeffer & Veiga, 1999). In a follow-up study (Huselid & Becker, 1997), shareholder wealth was found to be $41,000 higher per employee in companies with strong people management skills than in those with weaker management capabilities.

In a study of 60 Fortune 1000 firms, Hansen and Wernerfelt (1989) found that the ability to lead and manage effectively was twice as powerful in accounting for a firm's financial success as were hard economic variables such as industry profitability, firm market share, and size of assets. This finding was essentially replicated by Fulmer, Gerhart, and Scott (2003), who found that companies on Fortune's list of 100 Best Companies to Work for in America had more stability in their workforce and realized greater business success compared to the broader market. It seems evident that good managers positively influence employee behavior, and employees in turn produce stronger organizational performance and success.

From a database of over 20,000 leaders, Zenger and Folkman (2002) showed that effective leadership had a dramatic impact on every measurable dimension of organizational performance—employee commitment, retention, profit, customer satisfaction—and the differences were large, not trivial. Research by the Corporate Leadership Council (2005) on more than 11,000 employees and their managers found that high-quality managers (those who are personally and interpersonally effective and who can lead change, think strategically, and deal with complexity successfully) enhanced employee potential by as much as 37 percent. The results from these studies show why organizations invest such great effort to change and improve the effectiveness of their leaders.

What We Know About Behavior Change

As a discipline, psychology understands a good deal about behavior change. Therefore, a brief overview of relevant theory and research is instructive. Although it is not our intent to provide a comprehensive review of everything psychologists know, this section describes the best-supported theoretical contributions: these are the theories and schools of thought that are most useful for those interested in behavior change. The key operating mechanisms that lead to change in each approach are summarized in Table 8.1.

Psychodynamic Theory

Freud gets little attention in corporate life. Despite opinions one may have of Freud and his followers, many people would

Table 8.1. Contributions from Psychological Theory

Theory or Approach	Lessons for the Practitioner
Psychodynamic view	1. Behavior is often driven by a person's internal dynamics, which the person is unaware of or does not accurately understand.
	2. People are likely to be defensive when confronted with the need to change. Expecting and recognizing resistance and constructively confronting defensiveness can facilitate successful individual change.
Behaviorism	3. Reinforcing (for example, supporting, praising) success or efforts to change strengthens the likelihood that an individual will repeat and persist at those behaviors.
	4. Successful behavior change can be accomplished by shaping or guiding the individual through a series of steps that over time more closely approximate the desired outcome or behavior.
	5. The events or circumstances that trigger a particular behavior or reaction can be managed or changed to increase the likelihood that positive behavior or reactions will occur.
Cognitive behavioral psychology	6. People's thoughts influence the way they feel and subsequently behave. Change the way people think, and they will change the way they act.
Person-centered psychology	7. People will become more open to change when they are in a trusting, respectful, and supportive relationship (with a coach or consultant).

(Continued)

Table 8.1. Contributions from Psychological Theory
(*Continued*)

Theory or Approach	Lessons for the Practitioner
Adult learning and development	8. People want to control or decide what they will learn or try to change.
	9. Adults learn primarily through their experiences. Practitioners can help people learn by helping them make sense out of their experiences, especially when an experience is overwhelming or causes dissonance.
Work motivation theory	10. Setting effective goals for behavior change (those that are specific, challenging, and achievable) will facilitate learning and development.
	11. People cannot change without practice and feedback. Feedback helps people adapt and adjust their efforts so they can be more successful.
Social-cognitive theory	12. Confidence or self-efficacy is strongly related to a willingness to try new things. Practitioners need to help build clients' confidence that they can do new things.

acknowledge that his ideas are useful to them in some way. For example, HR professionals, psychologists, and executive coaches may often find themselves working with someone they believe is "defensive" about the ideas, suggestions, or feedback they offer to try to help them change and improve.

Psychodynamic theory proposes that behavior is the result of competing internal impulses and instincts. The id, the ego, and the superego all drive behavior in conscious and unconscious ways. The id propels an individual to seek pleasure and avoid pain, the ego makes a realistic assessment of what is possible, and the superego compels a person to live up to societal or parental ideals. Defense mechanisms protect the individual from dangerous thoughts or harmful impulses; they give people a way to interpret, adapt to, or ignore certain aspects of reality. Many of these forces and defense mechanisms operate in unknown ways; individuals are simply unaware of or do not accurately understand what drives their behavior (Peltier, 2001).

Confronted with a need to change, many people can become defensive. They make up explanations and excuses to defend against or resist changing their behavior. Consider the example of the CFO in a multibillion-dollar enterprise who had progressed in his career by being the brilliant expert with all the right answers. Convinced of his own superior intellect and afraid that showing any doubt or weakness would "prove" some lack of competence, he routinely ignored ideas from others and treated his staff as intellectually inferior. He was so defensive that to him even considering a coaching process implied that he was ineffective. Only when his executive coach (who was a psychologist) could help him see the relationship between his unconscious fears and his impact on people was he able to consider changing his behavior.

By expecting resistance and constructively confronting defensiveness, psychologists can help individuals become aware of unconscious forces that drive their behavior so they can then make better choices as leaders and learn to behave more effectively.

Behaviorism and Behavioral Approaches

Behaviorism is familiar to most people. It is based on the idea that behavior is a function of its consequences. With roots in the work of Pavlov, Watson, and Thorndike, modern behaviorism was primarily shaped by Skinner and is based on Thorndike's law of effect, which states that behavior that is reinforced or praised is more likely to reoccur. Reinforcement is pervasive and powerful in work settings: it affects, strengthens, or changes behavior daily. Other important behaviorist concepts are stimulus control (manipulating the circumstances so that desired behaviors are more likely to occur) and shaping behavior by successive approximation (reinforcing and rewarding small steps toward acquiring more complex, new behaviors).

Organizational behavior modification (OBM) (Komaki, 1986) is an application of Skinnerian behaviorism that specifies how to replace ineffective behaviors with more effective ones. Behavior change is accomplished by specifying the new behaviors that are desired, targeting and strengthening the preceding conditions that cue those behaviors, and then identifying and reinforcing the new behaviors in ways that are important to the individual and the organization (Goldstein, 1986; Weiss, 1992).

In brief, organizations and practitioners use behavioral concepts in several ways:

- To influence behavior change every day
- To help individuals understand the link between events and their reactions to those events and between their behavior and its consequences
- To reward the behavior they want people to show
- To praise or acknowledge behavior that is effective
- To track and measure behavioral change so individuals can see their own progress

These concepts are core to the individual change process. It is important for anyone who is in the business of helping leaders change behavior to consider two questions: How is current (ineffective) behavior being rewarded, and what reinforcers or incentives are needed to reward new, changed behavior?

Examples that demonstrate the power of reinforcement in changing behavior are common. The Vice President of Sales for a medical products company became concerned when he discovered that his Director of Asia Pacific sales was focused on achieving his own sales quota and giving too little attention to his direct reports. The Director's team members admitted to the Vice President that they felt ignored, that they received only limited support, and that their boss was slow to return their calls or e-mails. The Vice President identified two measures that he wanted to regularly review with his Director: a report on the sales calls he made jointly with his staff and a graph showing each of the Director's team members' progress toward their sales quotas. When the Vice President started to look at this information weekly, praised the progress made by the Director, and told the

Director that his raise would be contingent on his team's satisfaction with his leadership, the Director's behavior began to change.

Cognitive Behavioral Psychology

Change the way people think, and they will change how they act. Cognitive behavioral approaches evolved through the experiences of behaviorists as they learned about the role of thinking and cognition in the behavior change process. They had limited success in helping someone change behavior unless they took into account the individual's own evaluation and interpretation of the problem behavior and the events associated with it. Their success improved when they began to help their clients interpret events more objectively, choose different reactions to stressful events, and alter counterproductive thinking.

As an example, a newly promoted executive brought her fiercely competitive nature as a sales leader into her new role as general manager. With her team, she advocated competing against other divisions in order to win customers to achieve the largest gains in market share and to be the most profitable. Although that worked well for winning in the marketplace, her approach did not work for developing good relationships with her executive peers. Her relationships deteriorated so much that her peers even became reluctant to return her phone calls. "Why aren't they helping me win?" she wondered.

Her manager and an executive coach intervened. They helped her understand that senior-level jobs require one to be an executive at large. Although she needed to advocate for her own division's success, of equal importance was her responsibility to help all divisions to be successful. Once her coach helped her reframe her understanding of what she should be doing, she began to change her behavior. She started looking at the ways her peers were contributing to the success of the enterprise. She began to give her peers leads in the market and provided offers to help rather than just demands for service. As she found ways to support their success, they became engaged in helping her as well. Had someone told her just to be nicer to her peers, the behavior change would have been short-lived. Reframing the way she understood her role was the catalyst for her improved effectiveness.

Person-Centered Psychology

Behavior change may not result from just using the right techniques. Person-centered psychology maintains that behavior change happens through the quality of the relationship one individual has with another, for example, between a manager or external coach and the person he is trying to help change. When relationships are distant or when a person feels they are being judged negatively, then the person tends to refuse help, withdraw, or end the relationship.

Carl Rogers developed the person-centered approach based on his belief that people have enormous potential to grow and change provided they experience authenticity, acceptance, and support in their relationships with others (Peltier, 2001). The relationship itself is the vehicle for change. Providing direction, prescriptions, or advice is not the aim. The "active ingredients" are (1) helping an individual experience acceptance and unconditional positive regard, (2) accurately empathizing with the person, and (3) showing understanding in a climate that allows the individual to grow and become more fully functioning. The essential skill that is required is accurate and empathic listening so the other person discovers her own capacity to grow, change, and develop.

The person-centered approach underscores an essential condition for helping people change: establishing a positive and constructive relationship with the person who is being helped (Peltier, 2001). Most psychologists and executive coaches recognize that the quality of their relationship with their client is a foundation for change. Few practitioners would question the value or importance of this premise. Sometimes this is called "chemistry" and other times is described as the level of trust or respect that exists in an effective helping relationship.

The power of a good relationship was apparent to one CEO who worked with a coach on an ongoing basis. He described the value of coaching in this way:

> I bring issues or challenges I am facing or struggling with. She
> [my coach] listens, asks questions, draws out my hunches and offers
> insights of her own about the matter-at-hand without judging me. In
> the end, I come to my own conclusions and action plans, which are
> often different and richer than where I began. I believe without her
> listening and support, I would have chosen less effective solutions.

Adult Learning and Development

The field of adult learning has focused on the processes through which people make sense out of their life experiences. It is based on two fundamental assumptions. First, adults want to have control over their learning: they will determine what they need to learn, create and implement learning strategies, and assess their success (Knowles, Holton, & Swanson, 2005). Second, life experiences (rather than classroom training) are the primary source of learning for adults, provided those experiences are given good attention and reflection (Merriam & Clark, 2006). To explain the process of learning through experience, Kolb (1984) described a four-step process that begins with (1) having a concrete experience, which (2) leads to reflection, which in turn allows (3) the formulation of abstract concepts and generalizations and (4) the testing or use of these concepts in new situations.

Adult development, a closely related discipline, has extended the ideas of age and life stage progression, developed by Piaget, beyond adolescence into adult life. Life stage theories of adult intellectual, moral, ego, and social development have been proposed (see Hoare, 2006a). The common idea in adult development models is that people continue to change and develop as adults because their life experiences force them to do so. They acquire increasingly complex and effective means for making sense of and mastering their experiences, roles, and responsibilities.

Adults learn through experience by two processes: assimilation and accommodation. When people encounter new experiences that they can understand and comfortably make sense of, they will assimilate or fit those experiences into their existing mental models. However, when they encounter a new experience that their existing ways of understanding cannot adequately explain, they have to accommodate or restructure their way of thinking and understanding. As people assimilate and accommodate new experiences, they develop much more complex ways of understanding themselves and the world around them (McCauley & Hezlett, 2001).

Executive coaches typically support their clients' active involvement in the change process. When they work with individuals who are learning and changing, they frequently find themselves suggesting connections, explanations, and interpretations of experiences that the individual may not have considered. They also help individuals identify the things they want to learn and the ways in which they believe they will learn best. The Center for Creative Leadership's work on individual preferences for different learning approaches is relevant here. Some prefer to read, some want to learn from others, some want to learn by doing, and others learn by observing.

Consider the plant manager who told his coach that he wanted to learn how to be a better leader to his team but that he had no interest in reading books or attending classes. Together he and his coach designed several *learn-by-doing* activities and *learn-by-observing* opportunities. After each activity they talked about what worked, what did not work, and what could be done differently the next time. Over time, the plant manager realized that his team performed best when he involved them and facilitated their discussion to reach agreements and conclusions rather than when he told them what to do. He recognized that those who participated in developing solutions and plans had a deeper level of commitment to new ideas. By experimenting with and seeing his experiences in new ways, he learned how to be a more effective team leader.

Theories of Motivation

Why do individuals behave the way they do at work? The field of psychology has a deep body of research on motivation, and motivational theory has contributed much that is useful. This includes (1) the importance of establishing specific and challenging goals and (2) the central role of feedback (as information) in evaluating, adjusting, and adapting behavior.

A number of theories attempt to explain and predict motivated behavior in organizational settings (summarized nicely by Donovan, 2001). These include equity theory (Adams, 1963, 1965), expectancy theory (Vroom, 1964), and cognitive evaluation theory (Deci & Ryan, 1985). Equity theory states that individuals seek and expect fairness or equity in return for the input or effort they exert. Expectancy theory suggests that people's choices at work reflect their desire to maximize benefits to themselves while minimizing the downsides. In short, individuals will behave in ways that lead to outcomes they value, provided they believe they can successfully produce the necessary behavior. Cognitive evaluation theory suggests that intrinsic motivation—one's personal need or drive for competence and self-determination— is more powerful in explaining choices and behavior than rewards or anticipated outcomes. However, among theories of work motivation there are two that are most strongly substantiated by research: control theory and goal-setting theory.

Control Theory. Control theory focuses on how people regulate their behavior through feedback from the environment (Campion & Lord, 1982). In essence, it states that people actively monitor, evaluate, and regulate their behavior in relation to the goals and standards they have set. When feedback from their environment tells them how they are doing in relation to their goal, they engage in self-correcting thoughts and behaviors to close the gap, if there is one. In other words, when an important goal is not being achieved, it motivates them to try harder to get what they want (Donovan, 2001).

Goal-Setting Theory. One of the most well-researched motivation theories relevant to individual behavior change is goal-setting theory (Locke, 1968, Locke & Latham, 1990). Goal-setting theory and research has shown that goals improve performance when they are specific, challenging (but attainable), and participatively set (or at least accepted by the individual), and when feedback or knowledge of results is provided or available. These characteristics of goals and goal setting are among the most well established and widely accepted. Anyone who embarks on a behavioral change initiative would be well served by understanding and using effective goal setting to facilitate and sustain individual change and development.

Social-Cognitive Theory

Fundamentally social-cognitive theory states that people act intentionally and that they inherently want to control and make things happen through their actions. Believing that they can or cannot do something is the primary source for taking action or making decisions. Social-cognitive theory evolved from Bandura's social learning theory (Bandura, 1977, 1986) into a comprehensive view of behavior and behavior change. The central idea—the development and role of self-efficacy, that is, the beliefs one has about oneself—has been given widespread attention in psychological research and theory (Judge, Jackson, Shaw, Scott, & Rich, 2007). According to Bandura (2001) the core features of social-cognitive theory include:

- *Intentionality*—people act with purpose and make choices proactively.
- *Forethought*—people set goals, anticipate likely consequences, and create plans before taking action.
- *Self-reaction*—people evaluate the progress and success of their actions relative to the goals and standards they have set, and can adapt or change their effort based on their assessment.
- *Self-reflection*—a thought process that allows people to judge how well they are controlling their own behavior and external events.

Efficacy beliefs lead people to expect that they can or cannot realistically do something and to select strategies for taking action. A person with positive self-efficacy believes he can do what he set out to do, while individuals with negative self-efficacy believe that despite their best efforts, they will probably fail. Those who work in the field of leadership development should recognize that when individuals believe that they are able to change and become more effective, they are far more likely to change.

Consider the manager who was deathly afraid of public speaking. Convinced his fear was insurmountable, he routinely avoided giving public presentations, usually delegating this to one or another of his staff. In a leadership development seminar he attended, he was forced to participate in a module on giving high-impact presentations. After learning strategies for better managing his fears and other public speaking techniques he found helpful, he began to believe that he could be effective at making good presentations. Once he began to develop a positive sense of efficacy in his public speaking skills, he became more engaged in learning and changing, and eventually he was able to make reasonably effective presentations himself.

Factors Influencing Individual Change

Having explored how the field of psychology explains behavior change, our discussion now shifts to specific elements that influence the success or failure of individual behavior change efforts. Executive coaching is one of the most popular individual change interventions. The focus on behavior change in coaching is obvious; Kilburg (1996) was among the first to offer a definition:

> Executive coaching is defined as a helping relationship formed between a client who has managerial authority and responsibility in an organization and a consultant who uses a variety of behavioral techniques and methods to help the client achieve a mutually identified set of goals to improve his or her professional performance and personal satisfaction and, consequently, to improve the effectiveness of the client's organization [p. 142].

What should the industrial-organizational psychologist, consultant, or leadership development professional pay attention to during the coaching process? Many coaching approaches concentrate on who can change. However, other factors, such as the sequence of steps in the coaching process, the complexity of the learning task, qualities of the coach, and factors in the organization, are also relevant. The sections that follow explore a number of questions related to the change process:

- What steps are essential to behavior change and achieving a positive outcome?
- Which individual differences affect learning, and who will benefit the most from coaching or leadership development? Coaches use their knowledge of individual differences to decide whom to coach, how to coach, how to plan an intervention, and which methodologies to choose.
- What is to be changed or learned? Some researchers and many theorists have noted that behaviors vary in their complexity and malleability. Some behaviors or skills are easy to change, while others are more deeply entrenched and not easily altered.
- What environmental factors shape behavioral change and influence learning? Does the culture of the organization and the support of the individual's boss make a difference?
- What are the most important or helpful characteristics and skills of coaches—how is coach effectiveness measured?

A Model for the Change Process

Several efforts have been made to develop models of how people change by looking for common elements across theories. These models specify a sequence of steps through which people learn or change. For example, Hellervik et al. (1992) reviewed a number of theories and methods and proposed a five-stage behavior change process: (1) needs analysis, moves to (2) specifying desired new behaviors, that includes (3) formulating goals and specifying expectations, that calls for (4) learning, experimentation, and practicing new behaviors, and ends with (5) generalizing and maintaining the new behaviors.

McCauley and Hezlett (2001) considered individual change from a broader perspective. They compared approaches rooted in behavior change, self-directed learning, and adult development. Their synthesis also resulted in a process consisting of five common elements: (1) agreeing on the ways a person needs to change, (2) helping the person develop a belief that she can change, (3) participating in skill-building experiences, (4) exploring reactions to these experiences, and (5) recognizing that development leads to worthwhile outcomes.

Most models of executive coaching describe a similar process. In general, they propose that coaching begins with gaining agreement from an individual to participate, involves an assessment that helps to identify the person's change needs, includes an active coaching phase (usually the longest), and concludes with evaluating results. Practitioners who want to dig more deeply into the details of the coaching process can find several good resources (see, for example, Douglas & Morely, 2004; Flaherty, 1999; Goldsmith & Lyons, 2006; Hollenbeck, 2002; Peterson & Hicks, 1996; Ting & Hart, 2004).

A comprehensive model of individual change is presented in Figure 8.1 and shows behavioral change as a complex process that occurs over time. It incorporates stages in the change process and shows the influence of other factors, such as individual differences, the context (environment) in which change occurs, the qualities of the coach (if there is one), the role of the manager, and the need for measuring outcomes and sustaining change. This model serves as a frame of reference for the remainder

Figure 8.1. A Model of Individual Leader Change

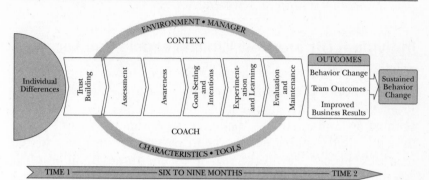

of this chapter. Individual behavior change depends on factors in the person, the environment, the coach, and the process.

The model reflects the lessons derived from psychological theory. A trusting relationship with a coach must be established. A trusted and skilled coach can assess and help a client increase his awareness of what behaviors need to change and why such change would be important. Goals for change and development that are specific and realistic are established with clients. This sets the stage for active experimentation, practice, and other learning activities—the heart of the change process—again in the context of a supportive, safe coaching relationship. In the ideal world, progress is evaluated (that is measured), and the coach and client identify ways the client can sustain his new and more effective ways of behaving.

Change process models like the one in Figure 8.1 are most often presented in a linear fashion, yet coaches frequently find they need to revisit earlier steps during coaching. Nonetheless, process models help practitioners understand where they are going and how to match methods and activities to the step or stage in the process. While the model provides a good way to understand individual leader change through a coaching process, it can apply to any individual behavior change initiative. Leadership development professionals can also use the model to increase the impact of group initiatives and team learning by considering the individual, the coach, and the context variables that support or reinforce new behavior.

Individual Differences: Which Leaders Can Learn?

Regardless of the models or theories of behavior change a practitioner adopts, there is no guarantee that a leader will change. Predicting who can change and how much they can change is both an art and a science. When an organization embarks on an initiative that requires executives to participate in a 360-degree feedback process or work with a coach, there is an implicit assumption that everyone has the capacity to change. But do they?

The psychology of individual differences plays a major role in predicting who (and what) can change. Differences in individual personality are related to leadership performance and the acquisition of leadership skills. Judge, Bono, Ilies, and Gerhardt (2002) demonstrated that most personality dimensions (emotional stability, extraversion, openness to experience, and conscientiousness) are related to both who emerges as a leader and leader effectiveness. Smither, London, and Reilly (2005) described five individual difference factors that correlated with improved performance following receipt of multisource feedback: leaders' motivation, feedback orientation (do I want or ask for feedback?), personality variables (extraversion, conscientiousness, locus of control, emotional stability), positive beliefs about change (self-efficacy), and the perceived need for change. The primary individual difference variables that are identified most frequently in both research articles and practitioner-oriented books are summarized below and in Table 8.2.

Motivation

An obvious predictor of change lies in an individual's desire to change. It does not matter whether that desire is intrinsic (I want to excel at everything I do) or extrinsically motivated (I want to change because I want to keep my job or please my boss). As long as an individual genuinely wants to change, that is enough. People who are avid lifelong learners and who constantly seek ways to improve their performance have an internal drive

Table 8.2. Individual Differences and the Capacity to Change

Variable	Illustrative Behaviors
Motivation to change	• Expresses genuine interest in becoming a stronger leader • Has made some significant changes in the past • Has a desire to advance or take on different roles in the future • Works hard to please his boss • Responds well to incentives or personal recognition • Will do whatever is needed to remain with the company
Intelligence	• Sees the world broadly rather than in highly structured terms • Deals well with complexity • Can move beyond formulaic solutions to making dynamic choices • Can think out several years into the future
Conscientiousness	• Actively follows through on goals and commitments • Pays attention to the demands of the organization or those of her boss • Displays personal responsibility and accountability for results
Openness to experience	• Often asks for feedback about personal impact as a leader • Can evaluate situations from multiple perspectives • Others describe him as nondefensive • Is a curious person and is personally adventuresome • Does not resist feedback or rationalize actions • Respects the expertise and knowledge of others

(Continued)

**Table 8.2. Individual Differences and the
Capacity to Change** (*Continued*)

Variable	Illustrative Behaviors
Learning orientation	• Is willing to try out new behaviors in real time • Has modified her style in the past based on the situation, culture, or context • Knows how to shift approaches to work effectively in multiple cultures • Takes personal risks; is willing to be vulnerable
Self-efficacy and beliefs about change	• Believes in her own capability to change • Expects to be able to affect others and the world around him • Has confidence that change is possible • Believes that leadership development is a never-ending process
Self-awareness	• Knows own strengths and development needs • Compensates for what she is not good at doing • Accurately assesses his impact on others • Is able to monitor self and change tactics within a situation • Takes personal responsibility for actions; neither blames others nor acts as a victim

to learn and grow that sustains them over the long term. Those whose motivation is externally focused (dependent on external rewards or approval) need regular attention to sustain their efforts to change and develop. Most books and articles written about creating change through coaching describe the importance of actively establishing, evaluating, and reevaluating motivation and commitment throughout the coaching process.

Intelligence

Intellectual ability correlates positively with success at all levels of leadership. Schmidt and Hunter (1998) bluntly concluded that the most valid predictor of future performance and learning is general mental ability. In a subsequent article, they reported that the correlation between intelligence and job performance averaged .55, and the relationship between intelligence and performance in training averaged .63 (Schmidt & Hunter, 2004).

The more highly positioned the leader is in the organization, the more that intelligence can help his ability to learn and change. Levinson (1982) noted the difference in cognitive demands between lower and higher levels of leadership: higher-level positions in organizations tend to require work that is more complex, ambiguous, and longer term. Hunter and Hunter (1984) reported that cognitive ability correlates .58 with performance in jobs with higher levels of complexity, while the correlation between cognitive ability and job performance decreases to .23 for jobs with the least complexity. Most experienced practitioners know that intelligence by itself is insufficient for guaranteeing leadership effectiveness or the ability to change. However, coaches need to understand the intellectual capacity of the individuals they are coaching. It would be a mistake to try to change an element of performance that the person is incapable of learning or to expect a rate of learning that is faster than what the individual can realistically accomplish.

Personality

Over the past 15 to 20 years, most research on the power of personality factors to predict job performance, training performance, or leadership effectiveness has relied on the Big Five Model of personality. The Big Five factors are: extraversion, emotional stability, conscientiousness, agreeableness, and openness to experience (Goldberg, 1990). Based on the results from several meta-analyses, it is generally accepted that at least four of the big five personality variables are relevant to leadership behavior (Hogan & Kaiser, 2005; Hough & Ones, 2001). However, it is important to understand which of the big five personality factors might be most predictive of an individual's capacity to change and develop successful leadership skills.

Extraversion
Extraversion is defined as energy, gregariousness, and the tendency to seek social stimulation and the company of others. It has been shown to be one of the strongest and most consistent

correlates of leadership emergence and effectiveness (Barrick & Mount, 1991; Hough, Ones, & Viswesvaran, 1998; Judge et al., 2002). Extraversion can help people learn and change because extraverts tend to be energetic and active; they seek out opportunities and experiences to learn from and then share their knowledge with others (Hoare, 2006b). For example, Smither et al. (2005) reported some tendency for extraverts to ask for more feedback than their introverted peers. Dominance, a facet of extraversion, has been found to be especially strongly related to leadership (Hough et al., 1998; Judge et al., 2002). Dominant people are forceful, influential, and persuasive. People with higher dominance have personal power and can take control of things, including the learning experiences and activities they initiate. It would be a mistake to assume that only extraverts can be leaders or develop leadership skills, but it would be natural for an extravert to engage in learning with and through others.

Emotional Stability

Neuroticism is the tendency to frequently or too easily experience unpleasant emotions such as anger, anxiety, or depression. The opposite of neuroticism is emotional stability. Good candidates for coaching have an absence of significant psychological issues or the presence of a high level of emotional stability. Emotional stability involves healthy adjustment, confidence, and self-esteem. Judge et al. (2002) found that emotional stability was significantly related to leadership effectiveness. Emotionally stable and confident people are more likely to tolerate their own failures and shortcomings, learn from mistakes, and appreciate feedback from others. Low emotional stability is associated with an inability to process information accurately or objectively and with lower self-efficacy (or confidence), which is essential for having the willingness to experiment with new behaviors. Clearly, low emotional stability interferes with learning. However, coaching is not therapy, and an effective coach needs to know when to refer an individual for psychotherapy (Levinson, 1996).

Conscientiousness

Conscientiousness involves the tendency to be self-disciplined, planful, and dutiful. Several studies have demonstrated that conscientiousness is related to job performance and leadership (Barrick & Mount, 1991; Judge et al., 2002; Schmidt & Hunter, 2004), but Hough et al. (1998) found achievement orientation to be more strongly related to leadership than dependability (both facets of conscientiousness). Individuals who score high on conscientiousness are more likely to follow through on the goals they set and more likely to feel obligated to work on their own development after receiving multisource feedback. Smither et al. (2005) summarized several studies that suggest highly conscientious individuals participate more actively in development activities than those who score lower on this trait. Responsible, disciplined, and goal-oriented people are likely to dedicate themselves to learning, establish more difficult goals for themselves, and learn more than their less conscientious coworkers (Clausen & Jones, 1998).

Agreeableness

Agreeableness is a tendency to be compassionate and cooperative in interactions with others. London and Maurer (2004) have commented on the value that organizations place on having effective interpersonal skills, and Russell (2001) found that good interpersonal and people-oriented skills were a strong predictor of executive effectiveness. However, no meta-analytic studies have shown that agreeableness predicts behavior change or that it is an important core trait of leadership effectiveness. One could speculate that agreeableness might be related to the ability to build a good working relationship with a coach, and improving interpersonal skills and interpersonal relationships is one of the most common goals of coaching assignments. However, the sheer number of stories from coaches who have worked successfully with strong-minded, aggressive executives suggest that agreeableness is not necessarily a prerequisite for behavior change.

Openness to Experience

This personality variable includes appreciation for adventure, having curiosity about the world, and being open to a wide range of experiences. Openness to experience describes people who are flexible, resourceful, imaginative, and intellectually curious. Judge et al. (2002) found openness to experience was related to leadership effectiveness, but results are more mixed in other meta-analyses

(Barrick & Mount, 1991; Hough et al., 1998). However, Hough and Furnham (2003) note that openness to experience may emerge as one of the more important factors in understanding performance in a rapidly changing world. Ackerman and Heggestad (1997) found openness to experience to be clearly related to continuous learning. London and Smither (2002) described this variable as "feedback orientation." Individuals with a high feedback orientation are not afraid of being evaluated, like and seek feedback, care about how others view them, and feel accountable for using the feedback they receive. Such qualities provide obvious advantages to those interested in learning, developing, and changing, especially when viewed in the context of the kinds of work roles and experiences most related to learning as a leader: new and unfamiliar responsibilities, creating and leading change, and roles with significant decision consequences (McCauley, 2001).

The opposite of openness to experience is inflexibility. Those who are not open to experience tend to be rigid, dogmatic, closed, and resistant to learning. They have little interest in looking at their world in different or more effective ways (Hoare, 2006b). To the extent that an individual leader remains closed and defensive in the face of feedback, there is little hope for changing behavior. At best, the inflexible or well-defended personality complies with learning new behaviors, but when the pressure is off, she reverts to old behaviors. Ludeman and Erlandson (2004) developed a defensiveness scale that they used to measure an individual's readiness to change and to participate actively in coaching. Defensiveness can be reduced by engaging the leader in designing the coaching or change process, including who should be surveyed for feedback and what should be asked. If a leader includes people whose opinions he cares about in the assessment phase, then it is more likely he will be open to their feedback.

Personality Derailers

Derailment factors were identified over 25 years ago by researchers at the Center for Creative Leadership (CCL) (McCall & Lombardo, 1983) and are well known in the leadership development field. In follow-up studies over the years, some new themes have emerged and some have disappeared, but one derailment factor that has remained consistent over time is the inability to adapt, develop, or learn from experience (Van Velsor & Leslie, 1995). Leaders who hope to remain successful over time are those "who can learn from their experiences and use that learning to develop a wider range of skills and perspectives so that they can adapt as change occurs and be effective in a wider range of situations" (Van Velsor, Moxley, & Bunker, 2004, p. 208).

Hogan and his colleagues have extended the derailment research and written extensively about the dark side of leadership and the factors that predict ineffective behavior in top executives (Hogan, Curphy, & Hogan, 1994; Hogan & Kaiser, 2005). Like the CCL findings, he has identified the causes of problems leaders have in getting along with others, getting things done, and getting ahead. The personality measure he constructed is designed to aid in assessing potential derailment factors (Hogan & Hogan, 1997). Evaluating these factors during the assessment phase of coaching is undoubtedly helpful in planning the coaching process. For example, coaching a highly self-centered, abrasive executive who believes the world revolves around him is different from coaching an executive who hesitates to make decisions until he is certain he has a perfect solution.

Self-Efficacy and Beliefs About Change

Related to motivation variables, self-efficacy encompasses personal confidence and belief in one's own ability to change. The work of Smither et al. (2005) showed that self-efficacy and internal beliefs about change were factors predicting the degree of change that occurred following multisource feedback. McCauley and Hezlett (2001) and London and Maurer (2004) include self-efficacy as an important factor that is related to an individual's ability to learn. Chen, Gully, Whiteman, and Kilcullen (2000) strongly endorsed self-efficacy as a predictor of performance. Judge et al. (2002) found self-esteem and locus of control (traits often associated with self-efficacy) were positively correlated with leadership, but more recent work (Judge et al., 2007) suggests that self-efficacy is more influential in learning or performing specific tasks rather than on overall performance.

Several studies have shown that self-efficacy for change or growth can be influenced. That is, a person's belief that he or she can change can be strengthened (Dweck & Leggett, 1988; Maurer, 2002). Knowing an individual's beliefs about change and learning can help the coach plan the intervention. A person who believes that change is not possible may appear defensive. In this instance, coaching efforts may have to address this issue before other work that is actually building new skills or changing behavior can proceed.

Self-Awareness

Self-awareness or self-insight is another individual difference variable that regularly emerges in the coaching literature. Self-awareness involves the accuracy of an individual's view of her own strengths and weaknesses and helps a person set realistic and relevant learning and development goals. It is seen as a prerequisite for leader development (London & Maurer, 2004; Ting & Hart, 2004). It includes self-identity or an awareness of the kind of person an individual wants to be, including the career objectives he wants to achieve. McCauley (2004) notes that self-awareness helps an individual know where and how to improve. Self-confidence (as a component of self-awareness) helps people solicit feedback and seek or adapt to new experiences.

Learning Orientation and the Ability to Learn

Individuals who show a desire to grow, seek novel experiences, and are self-directed and proactive in their approach to learning have a capacity that is described as a positive orientation toward learning (London & Maurer, 2004; McCauley, 2001). The coaching literature and organizational competency models include frequent references to learning ability and learning orientation, describing these as key predictors of success at all levels of management. Lombardo and Eichinger (2000) coined the term *learning agility* and defined it as an interest in first-time challenges, an eagerness to learn, and an ability to improve performance by incorporating new behaviors into one's repertoire of skills. Their research showed that higher ratings on a scale of learning agility were significantly related to a combined measure of performance and potential and to a measure of style, specifically, a propensity for staying out of trouble. Kaiser and Craig (2005) reported on the different success formulas required at different levels in an organization hierarchy and found that interest in learning and the ability to learn was the one consistent correlate of success across supervisory, managerial, and executive levels. These results suggest that learning ability or a positive learning orientation is important to change and growth.

Practitioners and HR professionals often state that they want to select senior leaders who have high levels of learning ability, but few seem able to clearly specify or measure it. The best and most useful definitions incorporate two elements: motivation to learn and ability to learn. These are the most salient parts of the definition, and the ability to learn has been shown to be related to career success, leadership effectiveness, and the capacity to prevent derailment (Yukl, 2006).

Individual Differences and Ability to Change: Implications for Coaching

Individual differences can have a dramatic impact on whether a person can change his leadership behavior. Table 8.2 incorporates all of the variables identified above, including illustrative behaviors related to each. Practitioners might use this as a rough outline to determine whether a potential coaching participant has a low, medium, or high readiness to change.

Table 8.3 shows how change readiness can affect a coach's actions and, subsequently, the outcomes of coaching. When readiness is high, the coach will be able to move more quickly to goal setting and implementation. When readiness is low, more time needs to be spent in the initial stages of the change process. If readiness remains low even after those efforts, a coach has to have the courage to stop the coaching process.

Differences in Leadership Level and Job Complexity

It makes sense that the complexity of the task or skill to be acquired would influence the change or coaching process. Mastering more complex tasks could require prolonged and

Table 8.3. Coaching Readiness, Actions, and Outcomes

Individual Readiness	Coach Actions	Possible Outcomes
Low: The leader has very few of the positive factors related to ability to change.	• Consider working directly on the individual's personal barriers to change. • Determine whether motivation can be increased through external pressure. • Spend considerable time on self-awareness and on activities designed to gain commitment. • Work on building trust, and determine whether the relationship itself can lead to positive change.	• Coaching may take considerably longer because the ability to change is initially low. • Coaching is discontinued because the likelihood of change is low and the investment is questionable. • The organization stops the coaching process because there is no visible change.
Medium: The leader has many of the elements that predict ability to learn and to change.	• Build on the positive elements, and use those to build commitment. • Determine whether any personal barriers need to be addressed first. • Help the individual see that more change may be possible than he imagines. • Create goals for coaching as soon as possible.	• Coaching will have an impact on behavioral change over the long term if the individual and the coach can build in feedback mechanisms to help sustain change. • Some positive change will occur, and it could be highly significant if both the individual and the coach create stretch goals.
High: The leader has most of the elements that predict ability to learn and to change.	• Move quickly into joint goal setting and action. • Define early on what role the individual wants the coach to play. • Ensure that the highest-impact goals (for the organization) are the focus because this individual may simply want to learn everything. • Coordinate coaching goals with the individual's manager.	• Coaching will have an impact for the leader; the coach needs to help the organization see quantifiable results. • It is energizing to work with high-readiness leaders. The coach may not want to terminate the relationship when goals have been met. • The leader is likely to become a stronger coach in her own leadership role.

more involved coaching; learning less complex skills might be accomplished through a simpler or shorter coaching process.

A way of conceptualizing task complexity is outlined in *The Leadership Pipeline* (Charan, Drotter, and Noel, 2001). In essence, this framework argues that different levels of leadership require substantially different leadership skills and activities. Higher-level positions in an organization involve broader and more complex responsibilities, and correspondingly require expanded and more complex skills. For example, setting strategy for and managing a portfolio of business units, an executive-level leader skill, is conceived of as more complex than assigning work to a team member—a supervisory-level skill. Table 8.4 summarizes the pipeline model and suggests that increasingly complex and broader skills are required as one moves from managing one's self into supervisory, managerial, and then into executive-level leadership roles.

Several studies support the notion that the skills needed to perform in increasingly broader or higher jobs increase in complexity as one moves up the organization hierarchy. Kraut, Pedigo, McKenna, and Dunnette (1989) showed that management tasks differed in importance at different levels in an organization. At the supervisory level, managing individual performance was most important. The most important work of middle managers was planning and allocating resources, coordinating interdependent groups, and managing group performance. The most important tasks of senior executives appeared to be the most complex: monitoring the business environment, identifying new business opportunities for the organization, and maintaining relationships with customers and other stakeholders.

Mumford, Marks, Connelly, Zaccaro, and Reiter-Palmon (2000) found that expertise, judgment, and problem-solving skills increased across six grade levels of military officers, with senior leadership positions requiring greater complex problem solving and creative thinking skills and a more balanced and mature approach to solving organizational issues. Kaiser and Craig (2005) found that different leadership levels in an organization do in fact involve different success formulas. Their results showed that supervisor success was most related to interpersonal effectiveness. Managerial success involved sound decision making, good execution skills, and the ability to effectively empower

Table 8.4. Skills Required at Different Levels of the Leadership Pipeline

Pipeline Level	Skills Required
Managing others	Planning work
	Hiring people
	Assigning work
	Motivating
	Coaching
Managing managers	Identifying and developing prospective managers
	Measuring people's progress as managers
	Coaching for development
	Strategic thinking
Function manager	Thinking broadly: Taking concerns of other functions into consideration
	Teamwork with other functional peers
	Blending functional strategy with business strategy
Business unit leader	Integrating functions
	Using staff functions effectively
	Adopting a profit perspective
	Balancing short-term and long-term thinking and goals
	Planning for the longer term
Senior executive	A well-developed external orientation that supports visionary thinking
	Evaluating strategy and allocating resources correctly
	Developing business unit leaders
	Managing a portfolio of business lines
	Building competitive organizational capabilities
	Managing external constituencies

Source: Adapted from Charan, Drotter, and Noel (2001).

subordinates. Executive success was most strongly related to a more thoughtful decision-making style and an ability to shoulder increasingly large amounts of responsibility.

It almost goes without saying that coaches need to help develop the skills that are the most relevant to their clients' needs, and studies on this topic give some guidance about where to focus. The complexity of the skills to be learned may also influence the amount of time required for the coaching engagement. If work at higher organization levels requires broader and more complex skill sets, setting realistic expectations about how long coaching may take would be important to establish so that coaching efforts have the best chance of being successfully completed.

Characteristics of the Coach

Coaches vary widely in their ability to facilitate behavioral change. Their personal qualities, skills, training, experience, and coaching approach are factors that influence their effectiveness. Much of the coaching literature emphasizes the importance of having strong relationship-building, communication, and interpersonal skills. Interpersonally effective coaches should be more effective at establishing trust with their coaching clients in the beginning stages of the coaching engagement (see Figure 8.1). The Corporate Leadership Council (2003) found that relationship factors were vitally important to achieving successful coaching outcomes. They reported that client perceptions that the coach was empathic, respectful, and shared an understanding of the goals of the coaching engagement were twice as important to achieving successful outcomes as the coach's technique or model.

In their review of the executive coaching literature, Kampa-Kokesch and Anderson (2001) note that many have advocated training in psychology as a preferred background for effective executive coaching. If behavior change is the goal, then psychologists seem uniquely qualified. Psychologists know a great deal about behavior change (see Table 8.1). They also know how to establish trusting relationships and confront individuals on the reality and impact of their behavior. Ineffective and psychologically unsophisticated executive coaches may do more harm than good (Berglas, 2002).

Knowledge of psychology and the ability to create a trusting relationship are necessary but not sufficient for effectiveness in coaching. Sherman and Freas (2004) suggest that the best coaches are grounded in their knowledge of behavior change and in their understanding of leadership and business. They are adept at understanding the client's work relationships and the values, goals, and dynamics of the client's business.

Hollenbeck (2002) states that coaching competence involves credibility. For him, credibility means the coach is competent in three areas: trustworthiness or absolute integrity, expertise (knowledge of business and knowledge of behavior change), and dynamism (or having the interpersonal skills to be able to successfully engage the coachee). This last point is significant. Data from the field of counseling psychology show that a client's involvement in the process of change is the strongest predictor of a successful outcome (Bachelor & Horvath, 2006).

One gauge of coach effectiveness comes from the opinions and observations of executives who have been coached. While such work has limitations (it is retrospective and subjective), it does shed some light on what resonates with executives. For example, Wasylyshyn (2003) conducted research with 87 executives to understand how they valued the coaching they received. Executives noted that they valued the following characteristics of their coach:

- Ability to form a strong personal connection (empathy, warmth, trust building, listening skills)
- Professionalism (intelligence, integrity, confidentiality, objectivity)
- Sound coaching methodology (delivering feedback constructively, contextual grounding, and unearthing core issues)

Several organizations and institutes publish competencies for coaches and offer training and certification programs. The International Coaching Federation (ICF) has identified eleven core competencies for professional coaching that include meeting ethical guidelines, establishing trust, active listening, creating awareness, planning and goal setting, managing process, and accountability. Certainly, demonstrating competence in these areas would be helpful. Although there is not one set of universally accepted or validated competencies for coaches, there is good agreement among practitioners and in the literature about key coaching skills and abilities, which are summarized in Table 8.5.

Table 8.5. Core Competencies of Effective Coaches

Skill or Competency	*Illustrative Behaviors*
Relationship-building skills	• Facilitates the individual's engagement in the coaching process • Listens actively • Understands the individual's intentions and goals • Displays empathy and acceptance • Initiates contact with the participant; does not wait to be asked • Relates effectively to others in the organization (boss, peers, and direct reports) • Personally supportive of the coachee • Builds a relationship based on trust • Willing to advocate for the person receiving coaching
Knowledge of business and organizations	• Actively learns about company strategy • Studies the industry to understand how success is attained • Knows the requirements of roles at different levels of leadership • Demonstrates a good grasp of organizational dynamics and learns the political atmosphere in the client's organization • Reads about business and relevant industries • Establishes and measures business outcomes for coaching

(Continued)

Table 8.5. Core Competencies of Effective Coaches (*Continued*)

Skill or Competency	*Illustrative Behaviors*
Personal courage	• Provides feedback in a straightforward and supportive manner • Brings potentially difficult issues to the table • Does the right thing for the organization and the individual being coached • Declines to remain involved when it is clear that progress cannot be made • Influences others to support or participate in the change process
Knowledge of behavior change	• Understands psychology and the factors that contribute to individual behavior change • Understands leadership and what it takes to be effective at all levels of the organization • Creates goals and objectives together with the coachee • Uses knowledge of the change process to plan activities • Brings in key organizational players or people in the individual's support system to assist with behavior change • Creates plans for maintaining behavior change
Personal integrity	• Maintains confidentiality for the coachee • Establishes boundaries with the organization in terms of what information will be communicated and what will not • Seeks feedback to improve own skills • Holds self accountable for coaching effectiveness • Maintains personal objectivity

Factors in the Organization

The context in which change occurs also plays a part. Vroom and Jago (2007) estimate that in most instances, the situation explains more variance in leadership effectiveness than stable individual differences do. Three situational factors outside the individual seem most relevant to influencing how a person might change: the individual's manager, the systems and processes in an organization, and the organization's culture.

Several authors have made the commonsense argument that an individual's manager can have a powerful impact on individual change. A boss who understands an individual's desire to change and develop could provide the support and reinforcement a person needs to make changes last (Yukl, 2006). McCauley and Hezlett (2001) cite studies that show support from supervisors or other senior staff encourages participation in learning and development activities. Informal and formal mentoring by a boss has a positive impact on the degree to which an individual learns and changes. A supportive boss is someone who:

- Participates in his direct report's change or coaching process
- Understands or corroborates the individual's objectives for change
- Provides feedback about the person's efforts and progress
- Designs or provides experiences that allow the individual to gain and practice new skills
- Helps the individual link new learning to other experiences
- Serves as an advocate for the individual to the rest of the organization

When an organization's systems facilitate and reward learning, individuals are more likely to make the time for learning and development. Training models (Campbell, 1988; Noe, 1986) have been explicit in specifying how transfer of training back to the participant's work occurs more frequently when organizations provide the opportunities for individuals to use their new skills or knowledge on the job. Several authors stress the need to embed development experiences in a "supportive organizational context" and provide "organizational learning boosters" for individual change and development. This means teaching managers the skills they need to develop others and ensuring that leadership development is integrated with other organizational processes, including succession planning, performance management, and reward systems (London & Mauer, 2004; Van Velsor et al., 2004).

The organization's environment can also influence individual learning and change. Organizations that value learning and development invest resources in training, have measures that track change, and reward managers who promote learning and development (Yukl, 2006). London and Maurer (2004) indicate that climate factors such as encouragement of innovation, setting expectations for development, and treating mistakes as learning opportunities facilitate development activity.

Events outside the organization can have an influence on learning and development. A turbulent external environment (economic downturns, unstable industry dynamics, and competitive pressures, for example) has the effect of reducing the individual's commitment to personal change. A recent study (Herold, Fedor, & Caldwell, 2007) found an interaction between the context and individual differences, which may explain the variance in a person's attitude toward change.

The organizational environment had an impact on a senior construction company executive. Although viewed as a highly talented executive, he struggled with his role as chief operating officer, which required him to lead (rather than micromanage) a team of strong performers. Yet he had a special talent in the area that fueled company growth: deal making and integrating acquisitions. The organization culture had never emphasized or rewarded development; historically, results were most important. Resistant to feedback and unaware of his impact on others, he nevertheless made a commitment to change because his boss made it clear that change was mandatory and his longer-term future with the company was at stake. He began learning about his impact and finding new ways to lead. Within six months, others began to see improvement in his ability to involve his team and change his controlling style. Then his environment shifted. His boss was promoted to a European-headquarters role so no one was any longer requiring change from him, and the U.S.-based company became consumed with the negotiations for the largest acquisition in its history. Factors in the organization—a new manager who did not emphasize the need to change—and disruption in the organization environment caused the executive to revert back to his *command and control* behavior.

Measuring the Effectiveness of Coaching

With the coaching industry exceeding the $1 billion mark, executives are naturally asking about the return on the investment and are looking for tangible evidence of results. There are four primary questions to be answered: What should be measured? Who should supply the measurements? How should change be measured? When is effectiveness best measured? Once evaluation efforts yield definitive outcomes, organizations will ask the question this chapter began with: How valuable is the change in behavior that has occurred, and what is the return on the investment (ROI)?

What Should Be Measured?

Kirkpatrick's (1998) framework for evaluation provides guidance on measurement categories. He categorizes training results into four useful dimensions: reactions, learning (improvement in skills or knowledge), behavior change, and outcomes (business impact or results).

Reactions are an easy place to start. Do the executives who receive coaching value it and think it mattered? Do they like the process well enough to participate again or recommend it to others? In one study, Smither, London, Flautt, Vargas, and Kucine (2003) found 86.3 percent of senior managers reported they wanted to work with an executive coach again. In Wasylyshyn's (2003) outcome study, all reported having made significant gains from coaching. One can infer a positive reaction to coaching from the experience of a Fortune 100 consumer products company. The organization embarked on an initiative to provide coaching to all of its senior leaders. They viewed the experience so positively that they cascaded coaching down to the next tier of leaders. Anecdotes like this are evidence that coaching has value.

The Corporate Leadership Council (2003) also found that executives highly valued coaching as a preferred development intervention, ranking it among the top five on a longer list of leadership development opportunities. Unfortunately, the fact that coaching is preferred or used repeatedly does not prove it is useful or effective in changing behavior. Its organizational value could be for something other than behavior change. One HR executive noted that his organization gained from coaching initiatives because "by paying attention to our leaders, we increase our ability to retain them."

Kirkpatrick's second category, learning or improvement in skills or knowledge, is relevant when coaching targets skill or knowledge acquisition. While group training for specific skills or knowledge is potentially more efficient than one-on-one training, skill or knowledge acquisition can be a legitimate goal of the coaching process. Consider the senior executive who faltered when making presentations to her board and investor groups. By developing improved formal presentation skills through rehearsal and video feedback, she significantly improved her ability to communicate clearly and powerfully in important settings. The board gained confidence in her leadership, and she gained comfort in handling an important senior executive task.

The third category, behavior change, lies at the heart of coaching and other individual interventions. Holt and Peterson (2006) reported on Peterson's 1993 study of 370 coaching participants who showed change of more than 1.5 standard deviations based on post-coaching rater perceptions of the individuals' behavior—the equivalent of moving from the 50th to the 93rd percentile. The Corporate Leadership Council (2003) found that aggregating the results of coaching across executives showed no significant impact on group performance, although for some individuals, coaching resulted in as much as a 54 percent impact on improving their individual performance.

Kirkpatrick's fourth evaluation category is measuring outcomes: the actual business results that can be linked to the intervention. Typical business outcomes include work team productivity, revenue growth, decreased turnover, faster time for bringing new products to market, enhanced profitability, increased customer satisfaction, stock price growth, and more engaged associates. Several studies have focused on these kinds of quantifiable outcomes. Olivero, Bane, and Kopelman (2001) compared productivity improvement from training alone to training paired with eight weeks of one-on-one coaching. Training increased productivity by 22.4 percent, and coaching paired with training increased productivity by 88 percent. McGovern et al. (2001) found that coaching was related to increases in productivity, quality, profitability, and retention, among other outcomes. The Corporate Leadership Council (2004) also cites evidence of dramatic increases in executive retention as an outcome of coaching interventions.

Unfortunately, there are too few studies that directly measure the business results of leadership development initiatives. Given the amount of money being spent by organizations on coaching, it is surprising that so few have looked at the correlation between individual leader change and business outcomes. Coaches need to routinely include business outcomes in measuring the results of coaching. Instead of executive coaches resting on their laurels and asserting, "Well, I must be effective; the organization continues to pay my fees," they should be diligent about measuring and communicating results.

Who Are the Best Judges of Change?

The question of who supplies the data to measure change is challenging. Practitioners and researchers have addressed this in multiple ways: they have solicited the judgments of the coach, the individual who received coaching, managers, direct reports, peers, and sometimes friends or family. Changes in behavior can be observed by different individuals in different settings. Having only the coach and the participant evaluate change seems subjective and self-serving. Asking direct reports, a boss, an HR professional, or peers to provide evaluation is reasonable and more objective. However, in a fluid business environment, these people often change jobs, making traditional pre- and postcomparisons problematic. To obtain the best and most objective evaluation of behavior change, common sense says to measure change from as many different perspectives as possible, which is generally consistent with the findings in the 360-degree feedback literature on rater accuracy (Murphy, 2004).

What Are the Right Measures of Individual Change?

The right measure of change is dependent on the behavior that an individual has decided to improve, add, or eliminate. Direct observation or testing would be especially useful when the goal of coaching is to improve a specific skill (like conflict resolution skills). Another reasonable approach to measuring the impact of coaching is to compare before and after behavioral measures or before and after qualitative interviews with people who have had the chance to observe the executive over time. Using personality inventories as pre- and postmeasures will likely be disappointing since personality inventory scores tend to be stable over time.

Some behaviors are also more easily observed than others. For example, if the executive who displays disappointment by launching into scathing tirades in meetings stops this behavior, it will be noticed! But it may be more difficult to see change in the executive who is trying to improve his ability to think strategically.

Measures of change should be comprehensive. While evaluation efforts need to be tied to the stated goals of coaching, coaching has both intended and unintended outcomes. For example, organizations that use coaching to improve executive retention may find additional benefits in improved relationships, better teamwork, and decreased conflict in the workplace (Holt & Peterson, 2006). Effective evaluation efforts need to provide ways to measure all the potential benefits of coaching.

The purpose for coaching and the nature of what is to be learned should also influence how outcomes are measured. Coaching may be remedial in focus (to stop or change behaviors that would lead to derailment), designed for accelerating readiness for a next-level role, provided in support of a significant leadership transition, focused on greater leadership effectiveness in one's current role, or used in conjunction with other training or development initiatives. If a person participates in coaching to help make a transition from manager to director, and does so successfully, how do we know that coaching was the cause? Would the transition have gone smoothly without the coaching intervention? Comparing a group of executives coached at the start of their transition to a control group of executives who received no coaching would provide an answer to the effectiveness question.

Of course, these would be expensive and somewhat impractical studies to design and implement, so answers to questions about coaching effectiveness tend to be based more on speculation and anecdotes than on research evidence.

When to Measure Outcomes?

In addressing the third question, when coaching outcomes should be measured, both Hellervik et al. (1992) and McCauley and Hezlett (2001) suggest that behavior change may not show up in measures until six or nine months after initiating the change process. Peterson (1993) found people changed when change was measured six to twelve months after the completion of coaching. Smither et al. (2003) used 360-degree feedback ratings one year apart and showed that managers who worked with an executive coach after receiving 360-degree feedback improved more than those who received the feedback with no coaching. Psychologists, coaches, and HR leaders need to be thoughtful about when to measure change, especially if the change measure is based on others' perceptions or ratings, since observable behavior change may require time to become apparent. Furthermore, if we intend to show the sustainability of behavioral change, then measurement should extend out beyond the one-year mark.

How Valuable Is It? A Look at ROI

Returns on the investment in coaching are difficult to calculate and highly variable. Inconsistency in coaching is an issue that makes it difficult to show returns. Organizations that use coaching report that they struggle with instances of poorly trained or mismatched coaches, unfocused coaching engagements, variable use of coaching across the organization, and poor integration between coaching and other leadership development efforts (Corporate Leadership Council, 2003). These issues influence the ability to accurately measure the real return on coaching for an organization.

Despite these measurement difficulties, there is some evidence that coaching can have impressive returns. McGovern et al. (2001) studied 100 executives who participated in 6 to 12 months of coaching and estimated that coaching was worth 5.7 times the initial investment on average. Research from the Corporate Leadership Council (2004) on the ROI of executive coaching includes references to a telecommunications organization that reported an ROI of 529 percent, as well as a six-to-one ROI ratio found at PricewaterhouseCoopers after a significant coaching initiative.

Because individual coaching often carries a hefty price tag, good coaches should be constantly looking for evidence of how they add value. Measuring ROI can be difficult, but there are resources that coaches can tap. Boudreau and Ramstad (2003) recommend using three measures of ROI for calculating the utility index of industrial-organizational psychology interventions: impact, effectiveness, and efficiency. Impact deals with business outcomes, effectiveness refers to whether the targeted change actually occurred, and efficiency relates to the costs (time, money, and resources) of producing the change. For the practitioner who is looking for practical tools, Anderson and Anderson (2005) provide worksheets for quantifying the results of coaching.

Small sample sizes and highly individualized coaching goals should not be an excuse for failing to measure impact and outcomes. Those who are engaged in the important work of behavioral change need to evaluate the effectiveness of individual change initiatives and share information about what works.

Implications and Lessons Learned

Changing individual behavior is a complex process influenced by a variety of factors that can help or hinder success. A good process can require substantial time and investment, not just on the part of the individual who is engaged in the process of change but also from those with whom he works. To ensure optimum results, there are important implications for both the organization and for those who practice or provide executive coaching services.

For the Organization

- Seriously consider the type of change required in the individual's leadership behavior. Some kinds of change—depending on the individual, her readiness, and the complexity of the change to be made—are more likely to be achieved through an individual intervention such as coaching. For other changes, a group intervention or training program may make more sense.

- Be a good consumer. Select consultants who have good professional knowledge, training, and breadth of knowledge. Link the need for coaching to organizational priorities and objectives.
- Qualify coaches and consultants to ensure they have good interpersonal skills, the ability to form relationships, business knowledge, and professional expertise. Beware of technique-dependent coaches.
- Expect and encourage coaches to conduct a thorough assessment of the individual's readiness to change, as well as a good diagnosis of other factors that will influence coaching success.
- Assess your organization. Consider whether the culture, the environment, the top leadership, and the business situation will support individual change.
- Use individual coaching to augment the value of 360-degree feedback interventions. Of the various tools and techniques employed in changing individual leader behavior, 360-degree feedback is among the most effective, but it is consistently improved when coaching and follow-up are included.
- Determine the desired results and business outcomes. Require coaches and consultants to recommend and establish measures of success at the outset of a change or coaching process.
- Recognize that a good coaching process takes time. Resist the temptation to insist on tangible evidence of change too early.

For Practitioners (Leadership Development Professionals or Executive Coaches)

- Organizations understand that leadership matters. Practitioners should be adept at making the business case for improving leadership effectiveness through coaching interventions.
- Keep current. Practitioners should make sure that they know and can demonstrate breadth of knowledge, training, and expertise in the art and science of individual behavior change.
- Sharpen and expand diagnostic skills. Individual differences contribute significantly to whether an individual will successfully change through coaching. Employ methods to assess the

motivation, intelligence, personality, potential derailers, and the confidence the individual has in order to determine his overall capacity to change.

- Use the entire change model when planning an intervention. Investigate factors other than an individual's willingness to participate that influence coaching success, including the complexity of the skill or task to be learned and the factors in the environment that will affect the acquisition and maintenance of new behavior.

- Have the courage to say "no." Sometimes organizations (or individual leaders) request coaching for the wrong reason. If you find yourself in the middle of a change process that is going nowhere, be willing to stop it.

- Understand the business results that the organization needs to achieve. Translate these into measures of success at the outset of the coaching engagement.

- Help organizations establish realistic expectations about the time required and the organizational commitment needed to receive a return on their investment in coaching.

Conclusion

Changing behavior is difficult, and there are few guarantees of success. When it works, the rewards are many for individuals and their organizations. Organizations and individuals who are willing to invest in effective individual behavior change efforts can achieve significant returns. Successful change and development can result in improved leader performance, more effective work relationships, increased job satisfaction and motivation, and career advancement.

Our aim in this chapter was to summarize what we know about the important work of facilitating individual leader behavior change. Our hope is that our discussion has provided help and guidance to practitioners and organizations in understanding and using best practices in their efforts to do so.

References

Ackerman, P. L., & Heggestad, E. D. (1997). Intelligence, personality, and interests: Evidence for overlapping traits. *Psychological Bulletin, 121,* 219–245.

Adams, J. S. (1963). Towards an understanding of inequity. *Journal of Abnormal and Social Psychology, 67,* 422–436.

Adams, J. S. (1965). Inequity in social exchange. In L. Berkowitz (Ed.), *Advances in experimental social psychology* (Vol. 2, pp. 267–299). Orlando, FL: Academic Press.

Anderson, D., & Anderson, M. (2005). *Coaching that counts.* Burlington, MA: Elsevier Butterworth-Heinemann.

Bachelor, A., & Horvath, A. (2006). The therapeutic relationship. In M. A. Hubble, B. L. Duncan, & S. D. Miller (Eds.), *The heart and soul of change* (pp. 133–178). Washington, DC: American Psychological Association.

Bandura, A. (1977). *Social learning theory.* Upper Saddle River, NJ: Prentice Hall.

Bandura, A. (1986). *Social foundations of thought and action: A social cognitive theory.* Upper Saddle River, NJ: Prentice Hall.

Bandura, A. (2001). Social cognitive theory: An agentic perspective. *Annual Review of Psychology, 52,* 1–26.

Barrick, M. R., & Mount, M. K. (1991). The big five personality dimensions and job performance: A meta-analysis. *Personnel Psychology, 44,* 1–26.

Berglas, S. (2002). The very real dangers of executive coaching. *Harvard Business Review, 80*(6), 86–92.

Bloom, N., Dorgan, S., Dowdy, J., Van Reenen, J., & Rippin, T. (2005). *Management practices across firms and nations.* London: Centre for Economic Performance and McKinsey & Company.

Boudreau, J. W., & Ramstad, P. M. (2003). Strategic industrial and organizational psychology and the role of utility analysis models. In W. C. Borman, D. R. Ilgen, & R. J. Klimoski (Eds.), *Handbook of psychology, Vol. 12: Industrial and organizational psychology.* Hoboken, NJ: Wiley.

Campbell, J. P. (1988). Training design for performance improvement. In J. P. Campbell, R. J. Campbell, & Associates (Eds.), *Productivity in organizations: New perspectives from industrial and organizational psychology* (pp. 177–215). San Francisco: Jossey-Bass.

Campion, M. A., & Lord, R. G. (1982). A control systems conceptualization of the goal setting and changing process. *Organizational Behavior and Human Performance, 30,* 265–287.

Charan, R., Drotter, S., & Noel, J. (2001). *The leadership pipeline.* San Francisco: Jossey-Bass.

Chen, G., Gully, S. M., Whiteman, J., & Kilcullen, R. N. (2000). Examination of relationships among trait-like individual differences, state-like individual differences, and learning performance. *Journal of Applied Psychology, 85,* 835–847.

Clausen, J. A., & Jones, C. J. (1998). Predicting personality stability across the life span: The role of competence and work and family commitments. *Journal of Adult Development, 5,* 73–83.

Corporate Leadership Council. (2003). *Maximizing returns on professional executive coaching.* Washington, DC: Corporate Executive Board.

Corporate Leadership Council. (2004). *ROI of executive coaching.* Washington, DC: Corporate Executive Board.

Corporate Leadership Council. (2005). *Realizing the full potential of rising talent.* Washington, DC: Corporate Executive Board.

Deci, E. L., & Ryan, R. M. (1985). *Intrinsic motivation and self-determination in human behavior.* New York: Plenum Press.

Donovan, J. J. (2001). Work motivation. In N. Anderson, D. S. Ones, H. K. Sinangil, & C. Viswesvaran (Eds.), *Handbook of industrial, work and organizational psychology* (Vol. 2, pp. 53–76). Thousand Oaks, CA: Sage.

Douglas, C. A., & Morley, W. H. (2000). *Executive coaching: An annotated bibliography.* Greensboro, NC: Center for Creative Leadership.

Dweck, C. S., & Legget, E. (1988). A social cognitive approach to motivation and personality. *Psychological Review, 95,* 256–273.

Flaherty, J. (1999). *Coaching: Evoking excellence in others.* Burlington, MA: Butterworth Heinemann.

Fulmer, I., Gerhart, B., & Scott, K. (2003). Are the 100 best better? An empirical investigation of the relationship between being a "great place to work" and firm performance. *Personnel Psychology, 56,* 965–993.

Goldberg, L. R. (1990). An alternative "description of personality": The big five factor structure. *Journal of Personality and Social Psychology, 59*(6), 1216–1229.

Goldsmith, M., & Lyons, L. (2006). *Coaching for leadership.* San Francisco: Pfeiffer/Jossey-Bass.

Goldstein, I. L. (1986). *Training in organizations: Needs assessment, development, and evaluation.* Monterey, CA: Brooks/Cole.

Hansen, G. S., & Wernerfelt, B. (1989). Determinants of firm performance: The relative importance of economic and organizational factors. *Strategic Management Journal, 10,* 399–411.

Hellervik, L. W., Hazucha, J. F., & Schneider, R. J. (1992). Behavior change: Models, methods, and a review of the evidence. In M. D. Dunnette & L. M. Hough (Eds.), *Handbook of industrial and organizational psychology* (2nd ed., Vol. 3, pp. 823–895). Palo Alto, CA: Consulting Psychologists Press.

Herold, D. M., Fedor, D. B., & Caldwell, S. D. (2007). Beyond change management: A multilevel investigation of contextual and personal influences on employees' commitment to change. *Journal of Applied Psychology, 92,* 942–951.

Hoare, C. (Ed.). (2006a). *Handbook of adult learning and development.* New York: Oxford University Press.

Hoare, C. (2006b). Work as a catalyst of reciprocal adult develop-
ment and learning: Identity and personality. In C. Hoare (Ed.),
Handbook of adult learning and development (pp. 344–380). New
York: Oxford University Press.

Hogan, R., Curphy, G., & Hogan, J. (1994). What we know about leadership. *American Psychologist, 49,* 493–504.

Hogan, R., & Hogan, J. (1997). *Hogan Development Survey manual.* Tulsa,
OK: Hogan Assessment Systems.

Hogan, R., & Kaiser, R. B. (2005). What we know about leadership.
Review of General Psychology, 9, 169–180.

Hollenbeck, G. P. (2002). Coaching executives. In R. Silzer (Ed.), *The
21st century executive: Innovative practices for building leadership at
the top* (pp. 137–167). San Francisco: Jossey-Bass.

Holt, K., & Peterson, D. B. (2006). *Measuring and maximizing the ROI of
executive coaching.* Paper presented at the 21st Annual Conference
of the Society for Industrial and Organizational Psychology,
Dallas, TX.

Hough, L. M., & Furnham A. (2003). Use of personality variables in work
settings. In I. B. Weiner (Ed.-in-Chief) & W. Borman, D. Ilgen, & R.
Klimoski (Vol. Eds.), *Handbook of psychology: Vol. 12. Industrial and
organizational psychology* (pp. 131–169). Hoboken, NJ: Wiley.

Hough, L. M., & Ones, D. S. (2001). The structure, measurement, validity, and use of personality variables in industrial, work, and organizational psychology. In N. Anderson, D. S. Ones, H. K. Sinangil, &
C. Viswesvaran (Eds.), *Handbook of industrial, work and organizational psychology* (Vol. 1, pp. 233–277). Thousand Oaks, CA: Sage.

Hough, L. M., Ones, D. S., & Viswesvaran, C. (1998). *Personality correlates of managerial performance constructs.* Paper presented at a symposium conducted at the 13th annual conference of the Society of
Industrial and Organizational Psychology, Dallas.

Hunter, J. E., & Hunter, R. F. (1984). Validity and utility of alternate
predictors of job performance. *Psychological Bulletin, 96,* 72–98.

Huselid, M. (1995). The impact of human resource management practices on turnover, productivity, and corporate financial performance. *Academy of Management Journal, 38,* 635–672.

Huselid, M., & Becker, B. (1997). The impact of high performance
work systems, implementation effectiveness, and alignment with
strategy on shareholder wealth. *Academy of Management Best
Papers Proceedings,* 144–148.

Judge, T., Bono, J., Ilies, R., & Gerhardt, M. (2002). Personality and
leadership: A qualitative and quantitative review. *Journal of Applied
Psychology, 87,* 765–780.

Judge, T. A., Jackson, C. L., Shaw, J. C., Scott, B. A., & Rich, B. L. (2007). Self-efficacy and work-related performance: The integral role of individual differences. *Journal of Applied Psychology, 92,* 107–127.

Kaiser, R. B., & Craig, S. B. (2005). *How is executive success different?* Paper presented at Leadership at the Top, the First Society of Industrial and Organizational Psychology Leading Edge Consortium, St. Louis, MO.

Kampa-Kokesch, S., & Anderson, M. Z. (2001). Executive coaching: A comprehensive review of the literature. *Consulting Psychology Journal: Practice and Research, 53,* 205–228.

Kilburg, R. R. (1996). Toward a conceptual understanding and definition of executive coaching. *Consulting Psychology Journal: Practice and Research, 48,* 134–144.

Kirkpatrick, D. L. (1998). *Evaluating training programs: The four levels.* San Francisco: Berrett-Koehler.

Knowles, M. S., Holton, E. F., & Swanson, R. A. (2005). *The adult learner.* Burlington, MA: Elsevier.

Kolb, D. (1984). *Experiential learning: Experience as the source of learning and development.* Upper Saddle River, NJ: Prentice Hall.

Komaki, J. (1986). Applied behavior analysis and organizational behavior: Reciprocal influences of the two fields. In B. M. Staw & L. L. Cummings (Eds.), *Research in organizational behavior: An annual series of analytical essays and critical reviews.* Greenwich, CT: JAI Press.

Kraut, A. I., Pedigo, P. R., McKenna, D., & Dunnette, M. D. (1989). The role of the manager: What's really important in different management jobs. *Academy of Management Executive, 3,* 286–293.

Levinson, H. (1982). *Executive.* Cambridge, MA: Harvard University Press.

Levinson, H. (1996). Executive coaching. *Consulting Psychology Journal: Practice and Research, 48,* 115–123.

Locke, E. A. (1968). Toward a theory of task motivation and incentives. *Organizational Behavior and Human Performance, 3,* 157–189.

Locke, E. A., & Latham, G. P. (1990). *A theory of goal setting and task performance.* Upper Saddle River, NJ: Prentice Hall.

Lombardo, M. M., & Eichinger, R. W. (2000). High potentials as high learners. *Human Resource Management, 39,* 321–329.

London, M., & Maurer, T. J. (2004). Leadership development: A diagnostic model for continuous learning in dynamic organizations. In J. Antonakis, A. T. Cianciolo, & R. J. Sternberg (Eds.), *The nature of leadership* (pp. 222–245). Thousand Oaks, CA: Sage.

London, M., & Smither, J. W. (2002). Feedback orientation, feedback culture, and the longitudinal performance management process. *Human Resource Management Review, 12,* 81–100.

Ludeman, K., & Erlandson, E. (2004). Coaching the alpha male. *Harvard Business Review, 82*(5), 1–10.

Maurer, T. J. (2002). Employee learning and development orientation: Toward an integrative model of involvement in continuous learning. *Human Resource Development Review, 1,* 9–44.

McCall, M., & Lombardo, M. (1983). *Off the track: Why and how successful executives get derailed.* Greensboro, NC: Center for Creative Leadership.

McCauley, C. D. (2001). Leader training and development. In S. J. Zaccaro & R. J. Klimoski (Eds.), *The nature of organizational leadership* (pp. 347–383). San Francisco: Jossey-Bass.

McCauley, C. D. (2004). Successful and unsuccessful leadership. In J. Antonakis, A. T. Cianciolo, & R. J. Sternberg (Eds.), *The nature of leadership* (pp. 199–221). Thousand Oaks: Sage.

McCauley, C. D., & Hezlett, S. A. (2001). Individual development in the workplace. In N. Anderson, D. S. Ones, H. K. Sinangil, & C. Viswesvaran (Eds.), *Handbook of industrial, work and organizational psychology* (Vol. 1, pp. 313–335). Thousand Oaks, CA: Sage.

McGovern, J., Lindemannn, M., Vergara, M., Murphy, S., Barker, L., & Warrenfeltz, R. (2001). Maximizing the impact of executive coaching: Behavior change, organizational outcomes, and return on investment. *Manchester Review, 6,* 1–9.

Merriam, S. B., & Clark, M. C. (2006). Learning and development: The connection in adulthood. In C. Hoare (Ed.), *Handbook of adult learning and development* (pp. 27–51). New York: Oxford University Press.

Mumford, M. D., Marks, M. A., Connelly, M. S., Zaccaro, S. J., & Reiter-Palmon, R. (2000). Development of leadership skills: Experience and timing. *Leadership Quarterly, 11,* 87–114.

Murphy, S. J. (2004). *A 360-degree feedback follow-up study: Effort to change is the key.* Unpublished doctoral dissertation, University of Minnesota, Minneapolis.

Noe, R. A. (1986). Trainee's attributes and attitudes: Neglected influences on training effectiveness. *Academy of Management Review, 11,* 736–749.

Olivero, G., Bane, K. D., & Kopelman, R. E. (2001). Executive coaching as a transfer of training tool: Effects on productivity in a public agency. *Public Personnel Management, 26,* 461–469.

Peltier, B. (2001). *The psychology of executive coaching.* New York: Taylor & Francis Group.

Peterson, D. B. (1993). *Measuring change: A psychometric approach to evaluating individual coaching outcomes.* Paper presented at the 8th Annual Conference of the Society for Industrial and Organizational Psychology, San Francisco.

Peterson, D. B., & Hicks, M. D. (1996). *Leader as coach: Strategies for coaching and developing others.* Minneapolis, MN: Personnel Decisions International.

Pfeffer, J., & Veiga, J. (1999). Putting people first for organizational success. *Academy of Management Executive, 13,* 37–48.

Pine, J., & Gilmore, J. (1999). *The experience economy: Work is theater and every business a stage.* Boston: Harvard Business School Press.

Russell, C. J. (2001). A longitudinal study of top-level executive performance. *Journal of Applied Psychology, 86,* 560–573.

Schmidt, F. L., & Hunter, J. (1998). The validity and utility of selection methods in personnel psychology. *Psychological Bulletin, 124,* 262–274.

Schmidt, F. L., & Hunter, J. (2004). General mental ability in the world of work: Occupational attainment and job performance. *Journal of Personality and Social Psychology, 86,* 162–173.

Sherman, S., & Freas, A. (2004). The Wild West of executive coaching. *Harvard Business Review, 82(11),* 82–92.

Smither, J. W., London, M. J., Flautt, R., Vargas, Y., & Kucine, I. (2003). Can executive coaches enhance the impact of multisource feedback on behavior change? A quasi-experimental field study. *Personnel Psychology, 56,* 23–44.

Smither, J. W., London, M., & Reilly, R. R. (2005). Does performance improve following multisource feedback? A theoretical model, meta-analysis, and review of empirical findings. *Personnel Psychology, 58,* 33–66.

Ting, S., & Hart, E. W. (2004). Formal coaching. In C. D. McCauley & E. Van Velsor (Eds.), *The Center for Creative Leadership handbook of leadership development* (pp. 116–150). San Francisco: Jossey-Bass.

Van Velsor, E., & Leslie, J. B. (1995). Why executives derail: Perspectives across time and cultures. *Academy of Management Executive, 9,* 62–72.

Van Velsor, E., Moxley, R. S., & Bunker, K. A. (2004). The leader development process. In C. D. McCauley & E. Van Velsor (Eds.), *The Center for Creative Leadership handbook of leadership development* (pp. 204–234). San Francisco: Jossey-Bass.

Vroom, V. H. (1964). *Work and motivation.* Hoboken, NJ: Wiley.

Vroom, V. H., & Jago, A. G. (2007). The role of the situation in leadership. *American Psychologist, 62,* 17–24.

Wasylyshyn, K. M. (2003). Executive coaching: An outcome study. *Consulting Psychology Journal: Practice and Research, 55,* 94–106.

Weiss, H. M. (1992). Learning theory and industrial and organizational psychology. In M. D. Dunnette & L. M. Hough (Eds.), *Handbook of industrial and organizational psychology* (pp. 171–221). Palo Alto, CA: Consulting Psychologists Press.

Yukl, G. (2006). *Leadership in organizations.* Upper Saddle River, NJ: Prentice Hall.

Zenger, J., & Folkman, J. (2002). *The extraordinary leader.* New York: McGraw-Hill.

CHAPTER 9

MANAGING LEADERSHIP TALENT POOLS

Ben E. Dowell

Do you have the talent to achieve or maintain competitive advantage? Where are your most highly talented people deployed? Do you have the talent to adapt to a new strategic reality? The answers to these questions can all come from the disciplined review and management of leadership talent pools.

Talent management is not what it used to be. More and more research suggests that fewer people are capable of meeting the demanding future needs of organizations (Michaels, Handfield-Jones & Axelrod, 2001; Charan, Drotter, & Noel, 2001; Wolfe, 2004). The Corporate Leadership Council (2005) identifies eight factors that are challenging organizations from a talent perspective: mergers and acquisitions, increasing business complexity, globalization, an aging workforce, competitive specialized talent markets, the need to manage global talent, leaner organizational structures, and the expectations for organization leaders to control costs while driving growth. These eight factors increase both the importance and the difficulty of managing critical talent pools.

In the past, when a position came open, you promoted the next person in line, and if you did not have the talent you needed, you bought it. However, increasingly, when you do find talent and bring the person into the organization, the chance is high that the person will not meet expectations (Dowell, 2002; Corporate Leadership Council, 2005; Groysberg, McLean, & Nohria, 2006). Within this context, organizations are facing the need to take a more proactive approach to managing their leadership talent pools. They are taking multiple paths to ensure they will have the talent they will need to meet current and future strategic needs. Some organizations focus on improving their ability to acquire external talent and integrate that talent into their organizations. Others are improving their capability to manage the internal talent they have. Some do both.

This chapter reviews the organizational process for choosing a talent management strategy to meet the future strategic needs of an organization. As with organization strategy, choosing an appropriate talent strategy requires organizations to have the capability to see future talent needs as they will be, the willingness to see the quality and depth of current talent as it is (not as management would like it to be), and the discipline to take the actions necessary to close the gap.

In some of the most effective organizations, the talent review process forms the third leg of the organization planning process, along with reviews of the organization's strategy and operating plans. Strategic plans and operating plans are critical to the talent planning process. Figure 9.1 illustrates the flow of these three organization processes that begins with the strategic plan. The organization's strategy provides the foundation for identifying

**Figure 9.1. Placement of Talent Reviews in
the Annual Planning Cycle**

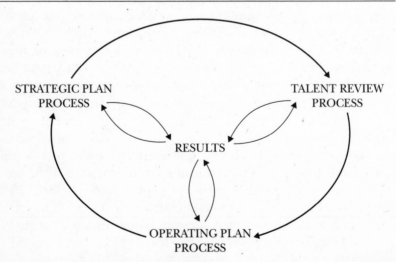

future talent needs, and the operating plan provides the mechanism for allocating resources (financial and human) to support the actions identified during the talent review process (such as new recruiting efforts, developmental programs for high potentials, and retention programs). Some business thought leaders assert that the strategy and operations planning processes of the firm are less important than future-oriented people processes, which identify and develop the leadership talent needed to execute the business strategy (Bossidy & Charan, 2002).

Organizations put their future at risk if they do not apply the same discipline to planning the development of their talent as they do to planning the development of products and services. The ability to formulate and execute strategy depends on having the necessary talent in place. An organization's talent is one of the sources of sustainable competitive advantage. When an organization has highly talented individuals in strategically critical positions this talent becomes a source of competitive advantage that is one of the most difficult to replicate by competitors.

The cycle of planning and executing the talent review process, illustrated in Figure 9.2, can begin once an organization's strategic

Figure 9.2. The Talent Review Cycle

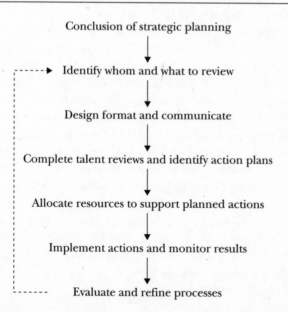

Conclusion of strategic planning

Identify whom and what to review

Design format and communicate

Complete talent reviews and identify action plans

Allocate resources to support planned actions

Implement actions and monitor results

Evaluate and refine processes

plan is established. With the conclusion of strategic planning, the design of the talent review process can begin with identifying who and what to review. An evaluation of the areas most critical to the successful execution of the organization's strategy should be the basis for these choices. Following the completion of the review and the development of action plans, the next critical step is to ensure that the necessary resources are available to execute the plans. The cycle continues with the implementation of the plans. In the most effective talent management systems, a continuing review of what is and is not working guides future actions.

The extent of the investment that organizations make in reviewing and managing their talent pools depends on the organization's internal and external environment. For some small organizations operating in a stable environment, an informal fifteen-minute discussion may suffice, while others may need a significantly higher investment of time and effort. This chapter presents the business case for purposefully reviewing and managing leadership talent pools and the critical factors in designing and executing the process.

The Business Case

Due to the baby boom in the 1940s and 1950s and the increasing participation of women in the workforce, there has been a relatively plentiful supply of leadership talent in the recent past. Over the past 25 years, the primary challenge in organizations has been to select the very best from among this extensive talent pool. In 1998 McKinsey & Company (Chambers, Foulon, Handfield-Jones, Hankin, & Michaels, 1998) caught the attention of the business community with the phrase *the war for talent*. McKinsey documented the shortage of qualified leadership talent in American business, and ongoing research over the past ten years has underscored this trend. As the need for more capable leaders is increasing, the supply is dwindling. The challenge of finding sufficient high-quality leadership talent is not just an American problem. The supply of quality leadership talent is an issue in Europe and Japan due to declining birthrates. China has similar shortages of leadership talent due to demographic and cultural issues (see Chapter 14 in this book by Elizabeth Weldon).

Wolfe (2004), citing multiple sources, paints an alarming picture of leadership shortages due to two demographic trends: an increasing number of senior managers will be retiring at the same time as the number of 35- to 44-year-olds, who would traditionally fill these vacated roles, will be declining. The combination of these trends will likely create shortages of quality leadership talent in many organizations. Historically organizations have addressed the issue of insufficient internal talent by going outside to recruit successors; however, there is a growing realization that this strategy is not working as well as it has in the past.

Although external hiring may bring fresh approaches to issues and executives who are not as bound by internal cultural constraints, hiring executives externally can be an issue. The business press regularly reports failures of executives brought in from the outside to run a business. Research suggests that the failure rate for executives recruited from the outside may be more than twice as high as the rate for executives promoted internally (Ciampa & Watkins, 1999; Dowell, 2002). Groysberg et al. (2006) suggest that these failures often occur because of a mismatch between the executive and the new organization. The reasons they identified for these failures include a lack of established relationships in the firm, poor understanding of the corporate culture and informal norms, and limited experience with company-specific systems and processes.

Recruiting senior leaders from the outside has another consequence that is frequently not recognized: the impact on executive turnover lower in the organization. Coyne and Coyne (2007) conducted research on turnover for proxy-level executives (the five highest-paid executives in a company) and all other executives following a change in CEO. Turnover was 50 percent higher among proxy-level executives (33 percent versus 22 percent) and 47 percent higher for all executives (25 percent versus 17 percent) when the new CEO came from the outside rather than from the inside. These are all factors that favor the insider over the outsider. Collins (2001), in his research on companies that evolved from being good companies to great companies, based on their record of financial returns, found that 10 of the 11 CEOs in the "great" companies came from the inside.

Frequently the resources required to build internal talent depth are limited, so organizations must choose where to invest.

A recent review of succession management practices (Corporate Leadership Council, 2003b) concludes that top-tier companies consider two primary factors in deciding where to make their talent investment. These high-performing companies invest in the talent pools that are most important to the successful execution of their strategic plan and in the talent that would be the most difficult to replace in the external labor market.

Foundations

We do not know when organizations began reviewing talent and managing leadership talent pools. Perhaps the ancient Chinese, as they managed the first civil service bureaucracy, might lay claim to being first. In contemporary times, PepsiCo and GE have probably had the most impact on the process of reviewing and managing leadership talent pools. These companies created many of the widely used processes associated with reviewing and managing talent. More important, both demonstrated the value of having a "talent mindset": the pervasive belief that organizational performance and competitiveness are achieved with better talent (Michaels et al., 2001). The senior line and human resource (HR) leaders who left these companies exported the processes and mindset to countless other organizations.

Most of the research on managing leadership talent pools has focused specifically on succession. Kesner and Sebora (1994) and Berke (2005) present excellent reviews of this succession literature. Although Kesner and Sebora wrote more than a decade ago, they framed many of the research questions that are still unanswered. These questions focus on clarifying the impact of succession practices on overall organizational performance:

- Does the source of successors, internal versus external, influence future organizational performance?
- How does the effectiveness of the succession process influence the performance of the organization following a leader transition?

Berke (2005) draws the distinction between replacement planning (the identification of replacements for key positions) and succession management (the deliberate development and preparation of identified successors). Succession management is one component of talent pool management. Other components are strategies for retaining existing talent, strategies for supplementing internal talent through external staffing, and programmatic development of talent in the feeder pools who may become future senior leaders.

The organization process that drives the management of leadership talent pools is referred to as the "leadership talent review." Practical guides for designing and implementing talent review processes can be found in Rothwell (2001), Dowell (2002), Byham, Smith, and Paese (2002), Corporate Leadership Council (2003a), Berger and Berger (2004), and Berke (2005).

Key Factors in Managing Leadership Talent Pools

The leadership talent review is the single most important element in managing leadership talent pools. An organization's approach to reviewing and managing talent typically evolves as the strategic issues change in the organization. Two critical factors that influence the approach to reviewing talent are the expectations for organizational growth and the predictability of the organization's external environment. Table 9.1 summarizes the impact of these factors.

For organizations facing short-term organizational growth issues (such as responding to a significant change, up or down, in demand for products or services), the focus is typically on the performance of critical individuals and meeting immediate staffing needs, with only a cursory review of longer-term talent issues. When the external environment is unpredictable, it is rarely worth the effort to conduct talent reviews deep into the organization and roll the results up to the top of the organization. In this situation, longer-term projections of talent requirements are rarely accurate. Inaccurate forecasts of future talent requirements frequently lead to the allocation of scarce resources to programs or actions that will not meet future needs. When the future of the organization becomes more predictable (based on moderate growth, a stable external environment, or more sophisticated planning processes), focusing on succession, internal

Table 9.1. Factors Influencing the Focus of Talent Reviews

	Predictability of the External Environment	
Organizational Growth	*High*	*Low*
Explosive growth	Focus on: Immediate next steps for internal talent Identifying recruiting needs to fill gaps	Focus on: Identifying external talent to fill immediate needs Retention of critical talent
Moderate growth	Focus on: Developing internal talent over the next two to three years Depth of current talent pools Identifying recruiting needs over the next year	Focus on: Developing internal talent over next 12 to 18 months Likely gaps requiring external talent
Slow growth	Focus on: Long-term (five or more years) development of succession candidates for critical positions Reviewing talent required to pursue new strategies	Focus on: Strategy implications for talent needs Performance of current talent
Decline	Focus on: Retention of critical talent Actions to address individuals who do not fit with future organization needs	Focus on: Performance of current talent Possible talent needs of a new organization strategy

development, and the broader talent pool in the organization is more likely to address future needs.

The strategic plan and ongoing talent metrics often indicate which talent pools should be included in a talent review, beyond the core of discussing the senior leaders and their successors. The principle of differential investment—investing resources more heavily in the areas of the organization that are most critical to future strategic success—should guide the effort devoted to the review and management of talent. Strategy elements that may influence which employees to review can include expansion to new markets, the rise of new technologies, the need to improve performance in one part of the organization, and changes in an organization's regulatory environment. In each of these circumstances, one or more areas of an organization may become significantly more critical to future strategic success.

HR metrics may also identify areas to review. For example, metrics that indicate a significant increase in turnover suggest that plans to retain critical individuals should be included in the talent review. The observation of a decline in internal promotions might lead to a decision to review the number of high potentials in critical internal talent pools and existing developmental processes. The periodic and disciplined review of leading indicators associated with critical talent, such as measures of the engagement of individuals identified as high potentials or the difficulty of recruiting individuals into strategically important areas, such as R&D, is essential to proactively managing talent pools.

Roles in the Talent Review Process

More than other talent management elements, effective management of leadership talent pools requires a true partnership between line management and human resources. If the management of talent pools is not an accepted practice in an organization, talent reviews will rarely be worth the investment of time and resources. Without strong leadership from line management, the alignment of talent reviews with the critical strategic issues and the follow-up actions required to translate plans into reality will rarely happen. Without strong HR support, the review process and follow-up actions will not have the discipline required for accurate assessment and effective execution.

Table 9.2 describes three roles in the talent review process: line management, HR generalists, and talent management specialists. Line management may perform all three roles in small organizations. Large organizations are more likely to differentiate the three roles. Larger organizations with sufficient scale may have a talent management specialist or may hire an external consultant for this role. Typically, an experienced industrial-organizational psychologist has the appropriate background to perform this specialist role most effectively.

Regardless of the size of the organization or the style of the talent review, the most successful reviews are led by the most senior line manager, who is responsible for ensuring that discussions of talent are objective and stay focused on relevant organizational outcomes. They also must ensure that specific action plans to address issues are established. Generally the line manager who is accountable for the individuals and organizations being discussed is the primary presenter of the assessments and plans. These line managers are responsible for objectively identifying the actions needed to build the quality and depth of talent in their organizations. HR generalists and talent specialists guide the discussion and provide supplementary information as required.

The human resource function has increasingly become a central player in the management of talent pools. PepsiCo was one of the first companies to expect this function to play a major role. Andrall Pearson (1987), a past president of PepsiCo, describes in some detail what executives should expect of human resources in managing talent in the organization: encouraging line executives to make more critical evaluations of their staff, take action on marginal performers, identify the best people in the organization for openings, and take risks on high-potential managers. For many HR executives, managing talent has become one of their most significant accountabilities.

As the expectations have risen for human resources, the quality of HR talent has also risen. Senior line managers increasingly expect human resource executives to be experts in executive assessment and development and, in turn, these HR executives have brought in talent management specialists to support them. These roles are supported by professional disciplines such as industrial-organizational

Table 9.2. Roles in Reviewing and Managing Talent Pools

	Designing the Process	Preparing for the Review	During the Review	Follow-up
Line management	Senior leadership: Establish connections to other organizational processes Identify and communicate the organizational imperative Identify the most critical strategic questions to be addressed in the reviews Identify individuals and talent pools to be discussed	All levels: Identify strategic talent needs based on the strategic plan Realistically assess individuals and organization capability Identify the critical gaps to be addressed Identify plan of action at both the individual and organizational levels	Presenter: Provide assessments and supporting evidence Discuss plans to address gaps Reviewer: Ask questions to test accuracy of assessments Identify critical actions to address identified gaps Communicate expectations for action	Presenter: Take agreed-on actions Report on progress Reviewer: Communicate expectations Follow up on commitments Periodically follow up to ensure plans are executed

(*Continued*)

Table 9.2. Roles in Reviewing and Managing Talent Pools (*Continued*)

	Designing the Process	Preparing for the Review	During the Review	Follow-up
HR generalist (HRG)	Work with line executives to identify critical strategic issues Work with line executives to identify critical individuals and talent pools Ensure that the organizational imperative is communicated to those involved in the reviews	All levels of HR: Independently assess talent and organization capability Help managers make accurate assessments Coach management on options to address gaps	HRG aligned with presenter: Provide supplementary answers to questions Contribute to discussions of alternative actions HRG aligned with reviewer: Ask questions to test accuracy of assessments Identify critical actions to address identified gaps	HRG aligned with presenter: Take agreed-on actions Ensure that presenter takes agreed-on actions Report on progress HRG aligned with reviewer: Check to ensure expectations are understood Ensure that reviewer takes agreed-on actions
HR talent specialist or external talent consultant	Design process including communications Identify talent assessment dimensions and process Design tools to prepare for the reviews Identify strategic issues based on talent metrics	Coach HRGs on assessment and developmental options Possibly conduct independent assessments Coach HRG on options to address gaps	Contribute to discussions of alternative actions Document discussed issues and action decisions	Generate metrics to track progress Develop and execute program solutions to address strategic gaps Report on progress

psychology, which has contributed significantly to knowledge of leadership assessment and development. As talent becomes scarce, organizations are expecting human resources to contribute independent talent assessments and take an active role in the development of high-potential talent.

Participation in talent reviews is generally limited to people with intimate knowledge of the organization and the individuals being discussed. One option is to include the peers of the presenter (line manager) as participants in the review. There are differing views on whether peers of the presenter should be present during the review. The advantages of including peers are (1) the greater ability to identify appropriate developmental roles for high-potential talent, (2) additional perspectives on the assessment of the individuals, and (3) a broader range of views on how to address individual or organizational issues. The disadvantages are (1) possibly reduced candor by the presenter in discussing sensitive issues, (2) a tendency for peers to offer assessments that might be based on hearsay or old data, and (3) the additional time required when more perspectives are discussed. As a rule of thumb, a minimum of five minutes of discussion time per individual is required when peers are not in attendance. The average discussion time more than doubles when peers are present.

Another important role, not usually mentioned, is for someone who is not directly involved in the discussions to take notes on the specific agreed-on follow-up actions. If someone is not assigned this role, the action steps are frequently not fully recorded because the discussion moves so rapidly.

Without CEO commitment to the process of reviewing and managing talent pools, the results of the process are rarely worth the time and resources committed to the process. Pearson (1987) provides a helpful guide to the roles for CEOs or other senior line managers in reviewing and managing talent pools. The most valuable role a CEO can take during a talent review is to be a coach and help others see issues and identify actions that need to be taken. Asking critical questions can be the most effective way to fulfill this role. Table 9.3 illustrates the types of questions that the most effective CEOs or senior line managers ask during a review.

Table 9.3. CEO and Senior Line Manager Questions

Discussion Area	Questions
Strategic environment	• What are the most significant strategic issues in your organization that drive your talent strategy?
	• Which part of your organization is most critical to your strategic success? What is the depth of talent in that area?
	• Which individuals in your organization would be difficult to replace if they left?
Discussion of second-level executives	• Who are your top performers? Are their behaviors consistent with the behaviors we want?
	• Do you have any marginal performers? What actions are you taking to raise the performance of these individuals? When will you take that action?
	• What are you doing to replace a marginal performer? How do you know your replacement is the best candidate?
Succession plans	• Why have you identified this person as a successor? How will the position change over the next five years? What are you doing to ensure the person will be ready for the position?
	• What are the person's career interests? How do these interests match your plans for his or her career?
	• What do they need to develop in order to be ready for the position? How can you accelerate their development?

High potential discussion

- Does the timing of their projected career moves coincide with succession needs? If not, what are the plans to accelerate their development in the next six to nine months?
- What are their career ambitions?
- How will we keep them challenged if they are ready before the next position opens? Do they have any personal limitations that might restrict developmental opportunities?
- Do we have any retention issues? What can we do to retain them in the organization? Do they have a mentor?

Concluding discussion

- What are the most critical actions that you need to take in the next year?
- Who are the individuals you are going to focus on during the next year?
- What support do you need from me to help you build the level of talent in your organization?

Characteristics of Successful Talent Reviews

The most important parts of the talent review process are the preparation for the review and the actions that occur following the review, not the review itself. The fundamental value of the review is to bring discipline to the overall process of managing talent pools and to assemble the key decision makers who are needed to make decisions and take action. The style of the talent review tends to mirror both the organization's culture and the style of other organizational reviews, such as strategy reviews and operating plan reviews. The style can vary along a continuum from formal stand-up presentations to informal discussions around a table. All styles can work as long as the review meets a few fundamental standards.

The most successful talent review discussions have four characteristics:

- *Relevance.* This standard is met when the discussion topics and the assessments are grounded in the organization's strategy.
- *Evidence-based assessment.* This standard requires that assessments of individuals be based on observed behaviors or other types of measures (such as cognitive skills or personality assessment) that have documented validity and reliability. The standard of evidence-based assessment of organizational issues (such as turnover, the success rates of newly hired employees, and the success of programs) also requires valid and reliable measurement.
- *An action orientation.* This standard is achieved when specific actions, accountability, and follow-up measures are agreed on to address specific issues identified in the review.
- *Disciplined follow-up.* This standard is met when there is an explicit assessment of whether action plans are being executed and whether the outcomes are successfully achieving objectives.

One key to a successful talent review is adequate preparation. The process will be more efficient when there is advance agreement on the strategic issues and the individuals who will be discussed, as well as the specific format for the review. Keeping the discussion focused on relevant information is critical to effectively using the time and ensuring that the process is worthwhile. It is also important for someone to maintain discipline during the review process. This individual, typically the senior human resources executive, can ensure that the four standards are met and that the review discussion stays focused.

The Architecture of a Talent Review

Organizations face a number of decisions when designing the talent review process: how frequently reviews should occur, which individuals should be included in reviews, and what is discussed in the reviews—essentially, when to review, whom to review, and what to review.

When to Review

One of the most important issues is deciding when to conduct reviews. If the talent reviews do not occur between the strategic plan and the operating plan, there will be a good chance that the strategic context for actions may be lost or the resources required to execute the talent plans may not be sufficient.

Another decision is agreeing on the frequency of reviews. Most organizations use an annual cycle that is consistent with other major organizational planning processes. It can be tempting to skip a year when the organization is facing difficult challenges. However, over a two-year period, changes in both individuals and the organization's external environment often lead to a significant loss of momentum in building leadership depth. An important cornerstone to establishing talent management as a sustainable competitive advantage for the organization is conducting reviews consistently year to year.

Whom to Review

The choice of whom to review is the primary determinant of how much time to set aside for the review process. These options include:

- Focusing on the top two organizational levels, discussing the incumbents in these positions and the talent who might have the potential to grow into those positions

- Identifying the most strategically important positions in the organization, regardless of level, and reviewing the current incumbents and successors for those positions
- Selecting a particular area in the organization (perhaps a function or geographic area) based on its strategic significance and then reviewing individuals at all leadership levels in that area
- Identifying individuals for discussion by using a nomination process by senior leaders, using assessed potential or other demographic factors (such as diversity status or geographic location) as the basis for nomination

Most reviews generally include more than one of these options, based on the strategic needs of the organization.

The time required to discuss an individual during a review is frequently underestimated. The discussion of an individual, including assessments, development plans, and possible career steps, typically requires 5 to 15 minutes. When an individual is being discussed in significant depth or when the discussion deals with a complex situation, the discussion can often exceed 30 minutes. The effectiveness of the discussion can be greatly enhanced when the time allocated to the reviews is consistent with the number of individuals selected for discussion.

What to Review

When choosing the content of a talent review, the most common element is a review of the performance of the current senior leadership and a discussion of actions needed to address any performance or fit issues (fit is the degree to which an individual's behavior is consistent with desired organizational norms). The second most common practice is to review the possible successors to these senior leaders and discuss plans to enhance the readiness of those successors.

Typically reviews of specific individuals include a discussion covering a number of common elements:

- *Demographics.* These generally include at least current position, time in company, and time in position. Other elements might be educational background and career history.

- *Contributions.* The best reviews look at significant accomplishments and failures over the past two to three years to reflect the individual's performance over time.
- *Leadership.* This is a summary assessment of strengths and developmental needs and is often based on a forward-looking leadership competency model.
- *Career interests.* This includes factors that might influence career choices or individual mobility.
- *Developmental actions.* This discussion identifies specific actions, including coaching support, project assignments, changes in position, or participation in formal programs to address identified needs.

These elements assist in keeping the review discussion focused and serve as a foundation for feedback to individuals after the review.

Leadership talent reviews can contain a variety of elements that may vary from year to year and organization to organization. Below are other content areas that might also be included in the review.

The Organization's Strategic Environment
A brief discussion of the strategic and operational issues facing the organization can provide a useful context for the evaluation of talent and can suggest the most appropriate developmental opportunities for individuals. One of the risks with including this segment is that a manager might be more comfortable discussing strategy and operations than discussing talent. As a result, he may allocate too much time to the strategic and operations discussion and not enough time to the discussion of people.

Senior Leadership Behavior
Organizations might discuss whether leaders demonstrate culturally desired behaviors or leadership competencies (such as collaboration and staff development) that can contribute to performance results. Due to changing expectations, past performance is frequently a poor predictor of future performance. Often a person's leadership behavior is the best indicator of potential.

In addition, this discussion helps to determine the degree to which senior leader behavior is supporting the desired culture of the organization. In many companies (such as GE, PepsiCo, and Bristol-Myers Squibb), a matrix is developed comparing assessments of behavior with achieved results in order to facilitate developmental action planning. For example, an individual who was seen as exceeding performance objectives but not demonstrating desired cultural behaviors might receive counseling and not be considered for increases in compensation or advancement until those behaviors change. One challenge is to ensure that these behavioral assessments are based on likely future standards. Research-based, organization-specific, forward-looking leadership competency models are the best approach to setting those behavioral standards. However, these models are time-consuming and costly to develop and must be continuously updated as the strategy of the organization evolves.

Performance-Potential Matrix

The assessments of an individual's performance over time and the person's potential to assume future roles of greater responsibility forms the basis for this matrix. This matrix helps senior leaders allocate scarce development and financial resources and make appropriate staffing decisions.

During a talent review, the vast majority of discussion time is spent on individuals in the lowest and highest categories of performance and potential. Here are some hypothetical examples of the discussions and decisions made on individuals using the matrix in Table 9.4.

Lowest Performance–Lowest Potential

Pat Jones was ranked among peers as the lowest in performance and in future potential. This was the second year that Pat was put in this category, and HR confirmed that Pat's manager had given Pat appropriate feedback and had worked to address performance deficiencies during the past year. The decision was made to terminate Pat's employment within the next three months.

Highest Performance–Lowest Potential

Kelly Smith was ranked as one of the highest performers among peers but was seen as not having the potential to move to more senior positions in the organization. The discussion focused on

Table 9.4. Performance-Potential Matrix and Likely Actions

		Potential to Assume Positions of Greater Responsibility		
		Lowest	Middle	Highest
Relative Performance over Time	Highest	Reward and retain— Kelly Smith		Create challenging career opportunities and reward to retain— Jon Forman, Chris Span
	Middle		Monitor performance and potential	
	Lowest	Provide remedial development or act to move or remove— Pat Jones		Accelerate development and monitor performance— Jess Brown

how valuable Kelly's performance was to the organization and how difficult Kelly would be to replace. The decisions included ensuring Kelly would get:

- Exposure to and positive feedback from senior management
- Challenging work assignments
- Appropriate development opportunities

In addition, HR was asked to review Kelly's compensation package to make sure that it was competitive and would reduce his interest in exploring other opportunities.

Lowest Performance–Highest Potential
Jess Brown had been in the organization less than two years and in her current role for six months. She was seen as having great potential but had not yet demonstrated a track record of high

performance because of her short tenure in the organization. The discussion focused on questions about her current assignment:

- Was it sufficiently challenging to accurately assess her performance?
- Were the experiences addressing her developmental needs?
- Was she getting the mentoring that would help her to integrate into the organization and be successful?

One of the decisions was to ask Kelly (the high performer) to get to know Jess and to look for ways to help Jess establish a track record of performance, possibly becoming Jess's mentor. In addition, Jess's manager would be asked to work with the talent management function to identify a series of career moves for Jess that would accelerate her development toward a senior operating committee role while also allowing her to demonstrate a performance track record. HR would be asked to review Jess's compensation package, with a particular focus on allocating long-term awards that would help to retain Jess in the organization.

Highest Performance–Highest Potential

Jon Forman and Chris Span were both seen as high performers with the potential to succeed as the senior vice president of technology development when the incumbent retires next year. The discussion focused on the questions that still remained regarding both of them. Jon was seen as technically strong and well respected by the organization, but there were questions about whether he had the leadership and strategic skills needed to take the technology organization to the next level of effectiveness. Chris was seen as a strong leader with excellent strategic skills but not strong technical skills; there also were questions about whether Chris would be accepted by the organization if appointed to the senior vice president role.

The decisions were to give each of them assignments that would answer the remaining questions about Jon and Chris within the next nine months. Jon will be asked to lead a small task force to develop a comprehensive five-year talent and organizational structure strategy for the technology organization. Chris will be asked to work with the heads of the technology groups to identify the technology innovations that will be required to give the organization a competitive advantage in the marketplace. In addition, the president of the organization will ask HR to work with the current senior vice president of technology development to identify alternative job placements that would retain both Jon and Chris regardless of who was appointed to the senior vice president role.

Using the Matrix

The Corporate Leadership Council (2003b) concluded that top-tier companies manage their talent pools by both rewarding the best performers and weeding out the worst performers. Lombardo and Eichinger (2001) provide a more detailed description of the possible uses of the performance-potential matrix.

One challenge in using this matrix is that the assessments of performance and potential can be subjective and may not be stable over time. Current managers may not have had the opportunity to observe an individual's performance over time, and judgments of potential may be inconsistent from manager to manager due to differing standards. Frequently there is not agreement on the meaning of *high potential* (that is, one person may think of high potential as the ability to move up one organization level, while another is thinking a high potential must be able to achieve the level of the Operating Committee). It is critical to agree on the meaning of *high potential* and take the time to discuss the evidence that supports the assessments in order to reach valid and reliable conclusions. It is likely that assessments will change as the context for the assessments changes (such as changes in the external environment dictating new or different standards). Labeling an individual as a "high potential" one year does not mean that that person will be still be seen as "high potential" the next year.

Retention Risk

Some organizations look at retention risk as part of their talent reviews. This includes an assessment of how critical an individual is to the success of the organization as well as how likely it is the individual will leave the organization in the future. A relative ranking of the value of individuals to the organization and a relative ranking of the probability that they will stay with the organization forms the basis for this risk assessment. A discussion of actions that can address the identified retention risks usually follows these assessments. Assessment of retention risk can help to efficiently use limited resources (such as compensation increases, stock options, developmental opportunities, personal relationships) to retain critical talent.

Including a discussion of retention risk in the review presents several challenges. The assessments can be subjective and inconsistent over time. Managers frequently have difficulty understanding what it would take to retain an individual. Finally, many organizations are unwilling to deliver differential rewards, such as compensation, developmental opportunities, or personal visibility, to a select group of individuals. An unintended consequence of rewarding individuals who are a retention risk may be to discourage other individuals who are loyal to the organization but not considered retention risks.

Replacement Planning and Succession Management

Replacement planning and succession management are not the same. As Berke (2005) indicates, replacement planning is quite different from succession planning or succession management. Replacement planning is simply listing the names of individuals who could replace specific individuals if they were no longer in their position. The more encompassing processes of succession planning or succession management are identifying possible internal replacements, discussing their readiness for the position, and identifying the developmental action plans needed to prepare them for the specific role. Succession planning and succession management may also include identifying external candidates and assessing their readiness. The challenge of including these discussions in the review is that they significantly increase the amount of preparation required in advance of the review, the discussion time during the review, and the follow-up efforts after the review.

Leaders frequently ask, "How many successors do we need?" or "How large does our feeder pool of high potentials need to be?" There are no easy answers to these questions. A variety of factors determines the needed number of successors or the number of high potentials in a feeder pool—for example:

- The likelihood of turnover among successors or the high potentials in the talent pool

- The number of individuals who are candidates for multiple positions
- The confidence in the accuracy of the assessments of potential
- The number of individuals whose development can be actively managed by the organization. Unless the organization acts to help individuals achieve their potential, putting a name on a chart labeled "succession candidates" or "talent pool" does little to meet an organization's future leadership needs.

Critical Indicators

A variety of statistics can be discussed that are indicators of the quality and depth of the talent in the organization: turnover rates, employee engagement measures from attitude surveys, and diversity indicators, such as time in current position, tenure in the organization, geographic origin, race, and gender. These indicators provide a basis for making systemic assessments of the organization and identifying areas where programmatic actions to build talent depth and diversity may be needed.

One problem associated with discussing critical indicators in the review is that the discussion may focus more on human resources programs than on specific individuals. Reviewing broad talent metrics is frequently not the best use of senior management time during the talent review. Using the metrics at the design stage to identify specific discussion topics for the review (such as actions to address turnover in a critical area) frequently leads to better use of senior management time.

Content of the Review

Ultimately the extensiveness of the reviews at the most senior level will depend on the time that the CEO is willing to invest in conducting the talent reviews. The areas where the CEO can gain or add the most value should guide the selection of elements for the review. Frequently the content of the review evolves over time, from a straightforward discussion of senior-level successors to a more robust discussion of critical talent pools. The perceived value of the review generally determines the evolution of the process. Exhibit 9.1 is an example of a typical review agenda,

Exhibit 9.1. Talent Review Agenda

I. Strategic Context (5 minutes)

The strategic issues that are the most relevant to managing talent

II. Organization Structure and Critical Positions (5 minutes)

Positions highlighted on the organization chart that are most critical to executing the business strategy

III. Past Plans and Actions (10 minutes)

Discussion of action plans identified during prior reviews and the results of actions taken

IV. Summary Assessment of Individuals in Critical Roles (10 minutes)

A summary assessment of individuals in critical positions in the form of a 3 × 3 chart assessing the degree to which behaviors are demonstrated consistent with the desired culture and the degree to which the individual has achieved her objectives

V. Developmental Review of Select Individuals (30 minutes)

An in-depth discussion of selected individuals to discuss strengths, developmental needs, work/life balance preferences, and developmental action plans, including next career steps. The time allocated is sufficient to review no more than five or six individuals.

VI. Succession Management (10 minutes)

Review of successors identified for critical positions

Action plans for all positions for which there is not a "ready now" successor and there is an anticipated opening and a transition must be managed between the current incumbent and a successor within the next year

VII. Retention Risk Assessment (10 minutes)

Assessment of retention risk for those individuals in critical roles

Retention action plans for individuals identified as being at risk

VIII. Summary of Action Plans (10 minutes)

Summary of plans to enhance leadership, talent depth, and retention with the approximate time needed for each segment. The areas discussed at the senior-most level of an organization frequently differ from those discussed at lower levels. Reviews at lower levels frequently are limited to the assessment and development of individuals without a discussion of the other elements.

Alternative Approaches to Talent Reviews

For a variety of reasons (the interests of the senior-most executive or urgent challenges facing the organization), the approach to reviewing talent may take a form other than a full talent review. An organization might choose to only review select talent pools, review talent strategy in the context of business strategy without a discussion of individuals, or only discuss talent that might be available external to the organization.

Reviews of Select Talent Pools

As an addition or as an alternative to the annual organization-wide talent review, an organization might focus on the assessment and development of a relatively small group of high-potential individuals. Dowell and Elder (2002) describe such a program developed within Bristol-Myers Squibb. In this example, 30 high-potential individuals were identified, assessed, given customized developmental opportunities, monitored for developmental progress, and mentored by a diverse organizational steering committee of senior leaders. The result was that members of this select group had significantly greater upward movement in the organization than a similar group of high potentials who were identified and developed through the typical talent review process. The challenge to this alternative is the high level of resources required to provide this intense focus for a relatively small group of individuals.

Talent Strategy Reviews

Some organizations separate the discussions of people from a more strategic discussion of programmatic approaches to building the quality and depth of talent. A review of the organization strategy and an evaluation of the availability and quality of internal and external talent form the basis for the talent strategy. Reviews of relevant demographic shifts and competitive talent practices heavily influence the evaluation of external talent availability. For example, to the degree other organizations are able to attract the best talent, your organization may be at a competitive disadvantage in the future. Critical internal talent measures, such as turnover, time in position, and retirement projections, and the culture of the organization influence evaluations of internal talent. These evaluations lead to an organization-specific strategy to manage talent. Possible elements of a talent strategy are presented in Table 9.5.

Review of External Talent Pools

Just as companies actively work to ensure a supply of raw physical materials, working to ensure an ongoing supply of external talent may also be an option. Important talent pools are the talent in other organizations and in educational institutions. Some organizations use search firms to identify and evaluate talent who are working in other organizations. Once talented individuals in other organizations are identified, senior leaders may look for opportunities to develop relationships with them that facilitate recruiting these individuals in the future. Many senior leaders also associate themselves with educational institutions to develop relationships with the most talented students and increase the chances that they can attract them in the future. An understanding of the quality of external talent may also lead to a better appreciation of the quality of internal talent. Many times a review of external talent leads to an increased focus on the development of internal talent.

Talent Assessment

Assessments of the future potential and the developmental needs of internal talent are central elements of talent reviews. Without valid and reliable assessments, all the benefits that come from talent reviews can be lost. There are different approaches to assessing the potential and diagnosing the developmental needs of individuals. These approaches base judgments on:

- The assessment of abilities and personality characteristics based on psychological assessments, such as cognitive complexity, assertiveness, sociability, and learning agility

Table 9.5. Sample Elements of a Talent Strategy

Strategic Element	Actions
Base talent decisions on results and behavior	• Retain individuals in roles long enough to demonstrate performance before moving to other roles. • Assess potential to progress based on assessments of performance over time and on learning agility.
Develop leaders from within	• Identify two successors for all positions critical to the organization strategy. • Initiate external recruiting to build depth when internal talent is not available.
Differentially invest in talent	• Invest more heavily in the development of leaders who are critical to executing strategy. • Focus development on the critical areas needed to address current and future organization challenges.
Rely on experience to develop talent	• Train managers to facilitate learning on the job • Train employees to better extract learnings from work experiences.
Hold managers accountable for developing talent	• Evaluate a manager's track record of developing talent when making compensation, hiring, and promotion decisions regarding that manager.
Retain high performers	• Create challenging developmental work experiences • Raise the leadership capability of managers to increase the retention of high-performing talent. • Differentially allocate rewards commensurate with performance contribution.

Note: The elements of any talent strategy will depend on the external and internal environment and the strategies of the organization. These are only example elements.

427

- The leadership competencies critical to executing the organization strategy, such as strategic thinking skills, team building, and staff development
- The strategic competencies needed to fulfill the organization strategy, such as experience in mergers and acquisitions, business start-ups in other countries, and talent development in developing markets

As the assessment approach varies from an assessment of basic abilities and personality to an assessment of the competencies required by specific organizational strategies, the ability to predict short-term performance increases. However, as organization strategies and the specific individual competencies required by those strategies tend to change over time, an assessment of basic abilities and personality may predict long-term performance more accurately. These basic abilities and personality attributes are likely to endure and better predict future performance even as the strategy of the organization evolves. Leadership competency assessments may fall somewhere in between these other two approaches. A combination of assessments may be the best approach, using one type of assessment for judging potential to assume specific roles in the short term and another assessment for judging the potential to assume future roles as the organization's strategy evolves over the longer term.

Outcomes of Talent Reviews

What happens after a review, not the review itself, largely determines the value of the review. Possible resulting actions or outcomes include:

■ ■ ■

- *Documenting individual and organizational plans.* Distributing a summary of the actions agreed to during the review and doing follow-up reviews of later progress greatly increase the likelihood that desired actions will be completed.
- *Providing feedback to the individuals reviewed.* There are different views on whether the individuals reviewed should receive

feedback from the reviews. Those receiving feedback often misinterpret the feedback. The possible actions discussed, such as promotions, the timing of moves, and participation in developmental programs, can be perceived by the individual as firm commitments by the organization to the individual rather than as possibilities. This can have a negative impact on the individual when the possible actions do not happen or do not happen in the expected time frame. Often feedback to an individual on the perceptions of the CEO or other senior leaders about the individual is magnified in the individual's mind and can lead to inaccurate conclusions. However, some feedback is generally better than none at all. More than one high-potential individual has left an organization because she did not know that the organization viewed her as having a promising future career there. The quality and nature of the feedback determine whether it will be useful to the individual. A good rule of thumb in providing feedback on the review is to provide an accurate description of the discussion and avoid sharing personal views of specific leaders or commitments to specific dates for developmental opportunities.

• *Resolving questions from the review.* Many times, there may be different views of an individual's performance or potential. Resolving these differences can be accomplished through a follow-up assessment, possibly by a third party, or by assigning a project that might provide additional information, such as asking the individual to develop a strategic plan on a specific issue in order to evaluate the person's ability to think through strategic issues. Other unresolved questions might be an individual's specific career interests, willingness to relocate to pursue developmental opportunities, or openness to a particular development role.

• *Determining the retention risk of identified high-potential individuals.* Following the talent review, HR may need to determine whether these individuals are receiving competitive compensation. HR may also need to speak individually with the targeted individuals in this group. During this follow-up, HR can ask individuals about their personal views of the organization. HR also can explore whether there are specific actions that could be taken that would increase the likelihood that the individual would stay. For example, is the person being mentored? What is his relationship with his current manager? Is he being challenged developmentally? Does he have an appropriate work/life balance?

- *Identifying the consequences of identified developmental moves.* Identifying needed developmental career moves during the review has little value unless the moves are completed. Following the review, there needs to be a realistic assessment of whether the identified developmental positions will naturally be available (such as through other planned moves, retirement, planned termination) or whether the organization needs to initiate action to make positions available (such as creating new roles, reorganizing the existing roles, or proactively moving an incumbent out of the position). A plan that coordinates the related moves and the needed communications should be developed once there is general agreement on the next career steps for the individual.

- *Creating staffing plans.* HR should create staffing plans following the talent review that include lists of internal candidates for critical positions. Candidate slates should include an evaluation of the developmental value a position would have for the different candidates. The staffing plans should identify areas where external recruiting is required to build depth of talent.

- *Following up with individuals where action needs to be taken.* Frequently there is a need to conduct follow-up reviews of individuals who are not meeting performance expectations in order to plan remedial action, such as developmental coaching, behavioral counseling, transfer, or termination. In most cases, someone needs to determine what previous feedback managers have provided to the individual before taking further action in order to ensure fairness to the individual.

- *Creating development programs.* Human resources may need to design new developmental initiatives based on the collective developmental needs of individuals discussed in the review. This may seem obvious, but many times organizations create general programs without regard for the specific needs of the critical talent in the organization. The Corporate Leadership Council (2003b) found a strong relationship between the degree to which development programs are aligned with specific talent needs and the strength of an organization's bench.

- *Pursuing other less common actions.* Other possible follow-up actions are decisions to outsource an organizational function or department when the collective judgment is that the internal talent is not capable of supporting the strategic direction of the organization. Another might be to revisit past strategic decisions. For example, the organization might need to abandon a planned acquisition if the talent review determined that there was insufficient internal talent to integrate the acquisition. Alternatively, an organization might supplement current internal talent by pursuing an acquisition that would bring needed additional talent into a strategically important geographic or functional area.

Lessons Learned

Just as there are attributes of individuals that lead to success in a position, there are attributes of management processes that lead to the success of the process. Based on my 25 years of designing and managing processes to review and manage talent pools, there are seven attributes that are critical to the success of that process.

Lesson 1: Hold Line Leadership Accountable for the Management of Talent Pools

Although it is tempting to delegate talent management to the human resources function, it does not work. Of course, HR is critical to the effective management of talent management processes and should be a strong partner to line management. Talent management plans are rarely executed without strong line management ownership. In the most effective organizations, line leaders are accountable for developing and executing plans to build the depth of talent, with consequences for both the success and failure of the plans.

Lesson 2: Make Talent Judgments Based on Standards Drawn from Strategic Plans

A thoughtful and disciplined look at the talent implications of the organization strategy is fundamental to meeting the future needs of the organization. The talent of tomorrow will be judged by the performance standards of tomorrow, not the standards in place today. An organization needs to anticipate future standards, and individuals need to be assessed and developed against those future standards.

Having talent with diverse skills and abilities is one of the key elements for successfully adapting to unpredictable future demands. This suggests that having future-oriented standards that allow some behavioral variance among individuals is more likely to produce a talent pool capable of responding to the variety of challenges the organization is likely to face in the future. Leadership standards that limit behavioral diversity may limit an organization's ability to meet unexpected demands. For example, setting a standard that all leaders need to be very strong in controlling costs and avoiding risk may be effective when adhering to governmental regulation and margin protection is critical. However, in a possible future where deregulation occurs and growth becomes the critical priority, individuals with different attributes may be required. In this example, setting standards that allow prudent risk taking (that is, risk taking that has been well thought through), instead of a standard that strictly limits any risk taking, would increase the likelihood of having the talent needed to compete in the future.

Lesson 3: Value Current Contributions and Future Potential

Identifying the talent and the development plans for the future leadership of the organization is strategically important. Focusing only on high-potential individuals to the exclusion of other individuals who are critical to leading the company in the short term can have serious negative consequences. These high-performing individuals, who are needed to achieve near-term results, represent another talent pool. High-performing individuals in strategically critical positions need to feel valued by the organization (such as knowing that they have visibility with senior leadership). If they are to grow and adapt to changes in the organization strategy, they also must have access to developmental opportunities. Frequently the perceived potential of individuals changes with continued development or when changes occur in the strategy of the organization. Not treating these high performers as a critical talent pool can lead to higher-than-necessary turnover and a loss of needed capabilities.

Lesson 4: Focus as Much on Development as on Assessment

Talent reviews provide an excellent opportunity to gain multiple assessments of the potential of individuals. However, this often is all that is accomplished. Obtaining accurate assessments is necessary to meet the future leadership needs, but it is not sufficient. Discussing the actions that need to occur based on the assessment, such as plans to address individual development needs or external staffing needs, is at least as important as the assessment. The multiple perspectives present in a talent review provide one of the best forums for the problem-solving discussion of what to do to address a development need.

Lesson 5: Include the Individual in the Planning Process

Focusing only on the needs of the organization and excluding the desires of the individuals involved is frequently a problem. The days are disappearing when individuals do whatever the organization asks of them in terms of making career moves. An integrated plan that involves coordinating a series of developmental moves can fall apart when one individual in the middle of the chain of events declines an opportunity. Knowing the career and work/life balance preferences of high-potential individuals can help the organization creatively meet its own needs while also meeting the needs of individuals.

Organizations can be very persuasive, and an individual may agree to take a position based solely on the needs of the organization. However, organizational coercion, whether based on promises of future benefits or threats of negative consequences, increases the risk that individuals will eventually pursue other outside opportunities once they refocus on their own needs.

Lesson 6: Emphasize the Dialogue over the Review Format and Technology

The role of the review format and information technology is to facilitate candid, accurate assessments and action plan discussions during talent reviews. An overemphasis on technology can get in the way of thoughtful preparation, honest dialogue, and effective follow-up. There are benefits to structuring reviews and using technology that simplify the preparation or follow-up. However, if technology costs or the time required to prepare a structured format are seen as excessive, senior management is likely to question the value of the process. In the end, it is the dialogue and resulting problem solving that are important, not the format of the review.

Lesson 7: Focus on the Follow-Up Rather Than the Review

A great review has little value if the plans end up in a professional-looking notebook sitting on a shelf. The follow-up to a review creates the greatest value for the organization. The actual content of a review has the least value. Without the execution of well-thought-out plans to address the individual and organizational gaps, the entire process of reviewing talent pools has marginal value for the organization.

The most effective organizations conduct a review midway through the annual review cycle to assess the progress on the plans identified during the comprehensive annual review. Many times the individuals who are accountable for executing specific plans may change. To maintain momentum, senior leaders need to ensure that as individuals change positions, the accountability for executing against plans is not lost.

Organizations need to step back periodically and identify what has worked and what has not in the review and management of talent pools. Those involved in the process, senior management and human resources, need to honestly ask and candidly answer the question, "Is our process for reviewing and managing our critical talent pools meeting our needs?" Great organizations regularly ask that question and take the appropriate actions to keep their talent management processes responsive to the strategic needs of the organization.

Future Directions in Research

The process of reviewing and managing talent pools has evolved through experience and practice. Researchers have systematically evaluated very few of the practices. Huselid (1995) concludes that a number of HR processes collectively contribute to successful organization performance. We do not know what part the process of reviewing and managing talent pools might play in driving successful organization performance. Furthermore, we do not have any systematic research that tells which approaches to reviewing and managing talent pools are most effective. The question becomes even more complex when the influences of organization size, organizational environment, and organization strategy are considered.

Research by Dowell and Elder (2002) demonstrated that when a small pool of high-potential talent received intense developmental focus, their upward movement in the organization exceeded the upward movement of a similarly identified group of high potentials who did not receive the same intense developmental focus. This development effort was resource intensive and not sustainable over the long run. Understanding which elements of managing talent pools contribute the most to success would improve the allocation of limited resources.

One area that receives much discussion but has received little systematic investigation is the impact of feedback on the individuals who are the subject of the reviews. The most frequent question is, "Does feedback to the individual regarding possible next career steps affect retention?" Another is, "How does the type of feedback [such as having the potential to advance—or not] affect engagement and performance?"

Another area of investigation relates to the social psychology of talent reviews. The process of reviewing and managing talent pools occurs in a social context. Theories and research from social psychology might provide insights into some problems that can occur in the talent review discussions. Research on interpersonal attraction, attribution, and small group decision making may all be relevant to the quality of the discussion and the accuracy of the assessments and predictions. Understanding the interpersonal processes that are occurring during talent reviews may identify the actions that would make this process more effective.

The research into interpersonal attraction suggests that individuals view more favorably those who are most similar to themselves. Do senior managers more positively evaluate others they see as being like themselves? Does an overly positive or negative relationship between the presenter and reviewer influence the way the reviewer perceives the assessments and plans? Does asking questions to ensure that there is behavioral evidence or alternative assessments increase the validity of a person's perceptions?

The attribution of individual competence is central to assessments of potential and the diagnosis of developmental needs. Attribution theory and research in other settings suggest that a number of factors may influence evaluations of a person's competence. Kendrick, Neuberg, and Cialdini (2007) cite research that suggests that a number of factors influence attributions of competence:

- Perceptions of whether the individual intended the action, the consequences were foreseeable, the action was freely chosen by the individual, or the results were achieved despite countervailing forces
- Consistency of behavior over time and the distinctiveness of the person's actions
- The number of possible causes for the behavior beyond the individual
- Culture (for example, Westerners are more likely than people from non-Western cultures to attribute results to the efforts of an individual), which might influence the discussions of talent pools in global companies

Each of these observations suggests areas for future research.

Small group decision-making research may also provide insights into the effectiveness of talent reviews. Questions that might be explored include:

- Do these small group discussions lead to more extreme positive or negative assessments?
- How do minority opinions influence the discussions?
- Does the phenomenon of groupthink compromise the quality of the process?
- What impact does increasing the size of the discussion group have on the quality of the discussion?

Conclusion

Organizations of all sizes are finding that the talent they need is becoming increasingly scarce, and they are looking inward to review and develop their internal talent pools and outward to identify pools of external talent. This chapter has explored the characteristics of successful talent review and management efforts, the roles individuals play, and the process design choices. Aligning the management of talent pools with the strategic needs of the organization, differentially investing in strategically important areas, and executing against plans are central to effective talent management.

References

Berger, L. A., & Berger, D. R. (2004). *The talent management handbook.* New York: McGraw-Hill.

Berke, D. (2005). *Succession planning and management: A guide to organizational systems and practices.* Greensboro, NC: Center for Creative Leadership.

Bossidy, L., & Charan, R. (2002). *Execution: The discipline of getting things done.* New York: Crown Business.

Byham, W. C., Smith, A. B., & Paese, M. J. (2002). *Grow your own leaders.* Pittsburgh, PA: DDI Press.

Chambers, E. G., Foulon, M., Handfield-Jones, H., Hankin, S. M., & Michaels, E. G. (1998). The war for talent. *McKinsey Quarterly, 3,* 44–57.

Charan, R., Drotter, S., & Noel, J. (2001). *The leadership pipeline.* San Francisco: Jossey-Bass.

Ciampa, E., & Watkins, M. (1999). *Right from the start: Taking charge in a new leadership role.* Boston: Harvard Business School Press.

Collins, J. (2001). *Good to great.* New York: HarperCollins.

Corporate Leadership Council. (2003a). *High-impact succession management: From succession planning to strategic executive talent management.* Washington, DC: Corporate Executive Board.

Corporate Leadership Council. (2003b). *Hallmarks of leadership success: Strategies for improving leadership quality and executive readiness.* Washington, DC: Corporate Executive Board.

Corporate Leadership Council. (2005). *Realizing the full potential of rising talent: Vol. 2. Strategies for supporting the development of high-potential employees.* Washington, DC: Corporate Executive Board.

Coyne, K. P., & Coyne, E. J. Sr. (2007). Surviving your new CEO. *Harvard Business Review, 85*(5), 62–69.

Dowell, B. E. (2002). Succession planning. In J. Hedge & E. D. Pulakos (Eds.), *Implementing organizational interventions: Steps, processes, and best practices.* San Francisco: Jossey-Bass.

Dowell, B. E., & Elder, E. D. (2002, April). *Accelerating the development of tomorrow's leaders.* Paper presented at the annual conference of the Society for Industrial and Organizational Psychology, Toronto, Canada.

Groysberg, B., McLean, A. N., & Nohria, N. (2006). Are leaders portable? *Harvard Business Review, 84*(5), 92–100.

Huselid, M. A. (1995). The impact of human resource management practices on turnover, productivity, and corporate financial performance. *Academy of Management Journal, 38,* 635–672.

Kendrick, D. T., Neuberg, S. L., & Cialdini, R. B. (2007). *Social psychology* (4th ed.). Boston: Allyn & Bacon.

Kesner, I. F., & Sebora, T. C. (1994). Executive succession: Past, present and future. *Journal of Management, 20*(2), 237–372.

Lombardo, M. M., & Eichinger, R. W. (2004). *The leadership machine.* Minneapolis, MN: Lominger.

Michaels, E., Handfield-Jones, H., & Axelrod, B. (2001). *The war for talent.* Boston: Harvard Business School Press.

Pearson, A. E. (1987). Muscle-build the organization. *Harvard Business Review, 65*(4), 49–56.

Rothwell, W. J. (2001). *Effective succession planning: Ensuring leadership continuity and building talent from within* (2nd ed.). New York: AMACOM.

Wolfe, I. S. (2004). *The perfect labor storm fact book.* Atlanta, GA: Creative Communications Publications.

CHAPTER 10

EMPLOYEE ENGAGEMENT

A Focus on Leaders

Jeff Schippmann

Employee engagement is one of those fascinating concepts that come along every few years in the human resource (HR) field that is fueled by an intense business need and is introduced into practice so quickly that it creates consternation and confusion in the research and academic communities. In this way, the "engagement" phenomenon is similar to the rush of interest and practice into competency modeling a few years ago (Schippmann et al., 2000). In the case of employee engagement, the burning platform has been the growing recognition that business and industry is facing a shortage of skilled employees at many levels of the labor market (Erickson, 2005; Frank & Taylor, 2004; Manpower, 2004; U.S. Department of Labor, 2003).

Indications that the metaphorical labor platform is on fire appear to be quite clear to the captains of business and industry. Many business leaders identify concerns about being able to attract and retain the talent they need to fuel growth plans among their top two or three business challenges (PricewaterhouseCoopers, 2004; Towers Perrin, 2004). This has created a receptive environment for engagement ideas and solutions targeting employee retention. It even appears that the confluence of engagement issues (the "new" job satisfaction) and retention issues (the "new" turnover), along with the emerging business focus on talent pipelines, human capital metrics,

I benefited from discussion and work by a number of colleagues during the preparation of this chapter, particularly Alan Colquitt, Ben Dowell, John Gibbons, and Rob Silzer.

and integrated human resource programs, has resulted in the creation of a new subfunction in HR: talent management.

Defining Terms and Some History

In broadest terms, employee engagement is the conceptual framework for understanding the connection between people and the companies that employ them. At a more specific level, it becomes difficult to determine the boundaries of the term, or, as Frank, Finnegan, and Taylor (2004) claim, "simple to understand yet more difficult to define and measure" (p. 15). Part of the challenge is in identifying the elements in the engagement framework and deciding how these elements are organized. Gibbons (2006), in a review of recent research for the Conference Board, organizes the components in three groups:

- Those that emphasize employees' cognitive connection to the work or the organization (such as career growth opportunities or compensation)
- Those that focus on emotional attachments (such as connection to one's boss or coworkers)
- Those that focus on behavioral outcomes (such as job search behavior or actual turnover)

Similarly, Macey and Schneider (2008), who provide a research platform for the engagement construct, organize the elements into three broad dimensions:

- Trait engagement (such as positive views of life and work)
- State engagement (such as feelings of energy and absorption)
- Behavioral engagement (such as extra-role behaviors like personal initiative or organizational citizenship)

In terms of measurement, many different instruments and approaches are used to assess engagement (Blessing White, 2005; Corporate Leadership Council, 1999; Gallup [see Buckingham & Coffman, 1999; Harter, Schmidt, & Keyes, 2003]; Hewitt Associates, 2005; Towers-Perrin, 2003), but most of them, in one way or another, focus on these core elements:

- Compensation
- Benefits
- Relationship with boss
- Relationships with coworkers
- Career growth and development opportunities
- Job support, fit, and autonomy
- Availability of flexible work programs
- Job demands (for example, hours, travel)
- Faith in top management
- Pride in the company

Of course, each of the core elements covered in a particular instrument may have a number of discrete parts. For example, the core compensation element may be further broken down into:

- Base pay
- Long-term incentives such as options and restricted stock
- Internal perceptions of pay equity
- External perceptions of pay equity

Taken together, these elements and the more discrete parts are considered antecedents to employee engagement.

For readers who have read the literature over the years, these elements of engagement look like the categories of job satisfaction that have been studied as part of job attitudes for many years (see Lawler, 1973; Locke, 1976; Steers & Porter, 1975). In terms of historical context, the engagement construct appears to have roots in the early needs-based work on employee motivation (Maslow, 1943; McGregor, 1960; Alderfer, 1969). Subsequent groundbreaking work in expectancy theory (Vroom, 1964) and goal setting (Locke & Latham, 1990) is also part of the deep historical base. More recent work on values is relevant as well. Locke and Henne (1986) describe values as being rooted in needs and providing a platform for goals. So while the needs described by Maslow and others are inborn, values are acquired through cognition and experience. Goals are similar to values except they are more specific and are mechanisms that help express values as behavior. Within this framework, research that examines values within expectancy-valence frameworks, to predict job search behavior, and other work-related choices is particularly relevant to engagement practice and research (Foreman & Murphy, 1996; Verplanken & Holland, 2002).

Of course, personal traits are also viewed as needs or drivers in the motivation literature. In fact, Schmitt, Cortina Ingerick, and Wiechmann (2003) conclude that personality is the primary predictor of the core elements of motivation. Underscoring this point of view, Mitchell and Daniels (2003) report that research on personality is the fastest-growing topic in the motivation literature. With specific reference to engagement, Macey and Schneider (2008) suggest that trait engagement is a key explanatory component of their model, where experiencing the world from a particular view is reflected as psychological state engagement.

From a different view, the research on workplace elements, as predictors or independent variables, is also part of the history of engagement. As such, the work on job characteristics clearly applies here (Hackman & Oldham, 1975). For example, Gustafson and Mumford (1995) have shown that the ability of personality to predict both performance and job satisfaction increases when the characteristics of a job are taken into account. However, this is only one example. Hundreds of studies have examined the characteristics of jobs as determinants of job satisfaction and behavioral outcomes (Ambrose & Kulik, 1999).

In sum, we have over 60 years of research demonstrating that a person's needs, goals, values, and personality drive job satisfaction, and these same needs, values, and personality variables affect, and are affected by, the job environment (Latham & Pinder, 2005).

What is new or different about engagement? Part of the difference is that engagement explains a heightened connection to a job or workplace or organization that goes beyond simple job satisfaction (Gubman, 1998, 2003). Specifically, definitions of engagement include a mix of cognitive, affective, and behavioral components, and as a result, engaged employees "feel" differently about their employers and the workplace, contribute differently than nonengaged employees do, and express a different level of desire to be part of the organization (versus going elsewhere to another company). The definition of *engagement* provided by the Corporate Leadership Council (2004) underscores the breadth of the concept: "Engagement is the extent to which employees commit to something or someone in their organization, how hard they work, and how long they stay as a result of that commitment" (p. 10a). This definition encompasses the extent to which employees believe their managers and organizations have their self-interest in mind and the extent to which employees value and believe in their jobs, managers, and organizations. Furthermore, the outputs of these two types of commitment are included in the definition in terms of performance or discretionary effort and retention or intent to stay. In this way, most current definitions of engagement are quite broad and include a mix of cognitive, affective, and behavioral components.

Another distinctive feature of the engagement concept is that not all of the various elements are considered equally important. In fact, most engagement research uses some mix of importance ratings, paired-comparison judgments, discriminant analysis, conjoint analysis, and so forth, to identify the relative value of each element, or subelement, to the overall engagement measure (for example, the importance or motivational value of each element multiplied by the individual's current level of satisfaction with each one). This information can then be used to prioritize possible HR engagement interventions and, more specifically, to guide the restructuring of an organization's "employment deal" or "employee value proposition" by providing a return on investment for each element. Regarding current employees, the "deal" refers to the value provided to employees through their employment and association with the company. Regarding the external labor market and prospective employees, the deal refers to the company's reputation and the communicated employment package.

Which Elements Matter Most?

There is no simple answer to the question of which engagement elements are most important. In part, this is because the predictive power of the different elements depends on how the elements are measured and how the desired engagement outcome is defined. That said, some useful general conclusions can be reached. For example, a large-scale research effort reported by

Buckingham and Coffman (1999) indicates that working for a supportive immediate boss is the most important single factor for engagement. Similarly, the Corporate Leadership Council (2004) reports that an employee's relationship with his boss had four times the impact on increasing discretionary work effort than a broad range of other potential drivers of engagement, including those related to pay, benefits, and working conditions.

A specific case involves a two-year investigation into the drivers of turnover among 80 high-potential executives with a large consumer product goods company (Schippmann, 2001a). These executives were identified as top talent based on a combination of top performance ratings for the previous two years and being prominently placed on succession planning slates. A third-party consultant evaluated the relationship each of these individuals had with her direct boss ("great"/"solid or medium"/"poor"). In addition, the extent to which each person was committed to the company was evaluated ("high commitment and no interest in engaging in a job search"/"medium commitment and some passive job search behavior"/"low commitment and actively searching for a job"). All individual-specific information was kept confidential by the consultant, and only aggregate results were reported back to the company in a way that preserved individual anonymity. The results were informative.

Each of the 20 high-commitment executives reported having at least a "solid" relationship with their boss, and most reported a "great" relationship. Conversely, 50 percent of the 60 executives with medium commitment and low commitment reported being dissatisfied with the quality of the relationship with their boss.

An interesting part of this research project included a broader group of executives. Again, the top talent group was composed of 80 mid- to senior-level leaders across the company. In addition, a midrange talent group (449 executives) and lower talent group (143 executives) were identified using the same classification criteria noted above. The differences in the commitment levels among these three segments of executives were a concern. In the top talent group (aggregating the data across the quality of boss relationship variable) 25 percent reported being highly committed to the organization and planned to be with the company for the long term, while 35 percent of the midrange talent group reported being highly committed to the organization. Finally, in the lower talent group, none of whom would have been classified as "regrettable turnover" if they had left the organization, 41 percent expressed a strong commitment and intent to stay. Clearly, hanging on to the best and brightest is more difficult than keeping second- or third-tier employees. Similar research results have been found by others (A. Colquitt, personal communication, September 30, 2007).

As above, most work on the formula of engagement includes some form of a multiplicative algorithm that combines individual satisfaction with the relative importance of the different elements. As a result, an employee who is extremely satisfied with the low-value elements of a current employment "deal" yet unsatisfied with the high-value elements would have a low overall level of engagement. Conversely, if the satisfaction ratings were distributed differently (very satisfied with the high-value elements and dissatisfied with the lower-value elements), the same individual would have a higher overall level of engagement.

Along these lines, work by the Corporate Leadership Council (1999) is a good example of typical research in the engagement field. With an impressive sample of 19 participating companies across the manufacturing, finance, retail, and technology sectors and 10,092 employees, they used a series of paired-comparison scenarios (presented online) to investigate the importance of 30 employment elements. At the top of the importance rankings were high-value elements such as:

- Manager quality
- Base salary
- External equity
- Health benefits

At the bottom of the list were relatively lower-value elements such as:

- On-site child care
- Company size
- Availability of telecommuting
- Availability of flextime options

The overall profile of importance values is interesting on its own. However, what is also interesting is that when the population is sorted by various demographic variables such as age, gender, and ethnicity, the resulting rankings on importance are substantially the same. While younger executives might generally value stock options differently than older executives, or female executives might value flextime opportunities differently than male executives, the overall relative profiles are similar.

A large proprietary study (Schippmann, 2001b) attempted to follow up on these findings using a sample of 1,323 top-performing managers and executives in a Fortune 100 consumer packaged goods company. The results were almost exactly the same as the importance profiles reported by the Corporate Leadership Council (with a correlation of .96 across 26 job elements). Further, the second-level analysis, which involved segmenting the population by demographic variables, yielded amazingly similar profiles. This was also true when the data were compared for U.S. and non-U.S. groups, for short- and long-tenure groups, and so forth. All of this consistency led one HR executive who reviewed the findings to throw up his hands in the middle of a meeting and lament, "Every way you look at it, the results are the same!? Are you telling us that everyone wants the same thing?"

The "Aha"

Of course people are motivated by different things. However, a limitation in much of the engagement literature involves incomplete analysis, which masks true variability across individuals. Rather than relying on standard demographic data and readily available company history data to segment the population, Schippmann (2001b) rotated the data set and conducted a series of inverse factor analyses, creating groups of managers and executives with similar importance profiles. The purpose of using the Q-factor procedure in this way was to cluster people, not variables, into similar groups (for a detailed description of the methodology see Schippmann, 1999). The results of this effort, when compared to the originally derived homogeneous importance or driver profiles, were dramatically different and more informative. Prior to this people clustering, based on the value of the element drivers, this large group of leaders appeared to have a common, indistinct set of core drivers. After the clustering, three large and very distinct groups of executives emerged.

Career Drivers

One of the "big three" clusters was a group of 389 managers and executives based on a review of their common driver profiles, a group clearly motivated by the career enhancement elements of the employment deal. These individuals were primarily focused on elements of the organization's employment offer that related to their career and their own development. Top-valued elements for this cluster of executives were:

- Manager quality
- Job fit
- Empowerment
- Promotion opportunity
- Base pay

Cash Drivers

The second of the big three clusters included 278 managers and executives who were motivated primarily by the potential wealth creation elements of the employment deal. These individuals were not overly concerned about the number of hours they worked during a week, they did not care about extensive travel requirements, it did not matter to them where they worked (geographically), and it did not even matter too much what the job was (perceived job fit). If the economic return matched their high expectations, they would run through walls to accomplish the work goals given to them. Their top-valued elements were:

- Base pay
- Stock options
- Bonus targets
- Empowerment
- Manager quality

Life Balancers

The third cluster included 390 managers and executives who, while not unconcerned about career or compensation issues, had an overriding emphasis on areas that were very different from all the other groups. More than the other manager and executive clusters, these employees displayed importance profiles that were more balanced or blended. Specifically, these individuals placed tremendous emphasis and value on:

- Hours (fewer is better)
- Travel (less is better)
- Location (where they live and work is important)
- External equity (fair return relative to external peers)

As is often the case in factor analysis (with either R-factor or Q-factor analyses), this research effort also yielded a number of much smaller and less readily interpretable factors (groups). In these cases, small groups of executives greatly overweighted, or underweighted, the value of some specific elements. However, in this study, the big three clusters of career drivers, cash drivers, and life balancers accounted for 85 percent of the 1,332 managers and executives included in the research.

Some confirmation of these results comes from a survey by *Fast Company* (2000) that asked readers: "You find yourself with five job offers. You are equally qualified for each job, but the pay, the hours, and the organizational culture are very different in each case. Which company would you choose to work for?" Here is a summary of the five choices and descriptions:

- Yahoo!—offers high base salary and lots of options; but the work hours are around the clock
- Goldman Sachs—offers high base salary and bonus; but the hours are intense and the culture is cutthroat
- Ben & Jerry's—offers modest salary, bonus, and stock; but the hours are reasonable and the culture is easygoing
- Procter & Gamble—offers nice base salary and modest bonus (no stock); but the hours are reasonable, and the workplace is stable and predictable

- Peace Corps—offers minimal base pay, no bonus or stock; but has the promise that your work, and the people you work with, will be fascinating

Which would you choose? The distribution across the respondents in this survey was as follows:

- Yahoo!: 24.0 percent
- Goldman Sachs: 8.9 percent
- Ben & Jerry's: 33.1 percent
- Procter & Gamble: 29.6 percent
- Peace Corps: 4.4 percent

While this survey effort was certainly not designed to be a scholarly study, the results are straightforward and help make a useful point. With some interpretive license, the Yahoo! and Goldman Sachs respondents would appear to be a mix of the cash drivers and the career drivers. On the other hand, the Ben & Jerry's respondents appear to be similar to the life balancers. The Proctor & Gamble respondents are likely a mix of the life balancers and the career drivers. And although the Peace Corps respondents do not clearly map to any of the big three, they are very similar to one of the much smaller factors ($n = 18$) in the internal research (Schippmann, 2001b).

The compelling insight, most relevant to this discussion, is that no single best employment offer works for everyone. Different people want different things, and the differences cannot be interpreted around simplistic demographic distinctions along age, gender, ethnic, or geographic lines. For example, in the Schippmann (2001b) research, executives of different ages, gender, and ethnicity were distributed across each of the big three clusters. Similar results have been found, though not broadly reported, in other internal and unpublished research programs from Global 1000 companies. Of course, these research findings are in conflict with articles in the popular press (for example, discussions about what elements are important to current or prospective employees based on generational differences).

Further, though based on anecdotal evidence and observations, it would appear that there are intra-individual variations as well.

A particular employee may want different things at different times in her career. We have all known executives who prefer a career driver or cash driver lifestyle at one point in their career, only to then look for something different once certain events in their life require a change (marriage, children, illness, caring for elderly parents, and so forth). The way these situational events often play out within the organization is that the person affected by these changes cannot make the current job, culture, and performance expectations fit with her new life realities. As a result, the person often leaves the organization to find a job and a culture that better fits her new motivation profile.

The concept of engagement cluster profiles is still emerging and clearly subject to further research and reporting. Although this direction seems particularly fruitful for future application and practice, it is also important to describe how current engagement results and practice are being operationalized.

Engagement in Practice

Initiating an organizational effort on engagement makes sense only if it is clearly linked to an important business outcome. Therefore the key findings from any engagement research should be prioritized against the strategies and operating plans of the business. The specific applications on the operational back end of the research (not to mention the target employee populations covered by an application) can be as varied and unique as there are companies participating in engagement research. So rather than trying to describe the full range of potential applications, it makes more sense to present several examples.

Using Performance Management to Support Development

Following the results of an employee engagement effort, PepsiCo diagnosed the need to improve a key aspect of its performance management process (PMP) (see Corporate Leadership Council, 2002, for background details). PepsiCo wanted to use its PMP to underscore the importance of manager accountability for people and leadership development. Throughout the 1990s, the company had succeeded as a portfolio business (with fairly independent business segments like Pepsi-Cola, Frito-Lay, and Tropicana), following a strategy that strongly emphasized execution and individual business results. This emphasis was clearly supported by a management-by-objective (MBO) PMP that focused exclusively on business results. However, significant turnover in the management ranks was beginning to create gaps in the talent pipeline that limited the ability to grow the business. The engagement research was used as a way to bring into focus some potential levers for changing the culture. The extent to which people management and people development was undervalued in various HR programs was surprising (for example, nominal emphasis in the PMP and light representation in the core leadership competency model), particularly when juxtaposed with the importance of these elements in predicting turnover in the company (Corporate Leadership Council, 2002).

While a number of changes and enhancements were made to various HR programs to support the reemphasis on people and development, the cornerstone of the change was a new dual-rating PMP that examined employee performance from two perspectives: (1) business results and (2) people results. The people results aspect was, like business results, an MBO-based format, where the "objectives" were built around growing talent, motivating teams, collaborating across organizational groups, making objectives clear for others, and so forth. In addition, the people results rating was made independently and kept separate from the business results rating at all times. As a result, these two ratings fed all downstream appraisal, feedback, and reward stages of the company's performance management process (that is, business results and people results are both important, and the ratings are never averaged or blended). So, using the company's 5-point rating scale (1 = significantly below expectations, up through 5 = significantly exceeds expectations), a particular manager might be a 4–3 (4 on business results and 3 on people results). A 4–3 in PepsiCo's new performance culture is just fine. Another manager having a 5 on business results and a 2 on people results would, if the two scores were combined, have the same overall score. However, a 5–2 performance at PepsiCo is most definitely not acceptable. Keeping the spotlight on both business and people objectives and outcomes was a fundamental part of a revised focus on people, development, and collaboration at PepsiCo, and this revised focus was in large part driven by the original engagement research.

Building an Employment Brand

For years branding has been a core concept in product marketing for winning customers in a crowded marketplace (Aaker, 1996; Kotler, 1999). The emergence of branding in the employment context (Ambler & Barrow, 1996; Hepburn, 2005; Hieronimus, Schaefer, & Schroder, 2005) seems like such a natural line extension it is surprising that the jump from product to people took so long. At the core of many employment branding efforts are employee engagement projects designed to understand, tweak, and clearly articulate a company's employment deal or employee value proposition. In other words, once an organization has a good grasp of the employment attributes that are currently "real" and important, then the attributes can get aligned (or changed to match) the messages that senior management wants to convey. Once established, the employment brand serves to differentiate the company's employment value proposition from those of other organizations competing for talent in the same labor market. At the core, an effective brand has a clear, compelling, and consistent promise so that in a crowded and noisy employment market, a meaningful message of differentiation can be heard.

Naturally a company's brand is built over time in the marketplace and supported through a variety of communication channels:

- Websites, job postings, and job fairs
- Employee and alumni networks
- Direct communications with current employees
- Onboarding and employee socialization materials for new hires
- Formal media campaigns

Perhaps the most influential aspect of a company's employment brand that is not on the list above is word of mouth in the marketplace. One of the reasons Yahoo!, Goldman Sachs, Ben & Jerry's, and Procter & Gamble were chosen as potential employment destinations in the Fast Company (2000) survey was because of the established brand associated with each company. The attraction and retention drivers for each company are both discernable and quite different.

A report by the Corporate Leadership Council (2001) provides a good overview of how companies like Johnson & Johnson, Blue Cross/Blue Shield, Eddie Bauer, and Kaiser Permanente go about defining their brand elements and managing brand activities. A nice supplement is an article by Caplan (2004) describing the evolution of the branding work at Dah Sing Bank as reported in *China Staff.* The work conducted at Philips is also useful to review (Van Leeuwen, Pieters, & Crawford, 2005), particularly in terms of their emphasis of the brand experience throughout the employment life cycle ("from the moment an individual looks for a job, until the moment they leave the company"). Related to the Philips perspective, it is worth noting that the Towers Perrin Global Workforce Study (2006) reports that company reputation was the only one of a wide range of organizational attributes that influenced all three phases of the employment life cycle: attraction, retention, and engagement.

Turnover Intervention Tool Kits

In response to the increased willingness of employees to search for a better employment fit and to bargain hunt for a better employment deal, many organizations are starting to provide retention tools to help managers try to better engage (or reengage) employees. Warning signs or early indicators of disengagement vary but typically include:

Personal Indicators

- Marriage
- Birth of children
- Health difficulties
- Death of a family member or spouse
- Caring for elderly parents
- The move to a duel-career household

Work and Performance Indicators

- Changing peer relationships
- New job or new boss
- Mentor or close friend leaving the company
- Limited available promotions
- Limited development opportunities
- Performance fluctuations
- High workload or excessive travel

Given the importance of the direct boss in the retention equation, many companies are building manager awareness of turnover warning signs by including modules in existing manager development programs (for example, PepsiCo included it as part of the PMP rollout described above). In these cases, managers are typically provided with some general supporting material or tip sheets. A typical tip sheet might include a list of warning signs to watch for and an associated list of questions or probes a manager might use as a way to check in, and if necessary, problem solve with an employee.

Still other companies, like Bristol-Myers Squibb (BMS), are taking the turnover intervention process a step further and creating specific programs and tool kits. BMS has developed a structured process for identifying (a) the "most critical" employees and (b) the "most at-risk" employees. The assessment of risk component includes a manager self-evaluation based on the framework of key retention elements. Sample questions include:

- Does this employee have a strong working relationship with you?
- Have you provided the employee with specific job or career feedback during the past 60 days?
- Does the employee have a good balance between work and personal time?
- Does the employee have a mentor or strong ties with others in the organization?
- Would this employee have difficulty leaving the organization to take a higher-paying role with another organization?

- Has the employee been recognized for his performance (for example, public acknowledgement, exposure to senior leaders) in the past year?

Based on a dichotomous scoring routine, employees are then plotted on a 3 × 3 matrix, a "criticality to BMS" by "risk of departure" grid. Individuals who appear in the combined high-value and high-risk cells of the grid are approached by their manager and asked to partner on a retention or reengagement action plan. Similar programs have been developed in other companies and described as "departure-risk management systems" or as "continuous sensing interviews" for high-risk employees (Corporate Leadership Council, 1998).

However, regardless of whether the turnover awareness and intervention program is more or less formalized, if an organization has a single fixed employment deal for all employees, efforts to problem solve and find unique solutions for individuals will be challenging.

The Future

Engagement research in companies around the world is proceeding at a rapid pace. This seems justified given the escalating competition for talent. Consequently, work to meaningfully define what a company "is all about," so the company can clearly include these elements in an employment deal, that is both useful and practical . . . to a point. The point of diminishing return for this work effort is determined by the pool of talent available to fuel the business. If an organization is full of talent and if there are no looming issues related to acquiring or retaining key personnel, then perhaps having a single employment deal may be a good strategy for continued success. But if finding and keeping enough talented people is a stark challenge for an organization, then perhaps the work needed to find the best employment formula (so they can modify their employment deal accordingly) is only a partial solution.

As noted, there is no single best mix of elements that works across the diversity of executive motivational profiles. That said, there would appear to be a huge benefit for those organizations that figure out how to be flexible in their employment deal to accommodate different clusters of people or people at different times in their careers. To be clear, this is not a question of part-time or flextime work (or telecommuting, or job sharing, or compressed work weeks, or other variations of flexible work arrangements). Instead, this proposal is much closer to a concept that appeared in the compensation area a few years ago around "my pay my way." That idea is that different people want a different mix of elements in building their overall compensation package. For example, some employees may wish to give up some of the riskier stock options in their company compensation package and instead choose a higher base pay or perhaps a smaller amount of sure-to-have-value restricted stock units. In this way, employees are able to move in and out of different packaged compensation offerings depending on what best fits their changing risk and wealth creation profiles.

Similarly, in the world of "my job my way," there would be a structured way for employees to sign up for different work and performance expectations that best fit with their motivational drivers. Of course, there would be trade-offs associated with different work and performance packages (for example, different levels of access to development opportunities, different positions on succession planning slates, different levels of bonus or variable compensation potential, and so forth). At the heart of this proposal is the ability to meaningfully and fairly set different levels of performance expectations within the same organization (versus maintaining and promoting the same standard of target performance for everyone).

As difficult as this sounds, several organizations are quietly testing these concepts in discrete segments of their business in an effort to gauge their potential for broader application. The goal is to create a platform for an individualized (within limits) versus homogenized employment deal that is attractive to a broader pool of talented executives and that changes as the motivational drivers for individual employees change over the course of their career. The payoff is the creation of engagement packages that are individualized (again, within limits) and that are maximally useful in attracting, motivating, and retaining leadership talent in a world where such talent is becoming a constrained resource.

References

Aaker, D. A. (1996). *Building strong brands.* New York: Free Press.

Alderfer, C. P. (1969). A new theory of human needs. *Organizational Behavior and Human Performance, 4,* 142–175.

Ambler, T., & Barrow, W. (1996). The employer brand. *Journal of Brand Management, 4,* 185–206.

Ambrose, M. L., & Kulik, C. T. (1999). Old friends, new faces: Motivation research in the 1990s. *Journal of Management, 25,* 231–292.

Blessing White. (2005). *Employee engagement report 2005.* Princeton, NJ: Author.

Buckingham, M., & Coffman, C. (1999). *First, break all the rules: What the world's greatest managers do differently.* New York: Simon & Schuster.

Caplan, J. (2004). Building a winning employer brand. *China Staff, 10,* 1–5.

Corporate Leadership Council. (1998). *Employee retention: New tools for managing workforce stability and engagement.* Washington, DC: Corporate Executive Board.

Corporate Leadership Council. (1999). *The compelling offer: A quantitative analysis of the career preferences and decisions of high value employees.* Washington, DC: Corporate Executive Board.

Corporate Leadership Council. (2001). *Employment branding initiatives.* Washington, DC: Corporate Executive Board.

Corporate Leadership Council. (2002). *Closing the performance gap.* Washington, DC: Corporate Executive Board.

Corporate Leadership Council. (2004). *Driving performance and retention through employee engagement.* Washington, DC: Corporate Executive Board.

Erickson, T. J. (2005, May 26). *Testimony submitted to the U.S. Senate Committee on Health, Education, Labor and Pensions.* Retrieved August 14, 2007, from http://www.gpoaccess.gov.

Fast Company. (2000, January–February). It's your choice. *Fast Company,* 200–212.

Foreman, P., & Murphy, G. (1996). Work values and expectancies in occupational rehabilitation: The role of cognitive variables in the return-to-work process. *Journal of Rehabilitation, 62,* 44–49.

Frank, F. D., Finnegan, R. P., & Taylor, C. R. (2004). The race for talent: Retaining and engaging workers in the 21st century. *Human Resource Planning, 29,* 12–25.

Frank, F. D., & Taylor, C. R. (2004). Talent management: Trends that will shape the future. *Human Resource Planning, 27,* 33–41.

Gibbons, J. (2006). *Employee engagement: A review of current research and its implications.* New York: Conference Board.

Gubman, E. (1998). *The talent solution.* New York: McGraw-Hill.

Gubman, E. (2003). *The engaging leader.* Chicago: Dearborn.

Gustafson, S. B., & Mumford, M. D. (1995). Personal style and person environment fit: A pattern approach. *Journal of Vocational Behavior, 46,* 163–188.

Hackman, J. R., & Oldham, G. R. (1975). Development of the job diagnostic survey. *Journal of Applied Psychology, 60,* 159–170.

Harter, J. K., Schmidt, F. L., & Keyes, C. L. (2003). Well-being in the workplace and its relationship to business outcomes: A review of the Gallup studies. In C. L. Keyes & J. Haidt (Eds.), *Flourishing: The positive person and the good life* (pp. 205–224). Washington, DC: American Psychological Association.

Hepburn, S. (2005). Creating a winning employer reputation. *Strategic HR Review, 4,* 20–23.

Hewitt Associates. (2005). *Hewitt engagement survey.* Retrieved August 14, 2007, from http://www.hewittassociates.com.

Hieronimus, F., Schaefer, K., and Schroder, J. (2005). Using branding to attract talent. *McKinsey Quarterly, 3,* 12–14.

Kotler, P. (1999). *Kotler on marketing: How to create, win, and dominate markets.* New York: Free Press.

Latham, G. P., & Pinder, C. C. (2005). Work motivation theory and research at the dawn of the twenty-first century. *Annual Review of Psychology, 56,* 485–516.

Lawler, E. E. (1973). *Motivation in work organizations.* Monterey, CA: Brooks/Cole.

Locke, E. A. (1976). The nature and causes of job satisfaction. In M. D. Dunnette (Ed.), *The handbook of industrial and organizational psychology* (pp. 1297–1349). Skokie, IL: Rand McNally.

Locke, E. A., & Henne, D. (1986). Work motivation theories. In C. L. Cooper & I. Robertson (Eds.), *International review of industrial and organizational psychology* (pp. 1–36). Hoboken, NJ: Wiley.

Locke, E. A., & Latham, G. P. (1990). *A theory of goal setting and task performance.* Upper Saddle River, NJ: Prentice Hall.

Macey, W. H., & Schneider, B. (2008). The meaning of employee engagement. *Industrial and Organizational Psychology, 1,* 3–30.

Manpower. (2004, April-June). *Global employment outlook.* Milwaukee, WI: Author.

Maslow, A. H. (1943). A theory of human motivation. *Psychological Review, 50,* 370–396.

McGregor, D. M. (1960). *The human side of the enterprise.* New York: McGraw-Hill.

Mitchell, T. R., & Daniels, D. (2003). Motivation. In W. C. Borman, D. R. Ilgen, & R. J. Klimoski (Eds.), *Handbook of psychology* (Vol. 12, pp. 225–254). Hoboken, NJ: Wiley.

PricewaterhouseCoopers. (2004, March 15). *Expecting sales growth, CEOs cite worker retention as critical to success.* Retrieved August 8, 2007, from http://www.pwc.com.

Schippmann, J. S. (1999). *Strategic job modeling: Working at the core of integrated human resources.* Mahwah, NJ: Erlbaum.

Schippmann, J. S. (2001a). *Executive retention at company X.* Unpublished report.

Schippmann, J. S. (2001b). *The employment deal at company X.* Unpublished report.

Schippmann, J. S., Ash, R. A., Battista, M., Carr, L., Eyde, L. D., Hesketh, B., et al. (2000). The practice of competency modeling. *Personnel Psychology, 53,* 703–740.

Schmitt, N., Cortina, J. M., Ingerick, M. J., & Wiechmann, D. (2003). Personnel selection and employee performance. In W. C. Borman, D. R. Ilgen, & R. J. Klimoski (Eds.), *Handbook of psychology* (Vol. 12, pp. 77–106). Hoboken, NJ: Wiley.

Steers, R. M., & Porter, L. W. (1975). *Motivation and work behavior.* New York: McGraw-Hill.

Towers-Perrin. (2003). *Working today: Understanding what drives employee engagement.* Stamford, CT: Author.

Towers-Perrin. (2004, January). *Reward and performance management challenges linking people and results.* Stamford, CT: Author.

Towers-Perrin. (2006). *Global workforce study.* Stamford, CT: Authors.

U.S. Department of Labor, Bureau of Labor Statistics. (2003). Retrieved October 4, 2007, from http://www.bls.gov.

Van Leeuwen, B., Pieters, J., & Crawford, T. (2005). Building Philips' employer brand from the inside out. *Strategic HR Review, 4,* 16–19.

Verplanken, B., & Holland, R. W. (2002). Motivated decision making: Effects of activation and self-centrality of values on choices and behavior. *Journal of Personality and Social Psychology, 82,* 434–447.

Vroom, V. H. (1964). *Work and motivation.* New York: John Wiley & Sons, 1964.

Part Three

Critical Issues

CHAPTER 11

BUILDING FUNCTIONAL EXPERTISE TO ENHANCE ORGANIZATIONAL CAPABILITY

Suzan McDaniel, Erika D'Egidio

In today's fast-paced and ever changing business world, companies face challenging business realities such as developing innovative products and accelerating their growth, competing in and shaping crowded global markets, producing shareholder returns during industry or economic downturns, and effectively understanding and adapting to the changing face of the customer, all while working with fewer financial and people resources. To face these realities effectively, many companies recognize that it is essential to have the right organizational capabilities and the right talent, with the right competencies, in the right job, at the right time. While many companies invest in building management and leadership capability, it is equally important to build deep functional capabilities. It is the combination of strong functional, leadership and management capability that establishes the solid foundation required for effective strategy execution.

Building functional capability is an investment for any company. Time and resources are spent creating, executing, and sustaining the elements of functional capability. Companies that are committed to building capability tend to do so in strategic areas that have the biggest impact on successfully executing the strategy. One important and common lever used to build functional capability is to enhance the level of functional expertise in the organization. While it has been more common to build functional expertise at the individual contributor level in organizations, the increased complexity of work has created the need to build functional depth at higher levels in the organization, including roles that involve managing people. Organizations are expecting individuals at all levels to actively contribute to meeting business objectives and making decisions using their functional expertise. Generalist managers whose primary role was to set objectives and coordinate the work of the group have been replaced by managers with strong leadership, management, and functional expertise.

Industrial-organizational psychology (I-O) practitioners and human resource (HR) professionals can influence and contribute significantly to building functional expertise as they create and execute people processes. A clear understanding of functional expertise and having a cogent method for building it can improve our effectiveness in enabling organizations to create strong functional capability and compete successfully in the marketplace.

This chapter presents a model and approach for building individual functional expertise to enhance organizational capability. It is organized around four key areas:

1. An overview of functional expertise, including definitions of key terms, a historical look at the field, and benchmark data from Fortune 500 companies
2. A method to build functional expertise in an organization, including potential elements of a functional talent system
3. Practical lessons learned from experience
4. Future trends and research in building functional expertise to enhance organizational capability.

Overview of Functional Expertise

Organizational Capability and Functional Expertise Defined

It is important to clarify the distinction we are making between the concepts of organizational capability and individual functional expertise. *Organizational capability* is the broader, more macro term that is defined at the organizational level. It represents the collective functional abilities that support executing a business strategy and is built through a combination of structure, process, tools, technology, and people. For example, for consumer goods companies such as Proctor & Gamble and Unilever, marketing capability enables them to develop and market products that meet customer needs. At an organizational level, this capability is created through an organizational structure that supports gathering data from customers quickly, consumer market research processes that outline how to conduct world-class market research, tools and technology that support building their brands, and talented people with in-depth marketing expertise. It is only through the combination of the marketing structure, processes, tools, technology, and people that a company successfully builds marketing capability.

Functional expertise is defined at the individual level and is a critical element in building organizational capability. It refers to the technical or functional knowledge, skills, and abilities that are required by a person to perform a job. For example, a focus on building in-depth functional expertise in marketing represents the people element of the equation, which can be created by defining functional standards and then sourcing, selecting, and developing people against those standards.

It is important that organizations strike the right balance between functional expertise and leadership competence. Too often, however, one trumps the other. Individuals can be selected or promoted based on their functional expertise to a level in the organization where the person's shortcomings in leadership become so significant that it is difficult for the individual to succeed in a leadership role. Other individuals are recruited or promoted for their strong leadership skills and may not have the functional depth to effectively contribute to the functional development of their team. While this chapter focuses on building functional expertise to enhance organizational capability, it is important to strike the right balance with also enhancing leadership competence.

Companies can have a competitive advantage in the marketplace by building strong organizational capabilities. However, successful companies can lose their growth momentum when there is a shortage of the organizational capabilities required for strategy execution.

A recent study conducted by Olson, van Bever, and Verry (2008) of leading corporations in the past half-century identified common "stall" factors that reversed a company's growth trajectory: "What stops growth dead in its tracks, however, is not merely a shortage of talent, but the absence of required capabilities—such as solutions selling or consumer marketing—in key areas of the company" (p. 58). To remain competitive in the marketplace, companies need to focus on critical organizational capabilities that are often tied closely to the level of individual expertise of employees.

History of Organizational Capability and Functional Expertise

There is limited discussion in the literature (that is, textbooks and professional journals) related directly to building functional organizational capability in an organization. Rather, the focus has been on building individual-level functional expertise either at the job level or person level. Job analysis is focused on defining the knowledge, skills, and abilities (KSAs) required to perform individual jobs or job families. Much of the literature in industrial-organizational psychology focuses on how to appropriately define the KSAs required to perform individual jobs (job analysis) and how to assess those KSAs for the purposes of selection, performance management, and development (Dunnette & Hough, 1991).

The training literature is another source of information on building functional expertise. This literature focuses almost entirely on methods of developing individual-level functional and leadership skills. These methods include a number of more traditional approaches to building functional expertise, such as apprenticeship programs, job rotational programs, on-the-job learning, community or technical college course work, four-year college course work, and formal learning programs (Goldstein & Ford, 2001). Depending on the industry and job, the type of training can vary, as well as the commitment of the company to buy or to build functional expertise for the organization. Other key considerations include whether one is attempting to build a broad base of cross-functional knowledge or build in-depth technical knowledge in a more focused area. Job rotational programs are a popular way to build cross-functional knowledge in an organization, while apprenticeship programs focus on building in-depth technical and functional expertise at the individual level. The number of formal apprenticeship programs in organizations has decreased over the years, and many organizations now primarily buy skilled talent from the external market. Most of the training literature is focused on building entry-level functional skills. However, the requirement for functional expertise is becoming more prevalent at upper levels within organizations. Executive searches increasingly specify the need to possess deep industry and functional expertise in candidate specifications, and the demand for specialist management development courses has grown much faster than demand for generalist courses (Nairn & Nicholson, 2006).

The limited references in the literature, the increased focus on functional expertise due to changing job requirements, and the importance of knowledge-based roles in the future economy suggest a need to identify practical approaches for increasing functional expertise within an organization (Nairn & Nicholson, 2006; Corporate Leadership Council, 2007).

Buying or Building Individual Functional Expertise

Companies can take two approaches to increase expertise within a function: buy it or build it. A buy strategy requires companies to have robust talent sourcing, recruiting, and selection practices that will help them find, identify, and hire people with deep functional expertise. Although this strategy often ensures that organizations are hiring employees with the necessary skills, it is generally not sufficient to meet the strategic needs of an organization. In many parts of the world, the talent demand far exceeds the talent supply. For example, in China, where there is fierce competition for talent and a limited supply of talent, "retention is a much cheaper solution than recruiting," according to Anthony Wu, head of accounting at Ernst & Young in Hong Kong and China ("China's people problem," 2005).

The U.S. Department of Education predicts that 60 percent of new jobs in this century will require skills possessed by only 20 percent of the current workforce (Glenn, 2000). The shortage of talent in the United States is expected to be particularly strong among the most educated and highly trained workers due to the increasing number of baby boomers reaching retirement age.

A talent supply shortage will be acute in certain functional areas.

- In the health care industry, the United States will have between 85,000 and 96,000 fewer physicians than needed by 2020 (Spotswood, 2006).
- Projections show that by 2020, the demand for oncology services will significantly outpace the supply of oncologists available to provide patient care (Hortobagyi, 2007).
- The oil services industry is facing a growing shortage of functional talent in petroleum engineering and geophysics ("Prospecting for petroleum engineers," 2000).
- In advertising, there is an acute shortage of individuals with skills in digital media (Atkinson, 2008).

The impending talent shortage coupled with existing business challenges is one reason companies also use a build strategy to create functional expertise. For several other reasons companies invest in building functional expertise rather than just buying it. First, many companies need more in-depth functional expertise as positions evolve into more complex, knowledge-based jobs. The critical knowledge, skills, and experiences needed for these positions are often specific to how the work is conducted within a particular company. This critical knowledge is frequently unique and creates a competitive advantage. For example, Google's search engine capability is a competitive advantage, and it is essential that the company has functional expertise in innovative software engineering and programming to maintain that advantage.

A second reason for building functional expertise in individuals lies in ensuring that the organization of the future has the strategic capabilities needed to compete effectively. As the external and internal business environments continue to evolve, companies are preparing for a marketplace that will look very different than it does today. More and more companies identify the capabilities needed to win in the future as part of a business strategic planning process. As a result, companies are looking to upgrade their existing functional talent to prepare them to meet increasing demands and levels of complexity. For example, to compete effectively in the war for talent, Human Resources (HR) functions will need to have greater organizational capability in talent management and workforce planning. As a result, some HR functions are outsourcing the transactional and administrative aspects of their work to enable a greater focus on these more strategic areas of HR that require greater functional expertise.

Finally, as mergers and acquisitions continue, companies face a need to establish common standards in a functional area across several businesses. This enables greater efficiency and effectiveness in the delivery of functional services to customers. For example, as banks continue to merge and consolidate, there is a significant need to have common performance standards and work practices for bank tellers, portfolio managers, and wealth management specialists to ensure the work is performed in a common and consistent way. These are some of the reasons why more companies employ both build and buy strategies for functional expertise to ensure they have the functional talent they need now and in the future.

Company Benchmarking

To get HR practitioners' views on how companies build organizational capability and functional expertise, we interviewed seven internal talent management practitioners and external talent management consultants to Fortune 500 companies across a variety of industries, such as consumer goods, financial services, pharmaceuticals, beverages, retail, and technology. We focused on two critical areas: (1) how they build functional capability at an organizational level and (2) how they build functional expertise at an individual level.

Functional Capability at the Organizational Level
In the majority of companies interviewed, there is not a clear link between defined organizational capabilities and the business strategy. Only two of the companies we interviewed identified the organizational capabilities that are needed today and in the future, as well as the levels of individual expertise needed to support

building the organizational capability. These companies identify organizational capabilities in two ways.

- Through a business strategic planning process that identifies the capabilities needed today and in the next three to five years for effective business performance
- Through dialogue with senior business and functional leaders that identifies the capabilities needed today and in the next three years to compete successfully in the marketplace

Once the organizational capabilities are defined, they serve as the starting point and the "North Star" for identifying the key areas of individual expertise needed for the organization.

Functional Expertise at an Individual Level

All of the companies invest in building functional expertise at the individual level. There were several similarities in how the companies approach developing functional expertise, including leveraging functional competency models as the foundation for functional talent systems. We identified five main interview themes related to functional talent systems.

1. Competencies are the Foundation for Developing Functional Expertise in Organizations

Most of the companies use competency models to establish the performance standards for a function. Many also have organizational competency models that define either leadership expectations or organizational values, or both. They noted that functional competency models and leadership and organizational competency models should complement each other rather than being redundant. Defining functional competencies by focusing solely on specific technical knowledge and expertise is the most effective way to reduce overlap and confusion with existing leadership or organizational competency models. Complementary functional and leadership competency models provide employees with a complete set of standards required to be successful in the organization that includes both the functional standards for the role and expectations for leadership performance.

Functional competencies are used for a range of purposes, for example:

- Setting the standards for functional performance—often used in combination with leadership competencies
- Developing curriculums for use in training and skill-building programs
- Identifying individual strengths and weaknesses that can be incorporated into individual development plans
- Serving as input into selection decisions when assessed through structured interview questions

Other less common uses are to embed functional competencies into career planning tools to describe the functional competencies that can be gained from a particular role or performance management processes that compensate people for the level of functional expertise demonstrated. Also, a few companies use functional competencies in talent reviews as a consideration for succession planning or to build internal candidate slates.

2. Business Imperatives Drive the Development of Functional Models
In almost all companies, the impetus to create a functional competency model was to address a business need such as expanding into new markets, upgrading talent in a function, or making sure functional expertise evolves with changes in the external environment and marketplace. For example, one company is expanding their global footprint by launching products in five new markets. The company sees the need to have a common approach to marketing and marketing standards in every market to ensure successful launches in the new markets. Another company realizes that because external competition and the company's target customer have changed drastically in the past three years, there is a need to build organizational capability in market research and analytics, and in proactively anticipating market and customer changes.

3. Business Leaders Lead the Development and Implementation of Functional Competency Models
All content development for the functional competencies is done by subject matter experts from the business and facilitated

by either internal or external talent management practitioners. In most companies interviewed, business leaders lead the implementation of programs using the functional competencies with support from the Human Resource professionals.

4. Launch Tactics Varied
Companies use multiple approaches to launch programs based on functional competencies, and the specific tactics depend on the company's culture:

- Senior business leaders introduce the competencies in town hall employee meetings or through e-mail communications.
- Paper-based and online materials and a marketing campaign are created to support the introduction of the competencies to the organization.
- Business leaders and HR generalists lead training sessions on the functional competencies and the functional talent system.
- Business leaders and managers review and present related materials during staff meetings.
- Online training modules are implemented.
- The functional competencies are posted on company websites.

5. The Impact Can Be Difficult to Measure
Most of the companies do not measure the business impact or the return on investment of functional talent systems. Two companies use employee surveys to measure the impact. For example, one company compared average employee survey ratings on employee engagement and employee development for groups that had functional talent systems with groups who did not. They found higher ratings on engagement and perceptions of development for the groups that had functional talent systems.

Methodology for Building Functional Expertise

This section builds on the literature on functional expertise, best practices, and benchmarking data to propose a method for building functional expertise in support of enhancing organizational capability. This methodology is designed to maximize the impact and value provided by the process. It is important to recognize that the specific approach a company uses to build individual functional expertise is dependent on a number of factors, such as the current business context, the available resources, the views of senior leaders, the company's talent strategy, and the current gaps in functional skills or the organizational capabilities that are required.

Figure 11.1 presents an eight-step model that incorporates the best practices and lessons learned from talent management practitioners who have experience using individual expertise to enhance organizational capability. It is based on several guiding assumptions:

- An organization seeks to ensure that work in functional areas is linked to the business strategy.
- An organization will differentially invest in functions critical to strategic success.

Figure 11.1. Model for Building Functional Expertise

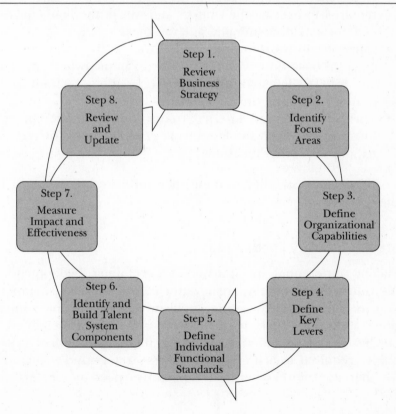

- The solution needs to be practical and pragmatic.
- The solution must be sustainable over time.

The proposed model is designed to help guide practitioners as they move through the key decision points related to building functional expertise to enhance organizational capability in key functional areas. Each step is described in more detail below.

Step 1: Review the Business Strategy

A critical first step in all talent-related decisions involves working with senior business leaders to fully understand these factors:

- Business strategy, needed capabilities, and workforce strengths and weaknesses—for example, the vision and key objectives of the business today and in the future, the key capabilities required to execute the strategy and win in the marketplace, and the workforce strengths and weaknesses
- Current and future trends (over three to five years) in the external business environment—for example, whether there are shifts in the market due to new regulations, technologies, or new entrants in the marketplace
- Current and future internal trends—for example, current turnover trends, possible internal consolidations, or combinations with other functions

A clear understanding of these areas informs the next steps in the process.

Step 2: Identify Focus Areas

Making differential investments in developing high-potential individuals is common in organizations; however, it is also important to consider making differential investments in some functional areas over others, particularly when resources are limited.

This can be initiated by defining the organizational capabilities required to achieve the business strategy and evaluating whether any of these critical capabilities need to be further developed or enhanced beyond the current state in order to deliver on the strategy. It also is important to identify any specific challenges related to a particular critical function (such as recent changes in legislation, changes in customer segments, or changes in technology or service delivery).

Decisions on where to invest should be based on an analysis of the business strategy and on the organizational capabilities that provide competitive advantage. In a world full of opportunities to outsource functions or hire external functional consultants, companies are making careful choices about where to maintain internal functions. These decisions are often based on whether the value provided by the function creates a competitive advantage in the marketplace. For example, in consumer goods companies such as PepsiCo and Procter & Gamble, the marketing function is usually seen as the primary critical function in the organization; if this function performs well, then the organization will be able to compete successfully. However, in the service and retail industries, such as Ritz-Carlton and Nordstrom, customer service is a critical function and an organizational capability that provides a competitive advantage in the marketplace. The outcome of this analysis should be the identification of the functional areas that are critical to the company's success, now and in the future. An example of identifying a critical functional area follows. For illustrative purposes, we are going to discuss the internal finance organization in hypothetical Company ABC:

> As a result of the collapse of Enron and other accounting scandals in the early 2000s, U.S. companies were forced to focus on key internal financial capabilities (driven by federal regulations such as the Sarbanes-Oxley Law enacted in 2002). Company ABC brought in a new chief financial officer whose first objective was to increase the overall capability of the finance function. She believed that a renewed focus on building the right set of functional capabilities and individual expertise in internal finance was critical to the organization. This increased focus would allow the organization to effectively respond to the increased scrutiny by government agencies, including new regulations around internal controls, and attract the best talent in an extremely competitive talent market.

Step 3: Define Organizational Capabilities

Once critical functional areas are identified, the next step is to define two or three key functional capabilities—broad macro-organizational enablers that are essential to executing the business strategy. Examples of these functional capabilities are described for Company ABC:

> As part of the strategic planning process in Finance, the senior finance leadership identified three key organizational capabilities that were critical for successfully executing current and future strategy:
>
> - *Financial stewardship:* Act as a guardian and control function; enforce and uphold finance policies, procedures, and controls; act in the best interests of shareholders.
> - *Business partnering:* Effectively partner with business leaders and other finance professionals to provide advice and counsel in support of the business strategy.
> - *Transaction processing:* Provide efficient and accurate processing of transactional activities in support of executing the business strategy.
>
> The reasons for each of these varied. Financial stewardship was seen as a critical capability of the finance organization in the new controls environment established by the Sarbanes-Oxley legislation. Business partnering was seen as a critical capability to the overall effectiveness of the finance organization, and transaction processing was a capability that needed to be enhanced in order to increase overall operational efficiency and reduce cost.

A definition of these capabilities should consider the strengths and weaknesses of the function and emerging trends facing the business. The identification of these organizational capabilities serves as the foundation for defining individual expertise by creating individual-level performance standards or competencies for jobs.

The senior leadership of a function typically identifies the critical capabilities that the function needs to deliver to execute the business strategy successfully. These leaders determine which functional areas will be needed for future success and how effective the current organization is in each area. This is frequently done as part of the strategic planning process. These functional capabilities can guide the creation of the individual-level performance standards within a function. They also can guide an organization in building or refining business processes and structures that support the function.

The following key questions can help identify the organizational capabilities and the quality of the talent needed in each area:

- What are the capabilities that will enable the organization to win in the marketplace and execute our business strategy?
- How strong is our functional talent in these areas?
- In what areas do our competitors outperform us?
- How well does our functional talent compare with our competitors' talent?
- Is there any functional area that we have to consistently source outside to obtain the needed talent?

The answers to these questions may indicate potential gaps in the critical functional areas that are needed to successfully compete and execute the strategy.

Step 4: Define Key Levers

Once the organization defines the organizational capabilities, the next step is to determine the appropriate approaches (levers) to build them. Some of the approaches used include:

- *People:* Taking actions to increase individual functional expertise, such as setting performance standards, identifying on-the-job development actions, and offering formal learning and skill-building programs
- *Structure:* Determining the organizational structure, roles, and responsibilities that align and support the functional capability
- *Process:* Building day-to-day work processes that help drive the functional work
- *Goals and objectives:* Aligning the functional goals and objectives with the business strategy
- *Leadership:* Ensuring that leader actions and key stakeholders support building the capability

We will focus on the use of people to build organizational capability. As mentioned, a key decision around people is whether the organization is going to buy or build the functional expertise that is needed to achieve the strategy. This decision impacts which programs and processes are built as part of the functional talent system. Some of the more common talent system components include:

- Structured selection processes
- Career development programs
- Talent assessments
- Formal learning and developing programs
- Functional competencies integrated with the performance management system
- Reward and recognition programs

Each of these components will be discussed in detail in step 6; however, each component typically requires functional standards to be defined at the individual level. The level of detail used to define individual standards and the level of validation is often determined by the talent components included in the system. For example, if selection processes are developed based on the functional standards, then a greater level of detail and validation may be required in order to ensure legal defensibility of the selection techniques than if the standards are used only for development programs.

While there is value in each of these components it is important to recognize that each approach requires the involvement of business/functional management and HR professionals and can be time consuming. Generally it is best to focus on the two or three system components that will have the most impact on building talent and then add other components later as needed. Regardless of the processes chosen, it is important to clearly define the functional standards for individuals. The most common question that employees ask after seeing the new or modified standards is, "How am I going to develop in these areas?" If you are creating new or modified standards, it is essential that you build development tools or programs that will help build those skills. An example of using people as a key lever to build organizational capability is described for Company ABC:

> In the finance organization example, a decision was made to both buy and build talent. The finance leadership recognized that there were new functional skills (for example, U.S. Securities and Exchange Commission knowledge) that needed to be brought into

the organization, since a depth of knowledge in those areas did not currently exist inside the company and it was knowledge that was not easily developed internally.

A career development framework was created to help build the overall effectiveness of all finance professionals. This framework communicated clear and consistent expectations, outlined how to build new skills through the day-to-day work, and identified potential career paths and principles that finance employees could use to guide their career choices

Step 5: Define Individual Functional Standards

Once the decision is made to invest in building organizational capability in a specific function and to use people as a key lever, the functional requirements need to be translated into job standards. Typically the process used to create these standards is determined by how the standards will be used (for selection or development, for example). Although it is tempting to focus only on the initial use for the standards, it is important to simultaneously consider all potential future uses of the standards. Each approach to developing standards has different requirements, and if all possible uses are not considered in the beginning, then other talent components, such as selection, might not be able to be easily added later. Generally the processes are identified through a partnership of business leaders and HR managers. We have found that the integration and implementation of functional standards is more straightforward if the functional standards focus solely on the functional-specific areas of jobs and do not overlap with existing leadership competencies or behaviors.

There are a number of alternative approaches to establishing standards. These options range in level of effort and complexity and include a number of advantages and disadvantages. Table 11.1 documents a number of options.

Standards can be established by:

- Creating a job profile by defining knowledge, skills, and abilities through traditional job analysis techniques
- Identifying functional competency models

Table 11.1. Approaches to Defining Individual Functional Standards

Method	Description	Complexity	Advantages	Disadvantages
Job profile	Traditional job description that includes areas of functional knowledge	Low	• Short development time • Job specific • Clear standards • Traditional format	• Difficult to build talent system • Narrow in scope • Lacks consistent terminology
Competency definition	Includes just the title and definition of the competency	Moderate	• Short development time • Easy to implement due to simplicity of model • Highlights key competencies required to deliver on organizational capabilities	• Limited information related to performance expectations • Individuals are required to determine how this relates to their own role

Competency matrix	Includes competency definitions along with expectations of proficiency by job role (see Table 11.2 for an example)	Moderate	• Less complexity than full competency model • Provides information related to expectations for various roles/levels	• Difficulty determining roles and levels if no natural groupings exist • Defines only one level of proficiency
Competency model with BARS	Includes competency definition, definitions of varying levels of expertise with standards linked to jobs, roles, or levels (see Exhibit 11.1 for an example)	High	• Provides most complete description of expectations • Outlines levels of proficiency required at various performance levels • Provides greatest opportunity to link to talent system	• Most complex to develop and maintain • Most resource intensive • Can be too complex to implement effectively

- Developing a functional competency matrix (see Table 11.2 for an example)
- Building a functional competency model with behaviorally anchored rating scales (BARS; see Exhibit 11.1 for an example)

Once the standards are defined, there is generally a desire in the organization to expand beyond its initial use. For example, managers often want to use within a short period of time a functional competency model that was created for individual development to select new employees or make promotion decisions. Therefore, it is important to be aware of possible future uses when a competency model is being created so that the appropriate validation approach is taken for all potential uses.

A Comment on Validation

Various validation methods are outlined in *Principles for Employee Selection* (Society for Industrial and Organizational Psychology, 2003) and industrial-organizational psychology textbooks (for example, content, criterion, and construct validation). The validation approach used is often based on the risks and benefits of each for the situation. For example, when a competency model is used for developmental discussions only and not for selection, the level of rigor used during the validation process may be less robust but still must establish that the functional competencies are representative of the job and needed for effective job performance. At a minimum, this may be accomplished by having senior business leaders who are knowledgeable about the job serve as content validation subject matter experts (SMEs) and confirm that the functional competencies are related to effective performance on the job.

When the functional competencies are used as input into a selection or promotion decision, a more robust content validation approach is needed. This can include having focus groups of high-performing subject matter experts (SMEs) define the competencies and administering content validation surveys of possible competencies to a different group of high-performing managers and incumbents to confirm the job relevance of the competencies. Later this may be followed with criterion-related validation studies.

Table 11.2. Functional Competency Matrix Example

Element/Job Group	Specialist	Senior Specialist	Associate Director	Director
Process knowledge	Applies a working knowledge of production processes and the work environment to the implementation of programs	Leverages an in-depth knowledge of production processes and the work environment to implement programs	Supports integration of best practices into production and business process planning and strategy	Leads the integration of best practices into production and business process planning and strategy
Applies knowledge	Applies working knowledge of facilities, equipment, and materials related to applicable production processes and the work environment to the implementation of programs	Uses detailed understanding of facilities, equipment, and materials to develop and implement procedures and directives	Uses detailed understanding of facilities, equipment, and materials to make decisions that develop and implement procedures and directives for controls	Leverages knowledge of facilities, equipment, and materials to ensure sound practices are incorporated into business decisions
Affects the business	Explains and reinforces to clients the importance of implications of production processes and the work environment	Recommends appropriate procedures and directives for clients that effectively support production processes and the work environment	Provides guidance to business partners on implications of production processes and the work environment	Provides direction to business partners on implications of current operations and strategic plans

Exhibit 11.1. Functional Competency Example with Behaviorally Anchored Rating Scale

Accounting and Reporting

- Demonstrates a current working knowledge of accounting theory, U.S. and local GAAP, and other relevant financial accounting standards; maintains an understanding of rules issued by the U.S. SEC and other relevant regulatory bodies, as well as policies, procedures, and work instructions, as it relates to position
- Maintains and updates accounting information and supporting documentation; performs transaction processing, analysis, reconciliation, and verification as appropriate to position
- Presents financial results impartially and in compliance with applicable standards that govern internal management and external statutory reporting
- Understands the flow of accounting information from transaction entry through reporting and its impact on the business

Basic	Proficient	Mastery
Applies relevant/current accounting standards, policies, and procedures to job responsibilities	Monitors the application of accounting policies and procedures to ensure compliance with current accounting standards	Serves as a subject matter expert on job-relevant accounting policies and procedures; ensures communication of changing standards and guidelines throughout the organization
Demonstrates familiarity with accounting and reconciliation concepts and performs tasks under supervision; maintains appropriate supporting documentation	Independently performs accounting and reconciliation tasks; reviews transactions and supporting documentation for accuracy, timeliness, and completeness	Spots variances and trends in accounting data; drives process improvements that reduce errors
Compiles information for internal and external reporting purposes	Produces internal and external reports as appropriate to position; articulates key differences between reports	Reviews internal and external reports for accuracy and ensures compliance with all applicable standards

Step 6: Identify and Build Talent System Components

It is important to embed the individual standards into a talent system as well as existing talent management processes to ensure sustainability and maximum impact. Some programs and processes require more time and resources than others. Table 11.3 presents a summary of potential components in a functional talent system organized by the resources and the work intensity that is needed to develop and implement each one.

Although the summary in Table 11.3 is not intended to be an exhaustive list of all possible components of a functional talent system, it does show a sample of the options that can be used when working with business leaders to build a functional talent system. Some of the key options include competency assessment, individual development actions, career paths, training programs, selection processes, new employee onboarding and integration processes, and promotion processes.

Competency Assessments

One approach to assessing talent against a standard that requires fewer resources is to simply have a discussion between managers and employees related to the standards. An approach that requires greater resources is to develop an online tool where managers and employees provide an assessment of the employee on the competencies. A benefit of using an online assessment process is that the data can be easily aggregated across individuals in order to identify the overall strengths and performance gaps for an entire function or subgroups within the function. This information is invaluable in shaping the formal learning and training agenda for the function and in identifying gaps in functional expertise on a team. This team assessment can be informative when selecting a new person for the team if you are trying to build a team with complementary skill sets.

Manager calibration meetings can be helpful when formally assessing individuals against functional standards for the first time to ensure that managers apply consistent standards across individuals. During a calibration meeting, managers identify and agree on a person who demonstrates the "gold standard" of performance for each competency, using specific behavioral examples

Table 11.3. Components of a Functional Talent System

Component	Resources Required[a]		
	Low	Moderate	High
Competency assessment			
• Self-assessment and manager discussion	X		
• Self- and manager assessment (on paper)		X	
• Self- and manager assessment (online)			X
• Calibration of assessments across groups			X
Individual and career development			
• Paired mentoring with functional subject matter experts	X		
• Development resource guide with suggested readings		X	
• Functional simulations or formal learning program focused on competencies			X
• Career development guides with suggested career paths for building functional expertise			X
Formal learning and training			
• Action learning projects		X	
• Formal training and development programs			X

Selection
- Competency-based interview questions   X
- Behaviorally based structured interview guides with behaviorally anchored ratings scales (BARS)   X

Integration
- Use of functional talent system in new manager and new employee orientation meetings to set standards   X

Promotion
- Promotional guidelines that include performance, standards for leadership competence and functional expertise   X

[a]Number of people and technology resources required to build, implement, and maintain.

to justify the choice. They agree on this standard and apply it subsequently to each person discussed. The following are some tips for conducting functional calibration meetings:

- Provide specific behavioral examples to support competency ratings that include a short description of (1) the situation, (2) the observable behavior by the individual, and (3) the outcome and impact of that behavior.
- When in doubt about a rating, go with the lower rating. Remember that the calibration process is not a performance discussion or a talent review; rather, it is used to ensure that consistent standards are applied across individuals.
- Evaluate individuals using the written competency definitions and behaviors. Do not compare people against each other, and do not discuss the traits or attitudes of a person.
- Managers need to take responsibility for the final ratings; the ratings are not a group consensus.
- Identify development actions that can be taken to close functional competency shortcomings.

Development Tools

Highlighting an employee's strengths and development areas in an individual development plan can be a meaningful way to ensure focus for key areas of development. Often this development plan is part of a broader performance management process. When assessing a person against a competency it is important to have tools and programs available to help the person develop in a specific area. One option that requires fewer resources is a competency development guide that links each competency to a set of developmental job activities, books, articles, and existing resources. Table 11.4 shows a sample page from a functional competency development guide for an HR competency. Another approach that requires more resources is to develop a functional training simulation or formal learning program that would help develop functional competencies. Creating career development guides that include potential career paths linked to specific functional competencies is also an effective tool to assist employees and managers during career planning discussions.

Table 11.4. Functional Competency Development Guide—Example for HR Professionals

Organization Diagnosis and Change Management

Developmental Experiences	
Actions	• Conduct a diagnostic or systems review of a client. Conduct a climate assessment (interview the front line, conduct focus groups, keep your finger on the pulse of the business).
	• Design or redesign a business process.
	• Support a new product launch.
	• Implement a program, process, or policy globally.
Activities	• Help design and plan a change initiative.
	• Lead an organization or regionwide HR initiative.
	• Take an assignment in a start-up organization.
	• Manage a cross-functional project or task force.
	• Manage a downsizing or organization restructure.
Assignments	• *For specialists:* Assume HR lead for distinct line of business or function.
	• *For generalists:* Assume an organization development specialist role.
Education and Training	
Training programs	• Driving execution formal training.
	• "Flawless Consulting."

(*Continued*)

Table 11.4. Functional Competency Development Guide—Example for HR Professionals (*Continued*)

Organization Diagnosis and Change Management

Academic courses and certification programs	Columbia University Teachers College (www.tc.columbia.edu) • Principles and Practices of Organization Development Program • Certificate in Advanced Organization Development & Human Resource Management Cornell University (www.cornell.edu) • Basic Tools of Project Management (one-day program) • Contemporary Leadership Part II—Adapting to and Leading Change (two-day program) • Problem Solving and Decision Making (two-day program) • Change Management: The Fundamentals (two-day program)
Other Key Resources	
Books	• *Champions of Change* by David Nadler • *The Heart of Change* by John Kotter and Dan Cohen • *Leading Change* by John Kotter • *Managing Transitions* by William Bridges • *Megachange* by William Joyce • *Organizational Capability: Competing from the Inside Out* by David Ulrich and Dale Lake • *Linkage Inc.'s Best Practices in Tools Guidebook* by Plotczyk, Jones, and Stimson
Websites	• Human Resource Planning Society (www.hrps.org/) • Linkage Incorporated (www.linkageinc.com/) • Organization Development Network (www.odnetwork.org/) • Six Sigma Forum (www.sixsigmaforum.com)

Selection Tools

Companies often use functional competencies in selecting new employees or promoting current employees into new positions internally. Exhibit 11.2 shows an example of a functional competency interview question with a behaviorally anchored rating scale to guide making an evaluation.

Promotion Tools

Another potential component of a functional talent system is focused on internal promotion decisions. Existing competency assessment data can be considered when making promotion decisions so that managers can assess the employee's performance against the competencies identified for the next level. However, it is important to validate the job relevance of the competencies before they are used to make promotion decisions.

Decisions on how functional talent systems integrate with other existing talent processes and systems need to be made prior to implementation so that the appropriate linkages can be made and communicated during implementation. ABC Company made these decisions and integrated these components with organizational talent processes:

> The intent of the chief finance officer was to raise the overall capability of the finance organization. The key talent approach was a development program, which included:
>
> - Defining performance standards for today and in the future.
> - Introducing an assessment process to assess the strengths and developmental needs of individuals.
> - Outlining potential career paths that would help an individual build financial expertise through job experiences.
> - Identifying additional development opportunities in key finance areas.
> - Building skill-based training for areas needing development.
>
> Due to the variety of roles in the finance organization and the desire to have a common language around functional standards, a competency model was developed to define the individual performance standards.
>
> The initial components focused on development and were launched at midyear to coincide with the performance management process. By integrating the approach with an

Exhibit 11.2. Functional Competency Interview—Question Example

Please describe a time when you used your understanding of customer data to solve a problem or to capitalize on an opportunity:

- What was the problem, and how did you identify it?
- What were the key elements?
- What was the outcome?

Notes:

Assessment Rating

Less Likely to Meet Standards		Likely to Meet Standards		Likely to Exceed Standards
☐ Translated customer feedback into action that did not meet customer expectations ☐ Lacked comprehension of gaps between what customers want and what currently delivering ☐ Described difficulty translating customer research results into unique market insights ☐ Did not demonstrate an ability to translate customer data		☐ Translated customer feedback into action that met customer expectations ☐ Addressed gaps between customer needs and current offerings by making appropriate changes ☐ Translated, or demonstrated understanding of how to translate, customer research results into unique insights and made actionable recommendations		☐ Translated customer feedback into action that exceeded customer expectations ☐ Drew unique conclusions about how to optimize customer data ☐ Sought information from a variety of common and novel sources to stay current on customer needs ☐ Applied unique knowledge of customer data and insights
1	2	3	4	5

already embedded process, the company capitalized on existing communications, and the approach was promoted as an enhancement of the existing performance management process. This alignment added greater depth to the development discussions than if it had been just an additional separate process.

Step 7: Measure Impact and Effectiveness

As companies invest in building organizational capability and individual expertise in functional areas, it is critical to understand the impact the function has on the business in order to demonstrate a return on investment. Intuitively, one would assume that if a company builds systems, tools, and processes to select, develop, and engage top functional talent and to close the gaps in critical organizational capabilities, there should be a positive business impact. However, it can be difficult to get an exact measure of the company's return on investment in this area since there are a number of variables that can confound the results, such as the external business environment, market forces, and the competition. A company can identify the areas that need to be improved or changed and establish qualitative and quantitative metrics that directionally indicate if the effort is having a positive impact.

It is important that the conversations identifying the desired outcomes and metrics occur in conjunction with the design of the talent system, and not after the system has been implemented. For example, when business or functional leaders describe the behaviors that demonstrate effective and ineffective customer behavior analysis as part of developing a competency, they should also describe the outcomes of highly effective customer analysis and how to measure it. This step is often overlooked during the development phase, and consequently the metrics either do not get defined or are defined poorly. The following questions can be used with senior business leaders to proactively identify the desired business and people impact of the functional talent system and how to measure it:

Business

- What are the business challenges in the next three to five years, and how will you know if this approach [for example, a talent system] has had a positive impact on these challenges? How would you best measure the impact?

- What does success look like from a business perspective if we successfully close the organizational capability gap or the individual expertise gap? How will you know when we are successful?

People

- What are the important people areas that we hope to change or improve [for example, engagement, turnover, selecting top employees, employee perceptions on a topic]?
- How will we know if we have been successful in these areas?

The business or functional leaders' answers to these questions will help pinpoint the areas that are important to them from both a business and a people perspective. Then the industrial-organizational psychology practitioner or HR professional can define the qualitative and quantitative metrics that will assess the impact in these areas. Table 11.5 offers examples of metrics that can give an indication of the impact. It is important to focus on outcome metrics (for example, "a 97 percent retention rate of key functional talent") as much as possible versus process metrics that track progress for completing a task (for example, "95 percent of employees have completed training").

Other business metrics that might be relevant (although the results might be harder to attribute to one cause) include successful product launches, the growth of a business, and increased sales. It is important to annually review the appropriateness of the success criteria and metrics and realign them with any changes in the business.

Step 8: Review and Update the Content

Functional talent systems, particularly those including functional competencies and performance standards, should be reviewed for relevance every two or three years, depending on changes in the business. The review may need to be more frequent in companies experiencing rapidly changing technology or significant changes in strategy. It is critical to establish the review and update time frame during initial implementation so that the needed resources for these activities are secured early while

Table 11.5. Metrics to Assess Impact

Area to Measure	Potential Metric

Level of engagement	• Conduct a pre- and post-assessment of employees' attitudes regarding:
	  Key engagement indicators
	  Career development opportunities
	  Clarity of job expectations

Manager and employee perceptions of impact of competency programs	• Conduct assessment of perceptions before and after implementation of the new talent system
Overall level of skill enhancement	• Conduct manager assessments of skills at defined intervals to assess skill level improvements
Internal talent movement	• Number of internal moves before and after implementation of the new talent system • Identify percentage of employees promoted before and after implementation of the new system • Review number of customer service complaints and commendations before and after implementation
Job performance	• Compare performance ratings for employees from before and after new system • Review leadership team's assessment of new product quality before and after implementation • Percentage market share and growth (recognizing that this could be confounded by other unrelated variables)
Retention	• Compare turnover rates from before and after implementation of the new talent system
Candidate selection	• Compare performance ratings of employees hired before and after the implementation of the new talent system

the project still has strong support among senior leaders. Also, it is important to identify who has the accountability for the review and update of the content. Usually placing the accountability with the function leaders increases the level of ownership felt by the function and the likelihood that they will continue to provide the necessary resources to maintain and update the system and programs.

Experience suggests that defining the functional performance standards is the easy part of the process, and sustaining the system and building organizational capability in the function tend to be more challenging.

Key Roles in Building Functional Expertise

Business leaders, HR generalists, and talent management practitioners all have important roles when building organizational capability and individual expertise in a function. It is important to clearly establish these roles and responsibilities up front to ensure successful execution and that the resources and commitment remain throughout the program implementation, and especially after implementation, to complete necessary periodic reviews and program evaluation.

The exact involvement of each role depends on the organization. Generally the business leader is the strategic thought leader and content expert in the function, the HR generalist gets involved in program execution and providing input into the content, and the talent management practitioner facilitates the development of content and is the process expert. In most organizations, all three groups work together as a team to develop functional expertise.

Business Leaders

Business leaders have a critical role in identifying the need for a functional talent system and in providing overall leadership in the design, execution, and sustainability of the functional system. With the HR generalist, they create the business case for why an organization should invest in building functional expertise and make the link to the overall business strategy. This step is critical for the long-term effectiveness and sustainability of the talent system. If the business case originates solely from HR professionals, then the chance for long-term sustainability of the system is significantly less. Experience suggests that the involvement of the leader in the business case solidifies the link between the business strategy and the talent system and enables greater line accountability for the implementation of the talent system.

Business leaders also need to identify the long-term organizational capabilities in the function that are needed to execute the business strategy and to determine whether to use internal or external resources to staff the level of functional expertise needed. The leaders of the function have an integral role in defining the level and type of individual functional competencies that are required in the function. They also serve as subject matter experts in content-validating the competencies, the career development principles, and other content.

HR Generalists

HR generalists in most organizations have a critical role in partnering with the business leader. They need to understand the internal and external workforce trends in the next three to five years, identify workforce implications, and propose potential actions that can be taken to close any expertise gaps. They also need to partner with the talent management practitioner in the development of content, processes, and tools to ensure the final product meets the needs of the business and is usable and valuable to the organization. In addition, the HR generalist drives the eventual implementation of the functional talent processes. If the HR generalist is more focused on transactional HR work versus strategic talent management work, then this responsibility may move to the talent management practitioner. Business leaders should be highly visible and lead the system development and execution, facilitated by human resources, and not the other way around, in order to sustain the system.

Talent Management Practitioners

Talent management practitioners often lead the process to develop and validate the content and tools. Given the technical requirements for this role, many talent management specialists have advanced degrees in industrial-organizational psychology or partner with external consultants who have specialized graduate degrees. They work closely with the business leader and human resource generalists and should facilitate the development process on behalf of the leader. They also advise leaders and recommend the right level of solutions for the organization. They ensure that the development and validation of content and tools are done appropriately and that the solution is an appropriate fit to desired business outcomes. They have an active role in defining the organizational capabilities and individual competencies, integrating available information, and ensuring that the final product is practical and adds value to the organization.

Talent management practitioners may also recommend not building a functional talent system if the functional gap may be more effectively and easily addressed with a different solution. For example, in one company, a leader in the market research function suggested to the HR generalist that he thought his group should create a marketing research functional talent system with a competency model, selection and promotion tools, and a development program to build functional skills and depth in market research. The market research group had 25 employees worldwide. The business leader and the HR generalist then met with their talent management consultant and explained the interest in developing a functional talent system. The talent management consultant asked four key questions:

- What is the overall business strategy, and how big of a role does the market research function play in the successful execution of that strategy?
- What is the business case for building the talent system?
- What are the current talent challenges in market research?
- Looking forward three to five years, what will be the talent challenges in market research?

Based on the discussion, they concluded that a functional talent system would add value, but the cost in terms of the time and people resources needed to develop the system would exceed the benefit the system would bring since the number of employees in the function was relatively small. The talent management consultant instead recommended establishing more detailed profiles for each level of position (see Table 11.1 for a description of job profiles) and facilitating a talent review and development discussion to identify possible job rotations within the market research function to help grow and develop the functional talent.

Key Lessons Learned

There is not one magic bullet or approach to successfully building individual expertise to enhance organizational capability. The key is to create a credible, sustainable system that maximizes the business value and minimizes the effort required to execute the system. In reflecting on our experiences building individual expertise and organizational capability in functional areas, the following are some of the key lessons we have learned:

- *Visible business leadership is essential.* The systems that are most successful are visibly led and championed by senior business or functional leaders. These systems create a legacy and impact that long outlast that leader's tenure with the function.
- *Start with organizational capabilities.* These act as the North Star when creating any talent system components and help ensure you are building talent and expertise you need now and in the future.
- *Show a clear link to the business strategy.* Directly tie the capabilities to the business strategy, and build the talent components that are needed to successfully execute the strategy. Functional talent systems that take a more strategic approach and identify the functional talent gaps in the workforce three to five years into the future also have greater long-term sustainability and credibility with business leaders.
- *Be practical, practical, practical.* The value from a functional talent system is only realized through execution. The keys to successful execution and sustainability are to create a development process that is efficient and to create tools and programs that are pragmatic, easy to implement and use, and transparent. Elaborate, complex systems are often more difficult to execute and sustain.
- *Other functions will want replicas.* Be aware that the design of a functional talent system in one function sets a precedent, and often other functions will want similar designs. It is important

to look at each situation individually and select the solution that best meets the needs of the business in the most practical way.

- *Use the language of the business.* Use the language of the business and corporate functions, not industrial-organizational psychology or human resources language. To be relevant, the language must be meaningful to the employees in the function. To help ensure this, it is good practice to have senior-level employees review all content and answer, "Does this match our language?"
- *Keep the end game top of mind.* Always keep in mind the desired business value, impact, and end state when developing the functional expertise or talent system components. This will help to ensure you are designing something that will be grounded in the business's needs.
- *All functions are not equal.* Differentially invest in areas that will have the biggest impact on executing company strategy. Not all functions need to create systems to enhance capability and build expertise. Establishing a competency model is not the universal solution.
- *Focus on implementation during development.* Defining the functional standards is the easy part of the equation; figuring out how to effectively implement, execute, and sustain the elements of the talent system is more challenging. Think through implementation and execution plans while you are creating the system to ensure you are designing workable and sustainable solutions.

Future Trends and Suggested Research

A workforce with deep functional expertise can create a competitive advantage for a company in the marketplace. Based on our experience working both inside and externally to business corporations, we think there are five key areas that need further focus to continue to progress in the field.

First, given the limited resources in many companies and the competing priorities for managers, we see an increased need to identify the most effective approaches to the successful implementation and sustainability of a functional talent system. We see simplicity of use as the key to sustaining functional talent systems.

Second, future research should focus on finding the discrete enablers for success and potential inhibitors of success—for example, the size of budget, CEO or head of function mandating use, or the impact of a new functional head coming to lead the group.

Third, because the usefulness or applicability of a functional talent system tends to be about three years, future research should identify rigorous yet expeditious approaches to content development and validation. When the external environment changes or the functional competencies have been in place for two or three years, companies will be hard pressed to spend six to nine months updating and revalidating the functional standards and functional talent system. Key questions we should push ourselves to ask are: As business strategies change, how do you refresh the functional talent system quickly to add value? and What are practical, efficient, and valid methods for developing the systems?

Finally, we see a need for further research related to quantifying the unique contributions of functional expertise, leadership competence, and management competence in predicting an organization's overall performance and success in achieving desired business outcomes such as growth in market share and revenue and profit. In addition, this research should explore the impact and effectiveness of various processes used in building functional expertise and determine if certain processes are more effective than others. For example, one could test whether a functional competency development program yields greater value than building a selection process around functional competencies.

Research in these areas will help human resource professionals and industrial-organizational psychology practitioners understand how to better develop functional expertise and the functional talent systems components that build organizational capability and are pragmatic and sustainable.

References

Atkinson, C. (2008, Sept. 22). Ad shops shift hiring tactics. *Advertising Age*. Retrieved October 17, 2008, from http://adage.com/talentworkscareerguide08/article?article_id=131032&search_phrase.

China's people problem. (2005, April 16). *Economist, 375*(8422), 53.

Corporate Leadership Council. (2007, May). *Maximizing the return on investment in technical expert pools*. Washington, DC: Corporate Executive Board.

Dunnette, M. D., & Hough, L. M. (Eds.). (1991). *Handbook of industrial and organizational psychology* (Vol. 2, 2nd ed.). Palo Alto, CA: Consulting Psychologists Press.

Glenn, J. (2000). *Before it's too late: A report to the nation from the National Commission on Mathematics and Science Teaching for the 21st Century.* Washington, DC: U.S. Department of Education. Retrieved November 3, 2008, from www.ed.gov/inits/Math/glenn/report.pdf.

Goldstein, I. L., & Ford, K. (2001). *Training in organizations: Needs assessment, development, and evaluation.* Florence, KY: Wadsworth.

Hortobagyi, G. N. (2007). A shortage of oncologists? The American Society of Clinical Oncology workforce study. *Journal of Clinical Oncology, 25*(12), 1468–1469.

Nairn, A., & Nicholson, J. (2006). *2020 vision: The manager for the 21st century.* Boston: Boston Consulting Group.

Olson, M. S., van Bever, D., & Verry, S. (2008). When growth stalls. *Harvard Business Review, 86*(3) 50–61.

Prospecting for petroleum engineers. (2000, October 11). *BusinessWeek.* Retrieved November 3, 2008, from http://www.businessweek.com/careers/content/oct2000/ca20001011_232.htm.

Society for Industrial and Organizational Psychology. (2003). *Principles for the validation and use of personnel selection procedures* (4th ed.). Bowling Green, OH: Society for Industrial and Organizational Psychology.

Spotswood, S. (2006, March). *Health care worker shortage a global phenomenon.* Retrieved November 3, 2008, from http://www.usmedicine.com/article.cfm?articleID=1280&issueID=85.

CHAPTER 12

MANAGING AND MEASURING THE TALENT MANAGEMENT FUNCTION

John C. Scott, Steven G. Rogelberg,
Brent W. Mattson

Leaders of top-performing organizations understand the significance of talent management in advancing business strategy, driving competitive advantage, and strengthening the long-term viability of their organizations. To achieve these outcomes, talent management must be completely aligned with an organization's mission, vision, and values and fully integrated into its long-term strategic planning. This may be a significant change for many organizations, which have generally considered workforce planning and people management as related but independent activities from business strategy. Furthermore, the successful integration of talent management processes into an organization's business strategy requires a paradigm shift within the human resources (HR) function. HR practice areas (such as recruiting, staffing, compensation, training and development, succession planning), which have been traditionally managed as separate operations with independent goals and strategies, need to be strategically aligned as a unified function.

Poorly executed talent management can have significant consequences on the long-term success of an organization. These consequences can range from the loss of hard-to-acquire talent to more extreme outcomes, such as a leadership vacuum created by the failure to prepare for the retirement loss of key executives or expensive class-action litigation. The best approach for realizing the full benefits of the talent management function is to develop a thorough understanding of what is required to meet the organization's business objectives and strategies and to evaluate talent processes and programs against those criteria. Based on the results of this evaluation, goals can be set, which can be used to monitor status and drive improvement to the strategy and results. High-performing organizations incorporate evaluation such as this as part of their strategic and tactical plans, making the evaluation of specific talent practice areas and outcomes (quality and depth and talent) an ongoing activity and priority.

This chapter explores how to leverage talent management evaluation as a strategic tool for driving business success and achieving competitive advantage. It is organized around three main topics: (1) laying the groundwork for effective evaluation (such as identifying key criteria for success), (2) defining relevant metrics (such as leading and lagging indicators), and (3) data collection and analysis (such as practical strategies for conducting organizational research). To illustrate this content, the chapter closes with an integrative case study.

Laying the Groundwork for Effective Evaluation

The field of program evaluation offers a well-established set of methods that are directly applicable to the process needed for effectively managing and evaluating an organization's talent management processes and programs. Program evaluation is a specialty area that gained prominence in governmental and educational institutions as a process for ensuring program accountability and continuous improvement. Kirkpatrick (1959a, 1959b, 1960a, 1960b) first introduced evaluation to human resources (HR) in the training arena. His framework and others' extensions of it (Phillips, 1997) have served to create a useful model for constructing an evaluation of any HR program. Edwards, Scott, and Raju (2003) have detailed the procedures for evaluating over 20 individual talent management practice areas.

Overview

Ideally talent management programs and their evaluation should be designed together (Davidson & Martineau, 2007). This helps ensure that the evaluation will be completed and also facilitates input into the process and greater acceptance of the outcomes by key stakeholders. The evaluation of the talent management system should start with determining the objectives and success criteria. Since talent management needs to be inextricably linked to organizational outcomes, it is necessary to define its objectives in strategic terms and metrics that speak the language of the stakeholders and decision makers. The focus needs to be on tying talent management solutions to valued organizational outcomes and building metrics that can be used to evaluate success.

The specific criteria used to evaluate talent management programs and processes vary by organization, but several key evaluation perspectives help to ensure optimal functioning and justify stakeholder investment. We recommend that any evaluation of talent management programs and processes should, at minimum, address four key perspectives:

1. *Strategic*—the alignment of the talent management system with the organization's strategic vision
2. *Operational*—effectiveness and integration of talent management practice areas and systems
3. *Customer*—stakeholder expectations regarding talent management design, strategies, and success criteria
4. *Financial*—contribution of talent management practice areas to strategic outcomes, such as market share, time to market, market expansion, and bottom-line profitability

This approach relies on a balanced scorecard framework (Becker, Huselid, & Ulrich, 2001) to ensure that the evaluation is comprehensive and meaningful to the organization. We recognize that these four perspectives are interconnected (for example, stakeholder expectations are both operational and strategic in nature); the reason for differentiating them is to ensure that they are all considered when designing the evaluation.

Evaluating the Strategic Objectives of Talent Management

The first step in the evaluation from this perspective is to clarify the business challenges and key strategic priorities that the talent management system is attempting to address. In identifying the overarching goals, it is important to work with the organization's leadership to understand the key organizational issues and priorities. Once the priorities have been established, a plan can be developed for how talent management can be leveraged as part of the overall strategy to advance the business. These priorities may include such initiatives as expanding into new markets, surpassing the competition, advancing profits and market share, and developing new products. The business challenge will be to ensure that the necessary talent exists in the organization to drive these initiatives in both the short and long terms. This becomes the crux of why the evaluation of talent management is itself a strategic priority.

Consider the case of a CEO from a Fortune 500 information technology company who is having trouble determining how long-term strategic plans will be executed due to the organization's inadequate mix of leadership talent, unacceptable level of turnover, and upcoming retirement of experienced leaders with a shallow bench of successors. Further exploration of this case reveals the following:

- Of the top executives 40 percent are slated for retirement in the next five to seven years, while only 15 percent of these positions have successors ready to move into these roles.
- Annual costs associated with poor selection and inadequate development of leaders are estimated at $3.5 million per year in lost sales and reduced productivity.
- Companywide turnover is at an all-time high (8 percent), and exit surveys indicate that the primary reason for departure is poor leadership (87 percent).
- Annual costs associated with turnover (time and replacement costs) of key talent are estimated at $1.2 million.
- Conservative costs associated with companywide turnover (time and replacement costs) are estimated at $3.6 million per year.

In this example, the organization's talent management processes and programs certainly can be more successfully leveraged to support the organization's goals. The question is what specifically needs to be done with the existing talent management process to address these issues. At minimum, an evaluation of the talent management process should cover:

- How are leaders being identified, developed, and engaged to meet short- and long-term organizational needs?
- How well aligned is the talent management process with the mission and strategic goals of the business?
- How much is the talent management function preparing for the upcoming retirements of key managers and executives?
- How can the tide of turnover be reduced at both the executive level and companywide?

Based on this evaluation, we find that the leadership competency model, which forms the basis of the selection and development programs, is significantly outdated and not aligned with the organization's newly revised strategic vision. In addition, the competencies that do exist vary by program—for example, those used for selection are different from those used to assess performance and potential. Another finding is that leadership development plans are not consistently designed, executed, or tracked. When these findings are combined with the high turnover rate and the shallow successor bench, clear opportunities for improvement are evident.

In this scenario, the selection, leadership development, and succession management practice areas require adjustment and realignment. A set of short-, medium-, and long-term objectives logically emerges from the evaluation that will help put the talent management processes and programs on a track to more directly support the business.

The talent management strategic objectives agreed on from this evaluation include:

- Base talent management decisions and strategy on an updated set of leadership competencies that are aligned with the organization's strategic vision.

- Incorporate common leadership competencies into selection, performance management, compensation, succession management, and development systems.
- Reduce voluntary turnover of top performers to 3 percent over the next year.
- Reduce companywide turnover to 5 percent over the next two years.
- Establish the talent pool for all critical leadership positions within 18 months.
- Increase cumulative sales revenues in selected leaders' areas by 30 percent within 12 months.

The means for accomplishing these objectives and establishing their connection to the organization's financial profitability will need to be clearly specified so that metrics can be established to track progress, to allow for midcourse corrections (including changing business strategy), and to ensure that long-term outcomes are realized. The approach for mapping out these connections and defining how objectives will be accomplished is outlined later in this chapter.

Evaluating the Operational Objectives of Talent Management

Talent management includes a number of previously independent practice areas that cover attracting, developing, engaging, leveraging, and retaining top talent. For talent management programs to succeed, each individual practice area must function successfully. At the same time, there must be effective and appropriate integration and support among practice areas. Consequently a comprehensive evaluation will need to cover both the operational aspects of the talent management program as a whole (the extent of integration across the individual practice areas) as well as each component part (individual practice areas).

The operational evaluation of individual practice areas comprising the talent management program has been presented in comprehensive detail (Edwards et al., 2003). More recently, Hannum, Martineau, and Reinelt (2007) presented an in-depth review of designs for evaluating leadership development and using the evaluation itself to increase business impact. These resources provide a foundation for designing the criteria and strategies for conducting an effective evaluation of the individual practice areas. A solid body of work also exists for many of the metrics that need to be incorporated into an evaluation of talent management. It will be important when conducting an evaluation to have a solid understanding of the metrics that have proven useful for determining the worth and value of the talent management components. These metrics have been extensively outlined by Fitz-enz (2000), Fitz-enz and Davison (2002), and Sullivan (2002).

One challenge in evaluating individual talent management practices lies in ownership and accountability. While the aspired-for model should be an integrated talent management function, the reality for many organizations is that individual practice areas still operate independently. While many practices report to the senior human resources leader, process evaluation strategies, if they exist at all, are often disconnected from each other. This makes it difficult to determine with any degree of certainty how aligned talent management practices are with one another and with the organization's short- and long-term strategy.

The business case for integrating the individual practice areas would logically start with a strategically driven evaluation that examines whether an integrated talent management function would deliver significantly greater bottom-line financial results and operational efficiencies over independently driven practice areas. Organizations wishing to assess the extent to which talent management practices are (or should be) integrated need to coordinate their evaluation efforts across each of the practice areas. Such efforts are often complicated for several reasons:

- Optimal timing for evaluating independent practice areas may differ; for example, the best time to assess succession planning may not be nearly the same as the optimal time to assess performance management practices.
- Audiences for the practice areas may differ (that is, the stakeholder or user group for one practice area is not always the same as the audience for another).

- Skilled resources within practice areas may differ.
- There will likely be general resistance to the evaluation by talent management practice owners.

The extent to which the individual practice areas are integrated can be evaluated in several ways. The first approach is to assemble those responsible for each of the practice areas (for example, program managers) and interview or survey these individuals about the current level of integration, support, and coordination across the practice areas. This review will help determine where inefficiencies exist between processes and show how aligned each practice area is with other areas. A more in-depth approach is to create cross-functional process examination teams that can examine practice operations by interviewing the consumers of talent management programs as well as program sponsors (executives responsible for the individual practice areas). This review will assess how well each practice area supports one another and the goals of the organization. These teams would chart key talent management processes that span practice areas in order to assess efficiency, appropriate coordination, and outcomes and to provide recommendations for tightening the integration across areas.

Stakeholder engagement will be essential for conducting the evaluation and building best-in-class, integrated talent management processes and programs. Edwards, Scott, and Raju (2007), Hannun et al. (2007), and Sullivan (2002) offer suggestions for building the business case for talent management evaluation and negotiating through the practical constraints, resistance, and politics associated with conducting a comprehensive evaluation.

Evaluating Customer and Stakeholder Objectives of Talent Management

Since talent management affects the business in so many ways, a number of customers and stakeholders will want to have input into the evaluation and ultimate direction of talent management efforts. It will be important to ensure that these stakeholder groups are carefully identified, subsequently involved in the evaluation planning process, and solicited for evaluation information. Some typical categories of stakeholders whose input and perspective should be considered are examined in the next sections.

CEO and the Executive Team

This group includes the key players in the evaluation and direction of the talent management function. They are primarily concerned with revenues, shareholder value, growth, and long-term sustainability. Since the current and future leaders will determine success in addressing these concerns, the focus of the CEO and the executive team will be on leadership selection, development, retention, and the talent pipeline. This group will expect a clearly defined, actionable strategy that may have both an immediate and long-term perspective. They may also have other goals or key business objectives that are not directly revenue focused but that will be addressed by talent management, such as the selection and development of diverse candidates, employee engagement, career rotation, and executive onboarding.

Line Management

This group is responsible for implementing business strategy and the execution of talent management systems and processes. The responsibilities for recruitment all the way through retention rest primarily with line management in the new talent management framework. To be successful, line managers need to secure and develop talent in their organizations. Effective retention, performance management, training, creation of career paths, and succession planning are all performance accountabilities that will differentiate top-performing managers from the others. These individuals are therefore key consumers of talent management programs and processes and can expect to play a critical stakeholder role in its evaluation.

Program Managers

HR is typically the manager of the talent management practice areas, although some organizations distribute the practice areas to business units outside of HR. Talent management program managers are responsible for the day-to-day program operations and need to be heavily involved in the evaluation process. They may have been involved in the design or integration of the practice areas and will be aware of the program's strengths and limitations. This group will be able to assist in creating metrics associated with each of the individual practice areas and in highlighting integration issues.

Employees

Employees, and in particular key talent and high-potential individuals, will be in large part the recipients of the talent management initiatives and will be a good source of information regarding the effectiveness of most practice areas (recruiting, onboarding, development, compensation, satisfaction with leadership, and others). Their input can be gathered through focus groups, interviews and surveys.

Job Candidates

Another good source of information regarding the effectiveness of the talent management programs and processes is the external candidate population. The organization can gather their insights regarding the fairness of the hiring process, the company's reputation as a good place to work, and diversity efforts.

Table 12.1 provides a sample of the expected goals, evaluation strategy, evaluation questions, and desired outcomes by stakeholder group. As the table shows, the focus of the evaluation will differ depending on the stakeholder group and their particular goals and expectations. We recommend that the evaluation of talent management processes and programs include multiple perspectives and follow a balanced scorecard approach (strategic, operational, customer, financial). This will ensure a comprehensive evaluation that will address the needs of each stakeholder group. That being said, there may be practical restrictions, such as time and resource limitations, which may limit the ability to implement a comprehensive evaluation. In these circumstances, it may be necessary to set priorities based on the purpose of the evaluation and the stakeholder agendas.

The ongoing engagement of these stakeholder groups will be required to maintain support for the evaluation processes and for subsequent decisions made on the basis of the evaluation information. For example, to engage its stakeholders, one Fortune 10 company links its talent management evaluation strategy to the company's ongoing planning and performance measurement process. Senior executives from each line of business are involved

Table 12.1. Evaluation Strategy, Evaluation Questions, Talent Management, and Organizational Outcomes by Stakeholder Group

Stakeholder Group	Evaluation Strategy	Focus of Evaluation Questions	Desired Talent Management Outcomes	Resulting Organizational Outcomes
CEO and executive team	Strategic and financial	• To what extent is talent management contributing to advancing business strategy, driving competitive advantage, and strengthening the long-term viability of the organization? • How well does the success profile of leaders match long-term business needs? • How effectively are we identifying, developing, and retaining potential talent to meet long-term business strategy?	• Industry competitive advantage in selection, development, and retention of high-potential talent • Rich talent pipeline with deep bench strength (two to three qualified successors identified for each of the 30 executive positions)	• A high-performing workforce that can drive revenues, shareholder value, growth, and long-term sustainability • A talent pipeline that supports the long-term success and growth of the organization

(Continued)

Table 12.1. Evaluation Strategy, Evaluation Questions, Talent Management, and Organizational Outcomes by Stakeholder Group (*Continued*)

Stakeholder Group	Evaluation Strategy	Focus of Evaluation Questions	Desired Talent Management Outcomes	Resulting Organizational Outcomes
Management	Strategic, operational, and financial	• How accountable and skilled are managers at identifying, developing, and retaining talent? • How can the existing practices be improved to better support and reward managers for executing their talent management accountabilities, including identification, development, and retention of high-potential talent?	• State-of-the-art systems and resources to support execution of talent management functions • Expert content knowledge and support from talent management program manager	• Execution of business strategy • Acquire and maintain a top-performing workforce • Enhanced operating performance
Program manager or sponsor	Operational	• How can the individual talent management practice areas be improved to better meet stakeholder needs? • How well integrated are the individual practice areas? • What feedback loops and metrics are in place to ensure a seamless operation and continuous improvement?	• Individual practice areas meet goals established by stakeholders • Individual practice areas are integrated and mutually supporting—relying on easily accessible metrics to operate effectively as an integrated function	• Talent management systems and practices that meet stakeholder needs and help achieve organizational goals

Employees	Operational		
		• What aspects of the talent management life cycle can be improved to more effectively recruit, develop, compensate, promote, engage, and retain top talent?	• Talent management systems are well established, transparent, and effectively used by managers and employees
		• How can manager training and accountability be improved to ensure superior and fair delivery of talent management components such as development, feedback, and career advancement?	• Managers are trained in use of talent management systems
		• How can employee accountability be improved for managing their careers and supporting overall business strategies?	• Ongoing and actionable performance feedback
			• Career advancement opportunities, incentives tied to performance
			• Satisfaction with leadership

in identifying the content of a talent management dashboard. A dashboard in this context is a graphical and text display presenting up-to-date information that outlines the key talent management indicators being tracked and current performance against the targets (see Table 12.2 for an example). After providing input into the most effective metrics to meet their decision-making needs, the executives agreed on the appropriate frequency for publishing the dashboard that would facilitate their review process. Through ongoing discussions with this key population, the talent management dashboard has achieved remarkable success in a very short period following its introduction and has fully engaged this stakeholder group. It has facilitated a change in the quality of the conversations around the health of the talent pipeline and precipitated regular discussions on organizational talent vulnerability, realistic succession planning, and individual development needs.

Evaluating Key Population Segments

Because of the breadth of talent management activities and practices, it is nearly impossible to evaluate every aspect of these processes. Decisions on what to evaluate are largely driven by the organization's overall talent management strategy. Some organizations adopt a general approach, focusing on metrics that apply to the entire organization, such as inclusion metrics, staffing metrics, and succession planning metrics. This approach has the benefit of providing a macrolevel view of the most important metrics and can illustrate key gaps; however, these strategies may create little actionable feedback because of their general focus.

For example, many organizations calculate the number of successors identified for specific leadership roles at an aggregate level (organization X has an average 1.5 successors for each leadership role). In the absence of other data about this population of leaders (such as trends in the data, relevant benchmarks, and quality of successors), this metric is meaningless. To illustrate, in terms of successor quality, few organizations evaluate the actual viability of potential successors for critical roles. Without an understanding of how many potential successors are actually chosen when openings appear, it is practically useless to calculate this successor ratio, let alone to compare it to a predefined external

Table 12.2. Sample Talent Management Dashboard

Metric	Current Performance	Target	Frequency
Roles with identified successors: Number of senior leadership roles with ready-now successors identified in talent management database	92%	Green: >90% Yellow: 75–90% Red: <75%	Quarterly
Top performer attrition: Percentage of voluntary terminations within senior leadership population	6.51%	Green: <10% Yellow: 10–15% Red: >15%	Monthly
Promotion rate: Percentage of top leadership population open roles filled with internal candidates	12%	Green: >15% Yellow: 10–15% Red: <10%	Monthly
Time to fill key roles: Mean number of days to fill open roles within senior leadership population	46 days	Green: <40 Days Yellow: 40–60 Days Red: >60 Days	Monthly
Quality: Mean percentage satisfaction on eight quantitative questions regarding the health of the senior leadership population	88%	Green: >90% Yellow: 80–90% Red: <80%	Annually

benchmark. In terms of being actionable, it is imperative to ask with any metric, "What decisions will we be able to make when we have these data?" In the case of the successor ratio, little guidance exists regarding potential actions an organization can take if it is higher or lower than its target.

To set priorities for evaluation, organizations facing specific strategic challenges frequently choose to evaluate only specific subgroups of talent, either on an individual or aggregate basis. One group that is commonly evaluated separately from the broader organization is high-potential talent. These individuals are generally viewed as having the potential to take on significant leadership or strategically important roles in the organization. As a result, the evaluation of the organization's efforts to develop, retain, and deploy these highly talented individuals is viewed as highly worthwhile and likely to provide a significant return on investment.

Some organizations focus on other strategically important subgroups. For example, in consumer and packaged goods organizations, the quality of marketing talent is critical for the organization's success. Certainly other functions are important for maintaining ongoing operations, but organizations in this industry view marketing talent as essential; in fact, the CEOs in these organizations often have extensive marketing backgrounds. As a result, these organizations frequently focus their evaluation efforts on their succession planning, recruiting, development, and retention of specific subgroups of the marketing function (for example, marketing analytics, pricing, promotion, product development).

One drawback to an organization's emphasis on evaluating the talent management activities related to strategically important subgroups is the potential to ignore the rest of the organization. While the war for talent has created an almost obsessive focus on the importance of attracting, developing, and retaining "high potentials"(also known as "HiPos"), other thinkers (DeLong & Vijayaraghavan, 2003) have suggested that core groups of employees must not be ignored. These "High Pros" "high professionals" are essential to the day-to-day operations of the organization. The long-term deterioration of attraction, development, and retention practices for these other essential individuals can limit organization performance over time. A more effective approach combines a focus on strategically important subgroups while simultaneously evaluating, at a broader level, the organization's talent management strategy for this high-potential group and other valuable contributors.

Evaluating the Financial Objectives of Talent Management

When evaluating talent management practices it is important to establish the connections to the organization's financial bottom line and business competitive advantage. This is more than simply establishing that a link exists; the evaluation helps to define how the business strategy will be accomplished and what competitive advantage will be achieved through talent management initiatives. One way of accomplishing this is to develop a logic model (W. K. Kellogg Foundation, 2003) that highlights how talent management processes and programs lead to the desired business outcomes.

The logic model presented in Table 12.3 shows how programs and processes can be designed to produce the long-term outcomes. This table focuses on talent management outcomes but also includes financial and strategic outcomes. Logic models are developed using the research, experience, and current thinking of the cause-and-effect relationships between interventions and outcomes. When developing a logic model, it is critical to identify the short- and medium-term outcomes in order to provide useful early information about the effectiveness of the talent management strategy and enable midcourse corrections. In addition, the assumed inputs in the first column are important in establishing the foundation for the success of the program. If any of these inputs is missing, the chances of a successful program decrease (Davidson & Martineau, 2007).

As can be seen from Table 12.3, one of the long-term goals for this particular organization focuses on creating a competitive advantage by ensuring a diverse, high-potential talent pool. The path for accomplishing this goal can be traced back through the medium- and short-term outcomes presented in the table. These intervening outcomes were established as milestones designed

Table 12.3. Logic Model for an Example Talent Management Solution

Assumed Inputs	Program Elements		Outcomes		
	Activities	Participation	Short	Medium	Long
Leadership and organizational support of talent management processes					
Diverse internal and external candidate pool	Development, validation, and maintenance of strategic competency models	HR, vendors, line subject matter experts	Core leadership competency model that aligns with organizational strategy	Identification and assessment of all high-potential managers across all divisions	Competitive advantage in selection, development, and retention of diverse, high-potential talent
Budget and resources are available to implement world-class talent management solutions	Sourcing, selection, development, and retention of organizational talent	Key stakeholders	Best-in-class assessment and development processes implemented to identify high potentials and establish actionable develop plans	Development plans created and shared with managers for all high-potential managers	Two to three qualified successors identified for all 30 key executive positions
Talent management functions are integrated under one practice leader or will be fully coordinated between practice leaders	Establishment of strategic and operational metrics and tracking mechanisms to ensure goal accomplishment	Diverse candidate population	All managers trained on talent management responsibilities	Compensation and performance management processes incorporate management expectations around talent management activities	
Tools are available to collect input from all stakeholder groups	Design and ongoing administration of talent management system		Key metrics and tracking system established for each talent management practice area		
			Stakeholder input and goals incorporated into processes and programs		

to lead to the accomplishment of the long-term objective. For instance, in order to create a competitive advantage for this organization, it is first necessary to ensure that all high-potential managers be assessed and that actionable development plans be put in place (medium-term outcome). In order for these medium-term outcomes to occur, it is necessary to implement a core leadership competency model that is aligned with organizational strategy and to build a best-in-class assessment process to identify the high potentials (short-term outcome).

The program elements in this example determine how these outcomes will be achieved and by whom. For example, it is necessary to involve subject matter experts from the line organization to create the core leadership competency model. The involvement of this stakeholder group is required to ensure that the competency model is meaningfully related to the organization's goals and realistically tied to employee performance expectations for driving the business. Finally, and some would say most important, the assumed inputs to this logic model must be specified. The organization in this example decided that the long-term goals can be achieved only if these elements are present:

- Full support for the talent management process by organizational leadership
- A diverse candidate pool
- An adequate budget to support world-class talent management solutions
- An integrated, or at least coordinated, talent management function
- Available tools for collecting stakeholder input

In addition to defining how the business strategy will be accomplished and how the competitive advantage will be achieved, the evaluation should also include an accounting of the value of talent management in quantitative and financial terms. The return on investment (ROI) resulting from this evaluation quantifies the value of the talent management process to the total organization and determines its relative worth as a strategic tool. A number of excellent sources for costing and measuring the value of the individual talent management practice areas are available (Cascio, 1992, 2000; Fitz-enz & Davison, 2002; Phillips & Phillips, 2007; Sullivan, 2002). Fitz-enz (2002) and Sullivan (2002) also provide metrics for measuring the overall talent management function. Fitz-enz's composite human capital scorecard provides a template for creating an integrated human capital evaluation across organizational levels and for displaying how an improvement in one of four human capital areas (acquiring, maintaining, developing, and retaining) affects the organization's operating and strategic goals. Sullivan provides four categories of metrics (HR dashboards, HR indices, self-improvement metrics, and alerts or warning metrics) for assessing the overall HR function and its impact on the organization's bottom line.

The ROI analyses should also include the risks of doing nothing or, worse, of having an ineffective talent management system (recent employment discrimination settlements have ranged from $42 million to as high as $190 million for a single company). ROI analyses will serve as one of several key criteria for determining the impact of talent management processes and programs. An example ROI chart is presented in Table 12.4 for a company that was proposing an integrated assessment center to select and develop managers.

ROI analyses can be used in conjunction with the elements presented in the logic map for determining where to invest scarce financial resources for talent management. These analyses should be forward looking and focus on leading indicators that will help forecast the chances of achieving the organization's strategic goals and revenue targets. For example, an ROI analysis of

Table 12.4. ROI Associated with Proposed Assessment Center

Project Outcome	ROI Years 1 and 2	ROI Year 3	ROI Year 4
Valid selection system	$ 376,000	$ 564,000	$ 940,000
Reduced turnover	1,400,000	2,100,000	2,800,000
Development	620,000	900,000	1,200,000
Cost of assessment center	(860,000)	(430,000)	(430,000)
Total	$ 1,536,000	$3,134,000	$4,510,000

Note: ROI = financial return on the investment.

Assumptions: *Valid selection system:* Productivity increase associated with valid selection system. Executive selection system assumes average salary at $180,000. Cost for assessment has been accounted for and subtracted from total. Calculations based on Brogden-Cronbach-Glesser equation as outlined in Cascio (2000). *Reduced turnover:* Assume the reduction in annual turnover to be 2 percent each year based on 350 executives. Assumes $100,000 replacement cost for one executive. *Development:* Productivity increase associated with development of 30 current leaders over the course of one year, accounting for decay in training over time. Calculations based on Brogden-Cronbach-Glesser equation (modified) as outlined in Cascio (2000).

the percentage and cost of voluntary separations in key population segments such as high potentials and high-performing executives will not only highlight the costs associated with losing and replacing this prized talent, but will also provide compelling data on how well the organization is positioned to meet its strategic goals. The Fortune 500 information technology company example presented earlier in the chapter revealed how this type of analysis can lead to targeted interventions.

ROI analyses should be just one of the many evaluations used for determining the impact of the talent management program and for building the business case for interventions. Sole reliance on ROI to make decisions should be avoided since it may result in the organization's overlooking critical connections between interventions and other important organizational outcomes. Beyond the financial or bottom-line perspective, the evaluation should also consider the impact of talent management on other valued organizational objectives. Talent management can also have other secondary benefits, such as employee engagement, diversity and inclusion, high-performance culture, or emphasis on development, which frequently link to important organizational goals. They provide leading indicators of the success of talent management processes and programs. The exact weight given to these elements in the evaluation should be determined by the nature of the organizational vision and strategies, as well as by stakeholder input.

Defining the Metrics

Metrics selected for evaluation should be aligned with the decision-making needs of talent management stakeholders. When formulating the criteria for an evaluation, it is useful to review the literature, including recent benchmarking or best practices studies, to help frame the evaluation questions for your own organization. Consortium or benchmark surveys, such as those conducted through the Conference Board and various vendors, can be quite valuable in highlighting key issues and trends. For example, a recent report on CEO challenges issued by the Conference Board (Rudis, 2006) found that among the 650 CEOs responding to the survey, top management succession was identified as either their greatest concern or among their chief concerns. This concern was shared among CEOs of both publicly traded and private companies. Clearly this aspect of talent management resonates across a broad range of leaders and organizations and should certainly be included as an important component of any evaluation.

Review of Related Research and Applications

A report by Hewitt Associates (Effron, Greenslaide, & Salob, 2005) examined the talent management factors that differentiate top-performing companies from the others. They found that the top 20 companies in their survey have these characteristics:

- CEO and Board involvement in leadership development
- Differentiation of high potentials in terms of compensation, developmental activities, and exposure to senior leaders
- Talent management practices that support the business strategy
- Leader accountability for talent management practices
- The use of the leader infrastructure to execute talent management practices

These differentiators, particularly leader accountability, are strongly correlated with superior financial performance. The differentiating criteria found in the Hewitt report provide additional insight when designing an evaluation and should be considered as important criteria against which to judge an organization's effectiveness in managing talent.

DDI's leadership forecast report (Bernthal & Wellins, 2005) provides additional criteria to consider when conducting a talent management evaluation. They studied over 800 organizations from 42 countries and included responses from over 4,500 leaders. Among other things, the objective of the study was to determine which leadership practices lead to improved organizational performance. This report presents 31 findings related to talent management practices. One key finding was that organizations with stronger leadership development practices and formal succession management programs had higher returns on equity and higher profits compared to their competitors. Interestingly, they also found that only 53 percent of leaders are satisfied with the development opportunities provided to them. Several other findings from the survey indicate that almost half of succession plans fail to support leader development and one-third of all succession plans are ineffective.

Some excellent strides have been made in quantifying the intangibles associated with talent management programs (Fitz-enz, 2000; Fitz-enz & Davison, 2002; Sullivan, 2002). For example, through research conducted by Fitz-enz and the Saratoga Institute, we are able to estimate with a good deal of precision the economic impact that a well-designed talent retention program can have on the bottom line (Fitz-enz & Davison, 2002). Similarly, we can readily calculate return on investment (ROI) figures for a valid selection system based on research that shows the relative worth in dollar terms of high-, average-, and low-performing employees. Credible metrics are available for most of the areas associated with talent management, including staffing, training, compensation, performance management, employee engagement, leadership development, and organizational effectiveness.

The critical point here is that there are a number of metrics now available to help quantify the worth of talent management programs and their role in strengthening and sustaining an organization's long-term viability and competitive advantage. In building the business case for an integrated talent management process, the first step should be to establish the relevant metrics against which success will be judged and to link these metrics to the organization's strategic goals and financial bottom line. The establishment of metrics is a fundamental element in managing and measuring the talent management function.

Despite advancements in measurement approaches across nearly all talent management practice areas, a Conference Board study of 268 HR leaders found that only 20 percent of the survey respondents rated their HR metrics as effective, and most perceived their metrics to be less effective than those of other corporate functions. The majority of respondents cited as their primary measurement challenges the identification of quantifiable links between HR performance and business goals and the identification of meaningful and value-added metrics (Conference Board, 2001). Reasons for the persistent lack of effectiveness of talent management evaluations include lack of alignment between stakeholder decision-making criteria and the reported measures, the complexity of the metrics, the lack of a connection to business results, and the poor credibility of the evaluation source (Mattson, 2003).

Leading and Lagging Indicators

When designing metrics, it is important to distinguish between leading and lagging indicators. Leading indicators are metrics that help predict future outcomes and provide data on how well the workforce is positioned for the future. Lagging indicators are metrics that confirm how well a talent management intervention has worked in the past; they focus on results at the end of a time period such as quarterly sales. Leading indicators are often considered the drivers of lagging indicators. Improved performance in a leading indicator (a high percentage of coaching and feedback sessions) generally results in better performance in the lagging indicator (increased productivity).

Key stakeholders are particularly concerned with the ability of the organization to meet future challenges such as attracting and retaining the right type of talent, having the right mix of competencies to win in the marketplace, and ensuring that key leaders have successors in the event of later attrition. Such concerns or questions can be best addressed with leading indicators. While a good evaluation will use a mix of leading and lagging indicators, organizational leaders will be particularly interested in as many relevant leading indicators as possible.

Fitz-enz (2000) describes five metrics that can serve as leading indicators for a workforce: competence (percentage of key employees who have met performance standards), preparedness (percentage of key positions with at least one fully qualified successor), job satisfaction, commitment, and voluntary separation. Wellins, Smith, and Rogers (2006) identified some additional leading indicators: (1) success profiles completed for value-creator positions (positions with an impact on revenue and profitability), (2) regular audit of talent against future business requirements, (3) development plans created and in place for high-potential talent and value creators, (4) manager accountabilities tied to effective talent management, (5) increased job satisfaction and engagement ratings, and (6) increased perception of career opportunities. Some additional examples of leading indicator metrics are shown by practice area in Table 12.5. Table 12.6 shows lagging indicator metrics by practice area.

The leading indicators provided in Table 12.5 can be useful in predicting the desired outcomes in the individual talent management practice areas. For example, the resource requirements and complexity of a talent management process are often indicative of how well the process will be embraced and used. Resource-intensive and complex systems are generally met with resistance and a variety of implementation obstacles. Similarly, perceptions of fairness and transparency can serve to support or sink a talent management initiative. In the succession planning practice area, one of the leading indicators, percentage of managers trained in the use of processes and support systems and tools, will have a direct impact on a number of the succession planning lagging indicators listed in Table 12.6, such as the percentage of key populations with eligible successors. Put in the context of the logic map, leading indicators are essentially short-term outcome metrics that are linked to and drive the long-term outcome metrics (lagging indicators).

As can be readily seen from Table 12.6, most of the lagging indicators listed for the individual practice areas can be easily turned into leading indicators for determining how well the overall talent management function has positioned the organization to achieve its strategic goals. For example, the first three lagging indicators under succession planning have to do with the retention of key talent, which in turn predicts the long-term health and sustainability of the organization. A review of the other lagging indicators across the individual practice areas reveals metrics that can be similarly positioned as leading indicators for desired organizational outcomes.

Great care should be exercised in selecting leading metrics since their ability to address a key talent question can be more easily questioned than a lagging indicator. Therefore, it is important to clarify the assumptions made in selecting particular metrics. For example, to address the question of leadership talent vulnerability, many organizations use projections of retirement eligibility. Despite the face validity and objectivity of this metric, retirement

Table 12.5. Leading Indicator Metrics Examples by Talent Management Practice Area

Recruiting and Staffing (Internal and External)	Compensation	Assessment and Development	Performance Management	Succession Planning	Talent Management Practice Alignment
1. Time to fill key roles	1. Time required to complete key milestones (dollar allocation, calibration across employee groups, final approval)	1. Assessment, selection, and development process implementation	1. Time required to complete key milestones (goal setting, reviews)	1. Time required to complete succession planning activities	1. Metrics and tracking systems established for each talent management practice area
2. Number of process steps required to hire internal and external candidates	2. Perceptions of compensation process fairness and transparency	2. Percentage participation in development activities	2. Percentage of goals completed that meet key criteria (specific, measurable, actionable, realistic, and timely)	2. Number of process milestones	2. Metrics established for evaluating overall, integrated talent management function and impact on bottom line
3. Cost per hire	3. Perceptions of compensation process complexity	3. Number of individuals with completed talent assessment profiles	3. Goal-setting process in place and used	3. Perceptions of process fairness and transparency	3. Talent management systems well established, transparent
4. Perceptions of process effectiveness by various subgroups (hiring managers, staffing personnel, internal and external candidates)		4. Regular audit process in place to assess overall talent against key business requirements	4. Development planning process in place and used	4. Percentage of managers trained in the use of processes and support systems and tools	4. Core leadership competency model aligned with internal practices and organizational strategy
			5. Perceptions of alignment between process and associated tools		

1. Cost of poor selection (productivity, revenue growth) 2. Percentage of external candidates on slates 3. Relative value difference between high-, average-, and low-performing employees 4. Number of experienced hires 5. Percentage of internal hires versus external hires	1. Percentage of compensation dollars distributed to high-, average-, and low-performing employees 2. Compensation practices incorporate management expectations around talent management activities 3. Total value of compensation shared with employees 4. Reported ability of compensation	1. Percentage of high potentials with completed and up-to-date assessments 2. Percentage managers trained on talent management responsibilities 3. Percentage movement of high potentials to new positions 4. Average time in high-potential pool before promotion 5. Internal movement across organization units	1. Average number of formal coaching and development sessions per employee 2. Percentage of performance goals aligned between senior management and individual contributors 3. Talent quality (performance ratings, values ratings, 360-degree survey ratings)	1. Percentage of retirement eligible employees by key population 2. Percentage retention of top performers 3. Percentage of regrettable talent lost 4. Percentage of key populations with eligible successors 5. Percentage of key positions filled from outside the organization	1. Link between integrated talent management practices and accomplishment of strategic goals 2. Talent management infrastructure that supports coordination between practice areas 3. Stakeholder satisfaction with talent management practices 4. Degree viewed as industry pacesetter

Table 12.6. Lagging Indicator Metrics Examples by Talent Management Practice Area

Recruiting and Staffing (Internal and External)	Compensation	Assessment and Development	Performance Management	Succession Planning	Talent Management Practice Alignment
6. Quantity of external talent in key populations 7. Quality of external hires 8. Strength of internal talent versus external labor market	practices to facilitate attraction and retention of key talent	6. Number and type of developmental assignments 7. Percentage of completed onboarding plans 8. Linkage of development efforts to achievement of business challenges 9. Skill or competency gaps existing in key populations 10. Percentage of high potentials satisfied with developmental opportunities	4. Degree of shared awareness of development needs or career interests between employees and management 5. Quality of coaching and mentoring relationships	6. Cost of turnover (time, replacement cost, opportunity cost) 7. Reasons for turnover regularly assessed 8. Retention and value discussions held with key contributors 9. Quality of successors for key positions 10. Impact of "regrettable" talent loss	in selection, development, and retention of high-potential diverse talent

eligibility is a limited predictor of vulnerability. Typically it is based on only two factors, age and tenure, and does not consider the wider range of factors that predict retirement such, as individual financial stability.

Application of Metrics

A well-crafted evaluation design contains an array of metrics that align with the broad talent management strategy and the information needs of stakeholders. For example, a large industrial-financial services conglomerate was concerned about its ability to grow the business organically (through internal growth). For years, the organization had grown largely through acquisitions and had recently lowered company expectations for long-term growth. The CEO suggested that the sales and marketing functions of the business had lost their concentration on the customer and were not focused enough on growing the business with existing customers or winning business from new customers. To address this issue, the organization's leaders identified four growth behaviors: (1) focus on the external market, (2) translate market strategy into concrete actions, (3) build commitment through inclusive leadership, and (4) exhibit the courage to execute on market strategies and the talent decisions made to support them.

A multi-year, multipronged approach involving annual assessments, feedback, coaching, and training and development programs was designed to weave these growth behaviors into the fabric of the organization. As part of formal talent management activities, the growth behaviors were assessed annually, and selection and promotion decisions for key commercial roles were based, in part, on these criteria.

To evaluate the impact of the growth behaviors as part of its talent management practices, the organization compared the financial performance (in revenue growth over two years) of each of its businesses in relation to combined measures of the growth behaviors for each senior leadership team. Although other process metrics (such as the number of diverse hires, talent potential, and performance rating differentiation) were assessed on an ongoing basis, the growth behavior assessment and development strategy was of critical importance given its key role in driving customer and shareholder value. Further, because leaders in the organization placed a premium on the use of data to drive business decisions, the linkage of these results to the initiative was readily accepted by the organization's senior leadership.

The example illustrates how an evaluation strategy was derived from a talent management initiative: that is, building growth leadership behaviors. The example also illustrates that evaluation can be multifaceted; although the evaluation of growth leadership practices was the most relevant element, it was not the only practice that was evaluated. Many evaluation efforts become diluted by an exuberant inclusion of multiple analytics and metrics that have little clear connection with one another. While such evaluation data can be interesting to talent management practitioners, they can easily become overwhelming for stakeholders.

Two questions must be considered when selecting an appropriate mix of metrics: "Which talent management practices or combinations of practices best address our organizational priorities?" and, "What other talent management practices do our key stakeholders want to include?"

Data Collection and Analysis

Once the focus of evaluation has been determined, strategies for data collection can be developed. Evaluation choices at this point include the type of assessment instrument or measure (using existing surveys or interviews, gathering quantitative or qualitative data), the type of data (using existing records or gathering new data), the appropriate level of data (individual versus group), and the specific data collection time period to best assess the evaluation questions.

Many talent management evaluation data collection efforts involve the use of either quantitative or qualitative measures. Quantitative measures include assessment instruments, surveys, and performance records. Qualitative metrics include data gathered from interviews (such as exit interviews), focus group results, responses to open-ended survey or performance record questions (for example, comments on specific strengths and development needs from a 360-degree feedback survey), and behavioral observations. Depending on the evaluation metrics employed, a combination of both qualitative and quantitative data is helpful when drawing conclusions and making recommendations to key stakeholders. Qualitative data can add context and color to quantitative results.

Another important source of talent management evaluation information is existing data, such as performance records or employee opinion survey responses. All data collection strategies should begin by mapping out what data exist currently in which sources of record and what, if any, issues exist in using the data from existing sources (for example, stakeholder perceptions of accuracy). Finally, evaluators must consider whether point-in-time data snapshots or longitudinal trends are appropriate for answering the questions asked by their key stakeholders. For example, understanding the change in the diversity of talent over time cannot be answered by a single data point. In such cases, trend data over time must be gathered. One important consideration in such cases is whether the available data were gathered using the same measurement system from time 1 to time 2.

Table 12.7 shows an example of a data collection planning template used to assess the Fortune 500 IT company example mentioned at the beginning of this chapter. Plans should have these key elements:

- A description of the outcome to be evaluated
- The type of outcome: strategic, perceptual, operational-process, operational-outcome (operational-process metrics gauge requirements of the talent management activities, such as user training, that must be accomplished to achieve the desired operational outcomes, such as lists of ready-now replacements)
- The time period in which impact will likely be apparent: short-, medium-, or long-term
- The operational definition of the metric used to assess the outcome
- The designation of the metric as existing or not
- A description of the type of instruments used (expert judgments, surveys, interviews, records)
- The measurement timing
- The data source of record

Table 12.7. Data Collection Planning Template

Outcome	Outcome Type	Impact Time Frame (Short-, Medium-, or Long-Term)	Metric (Operational) Definition	Existing Metric (Yes/No)	Instrumentation	Timing	Data Source
Core leadership competency model that aligns with organization strategy	Operational-process	Short-term	Model built and aligned	No	Expert judgment; interview	June 2009	HR executive
Best-in-class assessment and development processes implemented to identify high potentials and establish actionable development plans	Operational-process	Short-term	1. Validation: High-potential identification validated by Human Resources records 2. 100% have development plans	Yes	1. Expert judgment 2. Expert judgment; actionable development plans check sheet	June 2009	1. Consultant or HR executive 2. Performance management process owner
All managers trained on talent management responsibilities	Operational-process	Short-term	100% of eligible managers complete required talent management learning programs	Yes	Training course	Semiannual	Learning management system records
Key metrics and tracking system established for each talent management practice area	Operational-process	Short-term	100% of talent management practice areas have minimum of one metric, measurable on a quarterly basis	No	Records	Quarterly	Talent management system records; operational dashboards

Stakeholder input and goals incorporated into talent management processes and programs	Operational-process	Short-term	100% of key stakeholders identified and contributed input	No	Expert judgment; interview	June 2009	Senior leadership team
Identification and assessment of all high-potential managers across all divisions	Operational-process	Medium-term	100% of high-potential managers assessed within 12 months of identification	Yes	Records	Semiannual	Assessment system records
Development plans created and shared with managers for all high-potential managers	Operational-process	Medium-term	100% high potentials have current (within 12 months) strengths and development needs listed in performance management system	Yes	Records	Semiannual	Talent management system records
Compensation and performance management processes incorporate management expectations around talent management activities	Operational-process	Medium-term	Key compensation and performance management processes incorporate key stakeholder input	No	Expert judgment; interview	January 2010	HR executive

(Continued)

Table 12.7. Data Collection Planning Template (*Continued*)

Outcome	Outcome Type	Impact Time Frame (Short-, Medium-, or Long-Term)	Metric (Operational Definition)	Existing Metric (Yes/No)	Instrumentation	Timing	Data Source
Industry pacesetter in selection, development, and retention of diverse, high-potential talent	Strategic	Long-term	Selection, development, and retention practices judged as best-in-class	No	Expert judgment; interview	January 2011	HR leaders, external benchmarking
Two to three qualified successors identified for all 30 key executive positions	Operational-outcome	Long-term	Minimum of two successors listed for 30 key positions	Yes	Records	January 2011	Talent management system records
Reduce voluntary turnover	Strategic	Long-term	Enterprisewide voluntary turnover reduced to 5% within 12 months and 8% within 24 months	Yes	Records	Annual	Enterprise employee data system
Enhance cumulative sales production of targeted leaders' function	Strategic	Long-term	Increase sales production by 30%	Yes	Records	12 months	Finance sales tracking system

Using Quasi-Experimental Designs

In some circumstances, evaluators may wish to leverage quasi-experimental approaches to better understand the impact of various talent management practices on strategic metrics. Since true experimental conditions are seldom feasible in organizational settings, quasi-experimental designs offer an alternative for evaluators interested in assessing the impact of a talent management intervention. For example, a key stakeholder may be interested in understanding whether a particular practice (such as the use of a competency model to assess promotional candidates) is linked to stronger business results (perhaps increased revenue production). In this case, an evaluator could review at least two preexisting groups (one group who had been assessed using the competency model and another that had not) and analyze the difference in the dependent variable (such as revenue production). Although these two groups have not been randomly assigned, it is important that they have similar characteristics (for example, job tenure) to help ensure that extraneous influences did not affect the results. Another type of quasi-experimental design is the before-and-after comparison or pretest-posttest design. In this design, the criterion measures are compared before and after the intervention, and the group serves as its own comparison.

In most organizations, the quasi-experimental approach is the closest one can get to a true experiment. While a true experiment allows one to minimize threats to external and internal validity through the random assignment of subjects to treatment conditions, quasi-experiments, which often leverage naturally occurring subgroups such as training classes or intact work groups, do not eliminate all these threats. However, for the decision-making needs of most stakeholders, with the possible exception of the most scientifically rigorous stakeholders (senior leaders at an R&D company), quasi-experiments provide a reasonable way of assessing the impact of talent management practices.

Simplifying the Data Analysis

Once data have been collected, analyses can be conducted and the results can be organized. In general, the type of analysis should follow from the type of data gathered from the evaluation.

That is, quantitative data can be analyzed using descriptive statistics (measures of central tendency, variance, percentages, and frequencies) and related graphical representations (for example, Pareto graphs or scatter plots). Multivariate analyses (such as regression analyses and time-series analyses) should be used only when the assumptions underlying their conclusions (such as appropriate sample size, degrees of freedom, and instrument validity) are met. The challenge with these more complicated analyses is to meaningfully communicate the results to stakeholders. In the vast majority of cases, descriptive statistics will be sufficient to answer the evaluation questions.

At a fundamental level, data analyses represent collections of metrics and analyses that address stakeholder information needs. At a more advanced level, data analyses can be integrated to describe a comprehensive story about the organization's talent management efforts. For example, Bank of America creates an annual summary of its talent management process across the enterprise called the Talent Planning Executive Summary. This summary includes:

- A statement of the current business challenges and the implications for leadership talent
- Summary analyses of business growth and staffing trends
- Retirement vulnerability of key groups of associates
- Assessments of the depth of the leadership bench
- Analyses of individual and organizational capability
- Details of actions and recommendations to close key talent gaps

Each analytical element in the summary is crucial in telling the talent story and in building a business case for the following year's talent management focus. The summary is shared with the Chairman and CEO, as well as the Board of Directors and the senior leadership team.

Data can be collected and reported on an annual or semiannual basis. Many organizations, however, choose to do more frequent assessments. For example, one company has created a set of ongoing metrics that are measured and reported monthly to the Chairman and CEO. This index of measures includes indicators of talent vulnerability, key measures of executive staffing process efficiency and effectiveness, and a qualitative metric assessing senior leader opinions on the health of the talent bench within their organizations and across the overall enterprise. Data are analyzed and reported monthly in a simple dashboard format using frequencies and averages, along with lists of names corresponding to individual metrics where appropriate. While the overall measurement and analytical rigor associated with this set of talent management measures is strong, the regularity of reporting makes it a powerful tool in influencing the talent discussions across the organization in a consistent fashion. When using frequent measurements, it is important not to overreact to minor data fluctuations (such as seasonal ones) that may not be meaningful.

Bank of America Case Study

Bank of America's approach to evaluation demonstrates how strategic and operational evaluations of talent management practices contribute to the organization's mission and vision. Bank of America has a stated strategy of becoming the most admired company in the world. The bank's strategies for the selection, development, and retention of its associates are very clear and operate in a similar manner across its major lines of business. Each major line of business also has corresponding strategies that are specific to their business.

The primary strategic goal for evaluating Bank of America's talent management practices is to deepen and diversify the leadership talent bench to create a strong pipeline of leaders who are prepared to lead the bank to its desired status of being the most admired company in the world. This particular evaluation approach was initiated after the strategy had been implemented approximately two years earlier. The concept of deepening and diversifying the talent bench is integrated into the company's regular operating measurement process. Human Resources led the development of the set of metrics used to evaluate progress toward these goals with strong involvement and input from the senior leadership team. The primary challenge was to make the evaluation approach strategic, in terms of measuring long-term outcomes, and also design the approach to produce actionable data in the short term.

To achieve these objectives and provide an overall picture of Bank of America's "health of the bench," the evaluator, in consultation with clients, developed a set of fundamental evaluation questions that guided the development of metrics for the "health of the bench" indices. Some of the questions are:

- How effective is Bank of America in hiring, developing, and retaining talent?
- What is the quality of Bank of America's leadership development efforts? How effective are the programs in preparing leaders to assume larger and more complex roles?
- What impact does the strategy of deepening and diversifying the talent bench have on existing leaders and on leaders who are new to Bank of America?
- What is the value of Bank of America's selection, development, and retention efforts considering the investment of time, money, and other resources?

The creation of a logic map was helpful in making the evaluation strategic. The map illustrated how the various elements of the bank's talent management practices could work together to achieve long-term strategic goals (see Table 12.8). This logic map provides a framework for assessing the short-, medium-, and long-term impacts of a range of talent management practices. In effect, this evaluation approach captures the inputs, process, and outputs of the organization's practices. This triple focus can strengthen the conclusions reached about the overall effectiveness of talent management practices by identifying the links between immediate, intermediate, and long-term outcomes.

Using inputs as a starting point for the evaluation was useful in demonstrating the following necessary preconditions for long-term success of the Bank of America's talent management strategies:

- Leadership and organizational support for talent management practices
- Robust and diverse candidate pools
- Financial and human resource availability
- Coordination among talent management practice area leaders
- Tools available to collect stakeholder input

Table 12.8. Bank of America Talent Management Evaluation Logic Model

Assumed Inputs	Program Elements		Outcomes		
Support: Leadership and organizational support for talent management practices	Activities	Participation	Short-Term	Medium-Term	Long-Term
Talent Pools: Robust and diverse internal and external candidate pools	Development, validation, and maintenance of strategic competency models	Senior leadership and Human Resources subject matter experts	Up-to-date competency model aligned with business challenges, talent imperatives, and leadership implications	Assessment of high-potential talent across the enterprise	Pipeline of leaders who exceed the capabilities required to lead the enterprise to "most admired" status
Resources: Financial and Human Resources available to implement world-class talent management practices	Assessment, selection, development, and retention of organizational talent	HR subject matter experts, staffing, vendors	More than 95 percent of associates have clear understanding of goals: they receive regular coaching, feedback, and have career discussions with their manager	Associates perceive compensation as strongly linked to performance and view Bank of America where their career goals can be realized	Current associates perceive Bank of America as a great place to work and grow their careers ("Bank of Opportunity")
Integration and Coordination: Talent management practices are integrated and coordinated among practice leaders	Definition of role requirements for key leadership positions in each line of business	HR subject matter experts, staffing	100 percent of key roles documented with requirements in terms of experience, exposure, and education		Viewed as progressive in selection, development, and retention of high-potential talent. HR external candidates perceive Bank of America as a great place to work
Tools and Technology: Tools available to collect input from stakeholder groups	Talent mapped into talent pools based on key experiences	Associates, HR subject matter experts, staffing	Managers equipped to perform talent management responsibilities		Customers delighted by product and service offerings delivered by associates who are proud of working for Bank of America
	Established strategic and operational metrics and tracking systems	Enterprise leadership analytics function	Metrics in place for each talent management practice area		Investors and Wall Street view Bank of America as a great place to invest; corporate leaders view Bank of America as the most admired company in the world
	Ongoing administration of the talent management system and processes	HR talent management practice area owners	Stakeholder input and goals incorporated into talent management practices		Strong leadership reputation and outstanding financial performance create sustainable future growth and ability to grow investment in talent

541

The identification of these assumptions also helped to shape the vision for the future integration of talent management. The assumption of internal coordination and integration had always been an explicit goal. Stating it as a necessary precondition to achieve the organization strategy increased the awareness of some of the difficult challenges, such as tricky coordination, gaps, redundancies, unstated or unclear requirements, and other common problem areas. As a result, the logic map became the foundation of a business case to improve the overall talent management process and key practice areas.

Evaluating the overall benefit of Bank of America's talent management practices illustrated potential gaps in the existing measurement approaches used for each individual practice area (assessment, recruiting, performance management, associate development, and retention). The individual practice owners asked the company's leadership analytics function, a group within HR, to develop clear outcome and process-oriented measurements to drive performance improvement and to identify ways to better integrate processes, technology, and tools.

The process of improving tools and processes designed to operate across an enterprise of more than 220,000 associates is, almost by definition, a long-term effort; therefore, the evaluation approach was designed to be long term as well. The evaluation cycle for each of the practice areas is refreshed at the beginning of each year in order to integrate with the planning calendars for the bank's information technology partners and processes. Several process metrics in each area are tracked on a monthly basis, and associate data are gathered at multiple times during the annual cycle, depending on the specific talent management practice area:

■ ■ ■

• *Building a talent dashboard.* One additional outcome of this integrated effort was an enterprisewide talent dashboard. This dashboard reflected an integrated view of talent management practices as a continuous process, from human resources planning through assessment, selection (external hiring and internal promotions), onboarding, goal setting, feedback, coaching, associate development, pay for performance, and retention. This integrated approach served as the inflection point at which talent management began to be perceived as a collection of practices that reinforced and built on one another, as opposed to a series of independent HR-driven events. While the journey to evaluate and integrate talent management is a continuous one, with no clear end point, the change in the organization is significant. These changes range from the nature of the discussions about the business and the talent that drives it to the increased demand from senior executives and line managers for more robust assessment and development practices.

- *Shifting talent management accountability.* This change is one of the most notable hallmarks of an integrated talent management culture. The shift in accountability from HR ownership of talent to a shared ownership of talent among senior leaders and line managers is critical. Senior leaders are now accountable for the development of talent within their business. Through various practices, many senior leaders are accountable for talent across lines of business in order to drive the growth of talent capable of operating across the enterprise. Talent management accountability is ensured by pushing analytics into the lines of business and reporting overall outcomes on monthly scorecards that are reviewed and acted on by the senior leadership of the bank.

- *Health of the bench.* The most relevant metrics related to the growth of the leadership talent at Bank of America are summarized for the organization's monthly business review. This set of metrics, known collectively as "health of the bench," is a leading group of indicators designed to minimize leadership vulnerability within the organization. The metrics address three key areas: role vulnerability, talent management process efficiency, and senior leadership perceptions regarding the quantity and quality of existing talent in the organization. One of the strengths of the health of the bench is that its measurement approach is not solely quantitative. The final metric, leadership perceptions of talent quality, is measured by a set of questions administered annually in interviews with Bank of America's top leaders. These questions address the perceptions of the overall quantity and quality of talent within specific lines of business and across the enterprise, the bank's executive selection and development efforts, and the potential skill gaps looming that may have an impact on key strategies. The probing of attitudes that are underneath the surface perceptions is critical in building an understanding of what, how, and why various events and trends are happening in the organization. These indicators allow the talent management practice leaders to be better informed and to design better solutions that address perceived talent issues.

Health of the bench is a cornerstone of Bank of America's assessment of the primary talent management objective of deepening and diversifying the talent bench. The additional assessments of short-, medium-, and long-term outcomes provide the bank with a way to align outcome measures with talent management strategies and to determine which practices and processes are reinforcing the strategy. For example, one of the metrics in the health of the bench index relates to the quantity of external talent flowing into the bank. This metric is presented in the context of potential causes and the impact on other strategic metrics, such as the ability to build innovative products. The discussion around potential causes and the impact on the organization can lead to changes in practices and policies. These changes help to bring the metric in line with the target outcome over time, changing the target, or adjusting talent strategies to meet the changing business needs. In any case, it is the discussion generated by these metrics that is critical to the operation of the organization and to the continuing integration of Bank of America's talent management practices.

Conclusion

The case is made in this book that effective talent management is a leading indicator of the long-term viability of an organization. World-class organizations have learned that their competitive edge is driven by an integrated talent management strategy fully aligned with the business's mission and vision and meaningfully incorporated into its long-term strategic planning.

This chapter has focused on the strategic use of evaluation to define how organizational goals and competitive advantage can be achieved through talent management solutions. The evaluation of talent management, its specific practice areas, and its output (quality and depth of talent) must be an ongoing activity and priority to ensure its value as a key contributor to the organization's strategic priorities.

Five key points emerge from this chapter:

- Evaluation is an essential practice for managing, refining, and ensuring the success of talent management processes and programs.
- Talent management evaluation should address four key perspectives:
  - Strategic
  - Operational
  - Customer
  - Bottom line/financial
- Metrics included in the evaluation should be linked to the organization's strategic goals and bottom-line financial goals.
- The evaluation should be uniquely tailored to each of the customers' and stakeholders' goals.
- Ongoing communication and monitoring should be established through easily accessible vehicles such as dashboards.

The evaluation process outlined in this chapter provides a fundamental, systematic process for linking talent management solutions to critical business challenges and helping organizations achieve a competitive edge. This approach applies to all types of organizations and can be adapted to any business strategy. The use of a balanced scorecard framework ensures that all key stakeholders' input and agendas are taken into account.

As talent management evolves into an integrated function that influences an organization's long-term strategic planning, the evaluation process and its associated metrics must also evolve. Organizations are beginning to recognize the value of integrating the traditionally managed independent practice areas so that they work together rather than being at odds with each other. As such, a new set of metrics and creative evaluation strategies will be required to monitor and manage this newly coordinated function. One of the initial challenges here will be to overcome the turf battles that are likely to arise when program managers feel threatened by the evaluation of their area, particularly in those cases where the findings require changing roles and responsibilities. That said, once talent management program managers and stakeholders begin to incorporate evaluative thinking and practices, the connection between their responsibilities and the organization's priorities will become much clearer.

An increasing number of publications apply the field of program evaluation to HR, a field that is directly applicable to the process needed for effectively managing and evaluating an organization's talent management efforts. Recent work has detailed the procedures for evaluating individual talent management practice areas and for using evaluation as a strategic tool. Future research should concentrate on the evaluation of talent management as an integrated function and begin to assemble a body of evidence demonstrating its impact on an organization's bottom line and the accomplishment of valued organizational objectives.

References

Becker, B. E., Huselid, M. A., & Ulrich, D. (2001). *The HR scorecard: Linking people, strategy and performance.* Boston: Harvard Business School Press.

Bernthal, P. R., & Wellins, R. S. (2005). *Leadership forecast 2005–2006: Best practices for tomorrow's global leaders.* Pittsburgh, PA: Development Dimensions International.

Cascio, W. F. (1992). Assessing the utility of selection decisions: Theoretical and practical considerations. In N. Schmitt, W. C. Borman, & Associates (Eds.), *Personnel selection in organizations.* San Francisco: Jossey-Bass.

Cascio, W. F. (2000). *Costing human resources: The financial impact of behavior in organizations* (4th ed.). Cincinnati: South-Western.

Conference Board. (2001). *Exploring the measurement challenge: Results of a membership survey on HR metrics.* Washington, DC: Corporate Executive Board.

Davidson, E. J., & Martineau, J. W. (2007). Strategic uses of evaluation. In K. M. Hannum, J. W. Martineau, & C. Reinelt (Eds.), *The handbook of leadership development evaluation* (pp. 433–463). San Francisco: Jossey-Bass.

DeLong, T. J., & Vijayaraghavan, V. (2003). Let's hear it for B players. *Harvard Business Review, 81*(6), 96–101.

Edwards, J. E., Scott, J. C., & Raju, N. S. (Eds.). (2003). *The human resources program-evaluation handbook.* Thousand Oaks, CA: Sage.

Edwards, J. E., Scott, J. C., & Raju, N. S. (2007). *Evaluating human resources programs: A six-phase approach for optimizing performance.* San Francisco: Pfeiffer/Jossey-Bass.

Effron, M., Greenslaide, S., & Salob, M. (2005). *How the top 20 companies grow great leaders.* Lincolnshire, IL: Hewitt Associates.

Fitz-enz, J. (2000). *The ROI of human capital: Measuring the economic value of employee performance.* New York: AMACOM.

Fitz-enz, J., & Davison, B. (2002). *How to measure human resources management* (3rd ed.). New York: McGraw-Hill.

Hannum, K. E., Martineau, J. W., & Reinelt, C. (Eds.). (2007). *The handbook of leadership development evaluation.* San Francisco: Jossey-Bass.

Kirkpatrick, D. L. (1959a). Techniques for evaluating training programs. *Journal of American Society for Training and Development, 13,* 3–9.

Kirkpatrick, D. L. (1959b). Techniques for evaluating training programs; Part 2—Learning. *Journal of American Society for Training and Development, 13,* 21–26.

Kirkpatrick, D. L. (1960a). Techniques for evaluating training programs: Part 3—Behavior. *Journal of American Society for Training and Development, 14,* 13–18.

Kirkpatrick, D. L. (1960b). Techniques for evaluating training programs: Part 4—Results. *Journal of American Society for Training and Development, 14,* 28–32.

Mattson, B. W. (2003). The effects of alternative reports of human resource development results on managerial support. *Human Resource Development Quarterly, 14*(2), 127–152.

Phillips, J. J. (1997). *Handbook of training evaluation* (3rd ed.). Houston, TX: Gulf.

Phillips, J. J., & Phillips, P. (2007). Measuring return on investment in leadership development. In K. M. Hannum, J. W. Martineau, & C. Reinelt (Eds.), *The handbook of leadership development evaluation* (pp. 137–166). San Francisco: Jossey-Bass.

Rudis, E. V. (2006). *CEO challenge 2006: Perspectives and analysis.* New York: Conference Board.

Sullivan, J. (2002). *HR metrics, the world class way: How to build the business case for human resources.* Peterborough, NH: Kennedy Information.

W. K. Kellogg Foundation. (2003). *Logic model development guide.* Battle Creek, MI: Author.

Wellins, R. S., Smith, A. B., & Rogers, R. W. (2006). *The CEO's guide to talent management: Building a global leadership pipeline.* Pittsburgh, PA: Development Dimensions International.

CHAPTER 13

MANAGING TALENT IN GLOBAL ORGANIZATIONS

Thomas Ruddy, Pooja Anand

The world is changing. In fact the world already has changed and the pace of change continues to escalate. The technological explosion and proliferation of knowledge and information transfer via the Internet over the past 20 years has completely altered business functioning. For example, a chest X-ray taken by a laboratory technician in Boston may be interpreted by a radiologist in Bangalore, India, and the results sent to a cardiac specialist in California for a video consultation with the patient. All of this can occur in a span of 24 hours and at half the cost of traditional hospital procedures. This new world of globalization requires leaders who can manage the complexity of a global business landscape. However, only 47 of 115 executives surveyed by the Center for Creative Leadership (Criswell & Martin, 2007) had a well-defined succession plan in place to prepare the next generation of senior leaders. This is enough to give any CEO (chief executive officer) chest pains!

Over 25 years ago, Levitt (1983) defined globalization as a shift toward a more integrated and interdependent world economy with two key components: globalization of markets and globalization of production. Corporate employment trends support the contention that globalization already has occurred. For example, the United Nations (2000) reported 63,000 transnational corporations, with the top 100 firms employing over 6 million people. The Fortune Global 500 Report (Fortune, 2007) reports that

Wal-Mart alone employs 1.9 million people on a global basis. This trend is not expected to recede and may continue to escalate. A McKinsey Global Survey (McKinsey, 2006) indicates that business executives expect globalization to accelerate because it facilitates innovation in products, services, and business models; expands information and knowledge collection; and provides access to plentiful, cheap, and mobile capital. In addition, the survey indicated that 85 percent of respondents describe their business environment as either more competitive or much more competitive than five years ago.

Thomas Friedman (2005) discussed the impact of globalization on political, social, and economic dynamics in his best-selling book, *The World Is Flat*: "It is the triple convergence—of new players, on a new playing field, developing new processes and habits for horizontal collaboration—that I believe is the most important force shaping global economics and politics in the early twenty-first century" (p. 212). However, very little literature discusses how global organizations plan to manage the leadership challenge of this complex business environment. "The War for Talent," a series of articles by the McKinsey Group (Chambers, Foulon, Handfield-Jones, Hankin, & Michaels, 1998; Axelrod, Handfield-Jones, & Welsh, 2001) emphasized the need for effective executive talent management. They encouraged corporations to create a *talent mindset* and to continuously recruit and develop talent rather than simply fill open positions. They also highlighted the likelihood that changing demographics will create a scarcity of the best-trained people in developing nations.

Working in a global marketplace affects all Human Resources (HR) processes and requires that they be fully aligned. Access to talent across national boundaries and Internet-based job search sites vastly changes the recruitment process. Broader candidate pools across the global marketplace require changes in selection practices to account for regional legal variations and cultural differences. For example, before a job offer can be extended, issues concerning visas and other working permits must be addressed. Compensation systems also must have sufficient flexibility to ensure equity of pay across various currencies and economic conditions. Development systems may need to be tailored to local cultures to maximize knowledge transfer while respecting local traditions and business protocols. Finally, organizations need to develop retention mechanisms that consider local market conditions as well as the larger global labor needs of the organizations. Ultimately organizations that seamlessly integrate these processes in order to develop and retain future leaders for a rapidly growing global business will have a competitive advantage.

The corporate world recognizes these challenges. A 2004 McKinsey Global Survey of 7,300 senior executives found that hiring and retaining talent was the second highest concern of the executives, following only concerns about the overall global economic climate. Tucker, Kao, and Verma (2005) in *Next Generation Talent Management* reflect on the anticipated effects of globalization on workforce management and cite five critical trends that will transform the way work is done:

1. A smaller and less skilled workforce due to aging populations of workers
2. Increasing global workforces, with greater mobility and remote work access, enabled through technology
3. A highly virtual workforce that is dependent on online social networks and relationships
4. A vastly diverse workforce that includes more females and ethnic minorities
5. A more autonomous and empowered workforce that allows workers to switch employers at will

These trends are forcing global companies to rethink the way they find, develop, and move talent within their organizations.

This chapter discusses how companies deal with talent management issues for critical leadership positions on a global level. The focus is on the identification, development, and movement of talent in the context of these global challenges. Recent literature regarding global leadership models and global resources, including expatriate assignments, is reviewed. The chapter uses interviews with global talent management and succession planning professionals from a variety of transnational companies to illustrate the impact of globalization on workforce management. The focus is on commonly used techniques, important observations, and the lessons learned from real-world application of talent management.

Global Talent Management Strategy Framework

What does the term *talent management strategy* mean? McCauley and Wakefield (2006, p. 4) define talent management processes as "including workforce planning, talent gap analysis, recruiting, staffing, education and development, retention, talent reviews, succession planning, and evaluation." For the purposes of this chapter, we concentrate on several necessary components:

- Global strategic workforce planning through the identification of critical jobs linked to the business strategy
- Global leadership framework models used to define the performance and behavior characteristics the organization desires in its leaders
- Performance appraisal and management (for example, annual and midterm performance reviews) that facilitate the differentiation of individual performances
- Global talent assessment (for example, talent profiles, assessment centers, personality inventories, 360-degree feedback) to identify strengths and developmental opportunities for the future leaders
- Global talent reviews, including succession planning to identify critical talent and early high potentials within the organization and to identify individuals who can replace incumbents in global positions
- Strategic actions (for example, targeted recruiting, training, leadership development programs, and developmental international assignments) to reduce organization-wide talent gaps that could threaten future leadership and business success

The discussion of these elements of global talent management strategy provides the framework for this chapter.

Strategic Workforce Planning

Having a sound business strategy that leverages the organization's technical and human capital is one of the keys to being competitive in a global economy. Most successful global organizations complete annual human capital or workforce planning exercises to determine the future talent needs of the organization. These exercises

Figure 13.1. Business Strategy Competency Planning Matrix

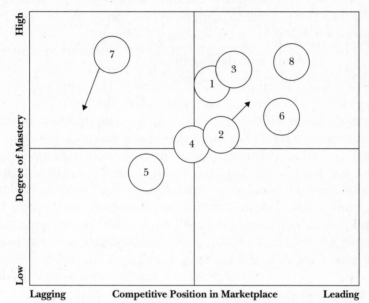

Number of Employees with Needed Competencies

Number	Competency	Current Number of Employees	Projected Number of Employees
1	Project management	64	78
2	Molecular imaging	45	100
3	Mergers and acquisitions knowledge	5	5
4	International resource management	24	22
5	Process management	52	58
6	Visual display technology knowledge	27	30
7	Electromechanical engineering	42	22
8	Global marketing strategy	6	10

usually include an assessment of the technical and leadership capabilities that are needed for the business to grow, an assessment of current employee competencies, and a gap analysis between these factors, resulting in strategy proposals to fill those gaps. A business strategy competency planning matrix (Figure 13.1) is one method used to facilitate this process. It plots various technical competencies on a grid indicating the organization's degree of mastery of that competency and its competitive position in the marketplace (better than, equal to, or below the competition).

This tool allows talent management professionals to plan and project head count associated with the forecasted competency needs and to determine critical skill gaps. The completion of a competency planning matrix helps talent management professionals determine if they should build (develop through training and experience), buy (through recruiting, mergers, and acquisitions), or reduce (through divestitures of noncompetitive parts of businesses, outsourcing) the various talent sets. For example, in 2006 Siemens decided to expand its medical imaging business to include more early detection medical diagnostics; however, the company did not have sufficient people with the required skills to enter this market. This analysis was one factor that led to the acquisition of Bayer Diagnostics, which had the needed expertise. In this way, the competency planning process assists business portfolio managers as they determine if they have the resources and skill sets to compete in the marketplace.

Corning provides another excellent example of the power of human capital planning on a global level. Corning has been an innovator in high-technology materials (among them, Pyrex glass, CorningWare, and optical fiber) for over 150 years. Globally Corning uses an extremely detailed human resource planning process to identify talent management implications for corporate and division business strategies. The process helps Corning determine the number, type, and quality of talent needed to execute the company's business strategy and enables line management to identify skill gaps that require action. Such actions include expanding specific roles, protecting and retaining certain roles, and shrinking, redirecting, or retraining various employees. Brush and Ruse (2005) provide a detailed review of this process.

Human capital planning benefits organizations by creating an awareness of the critical knowledge, skills, and abilities needed to run a business on a global basis. It also helps determine how to best identify and reallocate talent resources when developing new markets. This type of planning has helped Corning transition out of the struggling telecommunications industry and into the liquid crystal display (LCD) glass materials industry. Hank Jonas from Corning states that "human resource planning allows the human resource organization to play an important role in ensuring the success of the global business strategy by assisting in the determination of the roles that are critical to hire, retain, and develop in place" (H. Jonas, personal communication, July 20, 2007).

Global Leadership Models

Many corporations struggle to develop and retain leadership talent who can function optimally across geographic borders and various cultures. Chambers et al. (1998) state that "a more complex economy demands more sophisticated talent with global acumen, multi-cultural fluency, technology literacy, entrepreneurial skills, and the ability to manage increasingly delayered, disaggregated organizations" (p. 1).

The first step in creating a globally savvy team is to establish a standard model for assessing talent. The literature reviews many global leadership assessment models highlighting various leadership competencies and personality characteristics.

Spreitzer, McCall, and Mahoney (1997) provide an excellent review of early research literature on various aspects of global executive potential. They highlight as many as 14 leadership dimensions, including sensitivity to cultural differences, being culturally adventurous, insightfulness, risk taking, openness to criticism, and flexibility. Morrison (2000) provides a more recent review of important characteristics that includes factors such as global business savvy, integrity, ability to deal with uncertainty, and the ability to balance globalization and localization. Based on a global study, House, Javidan, Hanges, and Dorfman (2002) define leadership as the ability to influence, motivate, and enable others to contribute to the success of their organization. They examined the impact of national cultural dimensions, such as collectivism, power distance, and future orientation, on leadership skills and identified the following as core leadership attributes:

- *Charismatic or value based*—a decisive visionary with integrity
- *Team oriented*—a diplomatic team integrator
- *Participative*—a nonautocratic delegator

- *Humane*—modest with a humane orientation
- *Autonomous*—individualistic and unique
- *Self-protective*—a conflict inducer who pursues his own best interests, an attribute considered an impediment to outstanding leadership

These models also highlight the need to demonstrate performance results in a new global setting, as well as the specific behaviors needed to obtain that performance. Lockwood (2004) cites a study by the Society of Human Resource Management that highlights differences between the behaviors and skills for effective leadership in domestic (U.S.) versus international settings. The study shows that in an international setting, the most important factors for effective leadership, in order of preference, are performance, character, adaptability, persistence, and vision. Fulkerson (2002) provides a list of important global executive characteristics that emphasize the importance of adaptability (such as acknowledging and managing people's differences), willingness to learn and acquire new attributes and patterns of behavior, possessing cross-cultural empathy, and thinking across international borders. Cohen (2007) cites five critical categories of competencies for global leaders: business acumen, leadership characteristics (for example, emotional behaviors, self-assurance), worldwide awareness (for example, cultural awareness, adaptation), people leadership, and business leadership. A summary of some of the research studies on global leadership models is outlined in Table 13.1.

A review of Table 13.1 reveals a variety of dimensions and personal attributes identified in the literature that are important in global roles. Some common factors in effective global leadership clearly emerge: business and technical expertise, global perspective, balancing the pressure of global integration and local adaptation (duality), open-mindedness, learning ability, and integrity. In support of the literature, Cornelia Machnik, a Siemens global talent manager, summarized these concepts: "Really talented people can think outside the box, without any borders. For them, change is something positive. They want change and they drive it" (C. Machnik, personal communication, November 12, 2007). The research indicates that there are real differences in leadership dimensions, and their relative importance,

Table 13.1. Global Leadership Capabilities

	Integrity	Duality	Business and Technical Expertise	Global Perspective	Open-Mindedness and Flexibility	Entrepreneurial	Learning Ability
Adler & Bartholomew (1992)		X		X			
Alldredge & Nilan (2000) (3M)	X		X	X		X	X
Bingham, Felin, & Black (2000) (Procter & Gamble)		X	X	X	X		
Black, Morrison, & Gregersen (1999)	X	X	X	X			X
Brake (1997)		X	X			X	X
Caligiuri & DiSanto (2001)		X	X	X	X		
Chambers, Foulon, Handfield-Jones, Hankin, & Michaels (1998)		X	X	X		X	
Cohen (2007)			X	X	X	X	X

(Continued)

Table 13.1. Global Leadership Capabilities (*Continued*)

	Integrity	Duality	Business and Technical Expertise	Global Perspective	Open-Mindedness and Flexibility	Entrepreneurial	Learning Ability
Conner (2000)			X	X		X	
Fulkerson (2002)			X	X	X		X
House, Javidan, Hanges, & Dorfman (2002)	X		X			X	
Lockwood (2004)	X	X	X	X	X		X
Maznevski & DiStefano (2000)			X	X	X		X
McCall & Hollenbeck (2002)	X	X	X	X	X		X
Spreitzer, McCall, & Mahoney (1997)	X		X		X		X
Yeung & Ready (1995)	X	X	X	X	X	X	

between domestic and international management that should be addressed when developing a global leadership framework. Adler and Bartholomew (1992, p. 56) summarized these differences years ago by saying, "To be effective, transnational managers need both the culturally specific knowledge and adaptation skills required in international firms, and the ability to acquire a worldwide perspective and to integrate the worldwide diversity required in multinational firms. As a consequence, one of the transnational manager's primary skills is to exercise discretion in choosing when to be locally responsive and when to emphasize global integration." Today, being adaptive remains a critical factor for success as an international leader.

Recognizing Cultural Factors in Global Leadership Models

So how do global organizations implement leadership competency models? There are many factors that vary across organizations. Some develop a standardized global model of leadership, while others consider cultural differences by modifying the leadership model for various locations. Some organizations vary the importance and weight of leadership competencies geographically, while others treat all competencies equally across locations.

Interviews with people in various multinational companies indicate that most companies recognize cultural differences but ultimately develop a single global leadership model. These are often U.S.-based models with minor adjustments. Steve Walker, the former global head of talent management for JP Morgan Chase, summarized this view when he said, "When building our revised global leadership model, we were very aware of cultural differences. We selected the core competencies for our model with these differences in mind and attempted to make the competencies generic enough to minimize cultural issues" (S. Walker, personal communication, July 18, 2007). The company's leadership model includes competencies such as strategic thinking, client focus, execution, people management, and integrity, all of which apply across all cultures. Allan Church, the global head of talent management for PepsiCo, described a similar set of global competencies that cut across cultural barriers, such as "setting the agenda" (strategic thinking, innovation), "taking others with you" (developing others, teamwork), and "doing it the right way" (compliance, ethics) (A. Church, personal communication, July 19, 2007). It appears that the benefits of a single global model (for example, a common language for discussing talent in the organization, a common set of leadership competencies for evaluating talent, and common rating scales) outweigh the concerns about culture differences outlined in the literature. Since the research literature warns against a common global model, additional work is needed to determine the most practical and effective method for incorporating cultural differences into a global competency model that is both practical and effective.

Many of the companies interviewed base their higher-level leadership competencies on Lominger's 67 leadership architect competencies (Lombardo & Eichinger, 2004). Some models have leadership frameworks that consider both hard performance factors as well as the softer skills that lead to performance outcomes. Billie Hartless, Vice President of Human Resources in Nokia's Corporate Development Office, summarized it best: "We look at the *what* and the *how*, and both have equal weight in determining a person's performance and potential" (B. Hartless, personal communication, August 14, 2007).

On a global basis, the Siemens leadership framework (SLF) also considers both domains. The SLF defines the *what* as four performance results areas (financial, customer, employee, and process) and the *how* as five generic behavioral capabilities (edge, energy, energize, execute, and passion). The SLF assesses all leaders on the same performance and results platform to create a common view of all leadership talent in the organization globally.

These real-world examples indicate that the benefits of a common global talent evaluation model outweigh concerns regarding cultural differences. A global framework provides a uniform methodology for evaluating talent, determining the skill gaps, and implementing a plan for global talent development. Yet companies must be cognizant of cultural differences as they develop global leadership models and should be guided by the research as they select competencies to assess. Companies should use these models with caution since certain behaviors that are acceptable in one culture (for example, aggressiveness, interpersonal directness early in a business relationship, high sales orientation) may be misinterpreted as leadership deficiencies when viewed against a global leadership model.

Performance Appraisal and Management

Most talent management processes are based on an organization's annual performance appraisal processes. Organizations typically attempt to identify talented individuals (also known as high potentials, key talent, top talent, or critical talent) using performance reviews that evaluate individual achievement against defined performance objectives and behavioral criteria. The goal of this process is to identify individuals with the potential to succeed in more complex or higher-level roles within the organization. This approach always raises the question: Does past performance predict future performance in higher-level jobs? In fact, the Corporate Leadership Council (2005b) defines a high-potential employee as someone with the ability, engagement, and aspirations to rise to and succeed in more senior critical positions.

Organizations use various techniques (among them, performance reviews, assessment centers, leadership style assessments, and cross-organization project assignments) to clearly differentiate individuals with the potential to meet the future needs of the company. In 2006, Siemens launched a new global performance management process (PMP) to standardize performance feedback and increase differentiation among employees to identify future leaders. Performance results and capability ratings were changed to five-point scales from a former three-point system. The change was an attempt to increase the degree of differentiation of performance across employees in order to better identify the true top performers. More important, managers are held accountable to identify and develop talent within the organization. The PMP requires that all individuals above a certain grade level are discussed in calibration roundtable meetings, conducted by the manager and his peers to ensure the standardization of evaluations across managers. Mike Panigel, Senior Vice President of Human Resources for Siemens USA, summarized the importance of this process: "Identifying key individuals who can lead the organization in the future is a critical role of all managers. For this process to be effective on a regional and global level, you must have a standardization of the process and proper calibration of the ratings. The roundtable process creates a clear and open dialogue across managers, which improves talent evaluation accuracy" (M. Panigel, personal communication, November 26, 2007).

Several of the companies interviewed (including Nokia, Corning, Pepsi, and 3M) use calibration roundtables to evaluate talent and determine future potential while moving away from forced performance distributions. However, many organizations still follow a recommended distribution of 20 percent high performers, 70 percent steady performers/stay in place, and 10 percent needs improvement or change. This model, developed by General Electric, has come under legal scrutiny in recent years. In 2000, employees at Microsoft, Ford Motor Company, and Conoco filed suits against their respective companies, claiming that the rating systems are unfair because they favor some employee groups over others: white males over blacks and women, younger managers over older ones, and foreign citizens over Americans (Abelson, 2001). Even so, companies often defend the system as valid, and the concept is still used in many companies even if the exact percentage distribution is no longer strictly enforced. Ford Motor Company subsequently changed the company performance calibration system to have no required ratings distribution and to have three performance groupings: top achievers, achievers, and improvement required.

While the technique for calibrating performance varies among the organizations, many use some form of a nine-box grid that maps performance and potential. An example of such a grid is outlined in Figure 13.2.

The performance axis is usually defined by three anchors: "needs improvement," "meets expectations," and "exceeds expectations." The potential axis also has three anchors: "limited potential," "well placed or stay in place," and "high potential." Based on their performance reviews, individuals are mapped onto the grid, which is then used to identify the critical talent within the organization.

Figure 13.2. Talent Nine-Box Grid

		Needs Improvement (Bottom 10%)	Meets Expectations (Middle/Vital 70%)	Exceeds Expectations (Top 20 %)
P O T E N T I A L	High Potential	Move to new role (high potential but not performing)	Emerging leader (possibly early high potential)	High potential (potential for key global position)
	Moderate Potential	Inconsistent performer	Key performer	High potential (high professional or potential for other roles)
	Limited Potential	Improve or separate	Well placed	High professional (highly skilled in a specific area)

PERFORMANCE

Global Talent Assessment

Several factors affect the completion of the performance–potential grid on a global basis. First, who has the final decision in the placement of an employee on such a grid: the regional management or the global business unit management? Second, how do cultural differences influence the use of such scales? Third, who "owns" the talent: the region or the business unit?

Who Places the Employee on the Grid?

Most companies have an upward-flowing talent review process in which calibration roundtable meetings are first conducted at the local level by the manager and her peers to identify talent to be passed on to the next level of reviews. Candidate summaries are then combined at either the global business sector level (for example, power, industry, and medical at Siemens) or at the global technology platform level (for example, nanotechnology, safety, and security at 3M). The matrix nature of global organizations increases complexity by often requiring regional talent reviews, business sector talent reviews, and functional talent reviews. For example, at Siemens, key talent is reviewed using two parallel review processes—one based on geographic region and one based on business unit. Eventually both processes result in reviews with the global CEO. Because of the varying regional and business unit perspectives within the company, there might be confirming or conflicting views of a given individual's performance and potential. The individual might be considered top talent in the region but not fare well when evaluated within a global business unit. This tension can facilitate a more accurate identification of strengths and developmental opportunities for the candidates. In addition, it addresses cultural differences in perception, particularly regarding the personality fit of the individual. For example, an employee could be "too aggressive, not a relationship builder, or too sales and marketing focused for a leadership opening in East Asia."

The Corning talent review process provides another example of the complexity in a matrix global organization. They conduct four types of reviews:

- *Functional reviews*—review the talent for critical positions in areas such as finance or human resources
- *Business sector reviews*—focus on key general management positions within a business segment
- *Regional reviews*—focus on possible replacements for core positions within a specific geographic region such as a plant in China
- *CEO reviews*—discuss the top seven or eight global general manager roles

A single individual may be discussed in all four of these reviews for various positions, resulting in varying opinions of the individual's potential for the various jobs. Resolving the differences of opinion from the diverse perspectives is a complicated and time-consuming, but necessary, process. These analyses result in the individual's talent profile (discussed later in this chapter).

The discrepancies in evaluations of individuals are often resolved by the senior executive team during talent review sessions or solely by the CEO.

Cultural Differences

Calibrating performance and creating consensus about a person's "true" potential can be difficult when the discussion transcends geographic borders. Research on the impact of cultural differences on rating scales suggests that cultural factors must be considered in order to create a valid system. In some cultures, raters tend to use the extreme end points of the scales. Hui and Triandis (1989) found Hispanics have a stronger tendency for extreme ratings (about half the time, on the average) than non-Hispanics when five-point scales were used. In collectivistic cultures such as China, it is not culturally acceptable to give positive self-ratings, while in Western, individualistic cultures such as the United States, "individuals are motivated to view themselves as positively as possible" (Farh, Dobbins, & Cheng, 1991).

Interview data suggest that companies are aware of these differences but do little to accommodate them. Several of the executives interviewed indicated that they occasionally compare the performance rating distributions of leadership characteristics across various geographic regions and do see culturally influenced differences in the distributions. However, none of the companies interviewed made any adjustments for these findings.

Managers may evaluate individuals with more severity or leniency in some countries (or even business units) than others, but these differences may be balanced within the countries themselves. The global head of talent for one company, who asked to remain anonymous, cited Israel and China as an example of this conundrum. An underlying expectation in Israel is that all managers need to have strong business results and be able to challenge others. In contrast, managers in China tend to be less direct and confrontational, and there is great respect for higher authority. The talent manager said they do not directly address these discrepancies because it is assumed that the impact of cultural bias balances out when individuals are being evaluated by managers within their own country. However, this suggests that ratings may still not be comparable across countries. When asked if there are global differences in the way people are evaluated, several global talent managers stated that they see more differences across business units than they do across countries, with certain units being harsh in their ratings while others are more lenient. In summary, although differences in cultural ratings are important, it appears that companies that implement talent management globally ignore the differences across countries rather than apply complex mathematical or judgmental adjustment techniques that may create more issues than they resolve.

Who Owns Global Talent?

Another complex issue in global talent reviews is who owns the right to determine the next assignment for high potentials. The ultimate question is, Does the overall corporation control these talent assets, does the global business unit own them, or does the regional geographic area own them? Organizations vary in their answer to this important question. Business unit heads often stake their claim, believing the high-potential employees should not be made available to other business units because they are needed to deliver business results in their home organization. Yet this stance may not optimize the employee's usefulness to the organization as a whole. Based on our interviews, companies were almost equally split in their overall philosophy of talent ownership, with a third reporting business group ownership, a third reporting functional area ownership, and a third reporting geographic regional ownership. The majority of the companies reported having a small subgroup of global talent (top 200 to 400 people and early high potentials) or key global levels (top three to four job grade levels) that the organization considers "corporate assets" who are centrally managed and reviewed. Most businesses tended to shift power more toward the global business units when making final decisions about an individual's potential or placement in the organization. However, one global management head said that this balance of power shifts every time the organization shifts from a centralized to a decentralized approach to talent management decision making.

The variation in methods across organizations, and the reality that the talent management evaluation process is itself dynamic, highlights the fact that it is critical to keep the lines of communication open between regions, business units, and corporate headquarters to ensure successful coordination of talent moves. Clearly all organizations strive for this outcome from the talent review process, but transparent communications can be difficult to accomplish, in part because formal talent reviews are often only conducted annually or semiannually. Several companies, such as 3M and PepsiCo have moved toward more frequent (quarterly or even monthly) executive resource reviews, which involve the CEO, heads of business units, and HR to deal with rapidly changing business settings.

Global Talent Profiles

Annual performance reviews place employees on a nine-box assessment grid and help identify individuals with the potential to lead core functions. However, these processes will not succeed in the long term without excellent documentation on each individual. Documentation is critical to capturing the consensus decisions for future reference, especially since organizational and managerial changes occur frequently. What information should organizations document on these individuals, and how should they use this information to move and further develop talent? Almost all companies have some form of global talent portfolio that can be shared with managers and executives during talent management reviews. Exhibit 13.1 offers an example of a generic profile.

A review of Exhibit 13.1 highlights the most common components of global talent profiles including:

- Basic information, such as name and demographic details about the candidate (for example, current job position, date of hire, geographic location, knowledge of languages, education level, and citizenship)
- Work history or a brief résumé that outlines the various positions the employee has held
- Evaluation of job performance in the form of ratings as well as some descriptions of the results measured
- Evaluation of the leadership capabilities in a numerical format and sometimes as behavioral descriptions

Exhibit 13.1. Generic Talent Profile

DEMOGRAPHIC INFORMATION | PHOTO (Optional)

Name: Jeffrey Garcia

Group/Department: Business Solutions

Country: United States of America

Date of Hire: April 1, 2002

Function/Since: Audit, 4/2002

Position Level/Since: Director, 9/2005

Citizenship: USA

Degree/Specialization/Univ./Location: BA/Finance/University of Chicago/IL USA
MBA/Strategic Management/Finance/The Wharton School/PA USA

Knowledge of Languages	Level
English	Fluent
Spanish	Mother Tongue

EXPERIENCE

From	Location	Co.	Function/Job	Bus.	Job Family
2005/9	New York City, US	Global Corp.	Director, Finance	Pharma.	Finance
2002/5	New York City, US	Global Corp.	Sr. Manager, Audit	BioTech	Finance
1999/10	London, UK	Cooper Smith & Forbes	Sr. Manager, Audit	Bank	Finance
1995/3	New Jersey, US	Kesler & Holmes	Manager, Special Accounts	Bank	Finance
1992/6	Milwaukee, US	Kline & Kline	Staff Accountant	Pharma.	Finance

POTENTIAL/PERFORMANCE MATRIX

High Potential	X		
Well Placed			
Ltd. Potential			
	Needs Improvement	Meets Expectation	Exceeds Expectation

EXPERIENCE PROFILE

EXPERIENCE PROFILE	•	••	•••
International Experience		••	
General Management		••	
Variety of Business			•••
Variety of Function	•		

PERFORMANCE RATINGS

RESULTS	Not Achieved	Partially Achieved	Achieved	Partially Exceeded	Exceeded	REMARKS
Financials					Exceeded	Jeffery restructured budgets to realize a savings of over 25%. His score with his employee satisfaction survey declined 10% year to year, with teamwork being a key declining area. Customer satisfaction with financial reporting improved 3% to 88% satisfied. He has implemented 4 new finance and accounting processes based on six sigma techniques.
Employees		Partially Achieved				
Customers					Exceeded	
Processes			Achieved			
Overall Rating				Partially Exceeded		

CAPABILITIES	Unsatis-factory	Needs Improvement	Meets Expectation	Exceeds Expectation	Exceptional	REMARKS
Leadership		Needs Improvement				Jeffery has strong technical and analytical capabilities. He has great ideas for process improvement but is unable to bring together the team at the time of implementation. While Jeffery shows a high level of initiative, working long hours to ensure projects are delivered on time, he needs to do more to keep his team focused and assert himself as a leader.
Strategic Thinking				Exceeds Expectation		
Business Management			Meets Expectation			
People Management		Needs Improvement				
Partnership				Exceeds Expectation		
Integrity					Exceptional	

NEXT STEP AGREEMENTS

No Action	Expand Current Role	Move Laterally	Promote	Ready to Develop	Agreed Next Step	Mid-Term Function	Mid-Term Position	Succession Candidates
	X			1/2008	Sr. Director	Corporate Finance	VP Finance	Rosemary Simon Dylan Foster

EMPLOYEE PREFERENCES | RETENTION RISK

Geographical: USA/EU **Business:** All

Yes _X_ No ___

MENTOR

Bill Walton

Comments: Needs coaching/mentoring for further development of leadership skills. Technical skills have attracted offers from large consulting firms.

- Experience profile, which is typically a quantified version of types of experiences: variety of business, country, and functions
- A potential statement of possible next step positions for the individual
- Possible succession candidates if the individual was to move on
- "Ready to develop" date or a date when the person is available to take the next position; comments regarding the agreements made in calibration roundtables and talent reviews
- Employee comments regarding his desired next steps or any restrictions on his future development (for example, not available for relocation due to personal reasons)

The section detailing the employee's experience often documents the degree of international experience, general management experience, and the variety of businesses and functions that the high-potential individual has accumulated over his career. This information can be critical in determining the individual's potential for a global assignment. Some companies require that employees need to have experience in two countries, two functions, and two different businesses to get a top general management or executive assignment. When the individual's talent profile reveals that the candidate was raised, completed a college education, and worked for the last ten years in the same country, yet expresses interest in a global assignment, executives may question the individual's capability to "explore new situations and take risks." A review of the talent profile of Siemens top U.S.-based executives found that 85 percent of incumbents and 70 percent of individuals with potential for those positions had international experiences and experiences in a variety of functions throughout their careers.

Another controversial section on global talent portfolios is the inclusion of candidate photographs. Photographs help managers recall candidates with whom they have limited exposure. Based on our interviews, about half of the companies include photographs. The companies that do not include photographs cite legal concerns about age, gender, and race bias creeping into evaluations. Companies that do include photographs often have disclaimers indicating that the pictures are used for identification purposes only and that the company does not discriminate on age, gender, or ethnicity. Legal concerns about this topic are more of a U.S. issue since discrimination cases of these sorts are rare or nonexistent in other countries. In fact, Europeans are often amused at the American tendency to be conservative when considering factors such as age in business decisions. Age is often discussed in talent reviews that are conducted outside the United States. It is considered in some cases an important factor regarding how long a person will stay with the company and whether she is the right person for a specific long-term assignment in a given country. Since age cannot be discussed in U.S. talent reviews, the focus sometimes shifts to how long a person will continue to work for the company. This is often referred to as "the length of the runway left for the candidate." The legality of such discussions and the use of photographs will continue to be debated within HR organizations and legal departments, with the legal risk being balanced against the importance of accurate and relevant information.

In summary, our findings indicate that talent profiles look very similar across the globe. The process of developing and using talent profiles also is similar, but global talent discussions sometimes include information that is prohibited from the discussion in the United States. One constant appears to be that variety of experiences is an increasingly important factor in determining a person's readiness for global business assignments.

Global Talent Reviews

Most companies use global talent reviews to classify individuals by using a nine-box performance by potential grid (see Figure 13.2) into three key talent groups. The first group is high potentials: employees with the potential and aspiration to function in the highest positions within a global company (for example, global business unit head, region or country head, key functional roles such as CFO). These individuals often are considered corporate assets rather than being "owned" by a group or region, and they are expected to be globally mobile as part of global succession plans for critical assignments. The second group is emerging leaders/early high potentials: early career individuals who are seen as having the raw management skills to move up quickly in the organization and operate in larger and more complex business roles that may include international assignments. The third group is high professionals/key experts: individual contributors with deep technical expertise (for example, specialists in disease transmission, molecular imaging, or nanotechnology) that is critical to future business success and who have the potential to function as the global heads of specific research and development areas. These classifications guide the succession planning for critical positions around the world. Note that a large number of employees are often steady, solid performers who are central to an organization's success: these individuals are not typically the focus of talent forums since they are often labeled "meets expectation/well placed."

After completing reviews to identify the high-potential talent, how do organizations choose one person for each of the top global positions? Most organizations have well-designed succession plans that identify the top two to three candidates for each of the core positions, such as direct reports to CEO or heads of global businesses. An example of a typical global succession planning worksheet is displayed in Table 13.2.

These individuals, often referred to as the bench strength of the organization, are considered when a global position becomes available. Based on their succession plans, some companies put the top two or three candidates into "project assignments" for six months to validate their strengths and weaknesses prior to deciding whether they are ready for a global role. Although methodical succession planning that includes assessment using short-term job assignments is very beneficial, it may not always be possible when positions become open without warning. Unexpected turnover or the poor performance of an incumbent often creates emergency succession situations. In these unexpected situations, knowledge of possible succession candidates based on other methods often can contribute to the identification of candidates for an open position. Some of these methods are in-depth interviews, performance in assessment centers, feedback from 360-degree assessments (such as Lominger's Voices or Personnel Decisions International's Profiler), or even personality and

Table 13.2. Succession Planning Chart

Role	Current Incumbent	Possible Successors	Expected Readiness	Development Concerns or Questions	Move or Action Needed
Chief marketing officer	Kevin Scheff (likely to move within 12 months)	Candidates 1–2 years			
		Patty Manning	12 months	Needs exposure to general management role	Leadership role in a mergers and acquisitions assignment
		Fida Ayouby	18 months	Flight risk if not promoted	Promote or expand role
		Candidates 3–5 years			
		Peter Kirsch	36 months	Primarily sales background	Needs commercial marketing experience
		Tamara Jackson	48 months	Worked in only one business unit	Lateral move to another business

leadership-style inventories (such as the Hogan Personality Inventory or Saville Consulting's Wave Leadership Style Assessment).

In addition, timing also plays an important role when core positions come open. Some of the candidates on the succession plans may not be available in advance of their existing "ready to develop" date (business needs may require that the person stay in her current role) or may not be mobile at that particular time (perhaps personal desires not to go abroad due to children in high school).

Global Position Decision Making

While interviews, past experiences, and other assessment data influence promotion decisions, the head of the business or the CEO often has the final decision. One of the talent managers interviewed, who asked to remain anonymous, summarized this well: "Talent movement and placement many times appear to take place as a result of divine intervention. The person who actually gets the job is not always the most qualified, but is the one who is actually available at that time. He would be someone who possesses at least some of the critical skills that are needed, or would most benefit from the developmental experience, as determined by the CEO." In most of the companies we interviewed, the movement and placement of talent into top positions also has a political factor as part of the process: the CEO and the executive staff exert pressure on the organization to get individuals into specific high-level global assignments. Executive staff members often have legitimate and strategic reasons for these placements, but these reasons may not be transparent to the overall organization or to the candidates not selected for the position.

Selecting Local Talent

The final succession candidate for a core global position may come from the pool of globally available talent, but the trend is toward local talent filling local positions. For many years, companies were confident in the strength of their talent to run and expand their businesses globally. Companies either exported their U.S.-based talent to foreign countries or purchased talent, when needed, from other countries. However, in recent years companies have had increasing difficulty filling leadership positions around the world. Ben Dowell, former global head of talent management for Bristol-Myers Squibb, summarized this view: "Talent is not as plentiful as it used to be. The supply of savvy global leaders is limited, people are less willing to relocate around the globe, and it is increasingly difficult to go out and buy talent. Companies need to find new ways of developing talent locally" (B. Dowell, personal communication, November 1, 2007). Previously companies relied on large groups of expatriates who roamed the world imparting their wisdom to others in order to expand their multinational organizations. More recently, companies have scaled back the number of expatriates in key assignments and shifted to local development. Talent managers often cite the excessive cost of international assignments as the major reason for this shift because placing expatriates in international assignments is often three to four times more expensive than hiring local people.

The large failure rate of expatriates is an additional factor in companies' shift toward investing in local talent development. Ferraro (2002), in *The Cultural Dimension of International Business,* reports failure rates for international assignments that are up to 10 percent for Australian companies, 14 percent for Japanese companies, and 76 percent for U.S. companies. Local talent better understands the business community, language, culture, and local values. Eddy, Hall, and Robinson (2006) summarized interviews with 25 leaders of local business units from 21 global companies. The leaders concurred that "a successful strategy must integrate the nurturing of local leaders with broader localization effort, such as promoting education, building a supplier base, and improving the local business infrastructure." Companies often recruit international students from U.S. M.B.A. programs to return to critical roles in their home countries. Kuptsch and Pang (2006) provide an excellent overview of the shifts in global labor statistics that highlight the explosion of M.B.A. students from China and India in recent years. In addition, in a McKinsey study (Eddy et al., 2006), "more than two in five of the companies sampled have installed a local CEO or business unit leader and nearly as many have one or more nationals on the top executive team."

However, many of the companies that we interviewed indicated that it is very difficult for outside talent to succeed in top management positions because they struggle to learn the organization's corporate culture. To address this issue, companies often bring in new talent just below the corporate executive level to give them three to four years of experience in which to learn the corporate culture prior to entering top general management positions. Allan Church of Pepsi stated, "We have moved toward identifying more local talent for key positions, but we typically have them work in our global corporate offices to learn the company culture and establish networks that will be beneficial to their future success" (A. Church, personal communication, July 19, 2007). When there is not enough time for such a transition, companies often place an expatriate in the leadership role until they can identify suitable local talent. Companies reported having two objectives for expatriates when they are put into a key general management position in a country outside the United States: to get the business to be profitable in that country and to find a local individual to succeed her as the head of the business.

Although local talent is critical to the success of a company's global talent pool, companies tend to prioritize a fit with their corporate culture over a fit with the local culture. One executive stated, "We tend to look for local talent who display the same behaviors as our managers in the United States because that is how we define success, even if those behaviors are often not best suited for the local culture." Although companies seek to decrease a U.S.-centric view of leadership talent, this statement highlights the importance of leaders' ability to balance the company's corporate culture and the local country culture.

Strategic Actions to Develop Global Leaders

Once individuals have been identified for a position, they frequently need targeted development. Individuals often take on larger, more complex, international roles that expose them to a variety of developmental experiences. A study by the Corporate Leadership Council (2005a) suggests that the most effective methods for developing global business leaders are (1) long-term international assignments, (2) internal executive development programs, and (3) international cross-functional project teams.

In general, companies that we interviewed follow the 70-20-10 rule for developing global leaders: 70 percent development through job experience, 20 percent through coaching and mentoring, and 10 percent through formal training and development programs. According to Baird, Briscoe, Tuden, and Rosansky (1991), companies in Europe tend to rely on job assignments, expatriate activities, and technical development; North American firms focus on formal approaches such as executive development programs and job responsibilities; and Pacific Rim and Asian organizations resist formal approaches, preferring to instill learning into work processes rather than having separate activities. Based on this research and our interviews, we will focus on two of the most common methods of development: on-the-job learning through international job assignments and formal global development programs, which often include cross-functional global team projects.

Developing Leadership Through International Assignment

Research over the past twenty years indicates that there is no better way to develop people than learning by doing. McCall, Lombardo, and Morrison (1988) highlighted that firing people, working with managers, knowing how the business works, handling problems, dealing with office politics are the critical lessons of executive development. They highlighted the importance of assignments in which managers must learn new skills, deal with difficult bosses, and deal with various types of hardships (those with personal trauma, career setbacks, changing jobs, making business mistakes, and dealing with subordinate performance problems, for example) to help executives learn about themselves and prepare for future assignments. More recently, Carpenter, Sanders, and Gregersen (2000) suggest that early career international experiences lead to greater career advancement and may also create some competitive advantage for the company itself. Bingham, Felin, and Black (2000) interviewed John Pepper, CEO of Procter & Gamble, who stated, "There are few things that totally change your life, and taking my first international assignment in Italy was just that kind of experience." He personally felt that the international experience helped him learn to deal with uncertainty, know and understand customer needs, balance the tensions of global integration and local adaptation, and understand diversity by exploring new viewpoints, experiences, and cultures.

It would be prudent to recognize and acknowledge the cultural adjustment issues that are faced by home country expatriates (employees with the same nationality as the company headquarters working in a country other than their home country) as well as by third-country nationals (employees with a nationality different from the company headquarters and the country of assignment) when working in the local culture. This adjustment is particularly challenging for the third-country nationals who could be from a culture completely different from both the home country and the corporate host country. According to Shaffer, Harrison, and Gilley (1999), the complexity of the adjustment process has many elements, including the moderating effects of both individual adjustment factors (previous assignment experience and fluency in the host country language) and positional characteristics (hierarchical level, functional area, and assignment region).

It is difficult to quantify the importance of international experiences for developing leaders, but they are commonly cited in both the research literature and the interviews conducted for this chapter. For example, Erin Lap (E. Lap, personal communication, August 15, 2007) from Hay Associates stated that the key characteristics of global leaders primarily come from global experience. She noted that this experience helps managers:

- Develop a broader perspective to better understand complex business situations and trends
- Increase an organizational and cultural awareness of acceptable codes of conduct in given situations
- Cultivate a respectful curiosity that embraces the differences in the various cultures
- Build relationships and networking skills that help them understand both the business and the cultural perspectives of people in various countries

Oddou (1991) found that success in an international assignment depended on the following characteristics: "How easily the employee adapts to changes, how open-minded and diplomatic the employee is, does the employee enjoy meeting new people and learning about them, how self-confident or self reliant is the employee, how cohesive is the individual's family and does the employee deal effectively with stress" (p. 303).

Preparing Expatriates for Global Assignment

Although some of these factors reflect personality characteristics, the use of education and training, one-on-one executive coaching, and mentoring can help ease the transition. Several online tools and assessments (two are Globesmart and Culturewizard) have been developed in recent years to help individuals assess their readiness for international assignments and determine the gaps between their current culture and the culture in their new job assignment. However, Oddou (1991) notes that over 65 percent of expatriates receive no training to prepare for international assignments.

Open-mindedness and enjoying new experiences are critical to success in such assignments. Global managers need to embrace and appreciate the differences in cultures to truly learn and grow. Even simple things—like trying new foods, understanding the history of a country, or visiting a local marketplace—facilitate insight into how people live and their cultural beliefs. In turn these experiences can result in greater understanding and appreciation of the differences in how people work and make decisions. Individuals who do not embrace the culture during a global assignment (for example, they do not stray from expatriate compounds when not working) usually miss opportunities to learn and often fail in their international assignments. Beaman (2006) provides an excellent summary of the myths and mistakes in overseas assignments and concludes that expatriates need to move beyond superficial cultural differences and see the world through the eyes of the other culture to be successful on an international stage.

For expatriates to be successful and fully develop themselves, they must demonstrate learning agility: a willingness and ability to learn competencies required to succeed in first-time, challenging conditions and also be prepared to go against the grain of what they know and prefer to do (Lombardo & Eichinger, 2000). They should be ready to embrace the local culture and be open to new ideas and ways of living and operating a business. Companies must invest in the proper selection, education, and training of candidates prior to having them take international assignments in order to increase the probability of success.

Returning Home from Expatriate Assignments

It is also critical that companies help expatriates transition back home after completing their international assignments. Large global companies often fail to develop and advance their returning expatriates. In this regard, Oddou (1991) found in his study of 165 expatriates and HR directors in high technology and banking industries that nearly 40 percent of expatriates do not have a specific position identified for their return. As a result, they often languish in holding positions until a suitable new assignment can be found. According to Caligiuri and Lazarova (2001), most global firms recognize that the biggest benefit of successful repatriation to an organization is the increased global competence in the organization, and simultaneously acknowledge that the low retention rate of global assignees on repatriation is their greatest concern. According to Global Relocation Services (2006), 21 percent of the expatriates left the company during the international assignment, 23 percent within a year of returning, and 20 percent between the first and second year after returning. This is based on a survey of 125 organizations with offices located throughout the world, with 46 percent having their company headquarters located outside the United States. These expatriate attrition rates are double the rate of other employees. One cause of these disruptions is that expatriates may view a higher-level return work assignment as guaranteed, yet the company may not be able to fulfill their expectations. This reflects the importance of assessing the performance in the international assignment to determine the appropriate placement for those who are returning. Promotion to a higher-level position on repatriation cannot be guaranteed. Therefore, it is important to clarify the purpose of the expatriate assignment, and particularly the types of skills an individual is expected to develop from the experience.

All of the talent managers we interviewed commented on the challenge of deciding how to communicate this uncertainty to the outbound individuals regarding their return assignments. Their comments range from "we tell them nothing since there are no guarantees" to "we define specific jobs for them upon successful completion of the assignment." Gregerson and Black (1995) stated that truly strategic global talent management approaches select individuals for global assignments as part of their overall career development path and consider how globally acquired skills will be used on repatriation. Caligiuri and DiSanto (2001) cite eight global developmental goals for international assignments:

1. The ability to transact business in another country
2. The ability to change leadership style based on the situation
3. Knowledge of the company's worldwide structure
4. Creating a professional worldwide network
5. Knowledge of international issues
6. Openness
7. Flexibility
8. Reduced ethnocentrism

A clear business reason for an international assignment is a critical first step in developing global talent. An example was provided by George Nolen, CEO of Siemens USA, who said, "You need to get top talent working in emerging markets such as China and India very early in their careers. It is an expensive proposition for companies, but the firsthand knowledge of these markets and the relationships developed to get work done will be invaluable to any company" (G. Nolan, personal communication, October 31, 2007).

Developing Leaders Through Executive Development Programs

Global executive development programs are another common method to develop leaders. These programs further develop leadership and business skills and expose talent to top global executives and other potential leaders.

These programs give participants from around the world many types of development opportunities. They complete classroom-based learning (for example, globalization, marketplace trends, innovation), international travel to expose them to new business models (for example, Bangalore, India, to explore outsourcing, software development, and service call centers; China to explore low-cost electronic component manufacturing), and involvement in specific business improvement projects. After completing the programs, participants apply these skills back in their business setting, frequently with the support of ongoing coaching. Black and Gregersen (2000) provide an overview of goals and objectives for these programs. They conclude that exploring new concepts and contrasting experiences with others helps leaders develop a new set of global mental maps that facilitate future success. In addition, Neary and O'Grady (2000) reviewed the executive development program at TRW, a leading automotive supplier, and concluded that these programs increase leaders' flexibility and networking skills and enhance their cultural awareness.

Faculty for these programs often include internal leaders, who teach subjects based on their business experience, and outside academic professionals who are subject matter experts in their field. Siemens has a series of five executive development programs ranging from the CEO level down to the first line manager level. Individuals are placed into these programs within six months of their assignment to a new key global or regional position. These programs use the concept of leaders teaching leaders, allowing graduates of each program level to teach at the course level below. The courses develop leaders' skills in strategy development, market and business analysis, differentiation from competition, cross-business and cross-boundary collaboration, customer relations, change management, and effective leadership and communication techniques. Becton Dickinson and Company, a global medical technology company, has capitalized on this leader-as-teacher model to train over 500 leader-teachers around the globe. These leaders disseminate knowledge in the areas of business skills, leadership, sales, career development, and operational effectiveness.

Many organizations (for example, Corning, GlaxoSmithKline, and Siemens) also include action learning projects in which participants complete business improvement projects identified by the CEO and his executive staff. These projects reflect the typical challenges faced by organizations: such as developing a service business strategy or strategy for expanding into China, examining the impact of global warming on the business or the new pharmaceutical regulatory environment on sales, or trouble-shooting problems with quality and customer reactions due to outsourcing. Typically teams of global high potentials make recommendations regarding these issues. These project teams may work together for only a few days or as long as a year.

In addition to skill enhancements, the projects facilitate networking with current and future leaders of the organization to create relationships that can be extremely beneficial to participants as they develop their careers. These projects can help the participants apply their newly learned skills in a true business setting. Often the purpose of these exercises is not just developmental; the recommendations of the team are presented to the executive committee and many times shape the organization's future direction. For example, at Siemens, projects have ranged from developing a new global vision statement linked to the overall business strategy to developing a new monitoring device that can automatically transmit a person's heart rate and blood pressure readings to hospitals using a cell phone.

In summary, executive development programs provide senior executives with the opportunity to observe up-and-coming leaders and provide the potential future leaders with the opportunity to stretch and exercise their existing leadership skills in new and challenging environments.

How Do I Get Started?

The processes described in this chapter are complex, expensive, and resource intensive. How does a company, especially a small company with limited resources, begin to develop a global talent management strategy? The simplest way is to begin discussing talent in the organization. A critical element of talent management is to create a dialogue among senior management to identify the key individuals in the organization who have additional potential and can advance in the company. This dialogue does not require databases, talent profiles, or nine box grids. It requires only that senior management invest the time and energy to know the people in their organization, identify their skills and knowledge, and understand their aspirations for future assignments. Facilitating even just one or two meetings each year to discuss individuals and key positions can quickly start a talent management process. It is as simple as it sounds. Large organizations with numerous talent management resources may make the talent review process far more complex and time consuming than it needs to be. The dialogue, not the forms or the systems, is paramount.

Practical Advice from Practitioners

Here are some critical points from our experts.

Involve Senior Management

Involve senior management (CEO and her direct reports) in the review and assessment of talent to ensure they know the high potentials in the organization well. Annual talent reviews are not sufficient for them to know the people in this pool. Executives must have numerous opportunities to become familiar with the talent in the organization. Various activities facilitate the process, such as presentations by top talent to the executive committee, networking opportunities at top management meetings, business improvement projects, lunches with key executives, special project assignments defined by the executive committee, and observations of global talent in development centers and other settings. The more the executives personally know the talent in various cultures and countries, the more accurate their insight will be about these leaders—certainly beyond what words on a talent profile can provide. One global talent manager said, "The key is to give the top talent exposure to the core people who can give them the next job step in their career. This is what really moves and develops talent with an organization."

However, it is prudent that talent managers be realistic about the expectations for executive involvement. Steve Walker formerly of JP Morgan Chase stated, "It is important to tailor your programs and systems to appropriately meet the senior executive team's appetite for involvement. You want to establish a consistency of purpose in your talent management strategy and not have a lot of starts and stops" (S. Walker, personal communication, July 18, 2007). Talent managers may need to phase in new global programs over time based on the process capacity and mindset of the senior executive team.

Integrate the Talent Strategy

Ensure that the talent strategy is integrated into the overall business strategy. Hank Jonas from Corning said, "Organizations that start with a clearly defined business strategy and then derive their people strategy from this business perspective are more successful at driving and executing on their global talent initiatives" (H. Jonas, personal communication, July 20, 2007). Talent management cannot be viewed as a separate Human Resources initiative; it must be viewed as a business strategy that is driven by the managers and leaders of the organization. Human Resources provides the tools and enablers to identify talent gaps within the organization. However, the executive management team must create and support a "talent mindset," that is, a culture in which leaders in the organization constantly seek global talent both within and outside the organization. Managers and other leaders in the organization should be accountable for the development and success of the talent they place in key positions.

Develop a Global Leadership Framework

Develop a culturally sensitive, flexible, global leadership framework to evaluate and select talent that reflects behavioral competencies that are generic enough to be used globally. The challenge is to strike a balance between a framework that is too generic, and therefore not useful, versus a framework that is so specific and rigid that cultural factors will contaminate the consistency across the system. Billie Hartless from Nokia stated, "The framework must be specific enough to be able to provide effective developmental feedback to key talent, but if it becomes too specific. then cultural factors can distort the evaluation of your talent."

It is important to have a corporate culture, but you must recognize the relevance of the local culture. The old saying of *think globally but act locally* still holds. "Having a system that is 80 percent global but allows for 20 percent local customization may work best" (B. Hartless, personal communication, August 14, 2007). In most cases, companies must try to avoid imposing a North American or European view on other countries and cultures as they expand globally. A mutual cultural respect allows more successful collaborations.

Build Flexible Succession Strategies

Global succession and talent management strategies must be flexible and include alternative contingency plans. Due to a variety of factors, things do not always work out as planned. Allan Church from PepsiCo said, "You lay out plans with multiple global talent moves and then the first move itself does not work out and things start to fall apart. So, you need to explore multiple scenarios in order to be effective at managing global talent in real time" (A. Church, personal communication, July 19, 2007).

Implement Early Talent Identification Processes

The early identification of individuals with additional potential is critical to any effective talent management system. Identify talent early in their careers and move them to *stretch* assignments to help them develop. Managers must identify individuals who have the "basic DNA" to be global leaders: that is adaptability, learning agility, and open-mindedness. Early identification and job rotation programs assess individuals' ability to take on more challenging roles. Often the best time for people to learn is during the transition to a new position, before they establish their work processes and when they are more open to trying new things. Early career moves, including international experience, may be less disruptive to the individual's personal or family life. A senior executive summarized this nicely by saying, "The sooner you get high potentials out in the global business world, the better, since they need to see how things really work in other countries.

Now is the time to get them this experience, before their heads are filled with ill-defined preconceived notions."

Create a Nurturing Environment

Talent managers should focus on creating a nurturing environment for development rather than simply developing processes, systems, and assessments. Erin Lap from Hay Associates stated, "Managers and the top leaders of the organization need to create an environment that is professional and motivational for top talent management and development since leadership capabilities become more important as a company becomes more global" (E. Lap, personal communication, September 10, 2007). Talent managers may be prone to spending too much time ensuring that the global talent review processes and forms are completed correctly and lose sight of the purpose of these exercises: to identify and develop future leaders of the organization. All managers need to personally know the strengths, weaknesses, and career aspirations of the talent within their organization. They must be able to identify global job opportunities and project assignments to help talent grow and develop into future leaders. Michaela Buerger, head of Siemens corporate development, summarized this: "Managers must trust their employees, and have the courage to give them new tasks and not simply let them go on doing what they have always done, and generally done well. At the same time, employees must have the courage and flexibility to try out something new" (M. Buerger, personal communication, November 12, 2007). Managers must also help talented individuals understand their development needs and capitalize on their strengths. Valerie Gervais from GlaxoSmithKline encapsulated this: "Work with who people are, and take them on a journey of discovery. Do not try to make them into something that they are not. People can evolve and grow because everything that they need is already inside them" (V. Gervais, personal communication, September 13, 2007).

It also is important that people understand the rationale of specific assignments and the organization's expectations. Karen Paul from 3M said, "If you tell people why they are being given a specific global assignment and what they are expected to learn, then they tend to actually learn these key leadership skills and behaviors" (K. Paul, personal communication, August 16, 2007). Talent managers should recognize that global assignments are not the only way individuals learn and may not be right for everyone. Learning can occur in local project assignments, in short-term global assignments, through mentoring, and through exposure to different functions within the organization. Ben Dowell, formerly of Bristol-Myers Squibb, said, "A global job can be a very blunt instrument for developing talent, so you need to use these global job assignments wisely. Just putting someone in a job and hoping they learn something is not enough. Taking steps, such as setting expectations, honest feedback, and coaching are critical to ensuring individuals learn what you want them to learn" (B. Dowell, personal communication, November 1, 2007).

Develop Local Talent

Develop local talent within a country when possible. The use of expatriates to turn a business around or to open a new market is declining, mostly because of the cost involved and the limited success of expatriates in these assignments. Companies increasingly identify and develop local talent to lead their operations in new global markets. Clearly companies will still rely on expatriate talent to facilitate global expansions, but the shift is toward a limited use of such assignments and always in the context of finding local talent to succeed them. Allan Church from Pepsi said, "We are having more success with local home-grown talent than with expatriates, as they are better at managing within the local business culture. Expatriates often take three to five years to make an impact on the people they manage and then they move on again" (A. Church, personal communication, July 19, 2007).

Future Research

Our discussion has highlighted several issues that plague practitioners as they implement global talent management systems. Additional research is needed to clarify various issues and to optimize talent management and development implementation. First, future research should improve understanding of how global leadership models and assessment systems can be adjusted or modified to consider the impact of cultural differences. Many companies implement common global leadership competency models and rating systems but recognize that there are real cultural differences that have an impact on these evaluations. Researchers may be able to determine how competency and potential ratings vary across cultures and develop recommendations regarding strategies to minimize error variance when comparing individuals from different countries.

Second, future research should evaluate how to minimize failed expatriate assignments. Although a robust research literature has identified factors that lead to expatriate failure, the research offers few solutions other than education and training to minimize these risks. Organizations make a very large financial investment when moving high potentials to other countries, but research may indicate that some of this money may be better spent on validated evaluations and selection techniques that specifically screen for the characteristics necessary for success in various cultures. Some tools do exist for comparing an individual's leadership style against behavioral norms for a given country, but additional research and selection tools are needed. Related to this area, more research is needed on how career *derailers* identified in U.S.-based studies apply to expatriates working in various cultures. In addition, it would be helpful to better understand how organizations can ease the reintegration of expatriates into their home countries on their return, since many high-potential individuals leave organizations after expatriate assignments for a variety of reasons (for example, family issues, lack of professional challenges, dissatisfaction with decision authority in new role).

Third, research in real business settings is needed to determine the developmental impact and unintended consequences of action learning projects. While positive satisfaction ratings from project participants and senior executives support the use of these projects, a growing number of reports of participant burnout and dissatisfaction after project recommendations are not fully embraced and implemented reveal potential problems with their use. Research that clarifies how to maximize learning and development and minimize the unintended negative outcomes of such learning experiences could guide future practice.

Finally, talent management professionals often recommend that high potentials get international experience early in their careers. More longitudinal research is needed to determine if these early career moves are more effective at developing top leaders than later career moves. Researchers need to assess the balance of the lower cost and ease of moving early-career individuals against the knowledge, experience, and skills that later-career individuals bring to an expatriate assignment.

Conclusion

Talent managers must develop new global talent strategies that constantly advance and adapt to the rapidly changing global economy. The top executives of the organization must identify talent early, move people to learning assignments, and invest in the development of their people. Klaus Kleinfeld, the former global CEO of Siemens, said in a meeting with his top 400 U.S. managers: "When I look at leaders in the organization, I look at their overall business results first. But then I look at how many other leaders they have developed and moved within the organization. This tells me how good a leader they really are" (K. Kleinfeld, personal communication, October 13, 2007).

Exceptional global talent management depends on a culture that values learning for all levels of employees, whether it is experience for top management, job incumbents, candidates for top global positions, top talent who are still early in their careers, or global talent managers. All must continue to learn if they expect to lead this movement. This sentiment is best captured in the words of the late John F. Kennedy in a speech that he was to deliver on the day of his death in Dallas, Texas: "Leadership and learning are indispensable to each other." We all should strive to keep these words alive as we manage talent globally.

References

Abelson, R. (2001). Companies turn to grades, and employees go to court. *New York Times*. Retrieved March 19, 2007, from http://query .nytimes.com/gst/fullpage.html?res=9C03E7DC103DF93 AA25750C0A9679C8B63.

Adler, N. J., & Bartholomew, S. (1992). Managing globally competent people. *Academy of Management Executive, 6*(3), 52–65.

Alldredge, M. E., & Nilan, K. J. (2000). 3M's leadership competency model: An internally developed solution. *Human Resource Management, 39*(2, 3), 133–145.

Axelrod, E. L., Handfield-Jones, H., & Welsh, T. A. (2001). The war on talent, part two. *McKinsey Quarterly.* Retrieved August 10, 2007, from http://www.mckinseyquarterly.com/The_war_for_talent_part_two_10352.

Baird, L., Briscoe, J., Tuden, L., & Rosansky, L.M.H. (1991). World class executive development. *Human Resource Planning, 17*(1), 1–13.

Beaman, K. V. (2006). Myths, mystiques and mistakes in overseas assignments. In M. Foster (Ed.), *Global talent: An anthology of human capital strategies for today's borderless enterprise* (Vol. 1, pp. 35–73). Washington, DC: Human Capital Institute.

Bingham, C. B., Felin, T., & Black, J. S. (2000). An interview with John Pepper: What it takes to be a global leader. *Human Resource Management, 39*(2, 3) 287–292.

Black, J. S., & Gregersen H. B. (2001). High impact training: Forging leaders for the global frontier. *Human Resource Management, 39* (2, 3), 173–184.

Black, J. S., Morrison, A. J., & Gregersen, H. B. (1999). *Global explorers: The next generation of leaders.* New York: Routledge.

Brake, T. (1997). *The global leader: Critical factors for creating the world class organization.* Chicago: Irwin.

Brush, M. C., & Ruse, D. H. (2005). Driving strategic success through human capital planning. *Human Resource Planning, 28*(1), 49–60.

Caligiuri, P., & DiSanto, V. (2001). Global competence: What it is and can it be developed through global assignments? *Human Resource Planning, 24*(3), 27–35.

Caligiuri, P., & Lazarova, M. (2001). *Strategic repatriation policies to enhance global leadership development: Developing global business leaders.* Westport, CT: Quorum.

Carpenter, M. A., Sanders, W. G., & Gregersen, H. B. (2000). International assignment experience at the top can make a bottom line difference. *Human Resource Management, 39*(2, 3), 277–285.

Chambers, E. G., Foulon, M., Handfield-Jones, H., Hankin, S. M., & Michaels III, E. G. (1998). War on talent. *The McKinsey Quarterly.* Retrieved August 10, 2007, from http://www.mckinseyquarterly.com/Organization/Talent/The_war_for_talent_305.

Cohen, E. (2007). *Leadership without borders.* Hoboken, NJ: Wiley.

Conner, J. (2000). Developing the global leaders of tomorrow. *Human Resource Management, 39*(2, 3), 146–157.

Corporate Leadership Council. (2005a). *Realizing the full potential of rising talent, Vol. 2. Strategies supporting the development of high-potential employees.* Washington, DC: Corporate Executive Board

Corporate Leadership Council. (2005b). *HR organization's high potential employee management strategies survey.* Washington, DC: Corporate Leadership Council Research.

Criswell, C., & Martin, A. (2007). *Ten trends: A study of senior executives' views on the future.* Greensboro, NC: Center for Creative Leadership.

Eddy, J., Hall, S.J.D., & Robinson, S. R. (2006, August). How global organizations develop local talent. *McKinsey Quarterly.* Retrieved August 10, 2007, from http://www.mckinseyquarterly .com/How_global_organizations_develop_local_talent_1821.

Farh, J., Dobbins, G. H., & Cheng, B. (1991) Cultural relativity in action: A comparison of self-ratings made by Chinese and US Workers. *Personnel Psychology, 44,* 129–147.

Ferraro, G. P. (2002). *The cultural dimension of international business.* Upper Saddle River, NJ: Prentice Hall.

Fortune Magazine. (2007). *Global 500 report.* Retrieved September 19, 2007, from http://money.cnn.com/magazines/fortune/global500/2007/snapshots/2255.html.

Friedman, T. L. (2005). *The world is flat.* New York: Farrar, Straus & Giroux.

Fulkerson, J. R. (2002). Growing global executives. In R. Silzer (Ed.), *The 21st century executive: Innovative practices for building leadership at the top* (pp. 300—334). San Francisco: Jossey-Bass.

Global Relocation Services. (2006). *Global relocation trends, 2005 survey report.* Retrieved November 10, 2007, from www.gmacglobalrelocation.com.

Gregersen, H. B., & Black, J. S. (1995). Keeping high performers after international assignments: A key to global executive development. *Journal of International Management, 1,* 3–31.

House, R., Javidan, M., Hanges, P., & Dorfman, P. (2002). Understanding cultures and implicit leadership theories across the globe: An introduction to Project GLOBE. *Journal of World Business, 37,* 3–10.

Hui, C. H., & Triandis, H. C. (1989). Effects of culture and response format on extreme response style. *Journal of Cross-Cultural Psychology, 20*(3), 296–309.

Kuptsch, C., & Pang, E. F. (2006). *Competing for global talent.* Geneva: International Institute for Labor Studies, International Labor Office.

Levitt, T. (1983, May–June). The globalization of markets. *Harvard Business Review,* 92–102.

Lockwood, R. L. (2004, December). *Leadership styles in the global arena.* Retrieved September 9, 2007, from http://moss07.shrm.org/Research/Articles/Articles/Pages/Leadership_20Styles_20Series_20Part_20III__20Leadership_20Styles_20in_20the_20Global_20Arena.aspx.

Lombardo, M. M., & Eichinger, R. W. (2000). *The leadership machine: Architecture to develop leaders for any future.* Minneapolis, MN: Lominger.

Lombardo, M. M., & Eichinger, R. W. (2004). *For your improvement, a guide for development and coaching.* Minneapolis, MN: Lominger.

Maznevski, M. L., & DiStefano, J. J. (2000). Global leaders are team players: Developing global leaders through membership on global teams. *Human Resource Management 39*(2, 3), 195–208.

McCall, M., Lombardo, M., & Morrison, A. (1988). *The lessons of experience.* New York: Free Press.

McCall, M. W., Jr., & Hollenbeck, G. P. (2002). *Developing global executives: The lessons of international experience.* Boston: Harvard Business School Press.

McCauley, C., & Wakefield, M. (2006). Talent management in the 21st century: How to help your company find, develop, and keep its strongest workers. *Journal for Quality and Participation, 29*(4), 4–7.

McKinsey Quarterly. (2004, March). *McKinsey Global Survey of Business Executives.* Retrieved August 10, 2007, from http://www.mckinseyquarterly.com/The_McKinsey_Global_Survey_of_Business_Executives__March_2004_1411.

McKinsey Quarterly. (2006b). *McKinsey Global Survey of Business Executives: Confidence Index.* Retrieved August 10, 2007, from http://www.mckinseyquarterly.com/The_McKinsey_Global_Survey_of_Business_Executives__Confidence_Index_April_2006_1764.

Morrison, A. J. (2000). Developing a global leadership model. *Human Resource Management, 39,* 117–131.

Neary, D. B., & O'Grady, D. A. (2000). The role of training in developing global leaders: A case study at TRW Inc. *Human Resource Management, 39*(2, 3), 185–193.

Oddou, G. R. (1991). Managing your expatriates: What the successful firms do. *Human Resource Planning, 14*(4), 301–308.

Shaffer, M. A., Harrison, D. A., & Gilley, K. M. (1999). Dimensions, determinants and differences in the expatriate adjustment process. *Journal of International Business Studies, 30*(3), 557–581.

Spreitzer, G. M., McCall, M. W. Jr., & Mahoney, J. D. (1997). Early identification of international executive potential. *Journal of Applied Psychology, 82*(1), 6–29.

Tucker, E., Kao, T., & Verma, N. (2005). *Next-generation talent management.* Retrieved August 15, 2007, from http://www.cdi-tm.com/media/whitepaper_nextgentalenmanagement.pdf.

United Nations. (2000). *World investment report: Cross border mergers and acquisitions and development.* New York and Geneva: Author.

Yeung, A., & Ready, D. (1995). Developing leadership capabilities of global corporations: A comparative study in eight nations. *Human Resource Management, 34*(4), 529–547.

CHAPTER 14

MANAGING TALENT IN CHINA

Elizabeth Weldon

At a recent conference in Shanghai, a Human Resources (HR) director for a large Western multinational company (WMNC) in China was reflecting on her work. After sighing and taking a sip of tea, she said, "The success of my company is in my hands." Although she knew that she was exaggerating, there is a lot of truth in her statement. China is an important part of her company's growth strategy, and her job is to attract, motivate, develop, and retain the people the company needs to succeed. She feels a strong sense of responsibility for her company's success and is sometimes overwhelmed by the challenge.

Conversations with other HR professionals in China suggest that she is not alone. The challenges that she and other HR professionals face in China are described in this chapter. After a short overview of the activities of Western multinationals in China, several aspects of the Chinese context that create challenges for talent management professionals are described and the ways that some companies address these challenges are discussed.

Western Multinationals in China

China plays an important role in the global strategies of many WMNCs. According to *People's Daily*, China's state-run newspaper, 90 percent of the world's top 500 multinationals have some type of direct investment in China (Manpower China, 2006). For many companies, China serves as a low-cost center to produce goods for export and, as China's middle class grows, for the domestic market as well. In addition, many companies are building research and development capabilities in China to get closer to Asian markets and tap low-cost research and engineering talent. By 2006 there were between 750 and 800 foreign-invested research centers in China ("Foreign Investors," 2006), including IBM's software development center, PepsiCo's food and beverage center, and Rohm & Haas's center for developing paint additives. In addition, some companies have established global centers of excellence in China. For example, in 2006, IBM moved its global purchasing headquarters to Shenzhen (Comtex News Network, 2007).

For all these companies, building an effective local workforce is by far their biggest operating concern (American Chambers of Commerce Beijing & Shanghai, 2005; U.S. China Business Council, 2007). To conquer this challenge, HR professionals in WMNCs must determine how well their global talent management practices will transfer to China. They can transfer HR practices intact or adapt them to suit the Chinese context.

Transferring Talent Management Practices to China

Many managers believe that Western talent management practices can be, and should be, transferred intact to China. For example, Gary Dirks, the top executive at BP China, says that BP's HR policies are transferred with virtually no change: "The HR tools are the same we use anywhere. We apply them exactly the same way. Some of them are translated into Chinese. That's all" (Fernandez & Underwood, 2006, p. 42). Dominique de Boisseson, Chairman and CEO of Alcatel, says that the company's global HR practices are transferred with little adaptation, because "if we want to succeed in China, we must make sure the Chinese employees have a worldwide view and use best practices" (Fernandez & Underwood, 2006, p. 42). Similarly, at Royal Philips Electronics, the company's "One Philips" talent management system is used in China just as it is in other parts of the world (Bell, 2006), and at Wal-Mart China, managers and HR people work hard to transfer the company's existing HR practices into China. Gordon Orr, Director of McKinsey & Company's

Shanghai office, supports this approach. He says that WMNCs should use Western practices because they are a source of competitive advantage (Fernandez & Underwood, 2006).

HR professionals working in China usually agree that HR strategies and policies can be transferred to China, but most believe that some HR practices must be adapted to fit the Chinese context. There are four important aspects of the Chinese context that affect the successful implementation of talent management practices:

- The shortage of professionals and managers in China
- China's one-child policy
- The importance of maintaining face in Chinese culture
- The power distance, or respect for hierarchy

Of course, China differs from Western countries in many other ways, but these are the differences that most concern HR professionals.

The Chinese Context

This section describes the four elements of the Chinese context and their impact on talent management practices and the approaches that HR professionals are taking to adapt their talent management practices to deal with the China context.

Shortage of Professionals and Managers

The biggest problem that HR professionals face in China is the shortage of qualified people. These shortages are caused by three factors: the lingering impact of China's planned economy, the Cultural Revolution, and the nature of university training in China.

The Planned Economy

From 1949, when the People's Republic of China was founded by the Chinese Communist Party, until 1979, when Deng Xiaoping began a process of gradual economic reform, China had a centralized, planned economy (Zhou, Lu, & Jiang, 2005; Zhu, 2005). After almost 30 years of gradual reform and entry into the World Trade Organization, China's economy is now much more market driven, although the planned economy left a legacy that continues to affect talent management even today.

Under the planned economy, the government's central planning apparatus set economic plans that cascaded down to individual enterprises, indicating what each would produce and how they would produce it. These companies, all government owned, received allocations of capital, labor, and supplies, and their products were distributed according to the plan. In this system, enterprise managers implemented the plan with the resources they were given and sent the product on as directed. Enterprise managers did not generate plans or make decisions, and they had no incentive to pursue efficiencies or profit maximizing strategies.

In this system, workers were assigned to work units by central planning agencies, and most managers and professionals were appointed by the Communist Party. Each work unit provided lifetime employment and provided for employees' basic personal needs. Housing, cultural activities, recreation facilities, schools, and health care were all provided by the work unit. The work unit also controlled job transfers (people could not leave their jobs without official permission) and permissions to change residency, to travel, to get married, and to have a child.

Although people kept their jobs for life regardless of their performance, performance appraisals were used to determine promotions, to allocate welfare benefits, and to select model workers. Performance appraisals for blue-collar workers were sporadic and informal, and personal relationships with colleagues and enterprise leaders had the biggest impact on a worker's assessment. For the managers and professionals who were members of the Communist Party, performance appraisals were conducted by a department of the party's Central Committee, and the results relied heavily on political loyalty, ideological purity, and seniority. Training was centrally planned and focused primarily on ideology and political education rather than job requirements. Central planners also set wages and benefits. Wage increases were based on seniority, and there were few incentives to improve performance.

The Cultural Revolution

From 1966 to 1976, China was in chaos as Mao Zedong sought to reestablish his personal influence after the failure of his economic policies (Blackwell, 1999; World Encyclopedia, 2005). Expectations were high in 1958 when Mao launched his plan to transform China from an agrarian society into a modern industrialized country. But by 1960 it was clear that his "Great Leap Forward" had failed: people were starving, and industrial output was disappointing. As a result, many people in power felt that reform was required.

Mao relinquished his power to others, but in 1966, he launched the Cultural Revolution to reestablish his authority. Mao mobilized China's youth to struggle against people in authority and encouraged them to leave school to form revolutionary brigades, hold rallies, and conduct struggle sessions where intellectuals, landlords, and others suspected of "incorrect thinking" were subjected to physical abuse and public humiliation. Schools shut down, and 17 million students went to the countryside to experience manual labor in aid of the revolution. The turmoil and brutality of the Cultural Revolution destroyed many lives, and people who are now in their 40s, 50s, and 60s are often called the "lost generation" because of the chaos that reigned during their formative years.

The Legacy

The effects of the planned economy and the Cultural Revolution are still being felt through their impact on the availability of mature managers and professionals in China. As a result of working in the planned economy, many of the people now in their 40s, 50s, and 60s lack a deep understanding of market-oriented economies and profit-based business practices needed to perform in middle-level and high-level positions in Western multinationals. Furthermore, many adults today who should have been in school during the Cultural Revolution lack the basic education needed to learn new business practices quickly. This means that WMNCs in China must rely disproportionately on younger people to fill positions that would be filled by more senior people in other parts of the world.

University Training

Unfortunately only a small percentage of China's young people are suitable for managerial and professional positions in Western multinationals. Chinese schools, even at the university level, emphasize memorization rather than critical thinking and theory rather than practical application. To make matters worse, teaching materials at second- and third-tier universities are often out-of-date. As a result, most graduates lack the critical thinking skills and the practical action orientation needed by WMNCs. A McKinsey report estimates that no more than 10 percent of China's college graduates are able to perform professional and analytical work in foreign-invested enterprises (Economist Intelligence Unit, 2006). Another study found that only 3 percent of college graduates with a general degree (one not related to business or economics or to specific skills like engineering or information technology) were judged to be employable in WMNCs (Bannister & Learmond, 2007; McKinsey Global Institute, 2005).

Shortage of Human Resource professionals

Not surprisingly, HR professionals are also in short supply. Although many WMNCs bring in expatriates to fill high-level HR positions, most prefer to hire local people to fill lower-level roles (Law, Wong, & Wang, 2004; Tam, 2001; Zhou et al., 2005). This preference means that WMNCs must help local HR people develop the functional skills and strategic mindset expected of HR professionals today.

Summary

The planned economy, the Cultural Revolution, and the nature of university training combine to create a shortage of people with the skills that WMNCs need. This shortage increases turnover, drives up salaries, and limits companies' ability to grow. Although the situation may be improving, companies must work hard to recruit the right people and retain the people they already have.

The banking industry shows how difficult these conditions can be. After China fully opened its banking industry in 2006, Western banks began to expand ("Staff Turnover," 2007). According to PricewaterhouseCoopers, more than two-thirds of foreign banks in China now have annual staff turnover of more than 15 percent, and significant salary inflation plagues the industry. According to one expert, it is not unusual to increase the salary of a person who fills a key position by 50 to 100 percent or even more to retain him ("Staff Turnover," 2007). In spite of this difficult situation, Western banks hope to double their total workforce by 2010 ("Staff Turnover," 2007).

The "Little Emperors"

In 1979, China implemented the one-child policy to control population growth in its cities. This policy has produced a generation of young adults often called the "little emperors." Having grown up with the undivided attention of two parents and four grandparents, these "little emperors" are somewhat self-centered and hold themselves in high regard. They have high achievement aspirations and high expectations for material success.

According to HR professionals, these little emperors become impatient employees with inflated self-images and a sense of entitlement. They prefer short-term contracts to benefit from the personnel shortages that drive up pay and promotion opportunities, and they expect to be promoted every six months to a year. In addition, they resent any indication that a "bamboo ceiling" might exist, that invisible barrier believed to prevent Chinese managers from advancing to the highest levels in WMNCs (Manpower China, 2006; Ye, 2006).

Many HR professionals find that recruitment, retention, and development practices must be adapted to accommodate the expectations of these "little emperors." For example, in some companies, HR people create additional unofficial levels in the hierarchy to provide the frequent promotions these young people expect.

Face Concerns

In Chinese culture, giving and maintaining face is an important part of social behavior. Face (*mianzi*) refers to one's public image, including prestige, status, and reputation. Showing loyalty and respect and offering praise are behaviors that give face, and failing to show respect causes another person to lose face. As a result, Chinese people often deliver bad news and disagree indirectly, and they often use intermediaries in conflict situations (Gabrenya & Hwang, 1996; Gao, Ting-Toomey, & Gudykunst, 1996). People also behave in ways designed to maintain their own face. For example, Westerners find that Chinese employees are less likely to admit that they do not understand something, and they are less willing to take risks because they might make mistakes. Many HR people feel that face concerns must be considered when giving feedback, implementing performance management systems, and designing promotion and development processes.

Power Distance: Managers and Their Direct Reports

Several studies show that China is a high power-distance culture compared to Western cultures (Hofstede, 2003; Javidan, Dorfman, de Luque, & House, 2006). Power distance is the extent to which people in a culture accept hierarchical distinctions and accept that power is distributed unequally (Hofstede, 2003; Javidan et al., 2006). People in high power-distance cultures are more respectful of hierarchical position, more accepting of top-down decision making, and more accepting of one-way communication compared to people in low power-distance cultures.

Research shows that this cultural dimension affects the relationship between managers and their direct reports. In the West, the ideal manager is someone who empowers people, supports them, and coaches them to success. In contrast, Chinese managers are more authoritarian and directive. They tell people what to do, and subordinates expect to be told (Javidan et al., 2006). Although WMNCs could accept this cultural difference, most encourage Chinese managers to become more participative and their subordinates to become more proactive (Manpower China, 2006).

Talent Management in China

Together, the talent shortage, the one-child policy, power distance, and face concerns create real challenges for Human Resource professionals as they try to recruit, retain, motivate, and develop the people their company needs. This section describes the nature of these challenges in more detail and shows how HR professionals in China adapt their practices to meet those challenges. Table 14.1 provides an overview of this discussion.

Table 14.1. The Chinese Context Creates Challenges for HR Professionals

The Chinese Context	Business Challenges		The HR Challenges
Planned economy Cultural Revolution University education	Shortage of managers and professionals	→	*Recruitment:* Attracting enough qualified people *Retention:* Responding to salary inflation, offering frequent promotions, creating clear career paths *Development:* Volume and speed
One-child policy	Little emperors with high expectations and high aspirations	→	*Retention:* Removing the bamboo ceiling, managing expectations, creating unofficial levels in the hierarchy *Development:* Promoting people before they are ready
Power distance	Directive managers and submissive subordinates	→	*Development:* Building a coaching culture
Face concerns	Concerns about prestige and status	→	*Retention:* Promoting cohort simultaneously, creating unofficial job titles *Performance management:* Giving indirect feedback

Recruitment

Western multinational companies use a wide variety of recruitment activities to find qualified people. Most WMNCs recruit through university placement centers, job fairs, newspaper ads, company websites, and online recruiting agencies. In many companies, top managers take an active role by meeting with good prospects and visiting prominent universities to build connections. For example, the CEO of GE China visits Fudan University frequently to maintain GE's visibility (Gross & Connor, 2007).

In addition, many companies use hiring agents for technical and skilled labor and headhunters for professional and managerial positions. However, using agents can create problems. First, agents may not verify an applicant's qualifications. IBM, for example, has demanded refunds from a dozen of its hiring agents after firing scores of employees who had lied about their qualifications ("IBM Asks," 2006). Second, poaching employees is illegal under Chinese labor law. Therefore, when a company is hiring from another WMNC the company should verify that the candidate's past employment has ended before the person begins work or receives any compensation, including sign-on bonuses (Dessler, 2006).

Some companies employ more unusual activities to win the war for talent. DTZ, a global real estate adviser in Shanghai, stays in touch with former employees and invites them to attend alumni get-togethers. Eighty-five percent of its former employees are still working in the industry or in key positions in the value chain. DTZ uses this network to gather business intelligence, to collect referrals for vacant positions, and to check references when hiring for senior positions (Xu & Cheung, 2006).

L'Oreal, the world leader in the beauty industry, uses the L'Oreal Brandstorm International Marketing Award to attract young people from around the world, including China. Student teams play the role of a brand manager and analyze market trends, create product packaging, and develop a marketing campaign. According to Bocco Chen, recruitment and integration manager in Hong Kong, the Brandstorm award has been a very successful recruiting tool (Lui, 2006).

Google stages recruiting events that look more like rock concerts than job interviews. At a recent event in Beijing, a top executive "took the stage in the purple lights and smoke, with the song *Ain't No Mountain High Enough* blaring" in the background. The company also offers perks including free massages and funding for start-ups founded by employees (Liu, 2007). Google hopes that this approach will help them beat Beidu.com, the leader in the Chinese web search market.

Other companies participate in employer surveys, such as Hewitt Associates' *Best Employers in China* and Peking University's *Employer of Choice* surveys. Participation shows how companies score on the key factors that attract Chinese people, and when a company does well, the publicity works as a recruiting tool. Several recent studies show that learning and development opportunities, career progress, advancement opportunities, high-quality leadership, competitive compensation, pay-for-performance systems, and the degree to which the organization's work processes allow employees to be productive are key elements in the decision to join a company (Hulme, 2006; Manpower China, 2006).

At least one company has decided to do its own research to facilitate recruiting. Flextronics, a Fortune 500 company that designs, manufactures, and ships electronic products for leading brands such as Motorola, Sony Ericsson, and Microsoft, recently engaged a research firm to survey new graduates and midcareer professionals. The survey asked about their next career moves, their knowledge about the company, and how they would feel about living in the cities where Flextronics's largest operations are located. Flextronics will use the results to develop the employee value proposition, articulate a company brand, and tailor the recruitment and retention strategy.

Other companies try to leverage their consumer brand. For example, Wal-Mart China benefits because people in China know the Wal-Mart brand, and many young people prefer working in retail over manufacturing. However, people often underestimate the hard work and discipline required to work in retail, and they have difficulty adapting to the Wal-Mart culture.

Retention

Human resource professionals know from experience and from recent surveys that opportunities for growth and development, advancement, and compensation are the main reasons Chinese managers and professionals stay with or leave a company

(Manpower China, 2006). Many young people, and older people with marketable skills, feel entitled to development and expect promotions every six months to a year. They are also very aware of their market value and will leave if their pay does not seem fair to them. However, many will forgo a salary increase for development opportunities and a clear career path (Watson Wyatt Worldwide, 2006). One HR professional reported that the rule of thumb in her company is that development and career opportunities can neutralize a pay raise offer of up to 30 percent, but above that, people will leave.

To satisfy demands for development and promotion, many companies try to promote from within, as FedEx does. At FedEx, job openings are posted weekly for all employees to see. One result is that 91 percent of management appointments are internal promotions (Bell, 2005). In addition, most companies make sure that high-potential people get special attention, as they do at IBM China. In that company, 300 high-potential people receive special developmental opportunities, and clear road maps for career progress are created for them. Moreover, IBM's global resourcing system helps Chinese managers find opportunities outside China.

Although using development and promotion to retain people can be quite effective, it is not problem free. First, some managers resist developing people because their efforts are wasted when those people leave. Second, in some cases, people are promoted before they are ready for the next position, and they must be coached to help them develop quickly on the job. Third, companies must dispel any suggestion that a bamboo ceiling exists (Manpower China, 2006; Ye, 2006). Fourth, people lose face when others of about the same age and tenure are promoted before them. To overcome this, some companies simultaneously promote people of the same age and tenure.

To manage these challenges, the best companies try to manage expectations. When that does not work, some companies create unofficial levels in the hierarchy to allow more frequent promotions, and they allow people to use two titles: their official title for internal use and a more exalted title for their business cards. Third, some companies offer housing benefits, such as home loans and rent support, to retain good people. For example, Motorola China has built hundreds of condominium units that are sold to employees with a small down payment and affordable monthly mortgages (Gross & Connor, 2007).

But in the end, people do leave. When that happens, many HR managers try to look on the bright side: those who leave often join a customer organization or a partner firm, which strengthens ties and improves working relationships with those organizations.

Performance Management

Although in the early days some WMNCs in China had problems introducing performance-based pay because seniority-based systems were the norm, surveys show that Chinese people now prefer performance-based systems (Bacani & Sima, 2006; Baruch, Wheeler, & Zhao, 2004; Gross & Connor, 2007). These surveys also show that most WMNCs now link pay to performance (Hewitt Associates, 2005). In a survey of WMNCs conducted by Hewitt Associates, 78 percent of those surveyed reported using a performance management system involving goals, formal appraisals, and pay for performance, and a large majority said that appraisals were used to determine salary increases, coach employees, create development plans, and communicate expectations ("Performance Management," 2002).

Although these systems are generally successful, some companies adapt them to accommodate face concerns. Many HR professionals say that feedback must be less direct, and negative information should be tempered (Manpower China, 2006). As a result, one HR professional created new rating categories when she developed a performance management system for a semiconductor factory in China. In that system, the five rating categories are outstanding, successful plus, successful, successful minus, and improvement needed. These categories were perceived to be less negative than those used in other parts of the company.

Development

People familiar with Chinese culture often doubt that Western development practices can be used in China:

- Face and respect for hierarchy make it impossible to use upward or peer evaluations in 360-degree feedback.
- Chinese people lack the active learning skills required for stretch assignments and action learning projects.

- They do not believe that Western competency models are appropriate for Chinese leadership.

Although these are reasonable concerns, the evidence suggests that Western development practices and competency models can be used in China, but some adaptation may be required.

Development Processes

In one survey, 200 Chinese managers were asked how much they would like to participate in various developmental experiences. Results showed that the large majority of these managers were interested or extremely interested in stretch assignments, action learning projects, classroom education programs, overseas assignments, mentoring, coaching, and receiving 360-degree feedback (Weldon, 2005).

These results fit quite well with what WMNCs are actually doing. A recent review indicates that most WMNCs are using all or some combination of these developmental experiences (Law, 2006). In another survey, 25 percent of the respondents reported that they use internal management development programs, international assignments, mentoring and coaching, participation in cross-functional international teams, and action learning assignments to a great extent in their Asia Pacific operations (Bell, 2006). That same study showed that participation in cross-functional international teams, international assignments longer than two years, internal management development programs, short-term international assignments (less than six months), mentoring, and coaching were believed to be the most effective practices for developing leaders in Asia Pacific. These results show that mentoring, feedback, exposure to role models, and job assignments, particularly with an international focus, are important for developing Chinese managers.

Competency Models

Although academic research shows that Chinese leadership is different in some ways from leadership in the West (Javidan et al., 2006), most WMNCs use their global competency model to drive development in China. In a Conference Board survey of HR professionals working in the Asia-Pacific region, 83 percent of the respondents said that leadership skills and competencies are transferable across regions, and only 23 percent had developed competencies that vary by situation or geography (Bell, 2006). When competencies are added, they usually focus on three areas where Asia Pacific managers need additional development: cultural understanding and adaptation; collaboration, teamwork, communication, and alignment across boundaries; and people development and coaching skills (Bell, 2006).

Adapting Development Practices for the Chinese Context

Although Western development practices and global competency models can be used to develop Chinese managers, there are a few differences to consider. First, Chinese managers value classroom knowledge more than Western managers do (Fallon, 2005–2006). For this reason, Chinese managers may feel cheated when training does not include lectures by an expert. Second, when classroom instruction is used, WMNCs often develop separate Asia-Pacific programs rather than mix Asian managers with Europeans and North Americans. This tendency reflects the cost of travel and their different development needs, but also the concern that Western managers will dominate the program with their more assertive manner.

Third, in classroom discussion, Chinese managers like to discuss issues with their peers before stating an opinion. Fourth, Chinese managers often need help understanding Western business ethics and standards for professional behavior, as well as the dynamics of cross-functional, cross-business, and cross-country business processes (Law, 2006). Fifth, young Chinese managers are likely to feel that development is an entitlement, whereas Europeans and North Americans are more likely to believe that development must benefit both the individual and the organization.

Sixth, Chinese managers need more help and encouragement to build their coaching skills. For example, at Unilever China, leadership development efforts focus on getting managers to talk less and listen more and to be less directive and more supportive. In addition, direct reports were encouraged to use their bosses as sounding boards, to take responsibility for their decisions, and to learn from their failures as well as their successes (Bannister & Learmond, 2007). Of course, overbearing managers with poor listening skills are found in Western cultures as well. The difference is that most Western managers believe that managers should coach people, whereas Chinese managers may not.

Seventh, because WMNCs in China need to develop a lot of people, and they need to do it quickly, HR professionals are looking for ways to increase development volume and speed. One information technology services company leverages its IT knowledge to produce low-cost, high-volume e-learning programs. Others hope to expand and improve techniques believed to accelerate development, such as pairing junior talent with senior global executives in apprenticeship assignments; creating greater opportunities for global networking; providing more targeted feedback about performance and potential; and developing better ways to identify high-potential global leaders early in their careers (Kramer, 2007).

Future Research

Industrial-organizational (I-O) psychologists can help human resources people in China by conducting research in many of the areas discussed in this chapter. Western and Chinese industrial-organizational psychologists should work together to conduct this research so that English and Chinese language research and business publications can be reviewed and an indigenous view of the issues can be considered. Three areas of research, in particular, seem potentially fruitful.

First, studies of realistic job previews might be conducted. A realistic job preview (RJP) is the presentation of accurate job-related information, both favorable and unfavorable, to job candidates (Rynes, 1991). A large body of research in the United States has shown that realistic job previews can decrease turnover and produce other positive results (Rynes, 1991; Phillips, 1998). It would be useful to know if realistic job previews can have the same impact in China.

Second, studies on giving, receiving, and seeking feedback might be conducted. Although many HR professionals in China feel that the feedback process must be adapted to fit the Chinese context, there is little hard data to show how this should be done. A few studies of feedback processes and Chinese people have been reported, but these data are insufficient to draw firm conclusions.

Third, researchers might follow Chinese managers in international assignments to identify factors that influence their ability to learn quickly about job demands and their success in the assignment. Researchers might start with models of Western expatriate success (Black, Mendenhall, & Oddou, 1991) and see how well they apply to Chinese expatriates.

Conclusions

Human resource professionals in China are working hard to meet the challenges they face. They transfer Western talent management practices intact when they can and adapt them when required to meet the demands of the Chinese context.

Unfortunately, their jobs will not get easier anytime soon. First, recruiting and retaining good people may become even more difficult as domestic companies become better places to work. Currently many of the best young people in China prefer to work for WMNCs to learn the newest Western management practices and benefit from international experience. But that preference is waning as domestic firms like Lenovo, Hua Wei, and Haier build strong brands and global operations based on Western management practices.

Second, work/life balance is a growing concern in China. A recent study conducted by *Fortune* magazine found that 73 percent of the Chinese managers interviewed experience "obvious and extreme" stress, and 55 percent believe that stress interferes with their effectiveness at work ("China's Increasingly," 2007). In another study, Towers Perrin (2008) found that work-life balance was one of the top ten attraction drivers in China (Towers Perrin, 2006). While this concern about work-life balance creates another challenge for HR professionals, those who address it successfully will have a competitive edge. Nokia believes that working from home, flexible time, and well-being services, such as stress management workshops, help organizations attract and retain people (Bell, 2005). Similarly, workplace flexibility at IBM China motivates people to stay.

Third, as research and development operations ramp up, HR managers must develop ways to recruit, retain, develop, and motivate the science and technology people they need. Experts believe that these people need project management, teamwork, and English-language skills, and they must learn the value of intellectual property and the importance of protecting it for the company. They also need to build an understanding of the market and the business sense necessary for successful innovation (von Zedtwitz, Ikeda, Li, Carpenter, & Hämäläinen, 2007).

It seems that the HR professional's work is never done.

References

American Chambers of Commerce Beijing & Shanghai. (2005). *2005 business climate survey.* Shanghai, China: American Chamber of Commerce Shanghai.

Bacani, C., & Sima, K. P. (2006). *The great buy-out: M&A in China.* Hong Kong: Economist Intelligence Unit.

Bannister, J., & Learmond, D. (2007). *Bridging China's talent gap.* New York: Conference Board.

Baruch, Y., Wheeler, K., & Zhao, X. (2004). Performance related pay in Chinese professional sports. *International Journal of Human Resource Management, 15*(1), 245–259.

Bell, A. (2005). *Redefining the employee value proposition: New developments in Asia Pacific.* New York: Conference Board.

Bell, A. (2006). *Leadership development in Asia Pacific: Identifying and developing leaders for growth.* New York: Conference Board.

Black, J., Mendenhall, M., & Oddou, G. (1991). Toward a comprehensive model of international adjustment: An integration of multiple theoretical perspectives. *Academy of Management Review, 16*(2), 291–317.

Blackwell. (1999). *Cultural revolution (1966–76).* Retrieved July 17, 2007, from http://www.blackwellreference.com/subscriber/tocnode?id=g9780631209379_chunk_g97806312093794_ss1-36.

China's increasingly stressed-out execs. (2007, February 5). *Fortune,* 16.

Comtex News Network. (2007, April 19). *IBM invests half of spending on China in Shenzhen.* Retrieved July 17, 2007, from LexisNexis by Comtex News Network.

Dessler, G. (2006). Expanding into China? What foreign employers should know about human resource management in China today. *S.A.M. Advanced Management Journal, 71*(4), 11–25.

Economist Intelligence Unit. (2006, August). In E. Cheng (Ed.), *China hand: The complete guide to doing business in China.* Hong Kong: Author.

Fallon, M. (2005/2006). Maximizing rotational assignments in Asia Pacific. *China Staff, 12*(1), 1–3.

Fernandez, J. A., & Underwood, L. (2006). *China CEO: Voices of experience from 20 international business leaders.* Hoboken, NJ: Wiley.

Foreign investors select China as R&D base. (2006). *China Staff, 12*(2), 39.

Gabrenya, W., & Hwang, K. (1996). Chinese social interaction: Harmony and hierarchy on the good earth. In M. H. Bond (Ed.), *Handbook of Chinese psychology* (pp. 309–321). New York: Oxford University Press.

Gao, G., Ting-Toomey, S., & Gudykunst, W. (1996). Chinese communication processes. In M. H. Bond (Ed.), *Handbook of Chinese psychology* (pp. 281–293). New York: Oxford University Press.

Gross, A., & Connor, A. (2007). *China recruiting and retention issues.* SHRM Global Forum.

Hewitt Associates LLC. (2005, September 27). *Salary and turnover rates continue to rise* [press release]. Retrieved July 14, 2007, from http://www.hewittassociates.com/Intl/AP/en-AS/AboutHewitt/Newsroom/PressReleases/2005/11–23–05_malaysia.aspx.

Hofstede, G. (2003). *Culture's consequences: Comparing values, behaviors, institutions and organizations across nations* (2nd ed.). Thousand Oaks, CA: Sage.

Hulme, V. (2006). What distinguishes the best from the rest. *China Business Review, 33*(2), 22.

IBM asks recruiters for refund. (2006). *China Staff, 12*(8), 59.

Javidan, M., Dorfman, P., de Luque, M., & House, R. (2006). In the eye of the beholder: Cross cultural lessons in leadership from project GLOBE. *Academy of Management Perspectives, 20*(1), 67–90.

Kramer, R. J. (2007). *Becoming skilled at painting with two brushes: Asian and Western approaches to international leadership development.* New York: Conference Board.

Law, A. (2006). High-flying dragons in China. *T&D, 60,* 10.

Law, K., Wong, C., & Wang, K. (2004). An empirical test of the model on managing the localization of human resources in the People's Republic of China. *International Journal of Human Resource Management, 15*(4–5), 635–648.

Liu, J. (2007, July 26), Baidu and Google at loggerheads in China. *International Herald Tribune,* 16.

Lui, C. (2006). L'Oreal's "Brandstorming" unearths diamonds in the rough. *China Staff, 12*(5), 8–10.

Manpower China. (2006). *The China talent paradox: A Manpower China white paper.* Retrieved July 6, 2007, from http://www.manpower.co.uk/news/main_China_Making_your_business_work.asp.

McKinsey Global Institute. (2005). *The emerging global labor market.* Retrieved August 7, 2007, from www.McKinsey.com/mgi/publications/emerginggloballabormarket database.

Performance management and appraisal—China's first-tier cities. (2002). *China Staff, 40*(1), 40.

Phillips, J. (1998). Effects of realistic job previews on multiple organizational outcomes: A meta-analysis. *Academy of Management Journal, 41*(6), 673–691.

Rynes, S. L. (1991). Recruitment, job choice, and post-hire consequences. In M. D. Dunnette & L. M. Hough (Eds.), *Handbook of industrial and organizational psychology* (pp. 399–444). Palo Alto, CA: Consulting Psychologists Press.

Staff turnover hinders foreign banks in China. (2007, May 12). *International Herald Tribune,* 15.

Tam, T. (2001). Unsung heroes: Recognizing China's HR champions. *China Staff, 11*(2), 37.

Towers Perrin. (2006). *China global workforce study.* Retrieved July 24, 2007, from http://www.towersperrin.com/tp/jsp/hrservices_web-cache_html.jsp?webc=HRS/USA/2006/200605/GWS_china.htm.

U.S. China Business Council. (2007). *Best practices: Human resources: Strategies for recruitment, retention and compensation.* Retrieved July 17, 2007, from http://www.USChina.org/info/chops/2006/HR-best-practices.html.

von Zedtwitz, M., Ikeda, T., Li, G., Carpenter, R., & Hämäläinen, S. (2007). Managing foreign R&D in China. *Research Technology Management, 50*(3), 19–37.

Watson Wyatt Worldwide. (2006). *Work greater China: Commitment and beyond: Employee attitudes and commitment drivers in China, Hong Kong and Taiwan.* Arlington, VA: Watson Wyatt Worldwide.

Weldon, E. (2005). *Desire for development among Chinese managers.* Unpublished manuscript.

World Encyclopedia. (2005). Cultural revolution. *World Encyclopedia.* Retrieved July 17, 2007, from http://www.oxfordreference.com/views/ENTRY.html?subview=Main&entry=t142.e2998.

Xu, C. Y., & Cheung, E.K.C. (2006). DTZ's company alumni: Managerial flair and HR innovation exemplified. *China Staff, 12*(8), 2–4.

Ye, M. (2006). Coping with the "millennials." *China Staff, 12*(7), 19–21.

Zhou, Y., Lu, L., & Jiang, B. (2005). Study on staff management practice of multinational company affiliates in China. *Management Decision, 43*(4), 516–522.

Zhu, C. J. (2005). *Human resource management in China: Past, current and future HR practices in the industrial sector.* London: Routledge Curzon.

Part Four

Different
Perspectives

CHAPTER 15

TAKE THE PEPSI CHALLENGE

Talent Development at PepsiCo

Allan H. Church, Janine Waclawski

PepsiCo is a world leader in convenient snacks, food, and beverages. Founded in 1965 with the merger of Pepsi-Cola and Frito-Lay, the organization has delivered significant and consistent business growth over the past 40 years. In 2007, the organization posted a 12 percent growth in net revenues of $39 billion, with 18 megabrands that generated more than $1 billion each in annual retail sales. Some of these were Pepsi-Cola, Mountain Dew, Lay's potato chips, Doritos, Quaker Oats, Gatorade, Aquafina, Tropicana, and Walkers crisps. PepsiCo's iconic brands are available in nearly 200 countries and generate sales at the retail level of more than $98 billion.

If you had to summarize PepsiCo in a single word, it would be *growth.* It is the very first component of PepsiCo's corporate values statement ("Our commitment to deliver sustained growth, through empowered people, acting with responsibility and trust"), and is the core of the business strategy: "Performance with Purpose." Given this emphasis, it should come as no surprise that the growth and development of our people and our leaders represents a critical component to our success. Whether you are talking about PepsiCo's muscle-building framework of the 1980s (Pearson, 1986), leaders developing leaders in the 1990s (Tichy & DeRose, 1996), or more recently our dual-rating performance management process (Desrosiers & Church, 2007), PepsiCo is known for being an "academy" company (known for producing leaders that go on to successful careers in other companies) when it comes to talent development. In fact, many former PepsiCo leaders are now in leadership positions at other Fortune 500 companies, including seven CEO positions (Jones, 2008). Some might suggest that PepsiCo has been too successful in developing leaders for other firms. Nevertheless, it is clear that talent management and development are central to our growth agenda. In fact, the "Performance with Purpose" business strategy set by our CEO Indra Nooyi has talent sustainability as one of its three primary components. Talent sustainability is about having the right people, in the right place, at the right time, doing the right work, the right way.

With over 185,000 employees worldwide, however, providing tools, processes, and frameworks that support and sustain employee growth and development across both the enterprise and local levels is no simple task. Unless there is an extremely centralized organizational structure with a heavily staffed function in the corporate center, it is very difficult to manage talent across the organization. With more decentralized or matrixed organizational designs, such as PepsiCo's, there is a need to drive philosophical alignment, consistency of application, and a common set of tools and language for developing employees. In effect, the organization needs to ensure that talent management principles and capabilities are embedded in the culture itself.

This case study describes how talent management has been operationalized across PepsiCo over the past several years. This includes a review of our two primary conceptual models and how they are used to support internal development. Then we explore several trends and observations regarding talent management practices that have evolved both internally at PepsiCo and externally during this same period. Finally, we share some personal lessons learned. Throughout the chapter, we apply both an industrial-organizational psychology (I-O) specialist perspective and a human resource (HR) generalist perspective to our comments and observations.

Talent Management at PepsiCo

In our experience, *talent management* as a term or a construct can mean different things to different people. Some practitioners define talent management at its broadest application, encompassing virtually all aspects of employee development (including training, leadership development, 360-degree feedback, performance management, and executive coaching), while others define it more narrowly to just those interventions and actions that concern assessment, staffing, and succession planning. Whatever the definition, it is important to have a common philosophy and framework within a given organization in order to ensure consistent practices, systems, and decision criteria. PepsiCo approaches talent management from within the context of our talent sustainability framework. Talent sustainability is broader than talent management, although other practitioners might use a wider definition. The PepsiCo framework has four distinct planks:

1. *Talent acquisition:* Finding the right talent when needed and delivering a consistent candidate experience across the attraction, recruitment, hiring, and onboarding process
2. *Talent management and development:* Building bench strength for key leadership positions and delivering talent development opportunities and capability for employees
3. *PepsiCo University:* Developing a broadly accessible learning environment and course curriculum in support of global capability and employee learning
4. *Inclusive culture:* Shaping the PepsiCo culture and reinforcing the behaviors required to support the talent of the present and the future that reflects multicultural, multigenerational, and global needs

For this chapter, we focus on one element of the PepsiCo talent sustainability framework: talent management and development. Talent management and development relates to how PepsiCo conceptualizes bench building and developing broad-based talent capability (#2 above) versus the acquisition, training, and development of leadership, or cultural components (#s 1, 3, and 4 above), all of which are equally important but not our focus here. Although the talent sustainability framework was introduced relatively recently, in 2007, this approach to talent management itself has been in place both informally (in the fabric of our culture) and formally (through tools, training, and our people planning process) for many years. Although the templates and the language may have evolved over time to reflect current strategic priorities, the fundamentals of how we think about development remain steady. Essentially PepsiCo has a two-pronged approach to talent management and development. First is a widely disseminated conceptual model that is used for broad–based employee development (talent management for the masses). Second is a related but different model for more targeted succession planning processes.

Career Growth Model

The PepsiCo career growth model (CGM) is a foundational model that describes how we approach building a career at PepsiCo (Figure 15.1). It was developed in 2002, partly in response to organizational changes at the time, including the spin-off of Tricon (now Yum! Brands), the spin-off and initial public offering (IPO) of the Pepsi bottling system (the people who actually produce and distribute certain products), and the acquisition and integration of the Tropicana and Quaker organizations. In short, the model was created to articulate to employees (1) what factors leaders and HR consider when making internal

Figure 15.1. PepsiCo Career Growth Model

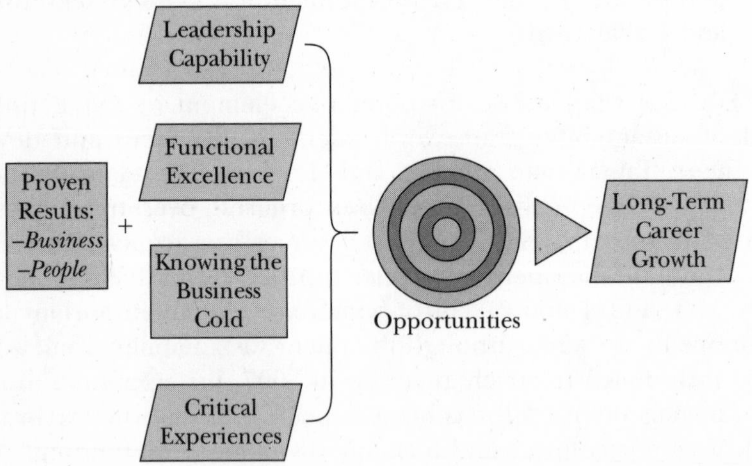

selection decisions, and (2) how employees should plan for their individual development with their managers and on their own. It reflects our fundamental cultural belief that all PepsiCo employees should have access to development.

The Career Growth Model (CGM) in Figure 15.1 describes five critical components for developing and managing talent broadly across the organization:

1. *Proven results* (both delivering business results and people results, which are weighted equally) are required to get you "in the game." Results are measured by our performance management process and reinforce the cultural emphasis on growth mentioned earlier. Business growth creates opportunities for individuals to grow as well.

2. *Leadership capability* reflects the competencies and behaviors that employees are expected to demonstrate. These behaviors are tiered in nature (that is, there is a set of behaviors for all employees that reflect PepsiCo Values, a set for midlevel leaders, and a set specifically tailored to senior leaders) and are measured through our 360-degree feedback process. We expect these competencies to increase in importance as individuals advance in their careers, and the organization places greater significance on the 360-degree results when considering senior leaders for new opportunities.

3. *Functional excellence* describes the basic building blocks of knowledge for any given role. These are supported through various functional competency models and training curriculum, for example, in sales, marketing, and finance. The key development message to employees is that we expect functional knowledge to be more of a focus for development (for example through job rotations or new assignments) earlier in one's career. As employees progress over time, leadership skills become more important to their success. This shift is important because it is one of the ways we bridge the gap from divisional capability and talent ownership (largely functional) to more senior-level talent management practices, such as using 360-degree results to inform decisions made during People Planning (that is, the PepsiCo talent review process.

4. *Knowing the business cold* means having a deep understanding of the various PepsiCo business models and go-to-market capabilities. Although some might question whether this category is truly needed (since most organizations naturally would expect their employees to learn their business), given PepsiCo's distinctly different divisions, product lines, and operating models, it has proven extremely useful to have this element codified in the model, and has been used at various levels of decision making. For example, the move to retain Mike White, CEO of PepsiCo International, when Indra Nooyi became chairman and CEO was all about retaining his deep knowledge of the business (Morris, 2008).

5. *Critical experiences* is the last component of the CGM. Based on the work of McCall (1998) and others over the years (Lombardo & Eichinger, 1989, 2002; McCall, Lombardo, & Morrison, 1998), PepsiCo believes strongly that providing individuals with the right set of experiences is one of the most effective ways of developing talent. Although there are many good generic lists of experiences available in the talent management literature (Lombardo & Eichinger, 2002, is one of them), we created a unique set of critical experiences for PepsiCo to allow individuals to map their prior experiences and to provide a common language around those experiences needed to attain higher leadership roles. For example, to be a well-rounded and fungible leader you need to have had experience in all three product categories (beverages, snacks, and foods) and understand how all three of our key go-to-market systems (franchise, warehouse, and direct store distribution) operate.

Finally, opportunities in the model are reflected as a target, suggesting that not everyone can reach the center of the target with any given assignment. It is important for people to understand that life and organizations are always shifting and changing, and that the dream job that an employee had been waiting for might be already filled by the time she becomes ready for it. The end result is long-term career growth, but it might not be exactly as planned. Talent management is a fluid process (yet a planful one when done well), but is far from being prescriptive, except in very specific functional tracks or industries.

Although the CGM is relatively straightforward in nature, its launch and subsequent institutionalization have proven to be quite successful over the past few years. It has become the unifying model for training, career development discussions, people planning, and functional career frameworks (Alziari, 2001; Church & Herena, 2003) and is now part of the formal lexicon. It is used both internally and externally for recruiting, and although it is not necessarily formulaic or prescriptive, it does in fact represent how PepsiCo leaders think through decisions on talent.

Talent Management Model

The second major development framework in use at PepsiCo is the talent management model (Oliver, Church, Lewis, & Desrosiers, in press). Introduced to the organization a number of years ago as well, it is also based on the importance of experiences following the work of McCall (1998) and Lombardo and Eichinger (1989, 2002). It is intended to define and communicate how we believe people are developed. This is typically used with a more segmented set of talent (such as the executive population, high potentials, and key feeder pools), often in conjunction with targeted leadership development programs and our people planning process. The talent management model (see Figure 15.2) outlines three phases:

1. *Identify*: The process by which individuals are identified as having additional potential to take on more senior roles in the organization. Getting this right (that is, the assessment of

Figure 15.2. Talent Management Model

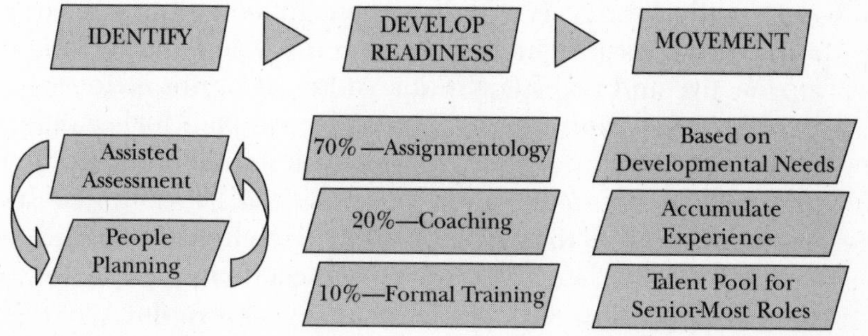

potential) is one of the biggest challenges in talent management (see Chapter 5 by Rob Silzer and Allan H. Church). At PepsiCo, this is typically done through the people planning process where talent is systematically reviewed and calibrated at successive levels in the organization, all the way up to final reviews with the CEO.

2. *Develop readiness*: This is based on the understanding that 70 percent of development occurs on the job or in the current role; 20 percent comes from coaching, feedback, and mentoring; and 10 percent is derived from formal training. Whether formally articulated (as it has been the past five years) or not, this has clearly been the operating principle at PepsiCo since the 1980s when Eichinger was involved in the talent function. PepsiCo currently uses this framework (as do many other organizations, as several recent Society for Industrial-Organizational Psychology conference sessions have noted) for development planning of key talent. The best approach here has proven to be an integrated one. For example, one of our very successful leadership development programs has effectively integrated formal training for our senior leaders with 360-degree feedback and results from the Hogan Assessment Suite (a collection of personality measures). Following the program, attendees are given extended follow-up coaching assignments (often over six to nine months) with PepsiCo-certified external coaches. This combination of all three development methods results in extensive career development planning as a means for accelerating high potential leaders (Oliver et al., in press).

3. *Movement*: This phase of the model is easier said than accomplished. If finding or identifying high potentials is one of the most difficult aspects of talent management (and we would argue it is), actually moving them is the other, particularly in a proactive and planful manner. At PepsiCo, this is done during the game planning process, where we plan for successive moves, capture "domino" moves (roles that become open and now need to be filled because a high potential has been moved out to a new position), track open roles, and note other issues, such as people who need to move somewhere else because they are blocking a key developmental role.

The objective here is that over time and through successive movement of high-potential talent the process allows you to build a talent bench for the future.

A Primer on People Planning

The concepts of both the career growth model and the talent management model are brought to life through the people planning process. The effective use of these models hinges on several critical factors. First is the ability of the leaders and managers in the room (sometimes with the guidance of the HR professional) to consistently and accurately assess talent against a series of criteria. Second is the extent to which the people in the meeting truly know their employees: This includes knowing their career aspirations, prior performance history, mobility constraints, the experiences that have been gained (both at PepsiCo and prior to their joining the organization), and those experiences that are needed to reach a particular future role. Third is the extent to which talent movement (decisions about who is going into what jobs) is done in a way that optimizes two objectives: (1) the match between the individual and the next job that will best deliver the experiences the person wants and needs and (2) the match between the job and the capabilities it will deliver to that leader based on the strategic needs of the organization. Figure 15.3 provides a snapshot of how the people planning process typically works.

The process begins with a release to the organization of a template, tool kit, and key messages for that year's execution (for example, these messages might reflect a greater focus on international movement, innovation capability, diversity and inclusion, or why some aspect of the process has changed). Next, talent is classified according to our internal high-potential model (see Table 15.1) and reviewed by managers with their peers in calibration meetings.

The intent here is for multiple people to be able to contribute to a given "talent call" (their classification of an individual), not just a single individual manager, much in the same way that calibration meetings are used to determine performance ratings. During the meeting, each manager reviews their direct reports. They present their initial talent assessment, discuss the strengths

Figure 15.3. Sample People Planning Process

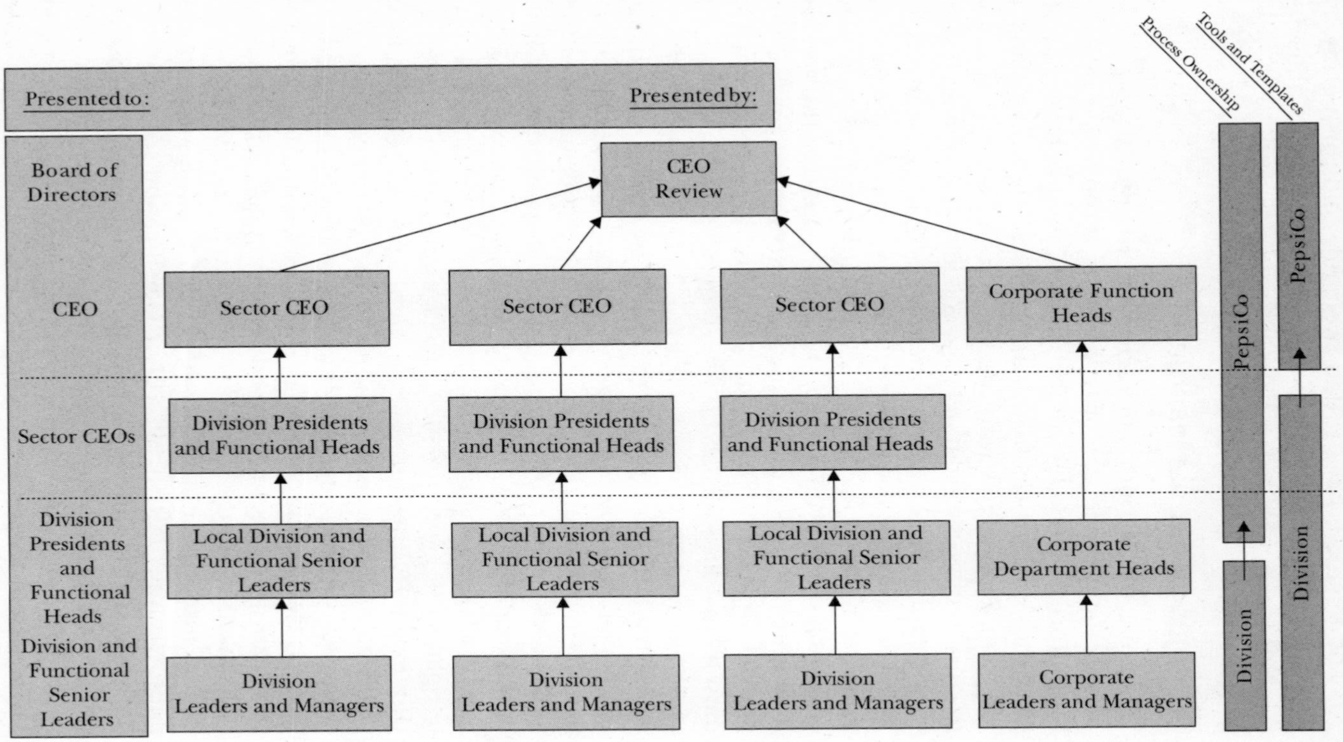

626

Table 15.1. Talent Call Model: Definitions

Talent Call	*Definition*
High potential	A highly valuable contributor with a great deal of stretch capability within the organization. Such individuals are typically promoted to higher levels beyond their current role, and a select few can be seen as leading the organization at the senior levels.
Key contributor	A valuable contributor to the organization with stretch capability. Such individuals may advance beyond their current role or can be considered for other roles at the same level. Capable of growing within the organization over time.
Critical professional	A highly valuable and experienced subject matter expert. Their career path has typically been in a specialized area or function, and they provide a critical role in leveraging their specialized skills. They are sought out by others, both inside and outside the organization, for their knowledge and advice.
Concern	Someone who meets one of several criteria requiring discussion—for example, performance issues, values issues, people management—or might be blocking key development roles needed for others.

and development opportunities of each individual, and talk about future roles, timing, and any concerns that might be present. Others in the room are invited to provide additional feedback, ask questions, and discuss future roles and opportunities. The outcome of the meeting is a set of aligned talent calls and potential plans for talent movement in the future.

These meetings continue at successively higher levels (that is an upward cascade from division leaders to division presidents), with the emphasis on higher and higher levels of talent being reviewed, until each organization and its key talent are eventually reviewed in-depth with the CEO. The information from this process then feeds into both the succession planning work for the future (including the board of directors review), as well Is the more immediate talent moves that need to be made. All in all it is an involved and comprehensive process and takes months to complete. Figure 15.4 provides a sample template page from the people planning process.

This tool is designed to provide all the information needed on a single individual to enable a comprehensive discussion during the talent review. It begins with some key information (for example, performance ratings, talent call, time in role) and then moves on to the key development question, the projected long-term role (how high up in the organization this individual can go), the next move and timing for that move, and the person responsible for ensuring action is taken. The bottom portion of the template focuses on experiences gained and needed, strengths and opportunities from a leadership perspective, and the key development actions for the individual over the next year. Essentially it combines an employee profile with a career planning tool.

Trends and Observations

Having worked in the area of talent management for a number of years and having served in roles as both designers and executors of these people processes, as well as having benchmarked with others externally, we have noticed some intriguing trends in this area over time. Some of these are unique to talent management, while others are perhaps simply a reflection of industrial-organizational psychology in this content area (one that has been given limited attention in the I-O psychology literature). We have highlighted a few of these below.

The Challenge of the Definition: What Is a High Potential?

Getting the talent call decision right and being able to differentiate the high-potential person from the average player is critical to successful talent management–related decision making. Although it is relatively easy to capture someone's history and

Figure 15.4. Sample People Planning Template Page

Name (PMP Ratings) • Title • Band • Time in Role • Talent Call • Mobility	Key Development Question	Target Long-Term Role (estimated timing)	Next Move (timing)	Person Accountable
• J. Pepsi (4/4) • Senior Manager Sales • Band 1 • 2 years • High Potential • No restrictions	• Demonstrate ability to add value to strategic agenda across broader range of customers • Be more open to others' ideas/perspectives and actively incorporate into win/win solutions	VP Sales (3–4 yrs)	Director Sales (Jan. 2009)	His Manager His HRD

Profile Summary

Critical Experiences	Senior Leadership Competencies
Gained	*Strengths*
• Developed high-growth market experience • Sales experience with Snacks and CSDs • Cross-functional experience in Operations	• Passionate sales leader, driven for results, good negotiator, strong motivator, great execution • Knowledge of carbonated soft drinks and operations
Gap	*Opportunities*
• Experience outside-of Plano • Foods • International	• Be more flexible, reflective when coping with pushback • Build new alliances outside of Plano • Work to better understand others' point-of-views • Continue to broaden perspective regarding PepsiCo overall

Key Dev. Actions

• Demonstrate ability to build new alliances, impact strategic direction, and influence alignment
• Deliver sales results for key customers
• Complete Hogan and 360 assessment/Read *Why CEOs Fail*
• Demonstrate ability to learn from and act on the feedback

Note: CSDs are carbonated soft drinks.

prior experiences, assessing the person's potential to perform in higher-level roles, and doing so with a high degree of precision, represents the talent management "holy grail" for many. This is in large part because there is no single or unifying definition of what exactly "potential" is or looks like. Multiple models and definitions exist in the field, largely driven by consulting firms, and most organizations have their own internal definition as well. This makes the identification process challenging because it is difficult to measure a construct when you cannot define it. This is also why organizations change their definitions every few years when a senior leader changes because much of the definition of potential is driven by the leader's own individual mental model.

Clearly there are many methods, models, and approaches available to practitioners (much of this book reviews these in detail) to help them identify and assess potential. What is interesting to us is the constant need, almost as if it is human nature, for leaders and managers to complain about the current approach, whatever it may be ("It is not precise enough," "It does not apply to my function," "I think it should be based on competencies") and want to try something new. It is also interesting to note that when the assessment data do not match the leader's own personal talent call decision, the discussion quickly turns to an opinion that "there must be something wrong with the tool." Clearly everybody thinks they are an expert at making talent-based assessments.

This is a common development in practice areas that are less well defined, particularly those where industrial-organizational psychology has not yet made a consistent impact. As external search firms (also known as headhunters) move to acquire their own high-potential assessment capability, and consulting firms continue to sell their own brand of assessment, the frequency with which organizations seem to be switching models and approaches seems to have increased over the past decade. While clearly some approaches may truly be more valid than others, we feel this need to constantly change the approach (presumably to win the war for talent) actually drives greater inconsistency in application overall. Every time a definition or model changes, there is a level of capability that must be developed in the organization before leaders and managers can take maximum advantage of the tools they are implementing. What many leaders fail to understand is that it takes time, practice using the tool or model, and enough data points to determine whether the approach is valid for a given organizational context. This is where I-O psychologists can help. Unfortunately they are often not the individuals in the talent management roles, although this is something that seems to be changing as well.

The Challenge of Metrics: What Metrics Should We Use for Talent Management?

Accountability in talent management is very important, but so is the adage that "what gets measured gets done." This is an age-old psychology issue, and one that has particular relevance for this area of practice. Although some would argue that HR metrics have been around for more than 30 years, determining the correct set of metrics for a given talent management system can be a challenge, and there really are no set standards in the industry yet. For example, some organizations, including PepsiCo, emphasize the notion of depth of the talent bench. The goal here is typically a bench "two or three deep"—that is, two or three potential successors for key leadership roles. This seems reasonable. Every leader would like to have at least two choices for successors.

The issue here is with the honest and accurate assessment of that depth. Typically it is determined by human judgment (usually by very senior leaders in an organization, if not by the CEO), as to whether certain individuals can effectively fill a given role if it were vacated. Sum up these judgments across key roles, and you have a metric. Of course, the efficacy of this decision is based on the ability of a senior leader to identify talent, which is in all likelihood a trait that is normally distributed. The other challenge here is that the bench assessment judgment made in the absence of a real selection decision to be made often differs significantly from reality when the time actually comes to make that move (that is, the actual selection decision regularly varies from the earlier judgments about people). We have found over the years that people can make bad assessment decisions in both directions. Sometimes they are too lenient and identify people as potential successors who would never actually be placed in that role. Other times they decide that an individual may not be bench talent for a key role, but when the time comes, the individual gets the job anyway for a variety of different reasons.

Another metric commonly used in organizations is the number of developmental moves that were made in a particular time period, whether within a specific business unit or perhaps across business units. We have used this measure internally as well. The issue with this metric is how to ensure that the moves were actually developmental in nature and that they will result in improved capability and stronger bench over time versus just a "shuffling of the deck chairs" or moving people across different roles for the sake of moving. This is why it is critical to understand the background and capabilities of the individual being moved and the characteristics of the role the person is going into well enough to ensure a truly developmental experience that will build bench for the long term. It is also important to ensure leaders are thinking about the long-term career path for their high-potential leaders so that when they need another experience, it can be well planned and executed. Sometimes this might even mean holding a key development role open for a period of time to ensure the right high-potential candidate gets identified or taking someone out of a role (who is blocking movement of others) in order to put in a high-potential person. The theme here is making bold moves to develop people. Unfortunately in practice, it is sometimes difficult to get leaders and managers to think beyond filling immediate open roles given the pressure of delivering immediate results.

Another type of metric is one that is meant to drive enterprise-wide accountability for movement. In this case, there is a shared goal among multiple leaders to move a certain percentage or number of individuals (usually high potentials, but in some cases, other talent pools might be considered) across borders, divisions, lines of business, or even countries. If implemented well with full accountability in place, this metric forces planned movement across the organization and should in theory help build bench. Similar to some of the other metrics, however, it does not address the quality of the move either—just the quantity. Even if all high potentials move into new roles every year, they still may not be gaining the right experiences to get them ready for more senior roles.

One final metric that we have seen employed in a number of organizations is a talent distribution model (for example, the percentage of high potentials often displayed by function, division, region, or country). Although this approach is helpful for developing a broad perspective of the talent available, unless all of the high potentials are equally fungible in nature, it says very little about their ability to reach certain critical key roles. Just because an organization has 15 percent high potentials in the finance function, for example, does not mean that all 15 percent have the same potential to become the CFO of the corporation (unless, of course, the definition of a high potential in finance includes that end-state goal as part of the criteria). In some organizations, we have even seen actual targets applied to talent distributions. This practice is dangerous because it can actually force leaders to make assessment decisions to meet the numbers.

You get what you measure. Determining the correct success metrics for a given talent management process is a significant challenge today, and there are no easy answers. It would be interesting to see I-O psychologists and other researchers address this issue in the future.

The Challenge of Ensuring Rigor: How Do We Get Leaders to Actually Execute on Plans?

All the best talent management tools, templates, assessment models, and career plans in the world are only as effective as the people executing them. You can spend months creating the most well-constructed succession plan, only to have the senior leadership refuse to pull the trigger on a key move. Sometimes this can be remedied (perhaps by a strategic outside hire or a replacement move), but in other cases, the carefully crafted plan may come to a full halt. This is where the role of the HR generalist or chief Human Resource officer (when dealing with C-suite-level moves) is critical. If HR is going to be a truly strategic business partner (Ulrich, 1997), guiding line leaders through an effective talent management process is critical for success. In addition, this is why having talent management metrics in place is critical, since many leaders tend to hoard their own high-potential talent, often at the expense of the enterprise (Capelli, 2008). It is also why the senior leaders of an organization need to take the process seriously. If everyone feels the process is just an exercise in order to say that you have a "plan," and it is never followed, the process is not doing the organization any good and it needs to be revisited.

The Challenge of a Changing Workforce: How Do Talent Management Systems Need to Change to Meet the Next Generation's Needs?

Much has been written about the changing nature of the workforce including the aging of the boomers, the rise of the relatively smaller Generation X into more senior roles, and the entrance of millennials (or generation "Y"), with potentially a totally different set of values and expectations (Benko & Weisberg, 2007; Dychtwald, Erickson, & Morison, 2006; Karoly & Panis, 2004; Smith & Clurman, 1997; Zemke, Raines, & Filipczak, 2000). Over the past several years, we have seen these changes impact both business and HR strategies in other organizations, and we are no exception. In fact, PepsiCo's *performance with purpose* business strategy, introduced in 2007, is an example of looking ahead and reflecting the corporate social responsibility–related values of future talent rather than looking behind (Bingham & Galagan, 2008; Morris, 2008).

For the talent management arena, however, these changes are likely to drive the need for a number of changes in how organizations operate. First, organizations will need to provide greater transparency in everything they do, including career paths, performance expectations, and even the sharing of talent calls with employees (telling people if they have been identified as a high potential or not). Interestingly, current practice in organizations is split in this regard. Some organizations believe in telling employees exactly where they stand, while others prefer to keep that information closely guarded for fear of what might happen: high potentials feeling entitled and non-high potentials leaving the company. Millennials, however, are far less accepting of not knowing where they stand and will demand the feedback.

Second, organizations will need to find ways to be more flexible in their work arrangements and how work gets done. For example, can a person truly work remotely with a team in another country and gain most of the experiences of an international assignment? Can organizations find new ways to leverage web technologies such as Facebook or MySpace to drive productivity? Millennials are focused on social networking, and organizations will need to adjust to this in the future.

Related to this issue is the fact that some leaders believe that if you are not mobile (that is, willing to relocate anywhere in the world for another) then you cannot be a high potential. That said, employees are less willing to move for the company than they were 30 years ago. As mobility becomes an increasing concern for many organizations, how do organizations address development of potential among people who are not open to moving? Given that we now have four generations in the workforce, organizations will also need to think more broadly in the future about life stages such as having children, dealing with aging parents, responding to illness, and going on extended leave for personal development and how these interact with career progressions. Finally, given the erosion of the psychological contract that started in the 1980s, organizations will need to be more accepting of job-hopping behavior, particularly among Generation "X" and "Y," with the implication that knowledge management becomes even more critical than it is today. Organizations have been able to ignore many of these issues in the past, but as the workforce shifts in composition, these trends will continue to have an impact on talent management practices as we go forward.

Lessons Learned

Aside from trends and observations, we can also clearly point to some important lessons learned from working in the talent management arena. Some of these are related to the issues we have already identified, while others reflect completely different aspects to consider.

1. Having clear lines of ownership in any talent management process is critical. It is a classic issue of role clarity. As noted at the opening of the chapter, ownership levels will likely vary by the structure (and degree of centralization versus decentralization) of the talent management function in a given organization.

Most organizations with which we have shared best practices have attempted to delineate clear lines of talent ownership, usually based on level in the organizational hierarchy. At PepsiCo, we have taken an approach that the top several hundred roles and the talent in them are owned by the enterprise, while divisions handle the significantly larger percentage of others, sometimes with support from the corporate center but not always; we also have centers of excellence in divisions that lead cross-divisional talent-sharing efforts. Having these roles and lines of account-ability clearly defined helps immensely in making talent deci-sions and executing these types of processes.

2. Do not assume that changing the definition of a high poten-tial in a tool will result in immediately enhanced talent calls. Whether it is the notion of adding new behavioral indicators, emotional intelligence, learning ability, cultural competence, leadership transition capability, or simply a measure of ambition to a talent differentiation model, the mere fact of incorporat-ing such changes will not automatically improve the talent data. Many leaders and managers believe in their own personal mod-els, and it takes time and practice with new constructs to truly drive toward a common language and a common set of high-potential selection criteria. For example, we recently moved from a typical hierarchical and level-based approach to iden-tifying future leaders (for example, "able to move two levels in an accelerated time period") to a more behaviorally based one ("seeks out opportunities for learning and building self-awareness and regularly works at acquiring new skills and abilities"). However, even after rolling out training materials and supporting tools, and a practice session with key leaders, it is still challenging for people to release their preexisting model of a high potential. Perhaps that is why it is so difficult to define what a high potential looks like: everyone has a personal perspective on what it takes based on their own experience.

3. Related to this point is that not every leader or manager is equally gifted in the ability to think strategically about the future capability needs of the organization and the career trajectories of their high potentials. Identifying a general high-potential indi-vidual is one thing, but identifying the potential needed for which specific long-term role is another thing altogether. Should this

high-energy M.B.A. be tracked toward a chief marketing officer role or a general management role, or both? We have found that this "future back" capability (that is thinking about the future and working backwards to current talent) is not easily or quickly developed. There is also a need to ensure that development plans have enough flexibility in them and that they will result in enough functional breadth in the high potential so that her career path is not narrowly targeted, and thereby potentially limited, if conditions or capability requirements in the future change dramatically.

4. While some people are very adept at spotting potential based on whatever definition they are using, others get caught in what we call the *performance-potential paradox*. This has been driven in part over the years by the use of grids that chart out performance versus potential. Most organizations use some form of "nine box" model, and consulting firms often promote these as well. Although these make sense conceptually, in practice we have found that when leaders are pressed to assess potential for future roles, they invariably use the current performance—often not even the complete past record of performance, which over time would be a somewhat better indicator—as the proxy. As a result of this practice, you often get linear progressions in performance by potential grids, so the effort becomes meaningless. We have also seen a number of instances where a high potential in a challenging business situation becomes a problem (versus perhaps moving them to another role or providing additional resources or coaching support to help them through the situation). We affectionately call this the "Hipo Alpo" effect (that is, one month the individual is identified as a high potential and the next month that individual is identified as a concern). In fact, this is common in many organizations. As HR generalists and talent management professionals, we must help leaders and managers avoid making these mistakes in judgment as we support the talent management process. In addition, given the tendency to base potential on current performance, from our perspective it is better to keep the formal performance management process and the talent management and future potential assessment cycles separate during the year. Although it may place more burden on the line clients to execute two processes instead of one, doing so increases the likelihood that these issues will not occur.

5. Another lesson learned is that forced ranking (similar to what is used in some organizations as part of their performance management process) should not be formally applied to talent management. Although the comparison of talent through what is known as a *slating process* (identifying people for specific future roles) makes complete sense (assuming you have the appropriate information regarding the knowledge, skills, and abilities of a given set of candidates), applying a fixed percentage-based distribution to a talent identification process can be misleading and potentially damaging. The proportion of talent in any given function, division, level, or organization will vary based on a host of factors, and although it might seem appealing to attempt to reach a required goal of 10, 15, or even 25 percent of high potentials, talent should be assessed independently, not based on a relative distribution. Otherwise you will not end up with a full understanding of the talent at hand.

6. Our final learning in this area is less about talent management and more about how these processes, particularly the definition of a high potential, can either support or conflict with organizational values or culture. It is important to remember that the people hired and promoted will ultimately shape the way things are experienced in an organization. If a specific profile is too rigidly applied (that is, to all roles and all levels in a given system), it can result in unintended consequences over time to the culture. Consider an example. As noted earlier, one of the four planks of PepsiCo's Talent sustainability strategy is about having an inclusive culture—one where people with different styles and approaches feel that they can bring their whole selves to work. This is an admirable goal. However, if care is not taken, applying a very specific and prescriptive approach to identifying high potentials can fly in the face of these cultural goals and innovation. For example, if the identification profile for a high potential includes being highly extraverted, the organization is likely to make talent decisions related to hiring, promotions, and special assignments on certain groups that are counter to the goal of being inclusive. Whether a high-potential profile is personality based, values based, or behaviorally based (or all of the above), it is not inclusive by definition. The answer we have found is somewhere in the middle. Talent management systems and processes need

to be flexible enough to determine which elements are necessary for cultural fit (at a broad level) and which are necessary for key strategic roles (that are the focus of Human Resource planning, such as CEO, CFO, Chief Marketing Officer and others). It is also equally important to determine where individual differences in style and approach should not be taken into account in the talent management process. In short, despite what many practitioners and consultants would tell you say, a "one size fits all"—high potential is probably not the best model in this context.

Conclusion

Talent management and development is a complex process that requires a number of conditions to ensure success. As described in this case, and as applied at PepsiCo, it is critical to have a common set of tools and processes that drive consistency in language and execution. In addition, the role of the HR generalist in this process in ensuring flawless execution and process integrity cannot be ignored. Although we do not have the definitive answer and continue to make changes and tweaks to our own processes and definitions, it is important to remember that this is a journey. Even as we change and evolve to meet the current requirements, talent management needs for future generations are right around the corner.

References

Alziari, L. (2001, December 17). One-on-one with Lucien Alziari. Building leadership innovation at PepsiCo: Leadership from Heidrick & Struggles [Special section]. *BusinessWeek*.

Benko, C., & Weisberg, A. (2007). *Mass career customization: Aligning the workplace with today's nontraditional workforce*. Boston: Harvard Business School Press.

Bingham, T., & Galagan, P. (2008, June). Doing good while doing well. *Training and Development*, 32–34.

Capelli, P. (2008). *Talent on demand: Managing talent in an age of uncertainty*. Boston: Harvard Business School Press.

Church, A. H., & Herena, M. R. (2003). The PepsiCo HR career framework: A data-driven approach to career development. *Organization Development Practitioner, 35*(4), 27–33.

Desrosiers, E. I., & Church, A. H. (2007, April 27). *PepsiCo's performance management process: Driving for results without running people over along the way.* Presentation delivered at the 22nd Annual Meeting of the Society for Industrial and Organizational Psychology, New York.

Dychtwald, K., Erickson, T. J., & Morison, R. (2006). *Workforce crisis: How to beat the coming shortage of skills and talent.* Boston: Harvard Business School Press.

Jones, D. (2008, January 9). Some firms' fertile soil grows crop of future CEOs. January 9, 2008. Retrieved September 9, 2008, from http://www.usatoday.com/money/companies/management/2008-01-08-ceo-companies_N.htm.

Karoly, L. A., & Panis, C.W.A. (2004). *The 21st century at work: Forces shaping the future workforce and workplace in the United States.* Santa Monica, CA: Rand Corporation.

Lombardo, M. M., & Eichinger, R. W. (2002). *The leadership machine.* Minneapolis, MN: Lominger.

Lombardo, M. M., & Eichinger, R. W. (1989). *Eighty-eight assignments for development in place: Enhancing the developmental challenge of existing jobs.* Greensboro, NC: Center for Creative Leadership.

McCall, M. W., Jr. (1998). *High flyers: Developing the next generation of leaders.* Boston: Harvard Business School Press.

McCall, M. W., Lombardo, M. M., & Morrison A. M. (1998). *The lessons of experience: How successful executives develop on the job.* Lanham, MD: Lexington Books.

Morris, B. (2008, March 3). The Pepsi challenge: Can this snack and soda giant go healthy? *Fortune,* 55–66.

Oliver, D. H., Church, A. H., Lewis, R., & Desrosiers, E. I.(In press). An integrated framework for assessing, coaching and developing global leaders. In *Advances in Global Leadership,* in press, Emerald Publishing.

Pearson, A. E. (1987, July-August). Muscle-build the organization. *Harvard Business Review,* 49–55.

Smith, J. W., & Clurman, A. (1997). *Rocking the ages: The Yankelovich report on generational marketing.* New York: HarperBusiness.

Tichy, N. M., & DeRose, C. (1996, May). The Pepsi challenge: Building a leader-driven organization. *Training and Development, 50*(5), 58–66.

Ulrich, D. (1997). *Human resource champions: The next agenda for adding value and delivering results.* Boston: Harvard Business School Press.

Zemke, R., Raines, C., & Filipczak, B. (2000). *Generations at work: Managing the clash of veterans, boomers, Xers, and Nexters in your workplace.* New York: AMACOM.

CHAPTER 16

INTEGRATED TALENT MANAGEMENT AT MICROSOFT

Paul R. Yost

Microsoft as a Business

Microsoft has experienced tremendous growth and change in the past 30 years. In 2007, revenue was over $50 billion, with the number of employees reaching almost 80,000. From the beginning, the company has made the recruitment, hiring, and development of top talent a high priority. The company has continued to be an employer of choice and is consistently ranked as one of the best places to work. One of the critical questions facing the company today is: Is what happened organically in the 1980s and 1990s sustainable as the company continues to grow?

Microsoft continues to compete in increasingly complex and competitive business markets, requiring multiple business models (for example, moving from product-focused business models to ones that focus on selling products plus services, the growth of online advertising markets, and the emergence of developing economies as key market segments). The maturing of some products means the company must move from operating solely as a start-up business to a business that can support products and services at various stages of market maturity. The value proposition to employees continues to evolve from the early days where employees joined a very small team to change the world, to the pre-dot-com days when people could work intensely for a few years and retire on their stock options, to today, when employees are focused on changing the world while maintaining a strong work/life balance.

Microsoft's culture provides a strong foundation to build a talent management system. The company has always taken talent seriously, and in recent years, it has begun to take talent management seriously. Microsoft has a smart, engaged workforce; strong functional leaders; a "get it done" attitude; and a pride in being a culture of meritocracy that places a premium on innovation and technology. However, with continued growth, new talent management challenges have emerged and include building strong, broad business leaders, moving employees from a focus on features and technology to solutions and services, managing a geographically dispersed workforce, and moving from an individual focus to collaboration in a complex and dynamic environment.

Talent Management at Microsoft

As noted throughout this book, talent management should always be considered in the context of the business strategy. The business strategy will determine the talent management processes that are most important, the key talent pools, and even the overall investment that is focused on talent management relative to other factors in the organization. At Microsoft, the people have been and will continue to be a strategic differentiator for the company, taking ideas and turning them into customer-focused solutions that help transform businesses and the way consumers interact with technology. In information technology, every employee counts. A newly hired software developer can be the person who sees the next big thing. A new sales manager can see the opportunities in emerging markets. In a highly dynamic environment, people are the only ones who can provide the foresight and agility to respond to, and even create, new market opportunities.

For these reasons, Microsoft has always invested resources and considerable time in talent management—from hiring practices, to career development, to the performance management system. Several key principles define Microsoft's approach to talent management:

- A systems approach to talent management
- Rigorous development and performance systems for everyone
- Frequent feedback and people reviews
- Living (not static) performance goals

This list is by no means comprehensive, but it highlights some of the key themes covered in this chapter. Three talent management systems will be discussed in more depth to illustrate some of the underlying principles that define Microsoft's approach to talent management:

- *Career models at Microsoft:* Career models, and the accompanying online talent management system, CareerCompass, serve as the underlying framework that employees at all levels across the company use to assess themselves and to receive feedback from their managers on the competencies, experiences, and results that are defined for each job level.
- *Performance management:* The performance management system is taken very seriously at Microsoft and is used to align employee goals with organizational strategy and to assess every employee at the end of the year on current performance and anticipated future contribution.
- *Leadership assessment, movement, and development:* The selection, assessment, and development of leaders in the company are considered dynamic processes that assume ongoing change in both organizational goals and individual capabilities.

Three underlying themes will be highlighted here: (1) the importance of linking talent management to the business strategy, (2) the importance of an integrated talent management system, and (3) how Microsoft has been able to leverage experience-based development throughout the system.

CareerCompass: Career Models at Microsoft

Over the past three years, Microsoft has built a talent management framework and online system to support talent management and career development across the company. The framework includes career models for 15 professions, covering all positions in the company. Within each profession, the critical competencies, experiences, and career stage results are defined. Leaders are also assessed against ten success inhibitors (derailers). The career models were built in partnership with leadership teams in each of the professions to identify the characteristics that differentiate the best from average employees based on the results they deliver. Although many companies have created similar systems using competency models as their framework, the Microsoft system differs in the fact that early on, it was decided that adding experiences and behavioral results would move conversations beyond just focusing on leadership characteristics to also focus on how employees develop (key experiences) and what the outcomes should be (career stage results). See Table 16.1 for examples of each of these dimensions.

Competencies include both behaviors and attitudes and are defined across four levels. One interesting distinction is that Microsoft has simply numbered the competency levels instead of using labels (such as "needs improvement" to "very strong") or linking them to management levels. In this way, the competency level can be determined for each role in the company independent of the official job title. This flexibility is important in a highly dynamic company. For example, it would not be unusual for a relatively junior leader of a small start-up project to need relatively advanced marketing skills. Numbered scales also allow for the possibility that some competencies, such as interpersonal awareness, should be high for all employees, regardless of their job level. In contrast, other competencies, such as organization agility, might be lower for lower-level leaders and only reach the highest level when they face more complex organizational challenges. Numbered scales are catalysts for employees and managers to discuss the competency proficiency levels required in a specific role, depending on where it is located in the company.

In the experience section of the framework, the key experiences for each profession are listed; for example, for leaders, the key experiences might include start-up business experience; sales, service, or marketing experience; and turnaround business experience, among others. Employees assess themselves against the experiences on up to nine jobs that they have held in the past using a four-point scale: not applicable, limited, moderate,

Table 16.1. Talent Management Framework at Microsoft

Career Development

Dimensions	Examples	Measures
Competencies	Building organizational capability Cross-boundary collaboration Impact and influence Developing senior leaders	Each competency is defined across four behaviorally defined proficiency levels.
Experiences	Start-up business experience Turnaround business experience Technical role Global role	Employees report the level of exposure they have had on each of the key experiences (limited, moderate, deep) for their current and past job assignments.
Success inhibitors	Lacking a track record of results Failing to learn and grow Not an attractor of talent	Leaders are rated by their managers against each of the success inhibitors on a three-point scale (not characteristic, somewhat characteristic, or characteristic).
Career stage results	Business results Management results Leadership results Customer/partner results Integration	Employees rate themselves and are rated by their managers on each result area. These are defined by career stage with each dimension rated on a three-point scale (developing, full, or exceptional).

Performance Management

Dimensions	Examples	Assessment
Commitment ratings	Each employee writes five to seven commitments for the year, including an execution plan and accountability measures for each	Three-point scale (underperformed, achieved, exceeded)
Contribution rankings	Assessment of the future contribution of the employee to Microsoft	Three-point scale (lowest 10%, middle 70%, upper 20%)

and deep. Taken together, these provide a snapshot of the kinds of experiences each leader has had. The information can be used to summarize and compare experience levels across leaders and organizations.

Ten success inhibitors are also rated by a leader's manager (for example, failure to build a strong network). These are rated on a three-point scale: not characteristic, somewhat characteristic, and characteristic. Career stage results areas are defined by profession, and employees rate themselves at their current career stage level on a three-point scale: developing, full, or exceptional against each of the dimensions.

Once a year, during midyear career discussions, employees are asked to articulate their career aspiration and then rate themselves on the competencies, update their experiences profiles, and rate themselves on the career stage results areas. Employees' managers also rate their employees on the competencies, on the results areas, and against the success inhibitors if the employee is in a leadership position.

This information allows a rich discussion between managers and employees about their strengths, gaps, development activities, and future career options. Employees can also use the career models in CareerCompass to find the requirements for success in other career paths they are considering. For example, the technical writer who is supporting the advertising group and considering moving into a marketing job can look up and understand what is required to succeed in the new career path.

At the organizational level, the CareerCompass system offers even greater possibilities for companywide talent management. First, it makes explicit and transparent to every employee what is required and the key differentiators in each profession so they can better self-direct their own careers. Second, when aggregated, the system provides data on the talent mix within an organization. Leaders can go beyond just the number of development engineers that are employed to ask more sophisticated talent management questions: In what competencies are our development engineers the strongest? In what areas are they weak? Where do they have deep experience, and where is experience light? How do these data compare against target levels? What will be needed to face emerging business challenges? How can we best invest our employee development dollars to grow employee capabilities to address future business needs?

Looking ahead the career model framework can provide the data that allow organizations to think about talent management in a dynamic environment. For example, the talent management requirements to meet emerging business challenges might change, but the underlying taxonomy can remain stable. That is, the list of competencies and experiences will remain the same, but some will become more important and others less important. For example, as a product group moves from selling software to selling software and services, the leadership team can use the career model framework to assess if the group has the people with the right set of competencies and experiences to meet the challenge. The same competencies and experiences will be important, but the mix of capabilities and experiences that are needed will change. In this way, senior leaders can assess not only the financials but the talent mix that will be needed in the new organization.

The data also allow more sophisticated talent management questions to be answered. For example, which competencies and experiences are most strongly related to business performance measures in each of the business groups? What is the relationship between the experiences and competencies; that is, do some experiences consistently lead to higher competency ratings? Do the critical competencies and experiences differ by leadership level; that is, what competencies might functional leaders need to let go of to be successful at the next level? Which professions and business groups will provide the greatest challenge, and hence the greatest development stretch, in each of the areas?

Performance Management at Microsoft

Microsoft has a culture where feedback and being self-critical are highly valued. This is particularly the case in the performance management process. At the beginning of the fiscal year, employees list five to seven commitments (performance goals). Commitments are cascaded through the organization to align them with organizational goals and strategy. For each one, employees include their execution plan (key milestones and dependencies) and accountabilities (success measures and metrics to evaluate the commitment). Commitments are taken seriously enough at Microsoft that employees often revise them throughout the year as new responsibilities emerge. For example, it is not uncommon for employees to renegotiate previous commitments when new ones are added. This is expected in the company because employees are held accountable to the commitments that they make.

At the end of the fiscal year, all employees are assessed against their commitments and on their projected future contribution. Commitment ratings are based on performance during the previous year with salary increases and bonuses tied to the results. Employees rate themselves and are rated by their manager on a three-point scale:

- *Underperformed*—Failed to achieve a significant or multiple commitments or expected results
- *Achieved*—Met all their commitments and expected results
- *Exceeded*—Achieved all commitments and exceptional results that surpassed expectations and consistently delivered the highest level of performance

Contribution rankings are used to assess the future contribution of employees and are linked to long-term compensation in the form of stock grants that vest over the next three to five years. Rankings are made using a forced distribution placing employees each year into one of three groups: lowest 10 percent, middle 70 percent, and top 20 percent.

Both sets of ratings are made by managers. This means that once a year, every employee receives feedback on his performance and an indication of his anticipated future contribution with the company. Many companies assess senior leaders on these dimensions, but it is less common for companies to assess all employees on both past and future contributions. The technology industry is dynamic enough that both types of feedback are important. Given the complexity that most companies today face, this is a practice other companies might want to consider. The feedback builds in a dynamic feedback loop that helps support talent management agility and alignment at the individual and organizational levels.

Leadership Assessment, Movement, and Development at Microsoft

Leadership remains a critical focus within the company. Considerable resources are invested, therefore, not just on senior leaders but on leaders throughout the pipeline, especially in the areas of assessment, talent movement, and development (see Table 16.2).

Assessment

Assessment is an important element of talent management at all levels in the company. Midyear development plan discussions include employee and manager ratings of competencies, experience levels, and career stage results areas. Several additional assessment processes have been added to support this process. For example, at the employee and manager levels, voluntary online developmental 360-degree feedback surveys are available and aligned to the professional and management competencies. At the midlevel management level, an online assessment has recently been introduced for leaders to assess themselves against leadership competencies that are required at more senior levels.

More formally, all managers, including senior leaders, are assessed during their performance review by their direct reports on a 45-item leadership behavior measure. These scores, in conjunction with standard business metrics (such as budget performance, customer satisfaction, execution against commitments) are used to assess the leader in the previous year.

External candidates and internal candidates moving into corporate vice president roles go through a behavioral event interview based on the Microsoft leadership competencies. Before moving into the most senior levels, leaders are required to go through the face-to-face 360-degree assessment where 15 to 18 senior leaders, peers, and the leader's direct reports are interviewed about the leader's strengths, weaknesses, and future development needs. The interviews include qualitative information from a series of open-ended questions and a card sort against the Microsoft leadership competencies and success inhibitors. Leaders are assessed on their managerial style and evaluated by their direct reports on the climate they have created for their team.

Table 16.2. Microsoft Talent Management and Development

Job Level	Assessments	Talent Movement	Development
Employees and Managers	• CareerCompass ratings (competencies, experiences, results areas) • Online 360-degree feedback • A manager feedback assessment during performance review • Annual performance ratings • Employee survey scores (used for development)	• Online job postings for employee and manager jobs • Culture that values regular job moves and taking on stretch assignments	• Yearly development conversations • Management, employee, and professional development offerings • Profession-based programs for High Potentials • Companywide mentoring program
Leaders	• All of the above plus: • Online assessment center	• In-business and within-function people review for positions two to three levels below senior-level jobs • Slating support for strategic leadership jobs	• Yearly development conversations • Leadership development offerings • Corporate bench programs for High Potentials • Companywide mentoring program
Corporate vice presidents	• All of the above plus: • Leadership behavioral event interviews for internal promotions and for all external candidates	• Corporate people review covering most senior leaders • CEO slating reviews for executive positions • Talent pools created for common roles	• Yearly development conversations • Leadership development program offerings including new-to-role CVP development program • Executive onboarding support
Senior leaders	• All of the above plus: • Face-to-face 360-degree assessment	• Corporate people review including succession plans for business presidents, their direct reports, plus two levels down in their organizations • CEO slating reviews for all senior roles	• CEO-approved career movement plan • In-business organizational consultant support to grow leadership capabilities within the context of role and business challenges • Executive coaching (as needed)

The process results in feedback that gets discussed with the leader and with her manager.

Talent Movement

Once a year, succession plans are reviewed and updated in the Microsoft people review process. This includes the CEO-led people review for corporate or senior leadership positions. All promotions and movement at the most senior levels are reviewed and approved by the CEO. People review meetings are also held within each of the business divisions focusing on the next two to three levels down.

Development

Employees and managers are encouraged to identify experience-based development and future stretch assignments as one of the best ways to develop their skills. For example, it is not uncommon for employees to change jobs every two years. To facilitate learning from others, new employees are often assigned mentors on their team. A companywide mentoring program is available through the company intranet to all employees that matches mentors and mentees. Formal training opportunities are also available, including technical, professional, and managerial classes.

At the functional leadership level, a program for High Potentials is available for midlevel leaders who may one day be promoted to functional leadership positions. Participants are in the program for one year where they receive targeted development and coaching and engage in special activities with senior executives. A two-year program for High Potentials is provided for more senior leaders who have been identified as having executive potential. The program includes targeted development, interactions with senior leaders, and additional developmental opportunities. For example, participants also attend a once-a-year strategy conference with Steve Ballmer, Bill Gates, and other senior leaders to wrestle with emerging issues in the business. Leaders may also be included in task forces to drive companywide strategic initiatives. There is special emphasis on how to navigate through and learn from the leadership challenges they are currently facing. Executive coaches are provided to all participants.

New corporate vice presidents attend a one-week program focused on how to build broad organizational capability that is not dependent on the leader. Onboarding support and coaching are provided for all new vice presidents. Senior-level leaders partner with organizational consultants in their business to grow their capabilities within the context of their role and business challenges. Executive coaches are available to senior leaders as needed.

Aligning and Integrating Processes

Special effort has been made to ensure the assessment, talent movement, and development processes are aligned. The leadership competencies serve as one of these alignment mechanisms. CareerCompass has also served as a key integration point. The same leadership model, including competencies, experiences, and results areas, is used to assess leaders at all levels. Alignment is not a one-time event but requires continuous attention. Are succession plans filled with people who have been identified as the high-potential leaders? Do people review processes put leaders in assignments that leverage their strengths and will also stretch them in areas where they need more development? The career models have been an important element in driving this alignment.

Lessons Learned

The journey has brought both confirmation of initial directions and several lessons learned along the way. Some of the initial design characteristics have proven to be particularly important. First, talent management at Microsoft was designed from a systems perspective, linking vertically to the business strategy and horizontally across the talent management systems to ensure they complement and reinforce each other. This required thinking about these issues from the start and daily vigilance to ensure they remain aligned. CareerCompass, including the career models and the online system, has proven to be an important underlying framework to drive this integration.

Another important lesson has been the importance of scalability. Considerable time was spent developing processes and systems that could generalize and scale across professions. CareerCompass was first launched with leaders and then scaled to other professions using the same underlying taxonomy (competencies, experiences, and career stage results). Leaders and all professions use the same online talent management system. The processes and programs also needed to be scalable. For example, development programs for high-potential leaders always beg the question, What is available for other leaders in the company? Having robust development ideas and opportunities for all leaders is important. At Microsoft, this includes yearly career and professional development discussions that are taken seriously, the expectation that people will regularly take new stretch assignments, and other "pull" options (such as online 360-degree feedback, a mentoring program, and leadership development classes with open enrollment).

A final design feature that has proved valuable is to link the talent management processes directly to experience-based development. The midyear career discussions emphasize on-the-job assignments as the best place to learn. The performance management system and other assessment processes provide constant feedback. Talent movement decisions are based on both who can perform a job most effectively and who will benefit from the job as a developmental assignment.

Other lessons have emerged along the way. Transparency has been an increasing priority. In CareerCompass, employees and managers see each others' ratings, leading to much more robust discussions. The discussions are not always easy, but the increased transparency has forced conversations into the open, giving employees and managers a chance to address issues and perceptions more directly.

A second lesson that has emerged is the importance of simple yet elegant solutions. Talent management is only one of a multitude of issues that leaders face. The systems are received best when they are simple and easy to use. This does not mean they have to be simplistic; in fact, they may be quite complex behind the scenes, but the user interface needs to be straightforward and easy to understand. As the company moves to the next level of providing talent management summary reports for leaders, interface issues are again being given considerable attention. The reports need to look simple even though they will summarize vast amounts of employee talent management data.

A third lesson is one that should never be forgotten. Talent management is hard work! It is not always glamorous, it requires continuous effort, and it is an evolutionary journey. Organizational change takes time. Key messages and elements need to be communicated, repeated, reinforced, and reemphasized as new people join the company. However, the payoff can be substantial. Talent management can make a difference both for people and for the company.

CHAPTER 17

THEY CAN DO IT! YOU CAN HELP!

A Look at Talent Practices at The Home Depot

Leslie W. Joyce

The Home Depot is the world's second largest retailer. With revenues in excess of $90 billion, it has the distinction of being the number one home improvement retailer in the world. Founded in 1979, The Home Depot has gained recognition as the fastest growing retailer to hit sales of $40 billion, $50 billion, $60 billion, and so on. At just 29 years old, The Home Depot is already an American icon, and the business is growing globally. The company began in the United States and grew into Canada, then Mexico, and most recently into China.

The Case for Talent Management

On average, The Home Depot places approximately 17,000 leaders into positions each year. This includes placements as first-line supervisors and continues all the way to placing executive vice presidents. Notably, more than 80 percent of leadership placements are internal promotions, and the vast majority of those placements are into key frontline management roles interfacing directly with customers every day. With a demand pipeline like that, The Home Depot has to take talent management very seriously.

Vacancies at the supervisor, assistant manager, and store manager levels are particularly important since these individuals have the greatest impact on the engagement level of The Home Depot's nearly 300,000 associates and on the shopping experience of billons of customers.

In addition to placing a large number of leaders, The Home Depot hires a significant number of hourly retail associates every year. Due to geographic dispersion, seasonality, international expansion, attrition, and new store growth, The Home Depot must source and hire tens of thousands of retail associates each year. This is especially true as the company prepares for its busiest season, spring, when sourcing and hiring can be at a fever pitch.

It has created multiple and diverse channels of entry into the organization and developed dedicated programs that build leadership and functional skills. The company works hard to attract top talent and then commits to supporting that talent while they prepare for upcoming leadership roles. This intense focus is the result of many things. Top among them are:

- Embedding the enduring importance of human capital to corporate success
- Internalizing the importance of engaged associates in creating a superior customer experience
- Experiencing unprecedented growth in challenging employment markets—our move to more rural stores with lower revenue volumes and other operational challenges
- Acknowledging significant changes in workforce and consumer demographics
- Understanding that talented associates tend to leave leaders, not companies, and therefore the competency and preparedness of leaders is paramount to ongoing success

This case study describes key talent channels that have been developed to meet the retail hiring needs and examines some of the leadership development programs that have been created to meet the leadership talent needs of the company. The information provided will be summary descriptions of actions and programs and not the design level of detail, to honor the proprietary and confidential nature of the talent processes.

Talent Channels

Early on, The Home Depot recognized that talent was the key competitive differentiator in a rapidly growing company that built its reputation and business case on knowledgeable associates, problem solving, and superior customer service. It would need a unique combination of service skills and product knowledge to meet and exceed the customers' expectations. As the company grew, the pool of talent with those high-level capabilities got smaller as the company's demand for them grew. In addition, The Home Depot realized it would need very capable leaders to inspire and engage very capable talent.

To those ends, the company has created multiple talent channels, each with a specific purpose or designated for a specific talent segment. Talent channels—the ways in which people are attracted and recruited to a company—include traditional sources like print media and job boards, as well as more creative sources like hiring partnerships and strategic alliances. The lesson to be learned from The Home Depot is that the more channels you have, the more likely your organization can source and hire talented people. Examples of talent channels include print, radio, and TV media; job boards; recruiting firms, partnerships, and strategic alliances; on-campus recruiting; and career websites. The Home Depot has been creative and innovative in a number of places, specifically in using hiring partnerships to create focused channels to key talent segments. It is through partnerships that The Home Depot is able to:

- Identify capabilities that are key to the success of the customer experience
- Determine the most productive channels for each talent segment
- Establish formal relationships with organizations or entities that serve as contact points to large numbers of candidates meeting the talent profile

On the leadership pipeline side, The Home Depot has many processes for managing and optimizing its leadership talent, including these key processes:

- Dedicated leadership pipeline programs that bring external talent into the company and accelerate their readiness to lead

- World-class development programs for High Potentials that invest in internal talent with the clear capability to lead at the executive level
- A comprehensive, mandatory leadership curriculum that provides a road map for success in the first six months of a leader's job
- Annual 360-degree assessments for all leaders at the manager level and above to provide timely feedback for improvement and to ensure alignment to the leadership expectations of the company
- A semiannual enterprisewide talent review process that ensures that all talent is reviewed and attended to in a purposeful manner

This case study focuses on the leadership pipeline programs, since these programs have been an essential element in preparing new hires to lead effectively.

Creating Successful Hiring Partnerships

The Home Depot hires large numbers of associates each year. Because these associates are the heart of the customer experience, it is imperative that they are knowledgeable and service oriented. They must also be plentiful, and that is where the challenge comes in. In 2001, The Home Depot was opening a new store about every 24 hours, and on average, a new store requires 150 to 200 new associates at grand opening.

The workforce planning process made it clear that reliable, sustainable pipelines of qualified candidates needed to be created. The company had learned a few things well: (1) older workers were proving more dependable and more service oriented than younger workers; (2) new associates with military backgrounds assimilated quickly, brought broad skill sets, and progressed more quickly than others; and (3) stores were struggling with reflecting and effectively serving the growing Hispanic customer base. These realizations led to a key decision: to establish hiring partnerships with organizations whose members or clients fit this talent profile, and through these partnerships establish The Home Depot as a preferred employer, one that members and clients considered first, above other options. These partnerships were targeted at two primary areas:

- Governmental organizations like the Department of Labor, whose local community-based outreach programs, workforce development organizations, and job training centers are a great source of local talent, and the Department of Defense, known for creating diverse, skilled workforces from which thousands of highly capable, vital people retire every year

- Nonprofit organizations, like the AARP (American Association of Retired Persons), whose members represent capable workforces that might be looking for flexible but meaningful work during retirement and community-based workforce advancement organizations, like the National Council of La Raza (NCLR) and the Hispanic Association of Colleges and Universities (HACU) whose constituents reflect members of the Hispanic community who may be underrepresented in other organizations and whose mission is to create opportunity for their constituents

These partnerships allow The Home Depot to reach out to the communities in which we operate, and provide the company with a broad range of qualified candidates with diverse backgrounds.

The Home Depot's first partnership, with the Department of Labor, was established in 2002. The primary purpose of this partnership was to identify The Home Depot as a key employer and expand the company's reach and approach to recruiting talent from a local to a national level. The second major partnership was the exclusive relationship created between The Home Depot and the AARP. The primary purpose of this partnership was to gain access to the millions of members of AARP, to make them aware of the incredible opportunities available at The Home Depot, and to underscore how valuable their skills and life experiences were in our high service environment. It was with this relationship that The Home Depot really began to develop its employment brand and articulate the value it placed on experience and the kind of environment that associates could expect to find when working for The Home Depot.

Next came Operation Career Front. At The Home Depot, we feel our support of the military sets the standard for corporate America. It is our belief that we must honor our military heroes where it matters most, not only in our thoughts and prayers, but also in our business practices, human resource policies, corporate giving, and volunteer efforts. In 2003, The Home Depot hired 10,000 veterans.

In September 2004, The Home Depot formed a joint hiring initiative with the U.S. Departments of Defense, Labor, and Veterans Affairs to provide career opportunities for America's military who are interested in transferring their unique skills, knowledge, and abilities into a successful second career. This partnership gave The Home Depot unprecedented access to thousands of members of the military as they began preparing for civilian employment when their military enlistments ended. This talent pool is rich in skills key to home improvement: areas like plumbing, electrical, building materials, and maintenance. It also was a great source of leadership talent, as we discuss below. In 2004 the company hired more than 16,000 former military personnel and far exceeded that number in 2005, having hired more than 13,000 by the end of September that year—a successful partnership by any measure.

In 2004, The Home Depot became a corporate partner with the Hispanic Association on Corporate Responsibility (HACR) and immediately began exploring ways to develop unique pro- gramming with its coalition partners. In February 2005, The Home Depot formed a hiring partnership with four of the country's leading Hispanic organizations: ASPIRA Association, Hispanic Association of Colleges and Universities (HACU), National Council of La Raza (NCLR), and SER–Jobs for Progress National. The Home Depot works with these organizations and their strong network of local offices and contacts to recruit candidates for full-time and part-time positions across the country. This was the first time ASPIRA, HACU, NCLR, and SER worked with a corporate partner on one hiring initiative.

The Hispanic partnership was a key element in the company's diversity strategy and a clear commitment to ensuring the com- pany made progress in its ability to meet the needs of the growing Hispanic customer population and reflect the diversity of the communities in which it operates. By working closely with the chief diversity officer, the staffing team led the creation of the Hispanic Advisory Board. This board comprised a number of senior lead- ers of leading Hispanic community organizations who agreed to work together with The Home Depot to establish relationships that would open The Home Depot up as a viable and valued employer in the Hispanic community. The board came together annually at the company's Atlanta headquarters to attend the Hispanic Summit to identify and discuss issues key to accelerating progress and building deeper partnerships.

So a clear business-focused talent acquisition strategy is a key starting point. From there it is a matter of determining where the talent is and how to get unique, exclusive, and visible access to that talent by creating new access channels before your competitors do.

The Home Depot places nearly 17,000 leaders into positions each year. Most of those are internal placements of talented people already employed by The Home Depot. One important source of highly regarded internal talent is through established leadership pipeline programs.

Creating Successful Leadership Pipeline Programs

For the purpose of this chapter, leadership pipeline programs are defined as those development programs designed specifically to hire and develop new external talent, who, on program completion, are placed in a leadership role with the company. Pipeline programs differ from other leadership development programs in that participants in pipeline programs are typically newly and externally hired individuals, who are targeted to fill upcoming and anticipated vacant entry-level to midlevel leadership positions in a couple of years.

The Home Depot has committed to leadership pipeline programs as an effective channel for developing high-potential talent into new leaders. In support of that commitment, they have developed and sustained multiple programs that hire new or soon-to-be graduates from the country's top colleges and universities into multiyear development programs that prepare these highly capable young people to take and succeed in what is often their first leadership role.

In addition, The Home Depot has taken what is a successful formula for early-career entrants and applied it to those who may be successful midcareer professionals looking to make a change in profession. In this instance, the targeted talent pools are successful professionals with many years of experience and demonstrated leadership proficiency who come to the company as a proven professional but without the requisite retail industry experience.

Two of the most successful and longest-running pipeline programs are the Internal Audit Leadership Program (ILP), which is focused on new career entrants, and the Store Leadership Program (SLP), which is focused on successful midcareer professionals looking to make a change. These two programs have important commonalities:

- Multi-hurdle, intense selection processes
- Cross-disciplinary rotational assignments of a duration sufficient to make a contribution to the business unit
- Centralized classroom learning as a cohort
- Unprecedented access to senior business leaders through multiple forums

These elements are widely regarded as the key success factors of The Home Depot's pipeline programs.

Internal Audit Leadership Program

This is an early-career entrant program, targeted at high-performing college graduates with degrees in accounting, process improvement and engineering, business administration, and consulting. They may come to the program with two to four years of work experience. The intent is to build internal business consultants capable of leading projects focused on optimizing business processes and ensuring compliance.

On completion of an extremely rigorous selection process, which includes well-defined program qualifications, interviews, and an assessment center that measures competencies core to leading at The Home Depot, participants are selected to enter the two-year program. They progress through the program as a cohort and graduate together at the same time. Key elements of the highly structured program are (1) rotational assignments in four critical business functions, which include operations, finance, IT, merchandising, operations, supply chain, and so on; (2) hands-on leadership experience in field operations, (3) high-visibility, team-based projects; and (4) presentation of results and recommendations to the executive leadership team.

Successful completion of the program results in placement into manager-level business consulting roles in the internal audit function as well as other areas of the business as needed. This program, which began around 2001, is one of the longest-running pipeline programs at The Home Depot It has an impressive placement rate in excess of 90 percent, and many of its graduates continue to progress through levels of increasing responsibility while maintaining their connection to the program that brought them to The Home Depot.

The Store Leadership Program

The Store Leadership Program (SLP) places individuals who are dynamic and driven with a strong foundation of strategic and technical skills on the fast track to coveted store manager positions. Candidates typically have up to ten years of previous work experience and a demonstrated record of leadership and business acumen.

Since the inception of the program in 2002, the company has enrolled almost 1,300 individuals, many of them former junior military officers or U.S. Military Academy graduates. Data suggest that after completing the program, graduates are as successful in their store manager roles as others with many more years of experience with the company.

The SLP program is a two-year rotational program. As with ILP, a rigorous assessment center is the foundation for selection into the program, and thousands apply for approximately 100 available positions. There are three primary rotations: operations, merchandising, and assistant store manager. In addition, there are centralized learning forums placed strategically at key points in the program to reinforce the on-the-job learning that occurs, as well as to stretch participants' thinking in areas of leadership and strategy. On graduation, participants are deemed "store manager ready" and await assignment to their new store. There are comprehensive processes in place to continue to support new graduates through their first year in the role.

SLP has been a successful program with consistent placement percentages and an impressive promotion acceleration profile for participants. It has also been a great learning experience for how to move new leaders into an existing leadership population and how to build a programmed experience that really builds work skills that can be immediately applied.

Lessons Learned

The lessons learned from innovating are often the most powerful. Here are some of the valuable lessons The Home Depot has learned so far about the important areas of talent channels and pipeline programs. These lessons focus on the elements that can differentiate you from other employers.

Talent Channels

1. *The more channels, the better.* Think critically about where the key talent segments are and find ways to get to them. The more channels you have and the more comprehensive your strategy, then the more likely talent continues to flow toward you, even in tight markets.
2. *Clear branding is the key to acceptance.* It is important to have a clear, differentiated message on what it means to work for your organization and how it differs from your competitors.
3. *Partnerships are key differentiators.* Partnerships can unlock enormous pools of qualified talent while lending immediate credibility to the employer. Creating the partnerships first, before others see the opportunity, provides competitive advantage.
4. *Success starts when the associate is hired.* The Home Depot has learned that the extent to which an associate is prepared, with knowledge and skill, to do their job is a key predictor of associate retention. Therefore, the resources expended to source and hire great talent are supported by the company's commitment to associate development. Once hired into The Home Depot, associates are provided with a comprehensive orientation and onboarding process and a learning curriculum built specifically for their particular role.

Lessons Learned—Pipeline Programs

1. *Get buy-in on the business need for the program.* It is critically important that leaders at all levels of the organization believe in and can articulate the business need that the program fulfills. These are large investments, often in employees with very little tenure, which can create resentment among existing employees.

2. *Do not make the participants too special.* Program participants are often afforded experiences that are not, or were not, available to incumbents. These include things as small as different work spaces, upgraded computers, and the ability to travel, to larger things, like access to coaches and mentors, exclusive learning opportunities and events, and exposure to senior executives. The more that program participants are treated as "special," the greater the likelihood of resentment among peers as they move into the new roles on program completion. And these are the peers whose support and assistance they will need to succeed. Also, it is important for program participants to experience a "real workplace" with real challenges, constraints, and barriers that must be overcome or else, at program completion, they will enter a workplace they have never experienced.

3. *Listen and respond to naysayers.* Pipeline programs are often big investments with high hopes and even higher visibility. This can make it difficult to hear constructive criticism and intervene early and appropriately for fear that changes may be seen as failures of design or commitment. Hear what people are saying, and listen objectively. Respond in a way that adds to the credibility of the program.

4. *Give the programs time to work.* By nature, pipeline programs are long-term investments. The impact horizon of a program does not even begin until the conclusion of the first cohort of participants, at which time there may be multiple cohorts in play, so setting realistic expectations for return on investment and overall business impact is critical.

5. *Invest in the talent you already have.* This may be the most valuable lesson learned. New programs and new talent are always exciting, and participants in programs are easy to focus on; however, to do this at the exclusion of existing internal talent is a potentially fatal mistake. Make certain that high-quality development opportunities are available for existing talent just as they are for program participants. Do not create a culture of "haves" and "have nots." Remember that leadership program participants will eventually be coworkers with incumbents, and those incumbents may hold the keys to their success.

The Home Depot's approach to talent management has significant strengths:

1. It ensures rich pipelines of leaders at all levels of the company.
2. It ensures that talent is guided, challenged, and supported.
3. It allows great talent to try a variety of roles and functions before making a career choice, resulting in a higher likelihood of true engagement with that career choice.
4. It encourages early intervention when issues arise around performance or organization fit.
5. It provides an opportunity for key leaders in the company to *preview* talent before making a commitment to hire. This allows a stronger connection to the new employee and greater certainty about the person's interests, abilities, and success.

As with all processes in organizations that are the size and scope of The Home Depot, there are challenges as well. Among them are funding, staffing, and managing the programs themselves and the ability to ensure placement of program participants:

- *Funding.* Two choices typically exist in terms of funding pipeline programs: Do you fund it centrally or do you distribute costs to the business functions that participate in the program or receive program graduates? With the decision to centrally fund the pipeline programs, which I believe is an essential element of success, come the benefits of ensuring adequate funding and program quality year after year, controlling costs throughout the program, allocating cost properly to the highest-valued activities, and making decisions quickly. These benefits are accompanied by the challenges of a single, large, centralized budget that makes it a very simple cost-reduction target in times of cost control.
- *Decentralizing the budget.* In my opinion this puts the program at risk from many sources, the first of which is the individual unit operator's choice of whether to invest at all, which makes consistent budgeting from year to year a challenge.
- *Staffing and managing the programs.* Programs of this size and complexity take infrastructure to succeed. Programs must be managed, activities and assignments arranged, and learning

events designed and executed. Participants must have consistent oversight and mentorship to navigate the organization and a consistent contact point for support and intervention in the event of ongoing struggles. Shortchanging infrastructure will lead to program degradation and participant disengagement.

Conclusion

The Home Depot is committed to a superior customer experience and understands the essential role of talented staff and extraordinary leaders in making that commitment an everyday reality. Significant strides have been made to take advantage of the riches available through all the talent sources available. Many of these efforts have worked out beautifully, and some have been valuable lessons in what to do differently. In learning, there is always progress.

CHAPTER 18

ALLSTATE'S "GOOD HANDS" APPROACH TO TALENT MANAGEMENT

An Interview with Ed Liddy and Joan Crockett

John W. Boudreau

A CEO's Personal Point of View on Talent Management

I have a twenty-four-year-old son who is just starting out in the business world, working for a financial fund. He was a fine athlete and played varsity basketball in college. Three or four months ago, he came to me and said, "Dad, I have a meeting set up for my six-month performance review. I'm used to getting my performance review by a red-faced coach in front of 3,000 or 4,000 people, who are screaming at me. Will it be like that?"

I laughed and said, "I know you have a job description, but do you also have a document that explains your job accountabilities and the kind of performance they are looking for or what expectations they have regarding behaviors?"

(Continued)

Thanks to Dave Groff, Jennise Henry, and Allstate HR leaders for advising and assisting with this chapter.

He said, "No, I don't think I have anything like that. We're a small company." So I pulled out Allstate's critical success factors for leaders and for frontline employees.

I said, "You know, when we do performance reviews, here's what we do. We go through these things, and we say, do you have leadership skills? Do you drive for a solution? Do you execute? Do you treat peers with dignity and respect and are you inclusive in your behaviors?" And he found it fascinating. My son is like most people. They want to do the right thing; they want to be successful. They just want some help in knowing where to go. Critical success factors helped us establish the kinds of behavior people should exhibit if they want to succeed.

. . . Over the past 35 years, I've thought a lot about human nature. At Allstate, we have leaders who believe that people are good and that they want to be successful; they want to do the right thing. They take personal satisfaction from working hard and achieving results. It's not clear to me that everybody believes that, but we do at Allstate, and I always have in my career.—Ed Liddy, chairman and former chief operating officer, Allstate

Allstate Background

Ed Liddy and Joan Crockett combine a deep respect for talent and the contributions of human resource (HR) practices with the healthy perspective of outsiders (Ed is an outsider to Allstate, and Joan a long-term Allstate line executive but an outsider to HR) who ask tough questions and expect a high level of specific results. Exhibit 18.1 shows how Ed Liddy sees the mission of Allstate going well beyond simply providing a return to shareholders, and how he articulates the larger mission to his employees.

Talent management at Allstate goes beyond Human Resources to embody a true decision science for talent (Boudreau & Ramstad, 2007). At the 2007 Human Resource Planning Society conference, Ed Liddy described Allstate this way:

Exhibit 18.1. Insurance Is the Oxygen of Free Enterprise

I have often described insurance as the oxygen of free enterprise. You never see it. You take it for granted. But without it, nothing thrives.

For example, you have a nice home or an apartment. But if you don't have homeowner's or renter's insurance, you can't live in that home because you can't get a mortgage. Every morning, you leave your home. You get in your car—but without automobile insurance, you couldn't drive. Or you got in the cab, or you got on a bus or a train or a tram, except that without three different kinds of insurance, none of those would be available to you.

You probably use airplanes. Those airplanes didn't get built, there was no pilot to fly them, and there was no airline company to own them if it wasn't for four different kinds of insurance.

You can stay at a beautiful hotel, which, of course, is not there if there are not five different kinds of insurance. You had a nice meal last night. . . . If there wasn't worker's compensation insurance and three different kinds of crop insurance, the food didn't get grown, it didn't get cut, it didn't get cooked, and it didn't get served to you.

Insurance, particularly property and casualty insurance, is the oxygen of free enterprise: it allows everything to grow.

We make that point to every single one of our employees. What you do is important. And helping people in their time of need is what the industry is so very good at.—Ed Liddy

---

Allstate is a great company. When I became President and Chief Operating Officer in 1994, and then Chairman, President and CEO in 1999, we had a lot of things going for us. We had enormous scale and size which, in the insurance industry, is very important. It gives us a strong competitive advantage. We had a great brand name— one of the most recognized not just in financial services or in the insurance industry, but anywhere in corporate America. We had 13,000 agents in offices across the country. They were professionals who know their business and really wanted to take care of people.

So, we had a lot to build on. But we were also at a crossroads in a number of areas. For the first 63 years of our existence we had been tucked under Sears Roebuck & Co. as a very large subsidiary of Sears. But in 1993 Sears announced that Allstate was to be spun off on its own, and the spin-off was completed in 1995. It is a different world when you have to justify your existence to shareholders every day, every quarter, every year. That was a very large change for us.

We had a great agency force. But it had grown up under a confusing patchwork quilt of contracts and relationships to the company. About two thirds of the agents were employees and about one third were independent contractors. We had multiple and different agent contracts with a variety of compensation and commission schedules. If we tried to introduce a new product, we were terribly hidebound in terms of how much do we have to pay people when you introduce it, because we were all over the lot. So we had some challenges. And for the most part it has worked out well. Today Allstate is the largest publicly traded personal lines insurer in the country.

We had 2006 revenues of just under $36 billion and almost $5 billion in net income. We serve 17 million households. We have approximately 37,000 employees and 14,600 exclusive agencies and financial specialists. And those people have another 31,000 folks who work in their offices. We've had an unbelievable run since becoming a public company. Our market capitalization has increased from $11 billion to $40 billion at the end of 2006. We had a return on equity of around 23 percent. We have repurchased about a third of our shares in the last 10 years while still paying our shareholders dividends in a range of $7 billion. If you were an investor in Allstate, for every single annual holding period from one year back 12 years, we have outperformed both the Standard and Poor's 500 stock index and the S&P property-casualty insurance stock index.

One way we were able to do that was by concentrating on people. And that's where Joan's role has been so very vital. In many ways, our approach to talent management reflects the priorities that drive decisions in other areas of our business. I believe strongly in a couple of things. I believe in segmentation. I believe in execution. I believe in focusing on those things that add the most value. Some of you may think of that as an 80/20 rule [a small proportion, say 20 percent, of the most influential elements account for a disproportional, say 80 percent, amount of the variation in system performance] but concentrating on the things that really add value and putting resources there instead of on the things that don't add value is a very important strategic imperative. So while we were concentrating on those things in all of our business initiatives, Joan and her team were doing pretty much the same thing in the HR world [Liddy and Crockett, 2007].

An Outsider Perspective on Talent and Human Resources

Ed and Joan are each unusual outsiders in their own way (see Exhibit 18.2). Ed was one of the few Allstate CEOs who did not have a career selling insurance. Throughout his career, he has

---

Exhibit 18.2. Background of Ed Liddy and Joan Crockett

Ed Liddy began his career at Ford Motor Company and held executive positions at G. D. Searle prior to moving to Sears for six years, the last three as CFO. As Chairman and CEO of Allstate from 1999 through 2006, Ed dramatically changed the business. He expanded the insurance giant's distribution channels beyond agents to include the Internet and call centers. He transformed the life insurance business with an array of savings and retirement products. Under his leadership, the company significantly improved its core competencies in pricing, product development, claims management, distribution, and marketing. During his tenure, as CEO and president, Allstate's market value more than tripled, from $11 billion to over $40 billion. Total shareholder return was 590 percent.

Joan Crockett, Senior Vice President of human resources at Allstate, joined the company right out of college. She has served in many positions including as an underwriter, selling commercial insurance, as a building inspector, and in the premium auditing department. Since 1994, she has led Allstate's Human Resources department under three CEOs, transforming the function into an insurance industry benchmark. She is a fellow of the National Academy of Human Resources, on the National Board of Jobs for America's Graduates, and a partner of the Center for Human Resource Management at the University of Illinois.

held a number of executive roles, but his main career path was through finance and the role of chief financial officer. When he assumed the role of Allstate's CEO, it marked quite a change for an organization in which firsthand experience in selling auto insurance had long been the prerequisite for joining the top team, let alone becoming CEO.

Joan Crockett has spent much of her career in the insurance industry and at Allstate, however, in many cross-functional assignments outside of HR. She has held several line leadership roles in areas such as underwriting, giving her a unique analytical and practical approach to the challenges of HR and talent management.

Allstate's strategic challenges, as Ed describes them, reveal an organization moving from being a subsidiary tucked comfortably within Sears, to an independent, publicly traded company, facing some profound changes in the customer base, sales channels, and public scrutiny, and confronting crises like the September 11, 2001, terrorist attacks on the World Trade Center and Hurricane Katrina. Allstate's approach to insurance has revolutionized the industry. It was one of the first to apply deep data analysis to customer segmentation in areas such as credit history and the first to offer "Your Choice" auto and home insurance, which allow the customer to select a customized package of insurance policy features and pricing. Your Choice Auto was launched in December 2004 and Your Choice Home was launched in 2006. The products were created by analyzing customer account-related data to give customers a more diverse choice of products with competitive pricing. For example, Allstate might use claims history to create differentiated products priced specifically to certain customers, as opposed to the traditional approach of a one-size-fits-all offer to customers, and commodity-like pressure to compete only on the price of the single offering.

When it comes to talent, some of Allstate's talent results are well known. Ed Liddy publicly said that he would replace 20 percent of Allstate's top executives. He completely reorganized the relationship between Allstate and its 13,000 agents—offering all agents the opportunity to be independent contractors who could own an economic interest in their own businesses rather than continuing the typical approach of having agents work as full-time employees.

Other strategic talent decisions were more subtle but equally profound, such as the development of critical success factors (expectations of leadership behaviors) that took Allstate beyond simply using prior job performance ratings as a prerequisite for executive advancement. Allstate also established a clear connection between talent and strategy throughout the company. One example is Allstate's redefinition of its talent pool to support the Your Choice approach to insurance features and pricing. This required the staff who establish prices to have unprecedented high levels of actuarial and statistical skills. Indeed, without executing this profound change in the role of insurance designers and pricers, the Your Choice offering would have been impossible.

From the beginning, Ed Liddy led with talent as his *strategic asset of choice*. He was deeply involved with, and the architect of, many game-changing and high-risk talent decisions. His Human Resources partner, Joan Crockett, and her team, supported Ed with an array of HR programs, expertise, and evidence-based analysis that demonstrate the power of the connection among strategy, talent, HR, and behavioral science. Allstate's success in talent management owes a great deal to the intangibles that are embodied in the close and respectful partnership between Ed Liddy in his role as CEO and Joan Crockett in her role as Chief Human Resources Officer.

Allstate's Commitment to Making Strategically Valuable Talent Decisions

Ed Liddy says that the insurance industry has two key assets— people and capital:

> There is a symbiotic relationship between strategy and human resources. Sometimes CEOs will dream up a strategy, and it may well be a wonderful strategy. But the organization is totally incapable of executing it. *People* execute a strategy. So leaders have to think in a coordinated way, "How do strategy and talent fit together?" That is what we have tried to do at Allstate.

> Here is a specific example. People are now buying and using financial services online to a much greater degree. The fastest-growing companies in our industry offer direct selling. So you can either choose to ignore that, or you can say, "There's something

happening here." Once you make that decision, the important thing becomes how to make the change in a way that supports cooperation and collaboration with what you already have. Allstate decided that when people buy our products over the Internet, they would pay exactly the same price as if they buy them from an agent. If we had set it up so that our Internet distribution channel was competing with the agent distribution channel, our agents would have legitimately opposed the idea.

But by doing it in a way that made sense, where we could explain it logically and consistently to the agents, we did not have too much difficulty with it. At first, some agents were worried that they would lose customers to Allstate.com. It doesn't work that way. People either tend to want to deal with you personally and locally, or they want to go to a national call center. So we believed that having a website would help us capture that second type of customer rather than losing them to another company. Of course, you have to test those views and go deeper in the organization to see whether you can actually execute that strategy. That one we executed fairly well. We are one of the few companies where you can buy insurance any way you want it. What's the Burger King ad? "Have It Your Way."

Talent Strategy at the Pivot Point: Agents as Entrepreneurs

Ed Liddy's maxim about the 80/20 rule means that talent management will focus its resources where they make the biggest difference. It is necessary to emphasize the return on the talent investment. While things like improved learning, bench strength, motivation, and performance are good, they are not equally valuable in every role, and it is not always worth it to try to improve them.

The same principles of segmentation that allow companies like Allstate to tailor service and promotion according to the strategic value of customer segments can also be applied to direct talent management in the talent areas where improvements have the greatest payoff (Boudreau & Ramstad, 2007). Consider the strategic imperatives of becoming accountable to shareholders, achieving growth through a more diversified set of products than just auto insurance, and enticing customers who increasingly demand a complete portfolio of insurance products.

Where would improvements in talent make the biggest difference to these goals?

Joan: You came from a CFO background, so when you became CEO, you might have started by allocating capital differently. You could have thought about different markets in which we might operate. Yet one of the first courageous moves you made involved our relationship with our agents. It was a "bet-the-company" move, because our distribution channel is so important to our success. You focused first on the talent side. Why?

Ed: At the tactical level we had a complex contractual relationship with our agents. Our field leaders had to manage agents who were both employees and independent contractors. It just did not work. We had many different contractual agreements. If you introduced a new product or you wanted to make a change in something, it was unbelievably cumbersome.

When people are independent contractors, they have a very visible and viable stake in the business. They have an equity interest. That's great motivation. It is in their best interests to make their book of business grow, to have the right risks in their book of business, to get good customer retention, and to take care of customers. It is much easier to drive behavior in that model than in the employee agent model, where, when you retire, Allstate distributes the book of business to other agents.

At that time we already were moving toward independent contractors—about two-thirds of our agents were independent contractors by mid-1999. Accelerating that trend gave agents an enormous economic upside in their book of business. They became more entrepreneurial. That made it easier for us to align their interests and our interests. It made it easier and more efficient for our regional management leadership team to lead the agent group, and we solved, once and for all, the unbelievably cumbersome and disparate organizational model that we had.

At the strategic level, agents are our face to the customer. That is the starting point of any business, and you have to get that right before you can do anything else. Starting there helped us determine how to price our products, how to develop our product portfolio, even how to organize ourselves based on the products we offer.

Joan: Was it a *bet-the-company* strategy?

Ed: I'm not sure it felt like bet the company. It was a bold move. It was, in some ways, frightening, but the business model was so compelling that it was the right thing to do. I thought it would be all okay in the long term.

And of course, there were doubters outside as well as inside the company. Remember, this was the height of the Internet bubble. A lot of people were convinced that anybody who sold a service through bricks and mortar was either dying or dead. We thought differently. Buying insurance is different from buying a book through Amazon.com. You are betting your future when you buy an insurance product, so we believed a lot of people would still want to deal with an agent. We just had to get agents to the point where they could benefit from that. At the same time, we also began selling Allstate over the Internet and through call centers because that is what other customers preferred. But we made that change in a way that was collaborative and cooperative with the agents, not in a way that was competitive with them. It was a big challenge for the first couple of years.

The tradition of selling auto insurance had led to some ingrained assumptions and habits that did not fit the future. For example, the existing agent incentive system rewarded only sales, yet the future company strategy emphasized that profitable sales was a key element in running a successful and profitable company. It was increasingly necessary to carefully choose where to sell for the long run and where not to sell, and to do that with an array of insurance products. This was very different from merely building a large book of auto insurance clients. There was a sense that the traditional agent talent-management approach motivated agents to build a sufficient client base to produce an annuity of insurance premium renewals that would support an agent's lifestyle, and then, after reaching a sufficient level of premium renewals, to stop growing and nurturing that existing client base. (The bulk of revenue and profits from insurance products, such as auto and home, come from the flow of premiums paid by customers after the initial policy is sold. This "annuity" of payments often lasts decades.) Many agents built their book of business to produce a yearly income sufficient to live comfortably in their small town. With the new competitive landscape and public investor scrutiny, that would not do any longer.

So the transition to the model where agents run a small business and own an interest in their own book of business was not an easy one. Many agents decided they would leave. Indeed, one result of this era was the emergence of agent advisory boards that provide agents across the country with a voice to the company on a number of important aspects of their Allstate relationship.

Ed: The change was positive over the long run. But it was difficult to get through in the short run. Agents had to make a decision: Do I want to stay with the company? Do I want to take a buyout offer? Do I view this as a good opportunity? Do I view it as a bad opportunity? Again, the business case was sufficiently compelling that people could see the wisdom of our decision. When your people think it makes some sense and you can articulate a vision and construct a path to realize that vision, and you just keep communicating it repeatedly, it seems to work. The folks who really did the brunt of that management work were our frontline supervisors, and the groups in our regional offices. They did a heck of a job.

Strategic Critical Success Factors for Leaders

The evolution of talent management for agents reveals the pivotal role of frontline supervisors. The changing strategy had an impact not only on the sales representatives but on leaders at all levels in Allstate. The new Allstate strategic imperatives would require leaders to be not merely great auto insurance salespeople, but also effective in leading and navigating the increasingly complicated business strategy and talent landscape.

In marketing, for example, Allstate had a vast and dispersed group of decision makers, often producing different advertising or promotional materials in different regions, with each region doing its own independent branding and marketing. Like so many other industries, there was a pattern of achieving early historical success by staffing, rewarding, and developing employees based on their technical prowess, in this case selling auto insurance, but later needing to put more emphasis on vision, execution, team building, and motivation. Like many other companies, one answer was to change the promotion criteria from one dimension—financial results—to two dimensions—financial results and leadership effectiveness (critical success factors). This added a second criterion for performance and promotion assessments, producing the familiar four-box decision framework of high-versus-low performance on both financial results and leadership effectiveness.

Ed: We spend a lot of time making sure people get the business results. But you have to get the business results in the right way. The basic question is, How do you lead an organization? We did not reduce our emphasis on operating measures or financial performance; we just added more to it. We said that if you are going to be a leader here, there's more to it than just hitting your numbers [achieving financial goals]. You also need to demonstrate the behaviors that Allstate expects of all leaders.

The Case of Changing Business Unit Leaders

Joan: Is it fair to say that the change you made in business unit presidents was driven by the change you made with the agents?

Ed: Yes, I think that's true. We had a very good fellow as a president who was retiring, and we had to find someone to replace him. The fellow that we chose had a very inclusive, engaging, and empathetic style. He was not afraid to lead, but he did it in an engaging way.

When you're going through those kinds of changes, it's good to have someone who can present the right face, meaning they can tell the story in a way that makes people understand that it is the best approach for everyone. And I think that also worked really well. The newly promoted president was the right leader at the right time. Yet the person we eventually chose wasn't at the top of our original list. This was not an easy talent decision. But we solicited input from the rest of the management team. Joan and I thought hard about the skill set we needed for the next couple of years. Who has that skill set? Who has the energy and the drive to be able to do it? This individual quickly got to the top of the list. But he was not the most obvious choice. In fact, he had decided he was going to retire within a couple of years, and we prevailed on him not to do that. He did a very good job for us.

He had managed large change efforts in the claims organization and we had seen him effectively lead change. There were 18,000 people in the claims department, and they had gone through a major philosophical change in terms of how we approached the claim process. This leader brought order and effectiveness to that whole change. So we looked at that, and said, here is an individual who has managed change very effectively in a different part of the Allstate organization, Let's have him apply those leadership capabilities in a different part of the company. We knew that he would be successful because he knew the company well and our people knew him well.

Codifying the "How" of Leadership with Critical Success Factors

Ed took a personal role in formulating and designing the set of critical success factors (CSFs) that would define the second dimension of leader quality. It was his way of articulating the "how" of leadership excellence, to complement the "what" that was represented by operating and financial results. What was the logic that caused Ed to see these CSFs as so important that he should attend to them first?

Ed: I think, overall, people want to do the right thing. They want to work for a winning company, and they want to work in a team environment. But if you don't know what you want people to do, and you don't know how you are going to evaluate them, then all of those positive aspects of human nature cannot come out.

So we developed the critical success factors. It took a few months to get them introduced. But it took much longer to get them fully integrated throughout the organization, so that they were being applied with the same rigor as performance results. I don't know any way to shortcut that process. You have to tell people how they're going to be evaluated, then the next year you have to evaluate them on those criteria, and then the following year you have to evaluate them again, so that they have a second crack at it. It takes time.

So it is important to stick with the criteria you developed. Don't keep changing them. For the first three to five years, we never changed anything, because I wanted the organization to get used to the critical success factors. Then, based on other strategic changes in the company, it was the right time to modify them a little. By then, people were used to these factors and to being specifically held accountable for them.

The eight critical success factors were:

- Establishes high-performance environment
- Thinks strategically
- Develops self and others
- Challenges and takes risks
- Leads change and innovation
- Works effectively with others and across boundaries
- Accountable for commitments
- Benchmarks internally and externally

Where did Ed Liddy's vision of the original eight critical success factors come from? Was this something he had experienced before?

Ed explains, "No. That was largely Joan, and Joan's team. The leadership expectations we selected were good and appropriate, but the most important thing was just selecting something and then using them consistently throughout our talent management processes. It was really important simply to start."

The factors were determined through focus groups using the senior management team, officers, and high-potential leaders. The eight factors were incorporated into development discussions for all officers in the first year. In the second year, a 360-degree feedback tool was introduced, and the assessment became half of their performance management rating (50 percent results and 50 percent CSF ratings) which is used to determine annual individual compensation. In year 3, the factors were cascaded to all bonus-level managers for use in performance management rating determinations.

Talent Management Goes Beyond Just the Numbers

It is interesting that a CEO of a major insurance company who came from a CFO background believed that his philosophy about talent management was even more fundamental to the business than the financial results themselves:

Joan: Ed does not see Human Resources as the police force. He assumes, of course, that leaders in the company will do the right things. So when he has talent reviews, he hears directly from the leaders, and if people are not doing what we ask, it shows up in their conversation. But a different leader might have wanted Human Resources' role to be much more of a police force: monitoring, reporting back on how many met the criteria and how many did not. HR would have played a different role if Ed had a different mindset.

Ed: I think that's right, Joan. You have to have monitoring processes in HR, as Joan says. Numbers are important. But starting with the right philosophy guides how you view the numbers.

Talent Management Synergy Through Integrated HR

It is well established that when Human Resource practices are aligned with organization strategy, the chance is greater that they will have strategic impact (Huselid, 1995; Huselid, Jackson, & Schuler, 1997; Lepak & Snell, 1999). The original eight critical success factors, after being used for several years, had the advantage of being familiar and understood by top leaders, and they were integrated into the core talent management processes that were applied consistently to leaders across the company. The Human Resources team realized that a systematic revision could develop critical success factors that were compatible with the original eight but were designed more rigorously by having top management define business imperatives from the strategies, identify the resulting critical talent roles and levels, and then outline the behaviors that might lead to success in these roles. As a result, the refined critical success factors (CSFs) were directly connected with top management's clear realization that future Allstate leaders would need to have an expanded range of capabilities to meet the specific strategic challenges facing the organization. Figure 18.1 shows the transition at Allstate to the new leader behaviors in the top half of the figure. The bottom half depicts how the new behaviors guide investments in building, hiring, and motivating leaders, which produces better role performance and eventually better business results.

Another key finding from research is that when HR practices reinforce and integrate with each other, they have greater positive impact (Ichniowski, Shaw, & Prennushi, 1997; MacDuffie, 1995). Joan and her HR team also recognized that the original eight CSFs were not defined specifically enough to build synergistic HR procedures and practices such as leader selection,

Figure 18.1. Allstate's Transition to New Critical Success Factors

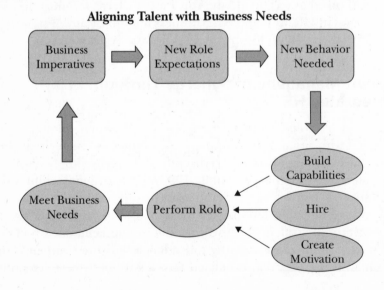

Aligning Talent with Business Needs

Business Imperatives → New Role Expectations → New Behavior Needed

Build Capabilities

Hire

Create Motivation

Perform Role

Meet Business Needs

development, rewards, and assessment. For example, one original CSF was "works across boundaries." This might encompass many things, but it provided few specific behaviors and results. A better version would specify that this involved "influencing others," "promoting collaboration," and "building relationships." Allstate HR leaders determined that they could build new critical success factors so that from the beginning, they would serve as an integrating framework for talent management practices, including performance management, rewards, career planning, coaching, and development.

As one Allstate HR leader describes it, "The original critical success factors were more like values to be held and used wisely, but now we embedded them in a specific decision infrastructure." The elegance of the new factors as a framework for synergy across HR practices and procedures became apparent to the top leadership team.

Ed: We introduced the critical success factors, and then we did 360-degree feedback assessments on all leaders. We used the feedback results in our individual compensation decisions, therefore putting higher priority on demonstrating those factors and developing them as a personal performance priority for leaders. That led to feedback that it was difficult for individuals to set personal performance goals because we didn't have sufficient standards for the critical success factors. So we revised the factors, enhanced the underlying behaviors, and improved the standards used to evaluate individuals against them. We added the revised factors to the 360-feedback surveys, added them to our talent management process, then went back and put them in the performance management process as personal performance development priorities. This provided some concrete things you could use—tools you could use to determine whether the critical success factors, the personal performance factors, were in fact being achieved or not.

Allstate's critical success factor CSF designers presented the rationale for changing the CSFs (see Exhibit 18.3). Notice how they emphasized the connection to business strategy, the improved precision in defining success, and the integration with

Exhibit 18.3. Allstate's Rationale for Enhancing Critical Success Factors

Refines, updates CSFs (add, modify)

Better alignment to current organizational imperatives, new business strategies

Enhances focus on requirements for success in "key roles"

Strengthens line of sight between leaders and business imperatives

Adds precision, clarity

- Eliminates overlaps, redundancies
- Eliminates nonbehavior and process components
- Incorporates level-appropriate behaviors
- Improves ease of assessing

Research-based, widely used, best-practice approach, takes science of human behavior into account

- Identifies behaviors "casually" related to job success

More predictive

Improved validity

Fully integrates/aligns with *new* tools (assessment, selection, development, training, coaching, etc.

Will be integrated with talent management processes/systems (recruiting, performance management, succession, etc.)

the tools and processes that were already being used to assess, reward, and develop Allstate's leaders.

Working with an external consulting firm, Personnel Decisions International (PDI), leaders inside and outside of Human Resources at Allstate defined the new critical success factors, realizing that it was important that they were compatible and aligned with the original eight factors to ensure that Allstate's leadership team accepted and understood the new ones. The Allstate team made sure that these connections were clear. Figure 18.2 shows the connections between the old and the new CSFs.

Figure 18.2. Connections Between Old and New CSFs

Critical Success Factor Mapping

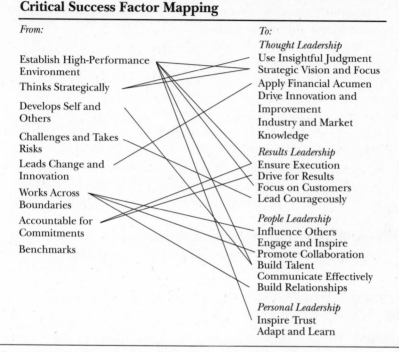

From:

Establish High-Performance Environment

Thinks Strategically

Develops Self and Others

Challenges and Takes Risks

Leads Change and Innovation

Works Across Boundaries

Accountable for Commitments

Benchmarks

To:

Thought Leadership
Use Insightful Judgment
Strategic Vision and Focus
Apply Financial Acumen
Drive Innovation and Improvement
Industry and Market Knowledge

Results Leadership
Ensure Execution
Drive for Results
Focus on Customers
Lead Courageously

People Leadership
Influence Others
Engage and Inspire
Promote Collaboration
Build Talent
Communicate Effectively
Build Relationships

Personal Leadership
Inspire Trust
Adapt and Learn

Source: Based on Personnel Decisions International research

The new competencies are divided into four "superfactors" of "Thought Leadership," "Results Leadership," "People Leadership," and "Personal Leadership." Dave Groff, Assistant Vice President for Talent and Chief Learning Officer, notes how the research-based material from PDI was used, but also was refined to fit Allstate's needs: "We adopted, with slight word modifications, some of the PDI standard competency set but only at the highest 'competency level.' With PDI assistance, we developed specific behaviors and standards for each competency based on Allstate's business imperatives and Allstate's role expectations."

For example, an identified business imperative was, "Build more consistency and discipline into the organization (including legal risk management)." The original thought leadership competency from PDI might include a generic critical success factor such as, "Create a clear, compelling vision of the organization's future." Allstate added a more specific factor: "Ensure that business unit strategies, decisions, tactics, and priorities are consistent with Allstate's broader strategies and long-term direction."

In presenting the new competency system, Allstate's HR team emphasized the following points:

- The 17 leadership competencies are aligned with Allstate's strategy and business imperatives. Therefore, these competencies should be predictive of future success.
- The four superfactors organize the competencies into groupings derived from years of research on human behavior (Howard & Bray, 1986; Likert, 1961; Sloan, Hazucha, & Van Katwyk, 2003; Stogdill, 1974). These competencies are the foundation for talent management processes: performance management, compensation, development, assessment, selection, and others.
- Each of these competencies is defined by specific behavioral expectations related to Allstate's business imperatives.

Beyond Scientific Rigor: The Change Process Must Reinforce Success

Allstate's Human Resources team worked closely with Ed Liddy and his executive team to ensure rigorous standards for both the content and the development of the new CSFs. It was equally important to take a sensitive and professional approach to the change process when introducing the new CSFs. Even the most rigorously designed competency system can fail if the leaders do not accept it and use it. Jennise Henry, former HR director at Allstate, describes it this way:

> There were some leadership success factors that had been successfully used by PDI in other organizations, but were too different from our original eight. We intentionally made some modifications so that the original and new success factors seemed a little more similar. While the revised factors were more rigorously derived than the original set of factors, we tried to convince others that we were not changing everything. We talked about them, not as an entirely new set of CSFs, but more as the reinvigorated original CSFs. It was about starting where we were and moving forward, as opposed to casting the old factors away. So in order

to gain acceptance and top leadership ownership of them, we massaged them a bit and took some liberties in modestly adjusting them from the strict results of our analysis.

Dave Groff, Assistant Vice President for Talent and Chief Learning Officer, explains it this way,

> There were occasions where Allstate's word to describe a particular critical success factor was similar to PDI's word, so there were occasions where we debated whether substituting Allstate's word substantially changed a meaning or its coherence with other components of either Allstate's model or PDI's taxonomy. On balance, if the effect was deemed slight, we favored using Allstate's word for continuity. That made the CSFs seem more compatible with the past while also taking us further. So we were trying to blend those two purposes.

Table 18.1 shows how Allstate's success factor designers express the contrast between how the success factors had worked in the past, in the Before column, and how they would work in the future, in the After column. Notice how candidly the team describes the limitations of the current system, noting disconnections between development and performance, the sporadic nature of coaching, and others. They plainly point out opportunities to improve what was already a well-accepted leadership development framework. Rather than accepting that Allstate's leadership team was reasonably content with the existing system, Allstate's talent management and leadership development designers set out to educate Allstate's leaders on how things could be better.

Making the New CSFs "Real" When It Comes to the Hard Decisions

A final ingredient for truly useful leadership factors is that they are actually applied in the organization. Working closely together, Ed and Joan made sure that the new CSFs drove decisions with real impact on careers, performance, and the leadership talent at Allstate.

Joan: What mattered more than anything was not that we had the critical success factors, but that we actually applied them. So when we had a leader who achieved good performance

Table 18.1. How New Success Factors Improve Leadership Development

Before	After
Created ad hoc, based on common sense and perceived need, often in a vacuum	Identifies the specific skills, knowledge, and capabilities that predict leadership success at Allstate
Different leaders have different levels of assessment. Feedback is primarily job related and limited frequency	Used to assess our existing leaders and provide feedback Provides basis of succession decisions about leadership
Coaching for our executive leaders has historically been sporadic	Provides focus for coaching
Internal training is most often job specific or general leadership topics	Prime focus for internal training content
Choice of external training is often random	Drives selection of external training courses
Development plans are often not linked to performances or succession	Drives individual development plans Enable performance assessments Development is continuous as is learning

results but who had the wrong leader behaviors, we did something about it. We slowly started using the performance management process to address those behaviors and then having some tough conversations with the individuals. Remember, these are leaders who were used to being told that getting results was enough to be successful in our organization. In some instances, we hired a coach to train the leader on the right leader behaviors. Our response escalated from there if the wrong behaviors continued. We wanted to send a signal in the organization that we were serious about realigning behaviors with the CSFs.

An example of applying the rejuvenated CSFs to a specific HR practice is in the area of hiring and interviewing. Before the success factor revisions, Allstate had used one standard behavioral interview guide for all interviews at all levels of management. It included questions organized around eight characteristics. For example, for the characteristic of integrity, a question was, "Tell me about the time you found it most difficult to follow a rule, policy, or decision." Under the new system, the interview guides are unique to each of five levels of management—individual contributor, first-line supervisor (attached), manager, director, officer—and each coincides with the four high-level factors shown on the right-hand side of Figure 18.2 discussed earlier. In addition, each interview question contained specific behavioral examples to anchor answer quality that was indicative of low, average, and high performance. An example is shown in Exhibit 18.4.

Strategic HR Partnership at Allstate

What is the practical reality of the strategic Human Resources partnership? It has as much to do with how leaders spend their time on talent management processes as with how they perceive their leadership role. Every leader must make choices about how much detail they attend to and how deeply they become involved in the talent process. Savvy HR leaders learn that a key to strategic talent success is the approach that key business leaders take to the talent issue.

How the CEO Allocates Time to Talent Management

Ed: There are only so many hours in the day. So my focus with Joan was primarily on the officers of the company. When I was CEO, I felt the officers were critical to the company's success, and therefore I had to invest time in them. Allstate has about 200 officers, 85 of whom were senior vice presidents or vice presidents. I spend more time on that group, a little less time on the next 100, such as assistant vice presidents. Who's on our list of high-potential people? Are they high potential this year and not last year? If they are high potential, what are we doing about developing them? What experiences or

Exhibit 18.4. Sample Allstate Interview Guide

Thought Leadership—Use Insightful Judgment: Identifies and analyzes information to make decisions and solve problems.

Question: Describe the last time you solved a complex problem that required a lot of thought and careful analysis on your part.

Probe:

a. Situation: What was the problem that required careful thought?

b. Behavior: How did you go about analyzing the problem? What alternative solutions did you consider? What solutions did you decide to try and why?

c. Outcome: How did you know your solution was successful?

Score Here:

High-Performance Behaviors	Average-Performance Behaviors	Low-Performance Behaviors
5 4	3	2 1
Consistently focuses on the big picture and long-term implications of issues, actions, and events as well as the detail, as appropriate to the situation	Typically focuses on the big picture and detail as appropriate to the situation	Occasionally gets too absorbed in the big picture or is distracted by unnecessary detail

Considers a range of potential future reactions, issues, and/or problems and fully prepares to address them	Considers potential reactions and issues in advance and prepares to address them	Focuses on current issues only, paying little attention to potential future issues, problems, or reactions
Fully defines and evaluates reasonable alternatives to resolve problems or make decisions, considering potential short- and long-term costs, risks, and benefits of each alternative	Defines reasonable alternatives to resolve problems or make decisions	Does not always fully evaluate costs, risks, and benefits of alternatives before resolving problems or making final decisions; focuses too quickly on a single solution, failing to adequately consider other alternatives
Consistently makes timely and effective decisions on problems or issues requiring immediate attention, balancing analysis with decisiveness	Typically makes timely decisions on problems or issues requiring immediate attention	Sometimes delays too long in addressing issues requiring immediate attention; analyzes issues too closely, thereby missing opportunities to act within critical time frames

Notes:

693

training do they need to get from where they are at a director level or a senior manager level to be considered for the pool of assistant vice presidents?

Dave Groff: The answers to such questions were unique to each individual's capabilities and developmental opportunities relative to role requirements and other performance expectations for the role. For example, a role might require, among other things, experience with state legislative processes, project management expertise, or a bias toward innovation. If an otherwise well-qualified high-potential individual is lacking these experiences or skills, a plan would be implemented to provide the appropriate development.

Ed: We spent a significant amount of time on talent conversations, including two in-depth sessions a year with each of the senior leaders focused on the talent implications of their business strategies. Joan would have very detailed and rigorous conversations, which included a focus on diversity goals. We needed to know we had the necessary talent pipeline of successors as backup for critical positions. It is absolutely a never-ending process.

I think as much as half my time is spent on people-related issues. Sometimes I feel like the company's internal headhunter. In the insurance business, we only have two assets: financial capital and people. You cannot buy our product on a shelf someplace, so how you put capital and people together very much determines whether you are successful or not. People-related issues in one form or another: that's 50 percent of my time.

Building Talent Management on the Foundations of Organization Culture

Certainly talent management and Human Resources practices can change and develop organization culture. Yet an equally important element of successful change is to recognize the existing organizational culture, norms, and values and make talent management efforts compatible with them. The metaphors used for talent management should reflect the metaphors that leaders use to understand their business and strategy. Organizational cultures can vary more across industries than among firms in the same industry (Chatman & Jehn, 1994). In the same way, leaders articulate strategic connections differently in different industries. For example, in industries that rely on anticipating fashion, the metaphors reflect design, merchandising, and creating a buzz around the new idea. In contrast, in industries that traditionally rely on engineering, the metaphors reflect process mapping, problem definition and solutions, and precise mathematical analysis. At Allstate, the metaphors reflect the insurance industry: they emphasize careful analysis of risk and return, deep customer segmentation, and a focus on the 20 percent of issues that drive 80 percent of competitive advantage.

Ed: The critical success factors and talent management have been reasonably successful here because we are an analytical organization, and we are very comfortable with segmentation. When an insurance claim comes in, we triage it. Does it have liability issues, or is it just physical damage? There's a great deal of rigor in how we think about our business. We applied the same philosophy to the segmentation of talent, and that made it easier for people to understand personal performance priorities. If you had tried to put a similar concept into place in an organization where they were not used to thinking in those terms, you might have met more resistance or have had less success.

Joan: If you're talking to people in a language they already speak, it makes it much easier for them to get on board.

We have seen examples of this throughout the chapter. The rationale for focusing on agents was that they were a small portion of the workforce that was affecting a very large amount of performance and agility. The rationale for the revision of the CSFs was the need for deeper segmentation of the vital elements of the leader's behaviors, which included more than just financial outcomes. Joan has also used the concepts of investment risk, return, and liquidity to communicate the idea of talent risk (such as turnover), talent return (such as performance levels), and talent liquidity (such as deploying individuals across a wider array of future roles or challenges).

The Importance of Leadership by Example: The Profit-Sharing Incentive Decision at Allstate

Even if CEOs cannot be involved in every talent decision, it is important that they lead by example when it counts. At Allstate, that pivotal moment came when making the decision about how widely to offer broad-based incentives.

Joan: Ed told people early on that when the company wins, everyone wins. So he made changes to profit sharing accordingly.

Ed: Approximately 85 percent of our employees participate in profit sharing. [The company matches up to $1.50 for every dollar nonbonus employees contribute for the first 5 percent of salary and up to $1.00 for bonus employees.] Our match is always in company stock, so to the extent that our company stock continues to appreciate in value, it is a gift that keeps on giving. I think people understood that early on. It is a way to get people to understand our different responsibility when we became a public company versus being simply a division or a subsidiary of Sears.

Joan: Ed's not taking enough credit. He wanted to make sure that nonbonus employees were well taken care of here. This is their avenue to accumulate wealth and be aligned with the shareholder. The decision to enhance profit sharing for nonbonus employees came from Ed. When he described his idea to the Allstate leadership, they gave him a standing ovation. Although the majority of Ed's time is spent on Allstate's leadership, he does still affect the talent decisions regarding all of our employees.

How Does the CEO Know Talent Management Is Working?

Of course, there is a vast variety of indicators and measures to formally evaluate talent management in organizations. That said, it is often the more intuitive and informal indicators that tell the story, in the mind of the CEO.

Ed: Here's how we know that the new CSF system is working. We have always held town hall meetings, where we spend an hour with employee groups and open the meeting up for questions. In 1998 a typical question would be, "How do I get my medical forms?" These questions were not strategic. Today in a town hall meeting, the questions are much more focused on customers, competition, the business environment. I am amazed at how much progress we have made fairly quickly. Maybe employees just got used to me; maybe they got more used to the process. But it has worked really well for us.

Strategic HR Partnership at a Personal Level: Learning How the CEO Learns

Joan: Early on, I realized I needed to learn how Ed learns. He is a very visual learner, so he responds strongly to visual imagery. Knowing that has made a big difference in how I work with him. If I can get it into a graph or a chart, he will look at it and quickly understand it. Lots of words on lots of pages is not his style at all. Knowing how many numbers he needs, how much evidence he needs, are the things you learn as you go.

Conclusion

The bedrock of Allstate's approach is a fundamental philosophy about talent management:

- Assume that people want to do the right thing.
- Provide tools to help leaders understand what that is and to guide and encourage their employees to do the right thing.
- Use the 80/20 rule to focus on the things that really make the biggest difference.

As Ed looks ahead to the future of Allstate under the new CEO, Tom Wilson, he suggests:

Strategy and talent management are both always evolving. In recent years our business strategy has focused on operating excellence and great capital management. Tom will keep those priorities in place, but also make us a more consumer-focused company. So now we will incorporate that into our thinking about human resources. Does our human resource process evaluate how well our leaders and employees relate to the customer?

You are never in one place; it is very much a journey, not a destination. Allstate's journey has been exciting. It seems to have worked well. Now they have to figure out how we get to the next level for the company. A lot of companies coast. They get someplace; then they coast. You cannot do that and continue to be successful. And Allstate will not do that.

References

Boudreau, J. W., & Ramstad, P. M. (2007). *Beyond HR: The new science of human capital.* Boston: Harvard Business School Press.

Chatman, J. A., & Jehn, K. A. (1994). Assessing the relationship between industry characteristics and organizational culture: How different can you be? *Academy of Management Journal, 37*(3), 522–553.

Howard, A., & Bray, D. W. (1990). Predictions of managerial success over long periods of time: Lessons from the management progress study. In K. E. Clark & M. B. Clark (Eds.), *Measures of leadership.* West Orange, NJ: Leadership Library of America.

Huselid, M. A. (1995). The impact of human resource management practices on turnover, productivity, and corporate financial performance. *Academy of Management Journal, 38*(3), 635–672.

Huselid, M. A., Jackson, S. E., & Schuler, R. S. (1997). Organizational characteristics as predictors of personnel practices. *Personnel Psychology, 42,* 727–786.

Ichniowski, C., Shaw, K., & Prennushi, G. (1997). The effects of human resource management practices on productivity: A study of steel finishing lines. *American Economic Review, 87*(3), 291–313.

Lepak, D. P., & Snell, S. A. (1999). The human resource architecture: Toward a theory of human capital allocation and development. *Academy of Management Review, 24*(1), 34–48.

Liddy, E. M., & Crockett, J. M. (2007, April 16). *Driving better talent decisions: That's Allstate's stand.* Keynote address at the Human Resource Planning Society Annual Conference, Fort Lauderdale, FL.

Likert, R. (1961). *New patterns in management.* New York: McGraw-Hill.

MacDuffie, J. P. (1995). Human resource bundles and manufacturing performance: Organizational logic and flexible production systems in the world auto industry. *Industrial and Labor Relations Review, 48*(2) 197–221.

Sloan, E. B., Hazucha, J. F., & Van Katwyk, P. T. (2003). Strategic management of global leadership talent. In W. Mobley & P. Dorfman (Eds.), *Advances in global leadership 3.* Amsterdam: Elsevier.

Stogdill, R. M. (1974). *Handbook of leadership: A survey of the literature.* New York: Free Press.

CHAPTER 19

A VIEW FROM THE TOP ON TALENT MANAGEMENT

An Interview with Warren Staley, Recently Retired CEO of Cargill Incorporated

Sandra L. Davis

During the past several years, Cargill has embarked on a significant transformation that began with a focus on leadership behaviors. When Warren Staley became CEO in 1999, Cargill had $45.7 billion in revenues, 90,000 employees in 56 countries, and earnings of $600 million. On his retirement from the company in the summer of 2007, it had grown to $88.3 billion in revenues, with over 158,000 employees in 66 countries worldwide, and earnings of $2.3 billion. This interview with Warren Staley presents his insights as a line executive of one of the world's largest privately held companies into the business case for leadership development, talent management systems, and the CEO's role in driving change.

■ ■ ■

Let's start at the beginning. What led you to focus on leadership when you began formulating your vision for Cargill in 1988?

I grew up in a working-class, blue-collar neighborhood in Illinois. As a young person, I was always curious, even in the neighborhood, why some people would step up and take charge and other people would always hang back. Watching my father, I saw a role model of a man with limited education who was always doing things for people. He had the courage to step out.

Growing up in Illinois, we also naturally studied and read about Lincoln from first grade on. He was the kind of leader I have studied all my life. He did not have a formal education, yet he taught himself and became a great president and leader. Observing my father and reading about Lincoln led me to conclude that leadership has little to do with formal education, which was an interesting thing for me to bring to Cargill. If leadership does not have much to do with education, then we ought to be able to cascade it down in the company. Everybody should have a chance to learn and practice leadership.

Then I thought through the role of experience in leadership. My intuition told me that some people seem to be born with leadership potential; for others it could be a result of their early experiences. My thoughts about leadership were mostly based on my own lifelong experiences, as I did not do much reading in the area of leadership until my later years.

Cargill employees all over the world come from differing experiences and backgrounds. My belief was that leadership could be taught, and the differences could be overcome.

I was curious enough about good leadership that I started compiling a list of the characteristics of good leaders. This is my own personal list [see Table 19.1] from my experiences, my observations, and my reading. I would hear something or notice something and compare it to my list. Over time it got to be a long list, but I think it works. And it inspired me. While I did not have an expectation of being a CEO, I thought if I were ever part of a small senior team that I would help the organization to understand leadership. I was convinced that leadership was the key ingredient that differentiates a merely good company from a great company. Greatness was not in strategy or in the products they made; I had seen all kinds of businesses with good products fail. They failed because of the lack of leadership, the lack of ability to lead change, and the lack of courage.

Table 19.1. Warren Staley's Personal Leadership List ("The Little Red Book")

Trust people, show support.

Challenge appropriately.

Coach/teach.

Delegate.

Encourage people; encourage risk taking.

Be ethical.

Have vision so people know who they are following; set direction.

Do my homework.

Invite dissent.

Stay composed at all times; stay balanced.

Simplify, clarify.

Keep learning; be a champion for change, and be open-minded.

Develop talent.

Listen/show respect (don't embarrass anyone).

Courage.

Resilience.

Communicator.

Credible/inspire trust.

Give direct, honest feedback.

Ensure consequences for behavior and performance are fair and rational.

Persistent/consistent—predictable.

■ ■ ■

Tell me about how you led change when you became CEO.

I wanted us to become the world-recognized leader in creating value solutions that made our customers more successful. I was convinced that would be a huge change and that most people in

Cargill had no idea what we were going to have to go through. I also knew that execution would be everything. A company could have a great strategy, but if they do not execute it, they might as well throw it in a trash can. If the strategy only comes out of the mind of a CEO and he tries to impose it, it will fail because people cannot execute something they do not understand or might not even agree with. So we needed to spend enough energy and create a process to bring people along and to involve them to get their buy-in. This would be the right thing to do for customer solutions.

The first thing I did when I became CEO was to think about the kind of organization and senior team I would need. There was no way I could get my arms around this company and keep track of everything by myself. I also thought that the other senior leaders needed to quit trying to run the businesses operationally. They were frustrating the business unit leaders by telling them how to manage their businesses. Business unit leaders needed the freedom to make decisions for and with their customers.

I selected seven other executives who became the corporate leadership team (CLT). That team—the CLT, as we called it— was told that they were going to immediately get out of operating responsibilities and that their roles were primarily to coach and teach, help to develop strategy, and allocate human and capital resources.

We wanted the business unit leaders to run their businesses. We produced a role document, published it in a white binder, and it became known as the "white bible." We thought if we were not prescriptive and did not spell out the roles for everybody, it would be too easy to go right back to where we used to be. There was a lot of dissension about going down this road; it was criticized as too soft and impractical. Some people even disagreed and said that it *is* the job of leadership to tell people how to do things. While there may be a time to intervene, it should probably be to put the right person in the job. We also dismantled the geographic matrix that had previously dictated geographic strategies for our product lines. The geographic overlay had worked in the past, but it had become too costly and too confusing. We said the role of the business leader is to decide where they should invest their capital and their resources; *they* need to decide

Exhibit 19.1. Warren Staley's Letter to Employees

From Warren Staley's June 18, 1999, letter to all employees:

Change is now our No 1 business partner. Sharing ideas, knowledge, concerns and successes is the best way to manage change while building trust. Please help me make all of our associates enthusiastic travelers with us in this transformation of Cargill.

the geographic strategies that make sense for their business. These changes pretty much turned things upside down. I was personally comfortable with that, keeping in mind what Henry Kissinger said about change: "For any student of history, *change* is the law of life. Any attempt to contain it guarantees an explosion down the road; the more rigid the adherence to the status quo, the more violent the ultimate outcome will be."

Under the heading of "Cargill can do better," we incorporated leadership characteristics in our model for the kind of employee we desired. One of the first task forces I put in place, even before I became CEO, was organizational behavior and leadership, which I led. Our goal was to tell the company about leadership—what it means and why we need to do it. We looked internally at the best of Cargill, our best-performing businesses, and we looked at the best businesses externally. We searched for what academic research and literature could tell us about organizational behavior and leadership. Ten days into my term as CEO, after four months of work, we published our thoughts—it was June 18, 1999 [see Exhibit 19.1]. What we concluded was that behavior is the key driver of high-performing organizations; that was the one sentence outcome. It is about behaviors.

We came up with six strategic intent behaviors:

1. Develop and leverage customer knowledge and insights.
2. Discuss, decide, champion.
3. Demonstrate respect, candor, commitment.
4. Pursue and reinforce collaboration.
5. Hold self and others accountable.
6. Challenge, innovate, change.

From some, the reaction was, "You spent four months and all you can tell us is that it's about behaviors?" In that paper, we wrote about the six behaviors and talked about the changes we expected to happen in the organization. I sent that white paper to all employees around the globe letting them know we were "transforming Cargill into a high-performing, customer-focused, solutions-oriented company."

People were told, up front, that they could be great performers and create terrific results for the company, but if they did not practice and champion these behaviors, they could not have a job at Cargill. I knew it would take three years before we would get traction, but the reason for making these changes was all about our customers. We all had to say it again and again at every opportunity all around the world.

■ ■ ■

What systems did you put in place to support the change?

There's some personal history in answering that question. I wanted to return to something that existed early in my career at Cargill. We had a high-potential management training program that not only rotated each of us through many areas of the company from merchandising to grain trading but also brought us to Minneapolis to meet with senior managers. We had a chance to explain to them what we were doing and what we were learning. These were conversations, formal and informal, that included not just the most senior leaders, but also some of the family owners and board members. I remember the whole experience as being energizing, invigorating, and impactful. I learned a lot from the mixture of people and areas of the company. I was disappointed when this program was discontinued later because it helped build relationships and a line of sight between high-potential performers and the senior team. I had always promised myself if I ever got a chance to be part of the senior team that I would find a way to bring back what I had valued in my training.

Over the course of the next three years, we crafted a goal that we called "building the common, shared mindset around leadership." With the help of our human resource team, we created the Cargill High Performance Leadership Academy. The CLT members were required to be the teachers. We felt that if we did not get involved as teachers, the change was not going to happen. We could not leave this to imagination. In addition, we instituted biannual leadership conferences where we bring together as many as 250 leaders within the world of Cargill at one time to focus attention on carrying out our leadership model.

The goal—building a common, shared mindset around leadership—was on the banner of our first worldwide leadership conference. We understood we needed to instill new vocabulary and interpret our strategic intent behaviors. We talked in detail in the conferences and in the academy classes, telling stories and discussing situations about when we saw these behaviors, or their opposites, in action. We did not want understanding at just the intuition level. We had to give this structure and rigor so there would not be 45 different interpretations of it. We wanted the strategic intent behaviors to be the same around the world. We respect cultural and religious differences, but as far as behavior and ethics go, there was to be one culture and set of standards for all who work here.

In all of these discussions, we kept bringing it back to the strategy the behaviors were directed at building: our strategy around customer solutions that was the reason for these changes. Another critical component was the three pillars of our strategy: innovation, high performance, and customer focus. To us it was clear: these are the three things that will make our business successful, and they are the purpose of our strategic intent behaviors. Changing leadership behaviors is not just about being good for goodness sake, but because they are the only way we can achieve our strategy. As one of my senior leaders said, "Throughout the organization, we need to be able to articulate clearly how each employee fits and why they matter." Employees around the world had to see what was in it for them. When a new, young employee looks around, they do not really focus on the corporate strategy. They want to know, "Where do I fit, what can I do, and why do I matter?" It is that simple!

It is important to understand that Cargill was not struggling financially at that time. We were not doing nearly as well as some of us believed we should be doing, but we were not in trouble; there was no crisis. But what we did understand was that the world outside Cargill was changing faster than the world inside. We knew we had to change. We told the organization that we would divest some businesses and go into some new areas. We said it was going to be different, and we knew it would make some people uncomfortable. Because we started by talking about leadership behaviors, we were able to engage the most people possible. We were going to do business differently and behave in accord with our goals.

One of the most disappointing things to me when I became CEO was the lack of collaboration across the company. We had taught people to act independently by telling them to be the best they could be and make the most money they could for their own businesses, even if that meant competing with other Cargill businesses. For business reasons, to leverage the breadth of Cargill, we wanted people to stop those actions and share their knowledge to help each other, which would then help our customers be more successful. That took some time to change. By building collaboration across our businesses and rewarding people for it, we have really improved our performance.

■ ■ ■

So the senior team became the teachers for leadership academy?

Every one of them—in the beginning, the CLT and a few others from the corporate center. Their initial reaction was often, "I don't know anything about teaching." I said that I did not either, but we needed to learn. One thing we all had working in our favor were great stories—people learn by stories—but stories have to have a teachable point. We had to learn how to tell a story that had a teachable point. That was hard for some of us. Our human resource team had to have the courage to say that while you are a very smart executive, you are not doing very well at teaching. In return, we had to give them permission to coach us to make us good teachers. The amazing thing is we all improved. We received the feedback, and we wanted to do well, so we adapted. In the end, I think everyone finds it is fun.

The leadership academy does not end when people go home. Now that we have conducted multiple programs, these groups of employees have built their own camaraderie. They are linked around the world; they even have their own internal websites.

■ ■ ■

How important have talent management systems been in driving your strategic goals?

Once an organization raises performance expectations for people, you need to be prepared to respond. That means you need to have everything aligned. We changed our recognition systems, including compensation. Given our commitment to leadership behavior, we had to begin using behaviors in performance management, selection, and succession planning. We have an annual performance management review that is individually based, goals oriented, and includes our leadership model and the seven key behaviors. (We had six originally, but we added a seventh: value differences.)

My biggest fear was that we would not develop the next generation of leadership from the inside of Cargill. I believe strongly that the best thing for the future of the company is to develop leaders from the inside. I think Noel Tichy is right in noting that the biggest failure of our corporate institutions is in not developing the next generation of leaders. I firmly believe that a company cannot go outside and buy leadership; it has to be built from the inside. Just look at the multiple failures related to bringing in outsider CEOs. Going outside at the top can be a short-term solution, but if there is competition out there that's been building leadership from the inside, they're going to win every time.

We needed to take a different approach to succession than we had in the past. In the past when there was an opening, we discussed an individual's technical skills, managerial capabilities, and job performance. If the senior people collectively did not know an employee's name, they probably were not on the list. Most important, though, we needed to begin considering leadership and character traits as part of evaluating whether an individual could rise to the next level.

Now we identify high-potential talent from around the world and bring them together for our High Performance Leadership Academy. We believe it is critical that we support people early in their careers so they have a chance to get to the next level of leadership. Our talent reviews bring people forward based on leadership skills, business results, and how well they demonstrate our values and behaviors.

In June 2007, we issued our first-ever talent declarations document [Exhibit 19.2]. It spells out for people how to do well in this company. It sets out our standards, our strategic reliance on talent management, and lists our commitments to action, which apply to all leaders. It includes actions like using the Cargill leadership model in selection. The most controversial item was stating that the majority of the members of Cargill's future senior leadership team will have a minimum of two years living and working internationally.

Exhibit 19.2. Cargill Talent Declaration

Cargill Talent Declarations

Strategic Significance: Talent Management is a top priority

High performance demands high standards/expectations and execution in talent management. Talent management is the selection, development and retention of the right people, in alignment with both the current and future business goals.

Standards/Expectations

- Exceptional coaching and developing of people
- Driving collaboration and connecting talent across Cargill
- Using inspirational leadership to increase engagement
- Selecting and deselecting the right people
- Practice accountability for talent management through rewards and consequences

---

■ ■ ■

What did you do to measure results? How do you know this focus had an impact on business performance?

If one considers individual Cargill business unit financial performance and engagement scores, there is a huge correlation. That data convinced us that one of the most critical things we can monitor is employee engagement. We do this about every 18 months around the world today. It is critical to continue to move the dial on employee engagement.

Remember, we set out in the beginning to make Cargill faster, more agile, high performing, and customer-solutions focused.

We want to build a company that people choose to work for and one with which customers choose to do business. At the end of the day, it is about our customers. They do not choose Cargill; they choose our employees because of great relationships built on high competence. That is true around the world. I believe, and the data show us, that Cargill's growth in revenue and continued high performance are because these customer-focused behaviors and strategies are working.

Keep in mind, we had a goal of enhancing the Cargill brand. We do not have consumer products, but we wanted Cargill to have a reputation for providing customer solutions based on our knowledge and insights, brought to bear through our competence and behaviors. Our measures show we have substantially increased the value of the Cargill brand. We are far better than we were eight or nine years ago. This has also been a source of pride for Cargill employees.

■ ■ ■

What advice would you give other CEOs who want to make a difference through leadership?

First, if you're not willing to spend a lot of energy, resources, and significant amounts of your own personal time, do not even begin. You have to hang in there and persevere for a long time— well past the resistance of employees thinking the initiative is just the "flavor of the month." Changing is a multiyear effort.

Second, I think you have to involve a sufficient number of people, certainly at the top. It was actually pretty easy to get Cargill employees' attention, but in other companies, it may be an uphill battle, and change will have to come in smaller bites. We worked on everything at once. Financially, things did not go well the first year or two. Then we finally gained traction, and things have gone quite well since. The CEO simply must have people around who will help the company go through dramatic change; it cannot be accomplished by a single individual. Be patient, and accept the fact that it will probably take three, four, or five years for people to really get it.

Then, the senior leadership team must go out, talk ad nauseam about the behaviors, and engage people in dialogue about them. When we would visit locations, we would not talk with them about operating results; that was someone else's job. When we held town hall meetings around the world, we warned people in advance that we would choose people at random and ask them to tell me about our credo, our behaviors, and what they personally have done to change. Their participation was amazing. I would often be warned in advance that people would not have the courage to open up to the CEO, but they stunned even their bosses. On some visits, we would still be there talking with employees until 1:00 in the morning, and it was clear that the change was catching hold. Every chance we had, we talked to people about customer solutions and leadership behaviors.

I received good advice when I was elected CEO. A former CEO told me that he saw me as a kind of perfectionist. He warned me that I would not be able to know everything, and if I tried, everything would fall down around my ears. So I just had to let go. I can tell you it is hard to do, and some CEOs cannot ever do it. But I kept in mind some advice I have distilled over the years from reading and hearing Peter Drucker. I have always been inspired by his admonishing executives to become learners and dismiss the notion that they know everything. I needed to recognize that sometimes my subordinates would actually become my teachers.

■ ■ ■

Looking back now on your tenure, what are you most proud of?

There are several things. One is that the company changed dramatically and is positioned for the future because of the great collective effort of the senior leadership team. Much of that was due to getting people to understand that in the long run, the behaviors, leadership, and customer focus mattered more than anything else. Of course, I am also proud of Cargill's financial performance. We have been able to help our employees understand that in the midst of ongoing change in our world, the only sustainable element is our strong leadership culture.

I am extremely proud of Cargill employees and of the collaboration and connections that occur across the company. Employees accepted the challenge and adapted to our new leadership culture. I am grateful to all Cargill employees for successfully working through the change that was necessary to continue to make Cargill a great company.

CHAPTER 20

CHIEF HUMAN RESOURCE OFFICER PERSPECTIVES ON TALENT MANAGEMENT

Marcia J. Avedon, Stephen Cerrone,
Mirian Graddick-Weir, Rob Silzer

Talent management is widely discussed as an organizing framework for many Human Resource (HR) systems and processes in organizations. This chapter draws on separate interviews with three highly seasoned Human Resource executives to understand the usefulness and application of talent management in organizations. Each of these executives has been the Chief Human Resource Officer (CHRO) for at least two major business corporations, and each holds a Ph.D. degree in industrial-organizational psychology. They bring a unique and highly experienced perspective, having seen the evolution of Human Resources over the years and across different corporations, and are willing to share their experiences and insight. Here are the three CHROs:

- Marcia J. Avedon is the Senior Vice President of Human Resources and Communications for Ingersoll Rand. Prior to this, Marcia was the Senior Vice President of HR at Merck and held senior HR positions at Honeywell, Allied-Signal, and Anheuser Busch.

All four authors contributed equally to this chapter and are listed alphabetically.

- Stephen Cerrone is the Executive Vice President of Human Resources for Sara Lee Corporation. Prior to this Stephen was the Senior Vice President of HR for retail financial services at JP Morgan Chase, Senior Vice President of HR for Bank One, and Executive Vice President for Worldwide HR at Burger King. He also has held senior HR positions at Diageo.
- Mirian Graddick-Weir is Executive Vice President of Human Resources for Merck. Prior to this, Mirian was Executive Vice President of HR at AT&T and held various senior HR and line management positions at AT&T.

The interviewer, Rob Silzer, also is an industrial-organizational psychologist. Rob has known each of these executives for many years and has had an opportunity to work with them on HR-related projects in their organizations.

Defining Talent Management

Rob: **Thank you for your willingness to share your experience and professional insights. Let's start with definitions. What does the term** *talent management* **mean to you?**

Marcia: Talent management to me is an integrated set of processes and procedures used in an organization to attract, onboard, retain, develop, and move talent, as well as to exit talent, to achieve strategic objectives.

Mirian: When I think of talent management at the highest level, I think of our ability to attract, develop, and retain key diverse talent to meet critical current and future business needs. It is also making sure that we have the next generation of leaders through the development of a robust pipeline of talent.

Stephen: The definition we use at Sara Lee is "attracting, retaining, and developing the right people with the right skills in the right roles." A big part of that is fit. And then, what are you doing to retain and develop them to drive business results?

Rob: **Do you distinguish between HR management and talent management?**

Mirian: HR management is broader than talent management. It can include benefit strategies, labor strategies, workforce

planning, change management, or other policies and programs that impact people. Talent management is primarily
focused on ensuring people have the right skills and capabilities to execute your business strategy.

Stephen: The way I describe the role of HR is giving managers the
information they need to make better decisions about their people. Those could be pay decisions, exit decisions, selection decisions, promotion decisions, motivation issues, and others. It is
about giving managers the information, experience, knowledge,
and tools to make decisions around talent. It is a very broad concept that involves a number of different things.

Talent is a part of HR management and specifically deals
with the right people, in the right role, with the right level of
support. It is an element of what we are trying to do in HR.
There are other things in HR, for example, our benefits strategy, that represent some of what we stand for as a company
but are not necessarily core elements of our talent strategy.
If you see the HR strategy from a broad perspective there is
an element that includes talent but also a number of other
elements (for example, OD [organization development],
compensation, and benefits) that are broader. Talent is more
focused on individual capability, whereas HR also focuses on
organizational capability, culture, and other areas.

Marcia: Talent management is not equal to HR management.
Talent management is largely at the individual level of intervention and does not include management functions that are
at the team or organizational development level. Certain aspects
of HR, such as compensation and benefits strategy, are not
directly part of talent management. However, these functions
have to support the talent strategy, but they are not one and
the same.

HR management includes building talent and capabilities, since
that is one of the central reasons that HR exists in an enterprise. But HR also includes driving organizational change,
employee engagement, and the processes and systems that are
required to run the people side of the business. These are the
four central priorities for HR. However, talent management
has become the most critical one from a strategic standpoint

for many companies. Surveys of CEOs have indicated that one of their critical concerns, or what keeps them up at night, is whether they have an ample supply of leadership talent to achieve their strategy. While there are other key priorities within HR around organization change, engagement, and processes, talent is on the top of the list.

Influences on Talent Management

Rob: **How do the business strategies in an organization influence talent management efforts?**

Stephen: There should be a talent strategy underneath each business strategy, so the talent strategy always has a business connection and business outcome. I have seen it in different organizations in different ways, and sometimes it is more explicit in some than in others, but it should always be driven by the business needs.

At Sara Lee, we are moving from a holding company mindset to one of an integrated operating company. So we need to build individual capabilities, but we now want to have one leadership group with a common set of values and a common mission, who are moving in the same direction. So our talent management efforts (for example, leadership competencies, talent review process) are influenced by that goal, including working on a common employment brand. As an integrated operating company, we want to leverage talent across our businesses and look at that talent on a global (versus line of business) basis; so as the business strategy has changed, we have dramatically changed our talent strategy.

Marcia: In determining where to start with talent management I always start by looking at the company strategy. First, I determine what the business is trying to achieve and then assess the current talent and capabilities in the organization versus the capabilities needed to execute against the strategy. So where are the key gaps in terms of the talent? How effective are the current approaches to deliver against the key gaps? It is not simply understanding the current company strategy and the talent implications, but also assessing if we will be able to meet the demand for talent in the next five years, our long-range planning cycle, if we just kept doing everything the way we are doing it now.

Mirian: The talent management strategies should always be aligned with your business strategy. An important part of our role as the CHRO is to help translate the business strategy into the critical skills and capabilities required for success. We should constantly be aware of the gaps that exist and ensure our recruitment, staffing, and development strategies are designed to close those gaps.

Rob: What is an example of how a business strategy influenced your talent management approach?

Mirian: In the past, Merck ran its business as three relatively autonomous divisions: research and development, marketing and sales, and manufacturing. There was almost no movement of talent from one division to another. Our current One Merck strategy requires the divisions to work in a more integrated manner to (1) shorten the cycle time between the discovery of a molecule and the launch of a product; (2) ensure that molecules being developed actually meet an unmet medical need from the consumer perspective; and (3) proactively anticipate the supply and demand of a particular product to be able to effectively manufacture the product at the time it is launched. For Merck, this translates into the need for more collaboration and teamwork across the various functional silos and the development of leaders who have general management skills and can lead horizontally across divisions. From a talent management perspective, we are moving more people across divisions and emphasizing leadership behaviors such as collaboration and teamwork and championing change in our performance management processes and reward systems.

Stephen: In one of our businesses, we are driving a turnaround and concurrently looking at how to build out the business geographically. So our talent management strategy has been a combination of *buy* and *build.* Internally, we have developed a program for incumbents (and for new hires) that develops the managerial skills we need to transform the business.

Concurrently, we are actively recruiting from outside the company since we really need employees who have experience in the industry and who understand how to drive growth. The business strategy is to have an infrastructure that can support a larger business, so we need more capable people in that space; therefore, the talent strategy is to improve the skills of incumbents and to hire individuals who can accelerate the turnaround and growth.

Marcia: In Ingersoll Rand, like many other global industrial companies, one of our key strategies is globalization. The growth in China is one of the most important economic opportunities in the world right now. Like many U.S.-based multinationals, we do not have a lot of depth of talent and people who have actually done business in China. Specifically, we need more people who understand everything from the regulatory issues, to workplace requirements, to the government relations, to the cultural norms and cultural requirements to be successful in China. It is important to learn not only how to acquire talent in China but how to retain talent in China. Retention is a huge problem, particularly because most multinationals are trying to grow their business in China. There is incredible labor market opportunity, which allows people to jump from company to company, which culturally is seen as perfectly appropriate.

China is a huge economic opportunity. What is required is that you develop your strategy for being an employer of choice and retaining people in that specific market. The business strategy of growth in China may be organic growth or through acquisition. Either way, there are talent management implications. When we acquire a business in China, we must address how we ensure the talent stays with Ingersoll Rand and so we can build the capabilities needed to sell, or manufacture, or provide service effectively, either for the local market or as an exporter. A critical piece of the talent management cycle for retention in China is development. We have learned that while compensation matters in China, learning and development is even more important. If people believe their employer will differentially invest in them and their skills, then they will stay. For example, we have opened a satellite branch of Ingersoll Rand University in Shanghai as a visible commitment to development for our employees in the Asia Pacific region. We have found that while training, development, and career opportunities are important throughout the world, they have a heightened sense of importance in China right now.

Sometimes talent management may influence your business strategy. One example is where we are trying to grow the business in developing countries. Where you locate a production site may be influenced by how proximal you are to universities or to the major metropolitan areas. Deciding which property we buy can be impacted by whether we can recruit and attract talent to that location. Which location would give us better talent in terms of the specific skills we need to be successful, such as engineers or managers? Another example of talent considerations driving strategy is when integrating a merger. Often, after a merger, we find we have more manufacturing capability than we need. In making the decision regarding which plants to keep, we often look at where there is better talent if their productivity and other metrics are essentially equal. These are cases where the talent availability and capability drive strategic decisions for the business.

I have even seen examples where businesses have been sold and the root cause was bad selection decisions. Leaders were put into jobs that they were either not ready for or not able to perform and were left in the position too long. The business then spiraled down in terms of performance, until finally the company either sells it or closes it. Publicly, these situations may be attributed to market factors, but certainly a key factor was poor talent management.

Rob: **What impact does the CEO have on the talent management direction?**

Stephen: They have a significant impact on the culture and talent of the company. First, how they spend their time is important, and great CEOs allocate a disproportionate part of their day to developing talent. Second, at the CEO level, there are always business trade-offs, and resources allocated to talent (people, money, time) are sometimes the first ones to get reduced if business performance suffers. CEOs who lead talent management efforts understand how critical those resources are, and they support and drive talent management as part of the long-term business strategy. In both the United States and in Europe, I have seen CEOs who understand the importance of both the culture and the talent plans to the future of the company, and they personally model the efforts and resist any efforts that might derail them.

Mirian: The time and attention paid to talent management in an organization is directly influenced by the CEO's perspective and whether he or she truly believes that attracting, developing, and retaining top talent is a competitive differentiator in the marketplace. That perspective gets translated into the amount of personal time they spend on talent issues and the amount of investment they are willing to make in people programs that drive value. It is never a good sign when the initial place executives want to cut costs is in the training and development arena. Our CEO instituted quarterly talent reviews in our executive committee meetings (focused on cross-divisional movement and career development), and he spent significant time this year with the divisional and functional heads conducting in-depth succession planning and talent reviews. These reviews culminated in an in-depth talent review with the board. The CEO also has significant influence on whether the company has a performance-based culture by setting high standards, by rewarding those who execute the strategy and role model the leadership behaviors, and by holding those accountable who do not.

Marcia: The CEO makes all the difference in the world between a successful, integrated talent management strategy and one that is programmatic. Everyone in the organization knows if people are simply going through the motions, or if talent management decisions and processes are seen as critical to the business, based on the CEO's personal behavior. The great CEOs spend enormous amounts of time personally evaluating leaders, selecting leaders for hiring or promotion, and determining who deserves the greatest rewards. They reinforce the principles and logic for talent management by the decisions they make and those they endorse or correct in managing others. Great CEOs create a mindset and culture of talent stewardship as a key component of being an effective leader.

Rob: **Since you have been the CHRO in several companies, are there a few specific differences between companies that directly influence your approach to talent management?**

Marcia: Several differences between companies seem to matter in determining the talent management approach that works best. First, where the company is in its life cycle and where the company is in its leadership life cycle both make a difference. How long has the CEO and the CEO's team been in place? Is the company at the beginning of a planned succession at the top, or, possibly, has a new leader just joined? The timing of senior leadership change can vastly change the talent management strategy because, in many ways, the talent management strategy is the CEO's people strategy. Your agenda in running talent management for the company is quite different if the CEO is very established in his or her job and has a strong point of view that has been in place for many years, compared to a new CEO who is coming on board and questioning whether he has the team he wants. New CEOs ask if the existing team embodies the behaviors and the cultural attributes that they want to drive for the new strategy. I have found that leadership life cycle is a key determinant in the approach to talent management as well as the priorities.

Regarding the company life cycle, it is critical to determine the stage of the company in terms of maturity. Is it at a point where it is very successful and established as a company and strategically making incremental improvements? Or, in contrast, is there a quite radical change in business strategy underway, like we have here at Ingersoll Rand? While our CEO has been here almost nine years, we are right in the middle of a portfolio transformation and radically changing the company, going from a cyclical heavy machinery company to a much more diversified industrial company with more predictable earnings and a greater emphasis on technology.

This has required significant acquisitions and divestitures, with many talent management challenges and opportunities to achieve the business transformation.

The talent implications are very different when you are going through a major redirection of the strategy versus when there are incremental bolt-on changes or small changes to the strategy. So the degree of change, either because of a change of leadership or a change in business strategy, can make the agenda very different across companies.

Mirian: At AT&T, as we evolved into a competitive marketplace, it became very clear to us that we did not have the required depth of marketing talent. When you are rooted in a monopoly, you can basically tell customers what they need. In a competitive marketplace, you need an in-depth understanding of your customer—what they value and what they are willing to pay for your products and services. We did not have the luxury of time to develop this capability, so we had to develop an external recruiting strategy designed to quickly acquire these skills. We had large profit-and-loss business units and had a plethora of general management talent. Here at Merck, we are just in the early stages of building leaders who can manage horizontally across the various divisions and who are more externally focused on meeting customer needs. Our goal is to begin to move people around from one division to build general management capabilities.

Stephen: In an organization like Burger King, the company has over 300,000 employees but only 30,000 who work directly as employees for the company. The remaining employees work for franchisees, so you do not control how they are hired, developed, paid, or managed. As the head of HR, you have to rely on your influencing skills by putting yourself in the shoes of the individual franchise owners and figuring out what is important to them. When we implemented a manager assessment tool, we chose owners who already understood talent management and welcomed the initiative. While this approach took longer and required more "selling," that was the nature of the business, and we had to manage within it. In other organizations, HR has direct control over

the employee population, so you can influence the key leaders, and it becomes much easier to implement systemwide
initiatives.

Rob: **Is the talent management approach different for critical
functions?**

Mirian: At Merck, the engine of the company is research and
development. Our success depends on our ability to have
scientists who can ensure we have a robust pipeline of drugs
that meet unmet medical needs. While we have a common
talent management process across the company, there are
unique requirements in attracting, developing, and retaining
very specialized scientific talent. Many of these individuals
are specialized in unique therapeutic areas (for example, diabetes and obesity) and there are not many of them in their
respective fields. So the competition for this talent is fierce.
We often have to think of unique ways to attract a tenure-
track department chair from the world of academia and
convince them to join the less certain world of working in a
publicly traded company. At the same time we are looking for
individuals in R&D with deep functional skills, we also need
people who have good leadership skills, particularly those
who lead people. So our leadership development programs
are applicable across functions.

At AT&T special attention was given to individuals in our
network group who had security clearance. This was a
unique and marketable skill set to have, because it often took
between 12 to 18 months for people to get through the government review process and obtain security clearance. We
came up with various retention strategies for these individuals because it was a hot skill set in the marketplace, especially with all the security concerns since U.S.-based terrorist
attacks in 2001.

Marcia: I think of these critical functions as dominant functions.
As you would expect in a pharmaceutical company, there is
a tremendous focus on the research and development and
the scientists. This includes not only the bench chemist who
hopefully is going to come up with the discovery for the next
cure for cancer, but also the person who is running the labs

and deciding how the labs are organized and where resources are focused. Do we have people who not only can discover great science but who can run a laboratory in a productive and effective way?

Every company has at least one, maybe a couple, of dominant functions. So at Merck, for example, "real guys" invent stuff and have breakthrough scientific discoveries. (Gordon Hewitt of University of Michigan introduced me to the notion of dominant functions as what people say "real guys" do in your company.) At Allied Signal during the 1990s, the "real guys" were finance guys, who knew the business numbers, and also general managers, who made the numbers. At Ingersoll Rand we are trying to move from being strong in productivity, cost, and internal process management to also being good at customer focus and innovation. So how do you change the dominant function in a company if you are trying to get stronger in growth, for example, versus productivity? It is difficult to broaden the number of dominant functions because the original culture and function is, typically, what has led to success in the company. It is similar to the career of an individual; sometimes what has made the person successful in the past is not what is going to keep making the person successful going forward. In organizations, the dominant function is what the company is really good at, and there is a reason why it is prized and favored, because it has been part of the value proposition of the company. So it is hard to change.

It is similar, in my mind, to why it is hard to integrate an acquisition that is markedly different from your own core competencies, in a way that does not squelch the very value for which you just paid a lot of money. This is because of the overwhelming power of culture. Culture is hard to permeate and hard to change. I think of dominant functions in the same way. It gets easier to change when the business strategy requires those other functions to be valued and there is a compelling business need.

An example, from Honeywell and Ingersoll Rand, is the development of general business managers. So rather than primarily focusing on the development of a single dominant function, a critical focus is developing broad business managers with multifunctional experiences who can run businesses. In diversified conglomerates, the number of businesses with separate profit and loss statements (P&Ls) in the company has an impact on the talent agenda. These companies have a great advantage in developing general managers who can aspire to and ultimately succeed at the highest levels, whether it is as a COO or president or CEO, because they have natural training grounds with various types and sizes of businesses. There are miniversions of those senior jobs all over the company. It is really fun to be in charge of talent management when you can see someone grow from running a small business with their first P&L, to running a global business that may have revenues of a billion dollars, to running a whole business sector, to ultimately being the president or CEO of the company.

Companies that do not have multiple P&Ls inherently are challenged in how to grow general managers. Years ago many companies created country manager and regional manager roles that really did not have a full P&L but companies pretended that they did. These roles became a grooming ground for larger positions. Although there was a developmental benefit, the organizational structure was expensive and inefficient. Many companies, pharmaceutical companies, for example, are struggling with this issue. How do we organize in a way that actually creates or simulates true P&Ls? So pharmaceutical companies are going to franchise organizational designs where someone is running a whole therapeutic area for the world with multiple functions included in that role, such as marketing, sales, and product development. It is a way to develop more of a general management mindset than a functional management mindset. That is why the diversified companies have a distinct advantage in developing general managers, since individuals can run a true P&L business early in their career, even if the business is quite small.

Rob: **What others factors influence your approach to talent management in an organization?**

Stephen: The board of directors has a role in talent management efforts involving the CEO, her direct reports, and our top 100 leaders. They are not yet aggressively driving an agenda around talent, but we provide them with talent profiles, assessments, and development plans for the key leaders so they understand how we are managing that population. Additionally, the evolution of the business drives the talent management efforts. I have been a part of an organization that was being sold, and the talent management effort revolved around retention and development until the sale was completed. After that, we significantly increased our efforts in recruiting since we launched a new business strategy that required new skills and behaviors. Finally, being public or private often influences the talent management efforts. Often, at private equity-owned firms, there is a shorter-term business strategy, and that impacts some long-term leadership and talent development efforts.

Mirian: Workforce demographics can impact your talent management strategies. Every company may have a different profile in terms of their demographics. For example, we had an aging workforce in the network group at AT&T and had to proactively manage a potential skill shortage over time. In addition, as younger people enter the workforce, most of them do not intend to stay with the same company for an entire career. Many will change jobs more than five times over the course of their careers. Finding ways to retain employees long enough to reap the benefits of your investment is an important part of a talent management strategy.

Marcia: Another concept that has impact on the success of talent management is the degree to which managers are actually accountable for talent management, or talent stewardship—which is what we call it at Ingersoll Rand. Do managers believe that their job is to be a talent steward, or is that really an HR function? Being an effective manager is doing talent management well, whether it is recruiting or developing. Great companies that have been very successful have embedded the notion that talent management is central to being a good manager. GE and Pepsi come to mind as examples because they have had long traditions of talent management as a key line management responsibility, equivalent in importance to budget management or strategic planning. How they manage talent might not be the same at these companies, and they use many different practices and approaches. But the degree to which there is a talent mindset that is broadly held in management is one of the key determinants of what makes talent management successful.

CHRO Influence on Talent Management

Rob: **As the Chief HR Officer (CHRO), what influence do you have in setting the talent management strategy?**

Mirian: One of the most significant ways CHROs can add value to the company is to ensure the company has a robust talent management strategy that is aligned with the business strategy. This is why we must be business partners at the table and make sure we have a good understanding of the business and leverage that knowledge to influence our recruitment, development, and retention strategies.

Stephen: The biggest impact is in developing and implementing a long-term people/organization strategy that describes how we will drive business results through our talent. That strategy gets discussed and agreed to with the CEO and her team, and that drives our three- to five-year priorities around talent. HR has a significant influence on the process, format, timing, and resources that are involved in attracting and developing our talent. For example, HR leads the process of identifying the management and leadership experiences that people need to drive our business strategy; with business input and direction, we develop and implement those experiences across the global organization and provide metrics that evaluate their impact.

Rob: **Which talent initiatives do you focus on early in your tenure in a company?**

Marcia: I really focus on the link to strategy. Talent management has to be seen as strategic and as part of the agenda on how we want to run the company—whether you call it a talent mindset or talent management or even the people strategy. One of the processes that I lead that is very powerful is our organization and leadership review (OLR). It is conducted on an equal level to the annual operating plan and the long-range strategic plan of the company. At Ingersoll Rand we call it the OLR, at Allied Signal we called it management resource review (MRR), and GE famously calls it Session C. The principle is that if a business manager is not thinking about how they are going to make their financial numbers in their annual operating plan, how they are going to strategically run the business for the long term, and whether they have the people and organizational capabilities to get there, then they are not running the business effectively. The third pillar, in addition to the strategic plan and the operating plan, is a talent management plan. It has to have an equal emphasis as the operational and strategic plans. Such a plan is more than succession or replacement plans and includes organization design, strategic staffing, leadership evaluations of both performance and potential, retention, and deselection. In the more sophisticated companies, these evaluations of performance and potential drive compensation decisions later in the cycle.

Stephen: The most important thing to do is to understand the critical issues in the business and how talent and organizational capabilities can be used to drive them. The thing to do is to try to find out where you can have a big impact on a business issue or problem. One way to do this is to spend a significant amount of time with senior leaders, and in the business, asking questions and listening to what keeps the business leaders up at night. In addition, I try to avoid looking for the perfect solution. Early on it is important to make an impact, and often you can do that by addressing a business need without attempting to find the perfect answer. Business leaders have a sense of urgency in getting their issues resolved, and addressing them quickly is important, especially early in your tenure.

Mirian: I try to first partner with the line organization and understand the business strategy, priorities, and organizational capabilities necessary to execute the strategy. You want to assess what talent gaps exist and determine ways to close those gaps. If we are trying to radically transform the business, it is important that the executive team understands that it takes time to dramatically change a culture. Three of our big cultural challenges at Merck are to get people to embrace change, collaborate across divisions, and become more externally focused. We have multiyear initiatives in place and a measurement strategy designed to close those gaps. On the other hand, if part of the strategy is to change the selling model for representatives, the goal would be to put an appropriate selection and training program in place to rapidly upgrade the skills in the sales force.

It is important to assess whether an intervention is easy to implement versus difficult to implement, or whether it will have a high business impact versus a low business impact. Early on, my advice is to focus on high impact and relatively easy projects to implement in order to gain credibility and momentum.

Rob: **What's the most difficult challenge you face as the SVP of HR?**

Stephen: One common challenge relates to the relationship you have with the CEO and her team. You absolutely must have a great relationship with the CEO because she trusts you and confides in you regarding a number of business and talent issues. That said, you also need to have a great relationship with your peers; they have to trust you enough so they can talk to you about each other and because you are often the only person who can be their confidant. It sounds strange but it can be isolating at times, and you have to manage the balance. You have to be a sounding board and keep a balance between the CEO and the team, and the way you do that is by talking about the business as a businessperson, not as an HR person.

Mirian: One of my most difficult challenges is time management. The CEO and the executive team require a lot of your time and attention, and you want to make sure that you stay very connected to them. Part of your effectiveness as a CHRO is based on the relationships that you build with that team. You have important board work associated with the compensation and benefit committee, and that requires enormous attention to detail throughout the year. You also have to lead the HR community, and many of us are in the middle of transforming our functions by reducing costs and strengthening the capabilities in the organization. Finally, it is important to stay connected with employee groups at all levels within the company and with customers. There are enormous demands on your time, and it is important to recognize the range of responsibilities, commitments, and roles we play and to balance them effectively.

Integration of Human Resource Functions

Rob: **How important is it to integrate HR functions around your talent management strategy?**

Marcia: HR is trying not to be so siloed. In most HR organizations, there is a disproportionate number of generalists to specialists. I expect every generalist to be thinking about talent management every day. The company's view or model on leadership talent should be widely held and understood by the entire HR function. I cannot think of a specialty area or center of expertise that should not be aligned, although some to a greater extent than others.

For example, benefits are typically not highly differentiated in a given company based on talent. Normally retirement plans and pensions would be the same for the majority of people except maybe for the very top executives. So a pension retirement planning specialist would not necessarily be thinking as deeply every day about talent. Paid time off is an interesting example. It is a benefit and part of the value proposition for talent that matters. If you remember back to the dot-com time period in the 1990s, certain benefits such as flexible work arrangements, time off, working from home, and telecommuting were part of the value proposition. Their proposition was that we will pay you less base pay and give you a bunch of stock options that may or may not pay off, but you can bring your dog to work, play Ping-Pong at lunch, and come and go as you please. So even work environment and new benefits can have a talent slant to them. Even relocation policies and administration, which is often the first onboarding experience, can matter; if it is a bad experience, then your critical talent may have a poor first impression of the company.

Mirian: It is very easy to send contradictory signals to the organization regarding what is important for success when your HR functions supporting your talent management strategy are not aligned. One example is when you define certain leadership behaviors as being critical for success, yet you promote people who are not strong leaders. Another example is to implement a state-of-the-art succession planning process, yet when it comes time to fill critical roles in the organization, the talent does not come from the succession planning roster. The bottom line is that it is critical to make sure your recruiting, staffing, compensation, performance management, succession planning, retention, and development strategies and systems are aligned.

Stephen: It is very important that they are integrated. We have a center of excellence in organizational development, and it includes five areas: talent acquisition, talent management, diversity, learning and leadership, and culture. We have made an effort to integrate everything and put it all under one person. Although he does not have responsibility for things like compensation, he can figure out what we need to do to bring people in, onboard them, and develop and retain them. The easy part is integrating functions here at corporate headquarters; the harder part, which is just as critical, is integrating across the businesses. We have to be clear about what the businesses are going to drive on their own and what we want to integrate across the businesses. We want businesses to coordinate with the corporate center of excellence, and when you get down to this level of integration, you need clarity of responsibility and accountability, and you need people to agree on who is going to do what.

The issue of integration also depends on the strategy and structure of the organization. Burger King, JP Morgan Chase, and Sara Lee each had a different structure, and the talent strategy was made easier or harder based on that structure. Burger King was in some ways a simple business that was challenging to execute across thousands of restaurants. Sara Lee is more complex and involves several different businesses with different strategies, issues, and margins. What you have to decide is what level of integration is important for the business, and that will vary across the different business structures.

Rob: How do you decide whether to buy or build talent?

Marcia: This is connected to the famous GE vitality index of 20-70-10, which says that you move the bottom 10 percent of people out every year. How aggressive should we be to deselect so that we make room to select new people? It is hard to generalize on that. There are huge cultural differences between companies. John Boudreau has been writing about "pivotal talent" (Boudreau & Ramstad, 2005). Where is the difference between an average performer and an exceptional performer most critical to your talent strategy and your business strategy? Where does it not matter much? How hard is it to develop the pivotal talent to get to the exceptional level? That is the sort of rigor we are starting to think about, and it helps to answer the buy-or-build question more precisely.

Buying versus building talent depends on a number of factors. First, there are some jobs that are very critical, and it takes too long to develop people for them. If you do not have a ready supply of talent, you have no choice but to select from the outside. Companies with legacies of great development of leadership talent hopefully do not find themselves in that position very often. However, sometimes even they still have to hire new talent if they want to go into a new market or if they need a technical skill set or familiarity with a new industry. Most companies want to create a robust internal talent development system so that you are not going outside the majority of the time. It depends on your strategy, how long you have been at it, and how good you have been in developing talent for the future needs of the company.

Rob: Are compensation and benefits getting more tailored to individual needs to support talent objectives?

Mirian: Benefits tend to be relatively core across the company (for example, pensions, 401K, health and welfare programs), except outside the United States, where they are customized to address local country needs and requirements. While we have an overall compensation framework, we have moved away from a homogeneous compensation structure toward one that recognizes important market differences across various job families. So we pay higher for certain jobs than others based on the market data. We also tailor retention strategies at the individual level based on a person's unique skills and criticality to the company.

Marcia: Normally the assessments of potential and performance are linked to rewards in different ways. For example, at Honeywell when I was there, performance in a given year drove annual bonuses, and long-term potential drove equity grants in terms of stock options and restricted stock. So the people who were seen as having tremendous potential for the long term were given significantly more long-term incentives in the form of equity. However, the company also believed strongly in pay for performance, so even if someone is not promotable to the next level and they had a tremendous year, we would still give them a big bonus. They both would still get equity, but not at the same level of reward. We did a lot of analysis to make sure we were executing against our strategy and that true high potentials were getting more equity than the people with less potential. Making these linkages clear and consistent is not always easy because it requires managers to differentiate employees.

In addition to tailoring rewards to performance and potential, there are also questions about both hot skills and hot markets. This involves how quickly a company adjusts to changing labor market dynamics. It ties back to how centrally or decentrally the company is managed and how these decisions get made. There is a question of how much autonomy you give to local HR managers to adjust the compensation ranges, such as hiring talent in China. It can be troublesome to respond in an agile manner when there is ambiguity or too much bureaucracy.

Rob: **What gets included in talent retention efforts?**

Mirian: We recently completed an employee survey that addressed a variety of compensation and retention issues. Not surprisingly, we found that the opportunity for people to realize their potential is a very important retention issue, in addition to having adequate training and development opportunities. The company culture is also a key aspect of retention. High performers are not attracted to staying in bureaucratic environments where it is difficult to get things done, while others want an environment where risk taking is valued and rewarded. Sometimes we underestimate the immediate impact that a supervisor or a work group has on the retention of individuals. The day-to-day interactions that people have with their supervisor and the quality of those interactions can definitely impact retention.

In today's environment, we find that more people want some degree of work/family balance. In the past, people were willing to relocate every few years for development. However, fewer people are willing to make those kinds of sacrifices, particularly when they are in a dual-career relationship. Offering programs such as child care and elder care support can make a difference in retaining top talent. While compensation strategies are important, there are numerous other factors that impact retention.

Predictors of High Potential

Rob: **How do you define high-potential talent?**

Marcia: Normally we are talking about leadership potential. Organizations try to assess an individual to determine how high the person can go in the leadership ranks based on what they have demonstrated to date. No matter how rigorous we try to be, at the end of the day it is a subjective assessment of how far we think this person can go and what we can do to get them there. In most companies, there is an assumption that if somebody is a high-potential person, they are performing adequately in their current job, although there is some debate about whether you can be high potential if you are not performing in your current job. But let us assume they are performing well. We usually assess leadership potential using the leadership model and competencies in the company.

One concern for me is *potential for what?* Running the research labs at Merck or running an HR organization? Potential is a generic designation, and by itself it is not that useful. However, within a certain talent pool, it is very useful. For example, it is very useful to identify our high-potential general managers who we think can run billion-dollar businesses. That is an interesting conversation because then I know what I am assessing for, and it is more than just general leadership capability. There are also some functional skills and capabilities that are very important.

We loosely use the term *high potential.* It is important to put people in pools in order to say who is in the potential pool for a certain job. The readiness concept is also interesting and usually comes into play with potential. So if someone has potential to be the SVP of HR, when will they be ready: Two years, five years, or ten years? Those are very different profiles. An early-career person who is just five years out of graduate school and who has potential to do my job requires a whole different set of actions than somebody who will be ready in two years. So there are several important variables to look at: high potential, growth potential at the same level, or mastery potential, which means they are staying at their current level.

Rob: **What are the characteristics of high-potential individuals?**

Stephen: While the characteristics are general in nature, we look for someone who embodies our values, who can assimilate new information quickly, and who has the energy and desire to move ahead in the organization. Having someone who has the ability to learn (that is, quickly absorb and understand new information) is important so you can move them to new positions and they can learn quickly. In our organization, it is important that they also understand the need to develop and leverage partnerships in getting results. Nobody, no matter how smart and driven, will succeed if it is at the expense of others. So high-potential employees who understand and embody that partnership will be more likely to be successful.

Marcia: There are some generic characteristics. For example, the Corporate Leadership Council (2005) has done some interesting work that discusses career aspiration as central to being high potential. Having a drive to achieve in your career certainly would be a generic characteristic of a high potential. Not only do people have to aspire, but they have to get something meaningful out of the variety and breadth of experiences they have, which is shorthand for learning ability— being introspective and learning from experience.

There are some people who are highly achievement oriented, who are career centered, and who want to keep getting better and keep learning. They are never satisfied that they have arrived. These are some base attributes that are important for career progression, irrespective of discipline or job. On the other hand, getting someone ready to be the head of HR is different from developing someone to be a general manager. They would need different experiences.

As people with leadership potential grow as leaders, it becomes less about them. As leaders move up the ranks, they must learn that their success is about others and developing others. We know a lot about leaders as teachers, and an important piece of leadership development is about others and not about self. Typically, early in a person's career there is the motivation and aspirational piece, which is still there in later stages. However, it becomes balanced with creating capability in others and surrounding oneself with people who are even more talented than you. The really exceptional high-potential leaders learn this lesson quickly, and people want to follow them.

Learning ability is more than just wanting to learn. Some people are able to adapt and learn on the fly. It is not just being eager to learn but actually being able to self-correct. When I coach people or give feedback to people, I find that some very talented people are "Teflon-like." You tell them something negative, and it just does not sink in. They will say they are eager to learn, but when they get the feedback, they really do not take it to heart, and they do not do anything about it. That is a potential derailer because they are not able to learn from mistakes, to handle tough feedback, or to be honest with themselves.

Often high-potential people do not wait for someone else to tell them that they performed poorly in some regard; rather they tell themselves that they could have done better. People with really high potential almost do that automatically. In *The War for Talent* study (Michaels, Handfield-Jones, & Axelrod, 2001), McKinsey noted that high-potential people really want feedback and create situations where success and failure are obvious. They are not just saying they want feedback; *they really want feedback.* Companies that differentially give high potentials more development, more stretch, more tough assignments tend to fulfill that need of asking themselves, *Can I do it?* So wanting challenges, testing oneself, and being honest with oneself are all characteristic of high potentials.

Another characteristic is resilience; maybe it is the incredible drive they have. It is not only what they learn from the setbacks and hardships, but the resilience to pick yourself up and say, *I am going to do it better the next time, and I am not going to let it sink me.*

International Challenges

Rob: **Does your talent management approach differ internationally?**

Marcia: The fundamentals of the talent strategy do not differ across countries, but the specifics do differ. For example, the degree to which leaders are willing to move their families geographically differs across countries and cultures. We also have some systemic barriers in HR to moving people internationally. For example, there are few global companies that have multinational pension plans, which allow movement of people easily across countries without hurting their retirement planning. We have barriers to doing what industrial-organizational psychologists have encouraged: giving people cross-cultural and diverse experiences and moving them rapidly and early in their career. But there are practical concerns and cultural issues. Some companies, such as Shell and Unilever, have identified a small pool of *global nationals,* who are people willing to move all around the globe, and then treat them differently in terms of compensation, benefits, and development.

Even teamwork differs across countries, depending on whether the culture emphasizes individualism or collectivism. To run a complex enterprise, information has to get shared and people have to work together for the collective good. Teamwork is a core value, but exactly what teamwork means and how teams work together varies greatly.

In China, U.S. multinationals have a fundamentally different value proposition from a local Chinese company. Many talented people in China, particularly at the managerial levels, want to work for multinationals so they can learn more about Western business practices and marketing practices. The more challenging question is, Why work for one multinational versus another? Most applicants are interested not only in the job you are offering them and the pay, but they are very interested in how you will develop them, what their career opportunities will be, and how quickly those opportunities will materialize. We have to be very clear about that and then deliver against it.

Stephen: The talent management strategy is similar, but the implementation is different. For example, how we treat cross-Europe assignments is different from how we treat an American moving to Barcelona. The entire area of cross-geography moves is challenging, since one size does not fit all issues. By way of example, we are considering three or four different expatriate levels so we can more readily move employees who have different needs—for example, schooling, child care, and housing. Regardless of whether the issues are the same, you need to understand and respect different cultures. People want to know that you are open to their cultural differences, and it's important to avoid assuming the U.S. approach will work for non-U.S. employees.

Measuring Talent Management Success

Rob: **How do you measure your success in talent management?**

Stephen: We look at retention and turnover at all levels, but particularly at a senior level. We also evaluate the percentage of positions where we have internal successors. Based on our talent review process, we track employees on the high-potential list, and we periodically review our retention rates for that particular group. We also do a compensation analysis to evaluate the differentiation of pay between performance levels, and we share and discuss that information with the senior teams. Finally, we track whether development plans and appraisals are completed, and we report on those data regularly so managers can help drive the process and behaviors in their teams.

Marcia: The depth of the key talent pools that are identified for the strategy, whether you call them high potentials or critical talent, is a clear measure of the success of talent management. Are we attracting them and retaining them? What percentage of high potentials is being retained? What is the selection ratio? How many applicants to hires do you have? Do you have a great pool of people coming into those critical, pivotal talent areas? Even the old-fashioned speed to fill or time to hire are still good measures. If you are getting that talent faster and they are effective, then you are at a competitive advantage. Evaluating the sources of talent that yield the highest acceptance rates and the highest retention multiple years later is also useful.

One measure that every company struggles with is readiness for taking larger roles or succession readiness. What portion of the key management positions has a ready-now successor or has a successor ready in one to two years? Every company I know does not have the percentage of *ready now* successors that they wish they had. What portion of key positions at any given time is vacant? It is a simplistic measure, but if you are running a sports franchise and you are missing people in a key position or two, you would not win the game. It is amazing to me that managers tolerate vacancies for very long.

Another area that interests me in terms of measurement is where we have differentially invested in talent. For example, at Ingersoll Rand we have a program we call the IR M.B.A. We have partnered with Indiana University to create a customized M.B.A. program for employees of Ingersoll Rand. It is targeted at high-potential midlevel managers who do not have an M.B.A. Our retention of those graduates five years later is a key metric of the return on our investment in them.

We should be treating them with particular care in managing their careers. since we have differentially invested in them. Are they progressing and getting ahead? Another example is our early-career accelerated development program, which is a two- or three-year rotational program in different functional areas for new graduates. A key metric is how many of them are still with us five years after graduating from the program.

Mirian: We have a company scorecard at Merck based on financial, customer, internal business drivers, and people/culture measures. Three of the people and culture measures are associated with talent management. The first is a measure of whether we are making progress in strengthening the diversity of our upper-management and executive team. The second measure is retention of our high performers, and the last measure focuses on having successors in place for key positions. Our annual bonus pool is funded based on the results of our company scorecard.

Lessons Learned

Rob: **What lessons have you learned about how to implement an effective talent management strategy?**

Mirian: One lesson I have learned is that you must have the support and sponsorship of the CEO and the senior team, and the programs must be viewed as adding value to the business. Everything we do in the talent management space must have a direct connection to the business strategy. Sometimes we have a tendency to develop state-of-the-art talent management programs even though they are not really utilized or valued by line managers. Senior executives must also be aligned around a development philosophy. For example, you cannot move people across divisions if the senior team does not believe that building general managers is important.

Another lesson is that the board must be fully engaged in the selection and development of the CEO and potential CEO candidates. Sometimes it is difficult for leaders to acknowledge that the person who might replace them needs to have a very different profile to be successful and have the ability to take the company to the next level. So boards play an important role and bring a level of objectivity that is critical.

A final lesson is that a significant barrier to effective talent management is the ability to give managers and executives open, candid, and honest feedback. It is a significant inhibitor to developing great leaders. It is important to have a culture where it is encouraged to be honest about an individual's strengths and developmental gaps. I have lived in polite cultures where people are told what they want to hear rather than what they need to hear. As a result, we avoid giving people honest feedback, and they often end up derailing, or, worse yet, we keep moving mediocre performers around the business. I have found that its gets more challenging the higher up you go in an organization, because egos get in the way of people being intellectually honest about performance. So my advice is to start giving candid feedback early in a person's career and create a culture where people are encouraged to provide and seek constructive feedback.

Marcia: One lesson is that it cannot be HR's talent management strategy. It has to be the way the company is being managed by all line managers and people managers. It needs to be a core process in the company that is owned by every manager, and it is part of how managers are judged on their effectiveness. Are they accountable? We can create all sorts of tools and processes, but if they are not part of the fabric of how the company is managed, they are not going to be successful.

I have also learned to avoid fads. Be focused on what is going to work in your particular culture and in your particular company, not only from a business strategy standpoint but even from the cultural view. For example, how much rigor and complexity will be tolerated in your culture? So you have to match the business need to the culture of your management. How do managers manage? How do the other management information systems work? Align what you are doing with the annual strategic management process. Give it the same rhythm, cadence, and complexity. Be sure to know and learn the culture. What works well in Microsoft will not work in The Limited. Do what will work in your company and what will be accepted in your company in order for it to be owned by the line management.

Stephen: One lesson is that you need clarity around the direction and future of the organization and what business strategies are critical to delivering on that. You need some clarity and consistency from the leaders in the company, and that needs to be communicated on a regular basis to others. Once you have that clarity, the talent management strategy should focus on the big business issues and on how to deliver them. I would focus on the three or four critical areas where you will make the biggest impact, versus trying to develop the ultimate solution. Finally, you should identify your most critical talent pools, measure their performance, and disproportionately allocate your talent management efforts toward those employees. One size does not fit all employees, and given we all have limited resources, you should focus on those employee groups that have the biggest impact on the organization's results.

Rob: **What lessons have you learned about how to be an effective CHRO?**

Mirian: The two most critical success factors in the CHRO role are credibility and trust. Credibility comes from having a solid knowledge of the business, ensuring that HR programs you implement add value to the business, and having the ability to build strong relationships with your colleagues. Establishing trust with the CEO and the senior team is so important. Without trust, you get shut out of critical discussions, especially involving talent management. You have to be a part of these important conversations in order to influence the outcome. We must also have courage in our roles to challenge the status quo and make sure behaviors are consistent with company values.

CHROs are under enormous pressure today to transform the HR function so we can keep costs aligned with competitive benchmarks, ensure we strengthen the capabilities in HR (particularly building strong business acumen), and proactively help line leaders solve important business problems. For me, having several years of actual line experience has been enormously useful, and I encourage others to obtain it, particularly early in their career.

Future Directions

Clearly these three seasoned professionals have a very broad range of talent management experience. They all have faced a wide range of significant business challenges as CHROs in different business organizations and often reach similar conclusions about talent management. For example they provide similar definitions of *talent management* as the processes and procedures used in an organization to attract, develop, and retain talent to achieve strategic business objectives.

They strongly underscore the importance of business strategies as the primary driver in their talent management efforts. Their examples throughout the chapter make it evident that different business strategies lead to different talent management strategies and HR programs and initiatives. It is critically important that talent management efforts fit the organizational culture and strategies.

They confirm the central role and influence of the CEO and the senior executive team on talent management efforts and note the importance of getting their support and sponsorship. But they also cite other important critical success factors, such as ownership by all line managers.

In addition, they discuss the value of coordinating and integrating their talent management efforts across various HR programs and systems, using business strategies as the integrating driver. It certainly makes sense for both effectiveness and efficiency reasons to make sure that all efforts are focused on the same objectives. It seems that many HR functions, including compensation and benefits, are now being fully integrated into talent management efforts.

They note the challenges they are facing in developing and implementing global talent management efforts. This seems to be a complex business challenge that CHROs need to address and solve. One key issue is balancing organizational culture and procedures with the cultural and business factors in various countries.

Clearly talent management efforts in organizations are now becoming more integrated and strategically driven. These CHROs are on the leading edge of these efforts. They give us an insightful view of the future direction of talent management in organizations.

References

Boudreau, J. W., & Ramstad, P. M. (2005, April). Where's your pivotal talent? *Harvard Business Review,* 23–24.

Corporate Leadership Council. (2005). *Realizing the full potential of rising talent.* Washington, DC: Corporate Executive Board.

Michaels, E., Handfield-Jones, H., & Axelrod, B. (2001). *The war for talent.* Boston: Harvard Business School Press.

Part Five

Future Directions for Practice and Research

CHAPTER 21

BUILDING SUSTAINABLE TALENT THROUGH TALENT MANAGEMENT

Benefits, Challenges, and Future Directions

Rob Silzer, Ben E. Dowell

Talent management systems and approaches are becoming widely used in many organizations, as this book demonstrates. In this book alone, over 40 companies are mentioned for their often leading-edge talent management programs or processes. We think there are some common themes, benefits, and challenges identified in the chapters.

Talent Management Themes

Several talent management themes or principles have emerged from this book across organizations, systems, and approaches. These are suggestions or approaches that have been proposed in various chapters for building effective talent management processes, programs, and systems. (See Table 21.1.)

Driven by Business Strategy

The most fundamental theme in this book is the importance of having business strategy drive and determine processes and

Table 21.1. Key Themes in Talent Management Approaches

1. Driven by business strategy
2. Requires differential investment
3. Accepted as a core business process
4. Integrated across HR practices and processes
5. Engrained as an organizational and cultural mindset
6. Practical, efficient, and easy to use
7. Includes relevant outcome measures
8. Future looking

programs for talent management. There is widespread agreement that the effectiveness of talent strategies and talent management approaches can be judged by whether they add value and help to achieve business strategies. Gone, or going, are the days when human resources (HR) could set itself, and its processes, apart from the business objectives and goals. This book contains many examples of how strategies can, and should, directly determine the design and implementation of talent strategies and approaches.

Of course, the talent processes must be designed and scaled to meet business needs and specific, measurable goals. They also must be adaptive as business strategies change for a variety of reasons, such as new competitors, changes in customer demands, acquisitions, mergers, market shifts, market globalization, technological advances, and others. They must take into account the availability of talent and the feasibility of a particular talent strategy. In addition, they need to be integrated with the talent strategies of the organization and other HR functions and processes.

Generally this means that there is no one best way to design and implement talent management. It must fit the business need, the talent objectives, and the organization culture. The talent management field is moving away from one-size-fits-all programs and toward tailored or customized approaches. While some basic components might be similar (such as starting a college recruiting program), the specific design and implementation plans need to closely fit specific organizational needs. For example, this may be why many corporations have designed their own internal executive leadership programs rather than use generic publicly offered university programs. Ultimately the selected talent management approach needs to add strategic value, and human resources needs to find ways to demonstrate that value to the leadership of the organization.

Requires Differential Investment

There is an emerging view that effective talent management requires organizations to differentially invest in various employee groups and not to invest equally in all employees. This is a logical extension from being strategy driven. Those businesses, organizational functions, and talent groups (such as high-potential individuals or scientists in a research-based organization) that are critical to achieving the business strategies need to receive a disproportionate share of resources to achieve the strategic goals.

In the days of limited resources, this means that some functions and talent groups will get a greater share of the resources, while other nonstrategic groups will receive a smaller share of the resources. In fact, some of these nonstrategic groups, such as call centers in some companies, are being outsourced and managed by external companies, often with the goal of reducing costs and company resources that are provided to them. This has raised some concerns about how far to go in differentially investing in some groups and not others. What is the right balance when deciding the extent of development resources to devote to high-potential talent versus the other 80 to 90 percent of employees? At what point do other employees realize that they are not getting a fair share of the resources and reduce their commitment or engagement or look for job opportunities elsewhere?

Simultaneously this puts greater attention on how to identify and invest in strategically important groups. Which groups or functions are more central to the business strategies than others? How do you decide who is worthy to join a high-potential pool? What level of invested resources is needed to build and sustain the talent, and at what point does investing more have diminishing value? What is the impact of investing in one group for a period of time and then shifting resources to another group as the organization strategy changes?

Accepted as a Core Business Process

In several companies mentioned in this book, the talent review and planning process has become a core business practice alongside the strategic planning process and annual operating plan reviews. These three are the core business practices that guide business decision making, work efforts, and investments. Only recently has the talent process started to be accepted as an equally important core business process. It needs to be aligned with the other business planning processes and might logically follow the business planning and precede the operational reviews.

Talent needs to be seen as a fundamental strategic business resource in the same way as financial assets. As we develop stronger measures of the strategic and financial impact of talent, it is becoming clear how central talent is to the success and survival of a business. In the years ahead, we anticipate that talent management will be valued and respected as much as financial management in business organizations.

Integrated Across Human Resource Practices and Processes

It is important that the talent management process, programs, and systems be coordinated and integrated with each other and with other human resource functions and programs. This is for both efficiency, so various efforts are not working against each other, and for effectiveness, so different program areas are collaborating to achieve shared goals. Often these shared goals are the execution of business strategies.

Engrained as an Organizational and Cultural Mindset

The highest level of effectiveness is often characterized by having an organizational or cultural mindset around talent management. This occurs when supervisors, managers, leaders, and executives have a commitment to effectively managing talent to achieve business strategies. They take responsibility and have accountability for building and retaining the needed talent in their own organization. Often this is accompanied by a set of organizational values and beliefs about the business need for talent.

It not only permeates management and executive decisions but also pervades the shared beliefs of the entire organization. It becomes a fundamental premise for the existence and success of the organization.

Practical, Efficient, and Easy to Use

Processes and programs designed to achieve talent strategies need to be practical. They need to be feasible to develop and implement. We hope that Human Resources is moving past the era of big, complex, and often prepackaged programs that do not actually meet a business need. These programs often deliver many extra features that are unnecessary and may lock the organization into an inflexible system or set of tools that is difficult to modify as strategies change. It is both costly and difficult to redesign complex programs that have linkages throughout the organization.

Many organizations are trying to design and execute talent management programs or processes that have a clear, strong link to a specific business need. That means that the program must efficiently focus on that need. Large, complex programs often include elements that are not needed and can divert the focus of the organization from what actually needs to be done.

Programs and processes should be easy to explain and use. Managers and leaders should be able to understand a program and see the value and benefit to their own business objectives. Our experience is that the closer a program is linked to the underlying business need, the more quickly managers and leaders will understand and implement it. Managers and leaders have a long list of their own work priorities, and a particular talent management program will get little attention or support if the business link and the program value are not readily apparent. Program implementation should be straightforward and easy. The process should be sustainable through normal business cycles and not put unrealistic demands on people. It should also be easy to maintain. For example, if the program relies on an underlying database, then that database should be easy to update and contain only the critical information (and not "the extra nice to have but difficult to update" information).

Includes Relevant Outcome Measures

Ultimately any talent management approach needs to deliver results that help to achieve a business strategy. This is perhaps the weakest link in the talent management process. Human Resources is now trying to identify the outcomes that need to be measured to determine if a talent program is effective or not. While there are outcomes that are frequently measured, such as voluntary and involuntary turnover and retention, it is important to identify the desired outcomes for specific strategies and particular organizations. The importance of measuring turnover and retention in a sales force may depend on the strategy of the company (for example, a company may want to retain only the very best sales representatives, not sales representatives in general). Using generic business or even industry benchmarks for these measures may not be helpful or relevant to a specific situation.

In addition, we need to develop better metrics for talent management programs. For example, some organizations invest a lot of resources into the development of high-potential talent. Historically there has been a reliance on measures of immediate manager reviews or a lack of failure by the individual to determine outcome success. However, these are very gross measures and do not usually provide a good measure of whether the person actually was developed in the experience. We need to develop better measures of actual development, such as setting and meeting specific learning objectives, demonstrating what was learned in a special project or assignment, or demonstrating through performance that real development had occurred.

The eventual success of talent management in organizations rests on identifying the important outcomes and developing accurate measures of those outcomes. Human resources needs to become more sophisticated in providing objective evidence that a program or process is actually delivering the desired outcomes. HR metrics need to be better designed and more data based. HR must hold itself accountable for proving the strategic value of the talent management programs and processes. Part of this effort should focus on evidence-based or data-based decision making. That evidence is often objectively collected data but might also include other sources of data, such as separation interview data or the collective experience of the recruiting team. The measures need to be determined ahead of time, collected in standardized ways, and objectively analyzed. A data-based approach can significantly improve the quality of the decisions and also raise the standards for programs and processes.

The decisions regarding programs should focus on what works and what does not. If something is not working, the talent professionals need to change it and consider other alternatives. Sometimes this may require trying several things to see which works best and letting the outcome data guide that final decision.

So it comes down to three basic steps: identifying the right outcomes for evaluating a program, developing the best possible measures of those outcomes, and making data-based decisions on the effectiveness of the programs and processes.

Future Looking

A paradox in most business decisions is that data-based decision making by definition is backward looking, relying on data collected on the past. Similarly, when talent management decisions are based on data collected on past events, the results capture the past, not the future. The future is inherently more ambiguous and unknown than the past. To predict future success, past data must be extrapolated into future situations and adjusted accordingly. This requires decision makers to consider what future situations might be like and take that into account when making business decisions.

Strategies are also inherently future oriented, focusing on how to approach future, anticipated business situations. The goal of business is to be successful in the future, not the past. This requires that decision makers, including talent professionals, consider data from the past, along with personal experience and insight, to predict what actions to take in the future. Ultimately talent decisions should reflect data-based judgment, being guided by data but using judgment to extrapolate to the future. This takes a deep understanding of the data as well as the judgment and courage to make predictions about the future.

The ability to make data-based judgments may not be widely distributed. Most people can probably learn to understand the data and to make short-term predictions about this afternoon or tomorrow. However, the ability to predict one year ahead is not common. And senior executives must make predictions about the longer-term future of the business, three to five years into the future. Some do this by sticking close to the data extrapolation, but the most effective executives have visionary skills and know how to adjust linear data predictions for a changing business environment. Similarly talent professionals will need to make similar data-based judgments about talent and predict their future effectiveness and contributions. It seems likely that the ability to make accurate, future-oriented talent predictions will be seen as just as valuable as the ability to forecast future business conditions and identify the strategies needed to address those conditions.

Benefits of Strategy-Driven Talent Management

The chapter authors have pointed out the benefits of various talent management processes, programs, and approaches. Here is a summary of the key benefits of taking a strategy-driven talent management approach:

- Directly supports the achievement of business strategies
- Facilitates strategic nimbleness and the ability to adapt quickly to changes in strategy
- Supports and pursues the efficient use of resources by selective investment, focused programs, and coordinated efforts
- Integrates and connects various efforts and programs to allow easy alignment and simple transitions from process to process
- Focuses everyone on pursuing shared company goals and objectives and encourages collaboration and teamwork
- Involves forward planning and focuses attention on future strategic needs
- Becomes a core business practice that provides a distinctive talent brand for recruiting and retention
- Becomes a mindset that permeates management decisions and holds managers and leaders accountable for talent resources
- Provides a durable competitive advantage in the marketplace
- Ensures strong links between talent decisions and business decisions

- Reinforces company focus and communication on business strategies
- Identifies and retains high-potential talent that fits strategic business needs
- Builds an organizational culture as well as values around talent
- Encourages and requires objective measurement of talent outcomes and impact on strategy success

As talent management becomes even more widespread, organizations should be able to document and measure these benefits.

Challenges to the Effective Management of Talent

Talent management offers a new approach to addressing many Human Resources issues. Of course, there are many challenges to strategy-driven talent management that need to be considered (see also Guthridge, Komm, & Lawson, 2008; Lewis & Heckman, 2006; Wellins, Smith, & McGee, 2006). Some challenges can be addressed directly, while others may require a more concerted long-term effort. Some challenges involve dealing with organizational issues while others deal with human issues. (See Table 21.2.)

Organizational-Level Challenges

Poor Alignment of Talent Management Programs with Strategy

In the past, senior executives in an organization often did not align talent efforts with the business strategy. Talent strategies and processes were seen as an afterthought, a "nice to have" program, or as unconnected with the business strategy. Fortunately that has changed for some organizations, where the CHRO has taken responsibility for getting senior executives to understand this critical link. Often this is done by using convincing outcome data that demonstrate this link. In other companies, it has occurred only after a business strategy has failed because of the lack of alignment.

Because of a rapidly changing business market or significant mergers or acquisitions, companies make significant changes in their business strategies. This may require a major shift in the talent strategy. For example, it may mean moving away from

Table 21.2. Organizational-Level Challenges to Talent Management (Order Based on Degree of Difficulty)

Poor alignment of talent management programs with strategy

Subjective talent decision making

Change in CEO

Sudden shifts in business markets or economy

Lack of alignment with organizational norms and values

Acceptance of differential investment in talent

Complex design

Breadth of talent management expertise required

Costs of talent management interventions

Poor introduction and execution

No consensus on definitions of *leadership* or *high potential*

Poor or no outcome measurement

Oversupply or undersupply of talent

Lack of transparency

Differences between talent management and business cycles

---

building a competitive internal information technology function and focusing instead on developing a six sigma operations focus. These shifts can undo years of effort and attention, as well as make the existing pipeline of IT talent less important. A solid talent management approach and habit provides the tools to focus quickly on the new business need and the development of appropriate talent strategies and processes. Managers and leaders who have a talent management mindset can leverage their knowledge and expertise to quickly refocus on the new strategies. However, these transitions can be highly disruptive to an organization, particularly when groups or functions that were formerly seen as strategic lose their status and are downsized or outsourced.

Subjective Talent Decision Making

Relying too much on the views and insights of a single individual, even if that person is the CEO, can be harmful to talent management efforts. Decisions need to be based on dispassionate reviews of results and the behavior that created those results. Our experience suggests that decisions tend to be better when discussions are based on data from multiple situations across time.

Many organizations have moved to group discussion and decision making, which is likely to prevent some of the poorest talent decisions dealing with both talent strategies and talented individuals. There is no substitute for multiple perspectives when making talent decisions. As talent metrics improve and the quality of the outcome data improves, there is an opportunity to significantly improve talent processes and the quality of the decisions about talent.

Change in CEO

Most CEOs and executives have developed their own talent framework and approach from their many years of business experience. When they begin their new executive role, they often want to install their talent values and approaches in their organization. The most effective executives work hard to first learn the culture and the current talent approach before making significant changes. However, HR and talent professionals, as well as the other executives, are often powerless to stop a radical change in approach to talent advocated by a new CEO. A well-designed talent management system should be able to provide the new CEO with some confidence that the current system works well in contributing to strategic objectives. In addition, an experienced Chief Human Resources Officer should be able to find opportunities to address the CEO's concerns about the existing talent management system while also being open to sound new ideas from the CEO. If the current system is well designed, efficient, and effective, it should be able to accommodate and adapt to a new CEO's specific objectives.

Sudden Shifts in Business Markets or Economy

Sometimes economic, social, or even political events can have a significant impact on an organization. An example might be the impact of political events in Nigeria on the oil industry there. Usually these are out of the control of the organization. Sometimes it might result in a change in strategy. At other times, it may require pulling back, slowing down, or eliminating some talent programs and processes. Of course, the specifics and seriousness of the situation usually determine the best course of action.

Frequently this precipitates a system and program review. Some programs can be pulled back to a minimal level and still keep operating; others may need to be put in temporary storage or even eliminated. The key is to not lose the basic talent management mindset and approach. While the strategies and programs may change, the basic fundamentals of how to effectively manage talent should be saved.

Lack of Alignment with Organizational Norms and Values

Talent management usually introduces values and objectives that may not always be consistent with existing company values. For example, talent systems often require a sharing of talent across the company to leverage that talent for organizational objectives. However, at the same time, managers and leaders throughout the company are held accountable for delivering monthly, quarterly, and annual results. Often they want to hang onto the talent that they have developed in order to achieve their own business objectives. This often leads to siloed structures where talent does not get shared across businesses or functions, and there is a lack of collaboration on talent. CEOs and senior executives are often asked to make talent decisions between two conflicting alternatives: leave the talent in a position where he can contribute to short-term results or move that person to possibly achieve longer-term business objectives. However, the quarterly pressure for showing strong financial results can make this a difficult choice for many CEOs. Usually the best decision is choosing to support the long-term business objectives. This becomes an easier decision if there is a sufficient supply of available talent so that openings that are created by talent moves can be quickly filled.

Another example is the choice between building a highly collaborative, respectful work environment that values every employee versus selecting a small group of employees for special development and differential investment. The move from a egalitarian talent culture to a more discriminating talent culture needs to be carefully managed.

Acceptance of Differential Investment in Talent

As organizations focus greater attention on select groups of high-potential talent or strategic talent, there will be fewer resources (that is, development, staffing, and retention resources) available for the remaining employees. This differential, or uneven, treatment may make sound business sense but may not be well received by the employees who are not getting these resources. One major company has started implementing a system where some employees need to pay (referred to as "investing") for their own development. This seems to be another step in the segregation of employee interests and organization interests. At some point these employees may take steps to make that segregation more official by leaving the company. If differential investment in talent benefits the company and a small select talent group, but results in other employees disengaging, then it may become a long-term detriment to the organization. Organizations may need to consider ways to strike a balance between investing in strategic talent while also investing sufficiently to keep other high-performing employees engaged and committed.

Complex Design

As in any other function, HR and talent professionals can get seduced by new fads, features, and designs. In the past, they often adopted new initiatives that were popular in other companies in order to demonstrate that they were on the leading edge of their field. Unfortunately this led to a "program of the year" approach or the introduction of highly complex, overengineered programs and processes that were neither effective nor useful and that had many unneeded features. The business need often got lost in the elaborate design. Many organizations have moved past *keep it simple* to *keep it narrowly focused on the business need.* A new program is no longer a virtue but often a sign of inefficiency and ineffectiveness.

Breadth of Talent Management Expertise Required

Well-developed and well-implemented talent management systems require talent professionals to have a breadth of expertise and skills. From talent recruiting at the front end through talent retention and outcome metrics, talent specialists need to be able to understand, manage, and evaluate a wide range of processes and programs. This includes skills in talent brands, recruiting, selection, assimilation, assessment, coaching, selection tool validation, development, engagement, retention, and others. In the future, it is likely to also include compensation and benefits. The talent professional must know how to use all the tools, techniques, and programs that are needed to achieve the talent strategies. While an individual may initially specialize in one area, ultimately she will need to know the full range of tools and techniques that can be used to achieve a strategy. The person must also know how to decide which ones to use and how to blend them into a coherent and unified effort. Individuals tend to use the tools that they know. So talent professionals need to gain experiences in a wide range of areas in order to build a talent effort that meets a specific business need.

Knowledge and skill in applying HR and talent management programs and processes is just the beginning. Talent management professionals also need to understand business strategy and a variety of business functions in order to effectively develop talent strategies to support the business.

Costs of Talent Management Interventions

An important criterion for effectiveness in the future will be the efficient use of resources. Talent programs and processes will need to demonstrate that the cost-benefit ratio to the organization is very high. Tightly managing resources, both financial and human, will be a central concern. Talent professionals will need to be creative in finding less resource-intense solutions to issues. This may mean fewer extra features or more tightly focused efforts or smaller target groups. As business costs in general increase, HR must demonstrate that it can be equally effective on tighter budgets.

Poor Introduction and Execution

Many talent programs and processes are poorly introduced and explained. Sometimes this is because of the technical or special language that is used; sometimes it is not presented well with clear, simple charts. In addition, there are some talent professionals who like to work on the design and development side and have little interest in ongoing implementation. This often results in programs that are more complex than necessary, that get a big splashy introduction, and that lack solid execution and follow-through. Many programs fail for this reason. As HR departments have moved away from administrative HR managers and more to HR consulting roles, there seems to be a diminishing commitment to ongoing execution and follow-through. Another concern is when the program or process gets handed off to new program managers. There is some evidence that with each transfer of responsibility, program guidelines and objectives become more ambiguous and execution becomes more free ranging and less standardized. As these programs and processes drift, they lose their effectiveness and their ability to address a business need. Ongoing implementation and execution need to receive even more attention and resources than program development. The real payoff for a talent program and process happens with careful ongoing execution and follow-through.

No Consensus on Definitions of Leadership or High Potential

Often executives and managers have their own unique intuitive definition of leadership and high-potential talent, which they have developed over their years of experience. This can present hurdles in trying to implement an organization-wide talent or high-potential program and can interfere with talent decisions and moves. An organization-wide model of leadership or high potential can help reduce the number of disparate personal definitions that are used to make decisions. Having shared definitions can significantly increase shared talent views and improve the effectiveness of the talent management system.

Poor or No Outcome Measurement

In the past, Human Resources gave little attention to developing and using strong outcome measures. This was partly due to a lack of measurement expertise in organizations and limited interest in a data-based approach to human resources. This has been changing since the late 1990s. Unfortunately most organizations still use weak or generic HR measures, such as general turnover data or average time to fill jobs. Although these are readily available, they lack the specific data needed to measure the effectiveness of specific talent programs and impact on strategic objectives.

What is needed now is a leap forward in HR metrics. The right outcomes need to be identified for each talent strategy, and objective data-based metrics need to be designed that best measure these outcomes. As strategy-driven talent management becomes widely adopted, there is likely to be a surge of interest in designing and using more rigorous and effective outcome measures. Organizations will need to be able to decide whether a particular program, process, or strategy is working. When there are no data and HR metrics are poor, then decisions are either avoided or made on someone's intuition. What is needed is a data-based approach to talent management.

Oversupply or Undersupply of Talent

The execution of a talent strategy can lead to several results: effective supply of talent, undersupply of talent, or oversupply of talent. The undersupply of talent is the most troublesome outcome because it can interfere with strategy achievement. Corrective action needs to be taken to change the talent programs and processes, change the talent strategy, or change the business strategy. However, there may also be some concerns with an oversupply of talent. Perhaps the costs associated with building this talent base may need to be reconsidered (see Cappelli, 2008). Also, the cost of retaining this talent may be problematic if there are insufficient career opportunities for members of this talent pool. Accurate and objective outcome data provide both an ongoing metric for the effectiveness of the talent effort and suggestions on how the programs and processes can be adjusted to be even more effective.

Lack of Transparency

Organizations vary on how much information is shared about specific aspects of the talent management system. How are people selected for various programs? Who has ultimate decision authority over the career of a talented individual? What information and decisions about an individual get shared with that person? Historically most companies have kept this information confidential and tightly controlled. However, in the past decade, there has been more organizational openness to sharing some information. How much gets shared with the individual is still a controversial issue. The procedures associated with various talent management programs, such as the high-potential nomination steps, are now more widely known by managers at all levels.

Organizations are becoming more transparent about talent processes and programs while still being very cautious about sharing judgments about individuals. Transparency is slowly taking root in corporations for the benefit of becoming a more effective organization and for the benefit of the individual.

Privacy concerns are limiting the sharing of information across national borders. For example, the European Union restricts the transmission of personnel data across borders without employee permission, which can create challenges for conducting effective talent reviews and sharing talent across an organization.

Differences Between Talent Management and Business Cycles

Typically the business planning cycle is often on an annual or even quarterly basis, while the strategic planning cycle is usually a one- to five-year cycle. Talent planning cycles tend to be more similar to longer strategy cycles. Once a business strategy is set, it often takes some time to identify, build, and implement talent strategies and programs. For example, creating a marketing function with competitive advantage in the market does not happen in one year. Although some short-term actions can be taken to get a strategic function up and running, it takes much longer to find and recruit the best talent, to build a superior performing function, and to fill the talent pipeline. Sometimes there may be some time cycle misalignment between business need and talent outcomes. Effective HR and talent professionals should carefully manage executive expectations and balance their expectations for results with the realities of the time required to develop and implement effective talent management efforts.

Employee-Level Challenges

In addition to the challenges at an organizational level are some challenges to effective talent management at the employee level. (See Table 21.3.)

Manager or Leader Resistance

Managers and leaders throughout the organization are being asked to adopt new talent management processes and programs, take responsibility for building talent for their unit and for the

Table 21.3. Employee-Level Challenges to Talent Management

Manager or leader resistance

Individual resistance

Lack of senior leader support

Consideration for life-balance issues

Engaging employees in nonstrategic areas

whole organization, and make talent decisions that are consistent with organizational values and norms. They are under pressure to take a much greater role in talent management and to do it in ways that are consistent and aligned with organizational talent systems. This often requires a significant change in behavior and thinking by managers and leaders.

Often managers and leaders are resistant to giving up their own habits and approaches to managing talent based on years of personal experience. They may hang on to outdated beliefs such as the "cream will rise to the top on its own" or that almost everyone (or no one) has the potential to advance in the organization given adequate development. These old beliefs are hard to change and can interfere with a consistent organizational approach to talent.

Some leaders and managers are more openly aware of their resistance, particularly when it is due to competing priorities. For example, they may be heavily focused on producing short-term results and do not see talent and development issues as a priority or are unwilling to "sacrifice" short-term results by sharing or moving talent. Often they are not measured or rewarded for attending to talent issues. Some resist identifying differences in the level of talent among their employees or are unwilling to address ongoing poor performance or underperformance, which undermines most talent development efforts.

On occasion some overly zealous line managers may want to develop and implement their own talent programs and processes. Sometimes these managers are talent champions and can pilot-test some corporate programs, and at other times their programs need to be reviewed to make sure they are consistent and aligned with organization-wide programs and processes.

Individual Resistance

Individual employees have their own set of values and beliefs about their work and careers. Sometimes they are not willing to put in the effort or make the organizational commitment that is required to advance their careers in an organization. An equally serious hurdle is when an employee does not see a need to further develop himself or sees this as the responsibility of the organization. This unwillingness to take personal responsibility for his development and to rely solely on the formal development efforts of the company (such as formal training programs) was a common characteristic in the past. However, now it is inconsistent with norms in many organizations and leads to stalled careers. As talent management introduces talent norms and values to the organization (such as individuals seeking and being open to feedback and coaching), individual employees are encouraged to follow and adopt those norms and values. Resistance to these values is often seen as a lack of commitment.

Lack of Senior Leader Support

Some CEOs and senior leaders have little personal interest in talent issues. They either see little value in the area or are much more interested in other areas, such as financial management or new business start-ups. Some hold on to narrow or outdated talent models or believe that people are born with talent and that development efforts are a waste of resources. This is not an uncommon view by executives who believe they have distinctive natural talents themselves and have built their career on it; they may not see the relevance of development to their own career and therefore have trouble seeing it as important for others. They may also be unwilling to "waste resources" investing in the development of young unproven talent.

Some CEOs do not make sufficient time for talent issues and either completely delegate them to someone else, give them superficial attention, or ignore them entirely. Sometimes this is because they have a lack of knowledge, a lack of interest, or are focused on other short-term strategic issues. Any of these can be addressed if the CHRO takes responsibility for educating the CEO and demonstrating the strategic importance of talent management.

Consideration for Life Balance Issues

An emerging view in organizations is that an individual's lack of mobility for career moves due to personal or family issues should no longer eliminate that person from future career opportunities. In the past, these individuals might be eliminated from the high-potential pool and not be reconsidered in the future for further promotions. However, now with the more limited availability of critical talent, organizations are more sensitive to situations that involve dual careers or to family issues (such as not moving children while they are in high school), which is requiring more flexibility by organizations. Another outcome is that this flexibility has complicated talent decisions and narrowed the options for moving highly talented individuals. Often an organization's plan for a series of talent moves gets disrupted because some individuals are unwilling to make a planned move. This has increased the importance of understanding individual situations and taking them into consideration in talent management decisions.

Engaging Employees in Nonstrategic Areas

As companies differentially invest in strategic talent, they need to identify ways to keep other employees engaged and committed to the organization. This may mean continuing to make some development and career investments in this population. This may be less of an issue in opaque organizations where few employees have information about talent practices and decisions. If employees know that they are not receiving development resources and career opportunities, they may decide to move to other organizations to pursue better options or where their talent is considered strategic to the company. The lack of investment may take different forms: lack of development resources and programs, reduced compensation, limited career advancement opportunities, or limited actions to retain employees. There is little research that discusses the impact of differential investment on employees in nonstrategic areas, and the potential impact remains a concern in some organizations.

Future Talent Management

Talent management will continue to grow in importance for organizations. It will increasingly be accepted as a core business practice that has a direct impact on business outcomes. Talent will be a core asset and treated as respectfully as financial assets. In the next decade, given the right tools and support, Human Resources will continue to evolve into a strategic department, and talent management will be the foundation.

Here are some characteristics of talent management in the future:

- Strategy driven and driving strategy
- A core business practice and highly visible business function
- Accepted as a core accountability of all managers
- Talent decisions that are rigorous, objective, and based on strategically important data
- Programs and processes scaled to the strategic issues identified and sustained through business cycles
- Talent accepted as a primary factor in creating a sustainable competitive advantage for the organization
- Talent management outcomes are measured with rigorous metrics that are incorporated into company evaluations by business and investment analysts
- Regarded as a critical career experience for high-potential executive talent
- Becoming a chief talent officer will require a broad set of experiences and a high level of skills, abilities, and education developed through advanced training in industrial-organizational psychology or new programs in talent management

Conclusion

In order to be effective, talent management needs active support and ownership from the CEO, executives, line managers, HR and talent professionals, and the talent itself. While this seems like a significant challenge, it becomes much easier when a talent mindset is engrained in the organization's culture.

The ultimate goal is to build sustainable talent for long-term competitive advantage. This will require hard work by executives, line and HR managers, and talent management professionals. It cannot be successful by pursuing fads or a program-of-the-year approach or by getting distracted by superficial issues. It must be focused on people, not process. The talent themselves must remain central to building an effective talent management system.

And finally the question gets raised of which comes first: good business or effective talent management? We think the answer is that both happen together and support each other. One boot-straps the other. Talent management can no longer be seen as separate from the business. It is as core to the business as finance, and perhaps even more so.

This book has covered a broad range of issues related to talent management. We encourage you to reflect on the important research questions in Chapter 22 and explore the Annotated Bibliography in Chapter 23. We also hope that this book will be a useful future reference for you on talent management.

References

Cappelli, P. (2008). *Talent on demand: Managing talent in an ago of uncertainty.* Boston: Harvard Business School Press.

Guthridge, M., Komm, A. B., & Lawson, E. (2008, January). Making talent a strategic priority. *McKinsey Quarterly.* Retrieved January 5, 2009, from http://www.mckinseyquarterly.com/Talent/Making_talent_a_strategic_priority.

Lewis, R. E., & Heckman, R. J. (2006). Talent management: A critical review. *Human Resource Management Review 16*, 139–154.

Wellins, R. S., Smith, A. B., & McGee, L. (2006, July). *The CEO's guide to talent management: Building a global leadership pipeline.* Pittsburgh, PA: Development Dimensions International.

CHAPTER 22

CRITICAL RESEARCH ISSUES IN TALENT MANAGEMENT

Rob Silzer

In general, research on talent management in organizations has been limited (see Gubman, 1998; Lawler, 2008; Lewis & Heckman, 2006), although much has been written about specific talent management components such as recruiting, selection, and performance management. Doing rigorous research in organizations is challenging because of the complexity of field research and the limited ability to hold some variables constant while others are studied. The field also lacks agreement on the appropriate type and level of outcome measures to use.

Many of the previous chapters make suggestions for future research in specific areas of talent management. This chapter discusses the talent management areas that would benefit from further research investigation (see Table 22.1).

Key Strategic Links

At the beginning of this book, we identified the key strategic links in how talent management can be ingrained in a business organization. While business managers have generally developed strong links among the business environment, the business strategy, and business results, this process in the past has often bypassed human resource (HR) and talent management systems. Business executives

Table 22.1. Talent Management Areas That Need Further Research

Strategic issues	Key strategic links
	Organizational talent strategy and talent models
	Talent as a driver of business strategy
Programs and processes	Talent model for individuals
	Talent programs and practices
	Talent pools and differential investment
	Talent decisions
Outcomes and cultural issues	Talent measures and outcomes
	Organizational acceptance
Talent expertise	Talent management talent

and human resource professionals are increasingly likely to see talent management as a core business process that has a major role to play in linking business strategy to business results. However, the links between these business elements are not yet well developed, and many of them are relatively weak (see Figure 22.1).

A critical area for research is investigating these links and identifying the factors that strengthen or weaken the links. We probably have better insight into the link between a talent strategy and talent programs and processes than for the other links in Figure 22.1. In this area, some HR and talent professionals are experienced and knowledgeable. But linking these at the front and back end with business practices is a relatively new field. For example, which changes in talent can directly result in strategic gains for the company?

Key research questions are:

- What is the most effective talent strategy for achieving a particular business strategy? What key factors are most important to consider when choosing a talent strategy (such as talent availability, business conditions, business strategy time frame, or others)?

Figure 22.1. Strength of Key Strategic Talent Management Links

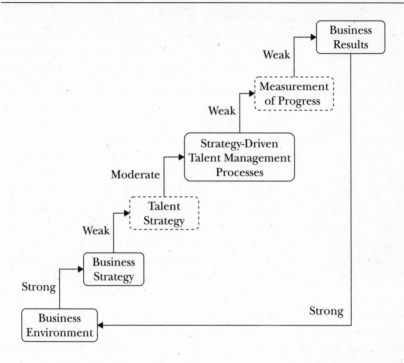

- How can we design the most efficient and effective talent programs and processes that have the greatest likelihood of achieving a talent strategy?
- How do we measure the impact of those talent programs and practices on achieving the talent strategy, and if they are ineffective, what diagnostic process should we use to identify and fix the underlying problem?
- How can we clearly understand the link between the success of talent programs and processes and the achievement of business results, achievement of the business strategy, and organizational success? What processes and conditions contribute to a stronger or weaker impact? What other variables (such as product development and technology) also contribute to these outcomes, and how can we identify the independent contribution of talent?

Organizational Talent Strategy and Talent Models

There has been some discussion in the HR profession regarding talent strategies, but frequently this gets reduced to focusing on specific talent programs and processes rather than choosing a broad approach to talent. There needs to be a greater understanding of which broad talent strategies are most effective for specific business conditions and strategies. For example, Leslie W. Joyce (see Chapter 3) presents a buy, build, borrow, or bind model of talent strategies and discusses the benefits of each. How can we measure the effectiveness of each strategy, and when should an organization switch talent strategies? Can we identify a talent ROI (return on investment) for each strategy (given specific objectives and business conditions)? What impact do limited financial resources or limited talent resources in a geographic location have on talent strategy choice? Many organizations have a broad cultural bias for selection or development approaches. What business conditions favor one approach over the other? What are the benefits and drawbacks of having a strong preference for one over the other, and how can we achieve the right balance?

Implementing and measuring the impact of various talent strategies are also areas of interest. How do we operationalize specific talent strategies in the most efficient and effective way? Some companies have talent strategies or talent brands that are well known. Do these talent brand strategies actually provide some competitive advantage by attracting the desired talent, or do they just provide marketing publicity? Most of the evidence here is self-report survey data. How do we more objectively measure the outcomes of a broad talent strategy and determine if the strategy is successful? If the organization is not achieving its business goals, how do we know whether to change the talent strategy or just the specific programs?

In thinking about broad talent management models (see Chapter 1 by Rob Silzer and Ben E. Dowell and Chapter 2 by Marcia J. Avedon and Gillian Scholes), can we confirm various stages in the development of an effective talent management system? What evidence is there for the effectiveness of different talent management models? What aspects of these models actually provide the most sustainable competitive advantage?

Key research questions are:

- What talent strategies are most effective, under what conditions, and for which business objectives and strategies?
- How can a talent strategy easily be converted into specific programs and processes that are effective and efficient?
- Is there a single general model of talent management across companies, or does it vary for different companies and business conditions?

Talent as a Driver of Business Strategy

Many organizations now see their internal talent as a competitive advantage that is critically important for delivering on existing business strategies. However, only a few see their internal talent as a major influence on driving or determining future business strategies. How can organizations evaluate current talent and build new business strategies around them? For example, Capital One Financial leveraged its existing internal fungible talent to pursue new businesses beyond the credit card industry. Human Resources is now being encouraged to step up to these opportunities and take a leadership role in shaping, rather than just responding to, business strategies. In this regard, Human Resources should be contributing to the company's strategic direction as much as finance and product development by leveraging current talent to identify new strategic directions.

Key research questions are:

- How can we identify the strategic opportunities that existing internal talent provides for the organization?
- What are the talent characteristics and business conditions that can be combined to create new strategic opportunities?
- What role can human resources take to exert influence on future business strategies?

Talent Model for Individuals

There has been a lot of emphasis on developing and implementing talent programs and processes, but there needs to be a greater understanding of the role of individual differences in program effectiveness. For example, what types of individuals (based on personality, ability, and motivational differences) benefit most from specific development interventions and learning opportunities? What are the person versus treatment versus situation interactions? Why do some individuals respond better in certain situations and not in others? How can we better match an individual to an effective learning experience? What are the core components and limits of talent fungibility (the ability to perform a variety of functions)? Can we outline a talent model for individuals based on individual differences that identify key matches to the work situations and talent programs? How can an individual's talent best be sustained or leveraged? What competencies or individual differences are foundational elements for other more complex skills and abilities?

Key research questions are:

- Can we develop a model of individual talent based on what we know about individual differences?
- How do individual differences influence the effectiveness of talent programs and processes (for example, does age affect learning ability in a development experience)?
- What are the core components of fungibility in an individual, and can we develop and nurture those characteristics in people?

Talent Programs and Practices

Designing and implementing talent systems, programs, and practices in an organization raises questions about:

- How to choose programs
- How to link them to the underlying strategies
- How to design programs to reflect the situation and business conditions
- How to implement and manage a program so it remains consistent with the original objectives
- How to integrate various talent programs and processes

First, we need research that identifies which programs and practices are most effective for specific purposes and conditions.

For example, when is starting a campus recruiting program or an apprentice program a good talent choice? How is the choice driven by the underlying business strategy? How simple or comprehensive does the talent approach need to be? When would a straightforward recruiting program be sufficient over an approach that includes recruiting, development, compensation, and retention components? When is it better to invest in a selection strategy over a development strategy?

Programs and processes may need to reflect the organizational culture, the business climate, and often the local geographic culture. How can they be designed to reflect these without losing program effectiveness? Which program aspects can vary, and which are essential to include? What is the necessary and sufficient level of design complexity to be effective?

Implementation issues are often ignored after the program developers have moved on to another project. How can programs and processes be implemented to best meet the original objectives? What periodic talent program reviews or updating are needed to make sure the program continues to meet those objectives over time? How can the program be designed to minimize the administrative resources that are needed but still maximize the outcomes?

Talent management integration is often cited as something that is important to achieve. What are the core characteristics of integration across talent programs and processes? Can we measure the degree of integration? Can we demonstrate that greater integration actually leads to more effective outcomes? How do we go about integrating existing programs, and what efforts bring the greatest payoff?

Often talent strategies discuss specific programs and outcomes but often seem to skip over discussing the specific characteristics of the talent involved. For example, a talent strategy might be to buy talent from the outside at above-market compensation rates, but how does this differentially apply to different talent groups? Some groups or individuals are likely to be more responsive to compensation inducements than others (for example, customer service representatives versus medical researchers). What are the key talent differences that make them more or less responsive to different programs and processes? How does a program need to adapt to the specific talent group?

Key research questions are:

- How can we make the best choices on which talent programs and processes to use to achieve specific business and talent strategies?
- How can programs be adapted to reflect local norms, situational factors, and business conditions without losing effectiveness?
- How can programs be managed over time to remain consistent with the original program objectives?
- How important is it to integrate talent programs and practices, and how can that be efficiently done?
- How much do individual or group talent differences affect the effectiveness of a program?

Talent Pools and Differential Investment

Currently there is great interest in the use of talent pools, such as high-potential talent, to identify and develop strategic talent. But we have little research on the effectiveness of talent pools and how they are identified and nurtured.

How do we know which talent groups in an organization are critical to achieving strategic objectives? Can we demonstrate that certain characteristics, such as hard-to-replace talent, actually matter? Perhaps "rare and hard to imitate" talent (Barney, 2001) is only a competitive advantage for a certain period of time before a competitor leapfrogs over that advantage to reframe the competition and capture a different type of talent. How long is specialized talent sustainable as a competitive advantage?

High-potential talent pools (see Chapter 5 by Rob Silzer and Allan H. Church) are so popular that in some organizations they seem to be an unquestioned talent program with little underlying thought and few clear objectives. What are the key characteristics of someone who is high potential? Can these characteristics be developed to increase a person's likelihood that he is seen as a high potential? How can we measure the outcomes and benefits of this program beyond just comparing promotional rates (a confounded variable)? How early in an individual's career can you identify her as a high-potential individual?

How can we evaluate the usefulness of differential invest- ment in talent? We should define and be able to measure the *talent return on investment* for a specific investment in talent. How should we make decisions on where to invest? What impact does differential investment have on the talent who get the resources and the other employees who don't? What is the impact on orga- nizational outcomes?

The composition of talent pools also needs further study. Typically organizations annually look for the best high-potential candidates for a specific talent pool but give little thought to what mix of talent or what number of individuals is needed. What combination of talent (potential level, performance mix, career stage) should be identified to have a sustainable talent pool over time?

What organizational resources should be included in the dif- ferential investment in talent? Are some investments (for example, compensation level, development experiences, or career advance- ment) more effective with certain individuals or at different career stages or in certain geographies? How much investment is suf- ficient? When does a particular investment provide diminishing returns? What is the appropriate level of talent investment to max- imize returns?

Key research questions are:

- How do we accurately identify the critical, strategic talent pools?
- What are the core characteristics of being high potential, and how early can they be identified in individuals? Can these characteristics be developed?
- Can we measure the *talent return on investment* of differen- tial investments in talent pools? What level and what type of investment is the most efficient and effective?
- What is the ideal mix of talent in a talent pool in order to have sustainable talent?

Talent Decisions

In the past, decisions regarding talent typically have been based on personal observations and experience. Often the most senior per- son in the room made the final call about an individual. However, we know that this type of decision making often has great potential for errors (Dawes, 1988; Hastie & Dawes, 2001; Tichy & Bennis, 2007). How can we build a decision-making process regarding talent that is data based and effective? Do we need to construct a talent decision-making science, as Boudreau and Ramstad (2007) have suggested, or can we improve the talent decisions by introducing objective decision-making techniques (Dawes, 1988; Hastie & Dawes, 2001) into the process? How can we improve the quality of each decision and also improve the overall decision-making process in the organization? What are the most important decision-making characteristics to include (such as making decisions based on objective data, getting others involved in the decisions, or focusing on the avoidance of typical decision errors)?

Key research questions are:

- How can we improve the quality and effectiveness of talent decisions?
- Can well-known decision-making techniques significantly improve these decisions?
- How important is it to first improve the quality and rigor of the talent data?
- How easily can managers and leaders learn and adopt these techniques?
- What outcome measures can we use to provide feedback to decision makers on the quality and effectiveness of their decisions?

Talent Measures and Outcomes

Most organizations now stick to basic talent metrics, such as turnover and time to fill a position, if they measure talent outcomes at all. These measures are very broad and may not be directly relevant to the specific talent programs and processes. There is emerging interest in developing more useful and precise talent metrics (see Chapter 12 by John C. Scott, Steven G. Rogelberg, and Brent W. Mattson). But what are the right outcome measures for talent management systems, programs, and practices? How do we measure achievement of program objectives, talent strategies, and business strategies?

Most current measures are either subjective or based on very general information. Can we develop more rigorous, relevant, and objective measures that also parcel out the influence of other related factors such as business and economic conditions? What are those other influential factors? How can we accommodate the dynamic nature of many talent programs and processes and still get a sound outcome measure?

The organizational level of the measure is also important. What are the complexities and limitations of measuring talent management effectiveness against broad organizational performance? What is the best organizational level to establish these metrics: organization-wide, business unit, department, work group, or specific talent group? Are some organizational performance criterion measures, such as profit margin, inappropriate to use because of the complex set of variables that can have an impact on them?

How rigorous do the measures need to be? What measurement standards, such as reliability and validity, should we insist on following in developing these measures? What type of data and data analysis capabilities are needed to provide high-quality, objective talent data? At what point does a focus on data analysis interfere with sound judgment?

How important is it to have a solid underlying model of talent management to guide the interpretation of the outcome results? How can outcome measures be most useful in guiding future talent decisions?

Key research questions are:

- What are the most useful and precise talent measures?
- Can we develop outcome measures that are objective and rigorous but still useful?
- At what levels in the organization should we measure talent outcomes and over what period of time?
- Should we rely on objective data-based outcome results or should they be interpreted using an underlying model of organizational talent as a guide?

Organizational Acceptance

Several chapters have noted the need for a cultural mindset for talent (see Chapter 1 by Rob Silzer and Ben E. Dowell) or a talent stewardship (see Chapter 2 by Marcia J. Avedon and Gillian Scholes) in order to have a highly effective talent management system. Also mentioned is the importance of installing talent management as a core business practice (see Chapters 1 and 2 as well as Chapter 9 by Ben E. Dowell). These assume an organization-wide acceptance of talent management.

This raises some important issues. What are the organizational readiness factors for gaining this broad acceptance? Are some organizations more ready than others? How critical is CEO support for establishing talent management as both a cultural mindset and a core business practice? Is CEO support necessary and sufficient? How do you introduce, communicate, and embed these organizational values? How do you maintain them over time? Do they require constant support and communication? What are the early signs that organizational acceptance is declining? Once accepted, what actions does an organization need to take to maintain acceptance? What is the impact of changing the allocation of resources to talent management?

Key research questions are:

- What are the key characteristics of a cultural mindset in practice?
- How can an organization introduce this concept, and are some organizations more ready than others than others to accept it?
- What factors, such as CEO support, are needed to embed a talent mindset in an organization?
- How can talent management get accepted as a core business practice? Is CEO endorsement and active support enough?
- How do you measure the impact of having a talent mindset in the organization?

Talent Management Talent

Over the years, HR professionals working in the area of talent have moved from being specialists in specific talent areas, such as staffing or training and development, to broader roles in management development and leadership development. More recently they have broadened their roles even further by working in organizational development or as an HR consultant to a business unit. Now some of them are being asked to step up to an even broader role as a talent director (or maybe in the future to chief talent officer) for a business unit. This requires knowledge (and preferably experience) in the full range of talent programs and processes but also an understanding of talent and business strategies and business in general. They will need to be partners with the senior business executive much as a chief financial officer is today.

These broader roles require talent professionals to have both a broader and a deeper background, which raises several questions that HR will need to address. How can an HR professional gain this breadth and depth? What individual characteristics (skills, abilities, motivations) are needed to operate effectively as a chief talent officer? Will they need to gain line management experience to fully understand the connection between business strategy, talent management, and business performance?

Key research questions are:

- How can we fully describe this broader and deeper talent management role?
- What skills, abilities, and motivations are needed to be effective in this critical role?
- How early in their careers can we identify individuals with potential for these roles?
- Should organizations develop a program for high-potential talent officers similar to ones found in finance, to build this critical talent pool?

Conclusion

A large number of questions regarding the effectiveness of talent management still need to be addressed. The most important priority may be to study how talent management efforts can be more directly linked to business strategies and outcomes. It is challenging to do nonsurvey-based research on talent management in organizations. But we need to find new ways to study these complex issues.

Readers are encouraged to review Chapter 12 on managing and measuring the talent management function for a better understanding of talent management metrics. In addition, relevant research issues have also been identified in most of the other chapters.

References

Barney, J. B. (2001). Is the resource–based "view" a useful perspective for strategic management research? Yes. *Academy of Management Review, 26*(1), 41–56.

Boudreau, J. W., & Ramstad, P. M. (2007). *Beyond HR: The new science of human capital.* Boston: Harvard Business School.

Dawes, R. M. (1988). *Rational choice in an uncertain world.* Orlando, FL: Harcourt.

Gubman, E. L. (1998). *The talent solution: Aligning strategy and people to achieve extraordinary results.* New York: McGraw-Hill.

Hastie, R., & Dawes, R. M. (2001). *Rational choice in an uncertain world: The psychology of judgement and decision making.* Thousand Oaks, CA: Sage.

Lawler III, E. E. (2008). *Talent: Making people your competitive advantage.* San Francisco: Jossey-Bass.

Lewis, R. E., & Heckman, R. J. (2006). Talent management: A critical review. *Human Resource Management Review, 16*, 139–154.

Tichy, N. M., & Bennis, W. G. (2007). *Judgment: How winning leaders make great calls.* New York: Penguin.

CHAPTER 23

TALENT MANAGEMENT
An Annotated Bibliography
Rob Silzer, Joshua B. Fyman

This annotated list of key talent management references identifies and briefly summarizes the most relevant articles, reports, and books in the field for readers who want to further explore certain topics. This list can be useful to human resource and talent professionals, researchers, and business managers who want a summary of the most relevant resources on a particular topic. The specific references were identified by the authors of Chapters 1 through 14, however we wrote the actual annotations.

Chapter 1: Strategic Talent Management Matters

by Rob Silzer and Ben E. Dowell

American Productivity and Quality Center. (2004). *Talent management: From competencies to organizational performance: Final report.* Houston: American Productivity and Quality Center.

This is the final report of a consortium benchmarking study conducted by APQC that involved 21 companies in three categories: sponsor, partner, and data-only organizations. The study surveyed these organizations on a range of talent management (TM) practices and highlighted five best practice organizations, which received site visits. Special emphasis was on TM components and accountabilities, senior leadership role, finding talent (competency models, talent gaps, recruiting and assessment techniques), delivering performance (development, performance management, retention), and talent metrics. The results are presented in summary bar charts and best practice descriptions.

The report presents eight general conclusions on what best practice organizations do, including integrating components into a TM system, focusing on the most valued talent, having committed CEOs and senior executives, and evaluating TM results. It is helpful to see the differences between the 16 sponsor and data-only companies and the five best practice companies in TM practices. In some areas, the differences are noticeable. The extensive case presentations of the best practice companies show how various TM components can be coordinated into a larger system.

This study shows how organizations differ on some key issues such as level of management involvement and which TM components, processes, and practices are included by different organizations. The study does not address why these differences exist, and like many other benchmark studies, it implies that other companies should use TM practices similar to the ones used in "best practice" companies.

■ ■ ■

Gubman, E. L. (1998). *The talent solution: Aligning strategy and people to achieve extraordinary results.* New York: McGraw-Hill.

Gubman starts with the basic premise that "connecting people to strategy to serve customers will build extraordinary results and long term value" and elaborates on this throughout the book. The basic components that he proposes for making this happen—alignment, engagement, and measurement—make up the three primary sections of the book. He also argues that communication is the number one problem cited by employees that needs to be addressed. In each chapter, he draws on his long career as an external consultant to provide numerous company examples. Gubman describes the Hewitt alignment model (aligning strategy with talent and outcomes) and uses it as a bridging framework across the chapters. Throughout the book, he makes a strong argument that there is a talent solution to many business problems and that talent "is the business."

The book is strongest when describing the links and showing the key business connections among strategies, talent, and customers. Gubman gives solid arguments for pursuing these connections and ways to improve strategy implementation in an organization, but not detailed descriptions of specific talent practices and approaches. The book would be helpful to readers who want to more fully understand the link between business strategy and talent management.

■ ■ ■

Lawler III, E. E. (2008). *Talent: Making people your competitive advantage.* San Francisco: Jossey-Bass.

Lawler proposes a talent-focused management approach to business and sees talent and organization as competitive advantages. He takes this further by advocating that companies create a human-capital-centric (HC-centric) organization. He defines human capital as the processes that create, manage, and organize talent. The book is organized around what a talent-focused organization looks like and discusses key issues such as organizational design, talent management, and performance management.

Lawler identifies the key features of an HC-centric organization—for example, business strategy is determined by talent considerations, the organization is obsessed with talent and talent management, performance management is one of the most important activities, and the HR department is the most important staff group. He uses company examples in the chapters and concludes by offering some suggestions on how to create a HC-centric organization.

Clearly the book is advocating for the centrality of talent to being a successful organization (although Lawler does point out a few possible exceptions). The strength of this book is in the solid reasoning and useful company examples. Lawler provides a broad understanding of talent in organizations without getting into specific detailed programs and practices.

■ ■ ■

Michaels, E., Handfield-Jones, H., & Axelrod, B. (2001). *The war for talent.* Boston: Harvard Business School Press.

This book is based on five years of extensive survey studies involving 120 companies by McKinsey & Company on why talent is a strategic business challenge and critical driver of corporate performance. The primary arguments are that talent is strategically important to companies because it can create enormous value and that there is increasing competition for limited leadership talent. The book is organized around the approaches that the authors propose for meeting and winning this challenge, particularly ways to attract, develop, and retain talent.

The book is organized around the five imperatives that the authors think are fundamental to this effort: embracing a talent mindset, crafting a winning employee value proposition, rebuilding the recruiting strategy, weaving development into the organization, and differentiating your people. Chapters contain useful survey data, relevant corporate examples, and solid arguments.

This book created a major stir in HR circles and is still seen as a seminal book on the strategic importance of talent and a useful framework for building an effective leadership talent management approach. It combines solid reasoning and business experience with relevant survey data and company examples. It clearly brought a fresh perspective to talent and human resources that continues to resonate in business corporations.

■　■　■

Morton, L. (2004). *Integrated and integrative talent management: A strategic HR framework.* New York: Conference Board.

This report is based on a study involving 35 companies in a Conference Board working group. The qualitative and quantitative data are from survey respondents, interviews, and discussions in these companies. Brief case studies are also provided for seven companies. The study tries to understand and provide a picture of integrated talent management (TM), with a focus on how various TM components can "fit together" and be "connected." Also discussed are internal and external factors that have an impact on TM integration and common approaches to integration such as performance management, recruitment, leadership, and high-potential development.

The study concludes that TM integration is relatively new and that companies that "see themselves as integrated have been so for only 10 years." Companies report that the glue that holds TM initiatives together includes "processes, management, CEO involvement, culture and accountability." The critical success factors for TM integration are "alignment with strategic goals, HR management and CEO participation."

The study takes a close look at how organizations are approaching TM integration. It also proposes a maturity model for how TM integration can grow over time. However, there is little discussion about aligning TM components with the business and talent strategies in an organization. This report might be particularly useful for organizations that are trying to better understand TM integration issues.

Chapter 2: Building Competitive Advantage Through Integrated Talent Management

by Marcia J. Avedon and Gillian Scholes

Boudreau, J. W., & Ramstad, P. M. (2002). *From "professional business partner to strategic talent leader": What's next for human resource management.* Working paper, Cornell University, Center for Advanced Human Resource Studies (CAHRS), Ithaca, NY.

This is a foundational paper for later articles and a book by Boudreau and Ramstad on the transition of human resources (HR) to a "decision science of talent" that they call *talentship.* It discusses why HR is at a transition point, moving from a professional business partner to a strategic talent leader. Boudreau and Ramstad want to link organizational talent to strategic success.

They model their approach to talent on the finance and marketing functions and argue that HR needs to follow a similar path to logical decision making. The article argues that HR needs to switch from a focus on talent programs to strategic talent decisions. They suggest that HR be held accountable for impact, effectiveness, and efficiency, and outline a human capital bridge framework for capturing their talent model.

This article provides an introduction to the Boudreau and Ramstad model and HR proposals that they further elaborate on in their book *Beyond HR.*

■ ■ ■

Hewitt Associates. (2005). *How the top 20 companies grow great leaders.* Lincolnshire, IL: Author.

In this benchmark study, the top 20 companies for leaders were selected by an independent panel of judges and compared with more than 350 other U.S. companies. The screening process involved reviewing responses to a survey, conducting in-depth interviews, and analyzing financial performance. Some of the top companies were 3M, General Electric, and Johnson & Johnson. The primary conclusion that set these companies apart from the larger group of companies was having "more rigor around developing their future leaders."

The study found that when compared to other companies, the top companies are more likely to focus on developing leaders, to have an actively involved CEO, and to hold their leaders accountable for developing their direct reports. They are also more likely to put teeth in their initiatives by tying a greater percentage of executive incentive pay to success in developing leaders. Top companies were also more likely to report that their leadership development efforts attract quality leaders to the organization.

The study provides insights into the approaches and programs that companies use to produce effective leaders. It should be noted that some of the companies in the larger pool also used some of these same programs, but perhaps not as systematically or comprehensively.

■ ■ ■

Michaels, E., Handfield-Jones, H., & Axelrod, B. (2001). *The war for talent.* Boston: Harvard Business School Press.

This book is based on five years of extensive survey studies involving 120 companies by McKinsey & Company on why talent is a strategic business challenge and critical driver of corporate performance. The primary arguments are that talent is strategically important to companies because it can create enormous value and that there is increasing competition for limited leadership talent. The book is organized around the approaches that the authors propose for meeting and winning this challenge, particularly ways to attract, develop, and retain talent.

The book is organized around the five imperatives that the authors think are fundamental to this effort: embracing a talent mindset, crafting a winning employee value proposition, rebuilding the recruiting strategy, weaving development into the organization, and differentiating people. Chapters contain useful survey data, relevant corporate examples, and solid arguments.

This book created a major stir in HR circles and is still seen as a seminal book on the strategic importance of talent and a useful framework for building an effective leadership talent management approach. It combines solid reasoning and business experience with relevant survey data and company examples. It clearly brought a fresh perspective to talent and human resources that continues to resonate in business corporations.

Chapter 3: Building the Talent Pipeline: Attracting and Recruiting the Best and Brightest

by Leslie W. Joyce

Hansen, F. (2006, December). Using social networking to fill the talent acquisition pipeline. *Workforce Management Online.* Retrieved August 21, 2007, from www.workforce.com.

The author opens the article with anecdotal evidence demonstrating the spread of social networking websites in recruiting talent and then briefly discusses case studies of Microsoft and Novell. Hansen ends by identifying a second benefit of social networking sites for HR practitioners: establishing the identity of leadership within an organization.

Social networking sites allow employers to broadcast competencies to a wide range of candidates and allow these candidates to connect to the organization. The authors suggest that joining networks of people with a particular group of competencies is an efficient way of publicizing personnel needs to others who are in those individuals' networks and who may possess the same competencies. Microsoft and Novell, two large organizations, are profiled as organizations that possess a very specific identity, which can be very useful in recruiting online.

The discussion of such sites as LinkedIn and other social networking outlets demonstrates the changing environment for job seekers and recruiters and illustrates how recruiters may have to adjust their approach in order to identify the best talent in today's talent pool.

■ ■ ■

Sartain, L., & Schumann, M. (2006). *Brand from the inside.* San Francisco: Jossey-Bass.

Directed toward an audience of executives and managers in organizations of all sizes, this is a handbook for developing a corporate culture that engages employees and reinforces their loyalty to their employer. The authors divide the lessons into three phases, within which are eight vital steps toward establishing a relationship with employees that maximizes what companies can achieve through their talent.

The first phase is becoming aware of the fundamentals of a corporate culture and how it can breed certain attitudes and behaviors in employees. The second phase is diagnosing a company's relationship with its employees and deciding on the form of the management-employee relationship. This process may entail organizational surveys and other steps to gauge the prevailing attitudes among employees at all levels of an organization. Based on the demands of the business and what must be expected of the talent, the organization must then outline the desired relationship with the employees. Finally, Sartain and Schumann introduce the third phase by describing four essential steps in implementing this new relationship with personnel.

The advice in this book is broad enough to apply to a wide range of organizational settings, and the essential steps give concrete examples for practitioners to follow. Numerous insights in the book explain efficient ways to increase employee satisfaction and establish a reputation as an employee-friendly organization.

■ ■ ■

Trank, C., Rhynes, S., & Bretz, R. (2002). Attracting applicants in the war for talent: Differences in work preferences among high achievers. *Journal of Business and Psychology, 16*(3), 331–345.

This study compares the work and career preferences of business students who have high cognitive ability and achievements with the career preferences of students with high social achievements.

Students are defined as high in cognitive ability and achievements by measures that include grade point average and scores on the Wonderlic Test. Social achievement was measured by extracurricular activities. Career preferences were measured by questionnaires that covered the students' desire for job flexibility, entrepreneurialism, contingent pay, and nine other variables. The results indicate that students high in cognitive ability cared most about individual pay, praise and recognition, organizational commitment, and pay level. Students high in social achievement, on the other hand, prefer contingent pay, promotional opportunity, fast-track opportunity, and entrepreneurialism.

The results of this study provide some insights for selection practitioners. Cognitive ability and social ability might now be used as predictors for which employees may be happier at jobs with different work variables and used as an insight into which employees will be most satisfied and have greater intentions to stay with the organization (*higher retention intention*).

■ ■ ■

Ulrich, D., & Smallwood, N. (2007). *Leadership brand: Developing customer-focused leaders to drive performance and build lasting value.* Boston: Harvard Business School Press.

The primary thesis of this book is that there is a significant relationship between how close a company's leadership style matches its brand identity and how successful the company will become. The authors outline six steps that companies can follow to develop and promote the leadership brand that they wish to project to employees and the prospective talent pool. These include creating a leadership brand statement, assessing leaders against the brand, assessing the brand, measuring return on leadership brand, building awareness for this brand, and preserving the leadership brand. The authors include one appendix that lists specific criteria for what constitutes a successful leadership brand and another that lists companies that have formed strong leadership brands to match the overall image that those companies project.

Beyond providing HR professionals and members of management with an outline for building a leadership brand that corresponds with the organization's image, Ulrich and Smallwood provide real-world examples through each step of the leadership brand–building process across several different types and sizes of organizations. These examples provide a reference point for practitioners to identify how their own organization can shape a leadership identity to match their organization's desired identity. The appendices are a useful addition to a book that helps HR managers and professionals work through an explicit brand–building process.

Chapter 4: Ropes to Skip and the Ropes to Know: Facilitating Executive Onboarding

by Seymour Adler and Lorraine Stomski

Aberdeen Group. (2008). *All aboard: effective onboarding techniques and strategies.* Retrieved April 4, 2008, from www.aberdeen.com/summary/report/benchmark/4574-RA-effective-onboarding-strategies.asp.

This research report is based on a survey of 794 participants (76 percent were working in Human Resources or related work) from a broad range of organizations. The study was designed to investigate the degree a formal onboarding program was being used, the structure and effectiveness of those programs, and the current use and benefits of the programs. Survey results compared three categories of companies: best in class (defined by three onboarding outcome criteria), industry average, and laggards.

The report provides numerous comparisons across these three groups with particular emphasis on the best-in-class group. The results show that the best-in-class organizations, when compared to the other groups, are 35 percent more likely to provide some form of new hire training as part of the onboarding, twice as likely to clearly define onboarding performance metrics, and 78 percent more likely to extend onboarding up to or beyond six months for executives (and 50 percent more likely to extend onboarding to regular employees). The results note that 62 percent of the participating organizations have a formal onboarding strategy.

The report includes data on a variety of onboarding issues and some suggested steps for improving onboarding efforts. The report is relatively brief but provides some guidance on how onboarding is designed, implemented, and measured. This is a useful article for companies interested in starting up an onboarding program or looking for ways to improve onboarding effectiveness.

■ ■ ■

Bauer, T. N., Bodner, T., Erdogan, B., Truxillo, D. M., & Tucker, J. S. (2007). Newcomer adjustment during organizational socialization: A meta-analytic review of antecedents, outcomes, and methods. *Journal of Applied Psychology, 92,* 707–721.

This meta-analysis examined the results of 70 studies that investigated what newcomer behaviors would best predict positive job attitudes and productive performance and behaviors. Newcomer information seeking and institutional socialization tactics were the newcomer behaviors measured, and the final outcomes examined were performance, job satisfaction, organizational commitment, intention to remain, and turnover. The model that the authors built also includes role clarity, self-efficacy, and social acceptance as mediators between the newcomer behaviors and the work outcomes.

Results of the meta-analysis demonstrated three direct relationships between newcomer behaviors and job outcomes. Newcomer information seeking, in which the new executive inquires about organizational procedures and culture, was shown to predict organizational commitment. Institutional socialization tactics, such as organized social events for employees or mentoring assignments, had a significant direct relationship with both job satisfaction and intentions to remain.

As the authors note, no single study had ever examined all of the relationships present in this study at once. This meta-analysis serves as a broad introduction to the effects of newcomer adjustment and socialization systems on newcomers' long-term success. The meta-analysis breaks down different types of newcomer socialization and discusses the implications for such programs in detail. Practitioners interested in maximizing the benefit of their onboarding systems could gain from this study.

■ ■ ■

Downey, K., March, T., & Berkman, A. (2001). *Assimilating new leaders: The key to executive retention.* New York: AMACOM.

The argument made in this book is that more than 70 percent of executives leave their new organizations in less than two years because they are ill prepared by the organization to take over operations at their new job. Part One of the book explains the importance of assimilating a new executive and presents a model for how to effectively assimilate new leaders. This model includes evaluating both the organization's and the new executive's potential for assimilation. Part Two describes the four-stage process of executive assimilation.

Stage 1 of the process, anticipating and planning, covers the pre-paratory stage and involves making arrangements for the new executive's transition into the job. Entering and exploring is stage 2, and this involves an executive's learning the organizational culture during the first weeks or months in the position. Building, the third stage, is when an executive begins incorporating herself into the culture and making adjustments tailored to her characteristics. It is at the fourth stage, contributing, that a new executive can operate at full speed. Within these chapters, the authors include prehiring strategies that help determine the fit between the executive and the organization, checklists for each of the stages, case studies, and workbooks for practitioners who use the book as a guide.

All of the tools included in the book combine to give HR professionals a comprehensive guide toward filling an executive vacancy and guiding a new hire into the position. This book provides information on handling executive hiring, organizational culture, and onboarding.

■ ■ ■

Watkins, M. (2003). *The first 90 days.* Boston: Harvard Business School Press.

Watkins's thesis is that adjusting to a new position, whether the result of a promotion or joining a new organization, is a teachable skill. Each of the ten chapters is titled after a key principle for being successful during the first 90 days in a new position. Instead of guiding readers chronologically through the stages of the transition, as most books on the subject do, this book names and discusses ten rules that the author suggests should be followed throughout an individual's transition.

The rules that Watkins discusses include guidelines for increasing readiness for a new position and separating from the patterns and habits that were only appropriate in the previous position. Among the principles discussed are assessing vulnerabilities, structuring learning methods, and increasing self-efficacy. Other principles, such as creating coalitions, building teams, and developing a relationship with a new boss, involve overcoming the interactional and social challenges of a new position. The conclusion brings all lessons together into a cohesive plan of action.

Although there is not a substantial amount of new information or research revealed in this book, Watkins does use existing knowledge and examples from case studies to articulate many of the challenges that face new job incumbents. These challenges are clearly expressed and may be the book's most valuable contribution. Managers and executives at all levels can find transition issues that they can relate to in this book.

Chapter 5: Identifying and Assessing High-Potential Talent: Current Organizational Practices

by Rob Silzer and Allan Church

Corporate Leadership Council. (2005). *Realizing the full potential of rising talent* (Volumes I and II). Washington, DC: Corporate Executive Board.

This two-part report attempts to address the question of how organizations should identify and develop high-potential employees. It begins by offering a model of employee potential that proposes three components of potential—ability, aspiration, and engagement—and then outlines a process for measuring potential.

Volume I reports the results of a high-potential management survey of 11,000 employees and their direct managers from 59 organizations and 29 countries. The study cites survey data to support their model of potential. The Council investigated 300 drivers of potential and found only 80 that have meaningful impact on improving potential. These drivers cluster into three themes: leveraging employee relationships, ensuring credible organizational commitment, and structuring challenges within job experiences. The rest of Volume I explores these three themes and outlines ways to leverage the drivers of potential in each area.

Volume II focuses on four key imperatives for developing high-potential (HiPo) employees: managing the HiPo pipeline, building sustainable professional networks, establishing credible commitment to HiPo development, and structuring job challenges to speed HiPo skill acquisition. Each imperative is supported by survey data and by company examples demonstrating specific leading-edge talent strategies.

The full report provides a data-based model and approach for identifying and developing high-potential talent. It might be particularly useful to organizations that want to take their high-potential programs to a new level of effectiveness.

■ ■ ■

Jeanneret, R., & Silzer, R. (Eds.). (1998). *Individual psychological assessment: Predicting behavior in organizational settings.* San Francisco: Jossey-Bass.

This is a seminal book on the use of psychological assessment in organizations for work-related purposes such as selection, promotion, and development. It includes some discussion of practical design and implementation issues, as well as underlying theoretical frameworks and organizational strategies. There is some emphasis on management and executive-level assessments.

The book is divided into four parts: frameworks (broad overview, underlying theory, research and legal issues), processes (design, character analysis, clinical approach, and providing results), strategies (assessment for new roles, across cultures, as an organizational strategy, and as part of leadership planning), and perspectives for the future. Jeanneret and Silzer, and most of the chapter authors, are highly experienced assessment psychologists who share their own assessment approaches and recommendations. The chapter authors discuss how assessment can and should be adapted to the strategies and context of an organization.

This book serves as a useful reference for the design and implementation of individual assessment. It provides expert guidance to assessment practitioners and human resource professionals and addresses key assessment issues faced by organizations. The need to accurately and objectively assess talent is a growing area of practice in industrial-organizational psychology and a core process of talent management in organizations. This book provides a comprehensive overview of a widely used assessment approach.

■ ■ ■

Lombardo, M., & Eichinger, R. (2000). High potentials as high learners. *Human Resource Management, 39*(4), 321–329.

Lombardo and Eichinger argue that one important characteristic of high-potential individuals is that they are learners who can learn in new ways and in different situations. It is based on the premise that people need to learn, grow, and change over time to be successful. The article presents a model for high potential based on studies conducted at Center for Creative Leadership.

Lombardo and Eichinger suggest that an individual demonstrates high potential by learning from experience. They propose the concept of learning agility, which they discuss as the willingness and ability to learn new competencies in order to perform under first-time, tough, or different conditions. They construct and describe four factors of learning agility: people agility, results agility, mental agility, and change agility. They also discuss implications for human resources.

In this short article, Lombardo and Eichinger introduce the concept of learning agility to human resource professionals. The concept has received a good deal of attention and has been included in high-potential characteristics by a few organizations. It outlines in a new way the importance of learning abilities and motivation in the changing business environment.

■ ■ ■

O'Connell, D. (1996). *High potential identification.* Boston: Executive
    Development Roundtable, Boston University School of Management.

This is a special report written for the Executive Development Roundtable based on interviews with 15 consulting firms and business companies and a review of selected literature. It provides a review of the current state of the identification of high potentials and compares the results with an earlier 1987 survey of 225 firms. It contains a discussion of findings and a selective annotated bibliography.

O'Connell concludes that there is no universal definition of *high potential* and that identification can begin at or near entry to an organization and is often a joint venture of operations and human resource professionals. He finds that organizations use a mix of formal and informal processes and that having top management commitment is important to ensure quality identification work. He also concludes that having a robust identification and development process can involve a major cultural shift in the organization.

Although relatively brief, the report discusses many of the key questions in the identification of high potentials It concludes with a list of principles and recommendations such as encouraging line ownership of identification. It provides a stimulating overview of important identification issues.

■ ■ ■

Spreitzer, M. S., McCall, M. W., & Mahoney, J. D. (1997). Early iden-
    tification of international executive potential. *Journal of Applied
    Psychology, 82*(1), 6–29.

The research presented in this article studies the ability to learn from experience using a multirater survey instrument and data from 838 lower-, middle-, and senior-level managers from 6 international firms and 21 countries. The authors describe the development of the instrument using primary and holdout samples. They compare survey dimension ratings (they resist calling them competencies) to current performance ratings and the immediate boss's determination that the individual was either a high-potential or a solid performer.

The results, although mixed, find that some of the survey dimension ratings (such as "brings out the best in people") were correlated with performance ratings in both samples, and the survey dimension ratings when combined had a 72 percent success rate in discriminating high-potential individuals from solid performers. However, "learning-oriented dimensions" (such as "seeks opportunities to learn") had little correlation with current performance and modest correlations with the decision about high potentials.

The authors provide a useful overview of the literature on learning from experience. Their study attempts to operationalize this construct and relate it to on-the-job measures of performance and potential. It is one of the few research studies that focuses on predicting who will be identified as high-potential individuals. Although the results are mixed, it provides a seminal research study in this area.

Chapter 6: Developing Leadership Talent: Delivering on the Promise of Structured Programs

by Jay A. Conger

Conger, J. A., & Benjamin, B. (1999). *Building leaders: How successful companies develop the next generation.* San Francisco: Jossey-Bass.

Individual skill development, promotion of organizational values, and strategic interventions are identified as the primary techniques of leadership development. The book covers a dozen case studies of these techniques by major corporations and discusses the resulting costs and benefits demonstrated in the case studies. A final section profiles action learning, as well as what the future of leader development may bring.

Conger and Benjamin assert that for too long, leaders have not been trained to lead others but to simply manage others' tasks and responsibilities. Best practices now are focusing more on teaching leaders how to integrate the workforce into the organizational culture and how to become more collaborative with employees at different levels of the organization. According to the authors, the more successful organizations now have leaders who are skilled at interacting intimately with employees at many levels.

This book offers a blueprint for converting an organization's outmoded leadership development methods into a system that fully considers the fluid and increasingly complex nature of organizations today. The introduction of action learning provides a detailed plan for teaching leaders how to handle their own projects while also becoming collaborators with others. This book can help develop leaders who are better equipped to excel in today's organizations.

■ ■ ■

Conger, J. A., & Riggio, R. (Eds.). (2006). *The practice of leadership*. San Francisco: Jossey-Bass.

Over a dozen contributors to this book discuss the leading trends and practices in leadership development. The book is divided into four parts: leader development and selection, the tasks of leaders, best practices, and leadership in today's world.

The different authors bring their own assertions and conclusions to this book, but some overarching themes tie their work together. First, the best organizations realize that selection involves more than looking at a candidate's hard skills or recent performance. The ability to succeed in a leadership role also requires cultural and emotional skills that must be assessed as they are being developed. Furthermore, entire organizations must be designed to foster leadership development. The authors argue that development cannot occur in a vacuum separate from the rest of the organization's operation.

The inclusion of many points of view gives readers an understanding of different approaches to common problems. The convergence of the ideas in this book provides readers with coherent conclusions about the state of leadership development. The book also can serve as a reference on some best practices.

■ ■ ■

Fulmer, R. M., & Conger, J. A. (2004). *Growing your company's leaders: How organizations use succession management to sustain competitive advantage*. New York: AMACOM.

The authors provide an overview of practices used by almost two dozen of the world's biggest companies in the major areas of succession management. Each area of succession management is covered in its own chapter. Overviews of practices are provided in talent identification, linking succession to development, monitoring long-term success, and other topics. A lengthy appendix provides detailed case studies of the succession management systems in six companies.

The book's driving argument is that executives too often are fast-tracked and overwhelmed once they reach executive ranks. The authors argue that the education of executives is too narrow and that they do not understand enough about their company's overall functions. Another executive failure is that CEOs are often externally hired and do not understand the company as well as internal veterans do. The authors suggest that a helpful practice would be to train talented employees in a wider array of organizational functions and then try to keep them from leaving the company. They argue as well that internal training and promotion is the best way to keep organizations stable and optimally efficient.

Fulmer and Conger state at the outset that they hope that organizations looking to improve the quality of their senior executives can learn valuable lessons about how their next generation of leaders can be discovered and developed. This guide was written to show organizations how to build internal talent so they do not have to go outside the organization for talent.

■ ■ ■

McCall, M. W., Jr., & Hollenbeck, G. P. (2002). *The lessons of international experience: Developing global executives.* Boston: Harvard Business School Press.

This book is based on an interview study with 101 global leaders from 16 companies and 36 countries. The focus is on investigating how companies develop global leaders. The authors code and summarize the interviews and provide a rich description of global executives and their life and work experiences. Case examples illustrate various points. This book extends previous work by McCall by identifying the lessons of experience in the global arena.

McCall and Hollenbeck identify seven core global executive competencies such as open-mindedness, cultural interest and sensitivity, and ability to deal with complexity. They outline the six key lessons gained from international experience, such as learning to deal with cultural issues, and identify the most widely reported development experiences described by global executives, such as a culture shock or business turnaround experience. They also discuss how global executives make sense of culture and how they handle derailment.

This book provides a comprehensive discussion of the challenges and issues faced by global executives and the organizations that are managing them. McCall and Hollenbeck clearly summarize the volume of interview data and provide suggestions on what organizations and the executives themselves can do to build global executive competence. Readers who are managing or developing global executives should find this book to be insightful and useful.

Chapter 7: Developing Leadership Talent Through Experiences

by Paul R. Yost and Mary Mannion Plunkett

Karaevli, A., & Hall, D. T. (2003). Growing leaders for turbulent times: Is succession planning up to the challenge? *Organizational Dynamics, 32,* 62–79.

The succession planning process of several companies is reviewed, based on interviews with 13 individuals in the field. Case by case, Karaevli and Hall identify the commonalities shared by organizations that are successful at developing leaders, as well as the shared deficiencies of the organizations that are experiencing difficulty with talent development. The article concludes with a list of 14 suggestions for designing better talent development strategies in today's environment.

The authors' primary conclusion is that many organizations are still using talent development methods that have been rendered obsolete by the changing work environment. They argue that more emphasis must be placed on the development of talent pools at early points in careers. Furthermore, emphasis must be shifted away from isolated succession events and toward an incremental approach.

The article not only provides a review of the state of talent development but also provides a tool to assess readers' own organizational talent development approaches. The checklist at the end of the article allows readers to examine how an organization measures up to the standards proposed by the authors. The article also offers a persuasive argument for why current talent development methods should be reevaluated.

■ ■ ■

Lombardo, M. W., & Eichinger, R. W. (2001). *For your improvement: A development and coaching guide.* Minneapolis, MN: Lominger.

The authors have compiled a leadership manual consisting of over 100 leadership competencies and how to improve performance in those competencies. The book is organized like an anthology of competencies; each entry describes not only a competency but the behaviors and work-related outcomes that can result from an individual's demonstrating either a mastery or a lack of skill in each competency. Following the competency listing are three additional sections covering performance dimensions for the competencies, career stoppers and stallers, and the international application of competencies.

Lombardo and Eichinger make the case that building leaders is based on building the core personal behaviors of individuals. With discussions on topics such as humor, approachability, and composure, emphasis is placed on developing personal traits that can make an individual adaptable in a variety of situations.

This book serves as a field manual for readers involved in developing talent. The competencies are organized so that readers can easily find a particular competency. Furthermore, the book offers helpful suggestions for competency development.

■ ■ ■

McCall, M. W. (1998). *High flyers: Developing the next generation of leaders.* Boston: Harvard Business School Press.

McCall argues for a transformation in the way that high-potential employees are identified and promoted within a company. In order to support this argument, the book is structured by the chronological order of the typical life cycle of a high-potential talent within an organization. The book demonstrates how high-potential talent often enter organizations and how specific employees are then targeted for grooming and development as the organization's next generation of leaders. At every step, McCall identifies some of the pitfalls that organizations face and suggests ways to fix them.

McCall theorizes that too much emphasis is placed on the experiences and the ready skills that young employees have. He argues that potential leaders can be better identified by looking at the latent traits that they possess, which means organizations need to develop better ways to assess employees. Furthermore, McCall asserts that because high potentials are too often considered ready for advancement by their employers, they are frequently given too much responsibility early on, and they subsequently burn out.

High Flyers makes a strong case, with examples and statistical data, for the benefits of a rigorous training program for high-potential employees instead of following the practice of simply plugging young talent into high-ranking positions. The book also identifies key attributes to look for in high potentials and how to systematically develop them to increase their chance of success.

■ ■ ■

McCauley, C. D. (2006). *Developmental assignments: Creating learning experiences for development in place.* Greensboro, NC: Center for Creative Leadership.

McCauley has developed a field guide that helps managers use developmental assignments to aid in the growth of high-potential employees. The first part of the book is an explanation of different approaches to developmental assignments and a discussion of the appropriateness of each type of assignment. The book then offers seven lengthy appendices. The first two provide examples of developmental assignments and exercises. The exercises help managers design assignments based on their employees' characteristics. The remaining appendices are cross-references of CCL resources related to the developmental approaches discussed in the book.

McCauley demonstrates with this reference work that a high-potential employee does not need to be removed from the work environment in order to develop into a leader. There are numerous activities and assignments that an employee can participate in during the course of his job that can prepare him for a future leadership role.

This book offers a wealth of exercises that can be generalized to a diversity of settings and employee types. The book walks the reader through procedures for using development tools such as 360-degree feedback, benchmarking, executive dimensions, and others. Leaders who want to develop future leaders without removing them from the work setting will find many useful resources in this book.

■ ■ ■

McCauley, C. D., & Van Velsor, E. (Eds.). (2004). *The Center for Creative Leadership handbook of leadership development* (2nd ed.). San Francisco: Jossey-Bass.

This handbook discusses a broad range of leadership development topics by prominent development experts. It is divided into three parts. The first part provides descriptions of specific techniques of leadership development currently being used. The second part discusses the contextual issues that may arise in leadership development, including racial and gender issues, developing leaders across cultures, and other situations in the modern workplace. Finally, the last part explains how to transform or adjust an organization in order to make it more conducive to leadership development.

One of the primary assertions the authors make is that there is a distinction between leader development, which is the development of individuals, and leadership development, which is the development of organizations in order to make them better at developing leaders. They argue that organizational development experts must be prepared to modify their practices to changing circumstances.

This book is a valuable source for discussing many relevant leadership development issues and offers important insights into several of the most vexing talent development issues. Many of the most popular development techniques are reviewed, which can be useful when weighing the relative benefits and costs of different approaches.

Chapter 8: Changing Behavior One Leader at a Time

by Sandra L. Davis and Robert C. Barnett

Goldsmith, M., & Lyons, L. (Eds.). (2006). *Coaching for leadership*. San Francisco: Pfeiffer/Jossey-Bass.

This edited book updates the 2000 edition and tracks developments in executive coaching. The book has four parts. The chapters in Part I discuss the nature of coaching and when it is and is not appropriate. Part II, "Building Blocks," identifies the basic tenets of a successful executive coaching program. Part III covers specific situations and topics that are involved in conducting a successful coaching process. Case studies constitute the final part of the book.

The chapters cover issues that examine the nature of executive coaching, as well as the different approaches that are used by different types of practitioners. Some of the authors discuss the psychological profiles of executives who are to be coached and how the temperaments and cultures of the executives and their organizations, respectively, are factored into their coaching approach. Aside from the case studies, the other chapters discuss key steps toward developing a rapport with coached executives, e-coaching, and other areas that have emerged in the field.

More than simply surveying trends in coaching, the book is organized to provide a comprehensive view of the nature of coaching, when it is applicable, and how it should be conducted differently across different settings and situations. Few of the topics covered break new ground, but best practices have been culled together to form a helpful guide to the coaching field.

■ ■ ■

Hoare, C. (Ed.). (2006). *Handbook of adult learning and development.* New York: Oxford University Press.

The editor has compiled a collection of chapters that explain in depth the cognitive, social, and emotional development in the human mind. The opening chapters provide a foundation for understanding adult cognitive and developmental psychology. The following six sections discuss overarching topics that have been the focal point of recent adult developmental psychology, with leading academics contributing their thoughts and findings.

In each section, several authors contribute their own perspective on topics that have fueled debate on cognitive adult development. Topics include the interplay of learning and development in the adult mind, the self system in adult learning, the context in adult development, and the mechanisms behind adult creativity and expression. The last part aims to identify measurements and applications to complement recent research.

For the purposes of changing behaviors in an organization, this book provides a unique contribution as a clinical tool for practitioners. Its scope and focus are intended for those with a psychology background; however, those without a psychology education may also benefit from this book. The essays offer a fresh perspective to motivating individuals and to modifying the habits of professionals who may need to adjust long-held habits.

■ ■ ■

Hogan, R., & Kaiser, R. B. (2005). What we know about leadership. *Review of General Psychology, 9,* 169–180.

Hogan and Kaiser conduct a review of leadership psychology and how the findings in the field have contributed to leadership selection and training. The article opens with a discussion of what leadership is, and then the authors explain how organizations have chosen leaders in the past. They provide a discussion of the leading theories of leadership and how each has been validated in clinical and applied settings. The practice of predicting leadership behaviors is covered next. Finally, the authors survey current trends and practices in leadership studies.

In defining leadership at the outset of the article, Hogan and Kaiser use the Yukl, Wall, and Lepsinger taxonomy that includes planning and organizing, problem solving, clarifying, informing, monitoring, motivating, consulting, recognizing, supporting, managing conflict and team building, networking, delegating, developing and mentoring, and rewarding. They then review the most common selection techniques for leaders, as well as evidence of each method. This discussion leads to the evaluation of leaders and which criteria for evaluation have proven to be most valid. The article discusses the prominence of personality testing in leadership selection and offers a lengthy review of the validity and practice of personality testing.

This article serves as a broad review of leadership theory and is useful as a quick reference. The article also cites almost 100 articles that explore the topics of leadership studies in more depth.

■ ■ ■

McCauley, C. D., & Van Velsor, E. (Eds.). (2004). *The Center for Creative Leadership handbook of leadership development* (2nd ed.). San Francisco: Jossey-Bass.

This handbook discusses a broad range of leadership development topics by prominent development experts. It is divided into three parts. The first part provides descriptions of specific techniques of leadership development currently being used. The second part discusses the contextual issues that may arise in leadership development, including racial and gender issues, developing leaders across cultures, and other situations in the modern workplace. Finally, the last part explains how to transform or adjust an organization in order to make it more conducive to leadership development.

One of the primary assertions the authors make is that there is a distinction between leader development, which is the development of individuals, and leadership development, which is the development of organizations in order to make them better at developing leaders. They argue that organizational development experts must be prepared to modify their practices to changing circumstances.

This book is a valuable source for discussing many relevant leadership development issues and offers important insights into several of the most vexing talent development issues. Many of the most popular development techniques are reviewed, which can be useful when weighing the relative benefits and costs of different approaches.

■ ■ ■

Peltier, B. (2001). *The psychology of executive coaching.* New York: Taylor & Francis Group.

Peltier takes a psychodynamic approach to the field of leadership development and addresses executive development and coaching from the point of view of a therapist. The opening chapters explain the potential connections between behavior modification in the workplace and traditional therapeutic techniques. Each successive chapter then proceeds to link a different psychoanalytical topic with leader and executive development.

The chapters explore topics such as how a person-centered approach can be used to mentor executives and how cognitive therapy can be used to diagnose and train leaders. There are also chapters that explain a place in leadership development for ideas borrowed from family therapy, social psychology, and hypnosis. Later chapters assert that many of these techniques are already being utilized in business and other applied fields, and discuss how they can be further used to improve leader training.

The intensely psychoanalytic focus of this book makes it rare in a field that is often driven by behavioral approaches. The chapters offer a clinical approach that provides insights into executives that most other books do not discuss.

Chapter 9: Managing Leadership Talent Pools

by Ben E. Dowell

Bossidy, L., & Charan, R. (2002). *Execution: The discipline of getting things done.* New York: Crown Business.

Bossidy and Charan argue for the importance of execution in an organization, explain what that includes, and then provide a tutorial on how to develop a better-executing organization. First, the argument is made that execution is needed by contrasting organizations that practice execution with those that do not. Next, the essential elements necessary for execution are discussed, such as: the necessary behaviors of leaders, the type of culture to establish, and the appropriate situations for delegating responsibilities. Finally, the three core processes of execution—people, strategy, and operation—are discussed.

The authors make the case that leadership is not a broad concept that simply involves setting agendas and establishing policy. The best leaders must dive into the details of a company and take an active role in day-to-day operations. Furthermore, there are some responsibilities, such as executive and manager selection, that should never be delegated. It is a leader's responsibility to be as familiar with his subordinates' jobs as he is with his own.

The guidance that this book offers about execution puts leadership in a new perspective. Managers may find fresh insights into their jobs as leaders that can transform stagnant organizations.

■ ■ ■

Corporate Leadership Council. (2003). *High-impact succession management: From succession planning to strategic executive talent management.* Washington, DC: Corporate Executive Board.

This report describes the practices of eight companies that are working to make the transition from traditional "names in boxes" replacement planning to a more strategic approach to managing executive succession. The authors suggest that organizations must build succession planning processes to address four succession risks: those resulting from key talent departures, underdeveloped successors, poor transition of executive talent into new roles in an organization, and the risks from not aligning talent with evolving business priorities.

The report summarizes four imperatives for organizations seeking to use succession management to improve executive bench strength. The first imperative is to focus succession efforts on the most vulnerable areas of the business by translating business strategy into a talent strategy. To illustrate this imperative, the report describes Johnson & Johnson's approach to executive talent reviews and Duke Energy's needs-based succession planning. The second key imperative is to accelerate executive development by matching the developmental needs of executives to experiences by balancing the short-term risks of stretch assignments with long-term benefits. The report describes IBM's approach to experience-based succession management, Schlumberger's nonobvious development moves, and Seagate's cross-business executive development forum as a means of illustrating practices that achieve this objective.

The third imperative is to overcome new-hire derailers by ensuring executives succeed in new roles by creating systems to identify needed behavioral changes for organizational fit and to successfully onboard executives. The report describes Shell's executive transition management and American Express's new-executive career launch. The fourth imperative described is maximizing strategic talent leverage by ensuring that talent is deployed in a manner that generates maximum return. The report describes Marriott's practice of using a strategic human capital review to align talent with the priorities of the organization.

■ ■ ■

Kesner, I. F., & Sebora, T. C. (1994). Executive succession: Past, present and future. *Journal of Management, 20*(2), 237–372.

Kesner and Sebora provide a review of the history of CEO succession management practices after an initial discussion of the importance and difficulty of replacing CEOs. Their review is broken into three phases. The first phase involves the emergence of succession management research in the 1960s. Key areas of research during this period focused on successor origin and rate of success. The 1970s, the second phase, are characterized as building on previous research while also focusing on successor traits and the board of directors' involvement in succession management. The final phase, the 1980s and 1990s, is characterized as a period of enormous growth, where the consequences of succession management were deeply explored and where advanced planning for succession took root.

After this review of the history, the authors conclude that the schism between applied and academic researchers, as well as between academics in different fields, led to an inconsistent model of succession planning—one that is still affecting succession management. One universally acknowledged conclusion, however, is that a more comprehensive approach toward succession planning that begins leadership development at onboarding must be adopted.

This review provides a rich historical perspective that allows readers to understand how the current situation came to be and how it can be improved. There is no specific advice for managers or executives, but an understanding of succession management research can help in developing successful plans in the future.

■ ■ ■

Pearson, A. E. (1987). Muscle-build the organization. *Harvard Business Review, 65*(4), 49–56.

This article proposes five changes that companies in any setting or sector can make to their organization in order to develop better leaders. Pearson begins by contrasting old, inefficient means of developing leaders with some more current and still relevant ideas that have gained traction among top organizations. The five steps to developing better leaders, with brief explanations, are then discussed.

Pearson asserts that an organization substantially increases its chance of developing high-quality leaders if it adheres to five tenets: (1) have high standards and continually raise them; (2) develop managers through fresh assignments and job rotations to ensure that they are always learning and to understand multiple facets of the organization; (3) facilitate and reward a manager's development; (4) infuse every level of the company with new talent in order to have more competition for management succession; and (5) use the human resources function as an active agent for change. These five tenets provide a useful checklist that can be monitored. The ensuing discussion offers examples of how each can be followed in different situations.

Chapter 10: Employee Engagement: A Focus on Leaders

by Jeff Schippmann

Corporate Leadership Council. (1999). *The compelling offer: A quantitative analysis of the career preferences and decisions of high value employees.* Washington, DC: Corporate Executive Board.

This research report studies employee preferences in employment offers and identifies the most leveraged attributes of a compelling job offer. It is based on an employee preferences survey of 5,877 high-value employees ("top performers who hold a valued skill and/or who have a high trajectory") from 19 companies. It tries to address how an employment offer or relationship can be made stronger or more competitive for high-value employees and views employment offers as a company product. The report is organized around three primary topics: understanding employee values, improving the offer fit in the high-value workforce, and crafting compelling offers. It also has useful appendices on the career decisions of information technology employees, Generation X employees, and women.

The report reaches 75 conclusions about employment offers supported by extensive survey data. It also identifies 12 key findings such as that there is an "alarmingly high intention to leave" among high-value employees, there is a disconnect between job satisfaction and retention, compensation factors are the most valued elements of the job offer, and manager quality is the single most important offer component.

This report provides extensive data and insights into understanding high-value employees and developing a compelling job offer for them. Readers who have responsibility for providing competitive job offers for these key employees will likely find this report useful in thinking through the range of effective offer options.

■ ■ ■

Gibbons, J. (2006). *Employee engagement: A review of current research and its implications.* New York: Conference Board.

This brief literature review and annotated bibliography focuses on defining employee engagement and identifying the factors that drive it. It discusses the impact of engagement on performance, customer service, and retention and points out a few interventions identified in the literature that can be initiated to enhance engagement. It also maps the key drivers to 12 primary published sources.

The report defines employee engagement as "a heightened emotional and intellectual connection that an employee has for his/her job, organization, manager or coworker, that influences him to apply additional discretionary effort to his work." Gibbons identifies 26 drivers and focuses on the eight that are most frequently mentioned in the literature: trust and integrity, nature of the job, connection between individual and company performance, career growth opportunities, pride in the company, coworkers and team members, employee development, and relationship with immediate manager.

The report provides a quick overview and summary of the relevant research reports and published articles on employee engagement. Readers who want to quickly get up to speed on employee engagement will find this to be a valuable resource.

■ ■ ■

Macey, W. H., & Schneider, B. (2008). The meaning of employee engagement. *Industrial and Organizational Psychology, 1,* 3–30.

This article offers a comprehensive review of the construct of employee engagement in an attempt to clarify the meaning and use of the term, as well as the antecedent and outcome variables that are related to engagement. Macey and Schneider review diverse literature and offer an integrative conceptual framework.

They also offer a series of fourteen propositions (conclusions) about psychological state engagement, behavioral engagement, and trait engagement that they believe are supported by the research on engagement. An example is that "job involvement, as traditionally conceptualized and assessed, is an important facet of the psychological state of engagement." In addition, they discuss the impact of job attributes and leadership on engagement and how relationships serve as a moderator of engagement. They conclude by reviewing the measurement of engagement, particularly through employee surveys.

Macey and Schneider provide a broad review of the engagement construct and cite relevant literature to support their conclusions. They purposefully stay away from discussing the related construct of motivation because of the "ambiguity associated with motivation" and their interest in "not confounding the issues." Readers who are interested in an in-depth discussion of employee engagement and the related literature will find this article informative and useful.

Chapter 11: Building Functional Competence to Enhance Functional Capability

by Suzan McDaniel and Erika D'Egidio

Corporate Leadership Council. (2003, October). *Functional knowledge competencies and training for general managers.* Washington, DC: Corporate Executive Board.

This report is formatted as a tutorial on core competencies and training methods for managers. The report is full of tables and illustrations that explain training and evaluation processes. At the outset, the report poses questions that ask what competencies are required of general managers, what areas of development training programs focus on, and what metrics are used to determine the success of such programs. Each question is discussed in its own section in the report.

Functional competencies have grown in importance as general managers have been asked to take on increasingly complex job duties. The report notes that the most common competencies and functions required for general managers are communication management, team building, management of innovation, development focus, relationship management, and strategic thinking and planning. However, a survey of the profiled companies also found that most companies today expect their general managers to have finance and marketing skills. General manager training at the profiled companies consists of a mixture of stretch roles, mentorship, and networking facilitation. An increasing trend is the practice of outsourcing training to outside vendors. Harvard, Northwestern, Dartmouth, and Stanford are among the leading providers of general manager training. The primary methods of training evaluation largely consist of performance evaluation of the manager, and the most common evaluation programs are detailed in the report.

This report serves as a good introduction to manager training, and the ample tables and appendices provide easy references for a review of current training trends for managers.

■ ■ ■

Corporate Leadership Council. (2007, May). *Maximizing the return on investment in technical expert pools.* Washington, DC: Corporate Executive Board.

The Corporate Leadership Council researched current knowledge and practice related to maximizing investment in technical expert pools by profiling and surveying five organizations. Aside from surveying human resource professionals from the five featured organizations, a literature review was conducted. The report opens with a discussion of various definitions of technical experts and technical expert pools. Once the differences and commonalities in the terms are clarified, twelve strategies for maximizing investment in technical talent are discussed. Most strategies are supplemented with case studies.

The introduction helps clarify three levels of technical experts: *expert* to describe an authority in a person's area of expertise within her segment of an organization; *senior expert* to describe a leading authority on a subject within an entire organization; and *fellow* to describe a recognized worldwide expert on a subject area. The report finds that experts are evaluated based on individual value, value they bring to their team (such as advising, coaching, and mentoring), and value they bring to the organization (such as creating knowledge bases and teaching classes). The report also found that performance management techniques used for experts with sometimes abstract skills are the same used for other personnel. For instance, objective and detailed evaluation criteria are used, as well as 360-degree feedback techniques. Customer feedback forms and self-assessment tools are also widely used. Finally, the report demonstrates how companies utilize development methods such as training classes and stretch assignments for their experts.

This study provides guidelines for managing the performance of a segment of the workforce whose performance may be difficult to quantify. The results of the research and surveys demonstrate that the best practice techniques for managing experts are similar to those used to manage the performance of others. There are subtle yet vital differences, however. The report demonstrates how to navigate the distinctions in order to properly tailor performance management to its experts.

■ ■ ■

Olson, M. S., van Bever, D., & Verry, S. (2008). When growth stalls. *Harvard Business Review, 86*(3), 50–61.

Olson, van Bever, and Verry argue that when most successful companies stall or even begin to regress, the root cause of the organization's decline is usually predictable and within the organization's control. In fact, they assert that in 87 percent of the cases they examined, the organization stalled because of reasons that the organization could have prevented. The article identifies the 12 most common internal reasons for stalling and examines how to predict and rectify each of them.

The authors claim that in 70 percent of cases of stalling, strategic factors are to blame. An examination of 50 organizations yielded a list of the most common stalling factors: poor premium position, innovation management breakdown, and abandonment of an organization's core principles. Aside from strategic problems, organizational shortfalls are also to blame. The authors identify the most common organizational problems as talent shortage in the talent bench and board inaction. Findings from the 50 organizations are used in examples to explain how each organization fell victim to one or more of these problems. The authors also identify the warning signs of such problems.

This study reveals warning signs for seemingly healthy companies and goes into depth about how stalling can be predicted while the organization still seems to be progressing. As the authors note, the profiled companies stalled because they did not heed such warnings. This article should be useful to organizational leaders to identify the warning signs and any preventive measures that should be taken before stalling happens to their organization.

■ ■ ■

Schippmann, J. S., Ash, R. A., Carr, L., Hesketh, B., Pearlman, K., Battista, M., et al. (2000). The practice of competency modeling. *Personnel Psychology, 53*(3), 703–740.

A project of the Job Analysis and Competency Modeling Task Force, this study aimed to better define the practices of competency modeling, a field that has been widely discussed and misunderstood, even within the discipline of industrial-organizational psychology. The authors discuss the processes they used during the study, including subject matter expert interviews and literature review. A comparison is made between competency modeling and job analysis, and a scale is devised to illustrate the distinctions between competency modeling and job analysis. Finally, the authors give examples of a theoretical job analysis and a theoretical competency model to demonstrate the similarities and differences.

Interviews, extensive literature review, and internal consultation among members of the task force were used to identify characteristics of accepted practices of job analyses and competency models. The authors broke down the findings into ten practices and measured the amount of rigor performed for each practice during a job analysis as opposed to the development of a competency model. The practices were method of investigation, type of descriptor content collected, procedures for developing descriptor content, detail of descriptor content, links to business goals and strategies, content review, ranking descriptor content, assessment of reliability, item and category retention criteria, and documentation. These practices are all explained in depth in the study. The review found that job analyses and competency modeling projects use approximately equal rigor in procedures to develop descriptor content and content review. For linking to business goals and strategies, however, competency modeling uses significantly more rigor. For the other seven practices, job analyses are significantly more rigorous than are competency modeling practices.

This study filled an essential knowledge gap in the field by clarifying and establishing the distinctions between competency modeling and job analysis. Even practitioners who had been clear on the distinctions can now review the criteria and their normal levels of rigor for ideas on how to perform more rigorous competency modeling or job analysis.

Chapter 12: Managing and Measuring the Talent Management Function

By John C. Scott, Steven G. Rogelberg, and Brent W. Mattson

Edwards, J. E., Scott, J. C., & Raju, N. S. (Eds.). (2003). *The human resources program-evaluation handbook*. Thousand Oaks, CA: Sage.

This edited book of 25 chapters covers program evaluation approaches for a wide range of human resource programs, processes, and systems, from staffing to evaluating and rewarding employees to employee and organizational effectiveness. The objective was to bring together the science of program evaluation with the practical considerations of conducting those evaluations in organizations. The chapter authors bring a wide range of academic and practitioner perspectives and experiences to their writing.

Each chapter provides an overview of the topic, such as selecting managers and executives, guidance on how to assess the effectiveness and efficiency of a specific program, some case examples, potential pitfalls, and a list of recommended readings. The authors integrate a broad understanding of the topic with practical evaluation suggestions. In addition, the book contains an overview of program management, a discussion of global HR metrics, an evaluation of HR information systems, and strategic planning for HR.

This book is an ambitious effort to bring science and practice together and outline ways to evaluate programs in a range of HR practices and programs. It can serve as a useful resource for HR professionals who want to build program evaluation into a specific HR process or across all of Human Resources.

■ ■ ■

Davidson, E. J., & Martineau, J. W. (2007). Strategic uses of evaluation. In K. M. Hannum, J. W. Martineau, & C. Reinelt (Eds.), *The handbook of leadership development evaluation* (pp. 433–463). San Francisco: Jossey-Bass.

This chapter opens by providing a broad definition of strategic evaluation and then including a section that introduces key technical terms and definitions related to the field. The authors explain the relationship between strategic evaluation and organizational goals and the process through which interventions can improve organizational operation. Case studies are provided to explain how the specific technique of strategic evaluation can benefit an organization. Finally, principles and conclusions are gleaned from the case studies.

The five primary elements of a strategic framework, according to the chapter, are an organizational vision, a mission statement, a set of overarching values, a set of strategies, and a set of strategic goals and actions. Examples from a government agency initiative and a health care initiative demonstrate how the principles of strategic evaluation can be used in various settings. The authors conclude by listing a set of best practices for strategic evaluation, including integrating evaluation from the start, employing not just content expertise but evaluation expertise, using multimethod or triangulation approaches, and employing comparison or control groups when possible. Potential challenges to strategic evaluation are mentioned, along with possible solutions to these challenges.

Strategic evaluation is a broad topic, and this chapter is a good primer. Best practices are discussed near the end of the chapter and can serve as an educational starting point for a practitioner looking to integrate evaluation into an organization's processes.

■ ■ ■

Fitz-enz, J., & Davison, B. (2002). *How to measure human resources management* (3rd ed.). New York: McGraw-Hill.

This guide is written for practitioners in human resource management to add both real value and perceived value to the HR department. The first part of the book explains why measuring Human Resources is important. Furthermore, the book makes the case that Human Resources must be measurable so that practitioners can demonstrate that HR is a value-added component of an organization. The following six parts explain the fundamentals for measuring different elements of Human Resources.

Part II discusses the measurement of hiring practices and includes topics such as recruitment and workforce planning. Part III discusses compensation and explains how outcomes can be linked to benefits and compensation packages and how these linkages can be communicated to management. Part IV is an extensive survey of training and development. It explains the basics of measuring training at each step of the process. Measurement of employee retention is the topic of the next section. Absenteeism and turnover are covered here, but so are other metrics that are not as commonly used. Parts VI and VII examine ways in which HR practice is changing and how measurement techniques will have to change with them.

This guide gives explicit instruction to HR practitioners on how to communicate the value of their services. Practitioners can learn from this book not only methods to improve their HR metrics but how to convey to non-HR professionals what HR practices can do to contribute to the operations of their organizations.

■ ■ ■

Sullivan, J. (2002). *HR metrics, the world class way: How to build the business case for human resources.* Peterborough, NH: Kennedy Information.

Sullivan has assembled a workbook for human resource practitioners that is divided into seven parts, each covering a broad area of HR practices. Each part contains a variety of chapters, some as short as a page. These chapters are sometimes assignments or checklists and are always highly specific to a certain topic. The broad topics covered are building a performance mindset, tools for assessing your talent, tools to energize your employees and increase productivity, strategies for retaining top performers, tools for attracting the best to your team, tools for communicating with your team, and measuring productivity and turnover.

Each chapter offers tips for increasing HR productivity by providing novel suggestions, some supported by anecdotal or statistical evidence. Checklists and graphs are common tools, and the writing style is more conversational than formal. For example, a performance appraisal system is introduced as the "How am I doing" graph. Checklists measure preferences for a supervisor, job rotations, goals for retention efforts, and more. The author often takes accepted theories and practices and repackages them into ideas that may be more applicable to practitioners without a research background.

Although this book does not introduce new research or paradigms, it does provide a wealth of exercises for HR professionals to use and makes theory applicable by distilling concepts into multiple checklists, graphs, and principles.

Chapter 13: Managing Talent in Global Organizations

by Thomas Ruddy and Pooja Anand

Beaman, K. V. (2006). Myths, mystiques and mistakes in overseas assignments. In M. Foster (Ed.), *Global talent: An anthology of human capital strategies for today's borderless enterprise* (Vol. 1, pp. 35–73). Washington, DC: Human Capital Institute.

This chapter discusses the multiple dangers and obstacles to successful international assignments. Beaman lists several myths, mistakes, and what are called mystiques involved in global assignments, and spends the second half of the chapter explaining strategies for overcoming these problems. Near the end of the chapter, empirical and applied findings are covered, with the author explaining how these findings can be used to succeed in overseas assignments.

The author identifies the most common myths involving international assignments, such as the assumptions that any smart employee can be an expatriate, that human resource professionals are effectively handling overseas assignments, and that there is a single trait that identifies a successful expatriate employee. The mystiques identified are that international assignments are glamorous and that Hollywood portrayals of different cultures are reliable and accurate. The authors also identify the three most prominent mistakes made by firms and individuals considering expatriate assignments: whatever works in the United States will work overseas, one must forget old ways in order to fit in, and one does not need to learn the language since "English is spoken by everyone." Several paragraphs are devoted to each myth, mistake, and mystique. Using both anecdotes and empirical studies, the author spends much of the rest of the chapter illustrating the errors in these assumptions.

The chapter works as an admonition to potential expatriates not to take such an assignment lightly and not to make the mistakes that so often doom international assignments. Individuals can also use the chapter as a preparatory guide to alert them to what they can expect on an international assignment. With its emphasis on cultural norms and personality types, the chapter can also offer some perspective to individuals who are considering an expatriate assignment.

■ ■ ■

Cohen, E. (Ed.). (2007). *Leadership without borders.* Hoboken, NJ: Wiley.

Cohen has compiled a comprehensive review of effective leadership for managers of multinational corporations and managers who are on assignment in international settings. Part One focuses on the wealth of knowledge currently available regarding identifying and measuring competencies for global managers. Part Two consists of contributed chapters from experts in global business. These chapters address specific areas for improving global leadership practices, such as global risk strategies and modifying leader development systems to fit different global settings. Case studies, such as chapters devoted to Vodafone and Booz Allen, are also included.

Almost all aspects of using leaders in multiple global settings are discussed, such as embedding the organization's culture into the local culture of the international setting. The case studies illustrate some main issues, such as merging operations from multiple worksites around the world into one cohesive operation and how an organization's core values may have to be adjusted when expanding into new territories.

With a combination of firsthand details and established practices, this book offers extensive coverage of global leadership practices. Its emphasis is more on practice than on research findings, and as a result would more likely benefit readers interested in applied management than those interested in empirical analyses.

■ ■ ■

Fulkerson, J. R. (2002). Growing global executives. In R. Silzer (Ed.), *The 21st century executive; Innovative practices for building leadership at the top* (pp. 300–334). San Francisco: Jossey-Bass.

Fulkerson provides an overview of the success factors and characteristics of global business executives and discusses approaches to growing and developing these executives. Fulkerson shares his insights based on his extensive career experience working on executive development in international and global enterprises such as PepsiCo.

The chapter is organized around five key steps, or frameworks, such as identifying global competencies, using global experience for development, and developing a cross-cultural mindset. He also provides global success factors, strategies for developing those success factors, and the characteristic differences between global executives and other executives. In addition to outlining the organization's perspective, he includes a matrix that describes global executives' views on their own development. To help make his point, he provides several executive case studies. Fulkerson concludes by providing experienced-based words of advice on how to grow and develop global executives.

How to develop global executives is a major concern for many corporations. As businesses increasingly operate in a world market, they need to decide how to effectively and efficiently build their global executive talent. Fulkerson provides extensive insights to this based on his years of global experience.

■ ■ ■

House, R., Javidan, M., Hanges, P., & Dorfman, P. (2002). Understanding cultures and implicit leadership theories across the globe: An introduction to project GLOBE. *Journal of World Business, 37,* 3–10.

House, Javidan, Hanges, and Dorfman introduce a new scale and a new system of measuring attitudes and job practices across cultures. The research program examining world cultures in business is called Global

Leadership and Organizational Effectiveness (GLOBE). Inspired by the culture studies of Hofstede, the authors describe the method by which they surveyed professionals in the fields of food processing, finance, and telecommunications and arrived at a new nine-factor scale for measuring cultures worldwide.

Numerous experts on global culture and work practices were consulted, and nine factors of culture are selected: uncertainty avoidance, power distance, social collectivism, in-group collectivism, assertiveness, future orientation, performance orientation, and humane orientation. Short descriptions of each factor are provided. The authors close by offering a set of propositions for future research. The propositions are expressed in a structural model, in which leader personality, organizational culture, and societal culture drive each other and organizational effectiveness.

GLOBE is a new direction in research that expands on ideas that have become central tenets of global leadership. The updated cultural factors can potentially alter the current understanding of culture's exchange relationship with multinational leadership. More empirical work must be done to verify the validity of many of the authors' propositions and ideas. However, some of these ideas could advance the conversation on what we currently know about the effects of intercultural interactions and their effect on global leadership.

■ ■ ■

McCall, M. W., Jr., & Hollenbeck, G. P. (2002). *Developing global executives: The lessons of international experience.* Boston: Harvard Business School Press.

This book is based on an interview study with 101 global leaders from 16 companies and 36 countries. The focus is on investigating how companies develop global leaders. The authors code and summarize the interviews and provide a rich description of global executives and their life and work experiences. Case examples are included to illustrate various points. It extends previous work by McCall by identifying the lessons of experience in the global arena.

McCall and Hollenbeck identify seven core global executive competencies such as open-mindedness, cultural interest and sensitivity, and ability to deal with complexity. They outline the six key lessons gained from international experience, such as learning to deal with cultural issues, and identify the most widely reported development experiences described by global executives, such as a culture shock or business turnaround experience. They also discuss how global executives make sense of culture and how they handle derailment.

This book provides a comprehensive discussion of the challenges and issues faced by global executives and the organizations that are managing them. McCall and Hollenbeck clearly summarize the volume of interview data and provide suggestions on what organizations and the executives themselves can do to build global executive competence. Readers who are managing or developing global executives should find this book insightful and useful.

Chapter 14: Managing Talent in China

by Elizabeth Weldon

Dessler, G. (2006). Expanding into China? What foreign employers should know about human resource management in China today. *S.A.M. Advanced Management Journal, 71*(4), 11–25.

Dessler provides a "practical understanding" of human resource management issues for foreign employers entering China. The literature from 2000 to 2005 is reviewed and includes research studies, consulting surveys, and journal and news articles. Past and current HR management practices in China are discussed, including recruiting, hiring, career development, training, appraisal, compensation, safety, unions, and employee relations.

Foreign companies are introducing Western HR practices into China, and "China business management practices are changing fast." But "vestiges of central planning" remain, and employers "confront cultural differences" when entering China. While incentive-based motivational programs and work/life benefits are being increasingly offered to attract the best workers in a competitive labor market, cultural differences between local and foreign business practices remain. In a face-saving culture like China's, performance evaluations must be handled carefully, and workers expect employers to treat them with family loyalty. Also, the Chinese government still exercises some control over personnel decisions and keeps a nationwide database of workers.

Dessler provides a useful review of important HR management and business challenges facing companies entering China. Although there is a long way to go to bridge the cultural divide, the transition to Western-style Human Resource management is under way.

■ ■ ■

Economist Intelligence Unit. (2006, August). In E. Cheng (Ed.), *China hand: The complete guide to doing business in China.* Hong Kong: Author.

The Economist Intelligence Unit prepares and regularly updates a comprehensive guide to conducting business in China, covering everything from trade, finance, and taxes to marketing, distribution, and politics. This chapter on human resource practices discusses labor market demographics, recruiting practices, education and training, workforce management, compensation and benefits, and labor legislation. It also reviews the influence of cultural issues and Western-style HR management on many areas, such as performance evaluations, job succession, and work motivation. Appendices report on workforce education, best colleges and universities, and the location of information technology professionals.

One key conclusion is that China's current manpower challenge is "a shortage of the right people," with acute shortages in senior management and sales promotion. Ironically unemployment among the well educated is increasing because of their lack of mobility due to government restrictions and family considerations. There is also significant skill deficit among laid-off state workers, which the government is addressing by providing educational resources.

China Hand offers a thorough guide to the key aspects of managing talent and human resources in China. This resource could be invaluable to businesses entering the Chinese market and to human resource managers developing and implementing HR practices in China.

■ ■ ■

Javidan, M., Dorfman, P., de Luque, M., & House, R. (2006). In the eye of the beholder: Cross cultural lessons in leadership from project GLOBE. *Academy of Management Perspectives, 20*(1), 67–90.

This team of researchers, under the overall direction of Bob House, has been reporting on GLOBE, a global study of leadership, over the years. Javidan, Dorfman, de Luque, and House describe a new metric for measuring the behavioral expectations that employees in different cultures have for work leaders. They create four hypothetical cases of an American firm operating with workforces in Brazil, France, Egypt, and China to illustrate cross-cultural differences.

Six dimensions of behavior, based on culturally implicit leadership theory (CLT), are identified: (1) charismatic/value based, (2) team oriented, (3) participative, (4) humane oriented, (5) autonomous, and (6) self-protective. They find that European and Latin American employees tend to expect more charisma and team-oriented behavior in their leaders, while Chinese and Egyptian workers expect leaders to show more self-protective behavior and autonomy. Some attributes are universally desired by employees, such as leaders who are trustworthy, have foresight, build confidence in subordinates, and are informed.

This cross-cultural study should help managers better understand cross-cultural employee expectations and help American companies improve communications and coordination with their workforces in other countries. The study also might help to determine what type of manager to assign to different countries.

■ ■ ■

Towers Perrin. (2006). *China Global Workforce Study*. Retrieved July 1, 2007, from http://www.towersperrin.com/tp/lobby.jsp?country= global.

This global survey by Towers Perrin provides an overview of the challenges in managing personnel in China. It surveyed 86,000 respondents in 16 countries, including 1,100 employees in China. The results illustrate how the Chinese workforce is becoming more like other workforces in the world, while still maintaining some distinctiveness.

The survey discusses Chinese workers' views on careers and organizations. For example, Chinese employees rate their supervisors more favorably than employees do in other countries. Chinese workers plan for the longer term when entering jobs, have lower turnover intentions, and are more attracted by learning and development opportunities than other employees. However, like other employees, Chinese employees list competitive pay and career advancement opportunities as chief drivers of career decisions. They are also increasingly interested in lifestyle benefits, work/life balance, and low-stress work environments.

This expansive study reviews the current work motivations of Chinese employees. Although the Chinese workforce still is unique, the most skilled individuals are beginning to seek the work benefits and amenities that have been reserved for their Western peers. As the Chinese workforce still is unique, continues to evolve, corporations will need to adjust how they can best appeal to this growing and increasingly talented workforce.

Name Index

Subject Index

A

Aberdeen Group, 160, 208, 789

Abilities, basing assessments on, 426, 428. *See also specific abilities*

Ability, defined, 260

Ability tests, 254–255, 267–268

"Academy" company, 617–618

Acceleration pools, 14, 228, 663

Accelerator roles, positions that are key, identifying, 329–330

Acceptance: organizational, research needed on, 777–778; of outcomes, 505; social, gaining, 167, 168, 171

Acceptance step, in the high-potential identification process, *233*

Accommodating new experiences, 359

Accountability: clearly defining, benefit of, 636; for the development and success of talent, 584; for experience-based learning, 338; of human resources, 750; influence of, perspective on, 724–725; for integrated talent management, 64; of leadership, and financial performance, 524; for managing talent pools, 431; onboarding, *184–186*, 206; for talent management practices, 509, 543. *See also* Responsibility

Accounting and reporting competencies, example of, *484*

Acquiring talent. *See* Attracting and recruiting talent; Executive onboarding; Selecting talent; Talent acquisition strategy

Acquisitions and mergers, 431, 469

Action learning, 285, 287, 306–309, 315, *487*, 488, 581–582, 588, 608

Action orientation standard, 414

Action steps, building experiences into, in the development plan, 333

Active sense makers, newcomers as, 169–170

Adaptability and flexibility. *See* Flexibility

Administrative assistant, new leader's, onboarding responsibilities of the, 181, 206

Adult development, *353*, 359–360

Adult learning theory, 289, *354*, 359–360

Affective engagement components, 440, 442, 443

Agendas, talent review, 423–425

Agilent Technologies, 177, 188

Agreeableness, 371

Alcatel, 596

Aligned stage, *31*, 32–33, 34

Alignment: benefit of, 683, 684; contradictory signals sent from lack of, 729; ensuring, 96, 652; failure to build underlying framework for, 319; importance of, 28, 65, 85, 111–112, 113, 154–155, 298, 550, 729; with organizational values, lack of, 756; poor, with strategy, challenge of, 753–754

Alignment model, 35, 45

Alignment tool, 88

All Aboard (Aberdeen Group), 789–790

M

Maersk, *220*

Management calibration meetings, 265

Management effectiveness, importance of, 350–352

Management metrics, 195–196, *197*

Management of talent. *See* Talent management

Management resource review (MRR), 726

Management training market, 349

Management-by-objective (MBO) performance management process, 451

Managerial leadership. *See Leadership entries*

Managers: awareness of, building, of turnover warning signs, 454–455; developing assessment skills of, 217–218; for the development and success of talent, 584; entrenched, issue of, 305; impact of, on individual change, 383; and job complexity, 377, *378*; mindset needed for, 41, 42, 43, 66, 81, 110; perspective on, 739; program, objectives of, addressing, in evaluating talent management, 511–512; relationships with, learning from, 106; resistance of, challenge of, 761–762; role in developing talent, 102–103, 104; shortage of, in China, contextual factors causing, 597–601; success factors for, 377, 379; and the talent review process, *626*; transnational, effective, 559. *See also* Line managers

Managing global talent. *See* Global talent management

Managing leadership talent pools: alternative talent review approaches for, 425–426, *427*; and the architecture of a talent review, 415–425; the business case for, 402–404; and characteristics of successful talent reviews, 414–415; conclusion on, 437; effective approaches to, research needed on, 435; foundations for, 404–405; future directions in research on, 434–436; key factors in, 405–407; lessons learned about, 431–434; and outcomes of talent reviews, 428–431; overview of, 399–402; relevant resources on, summaries of, 804–807; and roles in the talent review process, 407–411, *412–413*; and talent assessment, 426, 428

Managing talent in China: challenges of, addressing, 602, 604–610; and the Chinese context, 597–602, *603*; conclusions on, 611–612; introduction to, 595; overview of multinational companies and, 595–597; perspectives on, 716–717; relevant resources on, summaries of, 819–821; research needed on, 610–611. *See also* Global talent management

Managing Transitions (Bridges), *490*

Manpower, 439, 458

Manpower China, 596, 601, 602, 605, 606, 607, 613

Mapping: critical success factors, 686–687; and interviewing stakeholders, 191–192; the organization, as a transition task, 164, 187; performance and potential, 562, *563*

Market shifts, sudden, challenge of, 755–756

Market value: increased, example of, 672, 673; strong leadership and, 351

Marriott, *220*

Mastering the position, as a transition task, 164, 187

Maturity levels, and potential, issues concerning, 276

Maturity path approach, 93